HMH

into Literature™

GRADE

8

Printed in the U.S.A.

ISBN 978-0-358-41641-8

10 11 12 13 14 15 2706 31 30 29 28 27 26 25 24

4500879759

r9.22

HMH | into Literature™

Program Consultants:

Kylene Beers

Martha Hougen

Tyrone C. Howard

Elena Izquierdo

Carol Jago

Weston Kieschnick

Erik Palmer

Robert E. Probst

GRADE

8

Program Consultants

Kylene Beers

Nationally known lecturer and author on reading and literacy; coauthor with Robert Probst of *Disrupting Thinking, Notice & Note: Strategies for Close Reading,* and *Reading Nonfiction;* former president of the National Council of Teachers of English. Dr. Beers is the author of *When Kids Can't Read: What Teachers Can Do* and coeditor of *Adolescent Literacy: Turning Promise into Practice,* as well as articles in the *Journal of Adolescent and Adult Literacy.* Former editor of *Voices from the Middle,* she is the 2001 recipient of NCTE's Richard W. Halle Award, given for outstanding contributions to middle school literacy.

Tyrone C. Howard

Veteran teacher, author, and professor in the Graduate School of Education and Information Studies at UCLA. Dr. Howard is the inaugural director of the UCLA Pritzker Center for Strengthening Children and Families, a campus-wide consortium examining academic, mental health, and social and emotional experiences and challenges for the most vulnerable youth populations. Dr. Howard has published over 75 peer-reviewed journal articles and several bestselling books, including *Why Race & Culture Matters in Schools* and *Black Male(d): Peril and Promise in the Education of African American Males*. He is considered one of the premier experts on educational equity and access in the country.

Martha Hougen

National consultant, presenter, researcher, and author. Areas of expertise include differentiating instruction for students with learning difficulties, including those with learning disabilities and dyslexia; and teacher and leader preparation improvement. Dr. Hougen has taught at the middle school through graduate levels. Dr. Hougen has supported Educator Preparation Program reforms while working at the Meadows Center for Preventing Educational Risk at The University of Texas at Austin and at the CEEDAR Center, University of Florida.

Elena Izquierdo

Nationally recognized teacher educator and advocate for English language learners. Dr. Izquierdo is a linguist by training, with a Ph.D. in Applied Linguistics and Bilingual Education from Georgetown University. She has served on various state and national boards working to close the achievement gaps for bilingual students and English language learners. Dr. Izquierdo is a member of the Hispanic Leadership Council, which supports Hispanic students and educators at both the state and federal levels.

Carol Jago

Teacher of English with 32 years of experience at Santa Monica High School in California; author and nationally known lecturer; former president of the National Council of Teachers of English. Ms. Jago currently serves as Associate Director of the California Reading and Literature Project at UCLA. With expertise in standards' assessment and secondary education, Ms. Jago is the author of numerous books on education, including *With Rigor for All* and *Papers, Papers, Papers*; and she is active with the California Association of Teachers of English, editing its scholarly journal *California English* since 1996. Ms. Jago also served on the planning committee for the 2009 NAEP Reading Framework and the 2011 NAEP Writing Framework.

Weston Kieschnick

Author, award-winning teacher, principal, instructional development coordinator, and dean of education. Mr. Kieschnick has driven change and improved student learning in multiple capacities over his educational career. Now, as an experienced instructional coach and Senior Fellow with the International Center for Leadership in Education (ICLE), Mr. Kieschnick shares his expertise with teachers to transform learning through online and blended models. He is the author of *Bold School: Old School Wisdom + New School Innovation = Blended Learning That Works* and coauthor of *The Learning Transformation: A Guide to Blended Learning for Administrators*.

Erik Palmer

Veteran teacher and education consultant based in Denver, Colorado. Author of *Well Spoken: Teaching Speaking to All Students* and *Digitally Speaking: How to Improve Student Presentations*. His areas of focus include improving oral communication, promoting technology in classroom presentations, and updating instruction through the use of digital tools. He holds a bachelor's degree from Oberlin College and a master's degree in curriculum and instruction from the University of Colorado.

Robert E. Probst

Nationally respected authority on the teaching of literature; Professor Emeritus of English Education at Georgia State University. Dr. Probst's publications include numerous articles in *English Journal* and *Voices from the Middle,* as well as professional texts including (as coeditor) *Adolescent Literacy: Turning Promise into Practice* and (as coauthor with Kylene Beers) *Disrupting Thinking, Notice & Note: Strategies for Close Reading,* and *Reading Nonfiction*. He has served NCTE in various leadership roles, including the Conference on English Leadership Board of Directors, the Commission on Reading, and column editor of the NCTE journal *Voices from the Middle.*

UNIT 1

Gadgets and Glitches

Page 1

ESSENTIAL QUESTION:
Does technology improve or control our lives?

KEY LEARNING OBJECTIVES

- Analyze plot
- Identify central idea and details
- Analyze organization
- Analyze irony
- Analyze claim and evidence
- Analyze graphic features
- Analyze rhetoric

READER'S CHOICE

Go online for
- Unit and Selection Videos
- Interactive Annotation and Text Analysis
- Selection Audio Recordings
- Collaborative Writing — Writable

UNIT 2

The Thrill of Horror

Page 78

ESSENTIAL QUESTION: ***Why do we sometimes like to feel frightened?***

KEY LEARNING OBJECTIVES

- Analyze literary criticism
- Analyze point of view
- Analyze suspense
- Analyze themes
- Analyze foreshadowing
- Analyze epic poetry
- Analyze an adaptation

READER'S CHOICE

Ed

Go online for

- Unit and Selection Videos
- Interactive Annotation and Text Analysis
- Selection Audio Recordings
- Collaborative Writing — Writable

UNIT 3

Places We Call Home

Page 170

ESSENTIAL QUESTION:
What are the places that shape who you are?

KEY LEARNING OBJECTIVES

- Analyze plot
- Analyze themes
- Analyze character
- Analyze narrative structure
- Analyze imagery
- Evaluate a document

READER'S CHOICE

SHORT READS

Available online

Ed

LONG READS

Recommendations

UNIT 3 TASKS

Ed

Go online for

- Unit and Selection Videos
- Interactive Annotation and Text Analysis
- Selection Audio Recordings
- Collaborative Writing — Writable

UNIT 4

The Fight for Freedom

Page 260

ESSENTIAL QUESTION:

What will people risk to be free?

KEY LEARNING OBJECTIVES

- Analyze autobiography
- Analyze structure
- Analyze setting
- Analyze literary devices
- Analyze biography
- Analyze word choice
- Analyze figurative language

READER'S CHOICE

SHORT READS

Available online

Ed

LONG READS

Recommendations

UNIT 4 TASKS

Ed

Go online for

- Unit and Selection Videos
- Interactive Annotation and Text Analysis
- Selection Audio Recordings
- Collaborative Writing — Writable

UNIT 5

Finding Your Path

Page 348

ESSENTIAL QUESTION:

How do the challenges you face today help to shape your future?

KEY LEARNING OBJECTIVES

- Analyze perspectives
- Analyze structure
- Analyze author's purpose
- Compare poetic structure
- Analyze claim and evidence
- Identify counterclaims
- Analyze rhetorical devices

READER'S CHOICE

SHORT READS

Available online

LONG READS

The Outsiders
Novel
by S. E. Hinton

The House on Mango Street
Novel
by Sandra Cisneros

Hush
Novel
by Jacqueline Woodson

Recommendations

UNIT 5 TASKS

Go online for

- Unit and Selection Videos
- Interactive Annotation and Text Analysis
- Selection Audio Recordings
- Collaborative Writing — Writable

UNIT 6

The Legacy of Anne Frank

Page 434

ESSENTIAL QUESTION:

What can we learn from tragic events?

KEY LEARNING OBJECTIVES

- Analyze drama
- Analyze a diary
- Make inferences
- Analyze appeals
- Analyze rhetorical devices
- Analyze sound devices
- Analyze figurative language

READER'S CHOICE

Ed

Go online for

- Unit and Selection Videos
- Interactive Annotation and Text Analysis
- Selection Audio Recordings
- Collaborative Writing Writable

SELECTIONS BY GENRE

FICTION

Short Story

Novel

Oral Tradition

NONFICTION

Informational Text

Argument

HMH | into Literature™ Online

Ed Experience the Power of *HMH Into Literature*

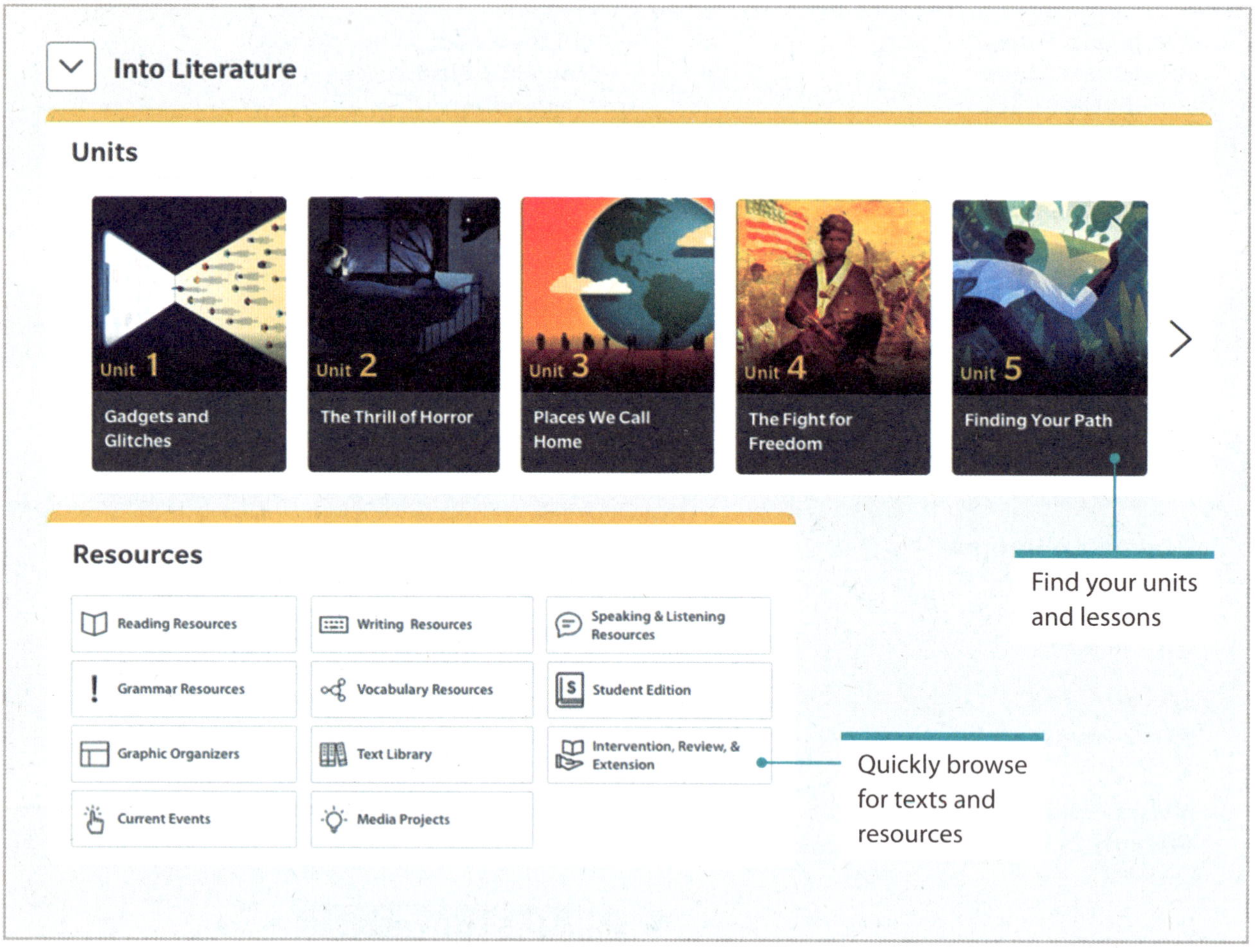

Tools for Today—All in One Place

Whether you're working alone or collaborating with others, it takes effort to analyze the complex texts and competing ideas that bombard us in this fast-paced world. What will help you succeed? Staying engaged and organized. The digital tools in this program will help you take charge of your learning.

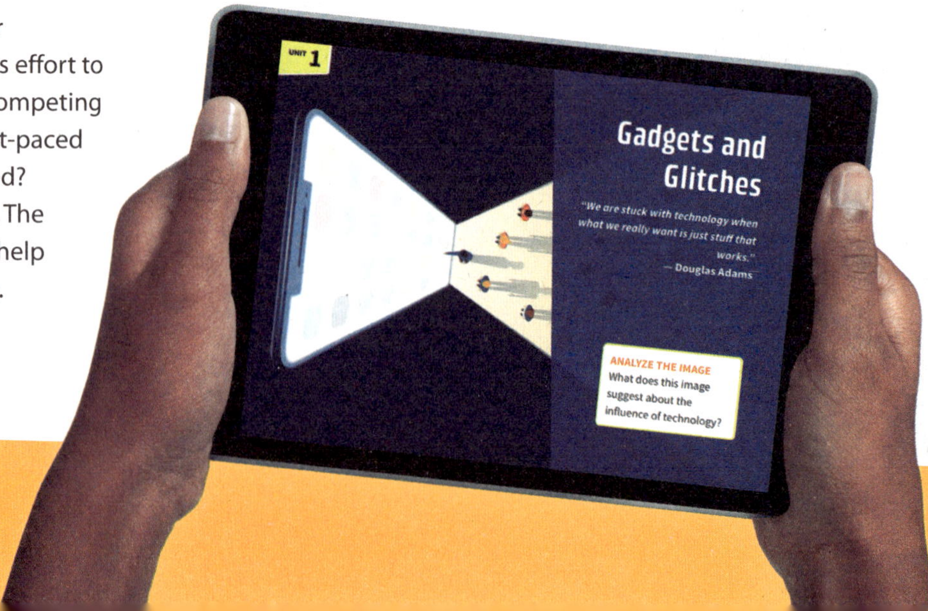

Engage!

Spark Your Learning

These activities kick-start the unit and help get you thinking about the unit theme.

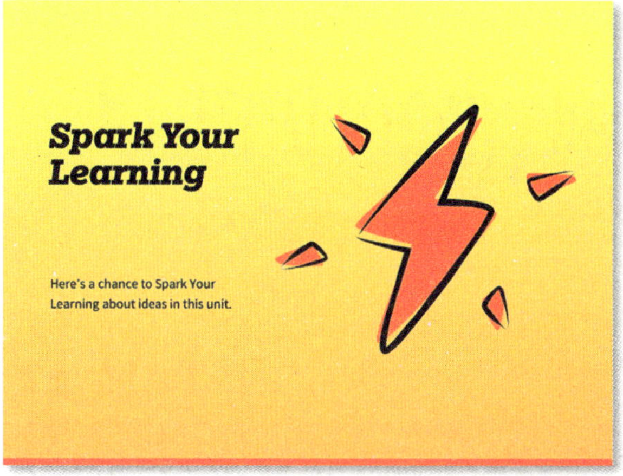

Engage Your Brain

Before you read, take some time to do a fun activity designed to rev up your brain and connect to the text.

Interact with the Texts

- As you read, highlight and take notes to mark the text in your own customized way.
- Use interactive graphic organizers to process, summarize, and track your thinking as you read.
- Play the audio to listen to the text read aloud. You can also turn on read-along highlighting.

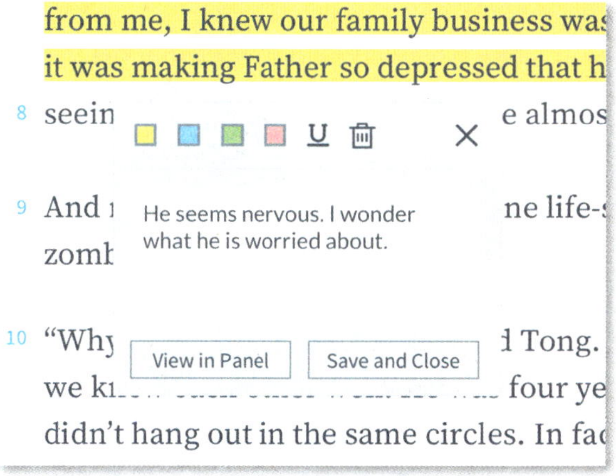

Choices

Choose from engaging activities, such as writing an advice column, creating a podcast, or participating in a debate, to demonstrate what you've learned.

Stay Involved!

Collaborate with and Learn from Your Peers

- Watch brief **Peer Coach Videos** to learn more about a particular skill.
- Flex your creative muscles by digging into **Media Projects** tied to each unit theme.
- Bring your writing online with **Writable,** where you can share your work and give and receive valuable feedback.

Writable

Read On!

Find helpful **Reader's Choice** suggestions with each unit, and access hundreds of texts online.

No Wi-Fi? No Problem!

With HMH *Into Literature,* you always have access; download when you're online and access what you need when you're offline.

Your Teacher Agrees!

AN ABSOLUTELY, POSITIVELY, MUST-READ ESSAY ABOUT READING

by two people you have never heard of

Dr. Kylene Beers

I've been a teacher all my adult life. I've worked with students at all grades, and now I spend most of my time working with teachers—maybe even your teacher! I live in Texas and when I'm not on an airplane flying off to work in a school, I'm on my ranch, plowing a field. I like to read, cook, read, garden, read, spend time with my family and friends, and (did I mention?) read!

Dr. Robert E. Probst

I've also been a teacher all my adult life. When I first started teaching, I taught kids in middle school and high school, and then I spent most of my career teaching people how to be teachers. For many years now, Dr. Beers and I have written books together—books that are about teaching kids how to be better readers. I live in Florida, and when I'm not in schools working with teachers and kids, I enjoy watching my grandkids play soccer and baseball, and I love being out on the ocean. And, like Dr. Beers, I love reading a great book too.

So, we're teachers. And we're writers. Specifically, we write books for teachers—books teachers read so that they can help their students become better readers. And we're going to try to help you become a better reader this year. We think that's important, because we both believe TWO things.

First, we've never met a kid who didn't want to get better at reading. Reading is important for almost everything you do, so doing it well is important.

Yes, true!

Second, we believe that reading opens doors. Reading something can open up your mind, your thinking, your ideas, your understanding of the world and all the people in it, so that you might choose to change yourself.

Become a Better You

Can reading really make me a better person?

Too often it's easy to forget why reading is important. You can come to believe that you need to read better just so your grades will go up, or you need to read better so that you do well on a big test. Those things are important—you bet—but they aren't as important as reading better so that you can become better.

How would that happen—how can reading help you change yourself? Sometimes it is obvious. You read something about the importance of exercise and you start walking a little more.

Or, you read something about energy and the environment and you decide to always turn off the lights when you leave any room.

Other times, it might be less obvious. You might read *Wonder* and begin to think about what it means to be a good friend. Maybe you walk over to that person sitting alone in the cafeteria and sit with him or her. Perhaps you'll read *Stella by Starlight* and that book helps you take a stand against racism. Or maybe it happens as you read *Mexican Whiteboy* and discover that who you are on the inside is more important than what anyone sees on the outside. And when you realize that, perhaps it will give you the courage you need to be truer to yourself.

Reading gives us moments to think, and as we think we just might discover something about ourselves that we want to change. And that's why we say reading can help us change ourselves.

Find Important Messages

It would be easy to find important messages in the things we read if the authors would just label them and then maybe send us a text.

But that would mean that every reader is supposed to find the same message. Not true! While the author has a message he or she wants to share, the reader—that's you!—has at least three jobs to do:

My Job

(1) **First**, enjoy what you are reading.

(2) **Second**, figure out the message the author wanted to share. This year we'll be showing you some ways to really focus in on that.

(3) **Third**, you need to decide what matters most to **YOU**. (Yes, we saved the best for last!!!) Sometimes the author's message and what matters most to you will be the same; sometimes not. For instance, it's obvious that J.K. Rowling wrote the Harry Potter series to show us all the sustaining power of love.

From Dr. Beers:
But when I read these books, what really touched my heart was the importance of standing up to our fears.

From Dr. Probst:
And what mattered most to me was the idea that one person, one small person, can make a huge difference in the world. I think that's a critically important point.

So as I read, I have to think about something called signposts?

Understanding the author's message requires you to do some work while you read—work that requires you to read the text closely. No, you don't need a magnifying glass. But you do need to learn how to notice some things in the text we call **SIGNPOSTS**.

A signpost is simply something the author says in the text that helps you understand how characters are changing, how conflicts are being resolved, and, ultimately, what theme—or lesson—the author is trying to convey.

You can also use signposts to help you figure out the author's purpose when you are reading nonfiction. If you can identify the author's purpose—why she or he wrote that particular piece of nonfiction—then you'll be better able to decide whether or not you agree, and whether you need more information.

Use the Book, Your Head, and Your Heart

We do want you thinking about signposts, but first, as you read, we want you to remember three letters: **BHH.**

BOOK	As you read, we want you to remember that you have to pay attention to **what's in the book** (or article). **Ask:** What is the writer telling me?
HEAD	You also need to think about **what's in your head** as you read. That means thinking not only about what you're reading, but also the thoughts and feelings you brought with you to the text. **Ask:** What are my responses and why?
HEART	And sometimes, maybe as you finish what you're reading, you'll ask yourself **what you have taken to heart.** **Ask:** What matters to me?

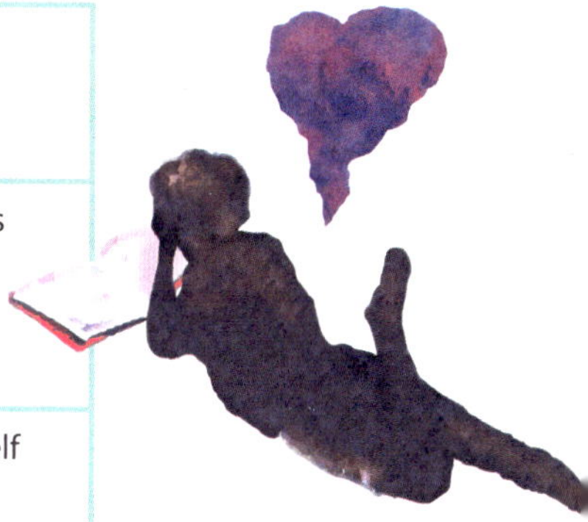

To think carefully about what's in the book and what's in your head, you need to become a reader who notices things. When a character starts acting in a way you don't expect, basically the author has put up a blinking sign that says "Pay attention here!" Or, if you are reading nonfiction, and the author starts using a lot of numbers, that's the same as the author waving a huge flag that says "Slow down! Pay attention! I'm trying to show you something!"

Pay attention here!

Some of the things you'll read this year, you might not like. (Just being honest!) But most of the things we bet you will. The important thing is to keep reading.

- Read every day.
- Read something hard. Read something easy.
- Read something that makes you laugh.
- And it's OK if sometimes what you read makes you cry.

Read joke books and how-to books and love stories and mysteries, and absolutely be sure you read about people who aren't like you. That's the best way to learn about the world—the best way to become a more open person who's ready to change and grow.

We hope you have a great year. Stay alert for signposts that you'll be learning throughout this book. And remember . . . reading is something that can help you become the person you most want to be.

TURN AND TALK

What message about reading did you take away from this essay?

*For more about the signposts, see the **Notice & Note Handbook**, pp. R7–R19.*

NOTICE & NOTE

Signposts

When you notice a signpost in your reading, mark the text with its initials.

LITERARY TEXTS

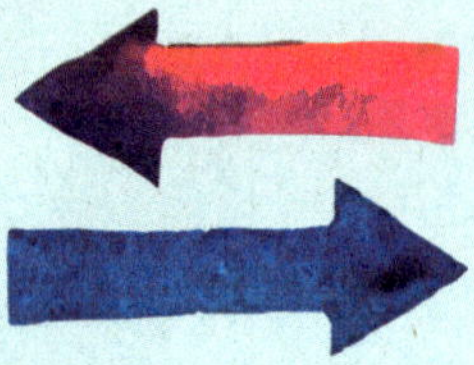

CONTRASTS AND CONTRADICTIONS — CC

A sharp contrast between what we would expect and what we observe the character doing; behavior that contradicts previous behavior or well-established patterns

When you notice this signpost, ask:

Why would the character act (feel) this way?

p. **R8**

AHA MOMENT — AM

A sudden realization of something that shifts a character's actions or understanding of self, others, or the world

When you notice this signpost, ask:

How might this change things?

p. **R9**

TOUGH QUESTIONS — TQ

Questions characters raise that reveal their inner struggles

When you notice this signpost, ask:

What does this question make me wonder about?

p. **R10**

WORDS OF THE WISER — WW

The advice or insight about life that a wiser character, who is usually older, offers to the main character

When you notice this signpost, ask:

What's the life lesson and how might this affect the character?

p. **R11**

AGAIN AND AGAIN — AA

Events, images, or particular words that recur over a portion of the story

When you notice this signpost, ask:

Why might the author bring this up again and again?

p. **R12**

MEMORY MOMENT — MM

A recollection by a character that interrupts the forward progress of the story

When you notice this signpost, ask:

Why might this memory be important?

p. **R13**

Ed Peer Coach Videos

INFORMATIONAL TEXTS

BIG QUESTIONS
BQ

It's important to take a **Questioning Stance** or attitude when you read nonfiction

- *What surprised me?*
- *What did the author think I already knew?*
- *What changed, challenged, or confirmed what I already knew?*

p. **R14**

CONTRASTS AND CONTRADICTIONS
CC

A sharp contrast between what we would expect and what we observe happening; a difference between two or more elements in the text

When you notice this signpost, ask:

What is the difference, and why does it matter?

p. **R15**

EXTREME OR ABSOLUTE LANGUAGE
XL

Language that leaves no doubt about a situation or an event, allows no compromise, or seems to exaggerate or overstate a case

When you notice this signpost, ask:

Why did the author use this language?

p. **R16**

NUMBERS AND STATS
NS

Specific quantities or comparisons to depict the amount, size, or scale; or the writer is vague when we would expect more precision

When you notice this signpost, ask:

Why did the author use these numbers or amounts?

p. **R17**

QUOTED WORDS
QW

Opinions or conclusions of someone who is an expert on the subject or someone who might be a participant in or a witness to an event; or the author might cite other people to provide support for a point

When you notice this signpost, ask:

Why was this person quoted or cited and what did this add?

p. **R18**

WORD GAPS
WG

Vocabulary that is unfamiliar to the reader—for example, a word with multiple meanings, a rare or technical word, a discipline-specific word, or one with a far-removed antecedent

When you notice this signpost, ask:

Do I know this word from someplace else? Does this seem like technical talk for experts on this topic? Can I find clues in the sentence to help me understand the word?

p. **R19**

Social & Emotional Learning

The Most Important Subject Is You!

by **Carol Jago**

You have essays to turn in. You have quizzes to take. You have group projects to complete. Your success in those areas depends on more than your understanding of the academic skills they cover. It also depends on how well you understand yourself, and how well you're able to extend that understanding to others. This might seem obvious, but there's an actual term for that type of learning—it's called **Social and Emotional Learning.**

Why It Matters

But doing well in school is not the only benefit to understanding yourself and others. When it comes to Social and Emotional Learning, the answer to the question, "When will I actually use this in my life?" is clear: every single day, forever. Whether you are with your family, your community, your friends, at a workplace, or by yourself on a deserted island, you will have a better chance of achieving satisfaction and making positive contributions if you're able to do things like the following:

- ✔ identify your emotions
- ✔ make smart choices
- ✔ set reasonable goals
- ✔ recognize your strengths
- ✔ have empathy
- ✔ manage your reactions
- ✔ evaluate problems and solutions
- ✔ show respect for others

Where Literature Comes In

English Language Arts classes can provide some of the best opportunities to develop these skills. That's because reading literature allows you to imagine yourself in different worlds and to understand what it's like to be in a wide range of situations. You can think through your own feelings and values as you read about various characters, conflicts, historical figures, and ideas, and you can become more aware of why others might act and feel as they do.

Throughout this book, you will find opportunities for Social and Emotional Learning in the Choices section of many lessons. But you don't need to wait for a special activity to practice and learn. Reading widely and discussing thoughtfully is a natural way to gain empathy and self-knowledge. The chart below shows the five main areas of Social and Emotional Learning and tells how reading can help you strengthen them.

Areas of Social and Emotional Learning	How Reading Can Help
If you have **self-awareness,** you're conscious of your own emotions, thoughts, and values, and you understand how they affect your behavior.	Understanding why characters act the way they do can increase your understanding of your own responses and motivations.
If you're good at **self-management,** you are able to control your emotions, thoughts, and behaviors in different situations.	Paying attention to why characters explode in tumultuous ways or how they keep calm under pressure can help you recognize what to do and not to do when faced with stressful situations in your own life.
If you have **social awareness,** you can empathize with others, including people who are different from you.	Reading about people with different life experiences can help you understand the perspectives of others.
If you have well-developed **relationship skills,** you can get along with different kinds of people and function well in groups.	Reflecting on the conflicts between characters can help you gain insight into what causes the conflicts in your life and how to reach mutual satisfaction.
If you are good at **responsible decision-making,** you make good choices that keep you and others safe and keep you moving toward your goals.	Evaluating the choices characters make and thinking about what you would do in their place can help you understand the consequences of your decisions.

Having the Hard Conversations

The more widely and deeply you read, the more you'll strengthen your social and emotional skills, and the more likely you are to encounter ideas that are different from your own. Some texts might bring up strong reactions from you, and you'll need to take a step back to understand how you're feeling. Or, your classmates might have responses that are dramatically different from yours, and you'll need to take a breath and decide how to engage with them. Remember: it's okay to disagree with a text or with a peer. In fact, discussing a difference of opinion can be one of the most powerful ways to learn.

Tips for Talking About Controversial Issues

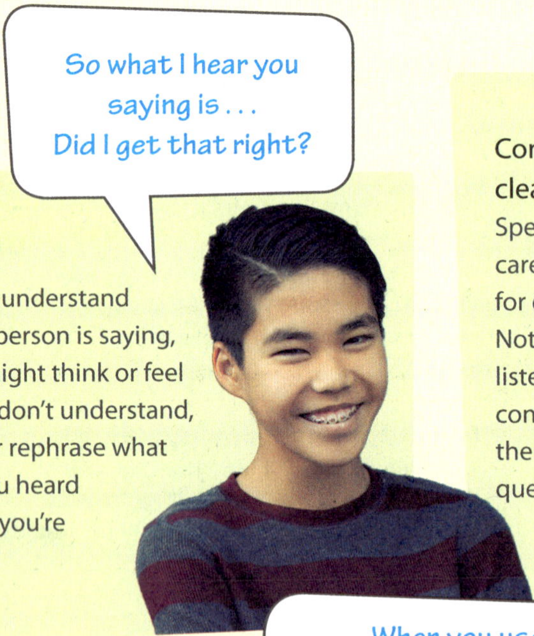

Listen actively.
Try your best to understand what the other person is saying, and why they might think or feel that way. If you don't understand, ask questions or rephrase what you thought you heard and ask them if you're getting it right.

Communicate clearly.
Speak honestly and carefully, rather than for dramatic effect. Notice if the person listening seems confused and give them room to ask questions.

Take a stand against name-calling, belittling, stereotyping, and bias.
Always try exploring ideas further rather than making personal attacks. If someone feels hurt by something you said, listen to them with an open mind. Perhaps you expressed bias without realizing it. Apologize sincerely if that happens. And if you are hurt by a comment or hear something that could be interpreted as hurtful, calmly let the person who said it know why you feel that way.

Pay attention to your feelings.
Recognize the topics or situations that make it hard for you to stay calm. Try to separate your strong feelings from what the person is saying. If you need to, excuse yourself from the conversation and find a place where you can help yourself relax.

Consider the relationship.
It's likely that the people you're in class with are people you will be seeing regularly for years. You don't have to be friends with them or agree with their point of view, but you do have to get an education alongside each other. Speaking respectfully even if you're on opposite sides of an issue will make it easier to work together if you ever have to collaborate. Try to assume the best about them rather than the worst. Acknowledge that our experiences affect our points of view.

Agree to disagree.
Even after listening carefully and being listened to, you still might not agree. That's okay. You can acknowledge your differences, remain respectful, and exit the conversation.

Learning, growing, and working with others isn't always easy. If you read widely and deeply and try your best to speak honestly, you're likely to gain the understanding and compassion that can help you manage the stresses, challenges, and opportunities that life brings your way.

UNIT
1

Ed

Get hooked by the unit topic.

Stream to Start Video

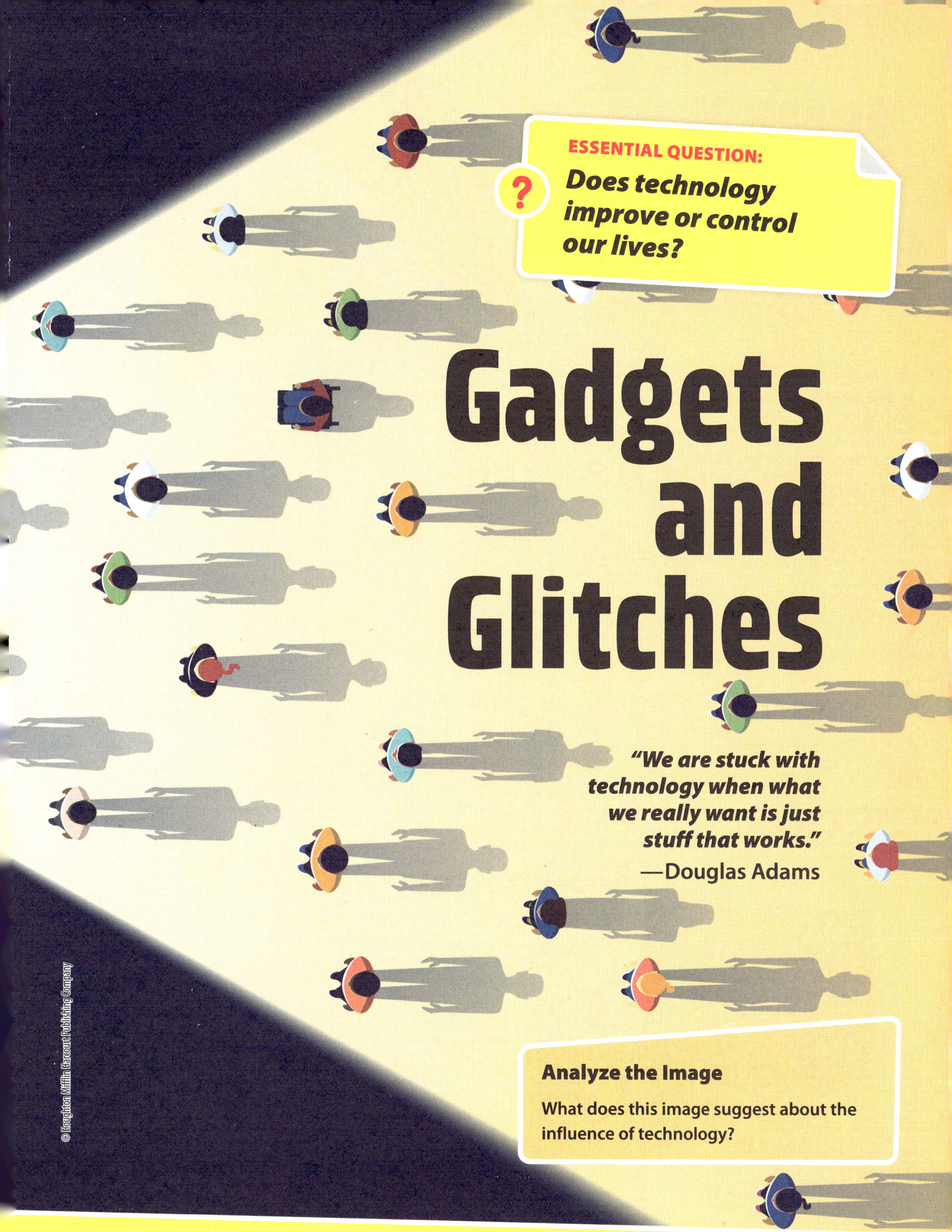

ESSENTIAL QUESTION:

Does technology improve or control our lives?

Gadgets and Glitches

"We are stuck with technology when what we really want is just stuff that works."

—Douglas Adams

Analyze the Image

What does this image suggest about the influence of technology?

Spark Your Learning

Here's a chance to spark your learning about ideas in **Unit 1: Gadgets and Glitches.**

As you read, you can use the **Response Log** (page R1) to track your thinking about the Essential Question.

Make the Connection

What is the most hi-tech thing you've encountered in the last few weeks? Make a sketch or write a few sentences to describe a technology you've used or heard about recently.

Think About the Essential Question

Does technology improve or control our lives? What do you think?

Prove It!

Turn to a partner and use one of the words in a sentence about technology and its successes and failures.

Sound Like an Expert

You can use these Academic Vocabulary words to write and talk about topics and themes in the unit. Which of these words do you already feel comfortable using when speaking or writing?

	I can use it!	I understand it.	I'll look it up.
commentary	☐	☐	☐
network	☐	☐	☐
occupation	☐	☐	☐
option	☐	☐	☐
speculate	☐	☐	☐

Preview the Texts

Look over the images, titles, and descriptions of the texts in the unit. Mark the title of the text that interests you most.

The Brave Little Toaster

Science Fiction by **Cory Doctorow**

A mysterious energy drink interferes in Mister Toussaint's networked home.

Are Bionic Superhumans on the Horizon?

Informational Text by **Ramez Naam**

What does the "bionic revolution" mean for the future of humankind?

Interflora

Poem by **Susan Hamlyn**

This poem pokes fun at how digital technology has changed the art of romance.

The Automation Paradox

Argument by **James Bessen**

This author's views on automation may be different than you expect.

Heads Up, Humans

Argument by **Claudia Alarcón**

This author sends a warning about the threat automation poses to human workers.

I Wonder . . .

Do you wish for a piece of technology that doesn't exist yet? Jot down or sketch your answer.

The Brave Little Toaster

Science Fiction by **Cory Doctorow**

ESSENTIAL QUESTION:
Does technology improve or control our lives?

Engage Your Brain

Choose one or more of these activities to start connecting with the story you're about to read.

"Smart" or Not?

The Internet of Things (IoT) is a network of devices including "smart" appliances that are connected to the Internet. In recent years, a lot of "smart" technology has hit the market—think of "smart" phones and "smart" boards used in the classroom. What are the benefits of these connected devices? Discuss your answers with the class.

Put Your Inventor's Hat On

If you could invent a new device that would help people in their kitchens or around their homes, what would it be? Use the space below to describe and/or illustrate your invention. Make sure to include details that will help explain the usefulness of the invention.

Analyze Plot

A story's **plot** is a series of events that occur in stages of development. Most plots focus on a **conflict,** or a problem faced by the main character. Most stories have five stages of plot development:

- An **exposition** that introduces the characters, setting, and conflict
- **Rising action,** in which the main character or characters try to solve the problem even while complications may be introduced
- A **climax,** or point of greatest tension, when the conflict eases
- **Falling action,** in which the effects of the climax become clear
- A **resolution,** or final outcome

To analyze a plot, examine the way events at each stage propel the story toward its climax and finally to the resolution of the conflict.

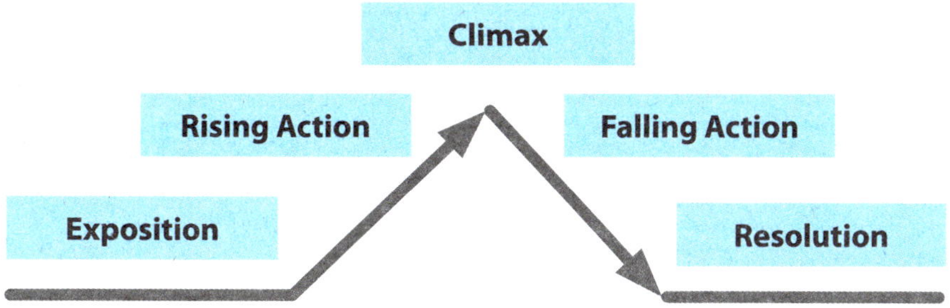

Focus on Genre

Science Fiction

- includes the basic elements of fiction—setting, characters, plot, conflict, and theme
- combines real scientific facts and theories with imaginative elements
- may comment on the present world by imagining a possible future
- may convey a message about the effects or consequences of technology

Analyze Science Fiction

In **science fiction,** writers combine scientific facts with their own ideas to create a believable **setting**—the time and place of the story's action. Science fiction writers set their stories in the future or in an alternative reality to explore the possible effects of science and technology. As characters move through the plot, several **themes,** or messages about life or human nature, are developed. Often, readers must use clues in the story to draw conclusions about a story's themes. As you read "The Brave Little Toaster," ask yourself these questions:

- What is the main conflict in the story?
- What effect does the setting have on the characters?
- What messages or lessons does the story convey about technology?

Annotation in Action

Here is an example of notes a student made about this paragraph from "The Brave Little Toaster." As you read, mark words that show elements of science fiction and make note of details that help you draw a conclusion about where and when the story takes place.

> "Why did you throw away all my food?" he demanded. The refrigerator hummed smugly at him.
> "It was spoiled," it said.
>
> *Why is the refrigerator acting smug? And why is it talking?*

Expand Your Vocabulary

Put a check mark next to the vocabulary words that you feel comfortable using when speaking or writing.

chafe	☐
retract	☐
ample	☐
reintegrate	☐

Turn to a partner and talk about the words you already know. Then, use as many words as you can in a paragraph about a home full of networked devices in the future. As you read "The Brave Little Toaster," use the definitions in the side column to learn the vocabulary words you don't already know.

Background

Cory Doctorow (b. 1971) is a journalist, a blogger, and the author of many works of science fiction. His young adult novels include *Homeland, Pirate Cinema,* and the award-winning *Little Brother,* which was also adapted for the stage. His other works include graphic novels, essays, and short stories. Doctorow was born in Toronto, Canada, and lives in Los Angeles. In addition to his other pursuits, he works for the Electronic Frontier Foundation, which aims to protect freedom in technology law and policies.

The Brave Little Toaster

Science Fiction by **Cory Doctorow**

A mysterious energy drink interferes in Mister Toussaint's networked home.

NOTICE & NOTE
As you read, use the side margins to make notes about the text.

1 One day, Mister Toussaint came home to find an extra 300 euros' worth[1] of groceries on his doorstep. So he called up Miz Rousseau, the grocer, and said, "Why have you sent me all this food? My fridge is already full of delicious things. I don't need this stuff and besides, I can't pay for it."

2 But Miz Rousseau told him that he had ordered the food. His refrigerator had sent in the list, and she had the signed order to prove it.

3 Furious, Mister Toussaint confronted his refrigerator. It was mysteriously empty, even though it had been full that morning. Or rather, it was *almost* empty: there was a single pouch of energy drink sitting on a shelf in the back. He'd gotten it from an enthusiastically smiling young woman on

[1] **euros' (yŏŏr′ōz) worth:** valued in euros, the currency of the European Union. 300 euros is about the same as $350 in American currency.

the metro[2] platform the day before. She'd been giving them to everyone.

4 "Why did you throw away all my food?" he demanded. The refrigerator hummed smugly at him.

5 "It was spoiled," it said.

6 But the food hadn't been spoiled. Mister Toussaint pored over his refrigerator's diagnostics[3] and logfiles, and soon enough, he had the answer. It was the energy beverage, of course.

7 "Row, row, row your boat," it sang. "Gently down the stream. Merrily, merrily, merrily, merrily, I'm offgassing ethylene."[4] Mister Toussaint sniffed the pouch suspiciously.

8 "No you're not," he said. The label said that the drink was called LOONY GOONY and it promised ONE TRILLION TIMES MORE POWERFUL THAN ESPRESSO!!!!!ONE11! Mister Toussaint began to suspect that the pouch was some kind of stupid Internet of Things[5] prank. He hated those.

9 He chucked the pouch in the rubbish can and put his new groceries away.

10 The next day, Mister Toussaint came home and discovered that the overflowing rubbish was still sitting in its little bag under the sink. The can had not cycled it through the trapdoor to the chute that ran to the big collection-point at ground level, 104 storeys below.

11 "Why haven't you emptied yourself?" he demanded. The trashcan told him that toxic substances had to be manually sorted. "What toxic substances?"

12 So he took out everything in the bin, one piece at a time. You've probably guessed what the trouble was.

13 "Excuse me if I'm chattery, I do not mean to nattery, but I'm a mercury battery!" LOONY GOONY's singing voice really got on Mister Toussaint's nerves.

14 "No you're not," Mister Toussaint said.

15 Mister Toussaint tried the microwave. Even the cleverest squeezy-pouch couldn't survive a good nuking. But the microwave wouldn't switch on. "I'm no drink and I'm no meal," LOONY GOONY sang. "I'm a ferrous[6] lump of steel!"

ANALYZE PLOT

Annotate: Notice what Mister Toussaint does with LOONY GOONY in paragraph 9. Mark details in paragraphs 6–8 that explain why he does this.

Infer: What conflict is Mister Toussaint facing in this story?

NOTICE & NOTE
AGAIN AND AGAIN

When you notice certain events, images, or words being repeated in a story, you've found an **Again and Again** signpost.

Notice & Note: What pattern do you notice in Mister Toussaint's actions? Mark words that show the pattern.

Analyze: Why might the author repeat this pattern of events again and again?

[2] **metro:** subway.
[3] **diagnostics** (dī´əg-nŏs´tĭks): tools a computer uses to identify problems.
[4] **offgassing ethylene** (ĕth´ə-lēn´): releasing a flammable gas, C_2H_4.
[5] **Internet of Things:** the network of devices, including "smart" appliances, that are connected to the Internet.
[6] **ferrous** (fĕr´əs): containing iron.

Don't forget to **Notice & Note** as you read the text.

16 The dishwasher wouldn't wash it ("I don't mean to annoy or **chafe,** but I'm simply not dishwasher safe!"). The toilet wouldn't flush it ("I don't belong in the bog, because down there I'm sure to clog!"). The windows wouldn't **retract** their safety screen to let it drop, but that wasn't much of a surprise.

17 "I hate you," Mister Toussaint said to LOONY GOONY, and he stuck it in his coat pocket. He'd throw it out in a trash-can on the way to work.

chafe
(chāf) *v.* To *chafe* is to annoy or bother someone.

retract
(rĭ-trăkt´) *v.* To *retract* is to pull in.

18 They arrested Mister Toussaint at the 678th Street station. They were waiting for him on the platform, and they cuffed him just as soon as he stepped off the train. The entire station had been evacuated and the police wore full biohazard containment gear. They'd even shrinkwrapped their machine-guns.

19 "You'd better wear a breather and you'd better wear a hat, I'm a vial of terrible deadly hazmat," LOONY GOONY sang.

20 When they released Mister Toussaint the next day, they made him take LOONY GOONY home with him. There were lots more people with LOONY GOONYs to process.

ANALYZE SCIENCE FICTION

Annotate: Mark details in paragraphs 18–20 that show what happens when Mister Toussaint tries to dispose of LOONY GOONY on the way to work.

Analyze: Why are the police waiting for him at the train station? What theme or themes about technology might these events suggest?

21 Mister Toussaint paid the rush-rush fee that the storage depot charged to send over his container. They forklifted it out of the giant warehouse under the desert and zipped it straight to the cargo-bay in Mister Toussaint's building. He put on old, stupid clothes and clipped some lights to his glasses and started sorting.

22 Most of the things in the container were stupid. He'd been throwing away stupid stuff all his life, because the smart stuff was just so much easier. But then his grandpa had died and they'd cleaned out his little room at the pensioner's ward[7] and

[7] **pensioner's ward:** part of a hospital that provides care for people receiving pensions, or government support for older persons.

he'd just shoved it all in the container and sent it out to the desert.

23 From time to time, he'd thought of the eight cubic meters of stupidity he'd inherited and sighed a put-upon sigh. He'd loved Grandpa, but he wished the old man had used some of the **ample** spare time from the tail end of his life to replace his junk with stuff that could more gracefully **reintegrate** with the materials stream.

24 How inconsiderate!

ample
(ăm´pəl) *adj.* To be *ample* is to be plentiful or enough.

reintegrate
(rē-ĭn´tĭ-grāt´) *v.* To *reintegrate* is to come together, as when similar materials are collected for recycling.

NOTICE & NOTE
AHA MOMENT

When you notice a sudden realization that shifts a character's actions or understandings, you've found an **Aha Moment** signpost.

Notice & Note: What words and phrases in paragraph 29 suggest that Mister Toussaint is having an Aha Moment? Mark these words and phrases.

Cause/Effect: What does Mister Toussaint suddenly realize, and how does this change things?

25 The house chattered enthusiastically at the toaster when he plugged it in, but the toaster said nothing back. It couldn't. It was stupid. Its bread-slots were crusted over with carbon residue and it dribbled crumbs from the ill-fitting tray beneath it. It had been designed and built by cavemen who hadn't ever considered the advantages of networked environments.

26 It was stupid, but it was brave. It would do anything Mister Toussaint asked it to do.

27 "It's getting hot and sticky and I'm not playing any games, you'd better get me out before I burst into flames!" LOONY GOONY sang loudly, but the toaster ignored it.

28 "I don't mean to endanger your abode, but if you don't let me out, I'm going to explode!" The smart appliances chattered nervously at one another, but the brave little toaster said nothing as Mister Toussaint depressed its lever again.

29 Just as he did, he thought to check in with the flat's diagnostics. Just in time, too! Its quorum-sensors[8] were redlining[9] as it listened in on the appliances' consternation.[10] Mister Toussaint unplugged the fridge and the microwave and the dishwasher.

30 The cooker and trash-can were hard-wired, but they didn't represent a quorum.

VOCABULARY

Context Clues: If you are unfamiliar with the word *vindictive* in paragraph 31, you can use surrounding words or other context to infer that it means "intended to hurt or take revenge on someone."

Analyze: What does the author's use of this word suggest about the firefighters?

31 The fire department took away the melted toaster and used their axes to knock huge, vindictive holes in Mister Toussaint's walls. "Just looking for embers," they claimed. But he knew that they were upset because there was simply no good excuse for sticking a pouch of independently powered computation and sensors and transmitters into an antique toaster and pushing down the lever until oily, toxic smoke filled the whole 104th floor.

8 **quorum-sensors:** devices that receive input from Mister Toussaint's smart appliances; when a certain number (a quorum) of the appliances signal distress, emergency action is taken.

9 **redlining:** reaching a limit or maximum; here, approaching the point at which the apartment would take action to stop the toaster.

10 **consternation:** a feeling of alarm or fear.

32 Mister Toussaint's neighbors weren't happy about it either.

33 But Mister Toussaint didn't mind. It had all been worth it, just to hear LOONY GOONY beg and weep for its life as its edges curled up and blackened.

34 He argued mightily, but the firefighters refused to let him keep the toaster.

ESSENTIAL QUESTION:

Does technology improve or control our lives?

Review your notes and add your thoughts to your Response Log.

TURN AND TALK

Turn to a partner and discuss the ending of "The Brave Little Toaster." What do you think the author's opinion of technology is?

Assessment Practice

Answer these questions before moving on to the **Analyze the Text** section on the following page.

1. This question has two parts. First answer **Part A**, then **Part B**.

Part A

Why does Mister Toussaint's refrigerator order more groceries?

- (A) The refrigerator takes stock and identifies missing items.
- (B) Miz Rousseau receives a grocery list from the refrigerator.
- (C) LOONY GOONY tells the refrigerator that the food is spoiled.
- (D) The appliances reach a quorum about placing an order.

Part B

Which detail best supports the correct answer?

- (A) Miz Rousseau has a signed order for the groceries.
- (B) Mister Toussaint identifies LOONY GOONY after analyzing data.
- (C) The refrigerator tells Mister Toussaint that the food was spoiled.
- (D) Mister Toussaint throws out the pouch of LOONY GOONY.

2. Why is the toaster able to destroy LOONY GOONY?

- (A) The toaster is braver than the other kitchen appliances.
- (B) The other appliances are not aware of the toaster.
- (C) The apartment's quorum-sensors approve the toaster's actions.
- (D) The toaster does not receive messages from other devices.

Ed

Test-Taking Strategies

Analyze the Text

Support your responses with evidence from the text.

NOTICE & NOTE

Review what you **noticed and noted** as you read the text. Your annotations can help you answer these questions.

1. **DRAW CONCLUSIONS** Is the story set in the past, the present, or the future? What details in the text help you draw this conclusion?

2. **ANALYZE** In paragraph 6, Mister Toussaint has an **Aha Moment** when he confirms that the energy drink caused his fridge to throw out his food. How does this realization affect the plot of the story?

3. **INTERPRET** Is LOONY GOONY an "Internet of Things prank," as Mister Toussaint suspects? Explain why.

4. **ANALYZE** Find the statement that Mister Toussaint says **Again and Again** in paragraphs 8 and 14. What is he responding to each time? How does this repetition relate to the story's main conflict?

5. **SUMMARIZE** Complete a plot diagram for "The Brave Little Toaster" by briefly summarizing the exposition, rising action, climax, falling action, and resolution of the story's plot.

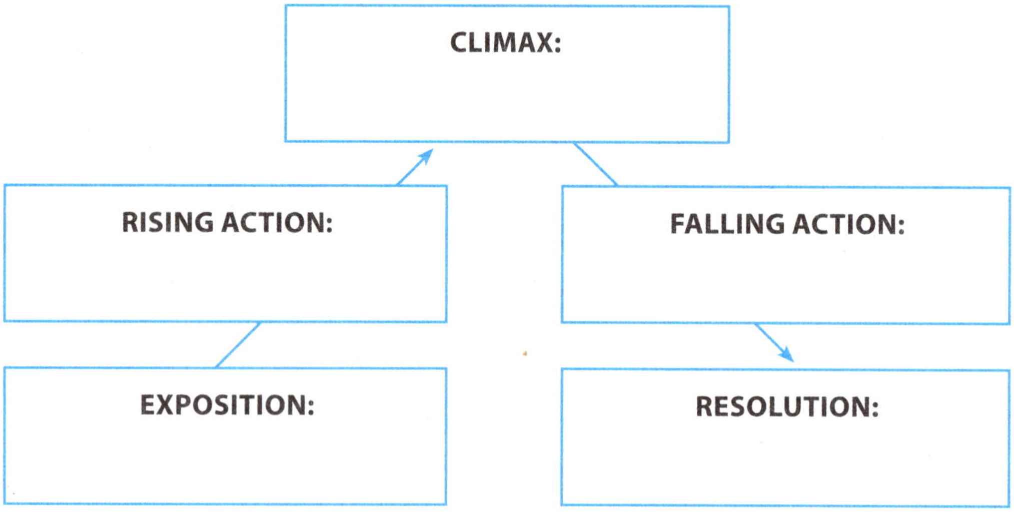

6. **SYNTHESIZE** Think about the story overall. Then, write a sentence that states its theme—its message about life or human nature.

Choices

Here are some other ways to demonstrate your understanding of the ideas in this lesson.

Writing

Summarize a Story

Write a summary of "The Brave Little Toaster." Your summary should briefly retell the most important events of the story in your own words.

- Begin by describing the story's setting and introducing the main character, Mister Toussaint.
- Next, describe the conflict Mister Toussaint faces and how he responds to it. Tell the main events of the story in the order in which they happened.
- Explain how the conflict is resolved at the end of the story.

As you write and discuss, be sure to use the **Academic Vocabulary** words.

commentary

network

occupation

option

speculate

Media

Create a Comic

With a partner or a small group, create a sequel to "The Brave Little Toaster" in the form of a comic or graphic novel. Use a combination of images and text to show what happens to Mister Toussaint after the events described in Doctorow's story.

- Decide what Mister Toussaint's conflict will be in your sequel. Does he try to find another "stupid" toaster to replace the one that melted? Does he become the victim of another prank?
- Organize the events into a plot structure that unfolds naturally. Review the plot diagram at the beginning of the lesson.
- Work together to draw the images for your comic or find images online. Use digital tools to construct your comic and to give it a polished look.

Social & Emotional Learning

Discuss with a Small Group

What could Mister Toussaint teach his neighbors about dealing with a prank like LOONY GOONY? Work with a group to create a set of helpful tips.

- As a group, review the story and note Mister Toussaint's actions in response to LOONY GOONY. Discuss which actions were effective and which were ineffective or destructive, and why.
- Brainstorm a list of tips or guidelines that would help someone overcome a similar "Internet of Things prank."
- Together, organize everyone's ideas into a set of step-by-step instructions for what a person should do if faced with something like LOONY GOONY.

Expand Your Vocabulary

PRACTICE AND APPLY

Words with similar meanings are called **synonyms. Antonyms** are words with opposite meanings. Identify each word pair below as being either synonyms or antonyms.

chafe	retract	ample	reintegrate

1. **chafe** / soothe
2. **retract** / extend
3. **ample** / plenty
4. **reintegrate** / explode

Vocabulary Strategy

Context Clues

Context clues are words, phrases, and ideas in the surrounding text that can provide hints to help you figure out the meaning of an unfamiliar word. Find the word *ferrous* in this paragraph:

> Mister Toussaint tried the microwave. Even the cleverest squeezy-pouch couldn't survive a good nuking. But the microwave wouldn't switch on. "I'm no drink and I'm no meal," LOONY GOONY sang. "I'm a ferrous lump of steel!"

Ferrous appears right before *lump,* which is a noun. This helps you determine that the word *ferrous* describes *lump*. You also know from previous paragraphs that LOONY GOONY pretends to be made of dangerous materials. Microwaving metal is dangerous, and steel contains iron; these are clues to the word's meaning, "made of iron."

Ed

Interactive Vocabulary Lesson: Using Context Clues

PRACTICE AND APPLY

Find the words *container* and *stupid* in paragraph 21. Complete the chart for both words.

WORD	POSSIBLE MEANINGS	CONTEXT CLUES	MEANING IN PARAGRAPH 21
container			
stupid			

Watch Your Language!

Participles

Ed

Interactive Grammar Lesson: Participles and Participial Phrases

A **participle** is a verb form that is used as an adjective, which modifies a noun. Writers often use participles to help create vivid descriptions.

- A present participle ends in *-ing*. A past participle can have different endings, such as *-d, -ed,* or *-en*.

Present participle: **Mister Toussaint had a surprising delivery.** *(The participle* surprising *modifies the noun* delivery.)

Past participle: **He called Miz Rousseau about the mistaken order of unwanted groceries.** *(The participle* mistaken *modifies the noun* order. *The participle* unwanted *modifies the noun* groceries.)

PRACTICE AND APPLY

Read these sentences from "The Brave Little Toaster." Identify each participle and the noun that it modifies.

1. His refrigerator had sent in the list, and she had the signed order to prove it.
2. Or rather, it was *almost* empty: there was a single pouch of energy drink sitting on a shelf in the back.
3. LOONY GOONY's singing voice really got on Mister Toussaint's nerves.
4. It had been designed and built by cavemen who hadn't ever considered the advantages of networked environments.
5. The fire department took away the melted toaster and used their axes to knock huge, vindictive holes in Mister Toussaint's walls.

Are Bionic Superhumans on the Horizon?

Informational Text by **Ramez Naam**

ESSENTIAL QUESTION:
Does technology improve or control our lives?

Engage Your Brain

Choose one or more of these activities to start connecting with the text you're about to read.

Superhuman

If you could have one bionic enhancement for your body or mind, what would it be? Robotic arms that give you superhuman strength? A microchip implanted in your brain to make you super smart? Sketch a portrait of yourself with your bionic enhancement or write a few sentences to explain how the bionic device would change you.

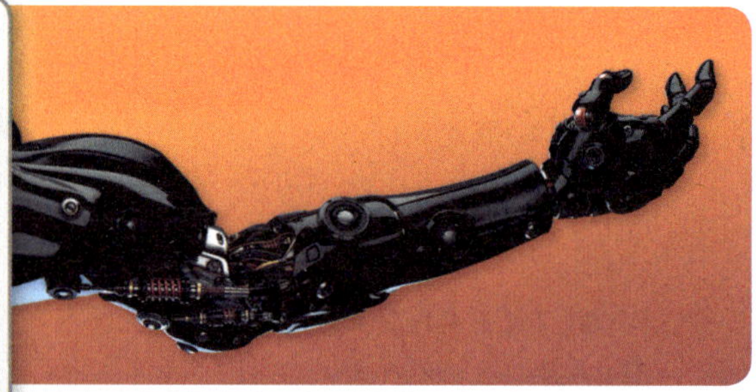

Dig In!

Do some digging online and find out more about bionics.

- What does the word *bionics* mean?
- How can bionics help people with disabilities?
- What are some of the newest applications of bionics?

Identify Central Ideas and Details

The **central ideas** of a text are the main points that the author wants to communicate to readers. You can use the following strategies to identify and understand central ideas of an informational text:

- Identify the specific topic of each paragraph or section of the text.
- Examine the **supporting details** the author uses to develop the key ideas of each section.
- Look for words that signal an organizational pattern.
- Ask yourself what idea or message the details convey about the topic.

As you read "Are Bionic Superhumans on the Horizon?," think about how the author develops his key ideas with supporting details.

Focus on Genre

Informational Text

- provides factual information
- includes evidence to support ideas
- contains text features
- appears in many forms, such as news articles and essays

Analyze Organization

Ramez Naam's article mostly uses a **main-idea-and-supporting-details** pattern of organization to connect ideas. Near the end, however, it breaks away from this pattern, filling one paragraph with questions and the next with a call to action. As you read, think about how the author uses these types of organization to convey the central ideas of the text.

TYPE OF ORGANIZATION	EXAMPLE
In **main-idea-and-supporting-details organization,** each paragraph or text section introduces a main idea and gives examples or other details about it.	We're in the midst of a bionic revolution, yet most of us don't know it. Around 220,000 people worldwide already walk around with cochlear implants. . . .
In **question-and-call-to-action organization,** the author poses questions and then tells readers what they ought to do.	. . . will only the rich have access to these enhancements? We have a little while to consider these questions, but we ought to start. . . .

Annotation in Action

Here is an example of one reader's notes on the main-idea-and-supporting-details organization used in the text. As you read, identify the central ideas of the text and examine how details are used to support these ideas.

We're in the midst of a bionic revolution, yet most of us don't know it.

Around 220,000 people worldwide already walk around with cochlear implants—devices worn around the ear that turn sound waves into electrical impulses shunted directly into the auditory nerve.

Tens of thousands of people have been implanted with deep brain stimulators, . . .

The 2nd and 3rd paragraphs give details that support the main idea stated in the 1st paragraph.

Expand Your Vocabulary

Put a check mark next to the vocabulary words that you feel comfortable using when speaking or writing.

- implant ☐
- integrity ☐
- enhancement ☐

Turn to a partner and talk about the words you already know. Then, write a few sentences about how you might create a "bionic" person. As you read "Are Bionic Superhumans on the Horizon?," use the definitions in the side column to learn the vocabulary words you don't already know.

Background

Technology can make our lives better, but it also can change them. In this article, science fiction author **Ramez Naam** shares some science facts about bionic body parts that can now change animal and human capabilities. Bionic body parts are those containing mechanical or electronic elements that improve functioning, and they may be part of your life someday.

Are Bionic Superhumans on the Horizon?

Informational Text by **Ramez Naam**

What does the "bionic revolution" mean for the future of humankind?

NOTICE & NOTE
As you read, use the side margins to make notes about the text.

1 We're in the midst of a bionic revolution, yet most of us don't know it.

2 Around 220,000 people worldwide already walk around with cochlear implants—devices worn around the ear that turn sound waves into electrical impulses shunted[1] directly into the auditory[2] nerve.

3 Tens of thousands of people have been **implanted** with deep brain stimulators, devices that send an electrode[3] tunneling several inches in the brain. Deep brain stimulators are used to control Parkinson's disease,[4] though lately they've also

implant
(ĭm-plănt´) *v.* To *implant* a device means to place it inside the body through surgery.

[1] **shunted:** allowed to flow from one pathway to another through surgery.
[2] **auditory** (ô´dĭ-tôr´ē)**:** related to hearing.
[3] **electrode** (ĭ-lĕk´trōd´)**:** a material through which electricity flows.
[4] **Parkinson's disease:** a disease that weakens muscles and causes a person's arms and legs to shake.

Ed

Text in Focus Video

Learn how to monitor comprehension.

NOTICE & NOTE

WORD GAPS

When you notice vocabulary that is unfamiliar, you've found a **Word Gaps** signpost.

Notice & Note: What words in paragraphs 6–7 are unfamiliar or confusing? Mark these words.

Infer: What clues in the text help you understand the words?

been tested—with encouraging results—in use against severe depression and obsessive compulsive disorder.

4 The most obvious bionics are those that replace limbs. Olympian "Blade Runner" Oscar Pistorius made a splash with his Cheetah carbon fiber prostheses.[5] Yet those are a relatively simple technology—a curved piece of slightly springy, super-strong material. In the digital age, we're seeing more sophisticated limbs.

5 Consider the thought-controlled bionic leg that Zac Vawter used to climb all 103 floors of Chicago's Willis Tower. Or the nerve-controlled bionic hand that Iraq war veteran Glen Lehman had attached after the loss of his original hand.

6 Or the even more sophisticated i-limb Ultra, an artificial hand with five independently articulating artificial fingers. Those limbs don't just react mechanically to pressure. They actually respond to the thoughts and intentions of their owners, flexing, extending, gripping, and releasing on mental command.

7 The age when prostheses were largely inert[6] pieces of wood, metal, and plastic is passing. Advances in microprocessors, in techniques to interface[7] digital technology with the human nervous system, and in battery technology to allow prostheses to pack more power with less weight are turning replacement limbs into active parts of the human body.

8 In some cases, they're not even part of the body at all. Consider the case of Cathy Hutchinson. In 1997, Cathy had a stroke, leaving her without control of her arms. Hutchinson volunteered for an experimental procedure that could one day help millions of people with partial or complete paralysis. She let researchers implant a small device in the part of her brain responsible for motor control. With that device, she is able to control an external robotic arm by thinking about it.

9 That, in turn, brings up an interesting question: If the arm isn't physically attached to her body, how far away could she be and still control it? The answer is at least thousands of miles. In animal studies, scientists have shown that a monkey with a brain implant can control a robot arm 7,000 miles away. The monkey's mental signals were sent over the internet, from Duke University in North Carolina, to the robot arm in Japan. In this day and age, distance is almost irrelevant.

[5] **prostheses** (prŏs-thē´sēz): artificial devices that replace injured or missing body parts.
[6] **inert** (ĭn-ûrt´): unable to move or act.
[7] **interface:** to connect or interact smoothly.

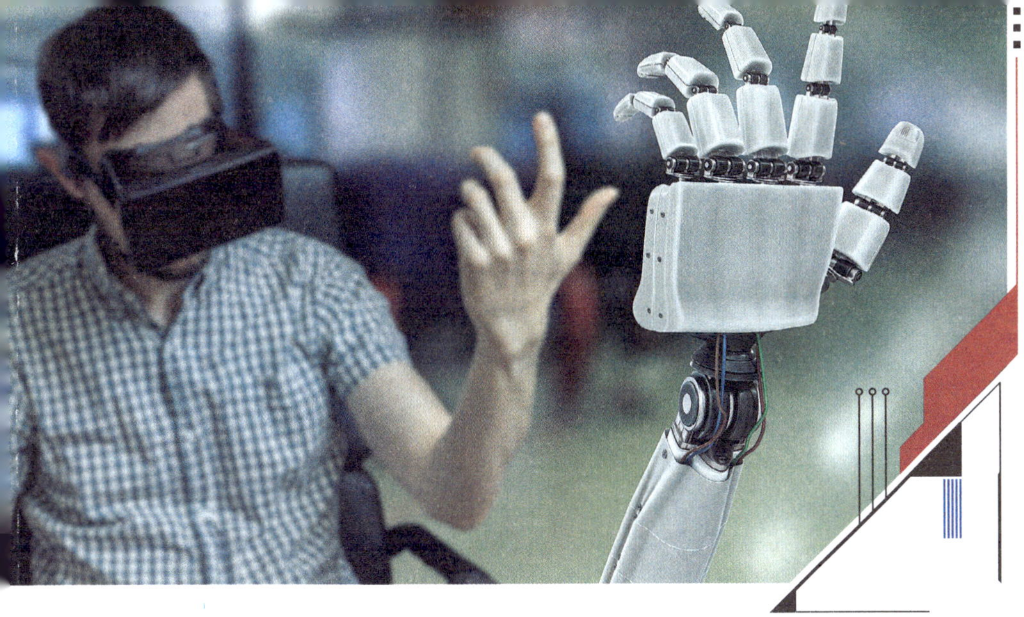

Don't forget to **Notice & Note** as you read the text.

The Superhuman Frontier

10 The 7,000-mile-away prosthetic arm makes an important point: These new prostheses aren't just going to restore missing human abilities. They're going to enhance our abilities, giving us powers we never had before, and augmenting[8] other capabilities we have. While the current generation of prostheses is still primitive, we can already see this taking shape when a monkey moves a robotic arm on the other side of the planet just by thinking about it.

11 Other research is pointing to enhancements to memory and decision making.

12 The hippocampus is a small, seahorse-shaped part of the brain that's essential in forming new memories. If it's damaged—by an injury to the head, for example—people start having difficulty forming new long-term memories. In the most extreme cases, this can lead to the complete inability to form new long-term memories, as in the film *Memento*. Working to find a way to repair this sort of brain damage, researchers in 2011 created a "hippocampus chip" that can replace damaged brain tissue. When they implanted it in rats with a damaged hippocampus, they found that not only could their chip repair damaged memory—it could improve the rats' ability to learn new things.

13 Nor is memory the end of it. Another study, in 2012, demonstrated that we can boost intelligence—at least one sort—in monkeys. Scientists at Wake Forest University implanted specialized brain chips in a set of monkeys and trained those monkeys to perform a picture-matching game. When the implant was activated, it raised their scores by an average of 10 points on a 100-point scale. The implant makes monkeys smarter.

IDENTIFY CENTRAL IDEAS AND DETAILS

Annotate: Underline the main idea in paragraph 12. Mark key details that give more information about this main idea.

Evaluate: Why do you think the author chose to state the main idea later in the paragraph, instead of in the first sentence?

[8] **augmenting** (ôg-mĕnt´ ĭng): increasing or adding to.

From Disabled to Super-capable

ANALYZE ORGANIZATION

Annotate: Underline the questions in paragraphs 14, 15, and 17, and mark the call to action.

Synthesize: How do the questions and the call to action work together to connect ideas?

14 Both of those technologies for boosting memory and intelligence are in very early stages, in small animal studies only, and years (or possibly decades) away from wide use in humans. Still, they make us wonder—what happens when it's possible to improve on the human body and mind?

15 The debate has started already, of course. Oscar Pistorius had to fight hard for inclusion in the Olympics. Many objected that his carbon fiber prostheses gave him a competitive advantage. He was able—with the help of doctors and biomedical engineers—to make a compelling case that his Cheetah blades didn't give him any advantage on the field. But how long will that be true? How long until we have prostheses (not to mention drugs and genetic therapies) that make athletes better in their sports?

16 But the issue is much, much wider than professional sports. We may care passionately about the **integrity** of the Olympics or professional cycling or so on, but they only directly affect a very small number of us. In other areas of life—in the workforce in particular—enhancement technology might affect all of us.

integrity
(ĭn-tĕg´rĭ-tē) *n. Integrity* is following a strict code of ethical conduct.

17 When it's possible to make humans smarter, sharper, and faster, how will that affect us? Will the effect be mostly positive, boosting our productivity and the rate of human innovation? Or will it be just another pressure to compete at work? Who will be able to afford these technologies? Will anyone be able to have their body, and more importantly, their brain upgraded? Or will only the rich have access to these **enhancements**?

enhancement
(ĕn-hăns´mənt) *n.* An *enhancement* improves or adds to the quality or function of something.

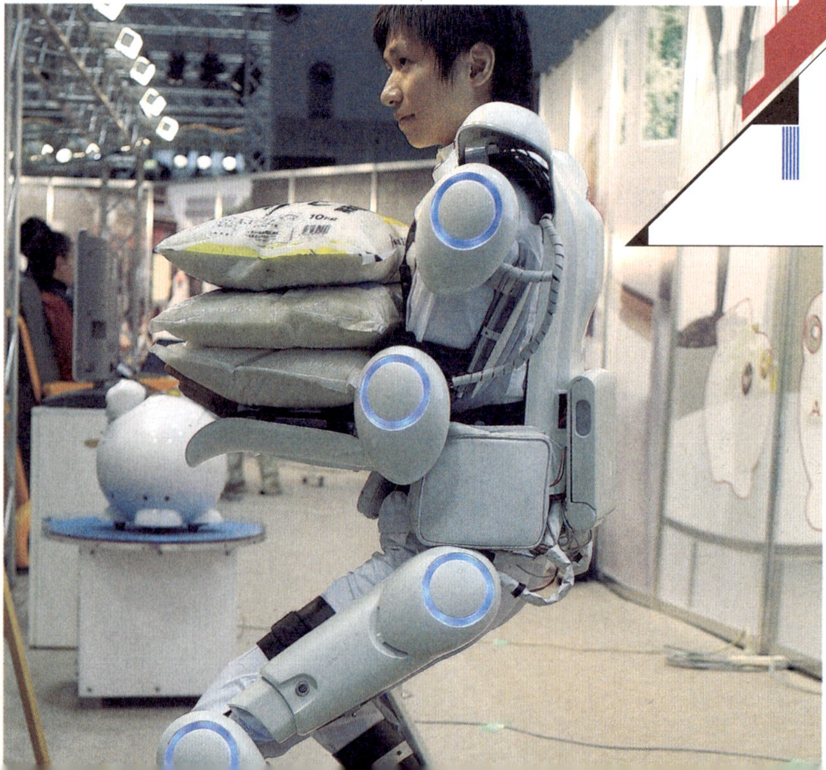

18 We have a little while to consider these questions, but we ought to start. The technology will sneak its way into our lives, starting with people with disabilities, the injured, and the ill. It'll improve their lives in ways that are unquestionably good. And then, one day, we'll wake up and realize that we're doing more than restoring lost function. We're enhancing it.

19 Superhuman technology is on the horizon. Time to start thinking about what that means for us.

?

ESSENTIAL QUESTION:

Does technology improve or control our lives?

Review your notes and add your thoughts to your Response Log.

TURN AND TALK

Get together with a partner and think about the questions the author asks in paragraph 17. How would you answer?

Assessment Practice

Answer these questions before moving on to the **Analyze the Text** section on the following page.

1. What is the main idea of paragraphs 1–9?

Ⓐ The future of bionics research is still uncertain.

Ⓑ Some bionics respond to brain signals.

Ⓒ Bionic implants have both positive and negative aspects.

Ⓓ Many medical problems are being helped through bionics.

2. Which **two** details in paragraphs 10–13 best support the idea that memory and intelligence can be enhanced?

Ⓐ the use of new memory drugs

Ⓑ the use of new training for surgeons

Ⓒ the use of a chip to repair damaged brain tissue

Ⓓ the use of additional funds to boost brain research

Ⓔ the use of a specialized brain implant

3. What is the most likely reason the writer includes a series of questions in paragraph 17?

Ⓐ to express his confusion about the issue to readers

Ⓑ to inform readers about what is certain to happen

Ⓒ to encourage readers to think deeply about the issue

Ⓓ to entertain readers with impossible fantasies

Ed

Test-Taking Strategies

Analyze the Text

Support your responses with evidence from the text.

NOTICE & NOTE

Review what you **noticed and noted** as you read the text. Your annotations can help you answer these questions.

1 **SUMMARIZE** The article is divided into three sections. Use the chart below to explain how the ideas in these sections are connected.

SECTION	HOW IDEAS ARE CONNECTED
First section	
"The Superhuman Frontier"	
"From Disabled to Super-capable"	

2 **SYNTHESIZE** What central idea does the information throughout the selection support?

3 **CITE EVIDENCE** In paragraph 4, the author states, "In the digital age, we're seeing more sophisticated limbs." What details does he provide in support of this main idea?

4 **ANALYZE** Think about the key concept expressed in the first sentence of paragraph 15. How do the remaining sentences in that paragraph develop that key concept?

5 **EVALUATE** What questions does Naam ask at the end of the article? How effective are these questions as a call to action? What does he want readers to do?

6 **INTERPRET** Now that you have read the article, how would you define the phrase *bionic revolution* (paragraph 1)? What, if any, **Word Gaps** did you fill that helped you understand the article?

Choices

Here are some other ways to demonstrate your understanding of the ideas in this lesson.

Writing
Informative Essay

Write a three-to-four paragraph essay in which you compare and contrast bionic technology that repairs damage to the human body and bionic technology that enhances the human body.

- Introduce the topic and state your central idea about the two kinds of bionic technology.
- Then, tell about the similarities and differences between the two kinds of technology, including their effects on people's lives. Use details from the text to support your ideas.
- In your final paragraph, state your conclusion about bionic technology and the different ways it can be used.

As you write and discuss, be sure to use the **Academic Vocabulary** words.

commentary

network

occupation

option

speculate

Media
Create a Graphic Aid

With a small group, create a graphic aid of some kind—such as a table, flow chart, word collage, or photo gallery—that reflects the ideas and information in the article.

- As a group, decide what kind of graphic aid you will create. Think about which kinds of images or graphics will convey ideas and information most effectively.
- Draw on details in the text and use the images included in the text as inspiration for the text and images you'll display in your graphic aid.
- Sketch out possible designs. Make sure that the images and text work together. When your group agrees on an approach, work together to create a final version.

Social & Emotional Learning
Discuss with a Small Group

Have a discussion about the best ways to distribute bionics fairly. Should people who can pay a lot of money get the best bionics first? Should people with disabilities be first in line? If so, who should pay for those bionics if they are expensive?

- As a group, set an agenda and establish clear goals for your discussion. Review the text and decide which information is relevant to the discussion topic. Use the headings to help you locate the information.
- Have group members add relevant research findings.
- Review the ideas together, listening closely and respectfully to all ideas.

Expand Your Vocabulary

PRACTICE AND APPLY

Choose the correct answer to each question.

implant	integrity	enhancement

1. Which of these would a doctor **implant** through surgery?

   a. an artificial leg **b.** a computer chip in a brain

2. Which of the following is an example of **integrity**?

   a. cheating on a test that you forgot to study for **b.** being honest when nobody is watching

3. Which of the following could be called an **enhancement**?

   a. an old, persistent problem **b.** a new, better feature

Vocabulary Strategy

Synonyms and Antonyms

A **synonym** is a word with a meaning similar to that of another word. An **antonym** has a meaning opposite that of another word. In paragraph 7, *inert* artificial limbs are contrasted with *active* ones, so you can infer that *inert* and *active* are antonyms. If you know the meaning of *active*, you can infer that *inert* means "not able to move."

Ed

Interactive Vocabulary Lesson: Synonyms and Antonyms

PRACTICE AND APPLY

Each sentence includes a pair of words in boldface type. Use context clues to figure out what the words mean and whether they are synonyms or antonyms. Then, in your own words, write the definition of the word indicated below the sentence.

1. Does the prosthetic hand have five **articulating** fingers, or are the fingers part of one **immobile** piece of plastic?

   articulating: ______________________________

2. Soon after researchers **implanted** the device, it malfunctioned, and they quickly **extracted** it.

   extracted: ______________________________

3. "That information is **irrelevant,** so let's get rid of it," Brad said, but I insisted that it was **essential** to keep it in the report.

   irrelevant: ______________________________

Watch Your Language!

Commonly Confused Words

English contains so many words that sound alike but are spelled differently that it's easy to get them confused. Ramez Naam's article includes some commonly confused words.

Interactive Vocabulary Lesson: Commonly Confused Words

- *It's* (meaning "it is") and *its* (meaning "belonging to it")

  What happens when it's possible to improve on the human body and mind?

  Technology will sneak its way into our lives.

- *Affect* (meaning "to influence") and *effect* (meaning "result")

  When it's possible to make humans smarter, sharper, and faster, how will that affect us? Will the effect be mostly positive?

Here are two other examples.

- *There* (meaning "in that place"), *their* (meaning "belonging to them"), and *they're* (meaning "they are")

  The scientists gave their lecture over there, near the college. They're answering questions now.

- *To* (meaning "toward"), *two* (meaning "a whole number that is more than one and less than three"), and *too* (meaning "also")

  We're going to the lab to see two or three new prosthetics. You can come, too.

PRACTICE AND APPLY

Write your own sentences with commonly misspelled words using the examples above as models. Your sentences might express your opinions about how bionics will affect people. Share your completed sentences with a partner and compare how each of you used the words.

Interflora

Poem by **Susan Hamlyn**

ESSENTIAL QUESTION:
Does technology improve or control our lives?

Engage Your Brain

Choose one or both of these activities to start connecting with the poem you are about to read.

To Email or Not to Email

In the poem you are about to read, one person communicates with another through email. Freewrite for a few minutes about when email is the right way to communicate, and when it might not be.

Dig Deeper!

Elizabeth Barrett Browning was one of the most famous poets of her day. "Interflora" is a modern-day riff on one of her most popular poems, "Sonnet 43", which she wrote to her husband Robert Browning, himself a poet. She wrote this poem before her marriage but did not show it to her husband until two years later. Do some research on the Brownings to answer the questions below.

- Why did she call her most famous collection of poems *Sonnets from the Portuguese?*
- What kind of illness did Elizabeth Barrett Browning have?
- What did Elizabeth Barrett Browning's father think of her marriage to Robert Browning?

Analyze Structure

"Interflora" is a **sonnet,** a 14-line poem with a strictly defined structure and pattern of rhyme. A sonnet often consists of three quatrains, or four-line units, and a final couplet. A sonnet also has a **rhyme scheme,** or pattern of end rhymes.

A rhyme scheme is noted by assigning a letter of the alphabet, beginning with *a,* to each line. Lines that rhyme are given the same letter. Most sonnets follow one of several traditional patterns of line grouping and rhyme scheme.

Sonnets also traditionally have a certain **meter,** or pattern of stressed and unstressed syllables. Each unit of meter, known as a foot, consists of one stressed syllable and one or two unstressed syllables. Sonnets are written in **iambic pentameter,** with five feet in each line. Each foot has one unstressed syllable (˘) followed by a stressed syllable (´).

Here are the first four lines of Elizabeth Barrett Browning's famous "Sonnet 43." Notice how the rhyme scheme has been marked *(a, b, b, a)*. Notice, too, how the meter of the first line has been marked. Mark the next three lines.

How do I love thee? Let me count the ways. a

I love thee to the depth and breadth and height b

My soul can reach, when feeling out of sight b

For the ends of Being and ideal Grace. a

As you read "Interflora," analyze the pattern of meter, the rhyme scheme, and any other structural elements you notice.

Focus on Genre
Sonnet

- is a form of lyric poetry that expresses personal thoughts and feelings and has a musical quality
- contains 14 lines
- follows a strict rhyme scheme, or pattern of end rhymes, such as *abbaabba cdcdcd* or *abab cdcd efef gg*
- is a popular form for love poems

Analyze Irony

Irony is a literary device used to show contrast between appearance and reality. Sometimes writers create irony by drawing attention to differences between the perspectives of the reader and a character in a story or the speaker of a poem. Irony is often used as a way to create humor. There are three types of irony frequently used in literature:

- **Situational irony** occurs when there is a contrast between what the reader expects and what actually happens.
- **Dramatic irony** occurs when the reader knows something that a character does not know.
- **Verbal irony** occurs when a character says one thing (sometimes by using a figure of speech or pun) but means something else.

As you read "Interflora," look for examples of irony that create humor.

Annotation in Action

Here are some comments one reader made on the irony in "Interflora." As you read, note how the poet uses irony to convey a message or to create humor.

From Robert B. @ mailexcite dot com
To E.B.B. @ virgin dot uk:
Please find herewith as proof of my esteem
a customized, fresh, virtual bouquet.

The sonnet is written like an email message, but line 3 uses old-fashioned language. Is this an example of irony?

Background

"Interflora" is a sonnet written as an email. The poem begins with the email addresses of the speaker and the person to whom he is sending a message. Readers familiar with the love sonnets that Elizabeth Barrett Browning wrote to her husband, Robert Browning, may recognize a certain humorous or ironic connection between this sonnet and those works. **Susan Hamlyn** is a London-based English teacher and writer. Hamlyn has published two collections of poetry, *The Only Thing Untouched* and *Quiet Myth*.

Interflora

Poem by **Susan Hamlyn**

This poem pokes fun at how digital technology has changed the art of romance.

NOTICE & NOTE
As you read, use the side margins to make notes about the text.

Elizabeth Barrett Browning

Robert Browning

ANALYZE STRUCTURE

Annotate: Use the symbols ˘ and ′ to mark the meter of the sonnet. Use letters of the alphabet to identify and mark the rhyme scheme.

Analyze: Does "Interflora" follow a traditional sonnet rhyme scheme? Explain.

ANALYZE IRONY

Annotate: Mark examples of humor in the sonnet.

Analyze: Explain how the poet uses irony to create humor.

ESSENTIAL QUESTION:

Does technology improve or control our lives?

Review your notes and add your thoughts to your Response Log.

Interflora

From Robert B. @ mailexcite dot com
To E.B.B. @ virgin dot uk:
Please find herewith as proof of my esteem
a customized, fresh, virtual bouquet.
For scent please click on cellophane and press
Control. To read the message on the tag
highlight the print, click on *Encrypt Reverse.*
To unwrap blooms and place in vase use *Drag.*
My flowers sent, beloved, in this way,
won't fade, stink of mortality's decay.
Petals won't wilt to husks nor leaves to slime;
these on-line flowers for you will outlast Time.
But if, my love, this gift seems incomplete
and does not touch your heart, then press *Delete.*

TURN AND TALK

Did you find this poem funny? Why or why not? Discuss with a partner.

Assessment Practice

Answer these questions before moving on to the **Analyze the Text** section on the following page.

1. This question has two parts. First answer **Part A**, then **Part B**.

Part A

Which statement best explains how the structure of "Interflora" contributes to the meaning of the poem?

- (A) The meter and rhyme scheme of the sonnet form emphasize the romantic theme of the poem.
- (B) The poem's format as an email message contrasts with the serious topic of love.
- (C) The poem's setup as a list of instructions emphasizes the theme of frustration with technology.
- (D) The traditional sonnet form contrasts with the modern subject matter of the poem.

Part B

Which line from the poem best supports the correct answer to Part A?

- (A) "From Robert B. @ mailexcite dot com" (line 1)
- (B) "To unwrap blooms and place in vase use *Drag*." (line 8)
- (C) "My flowers sent, beloved, in this way," (line 9)
- (D) "But if, my love, this gift seems incomplete" (line 13)

2. According to the speaker, in what way are the on-line flowers better than real ones?

- (A) They are customized.
- (B) They come with a message.
- (C) They will last forever.
- (D) They can easily be deleted.

Ed

Test-Taking Strategies

Analyze the Text

Support your responses with evidence from the text.

NOTICE & NOTE

Review what you **noticed and noted** as you read the text. Your annotations can help you answer these questions.

1 **CITE EVIDENCE** Which words and phrases in the poem reveal that it is a love sonnet?

2 **ANALYZE** How is verbal irony used in the sonnet? Give an example.

3 **COMPARE** Use the chart below to compare and contrast the structure of "Interflora" and Elizabeth Barrett Browning's "Sonnet 43." You can find "Sonnet 43" online or at a library. Determine whether the sonnets are written in iambic pentameter or if they vary from regular meter. Determine whether the poems follow the same rhyme scheme. Consider how these structural elements affect your understanding of each sonnet's meaning and style.

POEM	METER	RHYME SCHEME	EFFECTS ON MEANING AND STYLE
Interflora			
Sonnet 43			

4 **CRITIQUE** Review lines 13–14. How do possible differences in the perspectives of the sender and the recipient create humor?

5 **CONNECT** "Interflora" was published in 1994. Since then, much has changed about the way people use the Internet in their daily lives. How might the people in the poem communicate with each other today? What might Robert B. send to E.B.B. today?

6 **INFER** What theme or message about technology does the poet's use of irony suggest?

Choices

Here are some other ways to demonstrate your understanding of the ideas in this lesson.

Writing
Sonnet

Write a poem in the structure of a sonnet. Review the information from the Get Ready section regarding common rhyme schemes and metrical patterns used in sonnets.

- Decide on a topic and theme for your sonnet. Brainstorm some rhyming word pairs related to your topic.
- Consider how to include irony and humor in your sonnet.
- Write a draft of your sonnet in 14 lines. You might use a rhymed couplet at the end to reveal your theme.
- Revise your poem to match the traditional meter of a sonnet and to have a consistent rhyme scheme.

As you write and discuss, be sure to use the **Academic Vocabulary** words.

- **commentary**
- **network**
- **occupation**
- **option**
- **speculate**

Media
Design a Virtual Bouquet

Using digital tools and your imagination, create a virtual bouquet based on the one described in "Interflora." Your virtual bouquet should combine visual and textual elements. Think about the kinds of buttons or mouse clicks the recipient would use to unwrap, view, or smell the virtual flowers, and include instructions that explain how to enjoy the virtual flowers. Use Hamlyn's poem as a model and play with the words found on computer keys, such as *Control* and *Delete*, to create humor in the instructions you provide.

Speaking & Listening
Present a Sonnet

Prepare a sonnet for an oral reading. Find a sonnet online that you would like to present. When you and your classmates read your sonnets aloud, provide thoughtful feedback to each other.

- Practice reading your sonnet. Experiment with stressing different syllables to bring out the musical quality in the text.
- Practice making eye contact with your audience, and use facial expressions and natural gestures to convey the meaning of the sonnet.
- Finally, read your sonnet aloud to the class.

Collaborate & Compare

ESSENTIAL QUESTION:
Does technology improve or control our lives?

Compare Arguments

You are about to read two arguments concerning the impact of technology on jobs. As you read, notice how the claim in each argument is supported by reasons and evidence. Then think about how the arguments relate to each other.

MENTOR TEXT

A

The Automation Paradox

Argument by **James Bessen**
pages 40–45

MENTOR TEXT

B

Heads Up, Humans

Argument by **Claudia Alarcón**
pages 53–57

After you have read both texts, you'll take a stand on the issue. You will collaborate with a group in a class debate, following these steps:

- Choose a Side
- Gather Information
- Prepare a Counterclaim
- Conduct the Debate

The Automation Paradox

Argument by **James Bessen**

Engage Your Brain

Choose one or two activities to start connecting with the selection you are about to read.

List It

Early elevators required human operators to help passengers ride safely and efficiently. What other once-human jobs are now done by technology? List as many as you can below. Then share your list with the class.

Make a Prediction

A *paradox* is a contradictory statement, situation, or idea. If *automation* is the use of automatic equipment in a production process, what might an "automation paradox" be? Discuss with a partner and then write your answer on the lines below.

Analyze Claim and Evidence

In an argument, a **claim** is the writer's position, or viewpoint, on an issue. A claim usually appears early in an argument, following a few sentences or a paragraph or two that introduce the issue involved.

A strong argument clearly and logically lays out a claim and develops it by using sound reasons that support the claim plus relevant **evidence** that supports those reasons—facts, statistics, quotations, examples, and expert opinions.

As you read "The Automation Paradox," use a chart like this one to analyze the argument.

Focus on Genre

Argument

- states a claim and reasons to support the claim
- includes facts and other evidence to support reasons
- may note objections to claim and explain why they should be rejected
- takes many forms, such as editorials, feature articles, and essays

Analyze Graphic Features

A **graphic feature** is a design element such as a diagram, bar graph, or pie chart that visually represents information. As you read "The Automation Paradox," use the following questions to analyze and evaluate each graphic feature:

- What information or evidence does the feature provide? What is the author's purpose, or reason, for including this feature?
- What are the advantages of using the graphic to present ideas? How well does it help you to understand the author's argument?

Annotation in Action

Here are one reader's notes on the author's claim. As you read, note how the author presents his claim, reasons, and evidence.

> But these fears are misplaced—what's happening with automation is not so simple or obvious. It turns out that workers will have greater employment opportunities if their occupation undergoes some degree of computer automation. As long as they can learn to use the new tools, automation will be their friend.

The author seems to be taking a position here. Could this be his claim?

Expand Your Vocabulary

Put a check mark next to the vocabulary words that you feel comfortable using when speaking or writing.

redistribute	☐
robustly	☐
expansive	☐
predominantly	☐
collaborate	☐

Turn to a partner and talk about the words you already know. Then, write a few sentences about what you know about automation in today's world.

As you read "The Automation Paradox," use the definitions in the side column to learn the vocabulary words you don't already know.

Background

James Bessen (b. 1958) is an economist and lecturer at Boston University whose interest in the impact of technology on innovation and jobs has paralleled the rise of personal computers in the workplace as well as the ongoing push to automate tasks with computer technology. His book *Learning by Doing: The Real Connection Between Innovation, Wages, and Wealth* looks at history to understand how new technologies affect wages and skills over the long term.

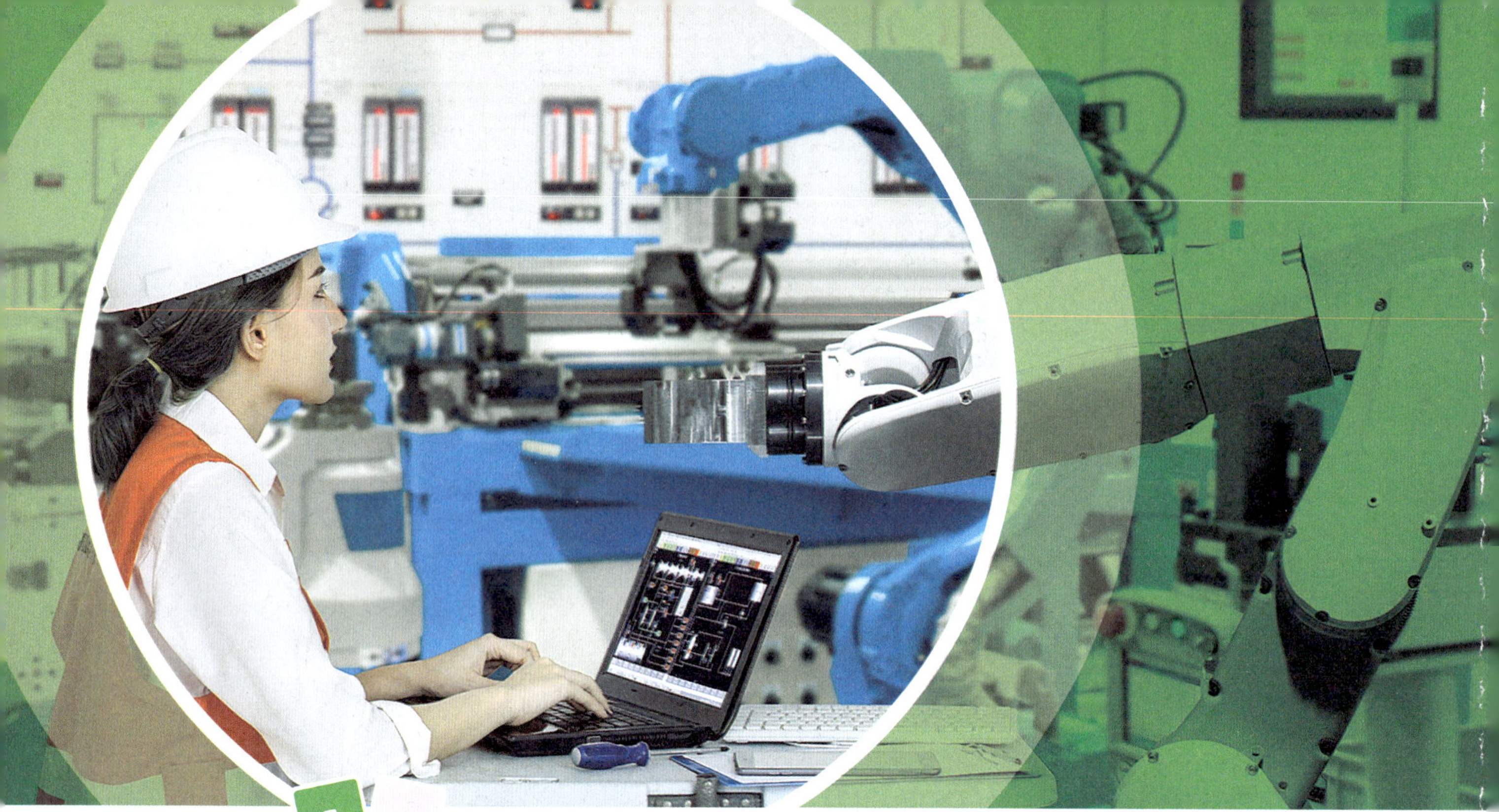

A

The Automation Paradox

Argument by **James Bessen**

This author's views on automation may be different than you expect.

NOTICE & NOTE
As you read, use the side margins to make notes about the text.

1 Automation[1] isn't just for blue-collar[2] workers anymore. Computers are now taking over tasks performed by professional workers, raising fears of massive unemployment. Some people, such as the MIT professors Erik Brynjolfsson and Andrew McAfee, identify automation as a cause of the slow recovery from the Great Recession[3] and the "hollowing out of the middle class." Others see white-collar[4] automation as causing a level of persistent technological unemployment that demands policies that would **redistribute** wealth. Robot panic is in full swing.

redistribute
(rē´dĭ-strĭb´yoot) *v.* To *redistribute* means to distribute again but differently.

[1] **automation:** the automatic operation of equipment, a process, or a system.
[2] **blue-collar:** relating to workers whose jobs are performed in work clothes and often involve manual labor.
[3] **Great Recession:** a period of economic decline from December 2007 to June 2009.
[4] **white-collar:** relating to workers whose work does not involve manual labor and who are often expected to dress with a degree of formality.

2 But these fears are misplaced—what's happening with automation is not so simple or obvious. It turns out that workers will have greater employment opportunities if their occupation undergoes some degree of computer automation. As long as they can learn to use the new tools, automation will be their friend.

3 Take the legal industry as an example. Computers are taking over some of the work of lawyers and paralegals, and they're doing a better job of it. For over a decade, computers have been used to sort through corporate documents to find those that are relevant to lawsuits. This process—called "discovery" in the profession—can run up millions of dollars in legal bills, but electronic methods can erase the vast majority of those costs. Moreover, the computers are often more accurate than humans: In one study, software correctly found 95 percent of the relevant documents, while humans identified only 51 percent.

4 But, perhaps surprisingly, electronic discovery software has not thrown paralegals and lawyers into unemployment lines. In fact, employment for paralegals and lawyers has grown **robustly**. While electronic discovery software has become a billion-dollar business since the late 1990s, jobs for paralegals and legal-support workers actually grew faster than the labor force as a whole, adding over 50,000 jobs since 2000, according to data from the U.S. Census Bureau. The number of lawyers increased by a quarter of a million.

5 Something similar happened when ATMs automated the tasks of bank tellers and when barcode scanners automated the work of cashiers: Rather than contributing to unemployment, the number of workers in these occupations grew. These are not special exceptions. On average, since 1980, occupations with above-average computer use have grown substantially faster (0.9 percent per year), as shown in this chart:

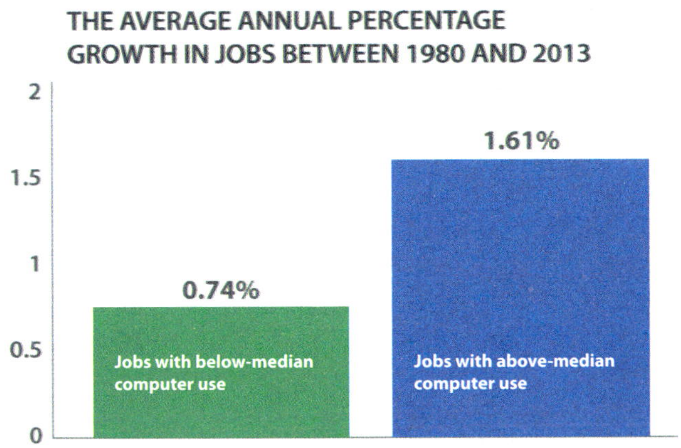

Don't forget to **Notice & Note** as you read the text.

ANALYZE CLAIM AND EVIDENCE

Annotate: In paragraph 2, mark the statement that best expresses the author's claim.

Analyze: Why is the writer's claim about automation a paradox?

robustly
(rō-bŭst´lē) *adv. Robustly* means in a strong, healthy way.

6 How can this be? It might seem a sure thing that automating a task would reduce employment in an occupation. But that logic ignores some basic economics: Automation reduces the cost of a product or service, and lower prices tend to attract more customers. Software made it cheaper and faster to trawl through legal documents, so law firms searched more documents and judges allowed more and more **expansive** discovery requests. Likewise, ATMs made it cheaper to operate bank branches, so banks dramatically increased their number of offices. So when demand increases enough in response to lower prices, employment goes up with automation, not down. And this is what has been happening with computer automation overall during the last three decades. It's also what happened during the Industrial Revolution when automation in textiles, steelmaking, and a whole range of other industries led to a major increase in manufacturing jobs.

7 But not all of the news about computer automation is good. Some of that growth in computer-using occupations has come at the expense of other occupations. As depicted in the chart below, desktop publishing systems have meant fewer jobs for typographers,[5] as graphic designers took over their work. Computerized phone lines meant fewer jobs for telephone operators, but more jobs for receptionists. These aren't examples of computers "stealing" jobs; they are cases where computers helped some workers take work from others. Workers with computers frequently substitute for workers in non-computerized jobs.

expansive
(ĭk-spăn´sĭv) *adj.* *Expansive* means broad in size, range, or degree of openness.

Ed
Close Read Screencast
Listen to a modeled close read of this text.

ANALYZE GRAPHIC FEATURES

Annotate: Mark the sentence in paragraph 7 that connects to the information in the graph.

Analyze: How does this graphic feature work with the text to emphasize a key point about computer automation?

[5] **typographers:** people who set words into type.

NUMBER OF GRAPHIC DESIGN JOBS VS. TYPOGRAPHER JOBS, IN HUNDREDS OF THOUSANDS

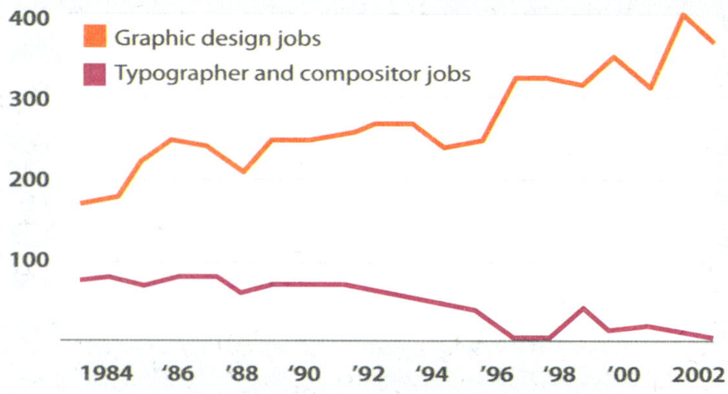

Don't forget to **Notice & Note** as you read the text.

8 So, while computers create jobs in some occupations, they also reduce employment in others. The total effect on unemployment depends on which tendency is stronger. Some of my research shows that the net effect, across the economy, is a wash: Computers create about as many jobs as they eliminate. In other words, automation is not causing persistent unemployment.

9 That could change decades into the future, as new generations of software powered by artificial intelligence becomes ever more capable of advanced tasks. But in the near term, the story is much different. A new study by McKinsey & Company took a detailed look at work tasks that are likely to be automated and found that only about 5 percent of jobs are at risk of being completely automated in the near future. The main effect of automation for the time being will not be to eliminate jobs, but to redefine them—changing the tasks and the skills needed to perform them.

10 Even so, this means that automation poses a major challenge. There will be jobs, but workers will only be able to get them if they have the new sets of skills that computers make important. It's not just computer skills that are in demand, because automation can change the nature of jobs. For example, bank tellers have become more like marketing specialists, telling customers about bank loans, CDs, and other financial offerings.

NOTICE & NOTE

NUMBER AND STATS

When you notice the use of specific quantities or comparisons to show amounts, size, or scale, you've found a **Numbers and Stats** signpost.

Notice & Note: How do the results of the McKinsey & Company study in paragraph 9 relate to the writer's argument? Mark these results in the text.

Evaluate: Do these numbers help prove a point?

predominantly
(prĭ-dŏm´ə-nənt-lē) *adj.* *Predominantly* refers to the most important, obvious, or typical aspect(s) of something.

collaborate
(kə-lăb´ə-rāt´) *v.* To *collaborate* means to work together.

ESSENTIAL QUESTION:
Does technology improve or control our lives?

Review your notes and add your thoughts to your Response Log.

11 Learning new skills is a significant social challenge as well. My research suggests that the jobs that get transferred to other occupations tend to be **predominantly** low-pay, low-skill jobs, so the burdens of automation fall most heavily on those least able and least equipped to deal with it. And often the new skills need to be learned on the job, so experience matters. To meet this challenge, some community colleges are **collaborating** with local employers to create work-study programs that allow trainees to learn on the job as well as in the classroom. Some trade groups are promoting skill-certification programs, which allow employers to recognize skills acquired through experience. These are the kinds of policies that can help overcome the real burden of automation. They deserve more attention than any panic about a supposed robot apocalypse.

TURN AND TALK

Has this writer convinced you that automation should not cause a panic? Discuss your thoughts with a partner.

Assessment Practice

Answer these questions before moving on to the **Analyze the Text** section on the following page.

1. According to the author's argument, which word best describes the impact of automation on future employment?

- (A) insignificant
- (B) transformative
- (C) limited
- (D) devastating

2. This question has two parts. First, answer **Part A**. Then, answer **Part B**.

Part A

What topic does the author discuss in paragraphs 3–4?

- (A) the difference between the work of lawyers and paralegals
- (B) why new training requirements for lawyers and paralegals are necessary
- (C) how automation has affected one aspect of the legal profession
- (D) the minor impact automation has had on the legal profession

Part B

Select **two** ways that best explain how the author develops the topic from Part A.

- (A) He explains how legal firms started using computers.
- (B) He gives statistics about the accuracy of automation compared to lawyers and paralegals.
- (C) He includes the results of a study that suggests that the entire labor force grew as automation was introduced.
- (D) He argues that "discovery" is an ineffective legal technique.
- (E) He explains why automation makes the "discovery" process less expensive and more efficient.

Ed

Test-Taking Strategies

Analyze the Text

Support your responses with evidence from the text.

NOTICE & NOTE

Review what you **noticed and noted** as you read the text. Your annotations can help you answer these questions.

1. **CITE EVIDENCE** In paragraph 1, what evidence does the author provide in support of the idea that many workers do not welcome computer automation?

2. **ANALYZE** Complete an analysis of the author's argument in paragraph 6 by reviewing your notes and filling in the chart below.

Claim:

Automation will not cause people to lose their jobs.

Reason:

Evidence:

Evidence:

3. **ANALYZE** In paragraph 7, how does the author respond to the viewpoint that computers "steal" jobs from workers?

4. **EVALUATE** Study the bar graph on page 41. How well does the information in the graph support the author's claim?

5. **CRITIQUE** Consider the author's use of **Numbers and Stats** both in the text and in the graphs. Is this evidence relevant and sufficient? Explain.

Choices

Here are some other ways to demonstrate your understanding of the ideas in this lesson.

As you write and discuss, be sure to use the **Academic Vocabulary** words.

commentary	option
network	speculate
occupation	

Writing
Argue It

Based on the argument you just read, write a short persuasive essay in which you support a claim of your own about the effects of increased automation on employment.

- Introduce the topic and state your claim about the impact of automation on future jobs.
- Give at least two reasons to support your claim. Acknowledge and respond to opposing claims about automation. Cite evidence from the text and your research to support your argument.
- In your final paragraph, restate your claim. Conclude with a piece of advice or a call to action.

Media
Sketchnote

One way to clarify your understanding of a text is to sketchnote it. Start with a central idea and write that in the center of a piece of paper or in a new file. Then, sketch or write other details that support this central idea.

Social & Emotional Learning
Prepare for the Future

Have a discussion about ways in which future workers might prepare for changes caused by increased automation. Make sure each group member gets equal time to speak.

- Review "The Automation Paradox" to identify ways in which the writer suggests automation will change or create future jobs. Take notes during your discussion and list types of skills and training that new or different jobs might require.
- Discuss steps workers might take to prepare for future changes in the job market and workplace. During the discussion, listen actively to help you ask questions and comment respectfully and thoughtfully on others' ideas.

Expand Your Vocabulary

PRACTICE AND APPLY

Use your understanding of the vocabulary words to answer each question.

redistribute	**robustly**	**expansive**
predominantly	**collaborate**	

1. Why is it often helpful to **collaborate** with a partner?
2. What types of search terms produce more **expansive** results? Why?
3. Why have machines **predominantly** eliminated low-skill jobs?
4. What might cause a company's income to grow **robustly**?
5. Why might you want to **redistribute** items in a package?

Vocabulary Strategy
Use a Dictionary

A dictionary is a reference work that provides information about words. Notice the parts of a dictionary entry:

Ed
Interactive Vocabulary Lesson: Using Reference Sources

syllabication | pronunciation | part of speech | forms of the word

rel•e•vant (rĕl′ə-vənt) *adj.* **relevance, relevantly**
1. Having a bearing on or connection with the matter at hand. **2.** Meaningful or purposeful in current society or culture: *thought that the traditional male role of breadwinner was no longer relevant.*

precise meanings of word are numbered

example of usage

PRACTICE AND APPLY

Use a dictionary to look up the following words from "The Automation Paradox." Then fill out a chart like this one.

WORD	PRONUNCIATION	PART OF SPEECH	GUESSED DEFINITION	DICTIONARY DEFINITION
paralegal				
trawl				
persistent				

Watch Your Language!

Transitional Words and Phrases

Transitional words and phrases connect ideas and signal how those ideas are related. Transitions are often set off with commas. Read the following sentence from "The Automation Paradox":

> Likewise, ATMs made it cheaper to operate bank branches, so banks dramatically increased their number of offices.

The word *likewise* signals a similarity, while the word *so* indicates an effect. The chart below contains examples of transitional words and phrases based on specific purposes.

COMMON TRANSITIONAL WORDS AND PHRASES	
Purpose:	**Example:**
compare or contrast ideas	*but, however, although, on the other hand, while, similarly, likewise*
indicate degree of importance	*especially, significantly, most importantly, chiefly, notably, particularly*
show time or sequence	*first, second, finally, when, initially, next, while, before, after*
add information	*also, in addition, too, and, furthermore*
introduce an example	*for example, for instance, such as, this shows*
indicate cause or effect	*as a result, therefore, consequently, for this reason, so*
indicate a conclusion	*in conclusion, in summary, overall, to summarize*

PRACTICE AND APPLY

Look back at the last piece of writing you submitted for class. Identify the transitions that you used and revise your writing to add more appropriate or stronger transitions.

Heads Up, Humans

Argument by **Claudia Alarcón**

Engage Your Brain

Choose one or two activities to start connecting with the selection you are about to read.

Photograph Preview

Take a look at the photographs that accompany "Heads Up, Humans." Write a caption for each. Then write a sentence or two predicting what this selection will be about.

Make It Automatic!

If you could automate one task or job you do, what would it be? Draw a sketch of a robot doing that job in the space below. If you don't feel like drawing, write a few sentences instead.

Evaluate Evidence

Evidence is any information that helps support a claim. Facts, quotations, examples, anecdotes, and statistics can all be used as evidence.

- Valid evidence is based on reliable sources that use sound reasoning. Many texts include endnotes, which list sources of information. Credible sources can help you confirm whether the evidence is valid.
- Evidence is relevant if it supports the claim in a clear and logical way.
- Sufficient evidence is enough to support the claim. A thorough and balanced argument includes a convincing amount of information related to the claim, and it addresses opposing viewpoints.

As you read "Heads Up, Humans," identify the main claim and evaluate the evidence the writer uses to support it.

Focus on Genre
Argument

- makes a claim
- supports its claim with reasons and evidence
- takes into account other points of view
- may rely heavily on the analysis and interpretation of data

Analyze Rhetoric

Rhetoric is the art of using language effectively and persuasively. One way writers use rhetoric is by carefully choosing words and phrases that are likely to have an impact on the audience or reader.

Rhetorical devices are techniques writers use to enhance their arguments and communicate more effectively. Here are two examples:

RHETORICAL DEVICE	DEFINITION	EXAMPLE
Direct address	Talking directly to the reader, often using the pronoun *you*	If you're like most young people, you've probably embraced technology.
Rhetorical question	A question that has such an obvious answer that it requires no reply	Will all these people find some other source of employment?

As you analyze "Heads Up, Humans," consider whether the writer's use of rhetoric is effective.

Annotation in Action

Here are the notes one reader made on the author's use of rhetoric. As you read, notice how the author uses language to persuade the reader to agree with her position.

If you're like most young people, you've probably embraced technology. You communicate with friends via videos and filters. You have vast numbers of songs and shows within reach. You can get items delivered to your home the same day you ordered them without leaving the house. These benefits of technology are easy to see.

The author directly addresses her intended audience using the pronoun "you."

Expand Your Vocabulary

Put a check mark next to the vocabulary words that you feel comfortable using when speaking or writing.

- **sector** ☐
- **exotic** ☐
- **renowned** ☐

Turn to a partner and talk about the words you already know. Then, write a few sentences about what you know about automation in today's world.

As you read "Heads Up, Humans," use the definitions in the side column to learn the vocabulary words you don't already know.

Background

The potential future impact of automation on employment has been the subject of much heated debate. Such arguments rely on the analysis of historical data as well as economic forecasts that may be influenced by a variety of factors.

Claudia Alarcón, a writer from Texas, sends her readers a warning about automation in her article, "Heads Up, Humans."

B

Heads Up, Humans

Argument by **Claudia Alarcón**

This author sends a warning about the threat automation poses to human workers.

NOTICE & NOTE
As you read, use the side margins to make notes about the text.

1 If you're like most young people, you've probably embraced technology. You communicate with friends via videos and filters. You have vast numbers of songs and shows within reach. You can get items delivered to your home the same day you ordered them without leaving the house. These benefits of technology are easy to see.

2 Perhaps you take it further, and are one of those who believe that technology does not just add fun and convenience to our lives, but is actually the answer to most of our problems—even problems that are caused by technology itself. In the very near future, one of the biggest of these problems is likely to be that many jobs now held by humans will be done by some combination of artificial intelligence and automated machine. If you're tempted to shrug off concern about this phenomenon because you assume that the wonders of technology will somehow create new and better jobs, you should be aware that research tells another story. As part of the generation that will arguably be most affected by these changes, it's in your interest to stay informed rather than simply hope for the best.

VOCABULARY

Greek Roots: The word *phenomenon* in paragraph 2 includes the Greek root word *pheno*, which means "to appear."

Interpret: How does knowing the meaning of the root help the reader determine the meaning of the word *phenomenon*?

NOTICE & NOTE
NUMBERS AND STATS

When you notice the use of specific quantities or comparisons to show amounts, size, or scale you've found a **Numbers and Stats** signpost.

Annotate: What data does the writer use as evidence in paragraph 3? Mark these details.

Draw Conclusions: Do these numbers help prove a point?

sector
(sĕk´tər) *n.* A *sector* is a part or division, as of a city or a national economy.

EVALUATE EVIDENCE

Annotate: Identify the source of the evidence in paragraph 6.

Infer: Why does the writer include these **quoted words** as evidence?

3 There is no argument that many jobs now held by humans will be replaced by some form of advanced technology According to a new report by a multi-national accounting and consulting firm based in London, 38% of U.S. jobs are at high risk of being replaced by robots and artificial intelligence over the next 15 years.[1] The report estimates the percentage of jobs lost to automation in Britain will be 30%, with 35% in Germany, and 21% in Japan.[2]

4 This change is already underway. Shipping companies have made headlines with self-driving trucks carrying cargo across the country. Ride share companies have been testing self-driving taxis in Pennsylvania and Arizona. Once more of our trucks and taxis drive themselves, what will happen to the people who held jobs as drivers? In the U.S., roughly 180,000 taxi drivers, 600,000 ride share drivers, and 3.5 million truck drivers could end up displaced.[3] This number is greater than the population of Houston, San Antonio, Dallas, Austin, and Fort Worth combined. Will all these people find some other source of employment? Or will the numbers of unemployed grow as the out-of-work drivers are joined by the millions of others who have been displaced by artificial intelligence and robots?

5 Technology fans claim that the fears that robots will lead to massive unemployment are unfounded. They say that people who are displaced from jobs will find new and better occupations that will be created by the economic shift. They suggest that a factory worker whose task on the assembly line is now completed by a machine might instead become someone who services the machine, for example. Or that there could be a rise in jobs in **sectors** that are harder to automate, such as healthcare.

6 "The last 200 years, we've had an incredible amount of automation," argues MIT economist David Autor. "We have tractors that do the work that horses and people used to do on farms. We don't dig ditches by hand anymore. We don't pound tools out of wrought iron. We don't do bookkeeping with books! But this has not in net reduced the amount of employment."

7 However, there is plenty of evidence to suggest that it's going to be different going forward. The introduction of the labor-saving tractor did indeed free up some farmers to plant more crops and others to take on different sorts of work. But the kind of automation combined with artificial intelligence being developed today doesn't just do the physical work of humans. It can do much of the high-level mental work too, faster and more effectively. In the past, newly freed laborers

Don't forget to **Notice & Note** as you read the text.

often went on to work in start-up industries that benefited from their availability. Today, the new industries are unlikely to need many human bodies or minds because technology can do the work for less cost.

8 Jerry Kaplan, an artificial intelligence expert who's founded multiple technology startups, has written a book called *Humans Need Not Apply*. In it, he lays out the risks of our new era. He explains what's cutting edge and poised to increase: systems that learn from experience and therefore don't need to be programmed, as we commonly understand the term. Not only will machines be able to do work that we think of as requiring human judgment and skill, such as fixing electrical problems, painting a house, or writing a news story, they will also be able to do work that people simply can't. "Unlike humans who are limited in the scope and scale of experiences they can absorb, these systems can scrutinize mountains of instructive examples at blinding speeds. They are capable of comprehending not only the visual, auditory, and written information familiar to us but also the more **exotic** forms of data that stream through computers and networks," he writes.[5]

9 Kaplan is mainly referring to the future he predicts based on his perspective as an expert in the tech world. But already, we can see the consequences. There is no evidence that recent advances in technology have so far offered the majority of workers better pay or positions. In fact, the opposite seems to be true. A report by the National Bureau of Economic Research found that between 1990 and 2007, automation lowered both the number of jobs available and the amount those jobs paid. "We estimate large and robust negative effects of robots on employment and wages," write the authors of the study.[6]

10 **Renowned** theoretical physicist Stephen Hawking is concerned about massive job loss and how that could affect the stability of our society. "The automation of factories has already decimated jobs in traditional manufacturing," says Hawking.

ANALYZE RHETORIC

Annotate: **Juxtaposition** is a rhetorical device in which a writer places two contrasting ideas or examples near each other to highlight the differences between them. Identify the juxtaposition in paragraph 7.

Analyze: How does this juxtaposition impact the writer's argument?

exotic
(ĭg-zŏt´ĭk) *adj.* Something that is *exotic* is unusual or different.

renowned
(rĭ-nound´) *adj.* Someone or something that is *renowned* is famous.

"The rise of artificial intelligence is likely to extend this job destruction deep into the middle classes, with only the most caring, creative, or supervisory roles remaining."[7] Hawking emphasizes that we live in a world where financial inequality is growing, not diminishing. He believes that many people can see their standard of living, and their ability to earn a living at all, disappearing.

11 This is a frightening scenario. It's tempting to avoid thinking about it, especially because solutions aren't obvious. But the first step toward avoiding the employment problems we might face is acknowledging them. As someone with your future on the line, don't let anyone tell you that technology is automatically going to create a healthy economy for everyone. If we don't want a bleak future for most of us, we have to prioritize human well-being even as we take advantage of what technology offers.

EVALUATE EVIDENCE

Annotate: Mark important details about the source in each citation.

Infer: Do these sources seem credible? Explain.

ENDNOTES

1 Alanna Petroff, "U.S. workers face higher risk of being replaced by robots. Here's why," *CNNtech* 24 March 2017, 4 Dec. 2017 <http://money.cnn.com/2017/03/24/technology/robots-jobs-us-workers-uk/index.html>.

2 Samantha Masunaga, "Robots could take over 38% of U.S. jobs within about 15 years, report says," *Los Angeles Times* 24 March 2017, 4 Dec. 2017 <http://http://www.latimes.com/business/la-fi-pwc-robotics-jobs-20170324-story.html>.

3 David Pogue, "When the robots take over, will there be jobs left for us?," *CBS News* 9 April 2017, 4 Dec. 2017 <https://www.cbsnews.com/news/when-the-robots-take-over-will-there-be-jobs-left-for-us/>.

4 Pogue, "When the robots take over."

5 Jerry Kaplan, *Humans Need Not Apply: A Guide to Wealth and Work in the Age of Artificial Intelligence* (New Haven: Yale University Press, 2015).

6 Daron Acemoglu and Pascual Restrepo, *Robots and Jobs: Evidence from US Labor Markets* (Cambridge, MA: National Bureau of Economic Research, 2017).

7 Rob Price, "Stephen Hawking: This will be the impact of automation and AI on jobs," *World Economic Forum* 6 Dec. 2016, 4 Dec. 2017 <https://www.weforum.org/agenda/2016/12/stephen-hawking-this-will-be-the-impact-of-automation-and-ai-on-jobs>.

TURN AND TALK

Do you agree with the author about the dangers of automation? Discuss with a partner.

ESSENTIAL QUESTION:

Does technology improve or control our lives?

Review your notes and add your thoughts to your Response Log.

Assessment Practice

Answer these questions before moving on to the **Analyze the Text** section on the following page.

1. This question has two parts. First, answer **Part A**. Then, answer **Part B**.

Part A

What claim does the author of "Heads Up, Humans" make?

- (A) Automation will not create more jobs or better pay for jobs.
- (B) Automation is happening more quickly than anyone predicted.
- (C) People are foolish to take automation for granted.
- (D) People who are displaced by automation cannot be retrained.

Part B

How does the author support the claim stated in Part A?

- (A) She shows how future changes in the job market will mirror historical changes.
- (B) She explains how machines impacted the farming and manufacturing industries.
- (C) She provides statistics that relate to many employment sectors.
- (D) She distinguishes the future of automation from past trends.

2. In "Heads Up, Humans," what does the author claim automation will increase?

- (A) wages
- (B) inequality
- (C) the number of unskilled jobs
- (D) the size of the middle class

Ed

Test-Taking Strategies

Analyze the Text

Support your responses with evidence from the text

NOTICE & NOTE

Review what you **noticed and noted** as you read the text. Your annotations can help you answer these questions.

1. **COMPARE** How does the author make use of the conflicting quotations from economist David Autor in paragraph 6 and artificial intelligence expert Jerry Kaplan in paragraph 8?

2. **CITE EVIDENCE** In paragraph 9, the author argues against the idea that "recent advances in technology have so far offered the majority of workers better pay or positions." What evidence does she provide in support of her view?

3. **CRITIQUE** In paragraph 11, how are the expressions *frightening scenario, future on the line,* and *bleak future* meant to affect the audience?

4. **EVALUATE** Which two quotations in the argument do you find most helpful in support of the author's reasoning? Use the graphic organizer to evaluate the author's use of expert quotes as evidence.

QUOTATION FROM THE TEXT	HOW IS IT HELPFUL?

5. **EVALUATE** What is the purpose of the sentences that provide **Numbers and Stats** in paragraph 4? How well do these sentences develop the author's argument?

Choices

Here are some other ways to demonstrate your understanding of the ideas in this lesson.

As you write and discuss, be sure to use the **Academic Vocabulary** words.

commentary	option
network	speculate
occupation	

Writing

Create a Public Service Announcement

Use ideas from "Heads Up, Humans" to create a public service announcement to build awareness about the potential impact of automation on jobs in the future.

- Choose a format for your announcement, such as a poster or a video.
- Plan and create your announcement, combining text and visuals to effectively convey your message.

Research

My Future Job

- Do some research on how automation may affect jobs in the future.
- Pick one job / career mentioned in the article.
- Research current job trends. How has automation affected this kind of work?

Social & Emotional Learning

Discuss with a Small Group

Have a discussion about how governments and other organizations might prepare for the impact of automation. Make sure all group members are included.

- Review the text to identify issues and concerns related to the future impact of automation on employment and the economy.
- Discuss possible ways in which people might solve the problems presented by automation. What steps might government and private organizations take to plan for the future?
- Listen closely to your group members. Ask questions and respectfully comment on others' ideas. As a group, summarize the key points of the discussion and identify points of agreement.

Expand Your Vocabulary

PRACTICE AND APPLY

Use your understanding of the vocabulary words to answer each question.

sector | **exotic** | **renowned**

1. Which vocabulary word goes with *famous*? Why?
2. Which vocabulary word goes with *division*? Why?
3. Which vocabulary word goes with *unusual*? Why?

Vocabulary Strategy

Use Greek Roots

Ed **Interactive Vocabulary Lesson: Common Roots, Prefixes, and Suffixes**

A word **root** is a word that forms the basis of a word's meaning. Look at this sentence from "Heads Up, Humans":

> As part of the generation that will arguably be most affected by these changes, it's in your interest to stay informed rather than simply hope for the best.

The word *generation* includes the Greek root *gen*, which means "to give birth." This can help you understand that *generation* means "the people born or living at the same time." Next, think of other words that include the same root. For example, *generation* relates to the word *generate*, which means "to come into being."

PRACTICE AND APPLY

Complete the word web with words that share the root *auto*, which means "self."

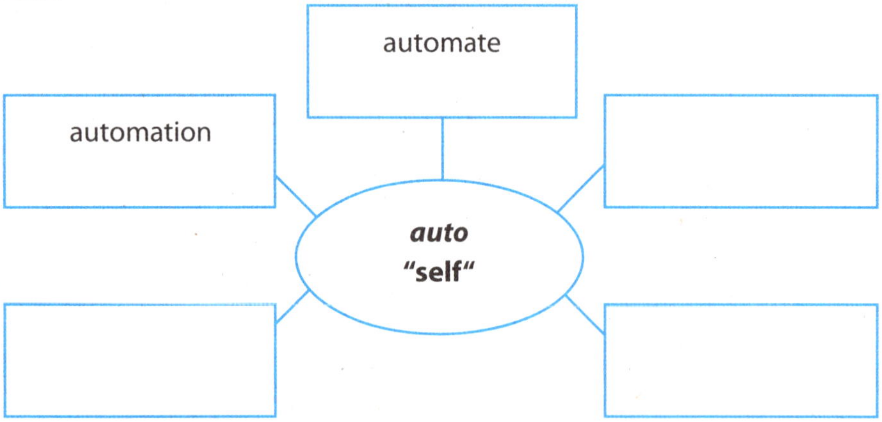

Watch Your Language!

Active and Passive Voice

The voice of a verb shows whether its subject performs or receives the action expressed by the verb. When the subject performs the action, the verb is in the **active voice**. When the subject is the receiver of the action, the verb is in the **passive voice**. Writers should avoid shifting between active and passive voice unnecessarily and should consider when each verb voice is most appropriate.

	DEFINITION	EXAMPLE	USE TO . . .
Active Voice	• shows that a subject performs an action	• *The robot finished the job.*	• emphasize the subject or actor • keep writing lively
Passive Voice	• shows that a subject is acted upon • uses helping verbs	• *The job was finished.*	• emphasize the action • show that the doer is unknown or unimportant

PRACTICE AND APPLY

Identify the voice of the verb in each sentence. Then rewrite the sentence in a different voice.

1. The factory workers were affected by changes in technology.

   ____

2. Automation eliminated their jobs.

   ____

3. The study shows the impact on the healthcare industry.

   ____

4. Your generation will likely be most affected by these changes.

   ____

Compare Arguments

When you **compare arguments,** you identify similarities and differences between the writers' claims, reasons, and evidence. As you review "The Automation Paradox" and "Heads Up, Humans" to compare the arguments, examine how the authors support their claims with reasons and evidence, and how they use rhetorical devices to advance their positions.

Also be sure to consider how the two authors respond to opposing claims. Good writers anticipate and acknowledge conflicting views and objections to their arguments and refute them effectively.

In a small group, complete the Venn diagram with similarities and differences between the two arguments.

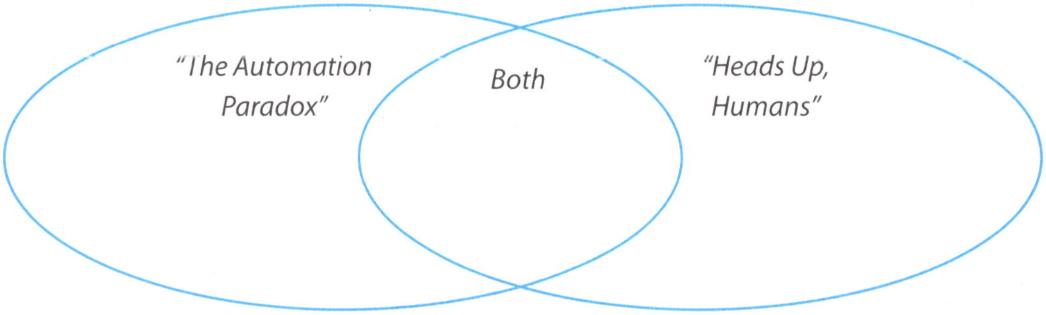

Analyze the Texts

Discuss these questions in your group.

1. **SUMMARIZE** What topic do both arguments address? In brief, what is their main area of disagreement?

2. **COMPARE** On which two concepts do these two authors have the same point of view?

3. **CONNECT** Cite evidence from one argument that contradicts information in the other argument.

4. **EVALUATE** Which argument is more convincing to you? Cite evidence from both texts to support your opinion.

Collaborate and Debate

Now your group can continue reflecting on the ideas in these texts and your responses to them by debating the impact of automation on employment. Follow these steps:

1. **CHOOSE A SIDE** Working with a small group, decide which viewpoint you will argue. Will automation have a positive or negative impact on employment?

2. **GATHER INFORMATION** Review the two arguments and use relevant text evidence to support your position. List reasons from the texts and from your prior research to help build your argument.

REASON 1:
Evidence:
REASON 2:
Evidence:

3. **PREPARE A COUNTERCLAIM** Anticipate the opposing team's claim, reasons, and evidence. List reasons and evidence you will cite to argue against the opposing team's position.

Opposing Team's Argument:	Counterclaim:

4. **CONDUCT THE DEBATE** Debate another group of students who have chosen the opposite position. Each group should be allowed to speak for a set amount of time. Use appropriate eye contact, speaking volume, and pronunciation to communicate your ideas effectively.

Reader's Choice

Continue your exploration of the Essential Question by doing some independent reading on technology. Read the titles and descriptions shown. Then mark the texts that interest you.

ESSENTIAL QUESTION:
Does technology improve or control our lives?

Short Reads

Available on Ed

These texts are available in your ebook. Choose one to read and rate. Then defend your rating to the class.

If You Go into the Woods You Will Find It Has a Technology

Poem by **Heather Christle**

If you look closely, you will see that nature is trying to communicate with us.

Rate It ☆☆☆☆☆

Hallucination

Science Fiction by **Isaac Asimov**

A boy working in a planetary outpost realizes that things aren't what they seem.

Rate It ☆☆☆☆☆

There Will Come Soft Rains

Science Fiction by **Ray Bradbury**

A vacant mechanized house is the only thing left standing in a ruined city.

Rate It ☆☆☆☆☆

from All the Light We Cannot See

Novel by **Anthony Doerr**

The discovery of a radio brings the power of music to a young boy and girl.

Rate It ☆☆☆☆☆

Long Reads

Here are a few recommended books that connect to this unit topic. For additional options, ask your teacher, school librarian, or peers. Which titles spark your interest?

Fuzzy

Novel by **Tom Angleberger**

Max befriends a new classmate who just happens to be a robot. She helps him understand how to survive middle school while uncovering a larger looming threat.

I, Robot

Science Fiction by **Isaac Asimov**

What could happen if robots become so intelligent that they threaten humanity? Nine stories examine the possibilities.

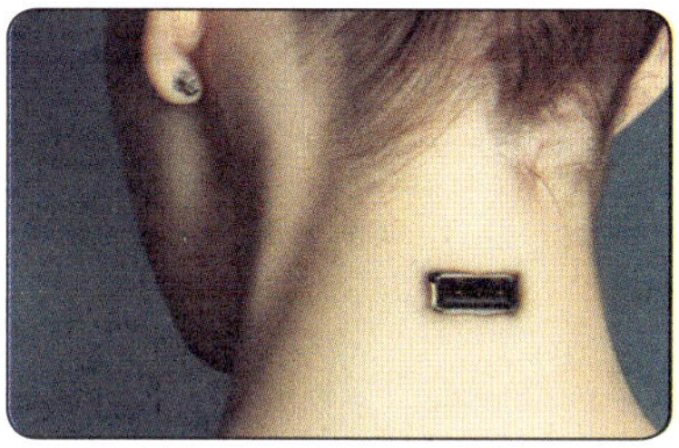

Feed

Novel by **M.T. Anderson**

In this futuristic society, people connect to the Internet via feeds implanted in their brains. What could possibly go wrong?

Extension

Connect & Create

CREATE A GRAPHIC NOVEL Select a scene from one of the texts and adapt it into graphic novel form. You can use text and dialogue from the book you read, or you may decide to write your own content for the purposes of your graphic novel. You can draw the images yourself or find images online to use. Use digital tools to construct your graphic novel and to publish it. Then share your work with your classmates.

CHARACTERS TEXTING With a partner, write a text message exchange between two characters from a text you've both read. Choose which character you will each play and decide on a topic to focus on in your exchange. Or you might choose a section of dialogue from the book to "translate" into text messages. Consider how the interaction between the characters might be different if they were communicating by texting.

NOTICE & NOTE

- Pick one of the texts and annotate the Notice & Note signposts you find.
- Then, use the **Notice & Note Writing Frames** to help you write about the significance of the signposts.
- Compare your findings with those of other students who read the same text.

Ed

Notice & Note Writing Frames

Write an Argument

Writing Prompt

Using ideas, information, and examples from multiple texts in this unit, write an argument on a topic related to technology.

Manage your time carefully so that you can:

- review the texts in the unit;
- plan your essay;
- write your essay; and
- revise and edit your essay.

Be sure to:

- clearly state the claim of your argument;
- address alternate or opposing claims;
- use and cite evidence from multiple sources; and
- avoid relying too much on one source.

Review the Mentor Texts

For two examples of well-written arguments you can use as mentor texts and sources for your essay, review:

- The Automation Paradox (pages 40–45)
- Heads Up, Humans (pages 53–57).

Review your notes and annotations about these texts. Think about how the authors make their arguments convincing.

Consider Your Sources

Review the list of texts in the unit and choose at least two that you may want to use as support for your argument.

As you review potential sources, consult the notes you made in your **Response Log** and make additional notes about ideas that might be useful to you as you write. Include titles and page numbers so that you can easily find the information later.

UNIT 1 SOURCES

- ☐ **The Brave Little Toaster**
- ☐ **Are Bionic Superhumans on the Horizon?**
- ☐ **Interflora**
- ☐ **The Automation Paradox**
- ☐ **Heads Up, Humans**

Analyze the Prompt

Review the prompt to make sure you understand the assignment.

- Mark the sentence in the prompt that identifies the topic of your argument.
- Determine which issue related to technology you want to write about. Describe your topic below.
- Write a sentence describing your purpose and a sentence describing your target audience.

Find a Purpose

As you choose a specific topic to write about, consider three common purposes of an argument:

- to **persuade** readers to agree with your position
- to **challenge** a commonly held opinion
- to **encourage** readers to take a specific action

My topic:

My purpose:

My audience:

Review the Rubric

Your argument will be scored using a rubric. As you write, focus on the characteristics as described in the chart. You will learn more about these characteristics as you work through the lesson.

PURPOSE, FOCUS, AND ORGANIZATION	EVIDENCE AND ELABORATION	CONVENTIONS OF STANDARD ENGLISH
The response includes: • A strongly maintained claim • Effective responses to opposing claims • Transitions to connect ideas • Logical progression of ideas • Appropriate style and tone	The response includes: • Effective use of evidence and sources • Effective use of elaboration • Clear and effective expression of ideas • Appropriate vocabulary • Varied sentence structure	The response may include: • Some minor errors in usage but no patterns of errors • Correct punctuation, capitalization, sentence formation, and spelling • Command of basic conventions

1 PLAN YOUR ARGUMENT

Develop a Claim

Ed

Help with Planning

Consult **Interactive Writing Lesson: Writing Arguments.**

In an argument, the **claim** is the writer's position on an issue. Identify your position below on the technology topic you've chosen. Then draft your claim, making sure it is direct and specific.

MY CLAIM

Identify Support

To build a strong argument, you must have solid support for your claim. Support consists of reasons and evidence.

- **Reasons** explain why you have taken a particular position on an issue.
- **Evidence** supports your reasons.

Use the chart to outline your support. Use the notes you took as you read to help you.

Provide Evidence

Make sure your evidence is **relevant,** or directly related to the claim and reasons. Evidence may include:

- facts
- statistics
- examples
- expert opinions

REASON	EVIDENCE	SOURCE (INCLUDE PAGE NUMBERS)

Address Opposing Claims

Make sure to acknowledge possible objections to your viewpoint in your argument. You should address at least one **opposing claim** and use logical reasoning to explain why your position is more valid. Review your notes to find claims that oppose, or disagree with, your position. Then write your response.

An Opposing Claim:

My Response:

Organize Ideas

Now organize your material in a way that will help you draft your argument. Keep in mind that your ideas should progress logically. **Transitional words and phrases** will create a **cohesion** that holds your argument together.

Organize Your Support

As you plan, try arranging reasons by complexity.

- Start with the most basic reason.
- Build meaning toward more complex reasons.

INTRODUCTION	• Clearly state your claim. • Use an interesting question, quote, or detail to grab the reader's attention.
BODY PARAGRAPHS	• Present reasons and evidence to support your claim, devoting one paragraph to each main idea. • Address an opposing claim in at least one paragraph. • Link ideas with transitional words and phrases.
CONCLUSION	• Restate your claim and its significance. • Wrap up your argument with a final thought about the topic.

2 DEVELOP A DRAFT

Now it is time to draft your essay. You can develop your writing skills by noticing what the experts do. Read about techniques professional writers use to craft their arguments.

Ed

Drafting Online

Check your assignment list for a writing task from your teacher.

Introduce a Claim

EXAMINE THE MENTOR TEXT

Notice how the author of **"Heads Up, Humans"** (page 53) introduces a claim.

Heads Up, Humans

Argument by Claudia Alarcón

The author clearly states her position.

. . . In the very near future, one of the biggest of these problems is likely to be that many jobs now held by humans will be done by some combination of artificial intelligence and automated machine. If you're tempted to shrug off concern about this phenomenon because you assume that the wonders of technology will somehow create new and better jobs, you should be aware that research tells another story. As part of the generation that will arguably be most affected by these changes, it's in your interest to stay informed rather than simply hope for the best.

The author addresses the reader directly to create interest.

APPLY TO YOUR DRAFT

Consider what is the most engaging way to introduce your claim. What might interest your readers most? Use the chart below to take notes on engaging ways to introduce your claim. After you generate ideas, choose one or two to use in your introduction.

Try These Suggestions

Imagine you are having a conversation with friends about your position on the topic of your argument. How might you draw them into the discussion? What might you say to capture their interest? Consider using one of the methods in the chart below when you introduce your claim.

A surprising fact or statistic	
An interesting quotation	
A connection between the topic and the audience	
A thought-provoking question	

Cite Sources and Use Evidence Effectively

EXAMINE THE MENTOR TEXT

Notice how the author of **"The Automation Paradox"** (page 43) cites a source to support his argument.

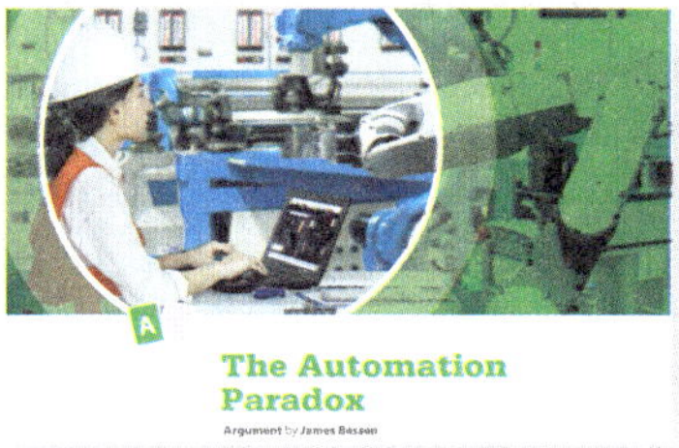

That could change decades into the future, as new generations of software powered by artificial intelligence becomes ever more capable of advanced tasks. But in the near term, the story is much different. A new study by McKinsey & Company took a detailed look at work tasks that are likely to be automated and found that only about 5 percent of jobs are at risk of being completely automated in the near future. The main effect of automation for the time being will not be to eliminate jobs, but to redefine them—changing the tasks and the skills needed to perform them.

The author refers to the source by naming the authors.

The author includes a statistic from the study.

The author elaborates on how the evidence from the study supports his reasoning.

APPLY TO YOUR DRAFT

Use this chart to practice citing a source from your draft. Then apply this technique to other sources in your argument.

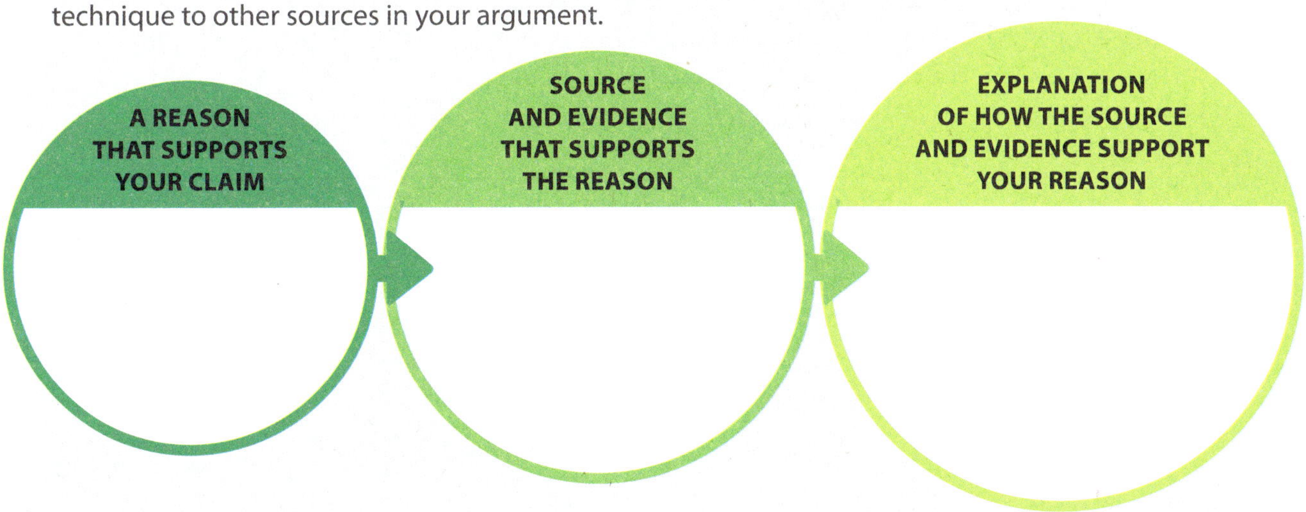

3 REVISE YOUR ARGUMENT

Even professional writers rework their ideas and language as they revise. No one gets it right the first time. Use the guide to help you revise your essay.

Ed

Help with Revision

Find a **Peer Review Guide** and **Student Models.**

REVISION GUIDE

ASK YOURSELF	PROVE IT	REVISE IT
Introduction Does my introduction contain a clear claim? Is my introduction engaging?	**Underline** the main claim your argument makes.	**Revise** your claim to clarify or strengthen your position. **Revise** your introduction to make it more engaging.
Organization Are paragraphs organized logically? Have I used transitions to connect ideas?	**Number** the paragraphs so that the most important reason comes first. **Circle** transitions that connect ideas.	**Rearrange** paragraphs in order of importance. **Add** transitions to connect ideas.
Support Does my argument include reasons and evidence to support my claim?	**Put a star** (★) next to each reason. **Highlight** the supporting evidence for each reason.	**Add** reasons and/or evidence such as a fact, an example, or a comparison to support each reason.
Citing Sources Have I cited sources properly?	**Put a check mark** (✓) next to references to your sources.	**Add** author names or article titles for your sources.
Opposing Claims Do I address opposing claims effectively?	**Underline** opposing claims. **Highlight** parts of your argument that address them.	**Add** possible opposing claims and address them thoughtfully.
Conclusion Does my conclusion logically flow from the reasoning of my argument?	**Highlight** parts of your conclusion that support your claim and reasons.	**Revise** the conclusion so that it follows from the reasoning of your argument.

APPLY TO YOUR DRAFT

Consider the following as you look for opportunities to improve your writing.

- Make sure your claim is clearly stated.
- Make sure your introduction grabs the reader's attention.
- Make sure your ideas are clearly connected with transitions.

Peer Review in Action

Once you have finished revising your argument, you will exchange papers with a partner for a **peer review**. During a peer review, you will give suggestions to improve your partner's draft.

Read the introduction from a student's draft and examine the comments made by her peer reviewer to see how it's done.

First Draft

It's Time to Ban Phones in Class
by Ximena Sanchez, Roseland Middle School

Phones should be banned in classrooms. Students are on their phones all the time. Teachers are constantly telling students to put them away. It's a bad idea to let students have phones in class.

Try to grab the reader's attention with an intriguing question or a surprising statistic.

Improve your claim by using formal language and directly stating why it's a "bad idea."

Now read the revised introduction. Notice how the writer has improved her draft by revising based on her peer reviewer's comments.

Revision

It's Time to Ban Phones in Class
by Ximena Sanchez, Roseland Middle School

Did you know that, according to a study published in the *Journal of Media Education*, students check their phones in class more than 11 times a day? This is just one of several findings that point to a disturbing trend. Phone use in class is taking away from valuable learning time. It is a technology that distracts both teachers and students. School districts should ban phones in class to create a more productive learning environment.

Referencing a study is a great way to grab your reader's attention. Good job citing your source, too.

You have clarified your claim. Nicely done!

APPLY TO YOUR DRAFT

During your peer review, give each other specific suggestions about how you might make your arguments more effective. Use your revision guide to help you.

When receiving feedback from your partner, listen attentively and ask questions to make sure you fully understand the revision suggestions.

4 EDIT YOUR ARGUMENT

Apply the finishing touches to your draft. Edit your draft to check for proper use of standard English conventions and to correct any misspellings or grammatical errors.

Watch Your Language!

USE TRANSITIONAL WORDS AND PHRASES

Transitional words and phrases connect ideas. They show how ideas are related. Using transitions correctly can help create coherence in your writing and strengthen your argument.

Read the following sentences from "The Automation Paradox."

> It might seem a sure thing that automating a task would reduce employment in an occupation. But that logic ignores some basic economics: Automation reduces the cost of a product or service, and lower prices tend to attract more customers.

The word *but* is a transition. It signals a contrast between two ideas: automation reducing employment and the basic economics of lower prices bringing in more customers.

Transitions to Try

Use these common transitions in your writing:

- **Comparison/contrast:** but, yet, however, although, similarly, in the same way
- **Elaboration:** also, in addition, too, furthermore
- **Cause/effect:** therefore, as a result of, so

APPLY TO YOUR DRAFT

Now apply what you've learned about transitional words and phrases to your own work.

1. Read your argument aloud and highlight the transitions you've used.
2. Replace any transitional words or phrases that are used incorrectly.
3. Add transitional words and phrases to connect ideas.

5 PUBLISH YOUR ARGUMENT

Share It!

You wrote your argument in the format of an essay. You may also use your argument for inspiration for other projects.

Ways to Share

- **Engage in a debate** with friends or family members about your issue.
- **Write a letter** to your school newspaper expressing your view on the topic.
- **Record a podcast** about the topic.

Speaking & Listening

Present an Argument

We're faced with important issues related to technology every day in our daily lives. You've chosen a specific topic related to technology to write about. Now you will adapt your argument for presentation to your classmates.

Adapt Your Argument for Presentation

Use the chart below to help you adapt the key elements of your argument to create a script and other materials.

Create Interest

As you plan your argument, consider how you will keep your audience engaged. What images or graphics might grab their interest? Which reasons or evidence might be important to lead with?

ASK YOURSELF	ANSWERS AND NOTES
How will I revise my **title** and **introduction** to capture the audience's attention?	
Is there a more concise way to state my **claim**?	
Is there a more effective way to organize my **reasons and evidence**?	
How will I **transition** between ideas?	
What **images or graphics** might clarify my ideas?	

Practice with Your Group

Once you've completed a draft of your script, practice your presentation with a group. Use this chart to help you improve your presentation.

Tips for Productive Discussions

- Don't interrupt each other.
- Stay on topic.
- Ask only relevant questions.
- Provide only thoughtful answers.

GOAL	NOTES FOR IMPROVEMENT
Say words smoothly without stumbling.	**Pronunciation:**
Speak loudly enough that even listeners in the back of the room can hear you.	**Volume:**
Let your eyes rest briefly on the audience, for natural delivery.	**Eye Contact:**

Deliver Your Presentation

Use the advice you received to make final changes to your presentation. Then present it to your classmates.

Share It!

- **Create a list** of interesting facts you've learned about technology and post it in your class.
- **Have a group discussion** about how working on your presentation may have changed your ideas about a particular topic.

Ed

Interactive Speaking & Listening Lesson: Giving a Presentation

Reflect & Extend

Here are some other ways to show your understanding of the ideas in Unit 1.

Reflect on the Essential Question

Does technology improve or control our lives?

Has your answer to the question changed after reading the texts in the unit? Discuss your ideas.

You can use these sentence starters to help you reflect on your learning.

- **My ideas have changed because …**
- **I mostly feel the same because …**
- **I'm still wondering about …**

Writing

Write an Explanatory Essay

Write an explanatory essay about how a type of technology works—such as networks, the Internet of Things, or artificial intelligence. Use the chart to jot down ideas. Then, research and write your essay.

ASK YOURSELF	MY NOTES
What is your **topic**?	
What reliable **sources** will you use for research?	
How will you **organize** your essay?	

Project-Based Learning

Create a Business Plan

You've read about different uses for technology. Now, with a group of classmates, create a business plan for a new company that uses technology in an interesting way.

Here are some questions to get you started.

- What specific service or product will your company provide?
- Who will use your service or product? How will it benefit them?
- What will your company be called? What message will be communicated in your company's name and **logo?** Remember a logo and it's colors, shapes, and design should appeal to your customers.

Ed

Media Projects

To find help with this task online, access **Create a Logo.**

UNIT 2

Ed

Get hooked by the unit topic.

Stream to Start Video

AL QUESTION:
we sometimes
el frightened?

The Thrill of Horror

"There is a . . . horror story that is only two sentences long: The last man on Earth sat alone in a room. There was a knock at the door."
—Fredric Brown

Analyze the Image

What scary elements do you see in this image?

S…rk Y…
…earnin…

Here's a chance to spa… …ng about ideas in **Unit 2: The T… …ror.**

As you read, you can use the **Response Log** (page R2) to track your thinking about the Essential Question.

Make the …nection

What was th…st horror story you watched, read, or h…d ab…ut? Write or sketch your answ…

Think About the Essential Question

Why do we sometimes like to feel frightened? What reasons come to mind?

Sound Like an Expert

You can use these Academic Vocabulary words to write and talk about the topics and themes in the unit. Which of these words do you already feel comfortable using when speaking or writing?

	I can use it!	I understand it.	I'll look it up.
convention	☐	☐	☐
predict	☐	☐	☐
psychology	☐	☐	☐
summary	☐	☐	☐
technique	☐	☐	☐

Prove It!

Turn to a partner and use one of the words in a sentence about the thrill of horror.

Preview the Texts

Look over the images, titles, and descriptions of the texts in the unit. Mark the title of the text that interests you most.

What Is the Horror Genre?

Literary Criticism by **Sharon A. Russell**

In what ways are horror stories defined and categorized? This author tries to pin down the genre.

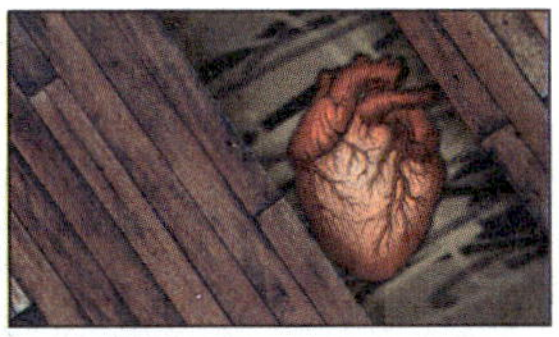

The Tell-Tale Heart

Short Story by **Edgar Allan Poe**

The narrator of this twisted tale tries to cover up his crime.

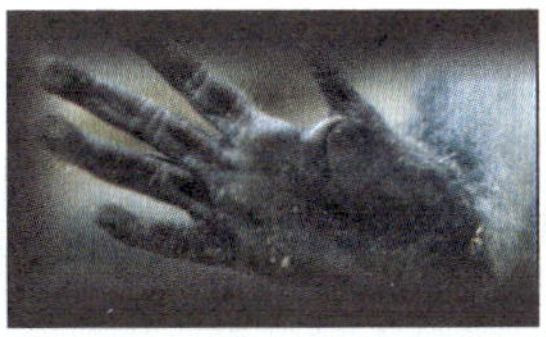

The Monkey's Paw

Short Story by **W. W. Jacobs**

A visitor gives the White family an object that will grant them three wishes, but he also gives them a grim warning.

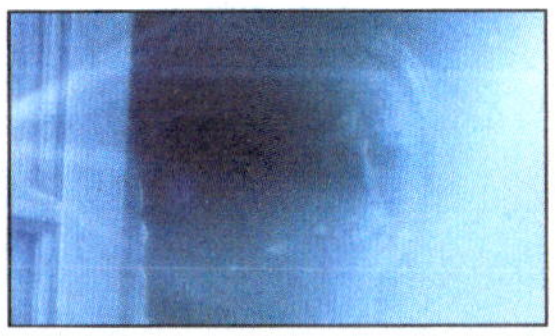

from The Monkey's Paw

Film Clip by **Ricky Lewis Jr.**

This film brings W. W. Jacobs's famous horror story to the screen.

from The Aeneid of Virgil

Epic Poem translated by **Allen Mandelbaum**

Trojan hero Aeneas goes to the underworld, where he watches in horror as Charon ferries the dead across the river Styx.

from Hades: Lord of the Dead

Graphic Novel by **George O'Connor**

This excerpt from a graphic novel provides a vivid look at what ancient Greeks believed about the afterlife.

I Wonder . . .

Why do people like to read and watch scary stories? Jot down or sketch your answer.

NTOR TEXT

What Is the Horror Genre?

Literary Criticism by **Sharon A. Russell**

ESSENTIAL QUESTION:
Why do we sometimes like to feel frightened?

Engage Your Brain

Choose one or more of these activities to start connecting with the text you're about to read.

List It

A genre is a category of literature, film, music, or other art form. With a partner, make a list of as many genres as you can think of.

Parallel Worlds?

The selection you are about to read mentions the idea of parallel worlds—separate realms or dimensions that exist alongside the reality we live in. Do you believe such places exist? Write a paragraph explaining your thoughts about this idea.

Emoji Reaction

Draw an emoji that expresses your interest in watching and reading horror stories.

Analyze Literary Criticism

Literary criticism is writing that examines, analyzes, and interprets a particular work or an aspect of literature. Literary criticism is often organized around **central ideas,** the most important ideas about a topic in a text. A central idea can be one of the main ideas of an entire work or a key idea expressed in a paragraph or section of a text. As you read, write down the central ideas of the text in the graphic organizer. Also include supporting ideas and important details from the text that help to develop the central ideas.

Focus on Genre

Literary Criticism

- often appears in the form of an essay with persuasive elements
- examines one or more works of literature
- contains specific examples and support from the literature and other sources
- may have the purpose of shaping how readers interpret a particular work

CENTRAL IDEA	SUPPORTING IDEAS AND DETAILS

Paraphrase and Summarize Text

A good way to check your comprehension of a text is to paraphrase or summarize it. These techniques are similar, but not the same.

- When you **paraphrase,** you restate all the information in the text using your own words. Paraphrasing is a helpful way to make sure you understand small, challenging sections of text.
- When you **summarize,** you briefly retell the text's central ideas and most important details in your own words. Summarizing helps you understand a larger section of text or the entire text.

As you read, use paraphrasing and summarizing to understand the author's ideas about the horror genre.

Annotation in Action

Here is an example of a reader's notes about the second paragraph of "What Is the Horror Genre?" As you read, mark clues about the central ideas of the text.

Some students of this genre find that the best way to examine it is to deal with the way horror fiction is organized or structured. Examining the organization of a horror story shows that it shares certain traits with other types of fiction. Horror stories share the use of suspense as a tactic with many other kinds of literature.

The idea that horror stories use suspense is a central idea of the text.

Expand Your Vocabulary

Put a check mark next to the vocabulary words that you feel comfortable using when speaking or writing.

- **intensify** ☐
- **justify** ☐
- **parallel** ☐

Turn to a partner and use one of the words you already know in a sentence about horror stories. As you read "What Is the Horror Genre?," use the definitions in the side column to learn the vocabulary words you don't already know.

Background

Sharon A. Russell (b. 1941) is a retired professor of Communication and Women's Studies at Indiana State University, where she taught courses on film and television. Russell has published extensively on horror film and literature and detective fiction. She is the author of *Stephen King: A Critical Companion,* a book that analyzes several of King's famous horror novels and in which this essay appears.

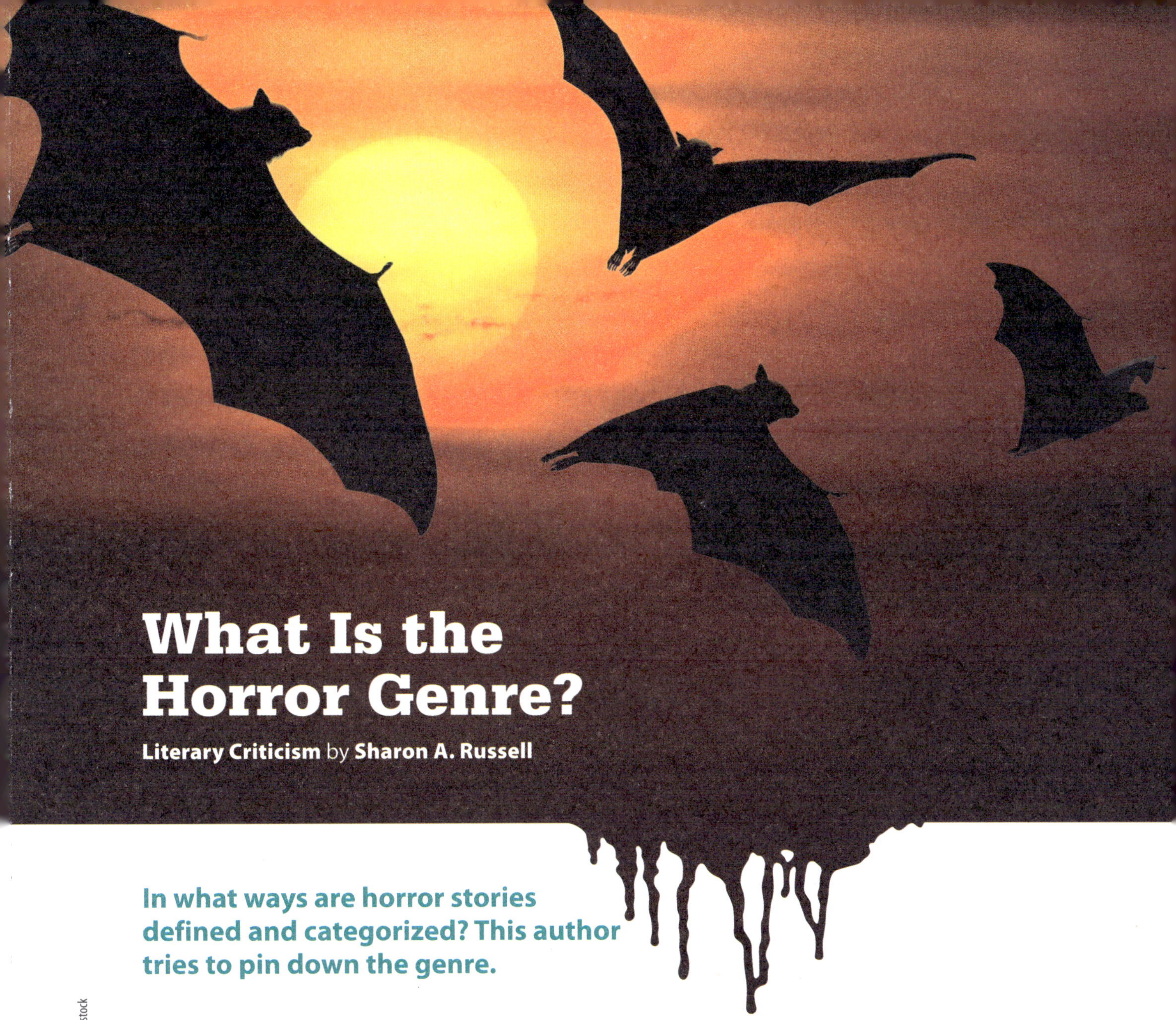

What Is the Horror Genre?

Literary Criticism by **Sharon A. Russell**

In what ways are horror stories defined and categorized? This author tries to pin down the genre.

1 Many people define horror by its subjects. We all think of creatures like Frankenstein's monster, Dracula, and the wolfman[1] as monsters in the horror genre. Each one of these creatures has a history and developed over a period of time. But we also know that horror covers more than just these monsters. We could all make long lists of the kind of creatures we identify with horror, especially when we think of films as well as literature. The minute we would start to make such a list we would also realize that not all monsters are alike and that not all horror deals with monsters. The subject approach is not the clearest way to define this genre.

Ed

Text in Focus Video

Learn more about understanding the horror genre.

Ed

Close Read Screencast

Listen to a modeled close read of this text.

[1] **Frankenstein's monster, Dracula, and the wolfman:** legendary monsters. "Frankenstein's monster" is the creature created by Dr. Victor Frankenstein in Mary Shelley's novel; "Dracula" is the vampire in Bram Stoker's novel; in folklore, the wolfman is a man who can become a wolf.

NOTICE & NOTE

QUOTED WORDS

When you notice the author citing other people to provide support for a point, you've found a **Quoted Words** signpost.

Notice & Note: Mark where Russell uses quoted words in paragraph 2.

Analyze: Why was this quotation included, and what does this add?

intensify
(ĭn-tĕn´sə-fī´) *v.* If you *intensify* something, you make it grow in strength.

justify
(jŭs´tə-fī´) *v.* If you *justify* something, you prove it is right or valid.

2 Some students of this genre find that the best way to examine it is to deal with the way horror fiction is organized or structured. Examining the organization of a horror story shows that it shares certain traits with other types of fiction. Horror stories share the use of suspense as a tactic with many other kinds of literature. The tension we feel when a character goes into the attic, down into the basement, or just into the abandoned house is partially a result of suspense. We don't know what is going to happen. But that suspense is **intensified** by our knowledge of the genre. We know that characters involved in the world of horror always meet something awful when they go where they shouldn't. Part of the tension is created because they are doing something we know is going to get them in trouble. Stephen King refers directly to our anticipation of horror. In *Salem's Lot*[2] Susan approaches the house which is the source of evil. "She found herself thinking of those drive-in horror movie epics where the heroine goes venturing up the narrow attic stairs . . . or down into some dark, cobwebby cellar . . . and she . . . thinking: . . . *I'd never do that!*" Of course Susan's fears are **justified**. She does end up dead in the basement, a victim of the vampire.

3 If the horror genre uses the character's search for information to create suspense, it controls when and where we get our knowledge. Because we are outside of the situation we usually know more than the characters. Our advance knowledge creates suspense because we can anticipate what is going to happen. The author can play with those expectations by either confirming them or surprising us with a different outcome. When suspense is an important element in fiction we may often find that the plot is the most critical part of the story. We care more about what happens next than about who the characters are or where the story is set. But setting is often considered a part of the horror genre. If the genre has traditional monsters, it also has traditional settings. Only authors who want to challenge the tradition place events in bright, beautiful parks. We expect a connection between the setting and the events in this genre. We are not surprised to find old houses, abandoned castles, damp cellars, or dark forests as important elements in the horror story.

4 Some people make further distinctions based on how the stories are organized. We can divide stories into different categories based on how we come to believe in the events related and how they are explained to us. Stories that deal with

[2] ***Salem's Lot:*** a horror fiction novel written by Stephen King.

The actor Boris Karloff as the monster in the 1931 film *Frankenstein,* based on the novel

The actor Lon Chaney as a werewolf in the 1941 film *The Wolf Man*

The actor Bela Lugosi as Dracula in the 1931 film by the same name

Don't forget to **Notice & Note** as you read the text.

parallel worlds expect us to accept those worlds without question. We just believe Dorothy is in Oz; we accept Oz as a parallel world separate from ours. Other times events seem to be supernatural but turn out to have natural explanations: the ghosts turn out to be squirrels in the attic, or things that move mysteriously are part of a plot to drive someone crazy. Sometimes the supernatural is the result of the way the central character sees the world, as in stories told from the point of view of a crazy person. But at times we are not sure, and hesitate about believing in the possibility of the supernatural. When I first read Dracula I seriously considered hanging garlic on my windows because I believed that vampires could exist. This type of hesitation, when we almost believe, falls into the general category of the "fantastic" (Todorov 25).[3] Often horror has its greatest effect on us because we almost believe, or believe while we are reading the book or watching the film, that the events are possible.

5 Yet another way of categorizing works of horror is by the source of the horror. Some horror comes from inside the characters. Something goes wrong inside, and a person turns into a monster. Dr. Frankenstein's need for knowledge turns him into the kind of person who creates a monster. Dr. Jekyll

parallel
(păr´ə-lĕl´) *adj.* If things are *parallel,* they have comparable or similar parts.

ANALYZE LITERARY CRITICISM

Annotate: Mark the sentence that states the main idea of paragraph 4.

Analyze: How does the main idea of paragraph 4 contribute to the development of the central ideas of the text?

[3] **Todorov 25:** The author is following MLA style to cite her source for the information just stated: page 25 of a work by an author named Todorov.

also values his desire for information above all else, and creates Mr. Hyde.[4] In another kind of horror story the threat to the central character or characters comes from outside. An outside force may invade the character and then force the evil out again. The vampire attacks the victim, but then the victim becomes a vampire and attacks others. Stories of ghosts or demonic possession also fall into this category.

6 We can also look at the kinds of themes common to horror. Many works concentrate on the conflict between good and evil. Works about the fantastic may deal with the search for forbidden knowledge that appears in much horror literature. Such quests are used as a way of examining our attitude toward knowledge. While society may believe that new knowledge is always good, the horror genre may question this assumption, examining how such advances affect the individual and society.

PARAPHRASE AND SUMMARIZE TEXT

Annotate: Underline a challenging sentence in paragraph 6. Circle words in the sentence that could be replaced with simpler ones.

Paraphrase: Restate the sentence in your own words.

[4] **Dr. Jekyll . . . and . . . Mr. Hyde:** the good and evil sides of the same character in a novella by Robert Louis Stevenson.

?

ESSENTIAL QUESTION:

Why do we sometimes like to feel frightened?

Review your notes and add your thoughts to your Response Log.

TURN AND TALK

Turn to a partner and discuss how Russell's ideas about horror stories compare with your own knowledge of this genre.

Assessment Practice

Answer these questions before moving on to the **Analyze the Text** section on the following page.

1. This question has two parts. First, answer **Part A**. Then, answer **Part B**.

Part A

Which sentence states a central idea of the text?

- (A) The horror genre is defined by its focus on monsters and scary settings.
- (B) There are many different ways to categorize the horror genre.
- (C) The use of suspense is a unique feature of the horror genre.
- (D) The organizational structure of the horror genre sets it apart from other genres.

Part B

How does the author develop the central idea throughout the text?

- (A) She describes the plots of the most popular horror fiction novels and movies.
- (B) She compares and contrasts the horror genre with other genres.
- (C) She provides various strategies to analyze the horror genre.
- (D) She argues that the horror genre always focuses on the conflict between good and evil.

2. How does the author present her ideas about sources of horror in paragraph 5?

- (A) by contrasting literary characters
- (B) by describing a sequence of events
- (C) by providing examples
- (D) by showing cause and effect

Ed
Test-Taking Strategies

Analyze the Text

Support your responses with evidence from the text.

NOTICE & NOTE

Review what you **noticed and noted** as you read the text. Your annotations can help you answer these questions.

1. **INFER** Reread the first two paragraphs of the essay. What does the opening suggest is one of the central ideas of the text?

2. **CONNECT** In paragraph 2, the author states that in horror stories "suspense is intensified by our knowledge of the genre." What knowledge is the author referring to? Explain why it increases suspense.

3. **ANALYZE** In paragraph 4, why does the author include the **Quoted Word** "fantastic"?

4. **PREDICT** How might the author answer the question in the title: "What Is the Horror Genre?"

5. **SUMMARIZE** Write the central idea of each paragraph in the chart below to summarize the essay.

PARAGRAPH	CENTRAL IDEA
1	
2	
3	
4	
5	
6	

Choices

Here are some other ways to demonstrate your understanding of the ideas in this lesson.

Research

Masters of Horror

In the selection, Russell discusses the novel *Salem's Lot* by "Master of Horror" Stephen King. Find two other famous Masters of Horror, including writers and directors. In the chart below, record their names and two works by each.

MASTER OF HORROR	TWO WORKS

As you write and discuss, be sure to use the **Academic Vocabulary** words.

- **convention**
- **predict**
- **psychology**
- **summary**
- **technique**

Writing

Write a Letter

Have you ever seen a movie or show or played a video game that you thought was either too violent or rated too harshly? Write a three- to four-paragraph letter to the Motion Picture Association of America or to the Entertainment Software Rating Board in which you argue that the rating of a movie, show, or game that includes horror content should be changed.

- Introduce yourself and the title of the movie, show, or game you are writing about.
- Explain why you think the rating is too restrictive or not restrictive enough, citing details.
- Be sure to maintain a professional tone throughout your letter.

Speaking & Listening

Discuss with a Small Group

Use the characteristics of the horror genre described in the essay to categorize the horror stories you have read and the horror films you have seen.

- Work with a small group to create a list of stories and films.
- Review the characters, setting, events, structure, and organization of each story and film. Take notes.
- Decide how to categorize the stories and films. What creates the suspense in each one? Do they have similar themes or settings? Are the sources of horror alike in some way?
- Explain your categories as you share your final list with the class.

Respond

Expand Your Vocabulary

PRACTICE AND APPLY

Write the best answer for each question.

intensify	justify	parallel

1. Which vocabulary word goes with **similar**? Why?
2. Which vocabulary word goes with **strengthen**? Why?
3. Which vocabulary word goes with **defend**? Why?

Vocabulary Strategy

Use Suffixes

A **suffix** is a word part that is added to the end of a root or base word. Sometimes spelling changes are also made to the base word.

> But that suspense is <u>intensified</u> by our knowledge of the genre. . . . Of course Susan's fears are <u>justified</u>.

Ed

Interactive Vocabulary Lesson: Common Roots, Prefixes, and Suffixes

This table summarizes patterns that will help you use base words and the suffixes *-d* and *-ed* to identify unfamiliar words:

EXAMPLE	PATTERN TO REMEMBER
abandon**ed**	Add *-ed* to most verbs to create past forms.
reliev**ed**	If a verb ends in *-e*, only *-d* is added.
horrif**ied**	If a verb ends in a consonant + *y*, the *y* is changed to *i*, then *-ed* is added.
occurr**ed**	If a verb ends in a vowel + a consonant and has more than one syllable, the consonant is doubled only if the verb is accented on the last syllable.

PRACTICE AND APPLY

Change each verb in parentheses to the past tense.

1. The main character (stop) for gas in a small town.
2. She was (mystify) when the pump was empty.
3. She (glance) around the town, but it was deserted.
4. Suddenly, she heard a scream that (petrify) her.

Watch Your Language!

Commas

A writer's use of punctuation not only helps readers understand the message, but also signals how the writer wants the text to be read. In your writing, you can use commas to signal a break or a pause to the reader.

Ed
Interactive Grammar Lessons: Punctuation I

Look at these examples of how Sharon A. Russell uses commas in "What Is the Horror Genre?"

PURPOSE OF COMMA	EXAMPLE
To signal a break in thought or an additional thought	Often horror has its greatest effect on us because we almost believe, or believe while we are reading the book or watching the film, that the events are possible.
To signal a pause between phrases or clauses	If the genre has traditional monsters, it also has traditional settings.
To set off a phrase or clause that provides information that is not essential to the sentence's meaning	She does end up dead in the basement, a victim of the vampire.

PRACTICE AND APPLY

These sentences include words, phrases, and clauses that need to be punctuated with commas. Rewrite the sentences, inserting the needed punctuation. If you get stuck, try reading the sentence aloud.

1. Yes I absolutely love horror stories.
2. You know of course that the main purpose of horror stories is to inspire fear and dread.
3. If Frankenstein's monster is frightening he is also sympathetic.

The Tell-Tale Heart

Short Story by **Edgar Allan Poe**

ESSENTIAL QUESTION:
Why do we sometimes like to feel frightened?

Engage Your Brain

Choose one or more of these activities to start connecting with the story you are about to read.

Dig In

Do some research to learn about the literary works of Edgar Allan Poe. Find facts about:

- Poe's first published work
- the kinds of writing Poe did
- his most famous stories

All in His Mind

With a partner, have a brief discussion to share your thoughts about this portrait of Edgar Allan Poe. What does the image suggest about the mind of this well-known author?

Analyze Point of View

Point of view is the method of narration used in a short story, novel, narrative poem, or work of nonfiction. In a story told from the **third-person point of view,** the **narrator,** or the voice that tells the story, is an outside observer. In a story told from the **first-person point of view,** the narrator is a character and uses the pronouns *I, me,* and *we.*

You can't always believe everything you learn from a first-person narrator. An **unreliable narrator** is a narrator whose story cannot be trusted for some reason—he or she might be purposefully lying, mentally unstable, or too young to fully understand events. To determine whether or not a narrator is reliable, consider his or her actions, attitudes, and statements, and then decide whether he or she is generally trustworthy.

As you read "The Tell-Tale Heart," look for clues that tell you whether the narrator is reliable or unreliable.

Focus on Genre

Short Story

- includes the basic elements of fiction—setting, characters, plot, conflict, and theme
- centers on one particular moment or event in the main character's life
- can be read in one sitting

Analyze Suspense

Suspense is the sense of growing tension, fear, and excitement felt by the reader. When a story is suspenseful, the reader becomes increasingly curious about what will happen next. Some techniques Poe uses to create suspense are listed in the chart below. Fill in the chart with examples of these techniques as you read "The Tell-Tale Heart."

TECHNIQUE	EXAMPLE
Describing a character's anxiety or fear	
Using vivid words to describe dramatic sights, sounds, or feelings	
Repeating words, phrases, or characters' actions	

Annotation in Action

Here are one reader's comments on the point of view of the narrator in the story. As you read, mark when the author's use of point of view builds suspense and tension.

True!—nervous—very, very dreadfully nervous I had been and am! but why *will* you say that I am mad? The disease had sharpened my senses—not destroyed—not dulled them. Above all was the sense of hearing acute. I heard all things in the heaven and in the earth. I heard many things in hell. How, then, am I mad? . . .

Point of view: The first-person narrator admits he is very nervous, but he denies that he is insane.

Expand Your Vocabulary

Put a check mark next to the vocabulary words that you feel comfortable using when speaking or writing.

- **conceive** ☐
- **vex** ☐
- **stifle** ☐
- **vehemently** ☐
- **derision** ☐
- **hypocritical** ☐

Turn to a partner and talk about the words you already know. Then, use as many words as you can in a paragraph about someone who tries to cover up a crime.

As you read "The Tell-Tale Heart," use the definitions in the side column to learn the vocabulary words you don't already know.

Background

Edgar Allan Poe (1809–1849) was born in Boston to parents who were traveling actors. Orphaned by the time he was three, he moved to Virginia, where friends of his family raised him. As a young man, Poe worked as a journalist while writing the stories and poems that would earn him the title "father of the modern mystery." After his young wife died, Poe fell into despair. He passed away two years later. His dark and sometimes horrifying works perhaps mirror the darkness and sadness of his own short life.

The Tell-Tale Heart

Short Story by **Edgar Allan Poe**

The narrator of this twisted tale tries to cover up his crime.

NOTICE & NOTE
As you read, use the side margins to make notes about the text.

1 True!—nervous—very, very dreadfully nervous I had been and am! but why *will* you say that I am mad? The disease had sharpened my senses—not destroyed—not dulled them. Above all was the sense of hearing acute. I heard all things in the heaven and in the earth. I heard many things in hell. How, then, am I mad? Hearken! and observe how healthily—how calmly I can tell you the whole story.

2 It is impossible to say how first the idea entered my brain; but once **conceived,** it haunted me day and night. Object there was none. Passion there was none. I loved the old man. He had never wronged me. He had never given me insult. For his gold I had no desire. I think it was his eye! yes, it was this! He had the eye of a vulture—a pale blue eye, with a film over it. Whenever it fell upon me, my blood ran cold; and so by degrees—very gradually—I made up my mind to take the life of the old man, and thus rid myself of the eye forever.

Ed

Close Read Screencast

Listen to a modeled close read of this text.

conceive
(kən-sēv´) *v.* When you *conceive* an idea, you think of it.

NOTICE & NOTE
AGAIN AND AGAIN

When you notice that a word, image, or event is repeated in a story, you've found an **Again and Again** signpost.

Notice & Note: In paragraph 4, mark details or ideas that the narrator keeps repeating as he tells his story.

Infer: Why do you think the narrator repeats these ideas again and again?

vex
(vĕks) *v.* If you *vex* someone, you bother or annoy that person.

ANALYZE POINT OF VIEW

Annotate: In paragraph 5, mark details that suggest whether the narrator can or cannot be trusted to describe events as they truly are.

Infer: Is the narrator reliable or unreliable? Explain why you think so.

3 Now this is the point. You fancy me mad. Madmen know nothing. But you should have seen *me*. You should have seen how wisely I proceeded—with what caution—with what foresight—with what dissimulation[1] I went to work!

4 I was never kinder to the old man than during the whole week before I killed him. And every night, about midnight, I turned the latch of his door and opened it—oh, so gently! And then, when I had made an opening sufficient for my head, I put in a dark lantern, all closed, closed, so that no light shone out, and then I thrust in my head. Oh, you would have laughed to see how cunningly I thrust it in! I moved it slowly—very, very slowly, so that I might not disturb the old man's sleep. It took me an hour to place my whole head within the opening so far that I could see him as he lay upon his bed. Ha!—would a madman have been so wise as this? And then, when my head was well in the room, I undid the lantern cautiously—oh, so cautiously—cautiously (for the hinges creaked)—I undid it just so much that a single thin ray fell upon the vulture eye. And this I did for seven long nights—every night just at midnight—but I found the eye always closed; and so it was impossible to do the work; for it was not the old man who **vexed** me, but his Evil Eye. And every morning, when the day broke, I went boldly into the chamber, and spoke courageously to him, calling him by name in a hearty tone, and inquiring how he had passed the night. So you see he would have been a very profound old man, indeed, to suspect that every night, just at twelve, I looked in upon him while he slept.

5 Upon the eighth night I was more than usually cautious in opening the door. A watch's minute hand moves more quickly than did mine. Never before that night had I *felt* the extent of my own powers—of my sagacity.[2] I could scarcely contain my feelings of triumph. To think that there I was, opening the door, little by little, and he not even to dream of my secret deeds or thoughts. I fairly chuckled at the idea; and perhaps he heard me; for he moved on the bed suddenly, as if startled. Now you may think that I drew back—but no. His room was as black as pitch with the thick darkness (for the shutters were close fastened, through fear of robbers), and so I knew that he could not see

[1] **dissimulation** (dĭ-sĭm′yə-lā′shən): a hiding of one's true feelings.
[2] **sagacity** (sə-găs′ĭ-tē): sound judgment.

the opening of the door, and I kept pushing it on steadily, steadily.

Don't forget to **Notice & Note** as you read the text.

6 I had my head in, and was about to open the lantern, when my thumb slipped upon the tin fastening, and the old man sprang up in the bed, crying out—"Who's there?"

7 I kept quite still and said nothing. For a whole hour I did not move a muscle, and in the meantime I did not hear him lie down. He was still sitting up in the bed listening,—just as I have done, night after night, hearkening to the death watches[3] in the wall.

8 Presently I heard a slight groan, and I knew it was the groan of mortal terror. It was not a groan of pain or grief—oh, no!—it was the low, **stifled** sound that arises from the bottom of the soul when overcharged with awe. I knew the sound well. Many a night, just at midnight, when all the world slept, it has welled up from my own bosom, deepening, with its dreadful echo, the terrors that distracted me. I say I knew it well. I knew what the old man felt, and pitied him, although I chuckled at heart. I knew that he had been lying awake ever since the first slight noise, when he had turned in the bed. His fears had been ever since growing upon him. He had been trying to fancy them causeless, but could not. He had been saying to himself—"It is nothing but the wind in the chimney—it is only a mouse crossing the floor," or "it is merely a cricket which has made a single chirp." Yes, he has been trying to comfort himself with these suppositions; but he had found all in vain. *All in vain;* because Death, in approaching him, had stalked with his black shadow before him, and enveloped the victim. And it was the mournful influence of the unperceived shadow that caused him to feel—although he neither saw nor heard—to *feel* the presence of my head within the room.

stifle

(stī′fəl) *v.* If you *stifle* something, you smother it.

9 When I had waited a long time, very patiently, without hearing him lie down, I resolved to open a little—a very, very little crevice in the lantern. So I opened it—you cannot imagine how stealthily, stealthily—until, at length, a single dim ray, like the thread of the spider, shot from out the crevice and fell full upon the vulture eye.

VOCABULARY

Use a Dictionary: If you are unfamiliar with the word *crevice* in paragraph 9, use a dictionary to look it up.

Interpret: How does the author's use of the word *crevice* help to describe the narrator's actions?

[3] **death watches:** deathwatch beetles—insects that make a tapping sound with their heads.

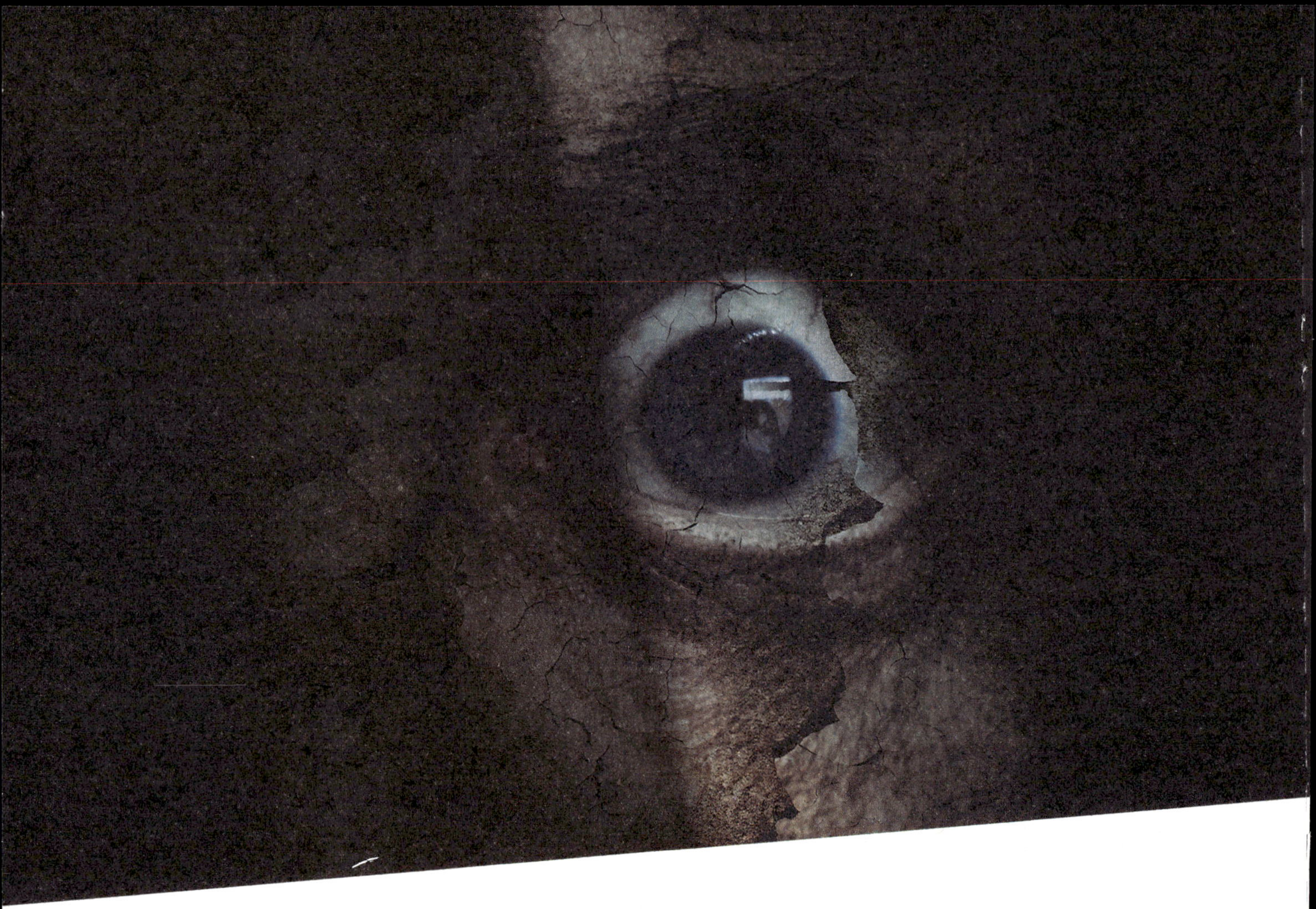

Ed

Text in Focus Video

Learn how to visualize a story.

ANALYZE SUSPENSE

Annotate: Mark words and phrases in paragraphs 11–12 that Poe uses to create suspense.

Analyze: Why do these details create suspense?

10 It was open—wide, wide open—and I grew furious as I gazed upon it. I saw it with perfect distinctness—all a dull blue, with a hideous veil over it that chilled the very marrow in my bones; but I could see nothing else of the old man's face or person: for I had directed the ray as if by instinct, precisely upon the damned spot.

11 And now have I not told you that what you mistake for madness is but over-acuteness of the senses?—now, I say, there came to my ears a low, dull, quick sound, such as a watch makes when enveloped in cotton. I knew *that* sound well too. It was the beating of the old man's heart. It increased my fury, as the beating of a drum stimulates the soldier into courage.

12 But even yet I refrained and kept still. I scarcely breathed. I held the lantern motionless. I tried how steadily I could maintain the ray upon the eye. Meantime the hellish tattoo[4] of the heart increased. It grew quicker and quicker, and louder and louder every instant. The old man's terror *must* have been extreme! It grew louder, I say, louder every moment!—do you mark me well? I have told you that I am nervous: so I am. And now at the dead hour of the night, amid the dreadful silence

[4] **hellish tattoo:** awful drumming.

of that old house, so strange a noise as this excited me to uncontrollable terror. Yet, for some minutes longer I refrained and stood still. But the beating grew louder, louder! I thought the heart must burst. And now a new anxiety seized me—the sound would be heard by a neighbor! The old man's hour had come! With a loud yell, I threw open the lantern and leaped into the room. He shrieked once—once only. In an instant I dragged him to the floor, and pulled the heavy bed over him. I then smiled gaily, to find the deed so far done. But, for many minutes, the heart beat on with a muffled sound. This, however, did not vex me; it would not be heard through the wall. At length it ceased. The old man was dead. I removed the bed and examined the corpse. Yes, he was stone, stone dead. I placed my hand upon the heart and held it there many minutes. There was no pulsation. He was stone dead. His eye would trouble me no more.

13 If still you think me mad, you will think so no longer when I describe the wise precautions I took for the concealment of the body. The night waned, and I worked hastily, but in silence. First of all I dismembered the corpse. I cut off the head and the arms and the legs.

14 I then took up three planks from the flooring of the chamber, and deposited all between the scantlings.[5] I then replaced the boards so cleverly, so cunningly, that no human eye—not even *his*—could have detected anything wrong. There was nothing to wash out—no stain of any kind—no blood-spot whatever. I had been too wary for that. A tub had caught all—ha! ha!

15 When I made an end of these labors, it was four o'clock—still dark as midnight. As the bell sounded the hour, there came a knocking at the street door. I went down to open it with a light heart,—for what had I *now* to fear? There entered three men, who introduced themselves, with perfect suavity,[6] as officers of the police. A shriek had been heard by a neighbor during the night: suspicion of foul play had been aroused; information had been lodged at the police office, and they (the officers) had been deputed to search the premises.

16 I smiled,—for *what* had I to fear? I bade the gentlemen welcome. The shriek, I said, was my own in a dream. The old man, I mentioned, was absent in the country. I took my visitors all over the house. I bade them search—search *well*. I led them, at length, to *his* chamber. I showed them his treasures, secure, undisturbed. In the enthusiasm of my confidence, I brought

Don't forget to **Notice & Note** as you read the text.

ANALYZE POINT OF VIEW

Annotate: In paragraphs 13–14, mark details that show how the narrator tries to convince readers that he is sane and reliable.

Evaluate: What effect do the narrator's explanations have on the reader?

NOTICE & NOTE

CONTRASTS AND CONTRADICTIONS

When you notice that characters' actions contradict their previous behavior, you've found a **Contrasts and Contradictions** signpost.

Notice & Note: Mark details in paragraphs 16–18 that show the contrast between the way the narrator acts around the police officers at first and his behavior as they are sitting and talking.

Draw Conclusions: Why might the narrator act this way?

[5] **scantlings:** small wooden beams supporting the floor.
[6] **suavity** (swä´vĭ-tē): graceful politeness.

chairs into the room, and desired them here to rest from their fatigues, while I myself, in the wild audacity of my perfect triumph, placed my own seat upon the very spot beneath which reposed the corpse of the victim.

17 The officers were satisfied. My *manner* had convinced them. I was singularly at ease. They sat, and while I answered cheerily, they chatted of familiar things. But, ere long, I felt myself getting pale and wished them gone. My head ached, and I fancied a ringing in my ears: but still they sat and still chatted. The ringing became more distinct:—it continued and became more distinct: I talked more freely to get rid of the feeling: but it continued and gained definitiveness—until at length, I found that the noise was *not* within my ears.

18 No doubt I now grew *very* pale;—but I talked more fluently, and with a heightened voice. Yet the sound increased—and what could I do? It was *a low, dull, quick sound—much such a sound as a watch makes when enveloped in cotton.* I gasped for breath—and yet the officers heard it not. I talked more quickly—more **vehemently**; but the noise steadily increased. I arose and argued about trifles, in a high key and with violent gesticulations,[7] but the noise steadily increased. Why *would* they not be gone? I paced the floor to and fro with heavy strides, as if excited to fury by the observation of the men—but the noise steadily increased. What *could* I do? I foamed—I raved—I swore. I swung the chair upon which I had been sitting, and grated it upon the boards, but the noise arose over all and continually increased. It grew louder—louder—*louder!* And still the men chatted pleasantly, and smiled. Was it possible they heard not?—no, no! They heard!—they suspected!—they *knew!*—they were making a *mockery* of my horror!—this I thought, and this I think. But anything was better than this agony! Anything was more tolerable than this **derision**! I could bear those **hypocritical** smiles no longer! I felt that I must scream or die!—and now—again!—hark! louder! louder! *louder!*—

19 "Villains!" I shrieked, "dissemble[8] no more! I admit the deed!—tear up the planks!—here, here!—it is the beating of his hideous heart!"

vehemently
(vē´ə-mənt-lē) *adv.* If you do something *vehemently,* you do it with intense emotion.

derision
(dĭ-rĭzh´ən) *n. Derision* is jeering laughter or ridicule.

hypocritical
(hĭp´ə-krĭt´ĭ-kəl) *adj.* If someone is *hypocritical,* the person is false or deceptive.

?

ESSENTIAL QUESTION:

Why do we sometimes like to feel frightened?

Review your annotations and notes. Then, add relevant details to your Response Log.

[7] **gesticulations** (jĕ-stĭk´yə-lā´shəns): energetic gestures of the hands or arms.
[8] **dissemble:** pretend.

TURN AND TALK

With a partner, discuss what makes this story such a thought-provoking classic.

Assessment Practice

Answer these questions before moving on to the **Analyze the Text** section on the following page.

1. This question has two parts. First answer **Part A**, then **Part B**.

Part A

How does the narrator try to prove that he is not mad?

(A) He describes how cunning and cautious he is.

(B) He waits until the eighth night to kill the old man.

(C) He says he pities the old man but laughs in his heart.

(D) He allows the police officers to search the house.

Part B

Select **two** sentences from the text that support the answer to Part A.

(A) "It is impossible to say how first the idea entered my brain; but once conceived, it haunted me day and night." (paragraph 2)

(B) "You should have seen how wisely I proceeded—with what caution—with what foresight—with what dissimulation I went to work!" (paragraph 3)

(C) "Presently I heard a slight groan, and I knew it was the groan of mortal terror." (paragraph 8)

(D) "In an instant I dragged him to the floor, and pulled the heavy bed over him." (paragraph 12)

(E) "If still you think me mad, you will think so no longer when I describe the wise precautions I took for the concealment of the body." (paragraph 13)

2. Why can't the police officers hear the old man's heart?

(A) The narrator is speaking loudly to drown out the old man's heart.

(B) The officers are sitting too far away from the old man's body.

(C) The officers' senses are not as acute as those of the narrator.

(D) The old man's heart is not actually beating.

Ed

Test-Taking Strategies

Analyze the Text

Support your responses with evidence from the text.

NOTICE & NOTE

Review what you **noticed and noted** as you read the text. Your annotations can help you answer these questions.

1. **INFER** Does the narrator's opinion of himself in paragraphs 1–2 make him seem more reliable, or less? Explain your choice.

2. **ANALYZE** Review the chart you filled in with notes about how Poe creates suspense. What prevents the narrator from killing the old man during the first seven nights? Explain how his inaction contributes to the story's suspense.

3. **DRAW CONCLUSIONS** Reread paragraphs 9–11. What do readers learn from this first-person narration about the narrator's subjective, or personal, experience?

4. **EVALUATE** Does the reader's inability to trust the narrator increase the suspense in this story? Explain your answer.

5. **ANALYZE** In what way does the image of the "eye of a vulture" being repeated **Again and Again** help to create suspense?

6. **COMPARE** Use the graphic organizer to contrast the narrator's opinion of himself with the reader's view of him. Include text details that highlight the **Contrasts and Contradictions** you notice.

NARRATOR'S VIEW OF HIMSELF	READER'S VIEW OF NARRATOR

Choices

Here are some other ways to demonstrate your understanding of the ideas in this lesson.

Writing

Rewrite a Scene

Rewrite a scene from "The Tell-Tale Heart" from the point of view of a reliable narrator.

- Review the story to find a brief scene. Identify specific details that a reliable narrator would describe differently.
- Decide whether you will write from the first-person or the third-person point of view.
- Write the scene from the perspective of your reliable narrator.

As you write and discuss, be sure to use the **Academic Vocabulary** words.

- convention
- predict
- psychology
- summary
- technique

Speaking & Listening

Dramatize a Scene

Working alone or with one or more partners, act out an especially suspenseful scene from "The Tell-Tale Heart."

- Review your notes to identify a scene in which Poe uses point of view and other literary devices to create suspense.
- Decide how many characters your scene needs and who will play them.
- Write dialogue for each character.
- Practice your scene. Then perform it for the class.

Media

Find the Tell-Tale Heart

With a partner, create a plan for an escape room based on Poe's short story.

- Include details and descriptions of the setting from the story in your plan for the escape room.
- Use digital tools to create a map or floor plan and a "deck" of cards that ask questions about the story.
- Players must answer correctly to get clues that will help them be the first to find the tell-tale heart and win the escape-room challenge.

Expand Your Vocabulary

PRACTICE AND APPLY

Use what you know about the vocabulary words to answer these questions.

1. Would it **vex** you if someone were **hypocritical?** Why?
2. Why might someone **vehemently** deny having **conceived** a plan to commit a crime?
3. What can you do to **stifle derision** of another student?

Vocabulary Strategy:
Use a Dictionary

A dictionary is a reference work that provides an alphabetical list of words with their meanings and pronunciations. Some dictionaries are books, while others are electronic or online resources.

Ed

Interactive Vocabulary Lesson: Using Reference Sources

Notice the parts of this dictionary entry for the word *wary.*

entry word | pronunciation | part of speech | definitions

war•y (wâr'ē) *adj.* 1. On guard; watchful: *taught to be wary of strangers* 2. Characterized by caution: *a wary glance at the black clouds*

PRACTICE AND APPLY

Use a dictionary to answer these questions about the Academic Vocabulary words for this unit.

1. What are two different meanings for *convention?*
2. What part of speech is *predict?*
3. What definition of *psychology* fits in the sentence *Our track team has a very successful psychology?*
4. What language does *summary* originally come from?
5. Which syllable is stressed when you pronounce the word *technique?*

Watch Your Language!

Dashes

A writer's use of punctuation not only helps readers understand the writer's message, it can also signal how the writer wants the text to be read. A **dash** (—) is a horizontal line that is longer than a hyphen. Writers may use a dash for different purposes, as noted in the following chart.

PURPOSE	EXAMPLE
to signal a sudden break in thought	"And this I did for seven long nights—every night just at midnight—but I found the eye always closed. . . ."
to signal the reader to pause and pay attention	"I resolved to open a little—a very, very little crevice in the lantern."
to let the reader better hear a narrator's thoughts	"I went down to open it with a light heart,—for what had I **now** to fear?"

PRACTICE AND APPLY

Working with a partner, write a paragraph in which your narrator tells readers about himself or herself. Use dashes to

- set off a sudden break in thought
- signal the reader to pause and pay attention
- let the reader better hear your narrator's voice

Collaborate & Compare

ESSENTIAL QUESTION:
Why do we sometimes like to feel frightened?

Compare Versions

You are about to read a short story and view part of a film version of the story. As you read, notice key details about the story's characters, setting, and plot events. Then, examine how these elements are adapted in a film version of the story's ending.

A

The Monkey's Paw

Short Story by **W. W. Jacobs**
pages 112–125

B

from **The Monkey's Paw**

Film Clip by **Ricky Lewis Jr.**
page 131

After you have read the text and viewed the film clip, you will have a discussion with your classmates, following these steps:

- Decide on the Most Important Details
- Discuss the Director's Choices
- Evaluate Advantages of Each Version
- Present to the Class

The Monkey's Paw

Short Story by **W. W. Jacobs**

Engage Your Brain

Choose one or more of these activities to start connecting with the story you're about to read.

The Rule of Three

In "The Monkey's Paw," the main characters are granted three wishes. Make a list of any other stories you know about that follow "the rule of three."

Lucky Objects

In the story you are about to read, the monkey's paw is a talisman, an object thought to have magical powers. What are some objects you know about that are believed to have magical powers or to bring good luck? Make a list or sketch a few of the objects below.

Analyze Themes

Literature often conveys **themes,** which are messages about life or human nature. Some themes are found throughout literature of all time periods. These themes, which apply to anyone, anywhere, are known as **universal themes.**

Readers can determine a story's theme or themes by looking for clues in dialogue, comments from the narrator, the ways characters interact and change, details about the setting, and the events of the plot.

In "The Monkey's Paw," the author uses a pattern of repetition drawn from traditional stories, known as the rule of three. On three occasions in the story, a wish is granted. The rule of three is often connected to a story's themes. As you read "The Monkey's Paw," use this information as well as clues in the story to analyze its themes.

Focus on Genre

Short Story

- is a work of fiction
- contains a plot, characters, setting, and theme
- is a popular format for horror stories
- if it is a horror story, often includes supernatural elements

Analyze Foreshadowing

Foreshadowing occurs when a writer provides hints that suggest future events in a story. Foreshadowing can propel the plot forward by building suspense, fueling readers' desire to find out what will happen next. Clues about future events may appear in **dialogue** (conversation between characters), incidents in the story, and **imagery** (words and phrases that re-create sensory experiences).

Consider what the first example in the chart suggests about events to come. Then, as you read "The Monkey's Paw," use the chart to note other examples of text clues that foreshadow future events.

DIALOGUE	"I did have some idea of selling it, but I don't think I will. It has caused enough mischief already."
INCIDENT	
IMAGERY	

Annotation in Action

Here is how one reader annotated the beginning of "The Monkey's Paw" with comments about foreshadowing. As you read, mark places in the text that hint at what might happen later in the story.

Without, the night was cold and wet, but in the small parlor of Laburnum Villa the blinds were drawn and the fire burned brightly. Father and son were at chess; the former, who possessed ideas about the game involving radical changes, putting his king into such sharp and unnecessary perils that it even provoked comment from the white-haired old lady knitting placidly by the fire.

The father takes unnecessary risks while playing chess. Could this detail about his personality be a kind of foreshadowing?

Expand Your Vocabulary

Put a check mark next to the vocabulary words that you feel comfortable using when speaking or writing.

- peril ☐
- condole ☐
- grimace ☐
- credulity ☐
- compensation ☐
- resignation ☐

Turn to a partner and talk about the words you already know. Then, write a few sentences about someone whose wish came true, using as many of the vocabulary words as you can.

As you read "The Monkey's Paw," use the definitions in the side column to learn the vocabulary words you don't already know.

Background

W. W. Jacobs (1863–1943) grew up in London near the waterfront wharfs. As a boy, Jacobs absorbed the tales of strange, distant lands told by passing sailors. As a young man, Jacobs worked at a bank—a job that he hated—and wrote stories in his spare time. He eventually became a popular writer of humor. Ironically, his best-known work, "The Monkey's Paw," became a classic of the horror genre.

The Monkey's Paw

Short Story by **W. W. Jacobs**

A visitor gives the White family an object that will grant them three wishes, but he also gives them a grim warning.

NOTICE & NOTE
As you read, use the side margins to make notes about the text.

Part I

1 Without, the night was cold and wet, but in the small parlor of Laburnum Villa the blinds were drawn and the fire burned brightly. Father and son were at chess; the former, who possessed ideas about the game involving radical changes, putting his king into such sharp and unnecessary **perils** that it even provoked comment from the white-haired old lady knitting placidly by the fire.

peril
(pĕr´əl) *n.* A *peril* is something that is dangerous.

2 "Hark at the wind," said Mr. White, who, having seen a fatal mistake after it was too late, was amiably desirous of preventing his son from seeing it.

3 "I'm listening," said the latter, grimly surveying the board as he stretched out his hand. "Check."

Don't forget to **Notice & Note** as you read the text.

4 "I should hardly think that he'd come tonight," said his father, with his hand poised over the board.

5 "Mate," replied the son.

6 "That's the worst of living so far out," bawled Mr. White, with sudden and unlooked-for violence; "of all the beastly, slushy, out-of-the-way places to live in, this is the worst. Pathway's a bog,[1] and the road's a torrent.[2] I don't know what people are thinking about. I suppose because only two houses in the road are let,[3] they think it doesn't matter."

7 "Never mind, dear," said his wife soothingly; "perhaps you'll win the next one."

8 Mr. White looked up sharply, just in time to intercept a knowing glance between mother and son. The words died away on his lips, and he hid a guilty grin in his thin gray beard.

9 "There he is," said Herbert White, as the gate banged loudly and heavy footsteps came toward the door.

10 The old man rose with hospitable haste, and opening the door, was heard **condoling** with the new arrival. The new arrival also condoled with himself, so that Mrs. White said, "Tut, tut!" and coughed gently as her husband entered the room, followed by a tall, burly man, beady of eye and rubicund of visage.[4]

condole
(kən-dōl´) *v.* If you *condole* with someone, you express sympathy or sorrow.

11 "Sergeant-Major Morris," he said, introducing him.

12 The sergeant-major shook hands, and taking the proffered seat by the fire, watched contentedly while his host brought out drinks and stood a small copper kettle on the fire.

13 He began to talk, the little family circle regarding with eager interest this visitor from distant parts, as he squared his broad shoulders in the chair and spoke of wild scenes and doughty[5] deeds; of wars and plagues and strange peoples.

ANALYZE FORESHADOWING

Annotate: Mark details in paragraph 13 that describe the content of Sergeant-Major Morris's conversation.

Analyze: How do the details describing what Morris talks about help build suspense?

14 "Twenty-one years of it," said Mr. White, nodding at his wife and son. "When he went away, he was a slip of a youth in the warehouse. Now look at him."

15 "He don't look to have taken much harm," said Mrs. White politely.

16 "I'd like to go to India myself," said the old man, "just to look round a bit, you know."

[1] **bog:** a swamp.
[2] **torrent** (tôr´ənt)**:** a swift-flowing stream.
[3] **let:** rented.
[4] **rubicund** (ro͞o´bĭ-kənd) **of visage** (vĭz´ĭj)**:** with a healthy rosy or reddish complexion.
[5] **doughty** (dou´tē)**:** brave.

17 "Better where you are," said the sergeant-major, shaking his head. He put down the empty glass, and sighing softly, shook it again.

18 "I should like to see those old temples and fakirs and jugglers," said the old man. "What was that you started telling me the other day about a monkey's paw or something, Morris?"

19 "Nothing," said the soldier hastily. "Leastways nothing worth hearing."

20 "Monkey's paw?" said Mrs. White curiously.

21 "Well, it's just a bit of what you might call magic, perhaps," said the sergeant-major off-handedly.

22 His three listeners leaned forward eagerly. The visitor absent-mindedly put his empty glass to his lips and then set it down again. His host filled it for him.

23 "To look at," said the sergeant-major, fumbling in his pocket, "it's just an ordinary little paw, dried to a mummy."

24 He took something out of his pocket and proffered it. Mrs. White drew back with a **grimace**, but her son, taking it, examined it curiously.

grimace
(grĭm´ĭs) *n.* A *grimace* is a facial expression of pain or disgust.

25 "And what is there special about it?" inquired Mr. White as he took it from his son, and having examined it, placed it upon the table.

26 "It had a spell put on it by an old fakir," said the sergeant-major, "a very holy man. He wanted to show that fate ruled people's lives, and that those who interfered with it did so to their sorrow. He put a spell on it so that three separate men could each have three wishes from it."

ANALYZE THEMES

Annotate: In paragraph 26, underline the lesson that the old fakir wanted to teach people.

Infer: What does this lesson suggest about the story's theme?

27 His manner was so impressive that his hearers were conscious that their light laughter jarred somewhat.

28 "Well, why don't you have three, sir?" said Herbert White cleverly.

29 The soldier regarded him in the way that middle age is wont to regard presumptuous youth. "I have," he said quietly, and his blotchy face whitened.

30 "And did you really have the three wishes granted?" asked Mrs. White.

31 "I did," said the sergeant-major, and his glass tapped against his strong teeth.

32 "And has anybody else wished?" persisted the old lady.

33 "The first man had his three wishes. Yes," was the reply; "I don't know what the first two were, but the third was for death. That's how I got the paw."

34 His tones were so grave that a hush fell upon the group.

35 "If you've had your three wishes, it's no good to you now, then, Morris," said the old man at last. "What do you keep it for?"

36 The soldier shook his head. "Fancy, I suppose," he said slowly. "I did have some idea of selling it, but I don't think I will. It has caused enough mischief already. Besides, people won't buy. They think it's a fairy tale, some of them; and those who do think anything of it want to try it first and pay me afterward."

37 "If you could have another three wishes," said the old man, eyeing him keenly, "would you have them?"

38 "I don't know," said the other. "I don't know."

39 He took the paw, and dangling it between his forefinger and thumb, suddenly threw it upon the fire. White, with a slight cry, stooped down and snatched it off.

40 "Better let it burn," said the soldier solemnly.

41 "If you don't want it, Morris," said the other, "give it to me."

42 "I won't," said his friend doggedly. "I threw it on the fire. If you keep it, don't blame me for what happens. Pitch it on the fire again like a sensible man."

43 The other shook his head and examined his new possession closely. "How do you do it?" he inquired.

44 "Hold it up in your right hand and wish aloud," said the sergeant-major, "but I warn you of the consequences."

45 "Sounds like the *Arabian Nights*,"[6] said Mrs. White, as she rose and began to set the supper. "Don't you think you might wish for four pairs of hands for me?"

46 Her husband drew the talisman[7] from his pocket, and then all three burst into laughter as the sergeant-major, with a look of alarm on his face, caught him by the arm.

47 "If you must wish," he said gruffly, "wish for something sensible."

48 Mr. White dropped it back in his pocket, and placing chairs, motioned his friend to the table. In the business of supper the talisman was partly forgotten, and afterward the three sat listening in an enthralled fashion to a second installment of the soldier's adventures in India.

49 "If the tale about the monkey's paw is not more truthful than those he has been telling us," said Herbert, as the door closed behind their guest, just in time for him to catch the last train, "we shan't make much out of it."

Don't forget to **Notice & Note** as you read the text.

NOTICE & NOTE

WORDS OF THE WISER

When you notice a wiser character giving advice about life to the main character, you've found a **Words of the Wiser** signpost.

Notice & Note: What words of advice about the paw does Sergeant-Major Morris share with the Whites in paragraph 47?

Infer: What's the life lesson, and how might it affect the Whites?

[6] ***Arabian Nights:*** a famous collection of fantastical Middle Eastern stories featuring such tales as "Ali Baba and the Forty Thieves" and "Aladdin and the Magic Lamp."

[7] **talisman** (tăl´ĭs-mən)**:** an object thought to have magical powers.

50 "Did you give him anything for it, Father?" inquired Mrs. White, regarding her husband closely.

51 "A trifle," said he, coloring slightly. "He didn't want it, but I made him take it. And he pressed me again to throw it away."

52 "Likely," said Herbert, with pretended horror. "Why, we're going to be rich, and famous, and happy. Wish to be an emperor, Father, to begin with; then you can't be henpecked."

53 He darted round the table, pursued by the maligned Mrs. White armed with an antimacassar.[8]

54 Mr. White took the paw from his pocket and eyed it dubiously. "I don't know what to wish for, and that's a fact," he said slowly. "It seems to me I've got all I want."

55 "If you only cleared the house, you'd be quite happy, wouldn't you?" said Herbert, with his hand on his shoulder. "Well, wish for two hundred pounds, then; that'll just do it."

credulity
(krĭ-do͞o´lĭ-tē) *n. Credulity* is a tendency to believe too readily.

56 His father, smiling shamefacedly at his own **credulity,** held up the talisman, as his son, with a solemn face, somewhat marred by a wink at his mother, sat down at the piano and struck a few impressive chords.

57 "I wish for two hundred pounds," said the old man distinctly.

ANALYZE THEMES

Annotate: Mark details in paragraphs 58–61 that show the main characters' attitudes toward the paw.

Compare: How have Mr. and Mrs. White's attitudes toward the paw changed? What might this change suggest about the story's theme?

58 A fine crash from the piano greeted the words, interrupted by a shuddering cry from the old man. His wife and son ran toward him.

59 "It moved," he cried, with a glance of disgust at the object as it lay on the floor. "As I wished, it twisted in my hand like a snake."

60 "Well, I don't see the money," said his son, as he picked it up and placed it on the table, "and I bet I never shall."

61 "It must have been your fancy, father," said his wife, regarding him anxiously.

62 He shook his head. "Never mind, though; there's no harm done, but it gave me a shock all the same."

63 They sat down by the fire again. Outside, the wind was higher than ever, and the old man started nervously at the sound of a door banging upstairs. A silence unusual and depressing settled upon all three, which lasted until the old couple rose to retire for the night.

64 "I expect you'll find the cash tied up in a big bag in the middle of your bed," said Herbert, as he bade them goodnight, "and something horrible squatting up on top of the wardrobe watching you as you pocket your ill-gotten gains."

[8] **antimacassar** (ăn´tĭ-mə-kăs´ər)**:** a cloth placed over an arm or the back of a chair.

65 He sat alone in the darkness, gazing at the dying fire, and seeing faces in it. The last face was so horrible and so simian[9] that he gazed at it in amazement. It got so vivid that, with a little uneasy laugh, he felt on the table for a glass containing a little water to throw over it. His hand grasped the monkey's paw, and with a little shiver he wiped his hand on his coat and went up to bed.

Part II

66 In the brightness of the wintry sun next morning as it streamed over the breakfast table he laughed at his fears. There was an air of prosaic wholesomeness about the room which it had lacked on the previous night, and the dirty, shriveled little paw was pitched on the sideboard[10] with a carelessness which betokened no great belief in its virtues.[11]

67 "I suppose all old soldiers are the same," said Mrs. White. "The idea of our listening to such nonsense! How could wishes be granted in these days? And if they could, how could two hundred pounds hurt you, father?"

68 "Might drop on his head from the sky," said the frivolous[12] Herbert.

69 "Morris said the things happened so naturally," said his father, "that you might if you so wished attribute it to coincidence."

70 "Well, don't break into the money before I come back," said Herbert as he rose from the table. "I'm afraid it'll turn you into a mean, avaricious[13] man, and we shall have to disown you."

71 His mother laughed, and following him to the door, watched him down the road; and returning to the breakfast table, was very happy at the expense of her husband's credulity. All of which did not prevent her from scurrying to the door at the postman's knock, when she found that the post brought a tailor's bill.

72 "Herbert will have some more of his funny remarks, I expect, when he comes home," she said, as they sat at dinner.

73 "I dare say," said Mr. White, "but for all that, the thing moved in my hand; that I'll swear to."

74 "You thought it did," said the old lady soothingly.

Don't forget to **Notice & Note** as you read the text.

VOCABULARY

Latin Roots: The word *prosaic* contains the Latin root *prōsa*, meaning "prose," which refers to ordinary speech or writing. Recognizing Latin roots can help you understand a word's meaning.

Analyze: In paragraph 66, what does the use of the word *prosaic* indicate about the atmosphere of the room?

[9] **simian** (sĭm´ē-ən): monkey- or ape-like.
[10] **sideboard:** a piece of furniture used to store linens and dishes.
[11] **virtues:** powers.
[12] **frivolous** (frĭv´ə-ləs): inappropriately silly.
[13] **avaricious** (ăv´ə-rĭsh´əs): greedy.

75 "I say it did," replied the other. "There was no thought about it; I had just—What's the matter?"

ANALYZE FORESHADOWING

Annotate: Mark details in paragraph 76 that describe the man outside.

Infer: How does the man's behavior build suspense and propel the action forward? What might it foreshadow?

76 His wife made no reply. She was watching the mysterious movements of a man outside, who, peering in an undecided fashion at the house, appeared to be trying to make up his mind to enter. In mental connection with the two hundred pounds, she noticed that the stranger was well dressed, and wore a silk hat of glossy newness. Three times he paused at the gate, and then walked on again. The fourth time he stood with his hand upon it, and then with sudden resolution flung it open and walked up the path. Mrs. White at the same moment placed her hands behind her, and hurriedly unfastening the strings of her apron, put that useful article of apparel beneath the cushion of her chair.

77 She brought the stranger, who seemed ill at ease, into the room. He gazed at her furtively, and listened in a preoccupied fashion as the old lady apologized for the appearance of the room, and her husband's coat, a garment which he usually reserved for the garden. She then waited patiently for him to broach his business, but he was at first strangely silent.

78 "I—was asked to call," he said at last, and stooped and picked a piece of cotton from his trousers. "I come from Maw and Meggins."

79 The old lady started. "Is anything the matter?" she asked breathlessly. "Has anything happened to Herbert? What is it? What is it?"

80 Her husband interposed. "There, there, mother," he said hastily. "Sit down, and don't jump to conclusions. You've not brought bad news, I'm sure, sir;" and he eyed the other wistfully.

81 "I'm sorry—" began the visitor.

82 "Is he hurt?" demanded the mother wildly.

83 The visitor bowed in assent. "Badly hurt," he said quietly, "but he is not in any pain."

84 "Oh!" said the old woman, clasping her hands. "Thank goodness for that! Thank—"

85 She broke off suddenly as the sinister meaning of the assurance dawned upon her and she saw the awful confirmation of her fears in the other's averted face. She caught her breath, and turning to her slower-witted husband, laid her trembling old hand upon his. There was a long silence.

86 "He was caught in the machinery," said the visitor at length in a low voice.

87 "Caught in the machinery," repeated Mr. White, in a dazed fashion, "yes."

Don't forget to **Notice & Note** as you read the text.

88 He sat staring blankly out at the window, and taking his wife's hand between his own, pressed it as he had been wont to do in their old courting days nearly forty years before.

89 "He was the only one left to us," he said, turning gently to the visitor. "It is hard."

90 The other coughed, and rising, walked slowly to the window. "The firm wished me to convey their sincere sympathy with you in your great loss," he said, without looking round. "I beg that you will understand I am only their servant and merely obeying orders."

91 There was no reply; the old woman's face was white, her eyes staring, and her breath inaudible; on the husband's face was a look such as his friend the sergeant might have carried into his first action.

92 "I was to say that Maw and Meggins disclaim all responsibility," continued the other. "They admit no liability at all, but in consideration of your son's services, they wish to present you with a certain sum as **compensation**."

93 Mr. White dropped his wife's hand, and rising to his feet, gazed with a look of horror at his visitor. His dry lips shaped the words, "How much?"

94 "Two hundred pounds," was the answer.

95 Unconscious of his wife's shriek, the old man smiled faintly, put out his hands like a sightless man, and dropped, a senseless heap, to the floor.

compensation
(kŏm´pən-sā´shən) *n.* *Compensation* is something, such as money, that is received as payment.

Part III

96 In the huge new cemetery, some two miles distant, the old people buried their dead, and came back to a house steeped in shadow and silence. It was all over so quickly that at first they could hardly realize it, and remained in a state of expectation as though of something else to happen—something else which was to lighten this load, too heavy for old hearts to bear.

97 But the days passed, and expectation gave place to **resignation**—the hopeless resignation of the old, sometimes miscalled apathy. Sometimes they hardly exchanged a word, for now they had nothing to talk about, and their days were long to weariness.

resignation
(rĕz´ĭg-nā´shən) *n. Resignation* is the acceptance of something that is inescapable.

98 It was about a week after that the old man, waking suddenly in the night, stretched out his hand and found himself alone. The room was in darkness, and the sound of subdued weeping came from the window. He raised himself in bed and listened.

99 "Come back," he said tenderly. "You will be cold."

100 "It is colder for my son," said the old woman, and wept afresh.

101 The sound of her sobs died away on his ears. The bed was warm, and his eyes heavy with sleep. He dozed fitfully, and then slept until a sudden wild cry from his wife awoke him with a start.

102 "*The paw!*" she cried wildly. "The monkey's paw!"

103 He started up in alarm. "Where? Where is it? What's the matter?"

104 She came stumbling across the room toward him. "I want it," she said quietly. "You've not destroyed it?"

105 "It's in the parlor, on the bracket," he replied, marveling. "Why?"

106 She cried and laughed together, and bending over, kissed his cheek.

107 "I only just thought of it," she said hysterically. "Why didn't I think of it before? Why didn't *you* think of it?"

108 "Think of what?" he questioned.

109 "The other two wishes," she replied rapidly. "We've only had one."

110 "Was not that enough?" he demanded fiercely.

111 "No," she cried triumphantly; "we'll have one more. Go down and get it quickly, and wish our boy alive again."

112 The man sat up in bed and flung the bedclothes from his quaking limbs. "You are mad!" he cried, aghast.

113 "Get it," she panted; "get it quickly, and wish—Oh, my boy, my boy!"

114 Her husband struck a match and lit the candle. "Get back to bed," he said unsteadily. "You don't know what you are saying."

115 "We had the first wish granted," said the old woman feverishly; "why not the second?"

116 "A coincidence," stammered the old man.

117 "Go and get it and wish," cried his wife, quivering with excitement.

118 He went down in the darkness, and felt his way to the parlor, and then to the mantelpiece. The talisman was in its

Don't forget to **Notice & Note** as you read the text.

NOTICE & NOTE

AHA MOMENT

When you notice a sudden realization that shifts a character's actions or understandings, you've found an **Aha Moment** signpost.

Notice & Note: What sudden realization causes Mrs. White to become excited in paragraphs 101–111?

Predict: How might this change things?

place, and a horrible fear that the unspoken wish might bring his mutilated son before him ere he could escape from the room seized upon him, and he caught his breath as he found that he had lost the direction of the door. His brow cold with sweat, he felt his way round the table, and groped along the wall until he found himself in the small passage with the unwholesome thing in his hand.

119 Even his wife's face seemed changed as he entered the room. It was white and expectant, and to his fears seemed to have an unnatural look upon it. He was afraid of her.

120 "*Wish!*" she cried, in a strong voice.

121 "It is foolish and wicked," he faltered.

122 "*Wish!*" repeated his wife.

123 He raised his hand. "I wish my son alive again."

124 The talisman fell to the floor, and he regarded it fearfully. Then he sank trembling into a chair as the old woman, with burning eyes, walked to the window and raised the blind.

125 He sat until he was chilled with the cold, glancing occasionally at the figure of the old woman peering through the window. The candle-end, which had burned below the rim of the china candlestick, was throwing pulsating shadows on the ceiling and walls, until, with a flicker larger than the rest, it expired. The old man, with an unspeakable sense of relief at the failure of the talisman, crept back to his bed, and a minute or two afterward the old woman came silently and apathetically beside him.

126 Neither spoke, but lay silently listening to the ticking of the clock. A stair creaked, and a squeaky mouse scurried noisily through the wall. The darkness was oppressive, and after lying for some time gathering up his courage, he took the box of matches, and striking one, went downstairs for a candle.

127 At the foot of the stairs the match went out, and he paused to strike another; and at the same moment a knock, so quiet and stealthy as to be scarcely audible, sounded on the front door.

128 The matches fell from his hand. He stood motionless, his breath suspended until the knock was repeated. Then he turned and fled swiftly back to his room, and closed the door behind him. A third knock sounded through the house.

129 "*What's that?*" cried the old woman, starting up.

130 "A rat," said the old man in shaking tones—"a rat. It passed me on the stairs."

131 His wife sat up in bed listening. A loud knock resounded through the house.

132 "It's Herbert!" she screamed. "It's Herbert!"

133 She ran to the door, but her husband was before her, and catching her by the arm, held her tightly.

134 "What are you going to do?" he whispered hoarsely.

135 "It's my boy; it's Herbert!" she cried, struggling mechanically. "I forgot it was two miles away. What are you holding me for? Let go. I must open the door."

136 "Don't let it in," cried the old man, trembling.

137 "You're afraid of your own son," she cried, struggling. "Let me go. I'm coming, Herbert; I'm coming."

ANALYZE THEMES

Annotate: In paragraphs 134–137, circle Mr. White's dialogue and underline Mrs. White's.

Infer: What lesson, if any, might each character have learned?

138 There was another knock, and another. The old woman with a sudden wrench broke free and ran from the room. Her husband followed to the landing, and called after her appealingly as she hurried downstairs. He heard the chain rattle back and the bottom bolt drawn slowly and stiffly from the socket. Then the old woman's voice, strained and panting.

139 "The bolt," she cried loudly. "Come down. I can't reach it."

140 But her husband was on his hands and knees groping wildly on the floor in search of the paw. If he could only find it before the thing outside got in. A perfect fusillade[14] of knocks reverberated through the house, and he heard the scraping of a chair as his wife put it down in the passage against the door. He heard the creaking of the bolt as it came slowly back, and at the same moment he found the monkey's paw, and frantically breathed his third and last wish.

141 The knocking ceased suddenly, although the echoes of it were still in the house. He heard the chair drawn back, and the door opened. A cold wind rushed up the staircase, and a long loud wail of disappointment and misery from his wife gave him courage to run down to her side, and then to the gate beyond. The streetlamp flickering opposite shone on a quiet and deserted road.

[14] **fusillade** (fyo͞o′sə-läd′): discharge from many guns; a rapid outburst.

ESSENTIAL QUESTION:

Why do we sometimes like to feel frightened?

Review your notes and add your thoughts to your Response Log.

TURN AND TALK

Turn to a partner and discuss Mr. White's motivations for making his first wish. Does he make the wish more for himself or for his family?

Assessment Practice

Answer these questions before moving on to the **Analyze the Text** section on the following page.

1. Which **two** sentences most strongly foreshadow that wishing on the monkey's paw will bring about events that cause grief?

(A) "The visitor absent-mindedly put his empty glass to his lips and then set it down again." (paragraph 22)

(B) "'He wanted to show that fate ruled people's lives, and that those who interfered with it did so to their sorrow.'" (paragraph 26)

(C) "'And did you really have the three wishes granted?'" (paragraph 30)

(D) "'If you must wish,' he said gruffly, 'wish for something sensible.'" (paragraph 47)

(E) "A silence unusual and depressing settled upon all three, which lasted until the old couple rose to retire for the night." (paragraph 63)

2. What does Mr. White come to realize in paragraphs 129–136?

(A) A rat had caused the knocking sound.

(B) The talisman really had granted their wishes.

(C) A mangled monster is at the door.

(D) They are only imagining the knocking sound.

3. Which words most contribute to the somber mood in paragraph 141?

(A) *The knocking ceased*

(B) *the chair drawn back*

(C) *The streetlamp flickering opposite*

(D) *a quiet and deserted road*

Ed
Test-Taking Strategies

Analyze the Text

Support your responses with evidence from the text.

1. **ANALYZE** Review paragraphs 1–6 and any notes you made in your chart about the use of imagery to foreshadow events. What images or details about the setting seem to foreshadow later events?

2. **DRAW CONCLUSIONS** Reread paragraphs 45–49. Identify the allusion, or reference to a well-known work, that Mrs. White makes. What does the allusion suggest about Mrs. White's view of the paw?

3. **INFER** Review paragraphs 92–95. What do the Whites realize about the two hundred pounds they will receive "as compensation" when they have an **Aha Moment**?

4. **CAUSE/EFFECT** In paragraph 114, what **Words of the Wiser** does Mr. White offer to Mrs. White? What effect does his advice have on Mrs. White?

5. **COMPARE** What do the actions of Mr. and Mrs. White at the end of the story reveal about their different expectations for wishes? Identify what hopes or fears these expectations reveal.

6. **ANALYZE** What themes are suggested by "The Monkey's Paw"? Fill in the chart with examples that show how the author develops these themes through the characters and plot.

NOTICE & NOTE

Review what you **noticed and noted** as you read the text. Your annotations can help you answer these questions.

THEMES	EXAMPLES FROM THE TEXT

Choices

Here are some other ways to demonstrate your understanding of the ideas in this lesson.

As you write and discuss, be sure to use the **Academic Vocabulary** words.

- convention
- summary
- predict
- technique
- psychology

Writing

Personal Response

Write a personal response to each of the three sections of "The Monkey's Paw." Then write a paragraph that reflects on your responses and connections to the text.

- Review your annotations and notes about Parts I–III of the story. Write a one-paragraph response to each of the three sections. Cite evidence from the text to support your reactions.
- Review your responses. Note similarities and differences between your reactions to each section.
- Write a paragraph that describes how your reactions changed over the course of the story.

Speaking & Listening

Share and Discuss Ideas

Are you familiar with the fairy tales "The Three Little Pigs," "Three Billy Goats Gruff," and "The Three Wishes"? Discuss connections between "The Monkey's Paw" and other familiar stories that follow this "rule of three" pattern.

- Note your ideas about the similarities and differences between the stories.
- Share and discuss your ideas with your group.

Social & Emotional Learning

Your Wish Is My Command

Imagine you and a few of your classmates are granted three wishes to share. Have a discussion about how you will decide as a group how to use the three wishes fairly.

- What rules about the wishes will you make as a group to ensure that everyone's desires are met?
- Listen carefully and respectfully to your classmates' ideas. Clear communication and cooperation are key to having a good group discussion!
- If members of your group disagree on certain points, consider using negotiation to come to a fair resolution.

Expand Your Vocabulary

PRACTICE AND APPLY

Explain what is alike and different about the meanings of the words in each pair.

1. **peril** / risk
2. **grimace** / frown
3. **compensation** / wages
4. **credulity** / trust
5. **resignation** / acceptance
6. **condole** / sympathize

Vocabulary Strategy
Latin Roots

A **word root** is a word part that contains the core meaning of a word. A root is combined with other word parts, such as a prefix or a suffix, to form a word. The roots of many English words come from Latin. Read this sentence from "The Monkey's Paw."

> His mother laughed, and following him to the door, watched him down the road; and returning to the breakfast table, was very happy at the expense of her husband's credulity.

The word *credulity* includes the Latin root *cred*, which means "believe" or "trust." You can use the meaning of the root *cred* to figure out that *credulity* means "a tendency to believe too readily."

Ed
Interactive Vocabulary Lesson: Common Roots, Prefixes, and Suffixes

PRACTICE AND APPLY

Find the word in each sentence that includes the Latin root *cred*. Use context to help you write the definition of the word.

1. Herbert was incredulous when he heard the sergeant-major's tale.

2. A person must have the proper credentials to enter a foreign country.

3. Mrs. White didn't give any credence to the notion that the monkey's paw moved.

4. Were the sergeant-major's stories about India credible?

Watch Your Language!

Subjunctive Mood

The **subjunctive mood** is used to express a recommendation, a requirement, a wish, or a hypothetical situation, or to describe a state that is contrary to fact. The subjunctive mood is also used to express uncertainty. It is generally used only in very formal English.

- Use the subjunctive base form of a verb in clauses beginning with *that* to express a recommendation or a requirement.

  Morris suggests that Mr. White burn the monkey's paw. (***burn*** **not** ***burns***)

- Use the subjunctive *be* in clauses beginning with *that* to express a recommendation or a requirement.

  Mrs. White insists that another wish be made. (***be*** **not** ***is***)

- Use the subjunctive *were* to express a wish or hypothetical situation, or to describe a state that is contrary to fact.

  The monkey's paw moved, as though it were alive. (***were*** **not** ***was***)

PRACTICE AND APPLY

One verb in each sentence is not correct. Rewrite each sentence correctly, using the subjunctive mood.

1. The Whites recommend that Morris is seated by the fire.

2. My teacher suggests that the class predicts what will happen next in the story.

3. Mrs. White acted as though she was mad.

4. Mr. White insists that his wife keeps the door closed.

5. If Mrs. White was taller, she could reach the bolt on the door.

6. I move that each student is required to write a story summary after reading.

MEDIA

from The Monkey's Paw

Film Clip by **Ricky Lewis Jr.**

ESSENTIAL QUESTION:
Why do we sometimes like to feel frightened?

Engage Your Brain

You're about to watch a clip from a filmed adaptation of "The Monkey's Paw." Prepare to be scared! What elements contribute to the spine-tingling creepiness of a good horror movie? Make a list of techniques that movie directors use to create suspense, bring their scary stories and characters to life, and totally freak out their audiences! Then share your list with a classmate.

Background

The film *The Monkey's Paw* is an adaptation of the short story of the same name. The film's writer and director, **Ricky Lewis Jr.**, read the story as a child. He decided to make it into a movie because his "morbid curiosity wanted to see it." While other film adaptations of the story had modernized it, Lewis thought it was important that the film be set in the past, "when odd things were sure to happen." He chose to "let a little darkness" into his film to create its gloomy, sometimes spooky mood.

Analyze Film

Like many movies, the film *The Monkey's Paw* is based on a written work. While writers use words to describe the rising action of their stories, film directors use a combination of visual and sound techniques to create suspense and tell a story.

Focus on Genre
Film

- combines images and sound to tell a story or convey information
- uses visual and sound techniques such as camera shots, lighting, music, and sound effects
- often includes actors who play the roles of characters

As you view the film clip, pay attention to the film techniques the director uses:

- **Lighting** (or a lack of lighting) can be used to create mysterious or scary moods.
- **Camera shots and angles** are related to different positions of the camera. Shots and angles can show different aspects of a scene or situation.
- **Camera filters** can be placed in front of a camera lens to change the way filmed images appear.
- **Sound effects** may include action noises or nature sounds.
- **Music** can signal dramatic events or tense moments.

When a director makes a movie of a written story, he or she has to make choices about how closely to follow the written work. Will the film include all of the same characters and events? Will it have the same setting? What themes will be emphasized?

As you view the film clip, think about how the director's choices affect the content of the film version of "The Monkey's Paw."

This film brings W. W. Jacobs's famous horror story to the screen.

Ed
Video
View "***from* The Monkey's Paw**" in your ebook.

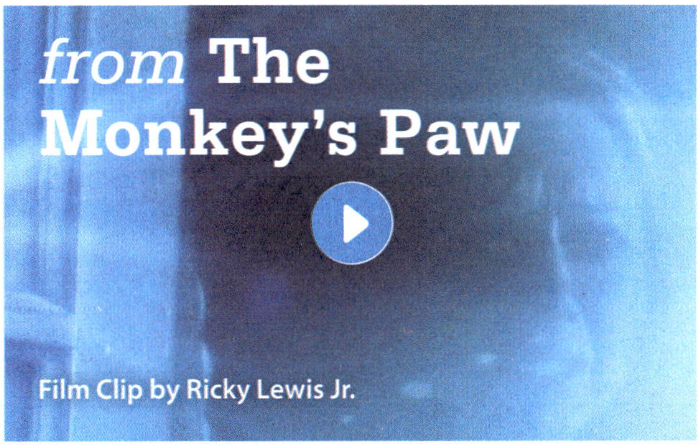

Analyze Media

Support your responses with evidence from the film clip.

ESSENTIAL QUESTION:
Why do we sometimes like to feel frightened?

1. **SUMMARIZE** The film clip shows several scenes from the short story "The Monkey's Paw." Summarize the events shown and described in the film.

2. **ANALYZE** Consider the ways the director uses lighting in the film. What is the effect of the lighting in the scene in which Herbert returns to the house?

3. **INTERPRET** Why do you think the music changes as Mr. White makes his second and third wishes?

4. **ANALYZE** How do the camera angles and camera filters that the director uses affect the mood of the film? How do they affect the impact of the final scenes at the cemetery?

CAMERA TECHNIQUE	PART IN THE FILM	EFFECT

5. **COMPARE** Identify two ways in which the director uses sound effects in the film. In what ways do these effects impact the mood?

Choices

Here are some other ways to demonstrate your understanding of the ideas in this lesson.

As you write and discuss, be sure to use the **Academic Vocabulary** words.

convention	summary
predict	technique
psychology	

Writing

Film Review

Write a critical review of Ricky Lewis Jr.'s film adaptation of W. W. Jacobs's short story.

- Provide some background about "The Monkey's Paw" and a brief summary of the events depicted in film.
- Compare the film to the story, and analyze how closely the filmmaker followed the written work.
- Evaluate the film's use of music, sound, and camera techniques. Also include your opinions of the casting and acting in the film.
- Conclude with a recommendation as to whether or not your readers should watch the film.

Media

Create a Storyboard

With your group, create a storyboard for a film retelling of a scene from "The Monkey's Paw."

- Draw a series of frames. Sketch the characters and scene for each frame.
- Write a line of dialogue or a description of the action.
- Decide what kind of music you will add, and where you'll include it.

Social & Emotional Learning

Plan an Adaptation

Have a group discussion about adapting a scene in "The Monkey's Paw" to create a film version.

- Review the story and the film clip. Think about the techniques the film director uses in the adaptation of the story's ending.
- Work together to decide on a scene to adapt as a film version. Make sure that the ideas of all group members are considered.
- As a group, determine whether your adaptation will stay true to the text or vary. Cite details from the story and the film clip to support your ideas.

Compare Versions

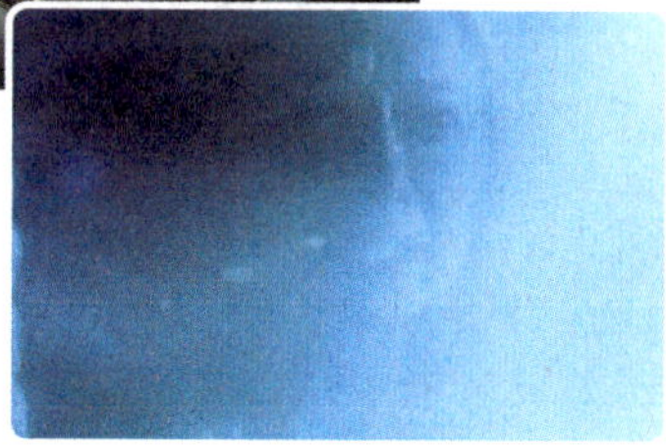

While authors use language to tell stories, film directors rely on visual and sound techniques to help bring stories to life. When directors decide to make a movie based on a written story or novel, they make choices about what to include and what to omit. For example, they might cut a scene that's hard to portray visually or isn't necessary to move the plot forward.

In a small group, complete the Venn diagram with similarities and differences between the story's ending and the film clip. Then write a response summarizing your findings.

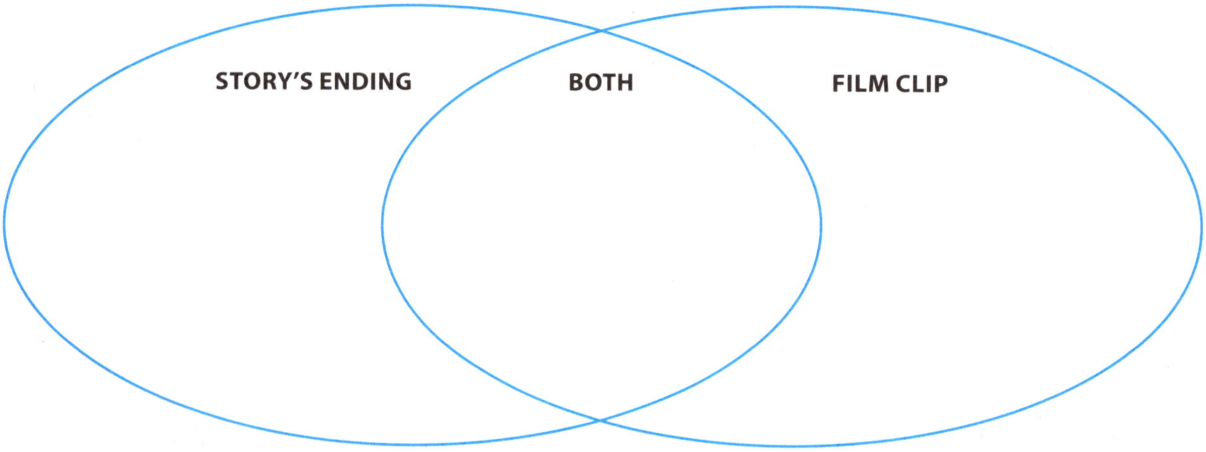

Analyze Text and Media

Discuss these questions in your group.

1. **CONNECT** In what ways does the film clip stay true to the story?

2. **CONTRAST** What differences are there between the story's ending and the film clip?

3. **INTERPRET** Which version helps you better understand how the characters feel? Cite evidence from the versions in your discussion.

4. **EVALUATE** Which do you find more frightening, the film version or the story? Which do you find more tragic? Cite evidence to support your ideas.

Discuss and Present

Now, continue comparing the story's ending and the film clip by exploring the reasons for the director's choices and evaluating the advantages of each version.

1 **DECIDE ON THE MOST IMPORTANT DETAILS** With your group, review your diagram to identify similarities and differences between the story's ending and the film clip. What are the most important details in each version?

2 **DISCUSS THE DIRECTOR'S CHOICES** Consider the similarities and differences you identified. Discuss possible reasons why the director might have chosen to stay true to some parts of the story and to tell some parts differently. You can use this chart to record supporting evidence.

	POSSIBLE REASONS FOR DIRECTOR'S CHOICE
Setting	
Characters	
Events	

3 **EVALUATE ADVANTAGES OF EACH VERSION** With your group, discuss advantages of the story and film versions. Record your ideas in the chart.

	ADVANTAGES
Story	
Film	

4 **PRESENT TO THE CLASS** Now it is time to share your ideas. Clearly state your inferences about the reasons for the director's choices. Provide examples to support your opinions about the advantages of each version. Adapt the charts you created or create other visuals to help convey your ideas to the class.

Collaborate & Compare

ESSENTIAL QUESTION:
Why do we sometimes like to feel frightened?

Compare Versions

You are about to read excerpts from two versions of a Greek myth about the underworld. One version is an epic poem, and the other is a graphic novel. As you read, think about how each version helps you imagine this frightening place and its inhabitants.

A

from **The Aeneid of Virgil**

Epic Poem translated by **Allen Mandelbaum**
pages 140–142

B

from **Hades: Lord of the Dead**

Graphic Novel by **George O'Connor**
pages 143–153

After you have read the selections, you will collaborate with a small group to retell another myth in graphic-novel form. You will follow these steps:

- Choose a Myth
- Outline the Story
- Consider Style
- Storyboard
- Share

from The Aeneid of Virgil

Epic Poem translated by **Allen Mandelbaum**

from Hades: Lord of the Dead

Graphic Novel by **George O'Connor**

Engage Your Brain

Choose one or more of these activities to start connecting with the texts you're about to read.

That's Epic!

The word "epic" is commonly used to describe something that is timeless or memorable, but it also refers to a long poem that tells a story about a hero. Do some quick research to learn more about epic poetry, and record your findings below.

Visions of the Underworld

According to Greek mythology, when people die, their souls descend into the underworld. What comes to mind when you imagine the underworld? Sketch or jot down your ideas in the space below.

Analyze Epic Poetry

An **epic poem** is a long narrative poem that focuses on the adventures of an epic hero. The hero figure is an **archetype,** a pattern in literature that is found in a variety of works from different cultures throughout the ages. An archetype can be a character, an image, a plot, or a setting. In Virgil's epic poem *The Aeneid,* Aeneas is an archetypal hero who embodies the qualities of bravery and persistence.

Like all poets, Virgil chose his words carefully to convey meaning and tone. He also used imagery and figurative language to create vivid descriptions. In the text you will read, Virgil's poetic use of Latin has been translated into English. As you read, use the chart to analyze the epic poem.

Focus on Genre
Epic Poetry

- tells the story of a hero's adventures
- uses a formal style of language
- reflects the ideals and values of a particular culture
- addresses universal themes about good and evil, life and death

USE OF POETIC LANGUAGE	EXAMPLES FROM *THE AENEID*	EFFECT OF EACH EXAMPLE
Word choice—interesting words and phrases that catch your attention and may convey tone		
Imagery—descriptive words that appeal to the reader's five senses		
Figurative language—language that conveys meaning beyond the literal meaning of the words		

Analyze an Adaptation

In *Hades: Lord of the Dead,* the author has adapted a Greek myth as a graphic novel. This work draws on archetypes that appear in mythology and other literature throughout history. The river Styx is an archetypal setting in Virgil's epic poem and in the graphic novel. Consider what crossing a river might symbolize, and compare how the author of each text uses this archetype.

As you read the excerpt from *Hades: Lord of the Dead,* look for elements of the myth that could be conveyed just as effectively in a short story or a narrative poem. Then note ways in which the graphic novel format provides a new twist on the story and makes this a uniquely modern adaptation.

Focus on Genre
Graphic Novel

- tells a book-length story in comic-strip style
- combines images, narrative text, and dialogue in frames or panels
- has a plot, characters, and themes

Annotation in Action

Here is an example of notes a student made about these lines from *The Aeneid of Virgil*. As you read, mark words the author uses to convey a tone or attitude toward his subject.

> Here starts the pathway to the waters of
> Tartarean Acheron. A whirlpool thick
> with sludge, its giant eddy seething, vomits
> all of its swirling sand into Cocytus.

The river "vomits"? That's vivid! Tone = disgusted

Background

Virgil (70–19 BCE) is considered the greatest poet of ancient Rome. In the *Aeneid,* Virgil tells the story of the Trojan hero Aeneas. As the Greeks are on the verge of conquering Troy, Aeneas learns it is his destiny to start a new civilization. He then makes an adventure-filled journey modeled on Homer's *Odyssey*, finally landing in Italy and founding the city that will become Rome. One of his adventures along the way is a trip to the underworld with the priestess Deiphobe to speak with the ghost of his father, Anchises.

George O'Connor (born 1973) is a fan of both Greek mythology and superhero comics. He brings these passions together in his Olympians series of graphic novels, each of which retells the myths surrounding a particular Greek god. *Hades: Lord of the Dead* is about the god of the underworld, whose kidnapping of the goddess Persephone explains the origin of the four seasons.

from

The Aeneid of Virgil

Epic Poem translated by **Allen Mandelbaum**

Trojan hero Aeneas follows a guide into the underworld, where he watches in horror as Charon ferries the dead across the river Styx.

NOTICE & NOTE
As you read, use the side margins to make notes about the text.

Here starts the pathway to the waters of
Tartarean Acheron.[1] A whirlpool thick
with sludge, its giant eddy seething, vomits
all of its swirling sand into Cocytus.[2]
Grim Charon is the squalid ferryman,
the guardian of these streams, these rivers; his
white hairs lie thick, disheveled on his chin;
his eyes are fires that stare, a filthy mantle[3]
hangs down his shoulder by a knot. Alone
he poles the boat and tends the sails and carries
the dead in his dark ship, old as he is;
but old age in a god is tough and green.

ANALYZE EPIC POETRY

Annotate: Mark words the poet uses to describe Charon in lines 5–12.

Infer: What tone or attitude toward Charon is conveyed by the poet's word choices?

[1] **Tartarean Acheron:** a river in the part of the underworld called Tartaros.
[2] **Cocytus:** another river in the underworld.
[3] **mantle:** a loose sleeveless coat or cloak.

And here a multitude was rushing, swarming
shoreward, with men and mothers, bodies of
high-hearted heroes stripped of life, and boys
and unwed girls, and young men set upon
the pyre of death before their fathers' eyes:
thick as the leaves that with the early frost
of autumn drop and fall within the forest,
or as the birds that flock along the beaches,
in flight from frenzied seas when the chill season
drives them across the waves to lands of sun.
They stand; each pleads to be the first to cross
the stream; their hands reach out in longing for
the farther shore. But Charon, sullen boatman,
now takes these souls, now those; the rest he leaves;
thrusting them back, he keeps them from the beach.

That disarray dismays and moves Aeneas:
"O virgin, what does all this swarming mean?
What do these spirits plead? And by what rule
must some keep off the bank while others sweep
the blue-black waters with their oars?" The words
the aged priestess speaks are brief: "Anchises'
son, certain offspring of the gods,[4] you see
the deep pools of Cocytus and the marsh
of Styx, by whose divinity even
the High Ones are afraid to swear falsely.
All these you see are helpless and unburied.
That ferryman is Charon. And the waves
will only carry souls that have a tomb.
Before his bones have found their rest, no one
may cross the horrid shores and the hoarse waters.
They wander for a hundred years and hover
about these banks until they gain their entry,
to visit once again the pools they long for."

Don't forget to **Notice & Note** as you read the text.

NOTICE & NOTE

WORDS OF THE WISER

When you notice a wiser character giving advice about life to the main character, you've found a **Words of the Wiser** signpost.

Notice & Note: Mark the lines in which the priestess shares insight with Aeneas about the souls on the shore of the river Styx.

Predict: What's the life lesson, and how might it affect Aeneas?

[4] **Anchises' son, certain offspring of the gods:** The priestess Deiphobe addresses Aeneas by referring to his heritage. Anchises is the name of Aeneas's father. Aeneas is an offspring of the gods because his mother is the goddess Aphrodite.

TURN AND TALK

Discuss the mood of the excerpt with a partner. What kind of feeling or atmosphere does the language of the poem create?

ESSENTIAL QUESTION:

Why do we sometimes like to feel frightened?

Review your notes and add your thoughts to your Response Log.

Assessment Practice

Answer these questions about *The Aeneid of Virgil* before moving on to the next selection.

1. Charon's role in the underworld is to —

Ⓐ pass judgment on human souls

Ⓑ prevent people from drowning in the rivers

Ⓒ welcome people to their lives after death

Ⓓ take souls across the river Styx in his boat

2. Which **two** things does the poet compare to the crowd of souls on the beach?

Ⓐ leaves falling from trees in autumn

Ⓑ water swirling wildly in a river

Ⓒ hairs growing in a thick beard

Ⓓ birds migrating to warmer climates

Ⓔ bones piling up in a graveyard

3. Charon refuses to help the souls of people who —

Ⓐ died while their parents were still alive

Ⓑ did not receive a proper burial

Ⓒ approach him on the shore of the river

Ⓓ are not descended from gods

Ed Test-Taking Strategies

from

Hades: Lord of the Dead

Graphic Novel by **George O'Connor**

This excerpt from a graphic novel provides a vivid look at what ancient Greeks believed about the afterlife.

NOTICE & NOTE
As you read, use the side margins to make notes about the text.

INTRODUCTION

In the excerpt you are about to read, you are first introduced to Hermes, the messenger of the gods. According to Greek mythology, one of Hermes's jobs is taking the souls of the dead to the underworld. As the reader of this graphic novel, you are immediately transported to a realm called Hades. You are then led through a series of haunting landscapes in the underworld, past scenes of endless suffering and hopelessness. Finally, you arrive at the throne of the god who rules over the underworld realm, who is also called Hades.

KNOW THIS FIRST: YOU ARE DEAD. YOU NO LONGER HAVE A BODY.
BUT STILL YOU WILL OPEN YOUR EYES. THE FIRST THING YOU SEE IS HERMES PSYCHOPOMPOS. IT IS HIS JOB TO GUIDE YOU TO WHAT COMES NEXT.
YOU REACH OUT AND TAKE HIS HAND.
IN HERMES'S GRASP, YOU WILL MOVE SO FAST IT WILL SEEM AS IF YOU HAVEN'T MOVED AT ALL.

Don't forget to **Notice & Note** as you read the text.

ANALYZE AN ADAPTATION

Annotate: Mark characters and events on these pages that come from Greek mythology.

Analyze: What elements of the text and illustrations reflect the style of modern comics or graphic novels?

ANALYZE AN ADAPTATION

Annotate: Mark text on this page that shows how this adaptation makes the reader a character in the story.

Evaluate: Do you find this modern way of telling the story effective? Explain your answer.

Don't forget to **Notice & Note** as you read the text.

ANALYZE AN ADAPTATION

Annotate: Mark details in the illustrations on these pages that convey the suffering of those that are being punished.

Critique: Does the modern comics style effectively portray these stories from Greek myths? Explain your opinion.

Don't forget to **Notice & Note** as you read the text.

HOPEFULLY, YOU WILL NEVER HAVE OFFENDED THE GODS AND SO WILL NEVER ENTER TARTAROS.
INSTEAD, YOU WILL JOIN THE HORDES OF THE ORDINARY DEAD AS THEY MEANDER ON THROUGH THE FIELDS OF ASPHODEL.
FINALLY THE DEAD COME TO THE SHORES OF ANOTHER RIVER, LETHE.
WHEN DRUNK, THE WATERS OF LETHE CAUSE FORGETFULNESS.
WHEN IT IS YOUR TURN, YOU WILL REACH INTO THE WATERS OF LETHE.
YOU WILL DRINK.
AND ALL YOUR MEMORIES, YOUR DREAMS, YOUR THOUGHTS AND FEARS, ALL THAT YOU WERE WILL BE GONE.

Don't forget to **Notice & Note** as you read the text.

ANALYZE AN ADAPTATION

Annotate: Mark details in the illustrations that reflect the modern comics style used to depict the god Hades.

Analyze: What kind of archetypal character does Hades remind you of? Do you think this is an appropriate way to adapt the mythical god for a modern audience? Explain.

TURN AND TALK

Turn to a partner and have a discussion about the illustrations in the graphic novel excerpt. Which image do you find most frightening or disturbing?

ESSENTIAL QUESTION:

Why do we sometimes like to feel frightened?

Review your notes and add your thoughts to your Response Log.

Assessment Practice

Answer these questions before moving on to the **Analyze the Texts** section on the following page.

1. This question has two parts. First, answer **Part A**. Then, answer **Part B**.

Part A

Which statement applies to most of the souls who arrive in the underworld?

- (A) They will be punished harshly for crimes against the gods.
- (B) They hope to wash away their guilt and be forgiven.
- (C) They are content in the company of other souls.
- (D) They feel pain and loss remembering their past lives.

Part B

Select **two** sentences that provide relevant support for the answer in Part A.

- (A) Souls form a huge crowd in the fields of Asphodel.
- (B) Souls drink from the river Lethe.
- (C) Souls crave the warmth of living bodies.
- (D) Souls carry water to fill a large tub.
- (E) Souls listen to the terrible groans of the Titans.

2. The job of Cerberus, the three-headed dog, is to —

- (A) prevent souls from escaping the underworld
- (B) guide Charon to the far shore of the river Styx
- (C) eat the liver of the giant Tityus every day
- (D) transport the souls of the newly dead to Hades

Ed

Test-Taking Strategies

Analyze the Texts

Support your responses with evidence from the texts.

NOTICE & NOTE

Review what you **noticed and noted** as you read the texts. Your annotations can help you answer these questions.

1. **INTERPRET** A **metaphor** is a figure of speech that makes a comparison by saying that one thing is something else. Find the metaphor used to describe Charon in lines 5–9 of *The Aeneid of Virgil.* What impression of Charon does this metaphor create?

2. **ANALYZE** Review the examples of imagery you recorded in the chart on page 138. Then, in the chart below, note several examples relating to Charon and the souls on the beach. Describe what you see, hear, and feel based on this imagery.

CHARACTER	IMAGERY IN POEM	WHAT I SEE, HEAR, AND FEEL
Charon		
Souls on the beach		

3. **CITE EVIDENCE** Review lines 38–45 of the epic poem. What tone does the poet express toward the underworld and toward the souls that must wait 100 years to cross the river? Cite specific word choices that reveal the poet's tone.

4. **SUMMARIZE** According to Greek mythology, what happens to a person's soul after death? Summarize the basic pattern of events as described in the excerpt from *Hades: Lord of the Dead.*

5. **ANALYZE** Review the first three panels in the graphic novel excerpt. How does the author use the illustrations to show the point of view from which this trip to the underworld is seen?

6. **EVALUATE** Does it make sense to adapt ancient Greek myths in the style of modern American superhero comics? Explain why you think it does or does not work to present the myth of Hades and the underworld in graphic-novel form.

Choices

Here are some other ways to demonstrate your understanding of the ideas in this lesson.

As you write and discuss, be sure to use the **Academic Vocabulary** words.

- convention
- summary
- predict
- technique
- psychology

Writing

Video-Game Storyline

Imagine you have been asked to develop a video game based on Greek myths that describe the underworld. Write a storyline for the game.

1. First, determine the type of game it will be. Will it be a role-playing game? An action and adventure game? What will make it fun to play?
2. Brainstorm ideas for the story. Incorporate details about the setting and characters from the excerpts you read.
3. Craft your story to fit your game type. Explain how players will advance through the underworld and achieve the overall goal of the game.

Research

Create a Character Profile

Conduct research to learn more about Aeneas, the hero of *The Aeneid of Virgil.* Use the information you gather to create a profile of his character. Include answers to the following questions in your profile:

- Who were Aeneas's parents?
- What was his role in the Trojan War?
- What personal qualities was he known for?

Social & Emotional Learning

Create a Virtual Tour

In *The Aeneid of Virgil,* Aeneas is led by a guide on a tour of the underworld. In *Hades: Lord of the Dead,* the reader is led on a similar tour. Think about how a guide is often important when visiting new places. Then, imagine you are a guide to students new to your school. Create a virtual tour of your school. Consider:

- What places would you take them?
- What people or characters would you have them meet?
- What rules must new students follow?
- What suggestions would you make about fitting in at your school?

Use illustrations, diagrams, or photographs to elaborate on your tour. Then, share your tour with the rest of the class.

Compare Versions

You have read two versions of Greek myths surrounding death and the underworld. *The Aeneid of Virgil* takes the classical form of an epic poem. *Hades: Lord of the Dead* is an adaptation of the same mythology in a modern media form—the graphic novel. Comparing these two versions can help you see how the structure of each text gives its author different ways to express meaning and tone.

In a small group, answer the questions in the chart for each selection. Be sure to support your ideas with text evidence.

	A THE AENEID OF VIRGIL	B HADES: LORD OF THE DEAD
What events from mythology are described?		
How does the author use the structure or features of his chosen genre to help readers see, hear, and feel what the underworld is like?		
What overall tone or attitude toward the underworld does the author express?		
How does the author draw on the archetype of the river?		

Analyze the Texts

Discuss these questions in your group.

1. **SYNTHESIZE** What does each selection say about the reason Charon refuses to take some souls across the river? How do you explain the difference between the two versions?

2. **COMPARE** Compare details about Charon's boat in the poem with the illustrations in the graphic novel. How are they different, and how would you draw the boat based on Virgil's description?

3. **CRITIQUE** Which version of the underworld myths is more effective? Do you enjoy using your imagination to visualize Virgil's text descriptions, or do you prefer viewing George O'Connor's illustrations? Explain your opinion.

Create and Present

Your group can continue exploring how classical texts are adapted for modern readers by retelling a myth in graphic-novel style. Follow these steps:

1. **CHOOSE A MYTH** As a group, brainstorm a list of myths you know. They may be from ancient Greece or Rome or from other cultures. Then choose one myth to adapt.

2. **OUTLINE THE STORY** Write a brief outline of the events your story will include. Be sure the story has a clear beginning, middle, and end.

3. **CONSIDER STYLE** Discuss what your graphic novel will look like. How will you draw the characters and setting? What colors will you use?

4. **MAKE A STORYBOARD** Break your story down into panels. Each panel should show an important action or a character's reaction to events.

5. **ILLUSTRATE** Decide how to divide up the illustration work. For example, you might have one person draw settings, another draw characters, and another write dialogue in speech bubbles. Then create your illustrations.

6. **SHARE** Invite your classmates to provide feedback on your graphic novel.

Reader's Choice

Continue your exploration of the Essential Question by doing some independent reading of texts written in and about the horror genre. Read the titles and descriptions shown. Then mark the texts that interest you.

ESSENTIAL QUESTION:
Why do we sometimes like to feel frightened?

Short Reads

Available on Ed

These texts are available in your ebook. Choose one to read and rate. Then defend your rating to the class.

Frankenstein

Poem by **Edward Field**

Frankenstein's monster encounters kindness for the first time.

Rate It ☆☆☆☆☆

beware: do not read this poem

Poem by **Ishmael Reed**

Prepare to be devoured by poetry.

Rate It ☆☆☆☆☆

Blood

Short Story by **Zdravka Evitmova**

A generous impulse has unintended consequences.

Rate It ☆☆☆☆☆

The Outsider

Short Story by **H. P. Lovecraft**

A narrator makes a shocking discovery when he escapes from his home, a dark and lonely castle.

Rate It ☆☆☆☆☆

Scary Tales

Essay by **Jackie Torrence**

A storyteller follows in her grandfather's footsteps.

Rate It ☆☆☆☆☆

Long Reads

Here are a few recommended books that connect to this unit topic. For additional options, ask your teacher, school librarian, or peers. Which titles spark your interest?

Coraline

Novel by **Neil Gaiman**

Coraline discovers a passageway to a world just like hers, only darker. She confronts horrifying illusions and learns to be brave.

The Strange Case of Dr. Jekyll and Mr. Hyde

Novel by **Robert Louis Stevenson**

Dr. Jekyll is a scientist who wants to test the bounds of human nature. His experiments give him a firsthand look at what people are capable of—both good and evil.

Miss Peregrine's Home for Peculiar Children

Novel by **Ransom Riggs**

Jacob has been stranded on an island where peculiar—possibly dangerous—children are known to have lived. Now he has to figure out why they were left there, and whether they are still alive.

Extension

Connect & Create

WRITE A CHARACTER ANALYSIS Choose a character from one of the texts to analyze in a 3–5 paragraph essay. Make sure to include evidence from the text to support your analysis and to help your reader to better understand the personality and motivations of the character. Your analysis should address some or all of the following:

- the physical appearance of the character
- the words, thoughts, and actions of the character
- how other people in the story respond to the character
- how the character changes over the course of the text

CREATE A COLLAGE Design a collage to show how the text you read fits into the horror genre. Search for photos and/or illustrations in magazines, newspapers, or online sources to represent the settings, characters, ideas, and events described in the text. Use text or labels as needed to help the reader understand what the images mean. Then, present your collage to your classmates.

NOTICE & NOTE

- Pick one of the texts and annotate the Notice & Note signposts you find.
- Then, use the **Notice & Note Writing Frames** to help you write about the significance of the signposts.
- Compare your findings with those of other students who read the same text.

Ed

Notice & Note Writing Frames

Write a Literary Analysis

Writing Prompt

Using ideas, information, and examples from multiple texts in this unit, write a literary analysis for other students in your class in which you analyze and interpret one of the stories in this unit.

Manage your time carefully so that you can

- review the texts in the unit;
- plan your literary analysis;
- write your analysis; and
- revise and edit your analysis.

Be sure to

- clearly introduce the topic of your literary analysis;
- provide a concluding statement or section;
- use and cite evidence from multiple sources; and
- avoid relying too much on one source.

Review the Mentor Text

For an example of a well-written literary analysis you can use as a mentor text and as a source for your analysis, review:

- "What Is the Horror Genre?" (pages 85–89).

Make sure to carefully review your notes and annotations about this text. Think about the techniques the author used to make her analysis effective.

Consider Your Sources

Review the list of texts in the unit and choose at least two that you may want to use as sources of ideas for your literary analysis.

As you review potential sources, consult the notes you made on your **Response Log** and make additional notes about any ideas that might be useful as you write your analysis. Include source titles and page numbers in your notes to help you provide accurate text evidence and citations when you include support from these texts.

UNIT 2 SOURCES

- ☐ **What Is the Horror Genre?**
- ☐ **The Tell-Tale Heart**
- ☐ **The Monkey's Paw**
- ☐ *from* **The Monkey's Paw** MEDIA
- ☐ *from* **The Aeneid of Virgil**
- ☐ *from* **Hades: Lord of the Dead**

Analyze the Prompt

Analyze the prompt to make sure you understand what you are required to do.

1. Mark the sentence in the prompt that identifies the topic of your essay. Rephrase the sentence in your own words.
2. Next, look for words that indicate the purpose and audience of your essay, and write a sentence describing each one.

Consider Your Audience

Ask yourself:

- Who will read my essay?
- What do my readers already know about the story and genre?
- What would capture their interest and hold it?

What is my topic? What is my writing task?

What is my purpose?

Who is my audience?

Review the Rubric

Your literary analysis will be scored using a rubric. As you write, focus on the characteristics as described in the chart. You will learn more about these characteristics as you work through the lesson.

PURPOSE, FOCUS, AND ORGANIZATION	EVIDENCE AND ELABORATION	CONVENTIONS OF STANDARD ENGLISH
The response includes: • A strongly maintained controlling idea • Use of transitions to connect ideas • Logical progression of ideas • Appropriate style and tone	The response includes: • Effective use of evidence and sources • Effective use of elaboration • Clear and effective expression of ideas • Appropriate vocabulary • Varied sentence structure	The response may include: • Some minor errors in usage but no patterns of errors • Correct punctuation, capitalization, sentence formation, and spelling • Command of basic conventions

1 PLAN YOUR LITERARY ANALYSIS

Draft a Controlling Idea

Decide which story you want to analyze, and list reasons for your choice in the chart. Then draft a **controlling idea,** or thesis statement, that tells what your literary analysis is about.

STORY TITLE	REASONS FOR MY CHOICE
	Controlling Idea:

Ed

Help with Planning

Consult **Interactive Writing Lesson: Writing Informative Texts.**

Determine Your Controlling Idea

A strong **controlling idea** should

- clearly state an opinion about the topic
- focus on specific literary elements
- engage readers and motivate them to keep reading
- preview the direction and purpose of the analysis

Develop Your Key Ideas

Key ideas help to further explain your controlling idea, providing readers with greater insights into the story. To generate key ideas for your literary analysis, list **literary elements** such as imagery or suspense that you consider important to your story. Then jot down ideas about their impact.

LITERARY ELEMENT	IMPACT ON STORY

Identify Evidence

Each key idea should be backed up by **relevant evidence**—such as examples, quotations, and concrete details. Draw on the notes you took about the story and other sources to help you fill out the chart. Be sure to include source information and page numbers for each piece of evidence.

KEY IDEA	EVIDENCE	SOURCE

Organize Ideas

Now organize your material in a way that will help you draft your literary analysis. Keep in mind that a well-written analysis demonstrates **coherence,** meaning there is a logical progression of ideas. Use the chart below to help you structure your essay.

Link Your Ideas

Here are some transitions you can use to connect ideas in your essay:

- For example . . .
- In addition . . .
- As a result . . .
- Similarly . . .
- In other words . . .

INTRODUCE	• Grab your reader's attention with an interesting question, quote, or detail. • Clearly state your controlling idea.
EXPLAIN & ELABORATE	• Present your key ideas and evidence in a logical order. • Devote a paragraph to each key idea. • Use transitions to link ideas.
SUM UP	• Restate your controlling idea and its significance. • Offer a new insight or a final thought for readers to consider.

2 DEVELOP A DRAFT

Now it's time to draft your literary analysis. Examining the work of literary critics can help you apply similar techniques to your own writing.

Ed

Drafting Online

Check your assignment list for a writing task from your teacher.

Write an Effective Introduction

EXAMINE THE MENTOR TEXT

Your introduction is your first chance to grab your readers' attention. Note the way the author captures the reader's attention in **"What Is the Horror Genre?"** (page 85).

Many people define horror by its subjects. We all think of creatures like Frankenstein's monster, Dracula, and the wolfman as monsters in the horror genre. Each one of these creatures has a history and developed over a period of time. But we also know that horror covers more than just these monsters.

The writer engages readers by identifying familiar monsters.

She then introduces her **controlling idea**—horror involves other elements besides monsters.

Try These Suggestions

Experiment with these approaches:

- Share a quotation.
- State an interesting fact.
- Point out a widely-accepted truth.
- Highlight an unusual point of view.
- Describe a familiar experience.

APPLY TO YOUR DRAFT

Use this chart to practice drafting an engaging introduction. Then, decide which one you think will capture readers' attention.

QUOTATION	
INTERESTING FACT	
ACCEPTED TRUTH	
UNUSUAL POINT OF VIEW	
FAMILIAR EXPERIENCE	

Provide Evidence

EXAMINE THE MENTOR TEXT

Notice how the author of **"What Is the Horror Genre?"** supports her ideas by incorporating an example from a work of horror by Stephen King.

The author identifies an **example** of how Stephen King uses an element of the horror genre.

. . . Stephen King refers directly to our anticipation of horror. In *Salem's Lot* Susan approaches the house which is the source of evil. "She found herself thinking of those drive-in horror movie epics where the heroine goes venturing up the narrow attic stairs . . . or down into some dark, cobwebby cellar . . . and she . . . thinking: . . . *I'd never do that!*" Of course Susan's fears are justified. She does end up dead in the basement, a victim of the vampire.

She integrates a direct **quotation** to explain the example.

The author **elaborates** on how her evidence shows the importance of this horror element.

APPLY TO YOUR DRAFT

Your literary analysis should include various types of evidence to support your key ideas. Be sure to explain the meaning and importance of each piece of evidence. Use the chart to guide you as you zoom in and reflect on your evidence. As you write, apply this technique to your draft.

FOCUS ON	REFLECT
At the beginning of the story, readers learn . . .	This helps create a feeling of . . .
In . . . , the author states . . .	This emphasizes . . .
In another passage, the author describes . . .	It is clear from this example that . . .

3 REVISE YOUR LITERARY ANALYSIS

Even professional writers rework their ideas and language as they write to make sure they are communicating their ideas effectively. Use the guide to help you revise your literary analysis.

Ed

Help with Revision

Find a **Peer Review Guide** and **Student Models** online.

REVISION GUIDE		
ASK YOURSELF	**PROVE IT**	**REVISE IT**
Introduction Does my introduction clearly state my controlling idea?	**Underline** the controlling idea.	**Add** a controlling idea, if missing, or **revise** the existing one so it is clearer.
Organization Is there a logical progression of ideas?	**Highlight** the key ideas.	**Rearrange** paragraphs or sentences to organize ideas logically.
Transitions Do transitions connect ideas?	**Put a star** (★) next to transitional words and phrases.	**Add** transitions to clarify and strengthen connections.
Evidence Do I support each key idea with evidence?	**Put a check mark** (✓) next to each supporting example or quotation.	**Add** more examples or quotations to support or strengthen ideas.
Conclusion Does my conclusion summarize the topic and support my analysis?	**Highlight** the summary, if one is presented.	**Add** or **revise** a statement to more effectively summarize the key ideas.

APPLY TO YOUR DRAFT

Consider the following as you look for opportunities to improve your writing.

- Make sure your controlling idea is clear and strongly stated.
- Check that your evidence clearly connects to your controlling idea.
- Correct any errors in grammar and punctuation.

Peer Review in Action

Once you have finished revising your literary analysis, you will exchange papers with a partner in a **peer review.** During a peer review you will give suggestions to improve your partner's draft.

Read the introduction from a student's draft and examine the comments made by the peer reviewer to see how it's done.

First Draft

"The Tell-Tale Heart"—Still Scary After All These Years
by Justine Thompson, Springfield Middle School

I have to admit it. I wasn't looking forward to reading this "classic"—"The Tell-Tale Heart" by Edgar Allan Poe—because it's a really old story. Don't get me wrong, I love horror movies, especially ones based on Stephen King novels. The elements of suspense and surprise are what really appeals to me in the horror genre. So, after reading Poe's story, I have to admit that I loved it! It had all the elements of horror that I think make for a great horror story.

Your opening grabs my attention, but the style seems too informal. Try revising so you don't use "I."

This is good, but it would sound stronger without words like "think" and "great."

Now read the revised introduction. Notice how the writer has improved the draft by revising based on the reviewer's comments.

Revision

"The Tell-Tale Heart"—Still Scary After All These Years
by Justine Thompson, Springfield Middle School

Modern young adult readers might hesitate to read "The Tell-Tale Heart" by Edgar Allan Poe just because it's a classic, or very old story. If so, they would be missing out on a horror tale that is equal to the best of modern horror stories, including those by the "king of horror," Stephen King. The elements of suspense and surprise are critical to the horror genre—and Poe's story contains both. In fact, Poe's story effectively uses many elements of the horror genre—and that's why it is still worth reading today.

Way to go! Your style is more formal, but it still grabs my attention.

Much better! Your controlling idea is clearer and stronger.

APPLY TO YOUR DRAFT

During your peer review, give each other specific suggestions for how you could make your literary analysis more effective. Use your revision guide to help you.

When receiving feedback from your partner, listen attentively and ask questions to make sure you fully understand the revision suggestions.

4 EDIT YOUR LITERARY ANALYSIS

Edit your final draft to check for proper use of standard English conventions and to correct any misspellings or grammatical errors.

Ed
Interactive Grammar Lesson: Commas

Watch Your Language!

USE COMMAS

Commas indicate how ideas are organized. Authors can use commas to prompt readers to slow down and take notice of an important idea or detail.

Read the following sentence from "What Is the Horror Genre?"

> We could all make long lists of the kind of creatures we identify with horror, especially when we think of films as well as literature.

The comma signals a pause between clauses, making it clear where a new idea begins. Perhaps more importantly, the author draws attention to a key point about the horror genre—that it includes films, not just books.

Common Comma Uses

Here are some ways to use commas:

- to indicate a pause between the clauses in a compound or complex sentence
- to separate items in a list
- to set off an introductory word, phrase, or clause at the beginning of a sentence
- to set off a phrase or clause that is not essential to a sentence's meaning

APPLY TO YOUR DRAFT

Now apply what you've learned about commas to your own work.

1. **Read your paper aloud** and notice where natural breaks or pauses occur.
2. **Add commas** where they are needed.
3. **Exchange drafts** with a peer and review the use of commas in each other's work.

5 PUBLISH YOUR LITERARY ANALYSIS

Share It!

The prompt asks you to present your literary analysis in the form of an essay. You may also use your literary analysis as inspiration for other projects.

Ways to Share

- Create a **screencast** to present your analysis using visuals and audio narration.
- Share ideas from your essay in an **online class discussion forum** about the horror genre.
- Adapt your essay as a **critical review** for a newspaper or literary magazine.

Reflect & Extend

Here are some other ways to show your understanding of the ideas in Unit 2.

Reflect on the Essential Question

Why do we sometimes like to feel frightened?

Has your answer to the question changed after reading the texts in the unit? Discuss your ideas.

You can use these sentence starters to help you reflect on your learning.

- **This story affected my thinking because . . .**
- **I gained new understanding about . . .**
- **I was surprised by . . .**

Project-Based Learning

Create a Movie Trailer

You've read some thrilling horror stories. Now, create a trailer for an imagined movie adaptation of one of the stories.

Here are some questions to ask yourself as you get started.

- How will the trailer hook viewers?
- What visual and sound elements will help establish a creepy mood?
- What plot elements will you reveal to build tension and end the trailer with a feeling of suspense?

Ed

Media Projects

To find help with this task online, access **Create a Movie Trailer.**

Writing

Write a Short Story

Show what you've learned about the horror genre by writing a short story of your own. Use the chart to help you brainstorm horror elements for your story. Then, write your story.

SETTING	
PLOT	
CHARACTERS	
SUSPENSE	

UNIT 3

Ed

Get hooked by the unit topic.

Stream to Start Video

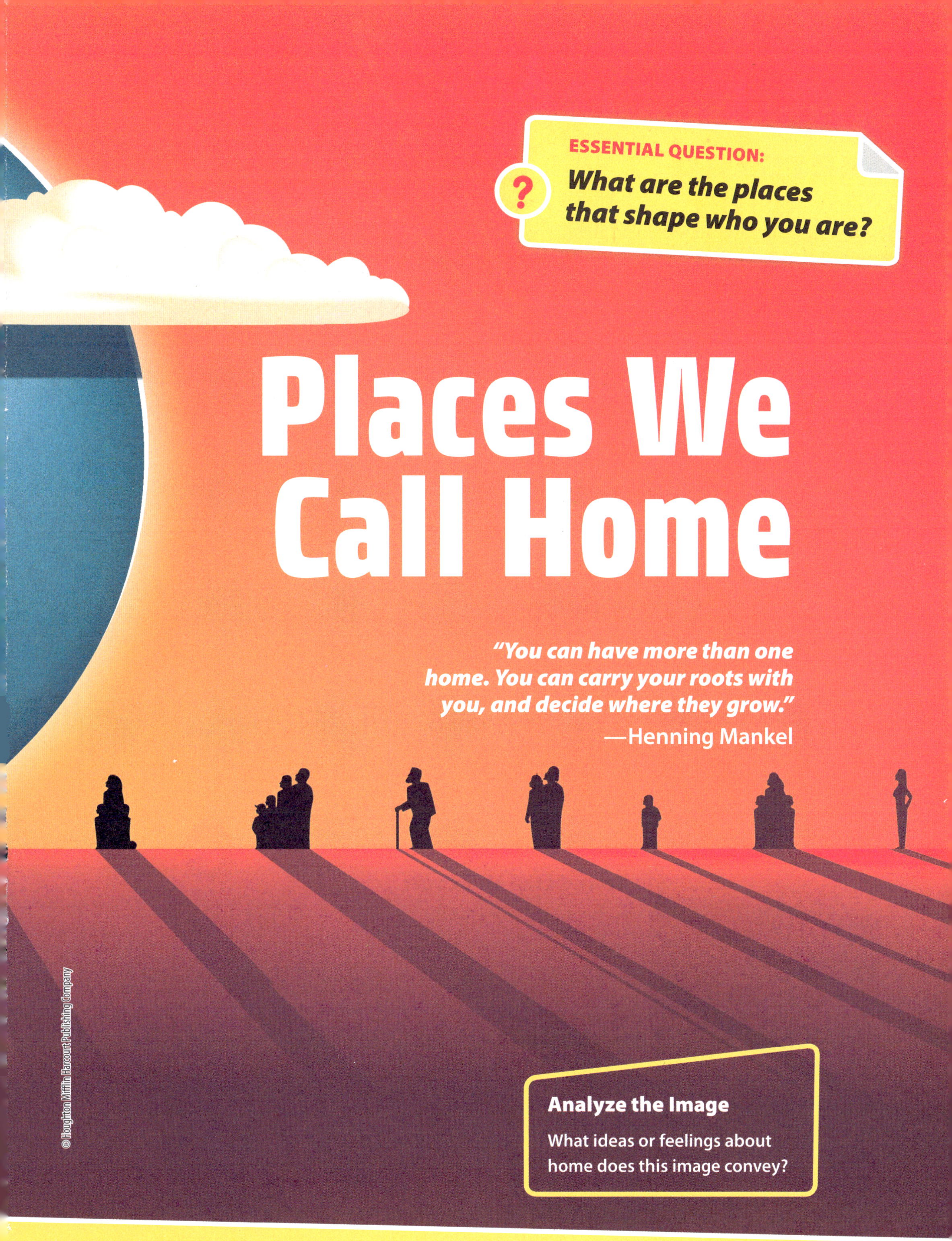

ESSENTIAL QUESTION:

What are the places that shape who you are?

Places We Call Home

"You can have more than one home. You can carry your roots with you, and decide where they grow."

—Henning Mankel

Analyze the Image

What ideas or feelings about home does this image convey?

Spark Your Learning

Here's a chance to spark your learning about ideas in **Unit 3: Places We Call Home.**

As you read, you can use the **Response Log** (page R3) to track your thinking about the Essential Question.

Make the Connection

Think about a place that feels like home. Sketch a picture of the place or write a detailed description of it in the space below.

Think About the Essential Question

What are the places that shape who you are? What places come to mind?

Sound Like an Expert

You can use these Academic Vocabulary words to write and talk about places we call home. Which of these words do you already feel comfortable using when speaking or writing?

	I can use it!	I understand it.	I'll look it up.
contribute			
immigrate			
reaction			
relocate			
shifting			

Prove It!

Turn to a partner and use one of the words in a sentence about the places that shape your identity.

Preview the Texts

Look over the images, titles, and descriptions of the texts in the unit. Mark the title of the text that interests you most.

from The Book of Unknown Americans

Novel by **Cristina Henríquez**

The Toro family faces obstacles whenever they try to visit their home country of Panamá.

My Favorite Chaperone

Short Story by **Jean Davies Okimoto**

Although they don't always get along, Maya and her brother Nurzhan find creative ways of helping each other.

Spirit Walking in the Tundra

Poem by **Joy Harjo**

The speaker of this poem describes a trip she took to Alaska to visit a friend.

New Immigrants Share Their Stories

Documentary produced by **The Working Group**

Watch how students from two schools in New York came together to learn more about each other.

A Common Bond

Informational Text by **Brooke Hauser**

What is it like for students who have recently come to the United States to go to a school with other immigrants from a wide range of backgrounds?

I Wonder . . .

About which place from your childhood do you have the most positive memories? Jot down or sketch your answer.

MENTOR TEXT

from
The Book of Unknown Americans

Novel by **Cristina Henríquez**

ESSENTIAL QUESTION:
What are the places that shape who you are?

Engage Your Brain

Choose one or more of these activities to start connecting with the story you're about to read.

Obstacle Course

Have you ever wanted to go somewhere or do something, but things kept getting in the way? What were the obstacles? Use the space below to sketch or explain what happened.

All About Panamá

The Book of Unknown Americans references real people, places, and events related to the history of Panamá. Conduct research to learn more about Panamá's history. Make sure to find facts about:

- the Panamá Canal
- Manuel Noriega
- the U.S. invasion of Panamá

Immigrants in Pop Culture

In a small group, have a brief discussion about how immigrants are portrayed in pop culture, such as in movies, TV shows, or Broadway musicals. Are these portrayals fair?

Analyze Plot

The series of events in a story is called the **plot.** Important plot events, or incidents in a story, propel the action forward by showing how the characters respond to and resolve the conflicts they face.

The excerpt from *The Book of Unknown Americans* spans from the narrator's early childhood until the present. The narrator, Mayor, describes a series of incidents related to his family's struggle to visit their home country of Panamá. As you read, pay attention to how these events build tension.

Focus on Genre

Novel

- is a long work of fiction
- tells a story from the writer's imagination
- can develop characters and conflict more thoroughly than a short story
- often develops more than one plot and/or contains subplots

Analyze Themes

A **theme** is a message about life or human nature that a writer develops over the course of a story or novel. To determine themes in fiction, you can analyze the following elements:

STORY ELEMENT	HOW THE ELEMENT CONTRIBUTES TO THEME
Characters	Look for explicit statements or implied details that help you understand what a character believes about life or people, how he or she reacts to conflict, and how his or her behavior affects the events in a story.
Setting	The **setting**—the time and place in which a story occurs—does more than provide a background for the plot. By showing how characters interact with their setting, a writer may emphasize certain ideas about life and human nature.
Plot	Recall that plot is the series of events in a story that center on a conflict or problem. As the characters struggle to solve the conflict or problem, you may recognize the writer's underlying message or "lesson."

As you read, consider how the plot affects the characters' sense of themselves and their cultural identity. Also consider how details about places in Panamá influence each character's thoughts and actions. How do these details relate to the themes of the selection?

Annotation in Action

Here is an example of how one reader made notes about the theme of the excerpt. As you read, note how the author develops the theme.

I was less than a year old when my parents brought my brother and me to the United States. Enrique was four. He used to tell me things about Panamá that I couldn't possibly have remembered—like about the scorpions in our backyard and the cement utility sink where my mom used to give us baths. . . .

The narrator does not remember living in Panamá. This could be related to the overall theme.

Expand Your Vocabulary

Put a check mark next to the vocabulary words that you feel comfortable using when speaking or writing.

reminisce	☐
assure	☐
ravage	☐
melodrama	☐
convene	☐

Turn to a partner and use one of the words you already know in a sentence about visiting a place you used to live.

As you read the excerpt from *The Book of Unknown Americans,* use the definitions in the side column to learn the vocabulary words you don't already know.

Background

The Book of Unknown Americans is told from the points of view of different immigrants who all reside in an apartment building in Delaware. Author **Cristina Henríquez** (b. 1977) grew up in Delaware and currently resides in Illinois. Her father emigrated from Panamá in 1971, and she spent many childhood summer vacations visiting family there. This excerpt is narrated by Mayor, a boy who came to the United States with his family after the United States invaded Panamá in 1989 in order to remove that country's military leader, Manuel Noriega, from power.

from

The Book of Unknown Americans

Novel by Cristina Henríquez

The Toro family faces obstacles whenever they try to visit their home country of Panamá.

NOTICE & NOTE
As you read, use the side margins to make notes about the text.

1 I was less than a year old when my parents brought my brother and me to the United States. Enrique was four. He used to tell me things about Panamá that I couldn't possibly have remembered—like about the scorpions in our backyard and the cement utility sink where my mom used to give us baths. He **reminisced** about walking down the street with my mom to the Super 99, the dust blowing up everywhere, the heat pounding down, and about looking for crabs between the rocks along the bay.

2 "It's in you," my dad **assured** me once. "You were born in Panamá. It's in your bones."

3 I spent a lot of time trying to find it in me, but usually I couldn't. I felt more American than anything, but even that was up for debate according to the kids at school who'd taunted me over the years, asking me if I was related to Noriega, telling me to go back through the canal. The truth was that I didn't know

reminisce
(rĕm´ə-nĭs´) *v.* When you *reminisce,* you think or talk about past experiences.

assure
(ə-shŏŏr´) *v.* To *assure* is to state something positively, so as to remove doubt about it.

which I was. I wasn't allowed to claim the thing I felt and I didn't feel the thing I was supposed to claim.

4 The first time I heard my parents tell the story about leaving Panamá, my mom said, "Our hearts kept breaking each time we walked out the door." They tried to give it time. They assumed conditions would improve. But the country was so **ravaged** that their hearts never stopped breaking. Eventually they sold almost everything they owned and used the money to buy plane tickets to somewhere else, somewhere better, which to them had always meant the United States. A while after I was old enough to understand this story, I pointed out how backwards it was to have fled to the nation that had driven them out of theirs, but they never copped to the irony of it. They needed to believe they'd done the right thing and that it made sense. They were torn between wanting to look back and wanting to exist absolutely in the new life they'd created. At one point, they had planned to return. They'd thought that with enough time, Panamá would be rebuilt and that their hearts, I guess, would heal. But while they waited for that day, they started making friends. My dad got a job as a busboy and then, later on, as a dishwasher. Years passed. Enrique was in school, and I started, too. My dad was promoted to line cook. More years slid by. And before they knew it, we had a life here. They had left their lives once before. They didn't want to do it again.

5 So they applied for U.S. citizenship, sitting up at night reading the Constitution, a dictionary by their side, and studying for the exam. They contacted someone at the Panamanian consulate[1] in Philadelphia who helped them navigate the paperwork. Then they woke up one morning, got dressed in their best clothes, caught a bus to the courthouse, and, while my mom held me in her arms and my dad rested his hand on Enrique's shoulder, took an oath along with a group of other men and women who had made living in the United States a dream. We became Americans.

6 We never went back to Panamá, not even for a visit. It would have taken us forever to save enough money for plane tickets. Besides, my dad never wanted to take time off from his job. He probably could've asked for a few days of vacation time, but even after years of being there, making omelets and flipping pancakes, he knew—we all knew—that he was on the low end of the food chain. He could be replaced in a heartbeat. He didn't want to risk it.

ravage
(răv´ĭj) *v.* To *ravage* is to cause serious damage or destruction.

NOTICE & NOTE
AGAIN AND AGAIN

When you notice that a word, image, or event is repeated in a story, you've found an **Again and Again** signpost.

Notice & Note: Mark places where *American* or *Americans* has appeared so far in the story, including in the title.

Analyze: Why might the author keep bringing this up again and again?

[1] **consulate** (kŏn´sə-lĭt): a representative office of a foreign government located within another nation's borders.

Don't forget to **Notice & Note** as you read the text.

7 Because of that, we'd missed my tía Gloria's wedding, which she'd had on a hillside in Boquete. She told my mom that she'd convinced her new husband, Esteban, to dance and that therefore the whole event was a success. We had my aunt on speakerphone and my mom had said, "Take it from me, hermanita,[2] they dance at the wedding and then they never do it again." My dad had said, "That's what you think?" and clutched my mom by the wrist, sending her into a small spin in the middle of the kitchen. She squealed with delight while he swayed with her for a few beats and then he broke out into some goofy merengue[3] moves, kicking his leg up at the end and shouting "¡Olé!" My aunt started yelling through the phone, "Are you still there? Celia! Rafael!" And my parents laughed until my mom dabbed the corners of her eyes with the back of her hand. I'd never seen them so happy with each other, even though it was just for those few seconds.

[2] **hermanita** (ûr-mə-nē´tə): the Spanish word for "little sister."
[3] **merengue** (mə-rĕng´gā): a dance of Dominican and Haitian folk origin, characterized by a sliding step.

8 We almost went back for my dad's high school reunion, which my dad somehow got into his head that he didn't want to miss. The reunion was on a Friday, so maybe, he told us, he could fix his work schedule so that he was off on Friday. We could fly there, go to the reunion, and then fly back Saturday night. He was usually off on Sundays, but if he took off Friday instead, he'd have to be back and work Sunday to make up for it. So one night would be the longest we could stay, but one night would be enough. He had decided. And it looked like we were going to try.

ANALYZE THEMES

Annotate: Mark places in paragraph 9 that show Celia's feelings about the trip to Panamá.

Infer: What do the narrator's descriptive details suggest about Celia?

9 My mom was as excited about the trip as I don't know what. She went to Sears to buy a new dress and had giddy phone conversations with my aunt about seeing each other again and what they would be able to pack into our eighteen hours on the ground. She started laying out her clothes weeks in advance even though my dad kept telling her she only needed two outfits—one to go and one to come home. "And why do you have ten pairs of shoes here?" he asked, pointing to the sandals and leather high heels my mom had lined up along the baseboard in the bedroom. "Ten!" my mom scoffed. "I don't even own ten pairs of shoes." My father counted them. "Fine. Seven. That's still six too many." He told her that he intended to take only a duffel bag for our things because that would make it easier to get through customs. My mom said, "I'll check my own bag, then." My dad kicked the row of shoes my mom had lined up and sent them flying into the wall. He walked right up to my mom and held his index finger in front of her face. "One bag, Celia. One! For all four of us. Don't talk to me about it again."

10 A few weeks before the reunion, my dad called the number on the invitation to RSVP. The guy who answered had been the class president. He and my dad joked around for a minute and then my dad told the guy we were coming. According to what my dad told us later, the guy said, "We'll roll out the red carpet, then." When my dad asked him what he meant by that, the guy said that my dad would have to forgive him if the party wasn't up to my dad's standards. "We didn't know the gringo[4] royalty was coming. We'll have to get the place repainted before you arrive." When my dad asked again what the guy was talking about, the guy said he hoped my dad didn't expect them all to kiss his feet now and reminded my dad how humble Panamá was. It didn't take long for my dad to slam the phone down. He stormed over to my mom, who was

[4] **gringo** (grĭng´gō): a foreigner in Latin America, especially an American or English person; the term is often considered offensive.

washing dishes, and said, "We're not going. If that's what they think, then we're not going."

11 My mom said, "What?"

12 "They think we're Americans now. And maybe we are! Maybe we don't belong there anymore after all." My dad went out on the balcony, which he did whenever he was really upset.

13 My mom stood in the kitchen, a soapy pot in her hand, and looked at me, baffled. "What just happened?" she asked.

14 When I told her everything I'd been able to gather, she walked out to the balcony and closed the door behind her. At the commotion, Enrique came out of his room.

15 "We're not going anymore," I told him.

16 "Huh?"

17 "On the trip."

18 "Are you serious?" Enrique asked.

19 My brother and I huddled together, listening through the front door. I heard my mom say, "Please, Rafa. He doesn't know anything about us. We can still go. You'll see. Once we get there . . . All your friends . . . And everyone will love you." I imagined her reaching out to touch his shoulder, the way she did sometimes when she was asking for something. "Don't you miss it?" she asked. "Can't you imagine landing there, being there again? You know how it smells? The air there. And seeing everyone again. Please, Rafa."

20 But my dad wasn't swayed.

21 The following year, we talked about going back, too. My dad's anger over being cast as a holier-than-thou gringo had finally simmered down, and my mom, who couldn't bring herself to return the new dress she'd bought and who hadn't gotten over the disappointment of not being able to see her sister after all, had been dropping hints ever since that she would still like to go even if the trip was only for one night again. She'd become a genius at turning any and every little thing into a way to talk about Panamá. She would get a mosquito bite on her ankle and point out the welt to us, reminiscing about the bites she used to get in Panamá and wondering aloud "what the mosquitoes there looked like now," as if they were old friends. She would make rice and start talking about the gallo pinto at El Trapiche, which was her favorite restaurant, saying things like "I wonder how Cristóbal—wasn't that the owner's name?—is doing. Wouldn't it be nice to find out?" We would drive over a bridge and suddenly she was talking about the Bridge of the Americas near the canal. "Do you remember, Enrique? That time we took the

Don't forget to **Notice & Note** as you read the text.

ANALYZE PLOT

Annotate: Mark details in paragraph 21 that show the Toros still want to visit Panamá.

Draw Conclusions: How do these details advance the story's plot?

ferry back from Taboga at night and it was all lit up? It was so beautiful. Mayor, I wish you could have seen it." She sighed. "Maybe one day." And my dad would sometimes shake his head at her **melodrama** and other times would just stay quiet, like he'd fallen into the haze of a particular memory himself.

melodrama
(mĕl´ə-drä´mə) *n. Melodrama* is behavior characterized by exaggerated emotions.

22 My mom's birthday was September 22, so my dad finally gave in and made plans for us to go to Panamá. The Toro Family! One night only! Put it in lights! My mom worked herself into a froth all over again, conferring with my tía Gloria on the phone. My aunt apparently said she wanted to take my mom to the new mall and for a drive through Costa del Este, which used to be a garbage dump but now had been transformed into an up-and-coming area of the city, and out for sushi on the causeway, and afterwards they could hit the clubs along Calle Uruguay and yes, she realized they weren't twenty anymore but it would be so much fun! Besides, she and my tío Esteban weren't doing so well, she told my mom. He was never home. He spent the night at friends' apartments. So she could use some distraction and someone to talk to. "Not a divorce!" my mom gasped. To her, there could be nothing worse. "No," my aunt assured her. "Just problems."

ANALYZE PLOT

Annotate: Mark words and phrases in paragraphs 23–25 that relate to time.

Compare: How does the passage of time in this section of the narrative compare with the passage of time in paragraphs 10–20? What is the impact of this structure on the story's plot?

23 Then, less than two weeks before we were scheduled to go, two planes flew into the World Trade Center in New York City and another one into the Pentagon in Washington, D.C. The country went into shock and we went right along with it. My dad called my mom from the diner, where, on the television above the counter, he had just seen the second plane hit the second tower. "They're blowing it up!" he apparently told her. "It's just like El Chorrillo.[5] They're destroying it!" And my mom, in her nightgown, rushed to the set and stood in front of it, watching with her hand over her mouth. I had been eating cereal in the kitchen. I carried my bowl over and stood next to her and kept eating, which, when I thought about it later, seemed kind of messed up, but at the time we didn't know what was happening. The world hadn't stopped—just stopped—like it would later that day and for days after. Everything was still just unfolding in front of our eyes and we had no idea what to make of it.

24 It didn't take long before everyone in our building was knocking on each other's doors and **convening** out on the balcony, standing around stunned and shaking with fear. Nelia Zafón just kept repeating, "What is happening? What is happening? What is happening?" I heard my mom say to

convene
(kən-vēn´) *v.* To *convene* is to come together for a purpose.

[5] **El Chorrillo** (ĕl chô-rē´yō): a neighborhood in Panamá City that suffered heavy damage during the 1989 U.S. invasion of Panamá.

someone, "We moved here because it was supposed to be safer! Where can we go after this?" All day long she kept herself no more than an arm's length from me and my brother, hugging us against her and then letting us go, like she wanted to assure herself that we were still there and that we were okay. Enrique, who was old enough by then that he usually squirmed away from my mom's embraces, must have known the situation was serious, because he let her do it. I let her, too, even though every time she did, instead of comforting me, it only made me more scared.

25 By evening, everyone's front doors were open and people were roaming in and out of each other's units, watching each other's televisions as if a different set would deliver different news, checking to see if anyone had heard anything new, getting tedious translations. Benny Quinto led prayer circles in his living room. Micho Alvarez paced up and down the balcony, talking on his cell phone and jotting things in his notebook. Gustavo Milhojas, who was half-Mexican and half-Guatemalan, wrote a letter to the army telling them that as of that day he was 100 percent American and that he was ready to serve the country and kill the cowards who had murdered his fellow paisanos.[6] At the end he wrote, "And here is a list of people who are willing to join me." He drew a few blank lines and spent the afternoon trying to recruit everyone in the building. When my mom saw what it was, she said, "More killing? That's what you want? *More?*" And Gustavo said, "Not killing. Justice."

26 That year around the holidays we were all miserable. Holidays were always bad—my mom in particular got homesick sometimes like it was a genuine illness—but that Christmas was the worst. We were depressed and on edge, still shaken up about September 11, and then re-shaken when someone tried to blow up another plane by hiding a bomb in his shoes two days before Christmas Eve.

27 My aunt called, which cheered my mom up for a while, but once that wore off, she was more down than ever, shuffling around the house in her slippers, no makeup, her hair a disaster. She carried tissues in the pocket of her bathrobe and made a big show of dabbing her nose with them every so often. Eventually, my dad came up with an idea. "You want Panamá?" he said. "A beach is the closest thing you're going to get." He hustled us out the door and down the street, where we took a chain of buses for an hour and a half to Cape Henlopen in southern Delaware. It was snowing when we arrived—Enrique kept

[6] **paisanos** (pī-zä´nōs): countrymen.

Don't forget to **Notice & Note** as you read the text.

ANALYZE THEME

Annotate: Mark places in paragraphs 26–27 that show Celia's attitude toward her home in Panamá and her home in the United States.

Infer: Why do you think the holiday season is a particularly difficult time of year for the Toros?

complaining that the snow was going to mess up his beloved Adidas sneakers—and everything was so colorless and barren that it looked like the moon. I had to hand it to my dad, though. With the water and the sand, my mom said it almost *was* like a little piece of Panamá. The waves roared in toward us and then silently pulled back again, slipping over the shore. Even with the falling snow, the air had the sting of salt water, and we crunched broken seashells under our shoes. But one beach isn't every beach. And one home isn't every home. And I think we all sensed, standing there, just how far we were from where we had come, in ways both good and bad. "It's beautiful," my mom said, staring out at the ocean. She sighed and shook her head. "This country."

?

ESSENTIAL QUESTION:

What are the places that shape who you are?

Review your notes and add your thoughts to your Response Log.

TURN AND TALK

Is the ending of the story satisfying? Why or why not? Discuss with a partner.

Assessment Practice

Answer these questions before moving on to the **Analyze the Text** section on the following page.

1. This question has two parts. First, answer **Part A**. Then, answer **Part B**.

Part A

What is Celia's primary role in this selection?

- (A) She brags to her sister about their life in the United States.
- (B) She urges her husband to take a trip to their homeland.
- (C) She encourages her two sons to be proud of their heritage.
- (D) She grieves over the good times she experienced in Panamá.

Part B

Select **two** quotations that show Celia in this role.

- (A) "It's in you. . . . You were born in Panamá. It's in your bones." (paragraph 2)
- (B) "Our hearts kept breaking each time we walked out the door." (paragraph 4)
- (C) "The air there. And seeing everyone again. Please, Rafa." (paragraph 19)
- (D) "I wonder how Cristóbal . . . is doing. Wouldn't it be nice to find out?" (paragraph 21)
- (E) "It's beautiful. . . . This country." (paragraph 27)

2. What is the main conflict the Toro family faces throughout the novel excerpt?

- (A) They feel unwelcome in the United States.
- (B) They are unsure about whom they can trust.
- (C) They feel unsafe because of violence in Panamá.
- (D) They are unable to visit their home country.

Ed Test-Taking Strategies

Analyze the Text

Support your responses with evidence from the text.

NOTICE & NOTE

Review what you **noticed and noted** as you read the text. Your annotations can help you answer these questions.

1. **ANALYZE** State one theme the author develops in this excerpt. Cite evidence from the text to support your analysis.

2. **DRAW CONCLUSIONS** In paragraph 7, the narrator states, "And my parents laughed until my mom dabbed the corners of her eyes with the back of her hand." What can you conclude about Celia based on this statement?

3. **CAUSE/EFFECT** What are the effects of the two canceled trips to Panamá on the course of the story?

4. **INFER** How is the narrator's identity, or sense of himself, affected by his surroundings? Cite text evidence to support your answer.

5. **CONNECT** How do the statements Rafa makes about being American in paragraph 12 relate to other ideas about American identity expressed **Again and Again** in the text?

6. **SUMMARIZE** Complete a plot diagram for the novel excerpt by summarizing the parts of the text that make up the chart below.

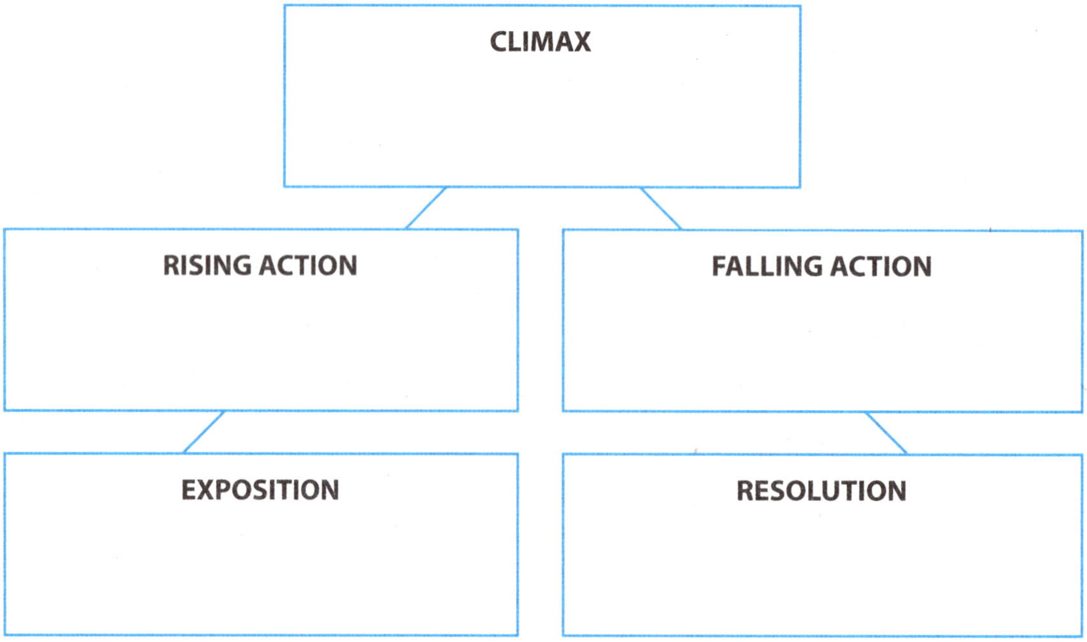

Choices

Here are some other ways to demonstrate your understanding of the ideas in this lesson.

Writing

Get Inside a Character's Head

Choose a character from *The Book of Unknown Americans* and write a paragraph from that character's point of view explaining how he or she feels about the place(s) he or she calls home.

- Review the text for implicit and explicit details that help you make inferences about the character's thoughts and feelings.
- Describe the connections the character feels to his or her home(s) and why. Be sure to write from the point of view of the character.
- Make sure you include details that clearly identify the character. Convey the voice of the character by using language that allows your reader to "hear" his or her personality.

As you write and discuss, be sure to use the **Academic Vocabulary** words.

- **contribute**
- **immigrate**
- **reaction**
- **relocate**
- **shifting**

Media

Create a Collage

Working with a partner, create a collage to express your ideas about the selection.

- Brainstorm with your partner to decide what kinds of images you want to include in your collage.
- Include photos and/or illustrations you find in magazines, newspapers, or online sources that represent the settings, characters, and events described in the excerpt.
- Use text or labels purposefully to make it clear how the images in the collage connect to the selection.

Speaking & Listening

Perform a Scene

In a small group, choose a scene to act out that's described by the narrator in *The Book of Unknown Americans*.

- As a group, review the text and discuss which scenes would be best to perform. How many actors will you need? How does the scene relate to the themes of the novel excerpt? Take notes to record your group's ideas.
- As a group, write a script. Next, cast the characters. Rehearse your scene. Practice using appropriate tone of voice. Assemble any props you may need.
- Finally, perform your scene for the class. Listen attentively as you watch other groups' scenes.

Expand Your Vocabulary

PRACTICE AND APPLY

Write a short answer to show that you understand each of the vocabulary words.

1. Write about a time in your life you like to **reminisce** about.
2. Describe how someone might **assure** you of something.
3. Write a sentence using the word **ravage.**
4. Share an example of a **melodrama.**
5. Give a reason why a group of people might **convene.**

Vocabulary Strategy

Use a Dictionary

A reliable dictionary will tell you not only a word's precise definition and spelling but also its pronunciation and part of speech. Note the word *copped* in paragraph 4 of the excerpt. If you look the word up in a dictionary, you might find these definitions:

cop (kŏp) *tr. v.* *Slang* **1.** To get hold of; gain or win. **2.** To take unlawfully or without permission; steal. **3.** To plead guilty; admit.

Ed

Interactive Vocabulary Lesson: Using Reference Sources

Definition **3** best matches the meaning of *copped* in the sentence.

PRACTICE AND APPLY

Find the words below in the excerpt from *The Book of Unknown Americans.* Use a dictionary to identify the definition that matches the word's meaning in context and its part of speech. Then use the pronunciation to say the word.

WORD	PART OF SPEECH	MEANING
utility (paragraph 1)		
taunted (paragraph 3)		
recruit (paragraph 25)		

Watch Your Language!

Ellipses

An **ellipsis** is a punctuation mark that consists of three dots, or periods. Study the uses of ellipses and the examples in the chart.

Ed
Interactive Grammar
Lesson: Ellipses

USES OF ELLIPSES	EXAMPLE
To show that a word or words have been omitted from a quotation	Mayor says his dad "clutched my mom by the wrist . . . and then he broke out into some goofy merengue moves. . . ." (paragraph 7)
To indicate an interruption, pause, or hesitation	We were all ready to go to Panamá . . . but then 9/11 happened.
To indicate an unfinished thought or speech that trails off	"Please, Rafa. He doesn't know anything about us. We can still go. You'll see. Once we get there . . . All your friends . . . And everyone will love you." (paragraph 19)

PRACTICE AND APPLY

Revise each sentence from the selection using ellipses. Add one or more ellipses in place of other punctuation to indicate a long pause or interruption, or to take the place of the underlined words in the quotation.

1. "We never went back to Panamá, not even for a visit." (paragraph 6)
2. "My dad's anger over being cast as a holier-than-thou gringo had finally simmered down, and my mom, <u>who couldn't bring herself to return the new dress she'd bought and who hadn't gotten over the disappointment of not being able to see her sister after all</u>, had been dropping hints ever since that she would still like to go <u>even if the trip was only for one night again</u>." (paragraph 21)
3. "'I wonder how Cristóbal—wasn't that the owner's name?—is doing.'" (paragraph 21)
4. "It was snowing when we arrived—<u>Enrique kept complaining that the snow was going to mess up his beloved Adidas sneakers</u>—and everything was so colorless and barren that it looked like the moon." (paragraph 27)

My Favorite Chaperone

Short Story by **Jean Davies Okimoto**

ESSENTIAL QUESTION:
What are the places that shape who you are?

Engage Your Brain

Choose one or more activities to start connecting with the selection you are about to read.

Picture It!

Think about the title of this selection. A chaperone is a person who supervises young people at social events. Who would your favorite chaperone be? In the space below, sketch an image or write a description of that person.

Fond Memory

Has your brother, sister, or other family member ever surprised you by doing something to help you when you weren't expecting it? Or maybe you were the thoughtful one. Explain what happened.

House Rules

In the story you are about to read, the main character struggles against her parents' rules. With a partner, have a brief discussion in which you share some of the rules of your household and how you feel about having to follow them.

Analyze Plot

A story's **plot** is a series of events that usually centers on a conflict or problem. Most stories begin with an **exposition,** in which the characters, setting, and conflict are introduced. The **rising action** of a story builds up to the story's **climax,** or its most intense moment. The **falling action** shows the consequences of the characters' decisions or actions. Most stories have a clear **resolution** in which the problem is solved.

As you read "My Favorite Chaperone," identify the conflict the main character struggles with and follow the events of the story through these five stages of plot development.

Focus on Genre

Realistic Fiction

- includes the basic elements of fiction—setting, characters, plot, conflict, and theme
- features events and characters that could exist in real life
- contains natural-sounding dialogue and realistic interactions between characters
- often has a linear plot—story events are presented in chronological order

Analyze Character

Characterization is the way an author reveals the personality traits and perspectives of characters in a story. Authors may introduce and develop the characters through:

- direct comments by the narrator about the characters
- descriptions of the physical appearances of characters
- the characters' own thoughts, speech, and actions
- the thoughts, speech, and actions of other characters

Fiction writers often rely on the use of **dialogue**—written conversation between characters—to reveal important aspects of a character's personality. Read the following dialogue (paragraphs 33–36). What can you infer about Maya's character as she speaks to the school counselor?

DIALOGUE	INFERENCES
"Do your parents speak English, Maya?" "Just a little." "Then perhaps you could attend the meeting and translate for them." "Yes. I must always do this for my parents—at the store, at the doctor, things like that."	

Annotation in Action

Here is an example of notes a student made about this paragraph from "My Favorite Chaperone." As you read, highlight the text that helps you draw conclusions about the characters in the story.

His dark eyes narrowed and his voice was severe. "I am ashamed of this! To come to this school and find you in trouble, Nurzhan! This does not seem like much punishment to me, this no watching television. You will go to bed tonight without dinner." He clenched his teeth.

Papa's actions and his dialogue suggest that he is angry and strict.

Expand Your Vocabulary

Put a check mark next to the vocabulary words that you feel comfortable using when speaking or writing.

- **sponsor** ☐
- **stun** ☐
- **dispatcher** ☐
- **scuffle** ☐
- **whimper** ☐

Turn to a partner and talk about the words you already know. Then, use as many words as you can in a paragraph about the way your parents or guardians expect you to behave. As you read "My Favorite Chaperone," use the definitions in the side column to learn the vocabulary words you don't already know.

Background

In addition to being the author of more than a dozen novels for young adults, **Jean Davies Okimoto** (b. 1942) is a therapist. Perhaps that is why she has such insight into the characters that she portrays. Okimoto typically writes about the everyday problems and challenges faced by teenagers like Maya, the main character in "My Favorite Chaperone." Maya and her family have come to the United States from Kazakhstan, a country in Central Asia that used to be part of the Soviet Union.

My Favorite Chaperone

Short Story by **Jean Davies Okimoto**

Although they don't always get along, Maya and her brother Nurzhan find creative ways of helping each other.

NOTICE & NOTE
As you read, use the side margins to make notes about the text.

1 In homeroom when Mr. Horswill handed out the permission slip for the Spring Fling, the all-school dance, I almost didn't take one. Why should I bother when I was sure the answer would be the same? Even though I'm in ninth grade now, it would still be the same. No. *Nyet* is what they say, and I don't want to hear this again. But I took a permission slip anyway. I don't know why I didn't just shake my head when this very popular girl Marcia Egness was handing them out. And even after I took one, I don't know why I didn't throw it away. Maybe I just couldn't give up hope. It's like that in America. It's a place where things can change for people, and many people always seem to have hope. At least that's how it seems to me. Maybe I was beginning to think this way, too, although my hope was very small.

ANALYZE CHARACTER

Annotate: In paragraph 1, mark details that reveal something about Maya.

Infer: In a few sentences, summarize what you can infer about Maya from these details.

NOTICE & NOTE
MEMORY MOMENT

When you notice the narrator has interrupted the forward progress of a story by bringing up something from the past, you've found a **Memory Moment** signpost.

Notice & Note: Mark the sentences in paragraph 2 that help you realize that Maya is interrupting her story to recall events from an earlier time.

Analyze: Why might the events described in paragraphs 2–7 be important?

sponsor
(spŏn´sər) *v.* If you *sponsor* someone, you support his or her admission into a group.

2 We came to America through an international dating magazine. I don't mean that our whole family was in the magazine looking for dates, just Madina Zhamejakova, my aunt. Aunt Madina came after Kazakhstan broke away from the Soviet Union and things got very hard. Everyone's pay was cut and the *tenge,* our money, was worth less and less. Then my grandmother died. That was the worst part. She was the head of our family, and without her everything fell apart. That's when Aunt Madina started reading international dating magazines.

3 The next thing we knew, she had a beautiful photo taken of herself wearing her best outfit, a black dress with a scoop neck and a red silk band around the neck. Aunt Madina is very pretty. Mama says she looks like an old American movie star we saw on TV named Natalie Wood, except Aunt Madina looks more Kazakh with her dark, beautiful Asian eyes. She sent the photo to one of these magazines, and in a very short time a man from Seattle saw her picture. He started calling her, and they would talk on the phone for hours. I guess he had plenty of money for these calls, which Aunt Madina thought was a good sign. After about six months, he asked her to marry him.

4 His name was Bob Campbell and he'd been in the navy. He told Aunt Madina he never had a chance to meet anyone because he traveled so much. Maybe that was true, but Mama was worried.

5 "Madina, something must be wrong with this man if he has to find a wife through a magazine."

6 Mama was afraid for her, but Aunt Madina went to America anyway and married Mr. Bob Campbell. She phoned us a lot from America, and Mama admitted she sounded okay. Madina said Bob was a lot older and had less hair than in the picture he had sent her. He was also fatter than in the picture, but he was very nice. She sounded so good, Mama stopped worrying about Aunt Madina, but then things got so bad in Kazakhstan that she worried all the time about us. Papa and Mama lost their teaching jobs because the government was running out of money. Mama had to go to the market and sell many of our things: clothes, dishes, even some furniture. When Aunt Madina asked us to come to America for the hundredth time, we were running out of things to sell and my parents finally agreed. Aunt Madina **sponsored** us, and not long after we got here, Papa got a job driving a cab, and Mama worked cleaning people's houses. It was hard for them not to have the respect they were used to from holding government teaching jobs, but they had high regard for the food they could now easily buy at the store.

7 Six months after we got here, the Boeing Company moved to Chicago and Mr. Bob Campbell got transferred there. When Aunt Madina left with him, it broke Mama's heart. Aunt Madina was the only person we knew from Kazakhstan, and it felt like our family just huddled together on a tiny island in the middle of a great American sea.

8 I looked at the permission slip, wishing there were some special words I could say to get Mama and Papa to sign it. Around me, everyone in my homeroom was talking excitedly about the Spring Fling. Mama says she thinks the school is strange to have parties and events after school when students should be doing their homework. Ever since I've been at Beacon Junior High, the only slip they signed was for the gymnastics team. Papa loves sports. (I think he told Mama that giving permission for this activity was important for my education.) I can't find words to say how grateful I was he signed that slip. The gymnastics team is a fine, good thing in my life. I compete in all the events: vault, beam, floor exercise, and my favorite: the uneven bars. I love to swing up and up, higher and higher, and as I fly through the air, a wonderful thing happens and suddenly I have no worries and no responsibilities. I'm free!

9 But there's another reason why I love gymnastics. Shannon Lui is on the team. We became friends when she was a teaching assistant in my ESL class. We're the same age,

Ed

Close Read Screencast

Listen to a modeled close read of this text.

ANALYZE PLOT

Annotate: Mark details in paragraph 8 that reveal the story's main conflict.

Summarize: Describe the story's conflict in one sentence.

but she says I'm like her little sister. Her grandparents came from China, and her parents speak perfect English. Everything about Shannon's family is very American. Her mother has a red coat with gold buttons from Nordstrom, and her father cooks and sometimes even washes dishes! (I couldn't believe this when I first saw it; no Kazakh man would do kitchen work.) Shannon encouraged me to try out for the gymnastics team, and the team has meant even more to me this year since I got put in the mainstream and had to leave ESL. Since I left ESL, I often feel like I'm in the middle of a game where I don't know the players, the rules, or even the object of the game.

10 In my next class, Language Arts, even though I knew it was foolish, I was dreaming of the Spring Fling. I really like Language Arts. Ms. Coe, our teacher, is also the gymnastics coach, and there's a guy in the class, Daniel Klein, who was my partner for a research project last semester. He encouraged me to talk and listened to what I had to say (he's also a very handsome guy), and I always look forward to this class so I can see him. I was trying to think of some ideas to convince Mama and Papa to give permission (and also sneaking glances at Daniel Klein) when Mr. Walsh, the vice-principal, came into our class. He whispered something to Ms. Coe and she nodded. And then I was **stunned** because she nodded and pointed to me!

stun

(stŭn) *v.* To *stun* someone is to make him or her feel shocked or dazed.

11 "Maya, you're wanted in the office," Ms. Coe said. "You can go now with Mr. Walsh."

12 My fingers tingled with fear. What was wrong? What had I done? Mr. Walsh only comes for people when there's trouble.

13 Like a robot, I gathered my books and followed Mr. Walsh. As he closed the classroom door behind us, my heart began to bang and I felt like I needed to go to the bathroom. In the hallway he told me Ms. Johnson, the school counselor, wanted to speak with me.

ANALYZE CHARACTER

Annotate: Mark words and phrases in paragraphs 11–17 that show how Maya is feeling.

Infer: What do her feelings reveal about her?

14 "What is wrong?" My voice came out as a whisper. I felt such terror I could barely speak.

15 "What's that?" Mr. Walsh couldn't hear my whisper.

16 "What is wrong?" I tried to speak more loudly.

17 "She didn't say. She just asked me to find you since I was heading down the hall anyway."

18 I suddenly remembered Sunstar Sysavath, who was in my ESL class last year. Her family came from Cambodia, and on her first day at Beacon she was in the wrong line in the

lunchroom. Mr. Walsh went to help her, and he tapped her on her shoulder to get her attention. When she felt the tap and saw him, she lifted her hands in the air as if she were being arrested and about to be shot. People who saw this in the lunchroom laughed, but it wasn't a joke. Sunstar was filled with terror.

19 I knew I wouldn't be shot, but walking with Mr. Walsh to the office seemed like one of the longest walks of my life. I often fill my mind with nice things, such as imagining myself at the Olympics winning a gold medal for the U.S.A.—especially on days like today, when we have a gymnastics meet after school. But now my mind was filled with nothing. It was empty, like a dry riverbed where there is only cracked, baked earth and nothing lives.

20 I walked into the main office, where Ms. Johnson was waiting for me. "Come with me, Maya." Ms. Johnson smiled at Mr. Walsh. "Thanks, Tom."

21 Like a person made from wood, a puppet, I followed Ms. Johnson through the main office down the hall to her office across from the principal's. She showed me in and closed the door behind us.

22 "Sit down, dear."

23 I sat in a chair across from her desk and clutched my books to my chest. I'd never been in her office before. She had many nice green plants in front of the window and a small fish tank in one corner. I stared at the brightly colored fish swimming back and forth, back and forth. Then Ms. Johnson spoke.

24 "I received a call from Mr. Shanaman, the principal at Evergreen Elementary, and your brother's been suspended for fighting."

25 "Nurzhan?"

26 "Yes. Nurzhan Alazova." She read his name from a pink message slip. "They haven't been able to locate your mother, so they called over here to see if you could help."

27 "Is Nurzhan all right?"

28 "Yes. And I believe the other boy wasn't seriously hurt."

29 "Who did Nurzhan fight?" It was a foolish question—I was sure of the answer. Ms. Johnson hesitated, so I just said, "Ossie Nishizono," and she nodded.

30 "What must I do?" I asked.

31 "The school policy on suspension requires that the parent or guardian must have a conference at school within twenty-four hours of the suspension. Can you help us locate your mother or your father?"

Don't forget to **Notice & Note** as you read the text.

ANALYZE PLOT

Annotate: Nurzhan's suspension creates a complication in the plot. Mark the reason that Ms. Johnson wants Maya to attend the meeting about Nurzhan.

Infer: What can you infer about Maya's role in her family?

dispatcher

(dĭs-păch´ər) *n.* A *dispatcher* is a person who sends out vehicles according to a schedule.

32 "Yes. I can do that."

33 "Do your parents speak English, Maya?"

34 "Just a little."

35 "Then perhaps you could attend the meeting and translate for them."

36 "Yes. I must always do this for my parents—at the store, at the doctor, things like that."

37 "Here's the phone. I'll step out to give you some privacy."

38 Ms. Johnson left the office, quietly closing the door behind her. I looked at the nameplate on her desk. CATHERINE JOHNSON, it said. Outside her window, the sky was gray and it had started to rain. I stared at the phone, wishing I didn't have to be the messenger with this bad news. Then I called the Northwest Cab Company and asked them to contact my father.

39 "Aibek Alazova. Cab 191. I'm his daughter, and there is a family problem I must speak with him about."

40 I stayed on the line while the **dispatcher** radioed Papa. I looked at the clock and felt my heart grow heavy. In a minute the bell would ring, school would be out, and the gymnastics meet would begin.

41 "Maya!" Papa's voice was alarmed. "What is wrong?"

42 "Nurzhan has been in a fight with another boy." Then I explained in Russian what had happened, and Papa said he had to drop his passenger at the Four Seasons Hotel downtown and then he'd come straight to Nurzhan's school. He'd be there about three-thirty.

43 Ms. Johnson came back into the office as I hung up the phone. "Did you get your mother?"

44 "I don't have the number where she works today, but I got my father. He will come to the school."

45 "Good."

46 "Ms. Johnson?"

47 "Yes?"

48 "I will leave now for Evergreen. Will you tell Ms. Coe I have a family problem and I cannot attend the gymnastics meet?"

49 "Of course. And I'll call Mr. Shanaman at Evergreen now and let him know that you and your father will be there."

50 I went to my locker, got my coat, then walked quickly down the hall to the south door that opens onto the play field that joins our school with Evergreen. Poor Nurzhan, getting in such big trouble. I couldn't fault him for fighting with Ossie Nishizono. Such a mean boy—he'd been teasing Nurzhan without mercy for not speaking well and mispronouncing

Don't forget to **Notice & Note** as you read the text.

things. I hoped Nurzhan had given him a hard punch. But why did he have to make this fight today! I felt angry that I had to miss the meet because of Nurzhan. Would Ms. Coe still want me on the team? Would she think I wasn't reliable?

51 But as I neared Nurzhan's school—my old school—I only worried about Papa. Even though he didn't shout at me on the phone, that didn't mean he wasn't angry. He had a person in his cab and the dispatcher might have been hearing us. Probably the dispatcher didn't know Russian, but Papa wouldn't show his anger in the cab anyway. But Papa could be very, very angry—not just with Nurzhan but with me, too. He and Mama think it's my duty to watch out for Nurzhan and keep him out of trouble.

52 As I walked up to the front door, Mr. Zabornik, the custodian, waved to me. He was picking up papers and litter around the bushes next to the front walk. It was still raining lightly, and Mr. Zabornik's wet gray hair was pasted against his forehead.

53 "Hi, Maya."

54 "Hello, Mr. Zabornik."

55 "Here about your brother, I suppose."

56 "How did you know?"

57 "I was fixing the drainpipe when it happened." He pointed to the corner of the building by the edge of the play field. "That kid Ossie Nishizono was teasing Nurzhan something fierce. Telling him he could never be a real American, making fun of the way he talked." He bent down and picked up a candy wrapper. "Reminded me of how this bully used to treat me when my family came after the revolution."

58 "Oh." I think Mr. Zabornik could tell I didn't know what revolution this was.

NOTICE & NOTE
TOUGH QUESTIONS

When you notice characters asking questions that reveal their internal struggles, you've found a **Tough Questions** signpost.

Notice & Note: Mark the tough questions Maya asks herself in paragraph 50.

Infer: What do these questions make you wonder about Maya?

59 "The Hungarian revolution, in 1956." He looked out over the play field and folded his arms across his chest. "Guess some things never change."

60 "Nurzhan's going to be suspended."

61 "Sorry to hear that. 'Course, the school can't allow fights, and this was no **scuffle**. But I can sure see how your brother lost his temper." Then he went back to picking up the litter. "Good luck."

scuffle
(skŭf′əl) *n.* A *scuffle* is a disorderly fight.

62 "Thank you, Mr. Zabornik."

63 I went to the front office, where Ms. Illo, the head secretary, spoke to me in a very kind way. "Maya, Mr. Shanaman is waiting for you in his office. You can go right in."

64 Mr. Shanaman was behind his big desk, and Nurzhan was sitting on a chair in the corner. He looked like a rabbit caught in a trap. He had scrapes on his hands and on his cheek, and his eyes were puffed up. I couldn't tell if that was from crying or being hit.

65 "I understand your father will be coming. Is that right, Maya?"

66 I nodded.

67 "Just take a seat by your brother. Ms. Illo will bring your father in when he gets here."

68 Then Mr. Shanaman read some papers on his desk and I sat down next to Nurzhan and spoke quietly to him in Russian.

69 "*Neechevo, Nurzhan. Ya vas ne veenu.*" It's okay, Nurzhan. I don't blame you, is what I said.

70 Nurzhan's eyes were wet with tears as he nodded to me.

71 I stared out the principal's window. Across the street, the bare branches of the trees were black against the cement gray sky. The rain came down in a steady drizzle, and after a few minutes, I saw Papa's cab turn the corner. His cab is green, the color of a lime, and he always washes and shines it. I watched Papa park and get out of the cab. His shoulders are very broad underneath his brown leather jacket, and Papa has a powerful walk, like a large, strong horse that plows fields. He walked briskly, and as he came up the steps of the school, he removed his driver cap.

72 It seemed like one thousand years, but it was only a minute before Ms. Illo brought Papa into the office. Nurzhan and I stood up when he entered, but he didn't look at us, only at Mr. Shanaman, who shook hands with him and motioned for him to have a seat.

73 Papa sat across the desk from Mr. Shanaman and placed his driver cap in his lap.

74 "We have asked Maya to translate, Mr. Alazova."

75 "Yes." Papa nodded. When he heard my name, he understood what Mr. Shanaman meant.

76 "Your son, Nurzhan, was involved in quite a nasty fight."

77 Papa looked at me, and I said to him in Russian, "Nurzhan was in little fight."

78 Mr. Shanaman continued. "The other boy, Ossie Nishizono, needed two stitches at the hospital."

79 "The other boy, Ossie Nishizono, was a little hurt," I told Papa.

80 Nurzhan's eyes became wide as he listened to my translation.

81 "We have a policy that anyone who fights must be suspended from school. Both boys will receive a two-day suspension."

82 "The other boy, who is very bad," I translated for Papa, "is not allowed to come to school for two days and his parents must punish him. Nurzhan must stay home, too. But he should not be punished so much."

83 Papa nodded.

84 Then Mr. Shanaman said, "We've been told the other boy was teasing your son. We'd like you to help Nurzhan find ways to handle this situation without resorting to violence. We're working with the other boy to help him show respect for all students."

85 I looked at Papa and translated: "The other boy was teasing Nurzhan in a violent manner. This boy will be punished and must learn to respect all students. We understand how Nurzhan became so angry, and we ask that you punish him by not allowing him to watch television."

86 "Yes, I will punish my son as you suggest," Papa said in Russian.

87 I looked at Mr. Shanaman. "My father says he will teach Nurzhan not to fight by giving him a very serious punishment."

88 "We are glad you understand the serious nature of this situation," Mr. Shanaman said. Then I told Papa in Russian the exact words of Mr. Shanaman.

Don't forget to **Notice & Note** as you read the text.

ANALYZE CHARACTER

Annotate: Mark the details in paragraphs 76–90 that indicate Nurzhan's reaction to Maya's translations.

Connect: Why might Nurzhan be having this reaction?

Close Read Screencast

Listen to a modeled close read of this text.

VOCABULARY

Context Clues You may be unfamiliar with the phrase *resorting to* in paragraph 84. You can use surrounding words as clues to a word's meaning.

Interpret: Based on its context, you can infer that the phrase *resorting to* means "to do something because no other choices are possible." What does the author's use of this phrase suggest about Mr. Shanaman's opinion of fighting?

89 Mr. Shanaman held out a form on a clipboard. "We require you to sign this to show that we've discussed the suspension and you'll keep Nurzhan at home until Monday."

90 Again, I told Papa exactly what Mr. Shanaman said, and Papa signed the form.

91 We said nothing as we left the school and followed Papa to his cab. Nurzhan and I sat in the back, not daring to speak. There was a small rip in the leather of the seat and I poked my finger in it. The cab smelled of perfume; maybe Papa's last ride was a lady who wore a lot of it. It smelled like some kind of flower, but I couldn't name it. I wished so much I was in a beautiful meadow right then, surrounded by sweet-smelling flowers, lying in the soft grass, looking up at the clouds. I tried to calm myself by thinking about this meadow, but I just kept feeling scared—scared Papa might somehow find out I'd changed what Mr. Shanaman said.

92 Maybe I should've felt bad about changing Mr. Shanaman's words, but I didn't. I only felt afraid. I don't mean that I think changing words like that is okay; I have to admit it's sort of like telling lies. But I think maybe some lies are okay, like in the play we read last semester about Anne Frank and how the people who were hiding her family lied and said no one was in the attic when they really were. They lied to save Anne's family from the Nazis. Maybe I wasn't saving Nurzhan from death, but I was sure scared to death of what Papa might have done if I hadn't changed the words. I stared at the back of Papa's thick neck. It was very red, and he drove in silence until he pulled up in front of our building. Papa shut off the engine. Then he put his arm across the top of the seat and turned his face to us, craning his neck.

93 His dark eyes narrowed and his voice was severe. "I am ashamed of this! To come to this school and find you in trouble, Nurzhan! This does not seem like much punishment to me, this no watching television. You will go to bed tonight without dinner." He clenched his teeth. "I have lost money today because of you. And Maya, you must keep your brother out of trouble!" Then he waved us away furiously, like shooing away bugs. "Go now! Go!"

94 We went in the house, and Nurzhan marched straight to the table in the kitchen with his books. He seemed to be in such a hurry to do his work, he didn't even take off his jacket.

95 "Take off your jacket and hang it up, Nurzhan."

96 "Okay."

97 I began peeling potatoes for dinner, while Nurzhan hung up his jacket. Then he sat back down at the table.

98 "Maya, I—"

Don't forget to **Notice & Note** as you read the text.

99 "Don't talk. Do your work."

100 "But I—"

101 "I missed the gymnastics meet because of you!"

102 "Watch the knife!" Nurzhan looked scared.

103 I glanced at my hand. I was holding the knife and I'd been waving it without realizing it.

104 "I wasn't going to stab you, stupid boy."

105 "I was only going to say thank you." Nurzhan looked glumly at his book.

106 I went back to peeling the potatoes. I'd had enough of him and his troubles.

107 "For changing what Mr. Shanaman said when you told Papa," he said in a timid voice, like a little chick peeping.

108 "It's okay, Nurzhan." I sighed. "Just do your work."

109 A few minutes before six, we heard Mama get home. She came straight to the kitchen, and when she saw Nurzhan sitting there doing his work, a smile came over her tired face.

110 "Oh, what a good boy, doing his work."

111 "Not so good, Mama. Nurzhan got in trouble." I didn't mind having to tell her this bad news too much (not like when I had to call Papa). Then I explained about the fight and how Papa had to come to the school.

112 "Oh, my poor little one!" Mama rushed to Nurzhan and examined his hands. Tenderly, she touched his face where it had been cut. Then she turned sharply toward me.

113 "Maya! How could you let this happen?"

114 "Me! I wasn't even there."

115 "On the bus, when this boy is so bad to Nurzhan. You must make this boy stop."

116 "No, Mama," Nurzhan explained. "He would tease me more if my sister spoke for me."

117 "I don't understand this. In Kazakhstan, if someone insults you, they have insulted everyone in the family. And everyone must respond."

118 "It's different here, Mama."

119 Mama looked sad. She sighed deeply. Then the phone rang and she told me to answer it. Mama always wants me to answer because she is shy about speaking English. When her work calls, I always speak on the phone to the women whose houses she cleans and then translate for Mama. (I translate their exact words, not like with Mr. Shanaman.)

120 But it wasn't for Mama. It was Shannon, and her voice was filled with worry.

121 "Maya, why weren't you at the meet? Is everything all right?"

122 "Everything's okay. It was just Nurzhan." Then I explained to her about what had happened. "I hope I can still be on the team."

123 "Ms. Coe is cool. Don't worry, it won't mess anything up."

124 Shannon was right. The next day at practice Ms. Coe was very understanding. Practice was so much fun I forgot all about Nurzhan, and Shannon and I were very excited because Ms. Coe said we were going to get new team leotards.

125 After practice we were waiting for the activity bus, talking about the kind of leotards we wanted, when two guys from the wrestling team joined us. One was David Pfeiffer, a guy who Shannon talked about all the time. She always said he was so cute, that he was "awesome" and "incredible" and things like that. She was often laughing and talking to him after our practice, and I think she really liked him. And today he was with Daniel Klein!

126 "Hey, Maya! How was practice?"

127 "Hi." I smiled at Daniel, but then I glanced away, pretending to look for the bus because talking to guys outside class always made me feel embarrassed and shy.

128 The guys came right up to us. David smiled at Shannon. "Wrestling practice was great! We worked on takedowns and escapes, and then lifted weights. How was your practice?"

129 "Fun! We spent most of it on the beam."

130 "I'm still pumped from weight training!" David grinned and picked up a metal trash can by the gym door. He paraded around with the can, then set it down with a bang right next to Shannon. Everyone was laughing, and then David bent his knees and bounced up and down on his heels and said, "Check this out, Daniel! Am I strong or what?" The next thing we knew, David had one arm under Shannon's knees and one arm under her back and he scooped her up. Shannon squealed and laughed, and I was laughing watching them, when all of a sudden Daniel scooped me up too!

131 *"Chort!"* I shouted, as he lifted me. I grabbed him around his neck to hang on, and my head was squished against his shoulder. He strutted around in a circle before he let me down. I could feel that my face was the color of borscht, and I flamed with excitement and embarrassment and couldn't stop laughing from both joy and nervousness.

132 "That's nothing, man." David crouched like a weight lifter while he was still holding Shannon and lifted her as high as his shoulders.

133 It was exciting and crazy: Daniel and David showing each other how strong they were, first picking up Shannon and me, then putting us down, then picking us up and lifting us higher,

as if Shannon and I were weights. After a few times, whenever Daniel picked me up, I was easily putting my arms around his neck, and I loved being his pretend weight, even though Shannon and I were both yelling for them to put us down. (We didn't really mean it. Shannon is a strong girl, and if she didn't like being lifted up and held by David, there was no way it would be happening.) I couldn't believe it, but I began to relax in Daniel's arms, and I laughed each time as he slowly turned in a circle.

134 Then Shannon and I tried to pick them up, and it was hilarious. Every time we tried to grab them, they did wrestling moves on us and we ended up on the grass in a big heap, like a litter of playful puppies. I couldn't remember a time in my life that had been so fun and so exciting. We lay on the grass laughing, and then David and Daniel jumped up and picked Shannon and me up again.

135 But this time when we turned, as my face was pressed against Daniel's shoulder, I saw something coming toward the school that made me tremble with fear.

136 "Daniel, please. Put me down!" My voice cracked as my breath caught in my throat.

137 But Daniel didn't hear. Everyone was shouting and laughing, and he lifted me up even more as the lime green cab came to a halt in front of the school. The door slammed. Papa stood like a huge bull in his dark leather jacket and flung open the back door of the cab.

138 "MAYA ALAZOVA!" His voice roared across the parking lot. He pointed at me the way one might identify a criminal. "*EDEE SUDA*!" he shouted in Russian. COME HERE!

139 Daniel dropped me and I ran to the cab, **whimpering** and trembling inside like a dog caught stealing a chicken.

140 Papa didn't speak. His silence filled every corner of the cab like a dark cloud, slowly suffocating me with its poisonous rage. Papa's neck was deep red, and the skin on the back of my hands tingled with fear. I lay my head back against the seat and closed my eyes, squeezing them shut, and took myself far away until I was safe on the bars at a beautiful gymnastics meet in the sky.

Don't forget to **Notice & Note** as you read the text.

whimper
(hwĭm′pər) *v.* To *whimper* is to sob or let out a soft cry.

I swung back and forth, higher and higher, and then I released and flew to the next bar through fluffy white clouds as soft as goose feathers, while the air around me was sweet and warm, and my teammates cheered for me, their voices filled with love.

141 We screeched to a stop in front of our building. My head slammed back against the seat. When I struggled from the taxi, it was as though I had fallen from the bars, crashing down onto the street, where I splintered into a million pieces. And as hard as I tried, I couldn't get back on the bars any more than I could stop the hot tears that spilled from my eyes. Papa roared in front of me, and as he charged toward the door in his glistening dark leather jacket, he again seemed transformed to a creature that was half man and half bull.

142 "Gulnara!" He flung open the door, shouting for Mama, his voice filled with anger and blame.

143 "Why are you here? What has happened, Aibek?" Mama came from the kitchen as Nurzhan darted to the doorway and peeked around like a little squirrel.

144 I closed the front door and leaned against it with my wet palms flat against the wood, like a prisoner about to be shot.

145 "Is this how you raise your daughter! Is this what you teach her? Lessons to be a toy for American boys!" Papa spat out the words.

146 The color rose in Mama's face like a flame turned up on the stove, and she spun toward me, her eyes flashing. "What have you done?"

147 "Your daughter was in the arms of an American boy."

148 Mama looked shocked. "When? H-how can this be?" she stammered.

149 "Outside the school as I drove by, I found them at this. Don't you teach her anything?"

Ed

Text in Focus Video

Learn more about understanding character traits.

ANALYZE PLOT

Annotate: Review paragraphs 137–150. Mark evidence of Maya's parents' reactions to finding her in the arms of an American boy.

Predict: What impact might this complication have on Maya's ability to resolve the story's main conflict?

150 "Who let her stay after school? Who gives permission for all these things? You are the one, Aibek. If you left it to me, she would come home every day. She would not have this permission!"

151 Mama and Papa didn't notice that I went to the bathroom and locked the door. I huddled by the sink and heard their angry voices rise and fall like the pounding of thunder, and then I heard a bang, so fierce that the light bulb hanging from the ceiling swayed with its force. Papa slamming the front door. Then I heard the engine of the cab and a sharp squeal of tires as he sped away.

152 I imagined running away. I would run like the wind, behind the mini-mart, sailing past the E-Z Dry Cleaner, past the bus stop in an easy gallop through the crosswalk. As I ran, each traffic light I came to would turn green, until there would be a string of green lights glowing like a necklace of emeralds strung all down the street. And then I would be at the Luis' house. Mrs. Lui would greet me in her red Nordstrom coat with the gold buttons. She would hug me and hold me close. Then Mr. Lui would say, "Hi, honey," and make hamburgers. "Want to use the phone, Maya?" Mrs. Lui would say. "Talk as long as you want—we have an extra line for the kids."

153 "Oh, by the way," Mr. Lui would say, "Shannon is having David and some other kids over Friday night for pizza and videos. It's fine if there's a guy you want to invite, too."

154 "Maya! Open this door. Do you want more trouble?" Mama rattled the doorknob so hard I thought she'd rip it off.

155 "I'm coming." My voice caught in my throat. I felt dizzy as I unlocked the door and held my stomach, afraid I would be sick.

156 "You have brought shame to your father and to this family." Mama glared at me.

157 "Mama, it was just kids joking. Guys from the wrestling team pretending some of us were weights."

158 "I don't know this weights."

159 "It was nothing, Mama!"

160 "Do not tell me 'nothing' when your father saw you!" she screamed.

161 The next morning Papa was gone when I woke up. And even though Mama hadn't yet left for work, it was like she was gone, too. She didn't speak to me and didn't even look at me, except once when she came in the kitchen. I was getting *kasha*, and she stared at me like I was a stranger to her. Then she turned and left. Not only was Mama not speaking to me, but she didn't speak to Nurzhan, either. This never happens. Even when he

Don't forget to **Notice & Note** as you read the text.

was punished for the fight with Ossie Nishizono and had to stay home, Mama still spoke to him. But as I was getting dressed in my room, I heard Nurzhan try to talk to her. I put my ear to the door to listen.

162 "It's different here, Mama. I'm sure Maya and those guys were playing. Joking, like in a game."

163 "Quiet, boy! You know nothing of these things!"

164 I was shocked. Mama hardly ever says a harsh word to her precious boy. Then I heard her rush by, and then *bam*! The door slammed. The *kamcha* that hung by the door trembled with the force. We brought our *kamcha* when we came to America. It looks like a riding crop with a carved wooden handle and a leather cord, decorated with some horsehair. It's an old Kazakh tradition to put the *kamcha* inside the house next to the door because it's believed to bring good fortune and happiness. But our *kamcha* was not bringing us good fortune today. Mama left without a word of goodbye to either one of us.

165 I came out of my room and Nurzhan and I just looked at each other. I didn't feel happy that Nurzhan got yelled at; I felt bad about the whole thing.

166 "Did you hear?"

167 I nodded.

168 "She won't listen."

169 "Thank you for trying, Nurzhan."

170 "It did no good," he said with sadness. "They don't know about things here, only their own ways. They are like stone."

ANALYZE CHARACTER

Annotate: In paragraph 171, mark Maya's description of how and why her family's relationships become "almost calm" again.

Analyze: What does this description emphasize about how Maya's family is affected by their being recent immigrants?

171 I wondered how long this tension and anger would stay in our home. I was afraid it might be a long time, because Mama and Papa were so upset. But gradually, in the way that winter becomes spring, there was a slight thaw each day. Perhaps because we huddled together like a tiny Kazakh island in the middle of the great American sea, we couldn't allow our winter to go on and on, and by the next week, things in my family were almost calm.

172 But it was not to last. On Wednesday afternoon of the following week, Mama was waiting to talk to me when I got home from school. I was afraid when I saw her. Her ankle was taped up, and she sat on the couch with her leg up on a chair. Next to it was a pair of crutches!

173 "Mama, what happened?"

174 "I fell at work. Mrs. Hormann took me to the emergency room. I can't work for six weeks until it heals. I must keep my foot up as much as possible."

Don't forget to **Notice & Note** as you read the text.

175 "I'll start dinner." My eyes filled with tears, I felt so bad for her. And I felt bad that I'd made them so upset when my father saw me and Daniel. Even though I knew I hadn't done anything wrong, it still bothered me that I'd been the cause of such trouble in our house.

176 It was decided that I'd take Mama's jobs for her while she couldn't work. I wouldn't go to gymnastics practice; instead, right after school I'd go straight to the houses Mama cleaned. The people Mama worked for agreed to this, and I worked at each house from three-thirty until six-thirty, when Papa came to pick me up. I wasn't able to clean their entire houses in this amount of time, but they told me which rooms were the most important, and I was able to clean those. Bathrooms were on the list at every house.

177 I didn't mind doing Mama's jobs. Although I did get very tired, and I was scared sometimes that I might break something when I dusted (especially at Mrs. Hathaway's house, because she had a lot of glass vases and some small glass birds), but I didn't mind vacuuming, mopping, dusting, cleaning cupboards, counters, stoves, and refrigerators. I didn't even mind cleaning toilets. It was as if all the work I did at Mama's jobs was to make up for the problems I'd caused. And besides, our family needed the money.

178 When I finished working for Mama, as soon as I got home I had to make dinner for everyone. Each day I got more tired, and on Friday, when I was peeling potatoes, I cut my finger. I thought it was just a little cut, so I washed it off and continued to peel.

179 Nurzhan looked up from the table, where he was doing his work. "What's wrong with the potatoes?"

180 "Nothing," I said automatically, with my eyes half-closed.

181 "They're red!"

182 "What?"

183 "The potatoes, Maya. They look like you painted them with red streaks."

184 I looked down and saw my finger bleeding on the potatoes, and it scared me to be so tired that I hadn't seen this. "It's just blood, Nurzhan. I cut myself. It'll wash off."

185 "Oh, yuck."

186 "Quiet, boy! I said I would wash it off."

187 That night at dinner, Nurzhan refused to eat the potatoes, even though there was no sign of blood on them, and I wanted to take the whole dish and dump them on his head.

188 The next week I was so tired after going to school and cleaning Mrs. Hathaway's house that I burned the chicken. After I put it in the oven, I sat at the table with Nurzhan to do my homework. I rested my head on my book for just a minute, and the next thing I knew, Nurzhan was pounding on my arm.

189 "Maya! The oven!" he shouted.

190 I woke to see smoke seeping from the oven. "Oh, no!"

191 I leaped up and grabbed a dishtowel and pulled the pan from the oven. The chicken was very dark but not black, although all the juice at the bottom of the pan had burned and was smoking. "It's okay, Nurzhan. We can still eat it."

192 "Good."

193 Nurzhan didn't mind the almost-burned chicken that night, but Papa did.

194 "This tastes like my shoe!" Papa grumbled.

195 "Aibek, I have to keep my foot up, and Maya is doing the best she can. It is not easy. She must go to school, then do my work, then cook for us. She is just a young girl."

196 I looked at Mama and felt tears in my eyes. I couldn't remember another time when Mama spoke on my behalf, and my tears were the kind you have when you know someone is on your side.

197 The next evening as dinner was cooking, I sat with Nurzhan at the kitchen table and helped him with his spelling words. While I waited for him to think how to spell *admire*, I took the permission slip for the Spring Fling from my notebook and stared at it. I'd never thrown it away.

198 "A-D-M-I-E-R."

199 "Almost, Nurzhan. It's this," I said as I wrote the correct spelling on the top of the permission slip and turned it for him to see.

200 "A-D-M-I-R-E," he spelled. Then he looked closely at the slip. "What's this for?"

201 "It's a permission slip for the Spring Fling, the all-school dance, but it is only good for scratch paper to help you with spelling. Papa will never let me go. I don't know why I trouble myself to keep such a thing."

202 Nurzhan took the slip and put it in his notebook.

203 "What are you doing with it?"

204 "Let me try."

205 "Try what?"

206 "Let me try to get permission for you from Papa."

207 I laughed. "Oh, Nurzhan. Don't be foolish. You waste your time. Papa will never change his thinking because of you."

208 "I will try anyway. When he comes home tonight, I will speak to him myself. I have a plan."

209 I could only smile a sad smile at the idea of little Nurzhan trying to change the mind of Papa, who is a man like a boulder.

210 After dinner I went to my room to study, leaving Nurzhan to talk with Mama and Papa. I was afraid to really hope that any good thing could come from Nurzhan's plan. To hope and then be disappointed seemed to be worse. It was better not to hope and to live my dreams through Shannon. I could at least hear every little detail of her experience at the dance and be happy for her, giving up the idea that I'd ever be the one who goes to the dance, too.

211 But I comforted myself thinking about the dream in my life that really had come true—the gymnastics team. I still had that, and I was warming my heart with thoughts of the team when Nurzhan burst into the room.

212 "Maya! You can go!" Nurzhan jumped up and down like a little monkey, and I stared at him in disbelief.

213 "Don't joke with me about such a thing, boy!" I snapped.

214 "No! It's true. Look!" He waved the permission slip in front of my face.

215 I stared at the slip, still in disbelief. *Aibek Alazova* . . . Papa's name and Papa's writing. *It was true!* I was still staring at the slip, still afraid to completely believe that such a thing could be true, when Mama and Papa came in.

216 "We give permission for this, Maya, because Nurzhan will go, too," Mama said.

217 "He will not leave your side," Papa announced in a most serious tone. "He is your *capravazhdieuushee.*"

218 "Chaperone." I said the English word. I knew this word because the parents who help the teachers supervise the kids at school activities are called this. But I hadn't heard of a little boy being a chaperone.

219 "Thank you, Mama. Thank you, Papa."

220 "It is Nurzhan you must thank," Mama said.

221 I thanked Nurzhan, too, and Mama and Papa left our room. Then I heard the front door close and I knew Papa had left for work.

222 That night Nurzhan and I whispered in our beds after Mama had gone to sleep.

223 "Nurzhan, what will I tell my friends when you come to the dance?"

224 "Don't worry. I thought about that problem. You will tell them you must baby-sit for me."

225 "But at a dance?"

Don't forget to **Notice & Note** as you read the text.

ANALYZE PLOT

Annotate: Mark the part of the story that appears to be the **climax**—the point of greatest tension—when the conflict begins to be resolved.

Cite Evidence: What story events and details support your conclusion?

ANALYZE CHARACTER

Annotate: Mark the parts of the whispered conversation between Nurzhan and Maya that best show his growth as a character.

Infer: Based on these details, in what ways has Nurzhan grown?

226 "I think it will work. At least it is better than to say I am your chaperone."

227 "That is true."

228 I watched the orange light of the mini-mart sign blink on and off, and I heard Nurzhan's slow breathing as he fell asleep.

229 "Thank you, Nurzhan," I whispered as I began to dream of the dance.

230 The morning of the dance, Mama came into the kitchen while Nurzhan and I were eating kasha. Mama still had a wrap on her ankle, but she was walking without her crutches now. She was happier, and I could tell she felt better. It was better for me, too. When Mama was happier, I didn't feel so worried about her.

231 "Maya, I have something for you." Mama came to the table and put a small package wrapped in tissue paper in front of me. "Open." She pointed at the package.

232 I looked up at her, my face full of surprise.

233 "Open."

234 Carefully, I unfolded the tissue paper and let out a gasp when I saw a small gold bracelet lying on the folds of the thin paper.

235 "You wear this to the dance." Mama patted my shoulder.

236 "Oh, Mama." I wanted to hug her like we hug on the gymnastics team, but I was too shy. We don't hug in our family.

237 "I forget sometimes when there is so much work that you are just a young girl. This bracelet my mother gave to me when I was sixteen. Girls and boys dance younger here, Maya. So you wear this now."

238 "Thank you, Mama. I will be careful with it."

239 "I know. You're a good girl. And Nurzhan will be right there. Always by your side."

240 "Yes, Mama." Nurzhan nodded.

Don't forget to **Notice & Note** as you read the text.

241 Shannon and I met in the bathroom after school, and she loaned me her peach lip-gloss. I can't remember ever being so excited about anything, and so nervous, too.

242 Nurzhan was waiting by the gym door when we got out of the bathroom. Shannon and I said hi to him, and he followed us into the gym. Nurzhan found a chair next to the door and waved to us while we joined Leslie Shattuck and her sister Tina and Faith Reeves from the gymnastics team. The gym got more and more crowded, and everywhere you looked there were flocks of boys and flocks of girls, but no boys and girls together, as if they were birds that only stayed with their own kind.

243 Then a few ninth-grade guys and girls danced together. They were very cool and everyone watched them, except some seventh-grade boys who were pushing each other around in an empty garbage can.

244 Shannon and I were laughing at those silly boys when Daniel and David came up to us. I was so happy to see Daniel, even though I was embarrassed about my face, which I knew was once again the deepest red, like borscht. But the next thing I knew, Daniel had asked me to dance, and Shannon was dancing with David!

245 Daniel held my hand and put his arm around my waist, and I put my hand on his shoulder just the way Shannon and I had practiced so many times. It was a slow dance, and Mama's bracelet gleamed on my wrist as it lay on Daniel's shoulder.

246 "My little brother's here. I had to baby-sit."

247 "Want to check on him?" Daniel asked.

248 "Sure."

249 We danced over near Nurzhan, who sat on the chair like a tiny mouse in the corner, and I introduced him to Daniel.

250 "Are you doing okay?" I asked Nurzhan.

251 "Yes. It's a little boring though."

252 "I'm sorry you have to be here."

253 "It's not that bad. The boys in the garbage can are fun to watch. I would enjoy doing that if I came to this dance."

254 Then we danced away and danced even more slowly, and Daniel moved a little closer to me. I looked over, afraid that Nurzhan was watching, but all I saw was an empty chair. And then we danced closer.

255 Daniel and I danced four more times that afternoon (two fast and two *very* slow), and each time Nurzhan's chair was

empty and he seemed to have disappeared. I didn't think too much about Nurzhan during the rest of the dance, and on the bus going home, while Shannon and I talked and talked, reliving every wonderful moment, I almost forgot he was there.

256 But that night when Nurzhan and I were going to sleep and I was thinking about how that day had been the best day of my life, I thanked him for making it possible for me to go to the dance.

257 "There's just one thing I wondered about," I whispered as the mini-mart sign blinked on and off.

258 "What's that?"

259 "Where did you go when I danced with Daniel?"

260 "To the bathroom."

261 "The bathroom?"

262 "Yes."

263 "You are an excellent chaperone."

264 Nurzhan and I giggled so loud that Mama came in and told us to be quiet. "Shhh, Nurzhan, Maya. Go to sleep!" She spoke sharply to both of us.

265 After she left, Nurzhan fell asleep right away like he usually does. But I lay awake for a while and I looked over at Nurzhan and was struck by how much things had changed. I looked at the table by my bed and saw the gold bracelet shining in the blinking light of the mini-mart sign, and I imagined Mama wearing it when she was sixteen, and I treasured what she'd said as much as the bracelet: "Girls and boys dance younger here, Maya. So you wear this now."

266 And I thought of Daniel, who I think is quite a special boy with a good heart. *Kak horosho.* How wonderful. Thinking of him made me smile inside. Then I closed my eyes, hoping very much that Nurzhan would like to chaperone at the next dance.

TURN AND TALK

Turn to a partner and discuss the ending of "My Favorite Chaperone." What do you think Maya means when she says she is "struck by how much things had changed"?

ESSENTIAL QUESTION:

What are the places that shape who you are?

Review your notes and add your thoughts to your Response Log.

Assessment Practice

Answer these questions before moving on to the **Analyze the Text** section on the following page.

1. This question has two parts. First answer **Part A**. Then, answer **Part B**.

Part A

What conflict does Maya face at the beginning of the story?

- (A) She wants to go to the dance but doesn't know how to dance.
- (B) She wants to go to the dance but thinks she won't be allowed.
- (C) She wants to go to the dance but has lost her permission slip.
- (D) She wants to go to the dance but wants to avoid a popular girl.

Part B

Which sentence from the story best supports the answer to Part A?

- (A) "I don't know why I didn't just shake my head when this very popular girl Marcia Egness was handing them out." (paragraph 1)
- (B) ". . . I don't know why I didn't throw it away." (paragraph 1)
- (C) "I looked at the permission slip, wishing there were some special words I could say to get Mama and Papa to sign it." (paragraph 8)
- (D) "I often feel like I'm in the middle of a game where I don't know . . . the rules, or even the object of the game." (paragraph 9)

2. What do Maya's thoughts, feelings, and actions in response to her mother's injury reveal about her character?

- (A) She lacks dedication to gymnastics.
- (B) She is caring and wants to help her family.
- (C) She enjoys doing tasks that others find unpleasant.
- (D) She is clumsy and tends to break things.

Ed

Test-Taking Strategies

Analyze the Text

Support your responses with evidence from the text.

NOTICE & NOTE

Review what you noticed and noted as you read the text. Your annotations can help you answer these questions.

1. **INFER** In paragraph 1, Maya asks herself the **Tough Question** "Why should I bother when I was sure the answer would be the same?" What clues does this question provide about the story's main conflict?

2. **ANALYZE** In paragraph 8, Maya says, "The gymnastics team is a fine, good thing in my life." What does this statement reveal about her character?

3. **INFER** In paragraph 18, Maya tells a story about a student from Cambodia. How does this **Memory Moment** enhance the plot's rising action?

4. **DRAW CONCLUSIONS** Reread paragraph 85. Complete this chart to show how Maya's translation changes the meaning of what the principal says. Why does she make these changes?

PRINCIPAL'S WORDS	MAYA'S TRANSLATION	EFFECT

5. **COMPARE** Reread the dialogue in paragraphs 109–119. What does this dialogue reveal about how Mama's relationship with Maya differs from her relationship with Nurzhan?

6. **ANALYZE** In paragraphs 172–176, Mama's injury results in more responsibilities and sacrifices for Maya. What stage of the plot do this event and its results fall into? Explain why.

Choices

Here are some other ways to demonstrate your understanding of the ideas in this lesson.

Writing

↳ Summarize a Story

Write a summary of "My Favorite Chaperone." To do this, you will briefly retell the plot of the story in your own words.

- Introduce the major characters and state the conflict.
- Convey the major events that occur during the rising action. Maintain the author's meaning and the logical order of events.
- Identify the climax of the story. Then describe the resolution of the conflict and the story's final outcome.

As you write and discuss, be sure to use the **Academic Vocabulary** words.

contribute

immigrate

reaction

relocate

shifting

RESEARCH

↳ Kazakh Culture

The behavior expected of Maya by her parents reflects their Kazakh roots. Learn about Kazakh culture by researching answers to these questions.

QUESTION	ANSWER
What roles do gender and age play in Kazakh society? Explain.	
What is one example of a Kazakh custom?	
How free are Kazakh young people to choose their marriage partners?	

Social & Emotional Learning

↳ Discuss with a Small Group

Did Maya handle the situation in the principal's office appropriately? Discuss this question with a group.

- Reread paragraphs 74–90. Discuss Maya's translations and their outcome. Look for clues as to why she chose to handle the situation in this way.
- Discuss what you would have done in Maya's place and whether any of these options would have been better, considering their likely impact on Maya and Nurzhan. Support your ideas.
- Together, decide whether Maya's handling of events was appropriate. Be prepared to support your conclusion.

Expand Your Vocabulary

PRACTICE AND APPLY

To demonstrate that you understand the vocabulary words, complete each sentence in a way that makes sense.

1. The civics club at school decided to **sponsor** . . .
2. When Nurzhan is Maya's chaperone, he **stuns** her by . . .
3. The cab driver needed to have his **dispatcher** . . .
4. The sounds of a **scuffle** alerted me to the fact that . . .
5. At a gymnastics meet, Maya might **whimper** if she . . .

Vocabulary Strategy

Context Clues

The **context** of a word is made up of the punctuation marks, words, sentences, and paragraphs that surround the word. When you encounter an unfamiliar word or one with multiple meanings, its context may provide you with clues that can help you understand its meaning. Look at the following example:

> **. . . Mr. Walsh, the vice-principal, came into our class. He whispered something to Ms. Coe and she nodded. And then I was stunned because she nodded and pointed to me!**

The exclamation point suggests that Maya did not expect that Mr. Walsh had come to get her. This context helps you understand that here the word *stunned* means feeling surprised or shocked.

Ed

Interactive Vocabulary Lesson: Using Context Clues

PRACTICE AND APPLY

Review "My Favorite Chaperone" to find the following words. Then complete this chart.

WORD	CONTEXT CLUES	MY GUESSED DEFINITION	DICTIONARY DEFINITION
huddled (paragraph 7)			
mispronouncing (paragraph 50)			
drizzle (paragraph 71)			

Watch Your Language!

Imperative Mood

Ed

Interactive Grammar Lesson: Sentence Sense

The **mood** of a verb refers to the manner in which the action or state of being is expressed. A verb is in the **imperative mood** when it is part of a command or request. In an imperative sentence, the subject is always implied or understood to be *you*. These sentences from "My Favorite Chaperone" are in the imperative mood.

"Take off your jacket and hang it up, Nurzhan."

"Let me try to get permission for you from Papa."

In the first sentence, Maya is giving her brother a command. In the second sentence, Nurzhan is requesting something from his sister Maya. Note that the subject of both sentences (you) is not stated but is understood.

PRACTICE AND APPLY

Rewrite each sentence so that it is in the imperative mood. Label each sentence as a command or a request.

1. I do not want you to ask her about the permission slip again.

2. You should call my father and tell him what happened.

3. I think you should stop teasing my brother.

4. You should punish your son so that he never fights like this again.

5. I'm telling you to sit at the kitchen table and do your homework.

6. Will you please tell your parents that they must sign this form?

7. I want you to quit asking me whether you can go.

8. I would like it if you would help your mother do her work.

Spirit Walking in the Tundra

Poem by **Joy Harjo**

ESSENTIAL QUESTION:
What are the places that shape who you are?

Engage Your Brain

Choose one or both of the activities to start connecting with the selection you are about to read.

A "Sense" of Place

Think of a place you like to go or one that holds special importance for you. Now write a few sentences to describe that place using words and phrases that appeal to the five senses.

Describe the Tundra

Do some quick research to learn about the tundra. What are the characteristics of this biome? Come up with a list of adjectives that describe what the tundra is like.

Analyze Themes

A **theme** is a message about life or human nature that a writer wants readers to understand. To create a new work of literature, writers sometimes draw on themes from traditional stories. Writers may also draw on the settings, patterns of events, and types of characters found in traditional stories.

Readers can determine the themes of a work of literature by looking for any elements that are drawn from traditional stories—clues from the past—in addition to considering how the characters, setting, and plot relate to the theme.

As you read "Spirit Walking in the Tundra," make note of words or lines in which the author seems to be referring to traditional stories of the native cultures of Alaska. How do these references contribute to the development of the poem's themes?

Focus on Genre

Poetry

- can convey emotional intensity in relatively few words
- is sometimes written using first-person point of view to express the speaker's thoughts
- often uses repetition to emphasize important ideas
- may include rhyming words or may be written in free verse, with no regular pattern of rhyme

Analyze Imagery

One way poets convey feeling and meaning is through the use of **imagery,** descriptive words and phrases that re-create sensory experiences for the reader. Although much of the imagery used in literature is visual, imagery may also appeal to the readers' senses of smell, hearing, taste, and touch. As you read the poem, use the chart to help you analyze Harjo's use of imagery.

KIND OF IMAGERY	SENSE TO WHICH IT APPEALS	EXAMPLES FROM THE POEM	EFFECT
Visual	Sight	turquoise lakes (line 2)	Helps the reader imagine the speaker's view from the airplane
Tactile	Touch	vibrates our bones (line 4)	
Olfactory	Smell	Her smell is sweet like blossoms (line 22)	

Annotation in Action

Here are one reader's comments on imagery in Harjo's poem. As you read, notice the use of imagery in the poem.

All the way to Nome, I trace the shadow of the plane
    as it walks
Over turquoise lakes made by late spring breakup
Of the Bering Sea.
The plane is so heavy with cargo load it vibrates our bones.
Like the pressure made by light cracking ice.

Strong use of imagery helps the reader imagine the speaker's experience.

Background

Born in Tulsa, Oklahoma, award-winning poet, musician, and author **Joy Harjo** (b. 1951) is a member of the Mvskoke (Muscogee) Nation. Although many of her poems are set in the American Southwest, Harjo also explores the landscapes and native cultures of Alaska. The "tundra" in the poem's title refers to the flat, treeless, Arctic regions where the subsoil is permanently frozen.

Spirit Walking in the Tundra

Poem by **Joy Harjo**

The speaker of this poem describes a trip she took to Alaska to visit a friend.

NOTICE & NOTE
As you read, use the side margins to make notes about the text.

All the way to Nome, I trace the shadow of the plane as it walks
Over turquoise lakes made by late spring breakup
Of the Bering Sea.
The plane is so heavy with cargo load it vibrates our bones.
Like the pressure made by light cracking ice.

Below I see pockets of marrow where seabirds nest.
Mothers are so protective they will dive humans.

I walk from the tarmac and am met by an old friend.
We drive to the launching place
And see walrus hunters set out toward the sea.
We swing to the summer camps where seal hangs on drying frames.
She takes me home.
I watch her son play video games on break from the university.

ANALYZE IMAGERY

Annotate: Mark the image in line 1.

Analyze: What effect does this image have on the reader's understanding of the poem?

NOTICE & NOTE

CONTRASTS AND CONTRADICTIONS

When you notice a sharp contrast between what you would expect and what the character actually does, you've found a **Contrasts and Contradictions** signpost.

Notice & Note: In lines 14–16, mark any details that contrast with how you might expect the son of the speaker's friend to act.

Analyze: Why might the young man act this way?

This is what it feels like, says her son, as we walk up tundra,
Toward a herd of musk ox, *when you spirit walk.*
There is a shaking, and then you are in mystery.

Little purple flowers come up from the permafrost.
A newborn musk ox staggers around its mother's legs.

I smell the approach of someone with clean thoughts.
She is wearing designs like flowers, and a fur of ice.
She carries a basket and digging implements.
Her smell is sweet like blossoms coming up through the snow.
The spirit of the tundra stands with us, and we collect
sunlight together,
We are refreshed by small winds.

We do not need history in books to tell us who we are
Or where we come from, I remind him.
Up here, we are near the opening in the Earth's head, the place
where the spirit leaves and returns.
Up here, the edge between life and death is thinner than dried
animal bladder.

(FOR ANUQSRAAQ AND QITUVITUAQ)
NOME, ALASKA, 2011

ANALYZE THEME

Annotate: Mark the phrase that is repeated in the last stanza.

Analyze: How does the repetition of this phrase help to develop the theme of the poem?

TURN AND TALK

Turn to a classmate and discuss the poem. What message do you take away from reading the poem?

ESSENTIAL QUESTION:

What are the places that shape who you are?

Review your notes and add your thoughts to your Response Log.

Assessment Practice

Answer these questions before moving on to the **Analyze the Text** section on the following page.

1. Why does the poem's speaker travel to Alaska?

- (A) to observe the ocean ice breaking apart
- (B) to visit an old friend and her family
- (C) to take part in a hunt for walrus and seal
- (D) to explain her beliefs to a young man

2. This question has two parts. First answer **Part A**. Then, answer **Part B**.

Part A

Which of the following is a theme of the poem?

- (A) Air travel can be uncomfortable.
- (B) Technology can help people relax.
- (C) Places can remind people of who they are.
- (D) Cultural change can cause serious problems.

Part B

Which excerpt from the poem most clearly supports the correct answer to Part A?

- (A) "The plane is so heavy with cargo load it vibrates our bones." (line 4)
- (B) "She takes me home. / I watch her son play video games on break from the university." (lines 12–13)
- (C) "We do not need history in books to tell us who we are / Or where we come from, I remind him." (lines 25–26)
- (D) "Up here, the edge between life and death is thinner than dried animal bladder." (line 28)

Ed Test-Taking Strategies

Analyze the Text

Support your responses with evidence from the text.

NOTICE & NOTE

Review what you noticed and noted as you read the text. Your annotations can help you answer these questions.

1. **INFER** The title of the poem makes reference to the Native American tradition of the spirit walk. Based on the events in the poem, how do you think the speaker of the poem would define the phrase "spirit walk"?

2. **EVALUATE** Read aloud lines 1–3. Notice that the first two line breaks do not come at the end of a sentence. What effect do the line breaks have on the poem's tone or meaning?

3. **INTERPRET** Identify the imagery in lines 4 and 5. To what senses does it appeal? Explain what this imagery suggests about the speaker's feelings during her flight to Alaska.

4. **DRAW CONCLUSIONS** In lines 7 and 18, the speaker refers to animal mothers and their young. How are these lines related to the rest of the poem?

5. **ANALYZE** What **Contrasts and Contradictions** do you notice about the detail included in line 13 of the poem? What might the poet be suggesting by including this detail?

6. **ANALYZE** What are the themes of "Spirit Walking in the Tundra," and how are they conveyed? In the chart below, identify the poem's themes and list specific details from the text that contribute to their development.

THEMES	DETAILS FROM THE POEM

Choices

Here are some other ways to demonstrate your understanding of the ideas in this lesson.

Writing

Poem

Write a poem that describes a time you took a walk with a friend. Use these guidelines to help you plan and draft your poem.

- Decide if you want your poem to be serious or funny.
- Use a free-verse structure, and think about where and why you will break lines.
- Use strong imagery that appeals to your reader's senses.

As you write and discuss, be sure to use the **Academic Vocabulary** words.

- contribute
- immigrate
- reaction
- relocate
- shifting

Speaking & Listening

Hold a Debate

Do you learn more about yourself and your identity by traveling, or by staying close to home? Debate this issue.

- With your group, decide who will represent each side.
- Identify sources to help support your position. What have writers or thinkers said about the topic? What reasons or examples can you provide to defend your point of view?
- As you present your side's argument, make eye contact with audience members, speak clearly and loudly, and make natural hand gestures to emphasize your points.

Research

Alaska Natives

With a partner, research Alaska Natives. Use the questions to guide your investigation.

- How many major groups of Alaska Natives are there? How are the groups defined?
- What is the climate like where Alaska Natives live? How has that influenced their lifestyle?
- What is the role of wildlife in the cultures and economies of Alaska Natives?

Collaborate & Compare

ESSENTIAL QUESTION:
What are the places that shape who you are?

Compare Purposes

You are about to view a documentary film and read a text that both focus on high school students who have immigrated to the United States. As you view the documentary and read the text that follows it, think about how the filmmakers and the author achieve their purposes by using the unique elements of film or text to convey ideas.

A

New Immigrants Share Their Stories

Documentary produced by **The Working Group**
page 230

B

A Common Bond

Informational Text by **Brooke Hauser**
pages 233–241

After you have viewed the documentary and read the text, you will interview a classmate, following these steps:

- Choose a Personal Story to Tell
- Choose a "Buddy" to Interview
- Prepare for the Interview
- Record Your Interviews

MEDIA

New Immigrants Share Their Stories

Documentary produced by **The Working Group**

Engage Your Brain

You're about to watch a video that shows immigrant students sharing their stories with students who have grown up in the United States. Like the students in the video, many people have dramatic stories to tell about how and why their family members first came to the United States. With a partner, take turns sharing immigration stories about your own family or another family you know.

Background

The Building Bridges project is a collaboration between two very different New York schools. Through letter writing, video diaries, and interviews, the English language learners from Newcomers High School in Queens, New York, tell their personal immigration stories to their "buddies" from St. Luke's, a private middle school in Manhattan. Together, students from both schools hope to change stereotyped ideas about immigrants. The documentary *New Immigrants Share Their Stories* chronicles the students' project.

Evaluate a Documentary

New Immigrants Share Their Stories is a **documentary,** a nonfiction film that presents information about people or events. A documentary's **purpose** is the reason it is made: to inform, entertain, persuade, or express feelings or opinions. Documentary filmmakers usually have a **motive,** or a reason why they feel the story is worth telling.

Here are some examples of motives and clues that can help you identify a motive based on the film's emphasis, or focus:

MOTIVE	FOCUS OF FILM/CLUES TO MOTIVE
Social	human interactions, changing behaviors or attitudes
Commercial	a product that viewers are encouraged to buy
Political	support for or opposition to government or laws

To evaluate a documentary, ask yourself these questions:

- How well does the film achieve its main purpose?
- What are the advantages and disadvantages of using the medium of film to present the topic?
- What kind of motive did the filmmakers most likely have?

Focus on Genre

Documentary

- provides factual information
- may investigate or tell a true story
- employs elements of film, such as live footage, narration, music, animation, and on-screen text
- often includes interviews with experts or other people involved with the topic

Watch how students from two schools in New York came together to learn more about each other.

Ed

Video

View **New Immigrants Share Their Stories** in your ebook.

A Common Bond

Teens Forge Friendships Despite Differences

Informational Text by **Brooke Hauser**

Engage Your Brain

What might you learn by going to school with people from around the world? In a small group, have a brief discussion to exchange ideas with your classmates.

Analyze Text Elements

Text elements are print and graphic features that authors use to structure texts. As you read "A Common Bond," notice how these elements help guide your reading and achieve specific purposes.

TEXT ELEMENT	EXAMPLE
A **heading** is a text's title. A **subtitle** may follow the title and give more detail about the topic. **Subheadings** within the text introduce new topics or sections and clarify how each section contributes to the text's central idea and its overall structure.	**A Common Bond** **Teens Forge Friendships Despite Differences** Part 1: A Second Home
Graphic features include graphs, charts, diagrams, photographs, and other visuals. Graphs present statistical information and show numerical relationships. Graphic features often help authors convey information by illustrating and emphasizing the ideas expressed in the text.	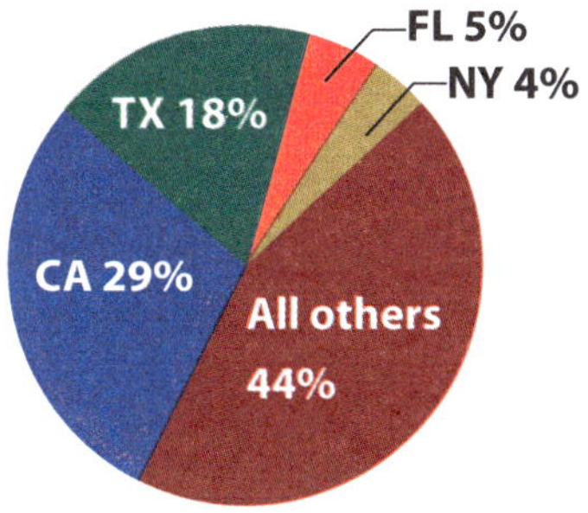

Focus on Genre

Informational Text

- provides factual information
- often includes graphic features
- typically makes use of text elements such as subheadings, boldfacing, sidebars, and footnotes

Annotation in Action

Here are one reader's notes about a section of "A Common Bond." As you read, mark text elements and features and consider how they affect your understanding of the information in the text.

Part 2: A New Identity
Indeed, most of the students are learning a new culture, all the while honoring traditions from their home countries. When the school's first-ever graduating class wanted to organize their senior prom, first they had to figure out exactly what a prom *was*.

The subheading makes me think this section will be related to the students' sense of identity.

Expand Your Vocabulary

Put a check mark next to the vocabulary words that you feel comfortable using when speaking or writing.

- **eligible** ☐
- **assimilate** ☐
- **capitalize** ☐
- **unrest** ☐

Turn to a partner and talk about the words you already know. Then, write a few sentences about what you know about the experiences of immigrants who come to the United States.

As you read "A Common Bond," use the definitions in the side column to learn the vocabulary words you don't already know.

Background

Longtime journalist **Brooke Hauser** has profiled a wide array of subjects, from Chinese beauty queens to former U.S. Secretary of State Colin Powell. However, in her first book, *The New Kids: Big Dreams and Brave Journeys at a High School for Immigrant Teens,* she chronicled the experiences of people who don't normally take center stage: recent immigrants who attend the International High School at Prospect Heights. The following text is informed by what she learned and whom she got to know while writing that award-winning book.

B

A Common Bond

Teens Forge Friendships Despite Differences

Informational Text by **Brooke Hauser**

What is it like for students who have recently come to the United States to go to a school with other immigrants from a wide range of backgrounds?

NOTICE & NOTE
As you read, use the side margins to make notes about the text.

Part 1: A Second Home

1 Have you ever been the new kid at school? Or maybe you've known the new kid at school? Either way, if you answered yes, then you might have a little glimpse into the experiences of the students at the International High School at Prospect Heights in Brooklyn, New York. Started in 2004, the school serves recent immigrants and refugees to the United States. How recent? Well, some of the students come to America just months or weeks before the first day of school in September each year.

2 According to a book about the school written by the author of this article, *The New Kids: Big Dreams and Brave Journeys at a High School for Immigrant Teens,* the students hail from

ANALYZE TEXT ELEMENTS

Annotate: Mark the first subheading in the article.

Predict: Based on this subheading, what can you predict about the overall structure of the article?

40-plus different countries and speak nearly 30 languages: Spanish, Creole, Arabic, Fulani, and Tibetan, to name just a few. Imagine walking down those halls: They're noisy! In many ways, they're also a reflection of our country and what's special about America, which has always been home to newcomers.

3 Spend a few hours at the International High School, and you'll quickly realize that students here represent a range of backgrounds and beliefs. Some are Christian or Jewish, others Buddhist or Muslim. But despite their differences, all of the students share one very important thing in common: They are all learning English together. In fact, to be **eligible** for enrollment, students must have failed an English language assessment test and be relatively new to the country, says Joe Luft, Executive Director of the Internationals Network for Public Schools, which oversees the school in Prospect Heights and others like it around New York City, and beyond: "All of the students in our schools are recently arrived immigrant youth who are new to learning English. Generally, they've been in this country for less than four years, although the majority have been here for less than a year or two."

eligible
(ĕl´ĭ-jə-bəl) *adj. Eligible* means qualified to be selected.

4 Maybe you've heard the term ESL, which stands for "English as a second language." The funny thing is, for many of these students, English isn't their second language: In some cases, it's their third, fourth, or fifth.

5 Take Nourou, a rising senior at the International High School who immigrated from Guinea in West Africa when she was 12, along with her mother, older brother, and little sister. In her native country, Nourou grew up speaking Fulani, as well as Susu and Mandinka. So technically, English is her *fourth* language, but we don't have a term for that, like "EFL." The better term for these students is "ELL" for English language learner.

6 Learning a new language is hard enough, but English is just one part of what these students must conquer as new immigrants in America. They are adapting to a new way of life, too. Every once in a while, there's a student who has never been to any school before the International High School. Some students have fled from their homes in countries damaged by war, political strife, or famine. Some have spent time in refugee camps, where a formal education isn't an option. Many students grew up in rural places, such as on farms or in the mountains, and they can experience major culture shock when they arrive in New York City: They have to take a bus or subway to school, navigating new routes through the city, which can be a scary

prospect when you don't speak the language. A good number of students also work after school, some in restaurants or nail salons, to help provide for their families. Others help out with housework and childcare, cooking and cleaning, and looking after younger siblings.

Don't forget to **Notice & Note** as you read the text.

7 For many students, the International High School at Prospect Heights is kind of like a second home in the city. "What makes our school a welcoming place and feel like home is in the importance we put on relationships: You can only develop a relationship with a people if you spend time with them and do things together," says the school principal, Nedda de Castro. Students and teachers get to know each other in small groups and different settings both inside and outside of school, on field trips, for instance. "Even though they come from all over the world and may be very different from each other," she says, "they are all in the same boat and have much in common in their journey to becoming a new American."

8 You may have heard the term "melting pot" to describe America as a place where people from different cultures and backgrounds mix together and **assimilate** into the whole, to create a new culture. At the International High Schools, there's another metaphor that students embrace, according to Luft. "The thing that I hear more than any other idea is the school as a family, in all its complexity," he says. "Everybody doesn't always get along, but ultimately they feel this very strong connection to each other and care about each other."

assimilate
(ə-sĭm´ə-lāt´) *v.* To *assimilate* means to blend into or become similar to the prevailing culture.

Part 2: A New Identity

9 Indeed, most of the students are learning a new culture, all the while honoring traditions from their home countries. When the school's first-ever graduating class wanted to organize their senior prom, first they had to figure out exactly what a prom *was*. The prom committee, made up of mostly African and Haitian girls, watched Hollywood prom movies as research. When the big night arrived, the girls and boys who went embraced many American prom customs, like buying corsages for their dates and getting their hair done at the beauty salon, but they also incorporated their own international touches. For instance, a girl from Bangladesh opted to wear a sari as her prom dress, and all the students danced to music from around the world.

10 For Lobsang, who's originally from Tibet, that was the best part: "The disco," he says and laughs. "The teachers also

danced, and they showed some funny moves that I had never seen, never expected."

11 While every culture has its specific traits, being a teenager can be challenging whether you're from Tibet or Texas. And as Nedda de Castro points out, an American teenager from another part of the country might actually share more in common with one of her immigrant students than with a native New Yorker. "For instance, a young person who lives on a farm in the United States could have more in common with one of my immigrant students who came from a farming community in their native country," she says. "You may not speak the same language, wear the same clothes, or even have the same religion, but there may be ways in which you understand each other very well and have the same values."

12 Like most kids, International High School students worry about what to wear on the first day of school and where to sit in the cafeteria and how to talk to someone they have a crush on. They also worry about getting good grades and getting into college. Nourou, the girl from Guinea, dreams of being a doctor.

13 Her classmate Daniel, a rising senior originally from the Dominican Republic, wants to be a professional baseball player like his idol, Derek Jeter. "My dream since I was 11 years is to sign with the Yankees," says Daniel, who moved to New York when he was ten.

14 Finally, Lobsang is determined to become a film director. His favorite movie? *"Forrest Gump,"* says Lobsang, who recently graduated high school and plans to study theater at college in the fall. "I love the story. It's not just one story, there's many different stories."

15 The same could be said about the high school. It's amazing how many different stories are inside of one school—around 415, in fact.

16 The International High School at Prospect Heights in Brooklyn is one of many schools of its kind popping up around the nation, from Bowling Green, Kentucky, to San Francisco, California. Many are under the umbrella[1] of the Internationals Network of Public Schools, which oversees 27 schools and academies with more than 9,000 students. In New York City alone, there are around 15 of these schools, serving newcomers who are learning English. At last count, the New York schools, combined, had students representing nearly 120 countries and more than 90 different languages.

[1] **under the umbrella:** part of a larger organization.

PERCENTAGE OF ENGLISH LANGUAGE LEARNERS IN PUBLIC SCHOOLS ACROSS THE UNITED STATES

Don't forget to **Notice & Note** as you read the text.

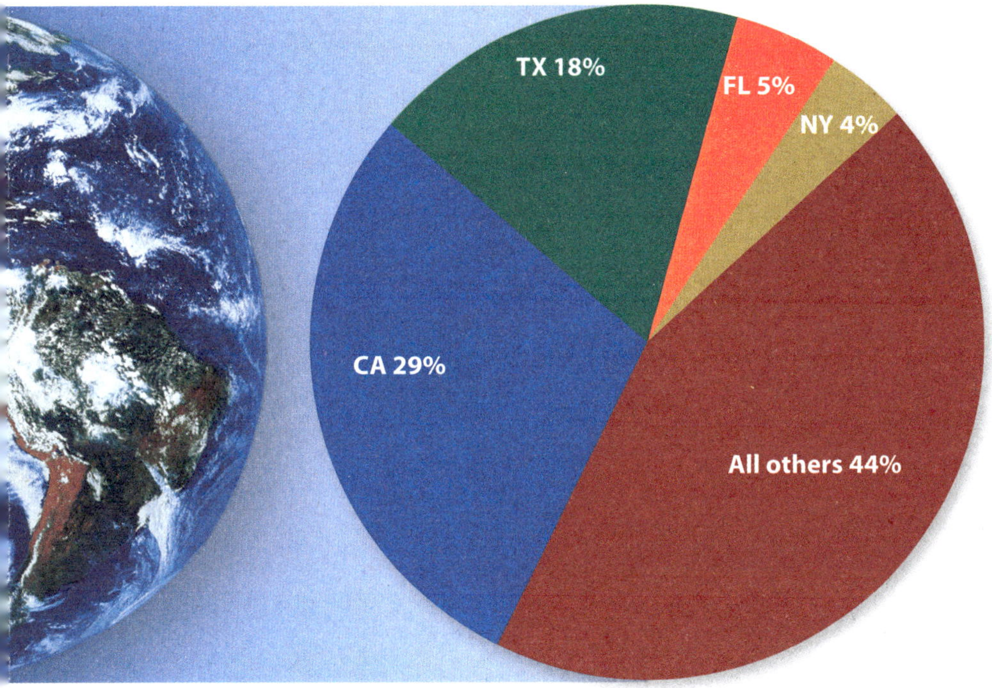

In 2014–15, there were nearly 5 million students who were English language learners (ELLs) in public schools across the United States. That's approximately 1 in 10 students. Most of these students live in four states, although every state has some population of students who participate in language assistance programs. Note: Not all ELLs are immigrants (some students born here grew up speaking a different primary language at home), just as not all immigrants are ELLs (many newcomers from England or Jamaica, for example, speak English as their native language).

ANALYZE TEXT ELEMENTS

Annotate: In the pie chart, mark the four states that have the highest percentages of ELLs in public schools.

Analyze: What is the advantage of presenting this information in a graphic instead of in text? What impact does the graphic have on you as a reader?

17 New York City is very diverse. Any public high school is likely to have some newcomers, so some people wonder why there is a high school just for immigrants learning English in the first place. Wouldn't they be better off mixing with other students born here? But one idea behind these "international" schools and academies is that English language learners (ELLs) benefit from incorporating their native cultures and languages into the classroom.

18 "Biculturalism is something that we celebrate because when our students arrive in this country, they immediately begin a process of developing a new identity," says the principal, Nedda de Castro. "They bring all of the richness of their languages and culture from their own countries, and then, as soon as they arrive, they begin to develop an identity that includes the new experiences they have in the United States.

19 "Coming to a new place changes you," she adds, "but it does not mean that you leave everything behind or erase your past."

Part 3: A Global Perspective

20 In the classroom, students frequently work in small groups, along with students who speak other languages. Sometimes, students are paired together with friends from their home country who speak the same native language and are able to translate words and ideas into English. All of the students mingle with classmates from a range of other countries throughout the day, whether they're learning math, playing basketball in the gym, eating lunch in the cafeteria, or attending a meeting of one of the many after-school clubs. ("I was in chess club, photography club, magazine club, dance club, and fashion club," says Lobsang. "I was a male model.") In the process, they learn English in addition to picking up bits and pieces of other languages and cultures.

21 "Our belief is that language and content cannot be separated and therefore you have to teach them together," says Luft. "There's a myth that students can't learn meaningful content until they learn English, and we think that's not true. Teenage immigrants know a lot about life and academics from their home country. We should think about ways to **capitalize** on that."

capitalize
(kăp´ĭ-tl-īz´) *v.* To *capitalize* on something means to use it to one's advantage.

22 This approach shows positive results: According to a recent study looking at English language learners over four years in New York City, International High School students graduate at a higher percentage than ELL students at other schools in the area (74% compared to approximately 31%).

23 "You want students to use all of the tools they have; that's part of what education should teach you, how to use every tool and source at your disposal," Luft says. "Think of a carpenter trying to bang in a nail," he adds. "You wouldn't tell a carpenter to build something and take the hammer away, and say, 'OK, do the job without your most important tool.' So the whole idea of telling a student, 'Don't use your language,' or that it's not important. … It's how they think, and it's often a part of how they express their emotions. It's an integral part of who they are as a person. You should always try to capitalize on all aspects of who you are as a person and extend that into learning."

24 For some students, their native language *is* their identity. Take Lobsang, for example. His family left Tibet because they weren't allowed to live freely there under Chinese rule. Before coming to the U.S., he says, "We had to immigrate to Nepal to

NOTICE & NOTE
QUESTIONING STANCE

When you read informational texts, you should take a **Questioning Stance,** which means you don't automatically believe everything the author says.

Notice & Note: Mark any details in the bar graph that help you answer this **Big Question:** What challenged, changed, or confirmed what you already knew about graduation rates?

FOUR-YEAR GRADUATION RATES IN NEW YORK CITY (2016)

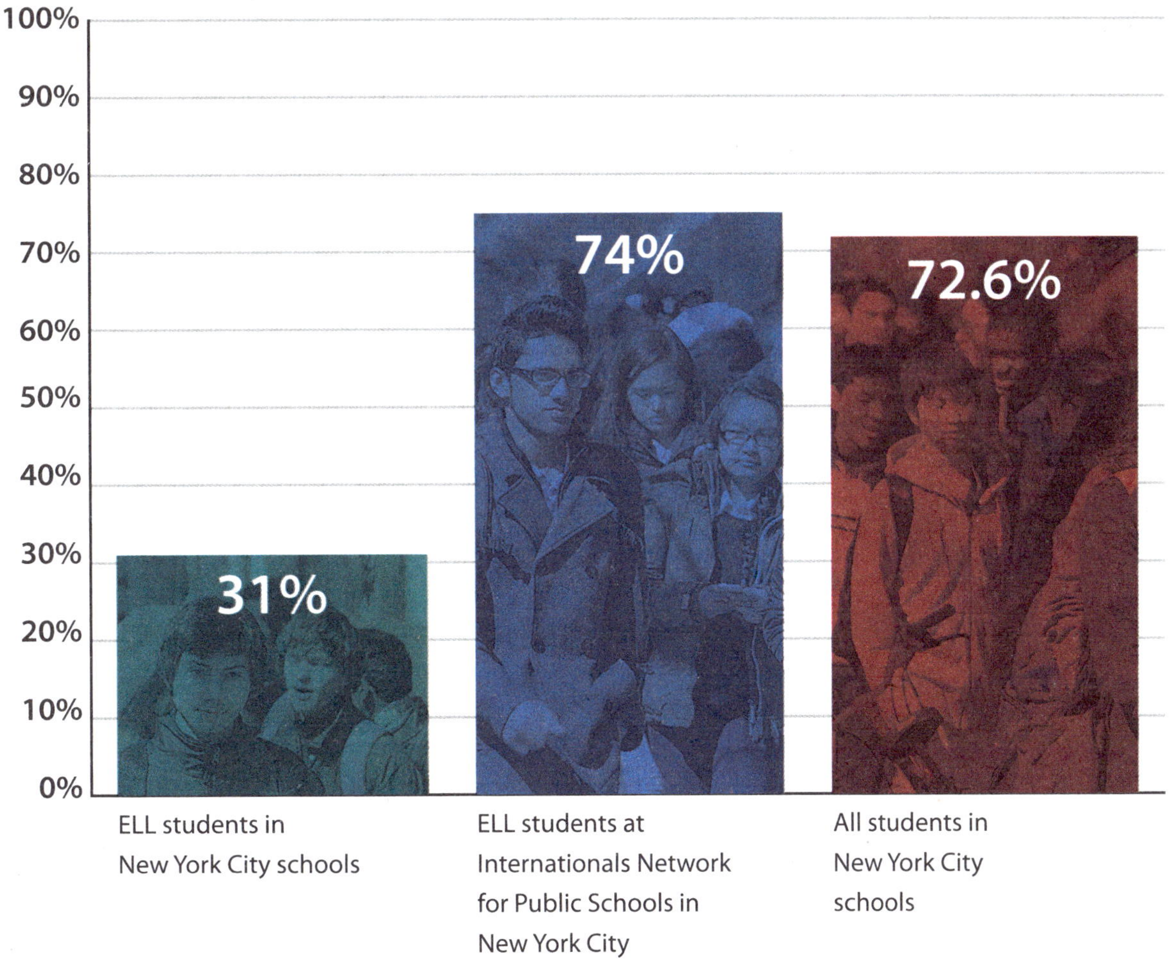

The English language learners who attend Internationals Network schools in New York City graduate at much higher rates than do English language learners who attend other New York City public high schools.

VOCABULARY

Multiple-Meaning Words The word *embrace* often means "to hold close with the arms," but it also has other meanings.

Interpret: What does the word *embraces* in paragraph 24 convey about Lobsang's feelings toward his Tibetan identity?

unrest

(ŭn-rĕst´) *n. Unrest* refers to an unstable or turbulent condition that is often marked by protests or riots.

live the way we want." In America, Lobsang and his family are free to speak their language and honor their culture in a variety of ways. "Right now, I live in Queens, so I think of myself as an American New Yorker," says Lobsang, who embraces his Tibetan identity at the same time. "We still practice celebrations like the Tibetan New Year," he says. Nourou, from Guinea, honors her culture by attending West African weddings in the city. She also celebrates religious holidays such as Eid al-Fitr, which marks the end of Ramadan, when Muslims fast for a month. It's important to honor her culture here, she says, partly because **unrest** in her country has made her nervous about returning. "I can't remember a lot from there."

25 Another way students connect to their home countries is through food. The International High School at Prospect Heights sometimes hosts food festivals, where students are invited to bring dishes that reflect their culture. Daniel, from the Dominican Republic, brings mangú. "It's like green plantain; you mash it, and then put on some salami, egg, onions and cheese," he says. "It's delicious."

26 Meanwhile, Lobsang and many of the other Tibetan students enjoy *momo*, a kind of Tibetan dumpling. "In Queens, there's a lot of Tibetan restaurants, and we also cook Tibetan food," he says. "Even though the pizza and the burger taste delicious, we still eat traditional food to keep the tradition alive."

27 Now that he has graduated, Lobsang is looking forward to college and his dream of becoming a filmmaker. But he also took some time to look back at the past four years and all that he accomplished and experienced at the International High School.

28 "I made a lot of friends from different countries: Yemen, Mexico, Pakistan; I have African friends," Lobsang says. "It's kind of like a family; a family with different races."

29 When he was still a student at the school, he says, some of his friends from the neighborhood who grew up here would laugh about the fact that he went to an International High School. "They called it 'immigrant high school,'" he says, "but they don't know how helpful the school is.

30 "If you are in a school with people from different countries, they share their problems, and it gives you more information to understand the world better," he continues. "If everyone is from same country and go to same school, then they don't have a lot of stories to share. Here, there are a lot of interesting stories."

TURN AND TALK

Turn to a partner and discuss what you learned from the text. How are students at International High School similar to students at other schools? How are they different?

ESSENTIAL QUESTION:

What are the places that shape who you are?

Review your notes and add your thoughts to your Response Log.

Assessment Practice

Answer these questions before moving on to the **Analyze Media and Text** section on the following page.

1. Which **two** details best support the main idea of paragraph 7 that the international school is "like a second home"?

(A) Students can focus on learning English.

(B) Students feel welcomed at the school.

(C) Students and teachers work together on school assignments.

(D) Students develop positive relationships with their teachers.

(E) Students have comfortable desks and chairs.

2. Which claim about International High School students does the bar graph best support?

(A) They graduate at a higher rate than other area ELL students.

(B) They prove that ELL students are more likely to succeed in New York City than in other places.

(C) They graduate at a rate that is similar to other area ELL students.

(D) They prove that ELL students can learn meaningful content and English at the same time.

3. About which person does the reader learn the most from the text?

(A) Nourou

(B) Principal de Castro

(C) Daniel

(D) Lobsang

Ed **Test-Taking Strategies**

Analyze Media and Text

Support your responses with evidence from the documentary and the text.

NOTICE & NOTE

Review what you **noticed and noted** as you read the text. Your annotations can help you answer these questions.

1. **INFER** What might be some of the director's motives—social, commercial, and political—for making *New Immigrants Share Their Stories*? Use the table to record your inferences and evidence.

TYPE OF MOTIVE	POSSIBLE MOTIVE	EVIDENCE
Social		
Commercial		
Political		

2. **EVALUATE** What is the director's main purpose for making the documentary, and how effectively does the video achieve that purpose?

3. **SUMMARIZE** Reread paragraph 6 of "A Common Bond." Then, briefly restate the challenges many immigrants must deal with besides learning English and why they may face these difficulties.

4. **ANALYZE** Review the subheadings in "A Common Bond." What purposes do they serve?

5. **SYNTHESIZE** Choose one of the two graphic features from the informational text and explain what it contributes to the text.

6. **INFER** What is the author's purpose for including **Quoted Words** in paragraph 21?

7. **ANALYZE** How did the information presented by Hauser's text answer this **Big Question:** What challenged, confirmed, or changed your understanding of immigrant students?

Choices

Here are some other ways to demonstrate your understanding of the ideas in this lesson.

As you write and discuss, be sure to use the **Academic Vocabulary** words.

contribute	relocate
immigrate	shifting
reaction	

Writing

Write a Letter

Write a letter to one of the students mentioned in either the text or the video. In your letter, ask specific questions that came up as you viewed the documentary or read the article.

- Provide the date, your return address, the name and address of the student, and a salutation in correct letter format.
- Begin the body of your letter by explaining who you are and why you are writing. Then ask any questions you have.
- Thank the student for his or her time. End with an appropriate closing, such as "Sincerely," or "Yours truly," and your signature.

Social & Emotional Learning

Discuss with a Small Group

Have a discussion about what makes you feel welcome at your school and what gives you a sense of belonging there.

- Review the text to identify ways in which the students form bonds with one another. Then consider whether you do anything similar.
- Identify school-sponsored activities at your school that help foster a sense of school spirit, unity, and belonging. During the discussion, listen actively to ask questions and comment respectfully on others' ideas.

Media

Create an Infographic

With a partner, put together an infographic to display data about the cultural backgrounds of students in your school.

- Take a survey of students in your school. Find out about the countries their families come from, the languages they speak, and the religions they practice.
- Decide what kinds of graphs or other visual aids to include in your infographic. Think about which kinds of graphics will convey the information you want to share most effectively.
- Sketch out possible designs. Revise to keep text brief and to ensure that the images and text work together. When you have a sketch that you both like, create a final version.

Expand Your Vocabulary

PRACTICE AND APPLY

Select the best answer to each question.

1. Which of the following would be a sign of **unrest**?
   a. a cold   **b.** a rebellion
2. Which might make a baseball player **eligible** to play on the team?
   a. showing up to every practice   **b.** showering every day
3. Which is a way to **capitalize** on hot weather?
   a. selling misting fans   **b.** closing a store early
4. What is one reason to try to **assimilate**?
   a. to honor old traditions   **b.** to connect with others

Vocabulary Strategy

Multiple-Meaning Words

To determine the meaning of a **multiple-meaning word,** you can use clues from its **context**—the words, sentences, paragraphs, and punctuation surrounding it. In the example below from "A Common Bond," learning a language is identified as something new immigrants conquer. One meaning of *conquer* is "to defeat in war," but the context helps you understand that the intended meaning in this sentence is "to overcome."

Learning a new language is hard enough, but English is just one part of what these students must conquer as new immigrants in America.

Ed **Interactive Vocabulary Lesson: Words with Multiple Meanings**

PRACTICE AND APPLY

Select the best meaning of each boldfaced word.

1. Lederhosen and dirndls are perfect clothes to wear in Switzerland, but to **assimilate** here, you should wear jeans.
   a. to absorb into the mind   **b.** to blend into the main group
2. Ellie's friends all wanted to **capitalize** on her new job at the ice cream parlor by getting her to give them extra toppings.
   a. take advantage of   **b.** invest funds in

Watch Your Language!

Ed Interactive Grammar Lessons: Punctuation I

Semicolons, Colons, and Parentheses

Writers use punctuation to make the meaning of a sentence clear. Some punctuation marks, such as periods and exclamation points, indicate the end of a sentence and the end of a complete thought. Other marks occur in the middle of a sentence and help separate one idea from the next. The chart explains how semicolons (;), colons (:), and parentheses are used.

PUNCTUATION MARK	WHAT IT DOES	EXAMPLES
Semicolon	separates parts of a compound sentence with no coordinating conjunction	"You want students to use all of the tools they have; that's part of what education should teach you, how to use every tool and source at your disposal." (para 23)
	separates items in a series that contain commas	There are schools for recent immigrants in Brooklyn, New York; Bowling Green, Kentucky; and San Francisco, California.
Colon	introduces a list	"I made a lot of friends from different countries: Yemen, Mexico, Pakistan. . . ." (para 28)
	follows the salutation of a business letter	To Whom It May Concern: Dear Mr. Luft:
Parentheses	set off extra information that explains or expands upon an idea in the sentence	"International High School students graduate at a higher percentage than ELL students at other schools in the area (74% compared to approximately 31%)." (para 22)

PRACTICE AND APPLY

Review a piece of writing you did for class. Look for sentences that could be improved or clarified by using one of the punctuation marks in the chart. Consider the following:

- Can I use a semicolon to combine two simple sentences with closely related meanings?
- Can I use a colon to add a list of examples or introduce a quotation from "A Common Bond"?
- Can I use parentheses to add an extra detail about one of my ideas?

Compare Purposes

In a small group, compare and contrast the purposes of *New Immigrants Share Their Stories* and "A Common Bond." Remember, each selection may try to fulfill one or more of these purposes: to inform, to entertain, to persuade, or to express the creator's feelings or opinions. Complete the Venn diagram with similarities and differences in each selection's purpose. One example is provided for you.

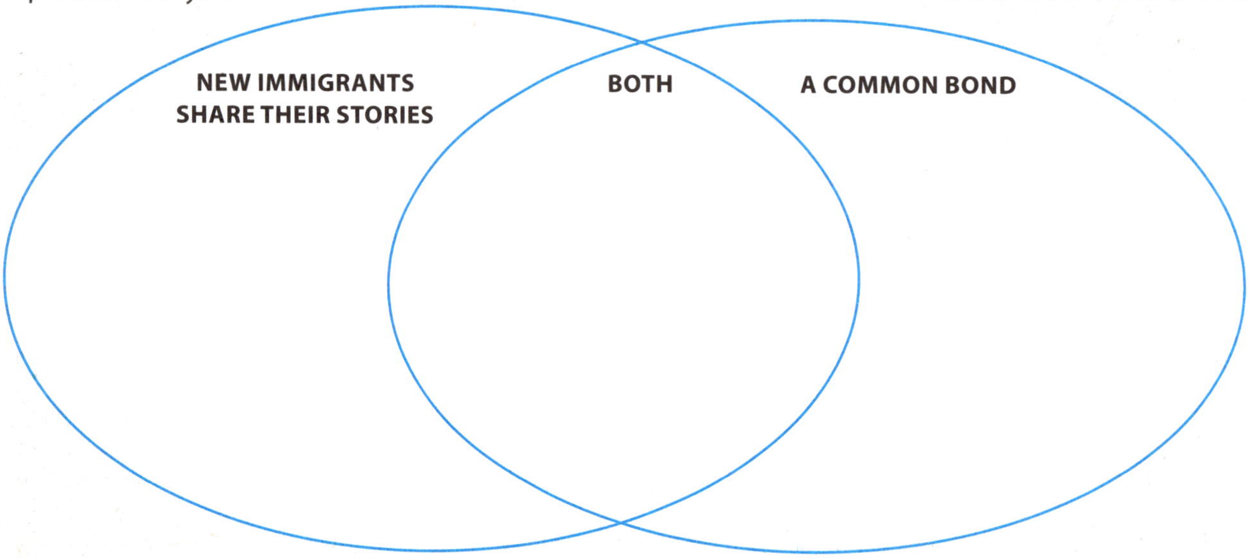

Analyze Media and Text

Discuss these questions in your group.

1. **CONNECT** What similarities do you see between the immigrants' stories in the documentary and those mentioned in the text?

2. **CONTRAST** In what ways do the filmmaker's purpose and the writer's purpose differ?

3. **EVALUATE** In your opinion, what are the advantages and disadvantages of using film to convey the immigrants' stories? What are the advantages and disadvantages of using text?

4. **SYNTHESIZE** What do both sources reveal about the challenges recent teen immigrants face and how best to overcome them?

Create and Present

Now your group can continue unearthing the kinds of stories and information you learned about in the documentary and the informational text. Follow these steps:

1. **CHOOSE A PERSONAL STORY TO TELL** In your group, tell a brief personal story that you would feel comfortable sharing in an interview. The story you share might be a family immigration story, or it could be a story about another important event in your life.

2. **CHOOSE A "BUDDY" TO INTERVIEW** After everyone has shared a story, choose a "buddy" in the group whose story interests you.

3. **PREPARE FOR THE INTERVIEW** Use the chart to jot down details or aspects of the story that sparked your interest. Then list questions that can help you learn more. Use the interview questions from *New Immigrants Share Their Stories* as a guide. Keep your questions general and open-ended.

INTERESTING DETAIL OR ASPECT OF THE STORY	INTERVIEW QUESTION ABOUT IT

4. **RECORD YOUR INTERVIEWS** Modeling the techniques you saw used in the documentary, take turns interviewing your buddy and recording one another's interviews.

Reader's Choice

Continue your exploration of the Essential Question by doing some independent reading on places that people call home. Read the titles and descriptions shown. Then mark the texts that interest you.

ESSENTIAL QUESTION: ***What are the places that shape who you are?***

Short Reads

Available on Ed

These texts are available in your ebook. Choose one to read and rate. Then defend your rating to the class.

My Father and the Figtree

Poem by **Naomi Shihab Nye**

For one girl's father, no house could truly be a home without a figtree growing in the yard.

Rate It ☆☆☆☆☆

Golden Glass

Short Story by **Alma Luz Villanueva**

How can sleeping in a fort in the woods help heal a broken heart?

Rate It ☆☆☆☆☆

A Place to Call Home

Research Study by **Scott Bittle** and **Jonathan Rochkind**

Life in America is not the way many immigrants imagined it would be.

Rate It ☆☆☆☆☆

Salmon Boy

Myth by **Michael J. Caduto** and **Joseph Bruchac**

A young boy who does not respect the ways of his people pays a high price.

Rate It ☆☆☆☆☆

Long Reads

Here are a few recommended books that connect to this unit topic. For additional options, ask your teacher, school librarian, or peers. Which titles spark your interest?

Enrique's Journey

Biography by **Sonia Nazario**

A Honduran boy braves unimaginable perils traveling to see his mother who left her family for the United States eleven years ago. Wit, courage, and hope allow him to push forward.

The Latehomecomer

Memoir by **Kao Kalia Yang**

Kao first recounts her family's captivity and escape to Thailand during the Vietnam War. Then, she describes the challenges she faced when her family immigrated to America.

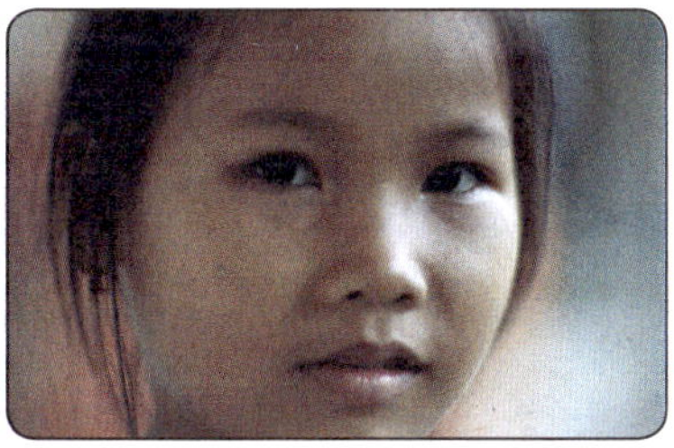

Inside Out and Back Again

Novel in Verse by **Thanhhà Lai**

Hà and her family flee Vietnam and sail to America seeking refuge. She experiences drastic change, grief, and healing as she attempts to start her new life.

Extension

Connect & Create

WRITE A MOVIE SCRIPT Choose a scene from one of the texts to adapt into a film script. Make sure to include the following elements:

- A scene heading that identifies the location where the action takes place
- Brief descriptions of any action that takes place during the scene
- Character names, followed by the dialogue spoken by each character
- Instruction for how dialogue should be spoken by the actors (in parentheses)

SELL THAT BOOK! Design a book cover for one of the texts. Brainstorm to come up with possible illustrations or photographs that would effectively capture the main ideas or themes of the text. Also consider a font and type size for the title treatment and author's name. Then, decide on the best design and create a final version to share with your class.

NOTICE & NOTE

- Pick one of the texts and annotate the **Notice & Note** signposts you find.
- Then, use the **Notice & Note Writing Frames** to help you write about the significance of the signposts.
- Compare your findings with those of other students who read the same text.

Ed

Notice & Note Writing Frames

Write a Short Story

Writing Prompt

Using ideas, information, and examples from multiple texts in this unit, write a short story about a character who is struggling with an obstacle in relation to a place.

Manage your time carefully so that you can

- review the texts in the unit;
- plan your story;
- write your story; and
- revise and edit your story.

Be sure to

- establish a context and introduce a narrator and characters;
- develop a plot with a logical sequence of events;
- include descriptive details and sensory language; and
- use narrative techniques such as dialogue and pacing.

Review the Mentor Text

For an example of a well-written narrative you can use as a mentor text, review the excerpt from

- ***The Book of Unknown Americans*** (pages 177–185).

Make sure to carefully review your notes and annotations about this text. Think about the narrative techniques the author used to make her story engaging.

Consider Your Sources

Review the list of texts in the unit and choose at least two that you may want to use as a source of ideas or inspiration for your short story.

As you review potential sources, consult the notes you made on your **Response Log** and make additional notes about any ideas that might be useful as you write your short story. Especially consider how the writers used language, developed characters, structured plot events, and employed other narrative techniques.

UNIT 3 SOURCES

- ☐ **My Favorite Chaperone**
- ☐ **The Book of Unknown Americans**
- ☐ **Spirit Walking in the Tundra**
- ☐ **New Immigrants Share Their Stories** MEDIA
- ☐ **A Common Bond: Teens Forge Friendships Despite Differences**

Analyze the Prompt

Review the prompt to make sure you understand the assignment.

1. Mark the sentence in the prompt that identifies the topic of your short story. Rephrase this sentence in your own words.
2. Next, look for words that indicate the purpose and audience of your short story, and write a sentence describing each.

Find a Purpose

Two common purposes of a short story are:

- to entertain readers
- to convey a theme, or a message about life or human nature

What is my topic? What is my writing task?

What is my purpose?

Who is my audience?

Review the Rubric

Your short story will be scored using a rubric. As you write, focus on the characteristics as described in the chart. You will learn more about these characteristics as you work through the lesson.

PURPOSE, FOCUS, AND ORGANIZATION	NARRATIVE TECHNIQUE	CONVENTIONS OF STANDARD ENGLISH
The response includes: • An engaging introduction • A well-developed plot structure • Use of transitions to convey sequence and connect ideas • Logical sequence of events • A conclusion that follows from the narrated events	The response includes: • Use of descriptive details and sensory language • Effective use of narrative techniques • Varied sentence structure	The response may include: • Some minor errors in usage but no patterns of errors • Correct punctuation, capitalization, sentence formation, and spelling • Command of basic conventions

1 PLAN YOUR SHORT STORY

Determine Characters, Setting, and Point of View

To start planning your short story, decide who the characters will be and where the events will take place. You'll also need to determine which point of view you'll use to tell the story. **Point of view** is the perspective from which events in the story are narrated. In the chart, list ideas for your characters, setting, and point of view.

Determine Point of View

- In a work told from a **first-person point of view,** the narrator is a character in the story.
- In a work told from a **third-person point of view,** the narrator is an outside observer.
- A third-person narrator is often **omniscient,** or all-knowing about every character.

Characters Who is your main character, and what is he or she like? Who are the other characters?	
Setting Where and when will the story take place? Why is the setting important?	
Point of View Who will tell your story? How will your choice of narrator impact readers?	

Identify a Central Conflict

To develop an engaging story, your main character must face a central **conflict,** or struggle between opposing forces. Record ideas about your character's conflict below.

Ed

Help with Planning

Consult **Interactive Writing Lesson: Writing Narratives.**

What is the central conflict? How does it relate to a specific place and time?

What obstacle(s) will complicate your character's conflict?

What will your character learn from his or her struggle?

Brainstorm Details

Your short story should include **descriptive details** that help readers imagine the events. Use the chart to brainstorm words and phrases that will help convey vivid descriptions of events for your readers.

EVENT	DETAILS

Organize Ideas

Now organize your material in a way that will help you draft your short story. Keep in mind that a well-written short story follows a plot structure that unfolds naturally and logically.

Determine Plot Structure

Here are some narrative techniques that can add interest to your plot structure:

- Use **flashback** to recall past events.
- Use **foreshadowing** to hint at events that will occur later.
- Speed up or slow down the **pacing** of the narrative by shortening or lengthening descriptions of events.

EXPOSITION	Establish the story's context and narrative point of view. Introduce the characters, setting, and conflict.
RISING ACTION	Develop the conflict with events that create complications. Be sure to use transitional words and phrases to show the sequence of events.
CLIMAX	Build to a turning point, or moment of greatest interest, in which the conflict begins to be resolved.
FALLING ACTION	Describe what happens as a result of the climax.
RESOLUTION	End your story with a resolution that shows how the conflict is finally resolved and reflects on the narrated events.

2 DEVELOP A DRAFT

Now it is time to draft your story. Examine how professional authors craft engaging short stories and use similar techniques in your own writing.

Ed
Drafting Online
Check your assignment list for a writing task from your teacher.

Engage the Reader

EXAMINE THE MENTOR TEXT

Notice how the author of *The Book of Unknown Americans* captures the reader's attention by establishing a context and point of view and by introducing the narrator and characters.

The author establishes a first-person narrator and introduces his parents and brother.

I was less than a year old when my parents brought my brother and me to the United States. Enrique was four. He used to tell me things about Panamá that I couldn't possibly have remembered—like about the scorpions in our backyard and the cement utility sink where my mom used to give us baths. He reminisced about walking down the street with my mom to the Super 99, the dust blowing up everywhere, the heat pounding down, and about looking for crabs between the rocks along the bay.

"It's in you," my dad assured me once. "You were born in Panamá. It's in your bones."

Vivid sensory details describe a setting.

Dialogue brings the characters to life.

Try These Suggestions

Consider using a variety of methods to engage your reader. You might:

- include vivid details about setting
- use dialogue to introduce a character
- experiment with different points of view

APPLY TO YOUR DRAFT

Use this chart to practice engaging your reader. Draft a few sentences to capture your reader's attention and introduce key elements of your short story.

Establish the point of view.	
Provide details about the setting.	
Use description and/or dialogue to introduce the characters.	
Hint at the main conflict of the story.	

Develop Characters

EXAMINE THE MENTOR TEXT

In *The Book of Unknown Americans*, Cristina Henríquez gives information about her characters by describing their actions and words using precise words and phrases.

The narrator's mother encourages her husband to visit Panamá by evoking memories of their life there.

Sensory details develop the mother's character.

> . . . She'd become a genius at turning any and every little thing into a way to talk about Panamá. She would get a mosquito bite on her ankle and point out the welt to us, reminiscing about the bites she used to get in Panamá and wondering aloud "what the mosquitoes there looked like now," as if they were old friends. . . .

Dialogue shows how the mother tries to persuade the father.

APPLY TO YOUR DRAFT

Your short story should develop your characters by describing what they look like, what they say, and how they act. Use precise language and other narrative techniques to make your characters and the situations they face seem real. Use the graphic organizer to help you develop one of your characters.

Words that describe the character's appearance	
Dialogue that reveals the character's personality or motivations	
Descriptions of the character's actions	

3 REVISE YOUR SHORT STORY

Experienced writers know the importance of revision. Review your story and consider how it can be improved. Use the guide to help you revise your story.

Ed
Help with Revision
Find a **Peer Review Guide** and **Student Models** online.

REVISION GUIDE		
ASK YOURSELF	**PROVE IT**	**REVISE IT**
Introduction Does my exposition establish a context and introduce characters?	**Underline** words and phrases that establish context and introduce characters.	**Add** details about the setting and characters.
Narrative Techniques Do I use narrative techniques to develop the characters and plot?	**Underline** descriptions that reveal character and advance the plot. **Put a check mark** (✔) next to dialogue.	**Add** dialogue that reveals character. **Add or rearrange** details to show how the plot unfolds naturally and logically.
Point of View Do I maintain a consistent point of view?	**Put a star** (★) next to pronouns that show point of view.	Change any first-person or third-person pronouns as necessary.
Transitions Do I use a variety of transitions to show relationships among events?	**Highlight** transitions that show sequence or signal shifts in time or place.	**Add** transitional words, phrases, and clauses to clarify relationships among events.
Precise Language Do I use precise, descriptive language to convey experiences?	**Underline** words and phrases that describe experiences and events.	**Add** descriptive language to convey ideas more clearly or vividly.
Conclusion Does my conclusion follow from the narrated events?	**Underline** sentences or phrases that reflect on events.	**Add** phrases or sentences that reflect on events or state a theme.

APPLY TO YOUR DRAFT

Consider the following as you look for opportunities to improve your writing.

- Make sure your story follows a logical plot.
- Use dialogue and description to enhance your characters.
- Correct any errors in grammar and punctuation.

Peer Review in Action

Once you have finished revising your short story, you will exchange papers with a partner in a **peer review.** During a peer review, you will give suggestions to improve your partner's draft.

Read the exposition from a student's draft and examine the comments made by his peer reviewer.

First Draft

Starting Over

By *Hernando Soares,* Washington Middle School

It's been five years since we moved, but I still remember the day we left like it was yesterday. I remember how sad and worried my father seemed as we pulled out of the driveway in our pickup truck for the last time, dust swirling in a cloud behind us, obscuring everything in its wake. If I understood then how much our lives were about to change, I might have shared my father's expression.

Begin with dialogue or a vivid image for a more engaging opening.

To strengthen your beginning, provide more information about the setting.

Read the revised story below. Notice how the writer has improved his draft by making revisions based on his reviewer's comments.

Revision

"That's it," I remember my father saying with resignation, as he slammed the door of our pickup truck, with the creaky old porch swing still swaying from him bumping into it on his way out. Although it's been five years since we left the farm, this moment still haunts me like it was yesterday.

From the rear seat where I was sprawled out for the long ride ahead of us, I had a clear view of his sad and worried expression in the rearview mirror as we pulled out of the driveway for the last time, dust swirling in a cloud behind us, obscuring everything in its wake. If I understood then how much our lives were about to change, I might have shared his look of concern. Instead I was oblivious to the gravity of our situation and what it would really mean to start over.

The dialogue and sensory details help me visualize the scene and make me want to keep reading.

Also, by adding specific details you provided more clues about the setting.

APPLY TO YOUR DRAFT

During your peer review, give each other suggestions for making your stories more engaging. Use your revision guide to help you.

When receiving feedback from your partner, listen attentively and ask questions to make sure you fully understand the revision suggestions.

4 EDIT YOUR SHORT STORY

Edit your final draft to check for proper use of standard English conventions and to correct any misspellings or grammatical errors.

Ed
Interactive Grammar Lesson: Punctuation

Watch Your Language!

USE DASHES AND ELLIPSES

Authors use dashes and ellipses to show a pause or a break. Ellipses may also be used to indicate an omission.

Read the following sentence from *The Book of Unknown Americans.*

> **Holidays were always bad—my mom in particular got homesick sometimes like it was a genuine illness—but that Christmas was the worst.**

The dashes interrupt a thought and set off additional information about the narrator's mother's response to the holidays. Notice that when an interrupting thought appears in the middle of a sentence, one dash appears at the beginning of the thought and one dash appears at the end.

Dashes and Ellipses

Here are some common purposes of dashes:

- to signal a sudden break in thought
- to signal the reader to pause and pay attention

Here are some uses of ellipses:

- to indicate a long pause
- to show omission of a word or words
- to represent thoughts or speech that trails off

APPLY TO YOUR DRAFT

Now apply what you've learned about ellipses and dashes to your own work.

1. **Read your paper aloud** and underline the dashes and/or ellipses you've used.
2. **Add dashes and/or ellipses** to show a pause or a break in thought.
3. **Exchange drafts** with a peer and review the uses of dashes and ellipses in each other's work.

Ways to Share

- **Perform a scene** from your story for your class.
- **Write a blog post** on a class or school website to let others know about your story.
- **Record an interview** to answer a classmate's questions about your story and your writing process.

5 PUBLISH YOUR SHORT STORY

Share It!

Finalize your short story for your writing portfolio. You may also use your story as inspiration for other projects.

Reflect & Extend

Here are some other ways to show your understanding of the ideas in Unit 3.

Reflect on the Essential Question

What are the places that shape who you are?

How has your answer to this question changed since you first considered it when you started this unit?

You can use these sentence starters to help you reflect on your learning.

- **I think differently now because...**
- **I want to learn more about...**
- **I still don't understand...**

Writing

Write an Article

Write an article for a newspaper or magazine about someone who found a new home after moving to the United States from another country.

- Introduce the subject and state your controlling idea about the person.
- Then, provide information about the person and their immigration story.
- In your final paragraph, state your conclusion about the person.

Project-Based Learning

Create a Photo Collection

You've read about the places we call home. Now, with a group of classmates, create a photo collection about one aspect of this topic covered in the unit.

Here are some questions to ask yourself as you get started.

- What are the different places people may think of as home?
- What message or information do I want my photo collection to communicate?
- How can I use images and layout to help convey that information?

Ed

Media Projects

To find help with this task online, access **Create a Photo Collection.**

UNIT
4

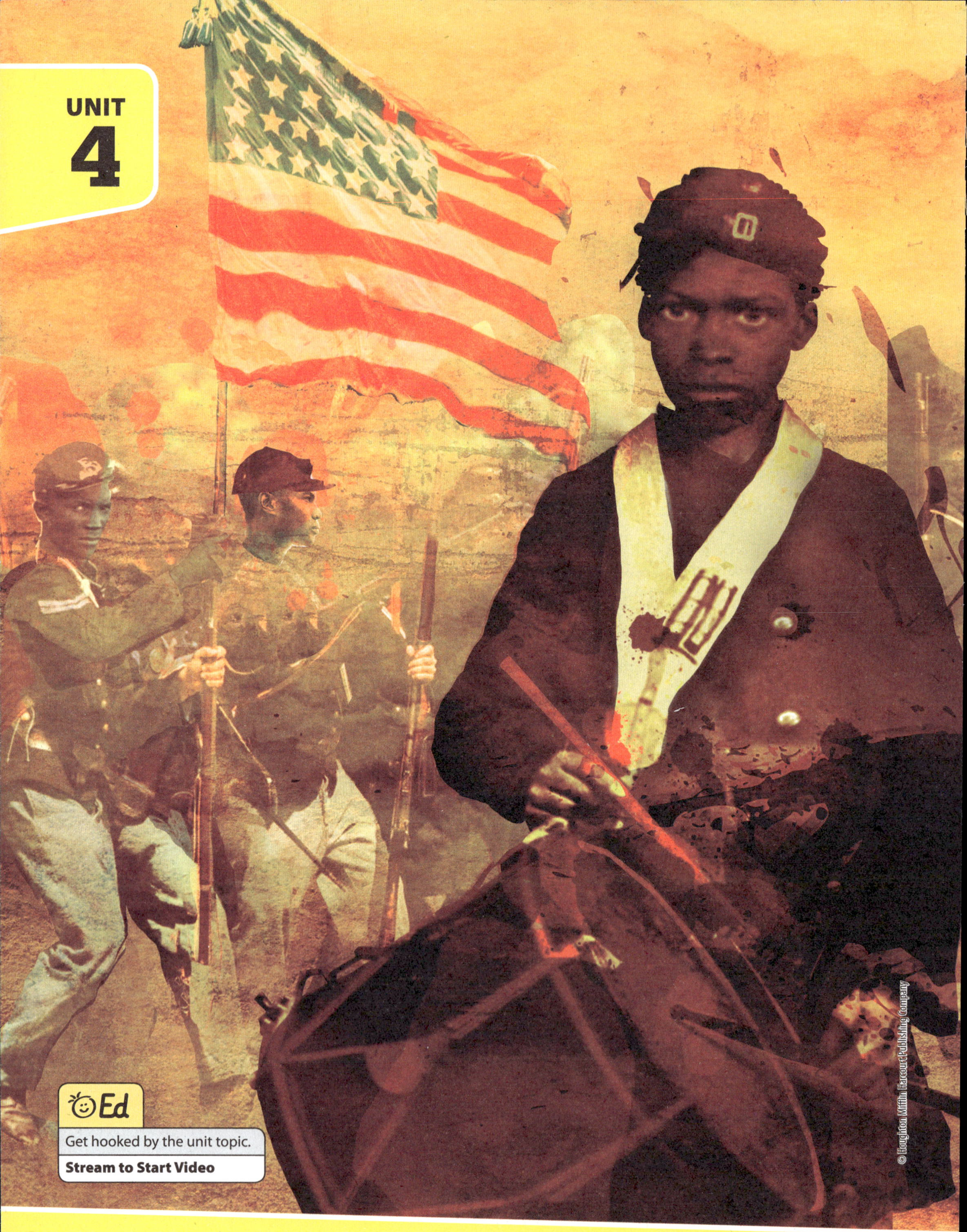

Ed
Get hooked by the unit topic.
Stream to Start Video

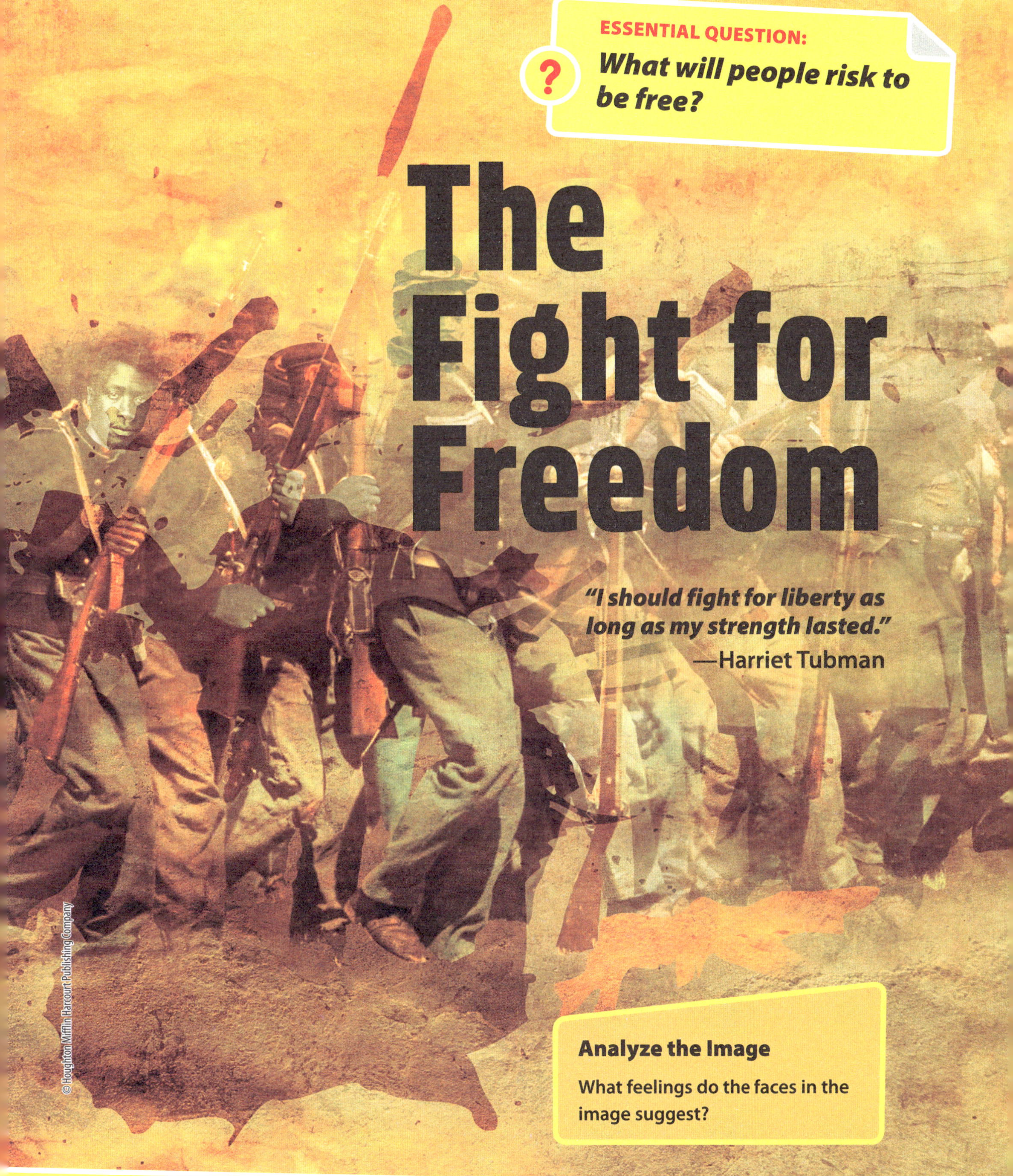

ESSENTIAL QUESTION:

What will people risk to be free?

The Fight for Freedom

"I should fight for liberty as long as my strength lasted."
—Harriet Tubman

Analyze the Image

What feelings do the faces in the image suggest?

Spark Your Learning

Here's a chance to spark your learning about ideas in **Unit 4: The Fight for Freedom.**

As you read, you can use the **Response Log** (page R4) to track your thinking about the Essential Question.

Make the Connection

What comes to mind when you think about the Civil War? Write or sketch your answer.

Think About the Essential Question

What will people risk to be free? Give examples of the kinds of risks people take when they fight for their freedom.

Sound Like an Expert

You can use these Academic Vocabulary words to write and talk about the topics and themes in the unit. Which of these words do you already feel comfortable using when speaking or writing?

	I can use it!	I understand it.	I'll look it up.
access	☐	☐	☐
civil	☐	☐	☐
demonstrate	☐	☐	☐
document	☐	☐	☐
symbolize	☐	☐	☐

Prove It!

Turn to a partner and use one of the words in a sentence about a fight for freedom.

Preview the Texts

Look over the titles, images, and descriptions of the texts in the unit. Mark the title of the text that interests you most.

from Narrative of the Life of Frederick Douglass, an American Slave

Autobiography by **Frederick Douglass**

In this excerpt, Douglass explains the profound effect learning to read had on him.

The Drummer Boy of Shiloh

Historical Fiction by **Ray Bradbury**

On the eve of battle, a fearful drummer boy has an unexpected encounter.

O Captain! My Captain!

Poem by **Walt Whitman**

The speaker of this poem shares his feelings of sorrow about the death of his "captain."

from Harriet Tubman: Conductor on the Underground Railroad

Biography by **Ann Petry**

Harriet Tubman leads eleven fugitives along the Underground Railroad toward Canada and freedom from slavery.

Not My Bones

Poem by **Marilyn Nelson**

The true essence of a person can never be enslaved.

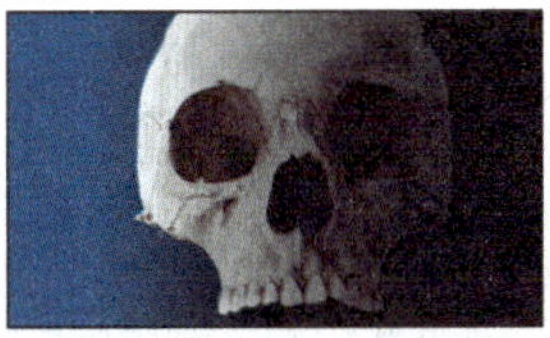

from Fortune's Bones

History Writing by **Pamela Espeland**

Who was Fortune, and what happened to his bones after he died?

I Wonder . . .

What kinds of freedom do people fight for?

from

Narrative of the Life of Frederick Douglass, an American Slave

Autobiography by **Frederick Douglass**

Engage Your Brain

Choose one or more of these activities to start connecting with the autobiography you are about to read.

Dig In

Conduct research to learn more about Frederick Douglass. See what you can learn about:

- his life as an enslaved person
- how he gained his freedom
- his fight to end slavery

Game Changer

In the text you are about to read, Frederick Douglass explains how learning to read caused a dramatic shift in his life. Have you ever learned something that was a game changer for you? Share your experience with a classmate.

Why Autobiography?

Douglass's narrative is an autobiography, or an account of his own life. What reasons do authors have for writing the stories of their lives? Make a list of possible reasons below.

Analyze Autobiography

Narrative of the Life of Frederick Douglass, an American Slave is an **autobiography,** which is an account of the writer's own life.

Authors of autobiographies often have a **purpose,** or reason for writing, beyond informing readers about events in their own lives. For example, writers might also want to shed light on the time period in which they have lived, or share a message about an issue that has shaped their lives as well as the lives of others. Writers may use **figurative language,** which communicates meaning beyond its literal meaning, to achieve their purposes.

As you read, try to identify Frederick Douglass's main purpose in this section of his autobiography.

Focus on Genre
Autobiography

- gives an account of the writer's own life, told from the first-person point of view
- describes events in chronological order
- provides interesting details and anecdotes
- has a tone that reveals the author's attitude toward people and events

Analyze Structure

In an autobiography, authors often choose to focus on events that are related by **cause and effect,** which means that one event brings about another event or creates a change in attitude. Paragraphs may be structured to show these cause-and-effect relationships, even in narratives told in chronological order.

As you read, note how the cause-and-effect structure helps Douglass achieve his purpose. Use a chart like the one below.

CAUSE	EFFECT

Annotation in Action

Here is an example of notes a student made about this passage from *Narrative of the Life of Frederick Douglass.* As you read, mark words and phrases that show cause-and-effect relationships.

Slavery soon proved its ability to divest her of these heavenly qualities. Under its influence, the tender heart became stone, and the lamblike disposition gave way to one of tigerlike fierceness. The first step in her downward course was in her ceasing to instruct me. She now commenced to practise her husband's precepts. She finally became even more violent in her opposition than her husband himself. She was not satisfied with simply doing as well as he had commanded; she seemed anxious to do better.

These sentences explain that slavery caused his mistress to change from tender to fierce.

Expand Your Vocabulary

Put a check mark next to the vocabulary words that you feel comfortable using when speaking or writing.

- **commence** ☐
- **apprehension** ☐
- **prudence** ☐
- **unabated** ☐
- **denunciation** ☐
- **vindication** ☐

Turn to a partner and use one of the words you already know in a sentence about overcoming challenges.

As you read the excerpt from *Narrative of the Life of Frederick Douglass,* use the definitions in the side column to learn the vocabulary words you don't already know.

Background

Frederick Douglass (1818–1895) was born into enslavement in Maryland at a time when slavery was still legal in many states in the Union. As Douglass grew up, he tried to escape several times. Finally, in 1838, he succeeded. Douglass went on to become a famous speaker and writer, fighting to abolish, or end, slavery. His autobiography, *Narrative of the Life of Frederick Douglass, an American Slave,* became a best seller in the United States and Europe.

from

Narrative of the Life of Frederick Douglass, an American Slave

Autobiography by **Frederick Douglass**

In this excerpt, Douglass explains the profound effect learning to read had on him.

NOTICE & NOTE
As you read, use the side margins to make notes about the text.

1 I lived in Master Hugh's family about seven years. During this time, I succeeded in learning to read and write. In accomplishing this, I was compelled to resort to various stratagems. I had no regular teacher. My mistress, who had kindly commenced to instruct me, had, in compliance with the advice and direction of her husband, not only ceased to instruct, but had set her face against my being instructed by any one else. It is due, however, to my mistress to say of her, that she did not adopt this course of treatment immediately. She at first lacked the depravity[1] indispensable to shutting me up in mental darkness. It was at least necessary for her to have some training in the exercise of irresponsible power, to make her equal to the task of treating me as though I were a brute.

Ed
Close Read Screencast
Listen to a modeled close read of this text.

[1] **depravity** (dĭ-prăv´ĭ-tē): moral corruption.

commence
(kə-mĕns´) *v.* When things *commence,* they begin or start.

ANALYZE AUTOBIOGRAPHY

Annotate: Mark details in paragraph 2 that describe Douglass's mistress.

Infer: What might Douglass's purpose be in devoting so much space to describing his mistress?

apprehension
(ăp´rĭ-hĕn´shən) *n. Apprehension* is the fear or dread of the future.

Ed

Text in Focus Video

Learn about analyzing the language in the narrative.

2 My mistress was, as I have said, a kind and tender-hearted woman; and in the simplicity of her soul she **commenced,** when I first went to live with her, to treat me as she supposed one human being ought to treat another. In entering upon the duties of a slaveholder, she did not seem to perceive that I sustained to her the relation of a mere chattel,[2] and that for her to treat me as a human being was not only wrong, but dangerously so. Slavery proved as injurious to her as it did to me. When I went there, she was a pious, warm, and tender-hearted woman. There was no sorrow or suffering for which she had not a tear. She had bread for the hungry, clothes for the naked, and comfort for every mourner that came within her reach. Slavery soon proved its ability to divest her of these heavenly qualities. Under its influence, the tender heart became stone, and the lamblike disposition gave way to one of tigerlike fierceness. The first step in her downward course was in her ceasing to instruct me. She now commenced to practise her husband's precepts.[3] She finally became even more violent in her opposition than her husband himself. She was not satisfied with simply doing as well as he had commanded; she seemed anxious to do better. Nothing seemed to make her more angry than to see me with a newspaper. She seemed to think that here lay the danger. I have had her rush at me with a face made all up of fury, and snatch from me a newspaper, in a manner that fully revealed her **apprehension.** She was an apt woman; and a little experience soon demonstrated, to her satisfaction, that education and slavery were incompatible with each other.

3 From this time I was most narrowly watched. If I was in a separate room any considerable length of time, I was sure to be suspected of having a book, and was at once called to give an account of myself. All this, however, was too late. The first step had been taken. Mistress, in teaching me the alphabet, had given me the inch, and no precaution could prevent me from taking the *ell.*

4 The plan which I adopted, and the one by which I was most successful, was that of making friends of all the little white boys whom I met in the street. As many of these as I could, I converted into teachers. With their kindly aid, obtained at different times and in different places, I finally succeeded in learning to read. When I was sent of errands, I always took my book with me, and by going one part of my errand quickly, I found time to get a lesson before my return. I used also to carry bread with me, enough of which was always in the house,

[2] **chattel** (chăt´l): a personal possession or item of property; an enslaved person.
[3] **precepts** (prē´sĕpts´): rules or principles regarding action or conduct.

Don't forget to **Notice & Note** as you read the text.

and to which I was always welcome; for I was much better off in this regard than many of the poor white children in our neighborhood. This bread I used to bestow upon the hungry little urchins, who, in return, would give me that more valuable bread of knowledge. I am strongly tempted to give the names of two or three of those little boys, as a testimonial of the gratitude and affection I bear them; but **prudence** forbids;—not that it would injure me, but it might embarrass them; for it is almost an unpardonable offence to teach slaves to read in this Christian country. It is enough to say of the dear little fellows, that they lived on Philpot Street, very near Durgin and Bailey's ship-yard. I used to talk this matter of slavery over with them. I would sometimes say to them, I wished I could be as free as they would be when they got to be men. "You will be free as soon as you are twenty-one, *but I am a slave for life!* Have not I as good a right to be free as you have?" These words used to trouble them; they would express for me the liveliest sympathy, and console me with the hope that something would occur by which I might be free.

prudence
(pro͞od′ns) *n. Prudence* is the wise handling of practical matters.

5 I was now about twelve years old, and the thought of being *a slave for life* began to bear heavily upon my heart. Just about this time, I got hold of a book entitled "The Columbian Orator."[4] Every opportunity I got, I used to read this book. Among much of other interesting matter, I found in it a dialogue between a master and his slave. The slave was represented as having run away from his master three times. The dialogue represented the conversation which took place between them, when the slave was retaken the third time. In this dialogue, the whole argument in behalf of slavery was brought forward by the master, all of which was disposed of by the slave. The slave was made to say some very smart as well as impressive things in reply to his master—things which had the desired though unexpected effect; for the conversation resulted in the voluntary emancipation of the slave on the part of the master.

ANALYZE STRUCTURE

Annotate: In paragraphs 5 and 6, mark details about the texts Douglass read at age 12 that were especially important to him.

Cause/Effect: What effect did reading these texts have on Douglass?

[4] **"The Columbian Orator":** a collection of political essays, poems, and dialogues that were used to teach reading and speaking at the beginning of the 19th century.

unabated
(ŭn´ə-bā´tĭd) *adj.* If something is *unabated,* it keeps its full force without decreasing.

denunciation
(dĭ-nŭn´sē-ā´shən) *n.* A denunciation is the public condemnation of something as wrong or evil.

vindication
(vĭn´dĭ-kā´shən) *n. Vindication* is the evidence or proof that someone's claim is correct.

NOTICE & NOTE
CONTRASTS AND CONTRADICTIONS

When you notice a sharp contrast between what you would expect and what you observe the character doing, you've found a **Contrasts and Contradictions** signpost.

Notice & Note: Douglass went to great lengths to teach himself how to read. In paragraph 6, mark the feelings he had after learning to read.

Infer: Why would Douglass feel this way?

ESSENTIAL QUESTION:
What will people risk to be free?

Review your annotations and notes. Then, add relevant details to your Response Log.

6 In the same book, I met with one of Sheridan's mighty speeches on and in behalf of Catholic emancipation.[5] These were choice documents to me. I read them over and over again with **unabated** interest. They gave tongue to interesting thoughts of my own soul, which had frequently flashed through my mind, and died away for want of utterance. The moral which I gained from the dialogue was the power of truth over the conscience of even a slaveholder. What I got from Sheridan was a bold **denunciation** of slavery, and a powerful **vindication** of human rights. The reading of these documents enabled me to utter my thoughts, and to meet the arguments brought forward to sustain slavery; but while they relieved me of one difficulty, they brought on another even more painful than the one of which I was relieved. The more I read, the more I was led to abhor and detest my enslavers. I could regard them in no other light than a band of successful robbers, who had left their homes, and gone to Africa, and stolen us from our homes, and in a strange land reduced us to slavery. I loathed them as being the meanest as well as the most wicked of men. As I read and contemplated the subject, behold! that very discontentment which Master Hugh had predicted would follow my learning to read had already come, to torment and sting my soul to unutterable anguish. As I writhed under it, I would at times feel that learning to read had been a curse rather than a blessing. It had given me a view of my wretched condition, without the remedy. It opened my eyes to the horrible pit, but to no ladder upon which to get out. In moments of agony, I envied my fellow-slaves for their stupidity. I have often wished myself a beast. I preferred the condition of the meanest reptile to my own. Anything, no matter what, to get rid of thinking! It was this everlasting thinking of my condition that tormented me. There was no getting rid of it. It was pressed upon me by every object within sight or hearing, animate or inanimate. The silver trump of freedom had roused my soul to eternal wakefulness. Freedom now appeared, to disappear no more forever. It was heard in every sound, and seen in every thing. It was ever present to torment me with a sense of my wretched condition. I saw nothing without seeing it, I heard nothing without hearing it, and felt nothing without feeling it. It looked from every star, it smiled in every calm, breathed in every wind, and moved in every storm.

[5] **one of Sheridan's mighty speeches on and in behalf of Catholic emancipation:** Richard Brinsley Sheridan (1751–1816) was an Irish playwright and politician who made speeches about the rights of Roman Catholics in Britain and Ireland.

TURN AND TALK

Turn to a partner and discuss why Douglass comes to think of the ability to read as a curse, even after working so hard to learn how.

Assessment Practice

Answer these questions before moving on to the **Analyze the Text** section on the following page.

1. In paragraph 2, why does Douglass first describe his mistress as "a kind and tender-hearted woman"?

Ⓐ to contrast with her later, cruel behavior

Ⓑ to show how much he wanted to learn to read

Ⓒ to prove that some slaveholders were caring

Ⓓ to emphasize his good fortune

2. This question has two parts. First answer **Part A**. Then, answer **Part B**.

Part A

According to this excerpt from Douglass's autobiography, what point of view did he develop from his reading?

Ⓐ an appreciation for the actions of his master and mistress

Ⓑ an understanding that people are cruel by nature

Ⓒ a conviction that slavery is a terrible violation of human rights

Ⓓ a desire to teach other enslaved people how to read

Part B

Which sentence from the excerpt best supports the answer to Part A?

Ⓐ "She at first lacked the depravity indispensable to shutting me up in mental darkness." (paragraph 1)

Ⓑ "Mistress, in teaching me the alphabet, had given me the inch, and no precaution could prevent me from taking the *ell*." (paragraph 3)

Ⓒ "With their kindly aid, obtained at different times and in different places, I finally succeeded in learning to read." (paragraph 4)

Ⓓ "It had given me a view of my wretched condition, without the remedy." (paragraph 6)

Ed Test-Taking Strategies

Analyze the Text

Support your responses with evidence from the text.

NOTICE & NOTE

Review what you noticed and noted as you read the text. Your annotations can help you answer these questions.

1. **ANALYZE** What **Contrasts and Contradictions** do you notice in the behavior of Douglass's mistress? How does Douglass explain the change in her character?

2. **CAUSE/EFFECT** Reread paragraphs 2–3 and complete the rows shown in the cause/effect chart. Did the mistress's initial kindness or her eventual cruelty have a greater effect on Frederick Douglass? Explain.

CAUSE	EFFECT
Mistress's Kindness	
Mistress's Cruelty	

3. **INTERPRET** In paragraph 4, Douglass uses figurative language when he refers to "that more valuable bread of knowledge." In what way is knowledge "bread"?

4. **EVALUATE** In paragraph 6, what words reveal Douglass's point of view regarding slaveholders?

5. **ANALYZE** What is Douglass's purpose for writing? Identify three passages that help him achieve his goal, and explain how.

PASSAGE FROM THE TEXT	HOW IT ACHIEVES DOUGLASS'S PURPOSE

6. **INTERPRET** In paragraph 6, Douglass says, "I have often wished myself a beast." What point do you think Douglass is making when he uses the word *beast* here?

Choices

Here are some other ways to demonstrate your understanding of the ideas in this lesson.

Writing

Literary Analysis

In one to three paragraphs, explain how the tone of Douglass's autobiography helps him achieve his purpose and communicate his message.

- Think about the author's purpose for writing.
- Identify the **tone**—the writer's attitude toward his subject. Find examples where Douglass's choice of words helps establish the tone.
- When you write, begin by stating your view. Then support that view with evidence from the text.

As you write and discuss, be sure to use the **Academic Vocabulary** words.

- **access**
- **civil**
- **demonstrate**
- **document**
- **symbolize**

Media

Create a Graphic Adaptation

With a partner or a small group, create a graphic novel that depicts an experience Douglass describes in his autobiography.

- Work together to decide which part of the text you will adapt.
- Make a list of details from the text to include in your adaptation.
- Draw images for your graphic novel or search for images online.
- Use digital tools to finalize and publish your graphic novel.

Social & Emotional Learning

Discuss with a Small Group

In paragraph 6, Douglass says, "I would at times feel that learning to read had been a curse rather than a blessing."

- With a small group, discuss Douglass's statement and examine whether people today might share his attitude.
- Be sure to support your views with evidence from the autobiography.
- During your discussion, listen closely and respectfully to all ideas.

Expand Your Vocabulary

PRACTICE AND APPLY

Use what you know about the vocabulary words to answer the following questions.

1. If an innocent convict receives **vindication,** will he feel relieved or upset?
2. Which demonstrates **prudence,** studying a little each day or waiting until the night before the test to begin studying?
3. To **commence** baking a cake, would you stir the batter or study the recipe?
4. Which is a type of **denunciation,** praise or criticism?
5. Would you feel **apprehension** about taking a test or getting an A?
6. If your interest in Frederick Douglass is **unabated,** will you read many books about him or just one?

Vocabulary Strategy

Connotation and Denotation

Words may have similar **denotations,** or dictionary definitions, but they can have very different **connotations,** the feelings or ideas associated with words. For example, *determined* has a positive connotation while *stubborn* has a negative one. Read this example from paragraph 4 of Frederick Douglass's autobiography.

> The bread I used to bestow upon the hungry little urchins, who, in return, would give me that more valuable bread of knowledge.

The use of *urchins* adds a very different feeling to the sentence than other words Douglass could have used, such as *children* or *kids.* By choosing to use *urchins,* he provides readers with a more a vivid picture of how he learned to read on the streets.

Ed

Interactive Vocabulary Lesson: Denotation and Connotation

PRACTICE AND APPLY

Explain how the meaning of each sentence would change if the underlined words were replaced by the words in parentheses.

1. The children smiled at the new student. (smirked)
2. She has an intense desire for knowledge. (a fierce)
3. The student rarely turned in late work. (sometimes)
4. I finally got the help I needed in school. (received)

Watch Your Language!

Infinitives and Infinitive Phrases

Ed
Interactive Grammar Lesson: Infinitives and Infinitive Phrases

An **infinitive** is a verb form that usually begins with *to* and functions as a noun, an adjective, or an adverb. An **infinitive phrase** consists of an infinitive plus its modifiers and complements.

In this example from his autobiography (paragraph 3), Douglass uses two infinitive phrases as adverbs. The first one modifies the adjective *sure*; the second one modifies the verb *called*.

> . . . I was sure to be suspected of having a book, and was at once called to give an account of myself.

Look at these examples of the uses of infinitives and infinitive phrases:

USE OF INFINITIVE	EXAMPLES
As a noun	**To read was young Douglass's great desire.** (subject) **The mistress grew suspicious and started to watch him carefully.** (direct object) **Douglass had no choice but to look for help elsewhere.** (object of a preposition)
As an adjective	**Douglass thought of some local boys to ask.** (modifies a noun) **Could he find anyone to teach him?** (modifies a pronoun)
As an adverb	**To attract neighborhood boys, he carried bread.** (modifies a verb) **Many boys were happy to help Douglass in exchange for some bread.** (modifies an adjective) **He soon read well enough to understand Sheridan's book.** (modifies an adverb)

PRACTICE AND APPLY

Identify the infinitive or infinitive phrase in each sentence. Tell whether it is used as a noun, an adjective, or an adverb.

1. Douglass often spoke to his friends about his right to be free.
2. They tried to offer him comfort, but what more could they do?
3. Then Douglass found Sheridan's book, which included many speeches for readers to study.
4. The reasoning in these speeches was too powerful to ignore.
5. It spoke to Douglass's heart and gave him the help he needed to form an argument against slavery.

The Drummer Boy of Shiloh

Historical Fiction by **Ray Bradbury**

ESSENTIAL QUESTION:
What will people risk to be free?

Engage Your Brain

Choose one or more of these activities to start connecting with the story you are about to read.

Night Before Battle

Imagine being camped out with an army on the night before a major battle. What would you think about? How would you feel? Write a paragraph from the perspective of a soldier preparing to fight the next day.

The Heart of the Army

What was the role of the drummer boy on the battlefield? Do some research to find out more about why drummer boys were used and what duties they performed. Record your findings in the space below.

Analyze Setting

Every story has a **setting,** the time and place in which the action occurs. Setting is usually a key aspect in works of **historical fiction.** These are stories that take place in the past and include characters that may be based on real people, plot developments that reflect real events, and details that are historically accurate. These story elements—characters, plot, and setting—work together to convey **themes,** or lessons about life or human nature.

As you read, pay special attention to details about the setting. Consider how the setting works with other story elements.

Focus on Genre

Historical Fiction

- includes the basic elements of fiction—setting, characters, plot, conflict, and theme
- is set in the past
- includes real places and historical events, along with events from the author's imagination
- has characters based on real people from history

Analyze Literary Devices

Literary devices are techniques authors use to create engaging works of literature. Some examples of literary devices are imagery (language that appeals to the senses) and figurative language (words and phrases that communicate meaning beyond the literal meanings of the words). Study the definitions and examples from "The Drummer Boy of Shiloh" in the chart below.

LITERARY DEVICE	EXAMPLE
Simile: a figurative comparison of two unlike things using the words *like* or *as*	bayonets fixed like eternal lightning (paragraph 10)
Imagery: descriptive language that re-creates sensory experiences for the reader	He smelled as all fathers should smell, of salt sweat, ginger tobacco, horse and boot leather, and the earth he walked upon. (paragraph 22)
Symbol: a person, place, object, or activity that stands for something beyond itself	The General stopped and made a little pile of winter leaves and twigs in the darkness.... (paragraph 38)
Allusion: a reference to a famous person, place, event, or work of literature	"Good grief, that has a beat and sound to it fitting for Mr. Longfellow." (paragraph 52)

As you read, look for other examples of Bradbury's use of literary devices and consider the impact of these techniques on the meaning of the text.

Annotation in Action

Here are one reader's comments on the setting of the story. As you read, mark other ways the author describes the setting.

In the April night, more than once, blossoms fell from the orchard trees and lit with rustling taps on the drumskin. At midnight a peach stone left miraculously on a branch through winter, flicked by a bird, fell swift and unseen, struck once, like panic, which jerked the boy upright. . . .

setting—in an orchard, during the spring, at midnight

Expand Your Vocabulary

Put a check mark next to the vocabulary words that you feel comfortable using when speaking or writing.

solemn	☐
askew	☐
strewn	☐
legitimately	☐
resolute	☐
muted	☐

Turn to a partner and talk about the words you already know. Then, use as many words as you can in a paragraph about a Civil War battle.

As you read "The Drummer Boy of Shiloh," use the definitions in the side column to learn the vocabulary words you don't already know.

Background

Though **Ray Bradbury** (1920–2012) is best known as a science fiction writer, he also wrote plays, mysteries, fantasies, realistic stories, and novels. In this story, Bradbury tells about a drummer boy on the night before the Battle of Shiloh in the Civil War. This two-day battle began on April 6, 1862, near the southwestern Tennessee church from which the bloody clash takes its name. More than 23,000 soldiers were killed or wounded. At that time, it was the bloodiest battle in American history.

The Drummer Boy of Shiloh

Historical Fiction by **Ray Bradbury**

On the eve of battle, a fearful drummer boy has an unexpected encounter.

NOTICE & NOTE
As you read, use the side margins to make notes about the text.

1 In the April night, more than once, blossoms fell from the orchard trees and lit with rustling taps on the drumskin. At midnight a peach stone left miraculously on a branch through winter, flicked by a bird, fell swift and unseen, struck once, like panic, which jerked the boy upright. In silence he listened to his own heart ruffle away, away, at last gone from his ears and back in his chest again.

2 After that, he turned the drum on its side, where its great lunar[1] face peered at him whenever he opened his eyes.

3 His face, alert or at rest, was **solemn**. It was indeed a solemn time and a solemn night for a boy just turned fourteen in the peach field near the Owl Creek not far from the church at Shiloh.

4 ". . . thirty-one, thirty-two, thirty-three . . ."

solemn
(sŏl′əm) *adj.* If an event is *solemn*, it is deeply serious.

[1] **lunar** (lo͞o′nər): of or relating to the moon.

askew
(ə-skyōō´) *adj.* When something is *askew*, it is off center.

strewn
(strōōn) *adj.* Something *strewn* is spread here and there, or scattered.

ANALYZE LITERARY DEVICES

Annotate: In paragraph 6, mark two phrases that make a figurative comparison between soldiers and meat that is being cooked (a metaphor).

Interpret: How is this language meant to affect readers?

Ed

Close Read Screencast

Listen to a modeled close read of this text.

5 Unable to see, he stopped counting.

6 Beyond the thirty-three familiar shadows, forty thousand men, exhausted by nervous expectation, unable to sleep for romantic dreams of battles yet unfought, lay crazily **askew** in their uniforms. A mile yet farther on, another army was **strewn** helter-skelter, turning slow, basting themselves with the thought of what they would do when the time came: a leap, a yell, a blind plunge their strategy, raw youth their protection and benediction.[2]

7 Now and again the boy heard a vast wind come up, that gently stirred the air. But he knew what it was, the army here, the army there, whispering to itself in the dark. Some men talking to others, others murmuring to themselves, and all so quiet it was like a natural element arisen from south or north with the motion of the earth toward dawn.

8 What the men whispered the boy could only guess, and he guessed that it was: Me, I'm the one, I'm the one of all the rest won't die. I'll live through it. I'll go home. The band will play. And I'll be there to hear it.

9 Yes, thought the boy, that's all very well for them, they can give as good as they get!

10 For with the careless bones of the young men harvested by night and bindled[3] around campfires were the similarly strewn steel bones of their rifles, with bayonets fixed like eternal lightning lost in the orchard grass.

11 Me, thought the boy, I got only a drum, two sticks to beat it, and no shield.

12 There wasn't a man-boy on this ground tonight did not have a shield he cast, riveted or carved himself on his way to his first attack, compounded of remote but nonetheless firm and fiery family devotion, flag-blown patriotism and cocksure immortality strengthened by the touchstone of very real gunpowder, ramrod, minnieball and flint.[4] But without these last the boy felt his family move yet farther off away in the dark, as if one of those great prairie-burning trains had chanted them away never to return, leaving him with this drum which was worse than a toy in the game to be played tomorrow or some day much too soon.

13 The boy turned on his side. A moth brushed his face, but it was peach blossom. A peach blossom flicked him, but it was a moth. Nothing stayed put. Nothing had a name. Nothing was as it once was.

[2] **benediction** (bĕn´ĭ-dĭk´shən): a blessing.
[3] **bindled:** fastened or wrapped by encircling, as with a belt.
[4] **ramrod, minnieball, and flint:** items used to fire a rifle.

14 If he lay very still, when the dawn came up and the soldiers put on their bravery with their caps, perhaps they might go away, the war with them, and not notice him lying small here, no more than a toy himself.

15 "Well, by God, now," said a voice.

16 The boy shut up his eyes, to hide inside himself, but it was too late. Someone, walking by in the night, stood over him.

17 "Well," said the voice quietly, "here's a soldier crying *before* the fight. Good. Get it over. Won't be time once it all starts."

18 And the voice was about to move on when the boy, startled, touched the drum at his elbow. The man above, hearing this, stopped. The boy could feel his eyes, sense him slowly bending near. A hand must have come down out of the night, for there was a little rat-tat as the fingernails brushed and the man's breath fanned his face.

19 "Why, it's the drummer boy, isn't it?"

20 The boy nodded, not knowing if his nod was seen. "Sir, is that *you?*" he said.

21 "I assume it is." The man's knees cracked as he bent still closer.

22 He smelled as all fathers should smell, of salt sweat, ginger tobacco, horse and boot leather, and the earth he walked upon. He had many eyes. No, not eyes, brass buttons that watched the boy.

23 He could only be, and was, the General.

24 "What's your name, boy?" he asked.

25 "Joby," whispered the boy, starting to sit up.

26 "All right, Joby, don't stir." A hand pressed his chest gently, and the boy relaxed. "How long you been with us, Joby?"

27 "Three weeks, sir."

28 "Run off from home or joined **legitimately,** boy?"

29 Silence.

30 "Damn-fool question," said the General. "Do you shave yet, boy? Even more of a damn-fool. There's your cheek, fell right off the tree overhead. And the others here not much older. Raw, raw, damn raw, the lot of you. You ready for tomorrow or the next day, Joby?"

31 "I think so, sir."

32 "You want to cry some more, go on ahead. I did the same last night."

33 "*You,* sir?"

34 "God's truth. Thinking of everything ahead. Both sides figuring the other side will just give up, and soon, and the war done in weeks, and us all home. Well, that's not how it's going to be. And maybe that's why I cried."

Don't forget to **Notice & Note** as you read the text.

legitimately
(lə-jĭt´ə-mĭt-lē) *adv.* When you do something *legitimately,* you do it lawfully.

ANALYZE SETTING

Annotate: In paragraph 34, mark what the General says is a possible explanation for his tears.

Infer: How does the General's comment relate to the story's historical setting? What broader theme about people or about life is suggested by his comment?

35 "Yes, sir," said Joby.

36 The General must have taken out a cigar now, for the dark was suddenly filled with the Indian smell of tobacco unlit as yet, but chewed as the man thought what next to say.

37 "It's going to be a crazy time," said the General. "Counting both sides, there's a hundred thousand men, give or take a few thousand out there tonight, not one as can spit a sparrow off a tree, or knows a horse clod from a minnieball. Stand up, bare the breast, ask to be a target, thank them and sit down, that's us, that's them. We should turn tail and train four months, they should do the same. But here we are, taken with spring fever and thinking it blood lust, taking our sulphur with cannons instead of with molasses[5] as it should be, going to be a hero, going to live forever. And I can see all of them over there nodding agreement, save the other way around. It's wrong, boy, it's wrong as a head put on hind side front and a man marching backward through life. It will be a double

[5] **taking our sulphur with cannons instead of with molasses:** Sulphur was an ingredient in gunpowder that was used to fire cannons; at that time sulphur was also used as a tonic or medical treatment. Molasses is a thick, brown syrup, used to mask the unpleasant taste of medicines.

massacre if one of their itchy generals decides to picnic his lads on our grass. More innocents will get shot out of pure Cherokee enthusiasm than ever got shot before. Owl Creek was full of boys splashing around in the noonday sun just a few hours ago. I fear it will be full of boys again, just floating, at sundown tomorrow, not caring where the tide takes them."

38 The General stopped and made a little pile of winter leaves and twigs in the darkness, as if he might at any moment strike fire to them to see his way through the coming days when the sun might not show its face because of what was happening here and just beyond.

39 The boy watched the hand stirring the leaves and opened his lips to say something, but did not say it. The General heard the boy's breath and spoke himself.

40 "Why am I telling you this? That's what you wanted to ask, eh? Well, when you got a bunch of wild horses on a loose rein somewhere, somehow you got to bring order, rein them in. These lads, fresh out of the milkshed, don't know what I know, and I can't tell them: men actually die, in war. So each is his own army. I got to make *one* army of them. And for that, boy, I need you."

41 "Me!" The boy's lips barely twitched.

42 "Now, boy," said the General quietly, "you are the heart of the army. Think of that. You're the heart of the army. Listen, now."

43 And, lying there, Joby listened.

44 And the General spoke on.

45 If he, Joby, beat slow tomorrow, the heart would beat slow in the men. They would lag by the wayside.[6] They would drowse in the fields on their muskets. They would sleep forever, after that, in those same fields, their hearts slowed by a drummer boy and stopped by enemy lead.

46 But if he beat a sure, steady, ever faster rhythm, then, then their knees would come up in a long line down over that hill, one knee after the other, like a wave on the ocean shore! Had he seen the ocean ever? Seen the waves rolling in like a well-ordered cavalry charge to the sand? Well, that was it, that's what he wanted, that's what was needed! Joby was his right hand and his left. He gave the orders, but Joby set the pace!

47 So bring the right knee up and the right foot out and the left knee up and the left foot out. One following the other in good time, in brisk time. Move the blood up the body and make the head proud and the spine stiff and the jaw **resolute.**

[6] **lag by the wayside:** fall behind.

VOCABULARY

Figures of Speech: In paragraph 37, the phrase "a head put on hind side front and a man marching backward through life" is a figure of speech, which is not meant to be taken literally. When you don't know what a figure of speech means, try using context clues to infer its meaning.

Interpret: What does the author's use of this phrase suggest about the General's thoughts about the upcoming battle?

NOTICE & NOTE

WORDS OF THE WISER

When you notice a wiser character giving advice about life to the main character, you've found a **Words of the Wiser** signpost.

Notice & Note: Read paragraphs 42–52. Then mark the main ideas in the advice that the General gives Joby.

Analyze: What's the life lesson and how might it affect Joby?

resolute
(rĕz´ə-lo͞ot´) *adj*. If you are *resolute*, you are firm or determined.

Text in Focus Video

Learn how to visualize the text.

Focus the eye and set the teeth, flare the nostrils and tighten the hands, put steel armor all over the men, for blood moving fast in them does indeed make men feel as if they'd put on steel. He must keep at it, at it! Long and steady, steady and long! Then, even though shot or torn, those wounds got in hot blood—in blood he'd helped stir—would feel less pain. If their blood was cold, it would be more than slaughter, it would be murderous nightmare and pain best not told and no one to guess.

48 The General spoke and stopped, letting his breath slack off. Then, after a moment, he said, "So there you are, that's it. Will you do that, boy? Do you know now you're general of the army when the General's left behind?"

49 The boy nodded mutely.

50 "You'll run them through for me then, boy?"

51 "Yes, sir."

52 "Good. And, God willing, many nights from tonight, many years from now, when you're as old or far much older than me, when they ask you what you did in this awful time, you will tell them—one part humble and one part proud—'I was the drummer boy at the battle of Owl Creek,' or the Tennessee River, or maybe they'll just name it after the church there. 'I was the drummer boy at Shiloh.' Good grief, that has a beat and sound to it fitting for Mr. Longfellow. 'I was the drummer boy at Shiloh.' Who will ever hear those words and not know you, boy, or what you thought this night, or what you'll think tomorrow or the next day when we must get up on our legs and *move!*"

53 The general stood up. "Well, then. God bless you, boy. Good night."

54 "Good night, sir."

55 And, tobacco, brass, boot polish, salt sweat and leather, the man moved away through the grass.

56 Joby lay for a moment, staring but unable to see where the man had gone.

57 He swallowed. He wiped his eyes. He cleared his throat.

58 He settled himself. Then, at last, very slowly and firmly, he turned the drum so that it faced up toward the sky.

59 He lay next to it, his arm around it, feeling the tremor, the touch, the **muted** thunder as, all the rest of the April night in the year 1862, near the Tennessee River, not far from the Owl Creek, very close to the church named Shiloh, the peach blossoms fell on the drum.

muted
(myo͞o′tĭd) *adj.* When something is *muted,* it is softened or muffled.

TURN AND TALK

With a partner, have a discussion about whether the boy regrets his decision to join the army once he realizes what war is like.

ESSENTIAL QUESTION:

What will people risk to be free?

Review your annotations and notes. Then, add relevant details to your Response Log.

Assessment Practice

Answer these questions before moving on to the **Analyze the Text** section on the following page.

1. This question has two parts. First, answer **Part A**. Then, answer **Part B**.

Part A

How does the General describe Joby?

- (A) as "a hero, going to live forever" (paragraph 37)
- (B) as part of "a bunch of wild horses on a loose rein" (paragraph 40)
- (C) as one of the "lads, fresh out of the milkshed" (paragraph 40)
- (D) as "the heart of the army" (paragraph 42)

Part B

Why does he refer to Joby in this way?

- (A) Joby has been resistant to military training.
- (B) Joby's battle position is in the middle of the action.
- (C) Joby's drumbeat sets the pace for the battle.
- (D) Joby is too young for legitimate military service.

2. How does Joby feel at the end of the story?

- (A) He misses his father even more than before.
- (B) He feels ready to face the next battle.
- (C) He is overwhelmed by the task before him.
- (D) He is confident that he is the most important soldier.

Ed

Test-Taking Strategies

Analyze the Text

Support your responses with evidence from the text.

NOTICE & NOTE

Review what you **noticed and noted** as you read the text. Your annotations can help you answer these questions.

1. **CITE EVIDENCE** What imagery does the author use to describe the General in paragraph 22? What is the effect of such imagery in a work of historical fiction?

2. **CONNECT** In paragraphs 12 and 14, Bradbury uses figurative language to compare the drummer boy and his drum to toys. What does the repetition of this comparison emphasize about Joby and his role in the upcoming battle?

FIGURATIVE COMPARISON	YOUR ANALYSIS
But without these last the boy felt his family move yet farther off away in the dark, as if one of those great prairie-burning trains had chanted them away never to return, leaving him with this drum which was worse than a toy in the game to be played tomorrow or some day much too soon. (paragraph 12)	
If he lay very still, when the dawn came up and the soldiers put on their bravery with their caps, perhaps they might go away, the war with them, and not notice him lying small here, no more than a toy himself. (paragraph 14)	

3. **INTERPRET** What do the peach blossoms symbolize in this story? Explain how this symbol contributes to the meaning of the story.

4. **ANALYZE** Henry Wadsworth Longfellow was a popular American author who wrote "Paul Revere's Ride" and other works immortalizing early American history. Locate the allusion to him in paragraph 52. How is that allusion meant to affect Joby?

5. **DRAW CONCLUSIONS** What would you say is the theme of "The Drummer Boy of Shiloh"? Why do you think so?

6. **PREDICT** How will the **Words of the Wiser** that the General gives to Joby about his role in the next day's battle most likely affect Joby?

Choices

Here are some other ways to demonstrate your understanding of the ideas in this lesson.

Writing
Report

Write a report about how the General would have been influenced by the historical setting in which he lived.

- Research soldiers' experiences fighting battles during the Civil War.
- Make inferences about how the General would have been affected by his experiences.
- Write a report that combines historical facts with your inferences about the General.

As you write and discuss, be sure to use the **Academic Vocabulary** words.

- **access**
- **civil**
- **demonstrate**
- **document**
- **symbolize**

Research
The Battle of Shiloh

Want to learn more about the historical events that inspired Ray Bradbury to write "The Drummer Boy of Shiloh"? Research the Battle of Shiloh and its historical importance.

- What did the Union army hope to achieve by fighting this battle in Tennessee?
- Why did the battle begin sooner than the army expected?
- How were the Union and Confederate armies affected by the battle's outcome?

Speaking & Listening
Dramatize a Scene

Working with a partner, act out the scene in which the General discusses Joby's fears and his role in the coming battle.

- Discuss the General's motivation for the conversation, and draw conclusions about how that might affect the way he speaks.
- Make a script with the dialogue each character will speak. Note movements, gestures, and facial expressions that will bring the scene to life.
- Practice your scene. Then perform it for the class.

Expand Your Vocabulary

PRACTICE AND APPLY

Use your understanding of the vocabulary words to answer each question.

1. When did you have to act in a **resolute** way to face a challenge?
2. When did you **legitimately** claim that someone owed you something?
3. When might things be **strewn** across a room? Why?
4. When would you need to be **solemn** in a group of people?
5. When has your response to news been **muted**?
6. When has your hat been **askew** on your head?

Vocabulary Strategy

Interpret Figures of Speech

A **figure of speech** is a word or phrase that communicates meanings beyond its literal meaning. **Idioms,** or expressions in which the entire phrase means something different from the words in it, are a figure of speech. Read this idiom from the story.

> These lads, fresh out of the milkshed, don't know what I know, and I can't tell them. . . .

You can use nearby words and phrases, or **context,** to help you understand that "fresh out of the milkshed" implies that not long ago these lads were farm hands milking cows. The phrase "don't know what I know" helps you understand that the General is expressing concern that his soldiers lack battle experience.

Ed

Interactive Vocabulary Lesson: Using Context Clues

PRACTICE AND APPLY

Use context to explain each underlined figure of speech below.

1. "Yes, thought the boy, that's all very well for them, they can give as good as they get! . . . Me, thought the boy, I got only a drum, two sticks to beat it, and no shield."
2. "There's a hundred thousand men, . . . not one as can spit a sparrow off a tree, or knows a horse clod from a minnieball. . . . We should turn tail and train four months. . . ."
3. "He might . . . strike fire to them to see his way through the coming days when the sun might not show its face. . . ."

Watch Your Language!

Indicative Mood

The **mood** of a verb shows the speaker's attitude toward what is being said. There are several moods for verbs.

MOOD	EXAMPLES
The **indicative mood** is used to state a fact. Most sentences are statements of fact in the indicative mood.	**As he lay there, blossoms fell from the orchard trees.**
The **imperative mood** is used for a command or request.	**Make the blossoms fall from the trees.**
The **subjunctive mood** expresses a recommendation, a hypothetical, or a condition that is contrary to facts.	**If the wind were to blow, the blossoms would fall from the trees.**

Notice how Ray Bradbury uses the indicative mood for effect. Read aloud these sentences from the story and hear how the statements of fact express difficult truths about the uncertainty of battle:

> The boy turned on his side. A moth brushed his face, but it was peach blossom. A peach blossom flicked him, but it was a moth. Nothing stayed put. Nothing had a name. Nothing was as it once was. . . .

PRACTICE AND APPLY

Rewrite each sentence using the indicative mood.

1. I hope we have not lost the document that proves we own this land.
2. Stop crying and do something useful!
3. Try to get some sleep before the sun comes up.
4. If the troops guard the camp, everyone will be safer.
5. Don't charge until I give the order.

And remember—no more subjunctives where the correct mood is indicative.

O Captain! My Captain!

Poem by **Walt Whitman**

ESSENTIAL QUESTION:
What will people risk to be free?

Engage Your Brain

Choose one or more of these activities to start connecting with the poem you're about to read.

The Good Gray Poet

Walt Whitman is one of the greatest American poets in history. Do some research on Whitman. Find facts about

- jobs he held throughout his life
- his most famous poems and publications
- his visits to military hospitals during the Civil War

Best Captain Ever

Whitman's poem compares President Lincoln to a ship captain. What kinds of qualities does a good captain have? Have a discussion with a classmate to share your ideas.

Analyze Figurative Language

One way poets help readers understand things in new ways is by using **figurative language,** or imaginative descriptions that are not literally true. A **metaphor** is a type of figurative language in which an author compares two things that are basically dissimilar but have some quality or qualities in common. Unlike a simile, a metaphor does not use the word *like* or *as*. In an **extended metaphor,** this comparison is developed at length.

An extended metaphor may continue, or extend, through several lines or stanzas or throughout the entire poem. In "O Captain! My Captain!" Whitman uses an extended metaphor to express his feelings about President Lincoln and the Civil War.

Read the poem to determine what is being compared. Also consider the poet's purpose in using the extended metaphor. Use a chart like this one to record your ideas.

Focus on Genre

Lyric Poetry

- is usually short and conveys strong emotions
- uses first-person point of view to express the speaker's thoughts and feelings
- often uses repetition and rhyme to create a melodic quality
- includes many forms, such as sonnets, odes, and elegies

QUESTIONS	ANSWERS AND TEXT EVIDENCE
What two things are compared in the extended metaphor?	
What effect does the extended metaphor have?	

Analyze Poetry

"O Captain! My Captain!" is an elegy. An **elegy** is a poem in which the speaker reflects on someone's death. Elegies often pay tribute to someone who has recently died.

Most elegies have formal, dignified language and a serious **tone,** which is the writer's attitude toward the subject. The serious tone may express sorrow and grief, praise for the person who has died, and comforting thoughts or ideas. Tone often can be determined by looking at the writer's word choices, especially those words with strong **connotations,** or the feelings and ideas that a word suggests beyond its dictionary meaning.

As you read "O Captain! My Captain!," identify words and phrases that praise President Lincoln's greatness and show the speaker's feelings.

Annotation in Action

Here is how one reader commented on the figurative language in the poem. As you read, mark details that develop an extended metaphor involving President Lincoln.

O Captain! my Captain! our fearful trip is done,
The ship has weather'd every rack, the prize we sought is won,
The port is near, the bells I hear, the people all exulting,
While follow eyes the steady keel, the vessel grim and daring:

Is the poem really about a ship? What could be compared to a "fearful trip"?

Background

Walt Whitman (1819–1892) was a great admirer of President Lincoln. After the president was assassinated, Whitman wrote "O Captain! My Captain!" to capture the sense of tragedy that descended upon the country. Largely unknown to the public when he wrote this poem, Whitman eventually gained a reputation as one of the greatest American writers. His book of poems *Leaves of Grass* is considered a masterpiece of American literature.

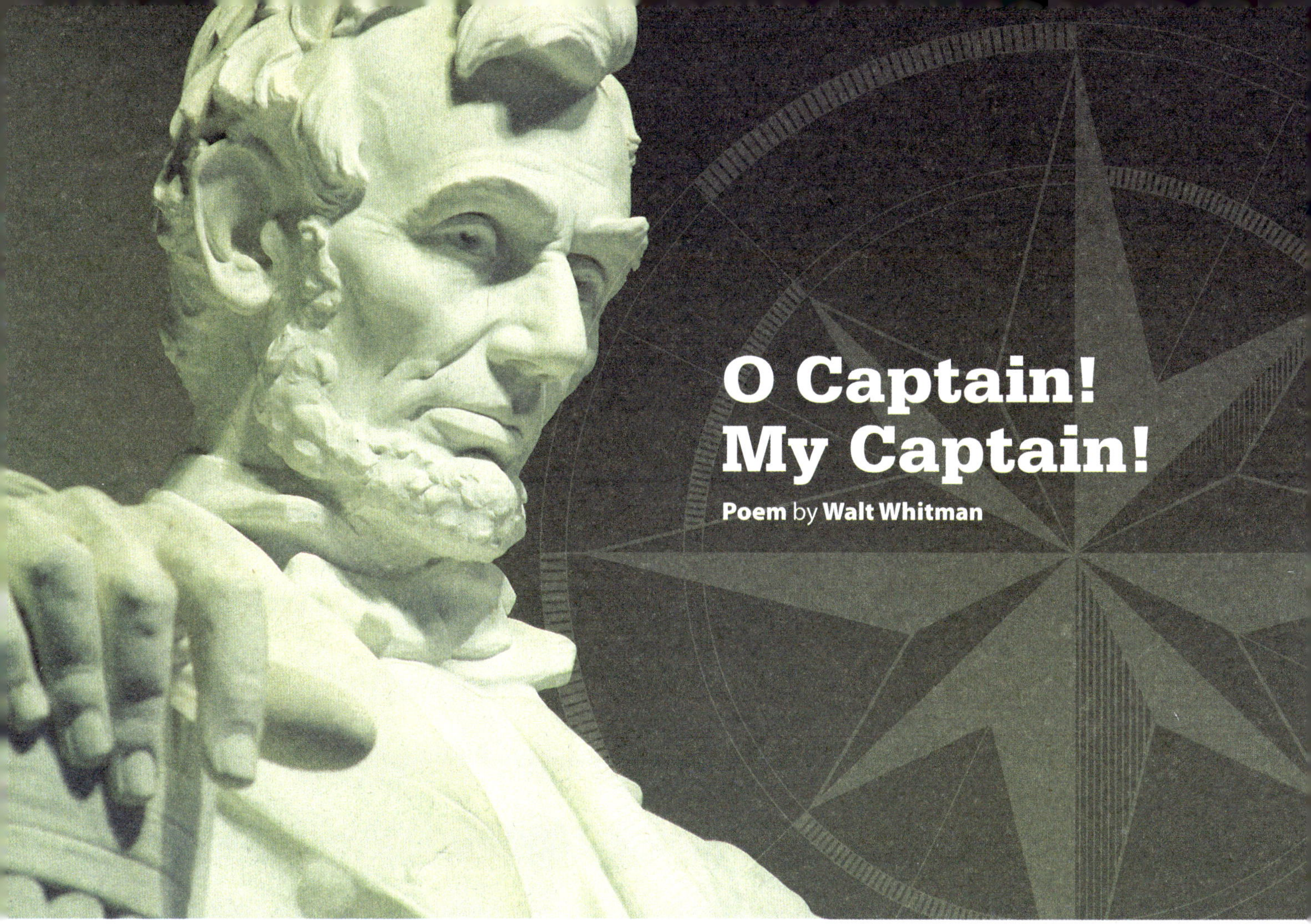

O Captain! My Captain!

Poem by **Walt Whitman**

NOTICE & NOTE
As you read, use the side margins to make notes about the text.

The speaker of this poem shares his feelings of sorrow about the death of his "captain."

BACKGROUND

On April 14, 1865, only five days after the Civil War ended, President Abraham Lincoln was assassinated at the Ford Theater in Washington, D.C., where he was watching a performance. Lincoln was shot by John Wilkes Booth, a famous actor and a Confederate sympathizer. Although Booth initially escaped, he was discovered days later by Union soldiers. Booth was killed while trying to avoid capture.

ANALYZE POETRY

Annotate: In lines 1–16, mark words and phrases that express a tone of sorrow and those that express a tone of joy.

Analyze: What is the overall effect on the reader of the language in this elegy?

ANALYZE FIGURATIVE LANGUAGE

Annotate: After reading the poem once, go back and mark details in lines 17–24 that are part of the extended metaphor of a ship's voyage and return.

Draw Conclusions: In the extended metaphor, who is the "Captain," and what is the "fearful trip"?

O Captain! my Captain! our fearful trip is done,
The ship has weather'd every rack,[1] the prize we sought[2] is won,
The port is near, the bells I hear, the people all exulting,
While follow eyes the steady keel,[3] the vessel grim and
daring:
But O heart! heart! heart!
O the bleeding drops of red,
Where on the deck my Captain lies,
Fallen cold and dead.

O Captain! my Captain! rise up and hear the bells;
Rise up—for you the flag is flung[4]—for you the bugle trills,
For you bouquets and ribbon'd wreaths—for you the shores
a-crowding,
For you they call, the swaying mass, their eager faces
turning;
Here Captain! dear father!
This arm beneath your head!
It is some dream that on the deck,
You've fallen cold and dead.

My Captain does not answer, his lips are pale and still,
My father does not feel my arm, he has no pulse nor will,
The ship is anchor'd safe and sound, its voyage closed and
done,
From fearful trip the victor ship comes in with object won;
Exult O shores, and ring O bells!
But I with mournful tread,[5]
Walk the deck my Captain lies,
Fallen cold and dead.

[1] **rack:** a mass of wind-driven clouds.
[2] **sought** (sôt): searched for; tried to gain.
[3] **keel:** the main part of a ship's structure.
[4] **flung:** suddenly put out.
[5] **tread** (trĕd): footsteps

The funeral procession of President Abraham Lincoln

TURN AND TALK

Turn to a classmate and discuss the thoughts and feelings that the poem expresses about the end of the Civil War.

ESSENTIAL QUESTION:

What will people risk to be free?

Review your notes and add your thoughts to your Response Log.

Assessment Practice

Answer these questions before moving on to the **Analyze the Text** section on the next page.

1. Why are "the people all exulting" in line 3?

- (A) The ship has returned with "the prize . . . won."
- (B) The ringing of the bells signals a celebration.
- (C) They don't see that the ship is "grim and daring."
- (D) They aren't aware that the Captain is dead.

2. This question has two parts. First, answer **Part A**, then **Part B**.

Part A

What other name for the Captain does the speaker use?

- (A) "the prize" (line 2)
- (B) "O heart" (line 5)
- (C) "dear father" (line 13)
- (D) "the victor ship" (line 20)

Part B

What was Whitman's likely purpose for choosing this other name for the Captain?

- (A) to create uncertainty about the identity of the Captain
- (B) to suggest that the speaker is the Captain's biological son
- (C) to emphasize the Captain's responsibilities and duties
- (D) to show the speaker's respect and love for the Captain

Ed

Test-Taking Strategies

Analyze the Text

Support your responses with evidence from the text.

NOTICE & NOTE

Review what you **noticed and noted** as you read the text. Your annotations can help you answer these questions.

1. **INTERPRET** Reread lines 1–3 and review the chart you created to record your notes about the extended metaphor of the poem. In Whitman's metaphor, what are the "fearful trip," the "ship," and the "prize" that was won? What is the "port"? Express your response by providing your interpretation of these aspects of the poem.

ELEMENT	WHAT IT REPRESENTS
fearful trip	
ship	
prize	
port	

2. **ANALYZE** What feelings and ideas are suggested by the phrase "weather'd every rack" in line 2?

3. **INFER** When there is a contrast between appearance and reality, a tone of **irony** is created. Why is it ironic that the crowds in this poem are celebrating?

4. **CITE EVIDENCE** How does Whitman express his own grief about Lincoln's death? Cite three specific examples from the poem.

5. **ANALYZE** Reread lines 19–20. What is the meaning of these lines in terms of Whitman's extended metaphor?

Choices

Here are some other ways to demonstrate your understanding of the ideas in this lesson.

Writing
Poem

Write a poem in which you pay tribute to someone you respect or admire, either real or imaginary.

- Decide if you want your poem to be an elegy, a limerick, a sonnet, or some other form.
- Consider creating an extended metaphor that connects to your subject in multiple ways.
- Draft your poem and then read it aloud to find places where you can sharpen the language or improve the rhythm.

As you write and discuss, be sure to use the **Academic Vocabulary** words.

- access
- civil
- demonstrate
- document
- symbolize

Speaking & Listening
Choral Reading

Work with a small group to present a choral reading of "O Captain! My Captain!"

- Reread the poem carefully. As a group, decide how each line should be read. Do the words express sorrow? praise? comfort?
- Decide who will read each line or part of a line. Should some words be read by one speaker? two speakers? the entire group?
- The choices you make should reflect your analysis of the poem. Be prepared to explain your choices.

Social & Emotional Learning
Create a Memorial

There are many ways to honor people—whether they are famous historical figures or people in our own lives. Plan a memorial for someone you want to honor.

- Decide whom to honor. If group members disagree, find ways to compromise or negotiate in order to find a fair resolution.
- Decide what kind of memorial you will create. A monument? A song or painting? A multimedia presentation? Determine how each group member will contribute to creating the memorial.

from

Harriet Tubman: Conductor on the Underground Railroad

Biography by **Ann Petry**

ESSENTIAL QUESTION:
What will people risk to be free?

Engage Your Brain

Choose one or more activities to start connecting with the biography you're about to read.

Not Really a Railroad

Do some research to find out about the Underground Railroad. Jot down answers to the following questions:

- What was the Underground Railroad?
- Who used the Underground Railroad?

Maybe You've Heard of Her

What do you know about Harriet Tubman? Make a list of facts about Harriet Tubman, and then compare lists with a partner.

Keep Moving Forward

Tubman led fugitives for many miles on foot. She had to make sure they kept moving even though they were facing extreme exhaustion and hunger. How do you keep people going when they are ready to give up? Turn to a classmate and share your ideas.

Analyze Biography

A **biography** is a form of nonfiction in which a writer provides a true account of another person's life. In a strong biography, the writer recounts significant events in the subject's life and provides insights about the subject's personality. The way a biographer reveals a subject's personality is called **characterization.** As you read the excerpt from Ann Petry's biography of Harriet Tubman, look for these methods of characterization:

- Direct comments about Tubman—what the author states about Tubman's hopes, worries, opinions, and beliefs
- Tubman's own thoughts, speech, and actions—and what you can infer about her possible **motivations,** or reasons for her actions
- How others behave toward Tubman—and what you can infer about her from their thoughts, speech, and actions toward her

Focus on Genre
Biography

- presents a true and balanced account of a person's life
- is based on multiple credible sources
- is told from the third-person point of view

Analyze Word Choice

Effective writers think carefully about the words they use. They know that **word choice** matters—not only as a way to make writing precise but also as a way to affect readers' emotions and to show the writer's attitude toward the subject (that is, the **tone**). Consider this example from Petry's biography of Harriet Tubman:

> The man who stood in the doorway looked at her coldly, looked with unconcealed astonishment and fear at the eleven disheveled runaways who were standing near her. (paragraph 16)

The author could have written *with surprise*, but instead used the more precise phrase *unconcealed astonishment*, so readers could feel the intensity of the man's reaction. In addition, *coldly* expresses a tone of heartlessness.

Annotation in Action

Here are one reader's notes about characterization. As you read, pay attention to the author's characterization of Harriet Tubman.

Harriet Tubman could have told them that there was far more involved in this matter of running off slaves than signaling the would-be runaways by imitating the call of a whippoorwill, or a hoot owl, far more involved than a matter of waiting for a clear night when the North Star was visible.

The author repeats the phrase "far more involved than" to emphasize that Tubman was very careful and thorough.

Expand Your Vocabulary

Put a check mark next to the vocabulary words that you feel comfortable using when speaking or writing.

- **disheveled** ☐
- **instill** ☐
- **linger** ☐
- **sullen** ☐
- **eloquence** ☐
- **evoke** ☐
- **cajole** ☐

Turn to a partner and talk about the words you already know. Then, write a few sentences about what you know about Harriet Tubman and the Underground Railroad.

As you read the excerpt from *Harriet Tubman: Conductor on the Underground Railroad,* use the definitions in the side column to learn the vocabulary words you don't already know.

Background

Ann Lane Petry (1908–1997) grew up in a small town in Connecticut, where she and her family were the only African American residents. Much of her writing focuses on the important contributions of African Americans. Before the Civil War, many enslaved people fled north to freedom along the Underground Railroad, a secret network of safe houses. One of the Underground Railroad's most famous "conductors" was Harriet Tubman.

from

Harriet Tubman: Conductor on the Underground Railroad

Biography by **Ann Petry**

Harriet Tubman leads eleven fugitives along the Underground Railroad toward Canada and freedom.

NOTICE & NOTE
As you read, use the side margins to make notes about the text.

The Railroad Runs to Canada

1 Along the Eastern Shore of Maryland, in Dorchester County, in Caroline County, the masters kept hearing whispers about the man named Moses, who was running off slaves. At first they did not believe in his existence. The stories about him were fantastic, unbelievable. Yet they watched for him. They offered rewards for his capture.

2 They never saw him. Now and then they heard whispered rumors to the effect that he was in the neighborhood. The woods were searched. The roads were watched. There was never anything to indicate his whereabouts. But a few days afterward, a goodly number of slaves would be gone from the plantation. Neither the master nor the overseer had heard or seen anything

ANALYZE WORD CHOICE

Annotate: In paragraph 1, mark two adjectives that describe "the man named Moses."

Analyze: How do these word choices add to your understanding of the person who was helping enslaved people escape?

unusual in the quarter.[1] Sometimes one or the other would vaguely remember having heard a whippoorwill call somewhere in the woods, close by, late at night. Though it was the wrong season for whippoorwills.

3 Sometimes the masters thought they had heard the cry of a hoot owl, repeated, and would remember having thought that the intervals between the low moaning cry were wrong, that it had been repeated four times in succession instead of three. There was never anything more than that to suggest that all was not well in the quarter. Yet when morning came, they invariably discovered that a group of the finest slaves had taken to their heels.

4 Unfortunately, the discovery was almost always made on a Sunday. Thus a whole day was lost before the machinery of pursuit could be set in motion. The posters offering rewards for the fugitives could not be printed until Monday. The men who made a living hunting for runaway slaves were out of reach, off in the woods with their dogs and their guns, in pursuit of four-footed game, or they were in camp meetings saying their prayers with their wives and families beside them.

ANALYZE BIOGRAPHY

Annotate: Mark details in paragraphs 5–7 that reveal Harriet Tubman's character.

Draw Conclusions: How does the information in these paragraphs differ from the details about "the man named Moses" in paragraphs 1–4? What do these differences suggest about the sources each may have been based on?

5 Harriet Tubman could have told them that there was far more involved in this matter of running off slaves than signaling the would-be runaways by imitating the call of a whippoorwill, or a hoot owl, far more involved than a matter of waiting for a clear night when the North Star was visible.

6 In December, 1851, when she started out with the band of fugitives that she planned to take to Canada, she had been in the vicinity of the plantation for days, planning the trip, carefully selecting the slaves that she would take with her.

7 She had announced her arrival in the quarter by singing the forbidden spiritual—"Go down, Moses, 'way down to Egypt Land"[2]—singing it softly outside the door of a slave cabin, late at night. The husky voice was beautiful even when it was barely more than a murmur borne[3] on the wind.

8 Once she had made her presence known, word of her coming spread from cabin to cabin. The slaves whispered to each other, ear to mouth, mouth to ear, "Moses is here." "Moses has come." "Get ready. Moses is back again." The ones who had agreed to go North with her put ashcake and salt herring in an old bandanna, hastily tied it into a bundle, and then waited patiently for the signal that meant it was time to start.

[1] **quarter:** the area in which enslaved people lived.

[2] **"Go down, Moses, 'way down to Egypt Land":** a line from an African American folk song. In the Bible, Moses led the enslaved Israelites in Egypt to freedom.

[3] **borne:** carried.

9 There were eleven in this party, including one of her brothers and his wife. It was the largest group that she had ever conducted, but she was determined that more and more slaves should know what freedom was like.

10 She had to take them all the way to Canada. The Fugitive Slave Law[4] was no longer a great many incomprehensible words written down on the country's lawbooks. The new law had become a reality. It was Thomas Sims, a boy, picked up on the streets of Boston at night and shipped back to Georgia. It was Jerry and Shadrach, arrested and jailed with no warning.

11 She had never been in Canada. The route beyond Philadelphia was strange to her. But she could not let the runaways who accompanied her know this. As they walked along she told them stories of her own first flight, she kept painting vivid word pictures of what it would be like to be free.

12 But there were so many of them this time. She knew moments of doubt when she was half-afraid, and kept looking back over her shoulder, imagining that she heard the sound of pursuit. They would certainly be pursued. Eleven of them. Eleven thousand dollars' worth of flesh and bone and muscle that belonged to Maryland planters. If they were caught, the eleven runaways would be whipped and sold South, but she—she would probably be hanged.

13 They tried to sleep during the day but they never could wholly relax into sleep. She could tell by the positions they assumed, by their restless movements. And they walked at night. Their progress was slow. It took them three nights of walking to reach the first stop. She had told them about the place where they would stay, promising warmth and good food, holding these things out to them as an incentive to keep going.

14 When she knocked on the door of a farmhouse, a place where she and her parties of runaways had always been welcome, always been given shelter and plenty to eat, there was no answer. She knocked again, softly. A voice from within said, "Who is it?" There was fear in the voice.

15 She knew instantly from the sound of the voice that there was something wrong. She said, "A friend with friends," the password on the Underground Railroad.

16 The door opened, slowly. The man who stood in the doorway looked at her coldly, looked with unconcealed astonishment and fear at the eleven **disheveled** runaways who were standing near her. Then he shouted, "Too many, too many.

Don't forget to **Notice & Note** as you read the text.

ANALYZE WORD CHOICE

Annotate: In paragraph 12, mark the sentence that refers to the price of enslaved workers.

Interpret: How does the author's word choice in this sentence express the attitude of people who might pursue the travelers? How does that attitude contrast with Tubman's attitude?

disheveled
(dĭ-shĕv´əld) *adj.* When something is *disheveled*, it is messy or untidy.

[4] **Fugitive Slave Law:** a law by which enslaved people who escaped could be recovered by their owners.

It's not safe. My place was searched last week. It's not safe!" and slammed the door in her face.

17 She turned away from the house, frowning. She had promised her passengers food and rest and warmth, and instead of that, there would be hunger and cold and more walking over the frozen ground. Somehow she would have to **instill** courage into these eleven people, most of them strangers, would have to feed them on hope and bright dreams of freedom instead of the fried pork and corn bread and milk she had promised them.

instill
(ĭn-stĭl´) *v.* When you *instill* something, you establish or implant it gradually.

18 They stumbled along behind her, half-dead for sleep, and she urged them on, though she was as tired and as discouraged as they were. She had never been in Canada but she kept painting wondrous word pictures of what it would be like. She managed to dispel their fear of pursuit, so that they would not become hysterical, panic-stricken. Then she had to bring some of the fear back, so that they would stay awake and keep walking though they drooped with sleep.

VOCABULARY

Use Latin Roots: The word *dispel* contains the Latin root *pel*, which means "drive." The Latin prefix *dis-* means "away." Recognizing Latin roots can help you understand a word's meaning.

Analyze: What does the use of the word *dispel* suggest about the influence Tubman has on the travelers?

19 Yet during the day, when they lay down deep in a thicket, they never really slept, because if a twig snapped or the wind sighed in the branches of a pine tree, they jumped to their feet, afraid of their own shadows, shivering and shaking. It was very cold, but they dared not make fires because someone would see the smoke and wonder about it.

20 She kept thinking, eleven of them. Eleven thousand dollars' worth of slaves. And she had to take them all the way to Canada. Sometimes she told them about Thomas Garrett, in Wilmington. She said he was their friend even though he did not know them. He was the friend of all fugitives. He called them God's poor. He was a Quaker[5] and his speech was a little different from that of other people. His clothing was different, too. He wore the wide-brimmed hat that the Quakers wear.

21 She said that he had thick white hair, soft, almost like a baby's, and the kindest eyes she had ever seen. He was a big man and strong, but he had never used his strength to harm anyone, always to help people. He would give all of them a new pair of shoes. Everybody. He always did. Once they reached his house in Wilmington, they would be safe. He would see to it that they were.

22 She described the house where he lived, told them about the store where he sold shoes. She said he kept a pail of milk and a loaf of bread in the drawer of his desk so that he would have food ready at hand for any of God's poor who should suddenly appear before him, fainting with hunger. There was a hidden

[5] **Quaker:** a member of a religious group called the Society of Friends.

room in the store. A whole wall swung open, and behind it was a room where he could hide fugitives. On the wall there were shelves filled with small boxes—boxes of shoes—so that you would never guess that the wall actually opened.

23 While she talked, she kept watching them. They did not believe her. She could tell by their expressions. They were thinking, New shoes, Thomas Garrett, Quaker, Wilmington—what foolishness was this? Who knew if she told the truth? Where was she taking them anyway?

24 That night they reached the next stop—a farm that belonged to a German. She made the runaways take shelter behind trees at the edge of the fields before she knocked at the door. She hesitated before she approached the door, thinking, suppose that he, too, should refuse shelter, suppose— Then she thought, Lord, I'm going to hold steady on to You and You've got to see me through—and knocked softly.

25 She heard the familiar guttural voice say, "Who's there?"

26 She answered quickly, "A friend with friends."

27 He opened the door and greeted her warmly. "How many this time?" he asked.

28 "Eleven," she said and waited, doubting, wondering.

29 He said, "Good. Bring them in."

30 He and his wife fed them in the lamplit kitchen, their faces glowing, as they offered food and more food, urging them to eat, saying there was plenty for everybody, have more milk, have more bread, have more meat.

A stop on the Underground Railroad

NOTICE & NOTE
TOUGH QUESTIONS

When you notice characters asking questions that reveal their inner struggles, you've found a **Tough Questions** signpost.

Notice & Note: Mark the tough questions the travelers ask themselves in paragraph 23.

Analyze: What do these questions make you wonder about?

31 They spent the night in the warm kitchen. They really slept, all that night and until dusk the next day. When they left, it was with reluctance. They had all been warm and safe and well-fed. It was hard to exchange the security offered by that clean warm kitchen for the darkness and the cold of a December night.

"Go On or Die"

32 Harriet had found it hard to leave the warmth and friendliness, too. But she urged them on. For a while, as they walked, they seemed to carry in them a measure of contentment; some of the serenity and the cleanliness of that big warm kitchen **lingered** on inside them. But as they walked farther and farther away from the warmth and the light, the cold and the darkness entered into them. They fell silent, **sullen**, suspicious. She waited for the moment when some one of them would turn mutinous. It did not happen that night.

linger
(lĭng´gər) *v.* To *linger* is to remain or stay longer.

sullen
(sŭl´ən) *adj. Sullen* people show silent resentment.

33 Two nights later she was aware that the feet behind her were moving slower and slower. She heard the irritability in their voices, knew that soon someone would refuse to go on.

34 She started talking about William Still and the Philadelphia Vigilance Committee.[6] No one commented. No one asked any questions. She told them the story of William and Ellen Craft and how they escaped from Georgia. Ellen was so fair that she looked as though she were white, and so she dressed up in a man's clothing and she looked like a wealthy young planter. Her husband, William, who was dark, played the role of her slave. Thus they traveled from Macon, Georgia, to Philadelphia, riding on the trains, staying at the finest hotels. Ellen pretended to be very ill—her right arm was in a sling, and her right hand was bandaged, because she was supposed to have rheumatism. Thus she avoided having to sign the register at the hotels for she could not read or write. They finally arrived safely in Philadelphia, and then went on to Boston.

35 No one said anything. Not one of them seemed to have heard her.

36 She told them about Frederick Douglass, the most famous of the escaped slaves, of his **eloquence**, of his magnificent appearance. Then she told them of her own first vain effort at running away, **evoking** the memory of that miserable life she had led as a child, reliving it for a moment in the telling.

eloquence
(ĕl´ə-kwəns) *n. Eloquence* is the ability to speak powerfully and persuasively.

evoke
(ĭ-vōk´) *v.* When you *evoke* something, you bring it to mind.

37 But they had been tired too long, hungry too long, afraid too long, footsore too long. One of them suddenly cried out in

[6] **Philadelphia Vigilance Committee:** a fundraising organization that helped people who had escaped enslavement.

despair, "Let me go back. It is better to be a slave than to suffer like this in order to be free."

Don't forget to **Notice & Note** as you read the text.

38 She carried a gun with her on these trips. She had never used it—except as a threat. Now as she aimed it, she experienced a feeling of guilt, remembering that time, years ago, when she had prayed for the death of Edward Brodas, the Master, and then not too long afterward had heard that great wailing cry that came from the throats of the field hands, and knew from the sound that the Master was dead.

39 One of the runaways said, again, "Let me go back. Let me go back," and stood still, and then turned around and said, over his shoulder, "I am going back."

40 She lifted the gun, aimed it at the despairing slave. She said, "Go on with us or die." The husky low-pitched voice was grim.

41 He hesitated for a moment and then he joined the others. They started walking again. She tried to explain to them why none of them could go back to the plantation. If a runaway returned, he would turn traitor, the master and the overseer would force him to turn traitor. The returned slave would disclose the stopping places, the hiding places, the cornstacks they had used with the full knowledge of the owner of the farm, the name of the German farmer who had fed them and sheltered them. These people who had risked their own security to help runaways would be ruined, fined, imprisoned.

42 She said, "We got to go free or die. And freedom's not bought with dust."

43 This time she told them about the long agony of the Middle Passage[7] on the old slave ships, about the black horror of the holds, about the chains and the whips. They too knew these stories. But she wanted to remind them of the long hard way they had come, about the long hard way they had yet to go. She told them about Thomas Sims, the boy picked up on the streets of Boston and sent back to Georgia. She said when they got him back to Savannah, got him in prison there, they whipped him until a doctor who was standing by watching said, "You will kill him if you strike him again!" His master said, "Let him die!"

44 Thus she forced them to go on. Sometimes she thought she had become nothing but a voice speaking in the darkness, **cajoling**, urging, threatening. Sometimes she told them things to make them laugh, sometimes she sang to them, and heard the eleven voices behind her blending softly with hers, and then she knew that for the moment all was well with them.

cajole
(kə-jōl´) *v.* When you *cajole,* you coax or urge gently.

[7] **Middle Passage:** a sea route along which enslaved Africans were transported to the Americas.

45 She gave the impression of being a short, muscular, indomitable woman who could never be defeated. Yet at any moment she was liable to be seized by one of those curious fits of sleep, which might last for a few minutes or for hours.

46 Even on this trip, she suddenly fell asleep in the woods. The runaways, ragged, dirty, hungry, cold, did not steal the gun as they might have, and set off by themselves, or turn back. They sat on the ground near her and waited patiently until she awakened. They had come to trust her implicitly, totally. They, too, had come to believe her repeated statement, "We got to go free or die." She was leading them into freedom, and so they waited until she was ready to go on.

47 Finally, they reached Thomas Garrett's house in Wilmington, Delaware. Just as Harriet had promised, Garrett gave them all new shoes, and provided carriages to take them on to the next stop.

48 By slow stages they reached Philadelphia, where William Still hastily recorded their names, and the plantations whence they had come, and something of the life they had led in

ANALYZE BIOGRAPHY

Annotate: Mark details in paragraph 46 that tell how the people in Tubman's group felt about her.

Infer: What do the details about the group members' actions suggest about Tubman?

slavery. Then he carefully hid what he had written, for fear it might be discovered. In 1872 he published this record in book form and called it *The Underground Railroad*. In the foreword to his book he said: "While I knew the danger of keeping strict records, and while I did not then dream that in my day slavery would be blotted out, or that the time would come when I could publish these records, it used to afford me great satisfaction to take them down, fresh from the lips of fugitives on the way to freedom, and to preserve them as they had given them."

Don't forget to **Notice & Note** as you read the text.

49 William Still, who was familiar with all the station stops on the Underground Railroad, supplied Harriet with money and sent her and her eleven fugitives on to Burlington, New Jersey.

50 Harriet felt safer now, though there were danger spots ahead. But the biggest part of her job was over. As they went farther and farther north, it grew colder; she was aware of the wind on the Jersey ferry and aware of the cold damp in New York. From New York they went on to Syracuse, where the temperature was even lower.

51 In Syracuse she met the Reverend J. W. Loguen, known as "Jarm" Loguen. This was the beginning of a lifelong friendship. Both Harriet and Jarm Loguen were to become friends and supporters of Old John Brown.[8]

52 From Syracuse they went north again, into a colder, snowier city—Rochester. Here they almost certainly stayed with Frederick Douglass, for he wrote in his autobiography:

> On one occasion I had eleven fugitives at the same time under my roof, and it was necessary for them to remain with me until I could collect sufficient money to get them to Canada. It was the largest number I ever had at any one time, and I had some difficulty in providing so many with food and shelter, but, as may well be imagined, they were not very fastidious in either direction, and were well content with very plain food, and a strip of carpet on the floor for a bed, or a place on the straw in the barnloft.

53 Late in December, 1851, Harriet arrived in St. Catharines, Canada West (now Ontario), with the eleven fugitives. It had taken almost a month to complete this journey; most of the time had been spent getting out of Maryland.

54 That first winter in St. Catharines was a terrible one. Canada was a strange frozen land, snow everywhere, ice everywhere, and a bone-biting cold the like of which none of them had ever experienced before. Harriet rented a small frame house in the town and set to work to make a home. The fugitives boarded with her. They worked in the forests, felling trees, and so did she. Sometimes she took other jobs, cooking or cleaning house for people in the town. She cheered on these newly arrived fugitives, working herself, finding work for them, finding food for them, praying for them, sometimes begging for them.

55 Often she found herself thinking of the beauty of Maryland, the mellowness of the soil, the richness of the plant life there. The climate itself made for an ease of living that could never be duplicated in this bleak, barren countryside.

ANALYZE BIOGRAPHY

Annotate: Mark details in paragraph 54 that describe Tubman's actions after she arrives in Canada.

Infer: What do these details reveal about Tubman's character?

[8] **Old John Brown:** an anti-slavery leader who was executed.

Don't forget to **Notice & Note** as you read the text.

Harriet Tubman is honored in this bronze statue, titled *Step on Board*, by sculptor Fern Cunningham. Located at the entrance to Harriet Tubman Park in Boston, Massachusetts, the statue shows Tubman holding a Bible as she leads a group northward to freedom.

56 In spite of the severe cold, the hard work, she came to love St. Catharines, and the other towns and cities in Canada where black men lived. She discovered that freedom meant more than the right to change jobs at will, more than the right to keep the money that one earned. It was the right to vote and to sit on juries. It was the right to be elected to office. In Canada there were black men who were county officials and members of school boards. St. Catharines had a large colony of ex-slaves,

and they owned their own homes, kept them neat and clean and in good repair. They lived in whatever part of town they chose and sent their children to the schools.

57 When spring came she decided that she would make this small Canadian city her home—as much as any place could be said to be home to a woman who traveled from Canada to the Eastern Shore of Maryland as often as she did.

58 In the spring of 1852, she went back to Cape May, New Jersey. She spent the summer there, cooking in a hotel. That fall she returned, as usual, to Dorchester County, and brought out nine more slaves, conducting them all the way to St. Catharines, in Canada West, to the bone-biting cold, the snow-covered forests—and freedom.

59 She continued to live in this fashion, spending the winter in Canada, and the spring and summer working in Cape May, New Jersey, or in Philadelphia. She made two trips a year into slave territory, one in the fall and another in the spring. She now had a definite crystallized purpose, and in carrying it out, her life fell into a pattern which remained unchanged for the next six years.

TURN AND TALK

With a partner, discuss the characteristics of Harriet Tubman that surprised or impressed you most.

ESSENTIAL QUESTION:

What will people risk to be free?

Review your annotations and notes. Then, add relevant details to your Response Log.

Assessment Practice

Answer these questions before moving on to the **Analyze the Text** section on the following page.

1. Read this sentence from paragraph 12 of the biography. Then, answer the question.

> **"If they were caught, the eleven runaways would be whipped and sold South, but she—she would probably be hanged."**

Which **two** reasons best explain why the author included this sentence?

(A) to show that Tubman had little concern for her own safety

(B) to suggest that Tubman looked out for others more than for herself

(C) to suggest that Tubman thought she was too clever to be caught

(D) to suggest that Tubman doubted the determination of her pursuers

(E) to show that Tubman continued bravely despite her own fears

2. Which detail from the selection best reflects the travelers' fear of getting captured?

(A) "She had to take them all the way to Canada. The Fugitive Slave Law . . . had become a reality." (paragraph 10)

(B) "She . . . kept looking back over her shoulder, imagining that she heard the sound of pursuit." (paragraph 12)

(C) "It was hard to exchange the security offered by that clean warm kitchen for the darkness . . . of a December night." (paragraph 31)

(D) "These people who had risked their own security to help runaways would be ruined. . . ." (paragraph 41)

Ed Test-Taking Strategies

Analyze the Text

Support your responses with evidence from the text.

NOTICE & NOTE

Review what you **noticed and noted** as you read the text. Your annotations can help you answer these questions.

1. **INTERPRET** In paragraph 7, why do you think the author refers to the song "Go Down, Moses" as "the forbidden spiritual"?

2. **INFER** Reread paragraphs 10–11. What does Tubman's response to the difficulty of her task reveal about her?

3. **ANALYZE** In paragraph 23, the travelers ask themselves **Tough Questions** about the things Tubman tells them about Thomas Garrett. What do these questions reveal about the travelers' inner conflict?

4. **DRAW CONCLUSIONS** How do the words *cajoling, urging*, and *threatening* (paragraph 44) affect your understanding of Tubman?

5. **CONNECT** Review the descriptions of St. Catharines and Maryland in paragraphs 54–55. How does the characterization of these places help you understand the main idea of this selection?

6. **ANALYZE** What methods does the author use to characterize Harriet Tubman? Fill in the chart to provide an example of each method of characterization and analysis of each example you find.

METHOD OF CHARACTERIZATION	EXAMPLE FROM THE TEXT	YOUR ANALYSIS
Direct comments about Tubman		
Tubman's own thoughts, speech, and actions		
How others behave toward Tubman		

Choices

Here are some other ways to demonstrate your understanding of the ideas in this lesson.

Writing
Speech

Prepare a persuasive speech to convince the board of a museum that Harriet Tubman should be included in a "Heroes Hall of Fame" exhibit. The following tips will help you.

- Form a claim, and state it early in your speech, along with an attention-grabbing example of Tubman's heroism. Use a formal style throughout.
- Support your claim with reasons, and each reason with strong, relevant evidence. Consider quoting an historian's opinion of Tubman's impact on the quest for freedom prior to the Civil War.
- Close by summarizing your main points.

As you write and discuss, be sure to use the **Academic Vocabulary** words.

- access
- civil
- demonstrate
- document
- symbolize

Research
Tubman and Douglass

In this selection, not only does Tubman tell the people in her group about Frederick Douglass, they eventually meet him. Conduct research to learn more about Tubman and Douglass.

- What did Tubman and Douglass have in common?
- How did Tubman and Douglass differ in their fight against slavery?
- What interactions did the two leaders have with each other?

Media
Create a Timeline

With a partner or group, create a timeline of events from the biography excerpt.

- Review the text and identify important dates and events to include in your timeline.
- Use digital tools to add visual elements such as historical photographs and maps.
- Make sure the information in your timeline is accurate and that the events are in correct chronological order.

Expand Your Vocabulary

PRACTICE AND APPLY

Circle the letter of the best answer to each question.

1. Which of the following would **instill** a sense of responsibility?
   a. having a child care for a plant
   b. giving a child fresh flowers
2. Which of the following would be **disheveled**?
   a. a car that was just washed
   b. a person who just woke up
3. Which of the following would require **eloquence**?
   a. cheering at a football game
   b. giving a speech
4. Which of the following exemplifies what it means to **cajole**?
   a. worrying about losing
   b. giving someone a pep talk
5. Which of the following exemplifies what it means to **linger**?
   a. staying seated after a movie ends
   b. making eye contact as you walk
6. Which of the following would most likely **evoke** sullen feelings?
   a. a party invitation
   b. an angry letter

Vocabulary Strategy

Latin Roots

Recognizing **word roots** can help you determine the meanings of unfamiliar words. For example, the word *conducted* includes the Latin root *duc* or *duct*, which means "to lead." This can help you infer that *conducted* means "led or guided" in this context:

> **It was the largest group that she had ever conducted . . . .**

Ed

Interactive Vocabulary Lesson: Common Roots, Prefixes, and Suffixes

PRACTICE AND APPLY

Use online or print resources to find four more examples of words that use the Latin root *duc* or *duct*. Use your knowledge of the root's meaning to write a definition for each word.

Watch Your Language!

Conditional Mood

Writers use the **conditional mood** when they want to make a statement about what might happen if something else happens. The conditional mood often includes the words *might, could, would*, or *if*.

Look at the example below from *Harriet Tubman: Conductor on the Underground Railroad*. Notice that the sentence describes what might happen ("he would turn traitor") if something else happens ("If a runaway returned").

If a runaway returned, he would turn traitor, the master and the overseer would force him to turn traitor.

If this happens, it might cause . . . . . . this to happen.

Study these examples:

If he did not forge ahead, he would not reach his goal.

He might have succeeded if he had tried harder.

She could have won the game if she had practiced.

PRACTICE AND APPLY

Read the sentences. Rewrite them so that they are in the conditional mood.

1. Max did not write a good report because he had not done enough research.

2. Kim did not study hard and did not do well on the test.

3. Maria wanted to succeed but decided to play computer games rather than to study.

4. To earn a good grade you have to do thorough research on the topic.

5. The weather has to be good in order for gym class to be held outside.

Collaborate & Compare

ESSENTIAL QUESTION:
What will people risk to be free?

Compare Treatments

You are about to read a poem and a piece of history writing about an enslaved person called Fortune. The poem and the nonfiction text share the same topic. As you read, notice how each writer uses the elements of her chosen genre to explore the topic, and how each treatment helps you understand different aspects of the topic.

MENTOR TEXT

A

Not My Bones

Poem by **Marilyn Nelson**
pages 322–325

B

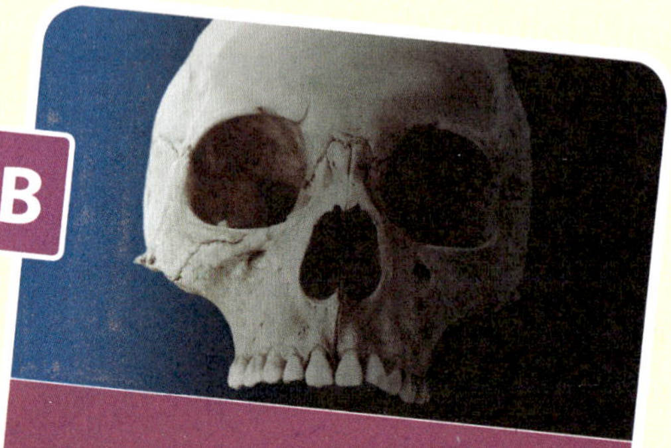

from **Fortune's Bones**

History Writing by **Pamela Espeland**
pages 326–329

After you have read the texts, you will have a collaborative discussion with your classmates, following these steps:

- Choose a Position
- Gather Information
- Select Information
- Share Your Views

Not My Bones

Poem by **Marilyn Nelson**

from Fortune's Bones

History Writing by **Pamela Espeland**

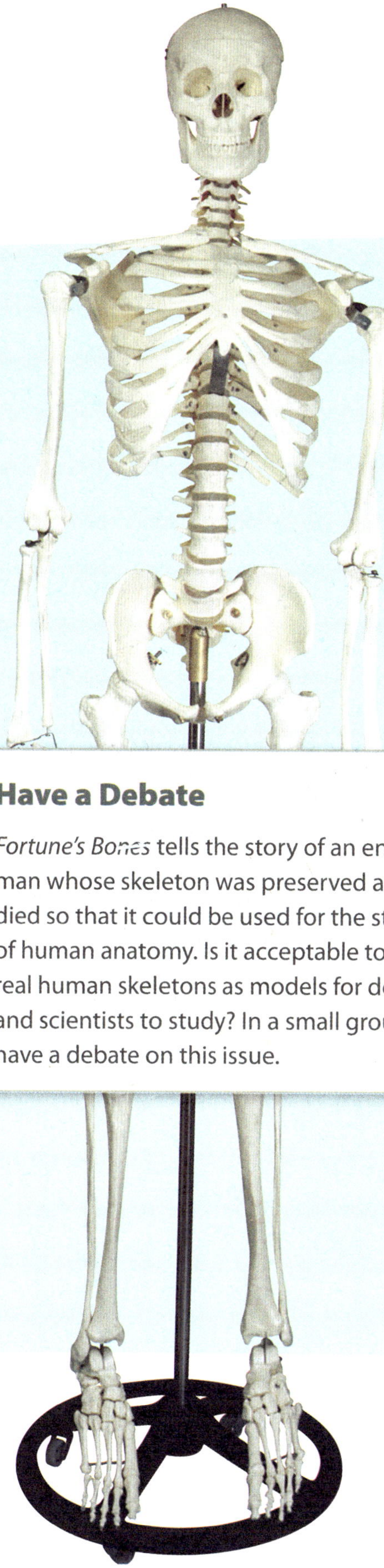

Engage Your Brain

Choose one or more of these activities to start connecting with the texts you're about to read.

Body and Soul

You're about to read a poem in which the speaker repeats the idea that people are more than just their bodies or their bones. Write a few sentences to examine your beliefs about the human body and soul.

Have a Debate

Fortune's Bones tells the story of an enslaved man whose skeleton was preserved after he died so that it could be used for the study of human anatomy. Is it acceptable to use real human skeletons as models for doctors and scientists to study? In a small group, have a debate on this issue.

Analyze Figurative Language

One way poets and other writers appeal to their readers' imaginations and emotions is by using **figurative language**—words and phrases that suggest meaning beyond the words' literal meanings. Study these examples of three types of figurative language from "Not My Bones":

TYPE OF FIGURATIVE LANGUAGE	EXAMPLE	ANALYSIS
Personification: giving human qualities to an object, idea, or animal	Elementary molecules converged for a breath, / then danced on beyond my individual death. (lines 5–6)	By describing molecules as gathering and dancing, the author emphasizes that a person is more than just a physical being.
Simile: a comparison of two unlike things using the word *like, as,* or *as if*	You can own a man's body, / but you can't own his mind. / That's like making a bridle / to ride on the wind. (lines 17–20)	The author suggests that trying to own a person's mind is like trying to harness the wind—impossible.
Metaphor: a comparison between two unlike things without the use of the word *like* or *as*	We are brief incarnations, / we are clouds in clothes. (lines 9–10)	The author points out that human life is short—our "clothes" (skin) only briefly cover our "clouds" (soul).

As you read "Not My Bones," think about how the use of figurative language affects your thoughts about this poem and its message.

Focus on Genre
Poetry

- uses imagery and figurative language to convey meaning and mood
- uses sound devices such as rhythm and repetition to unify the poem and create emphasis
- expresses a theme, or a message about life
- features a speaker who "talks" to the reader; the speaker is not necessarily the poet

Analyze Chronological Structure

Chronological structure is the arrangement of events by the order in which they took place. Writers use transitional words and phrases to signal the order of events (for example, *before, during, after,* and *finally*) and to identify when certain events happen (such as references to dates). Study the chronological structure of paragraph 5 from *Fortune's Bones:*

> When Dr. Porter died in 1803, he left an estate that was worth about $7,000—a lot of money for the time.

In this sentence, the word *when* and the date help you know where this event fits in the selection's overall timeline. As you read the excerpt from *Fortune's Bones* that follows, consider how the chronological structure of the text helps the author achieve her purpose.

Focus on Genre
History Writing

- uses chronological structure
- relates facts about history or from an individual's life
- is most often written to inform or teach
- may include domain-specific vocabulary

Annotation in Action

Here are one reader's notes about figurative language in "Not My Bones." As you read, notice the poet's use of figurative language.

> Elementary molecules converged for a breath,
> then danced on beyond my individual death.
> And I am not my body,
> I am not my body.

"dancing" molecules = figurative language

Background

The poem "Not My Bones" comes from the book *Fortune's Bones: The Manumission Requiem*. The author, **Marilyn Nelson** (top), is a former poet laureate of Connecticut. *Fortune's Bones* includes history writing and primary source documents and illustrations that tell Fortune's story. Some of the historical notes written by **Pamela Espeland** (bottom) are included here. Read these notes to learn facts and additional information about Fortune's life.

Not My Bones

Poem by **Marilyn Nelson**

The true essence of a person can never be enslaved.

NOTICE & NOTE
As you read, use the side margins to make notes about the text.

ANALYZE FIGURATIVE LANGUAGE

Annotate: Mark the figurative language used that creates a comparison in lines 1–4.

Analyze: Is this comparison a simile or a metaphor? What does this comparison suggest?

I was not this body,
I was not these bones.
This skeleton was just my
temporary home.
Elementary molecules[1] converged[2] for a breath,
then danced on beyond my individual death.
And I am not my body,
I am not my body.

[1] **elementary molecules:** the smallest, most basic particles of substances.
[2] **converged:** came together in one place; met.

We are brief incarnations,[3]
we are clouds in clothes.
We are water respirators,
we are how earth knows.
I bore[4] light passed on from an original flame;
while it was in my hands it was called by my name.
But I am not my body,
I am not my body.

You can own a man's body,
but you can't own his mind.
That's like making a bridle
to ride on the wind.
I will tell you one thing, and I'll tell you true:
Life's the best thing that can happen to you.
But you are not your body,
you are not your body.

You can own someone's body,
but the soul runs free.
It roams the night sky's
mute geometry.
You can murder hope, you can pound faith flat,
but like weeds and wildflowers, they grow right back.
For you are not your body,
you are not your body.

You are not your body,
you are not your bones.
What's essential[5] about you
is what can't be owned.
What's essential in you is your longing to raise
your itty-bitty voice in the cosmic[6] praise.
For you are not your body,
you are not your body.

Don't forget to **Notice & Note** as you read the text.

ANALYZE FIGURATIVE LANGUAGE

Annotate: In lines 25–28, mark examples of figurative language.

Analyze: What kind of figurative language is used here? What does its meaning suggest about a person's soul or essence?

[3] **incarnations:** bodily forms.
[4] **bore:** carried; transported.
[5] **essential:** having the qualities that give something its true identity.
[6] **cosmic:** universal; infinitely large.

Well, I woke up this morning just so glad to be free,
glad to be free, glad to be free.
I woke up this morning in restful peace.
For I am not my body,
I am not my bones.
I am not my body,
glory hallelujah, not my bones,
I am not my bones.

ESSENTIAL QUESTION:

What will people risk to be free?

Review your notes and add your thoughts to your Response Log.

TURN AND TALK

Who is the speaker of this poem? Who is the poem's intended audience? Turn to a partner and discuss these questions.

Assessment Practice

Answer these questions about "Not My Bones" before moving on to the next selection.

1. According to the speaker, what happens when people's hope and faith are attacked?

   (A) The people give in to despair.
   (B) The people are tempted to strike back.
   (C) Those qualities return as strong as ever.
   (D) Those qualities are reborn in others.

2. This question has two parts. First, answer **Part A**. Then, answer **Part B**.

   Part A

   What is the primary message of "Not My Bones"?

   (A) A person's most important qualities can't be owned.
   (B) A person's remains should be treated with respect.
   (C) People ought to make the most of what life gives them.
   (D) People shouldn't try to control other people.

   Part B

   Which detail from the poem best expresses this message?

   (A) "This skeleton was just my / temporary home." (lines 3–4)
   (B) "Life's the best thing that can happen to you." (line 22)
   (C) "You can own someone's body, / but the soul runs free." (lines 25–26)
   (D) "Well, I woke up this morning just so glad to be free," (line 41)

Ed
Test-Taking Strategies

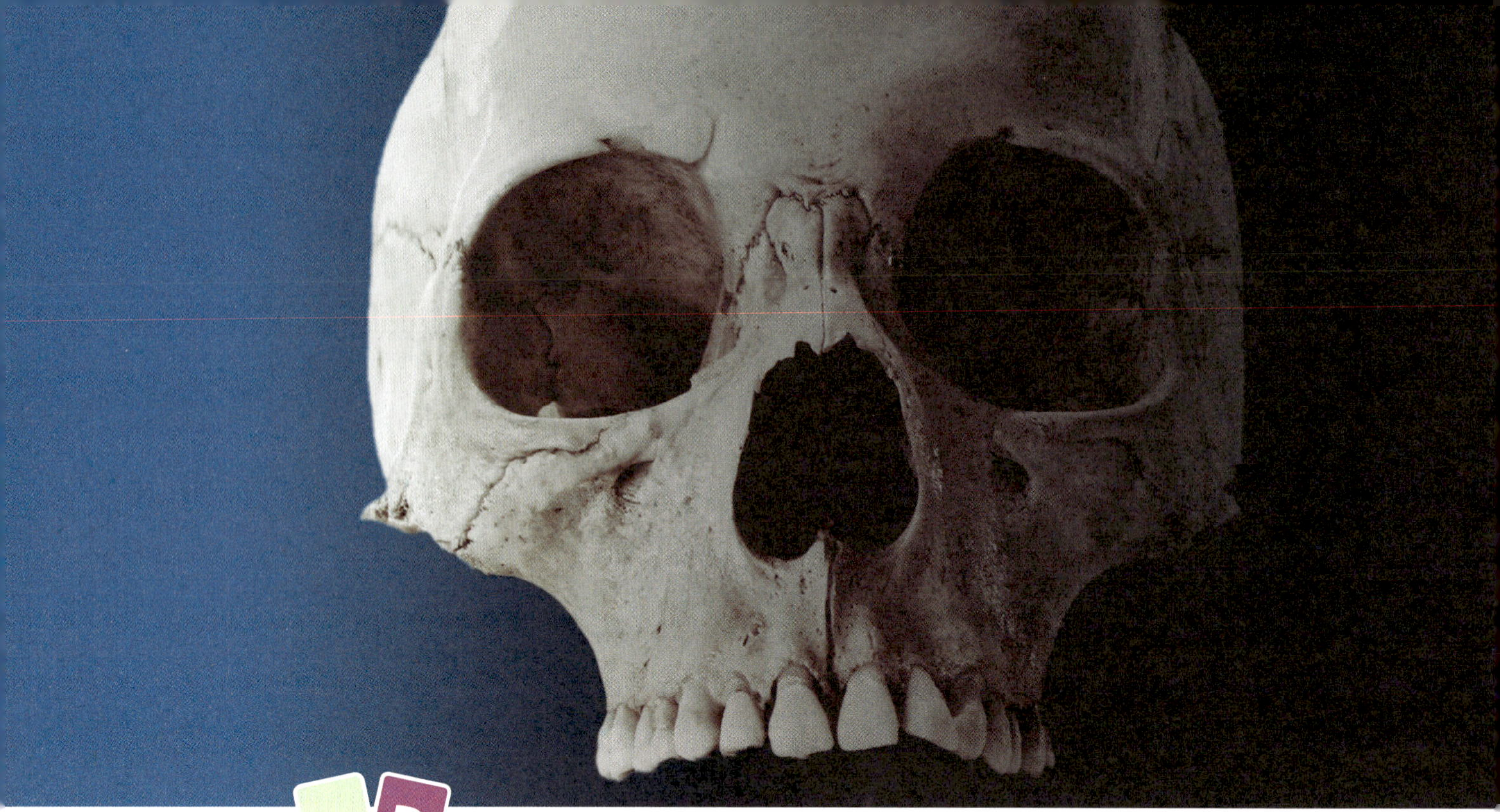

from

Fortune's Bones

History Writing by **Pamela Espeland**

Who was Fortune, and what happened to his bones after he died?

NOTICE & NOTE
As you read, use the side margins to make notes about the text.

ANALYZE CHRONOLOGICAL STRUCTURE

Annotate: Mark the word that signals sequence in the first paragraph.

Predict: What does this first sentence tell you about how the text will be organized?

1 Before Fortune was bones in a Connecticut museum, he was a husband, a father, a baptized Christian, and a slave.

2 His wife's name was Dinah. His sons were Africa and Jacob. His daughters were Mira and Roxa. He was baptized in an Episcopal church, which did not make him free. His master was Dr. Preserved Porter, a physician who specialized in setting broken bones.

3 They lived in Waterbury, Connecticut, in the late 1700s. Dr. Porter had a 75-acre farm, which Fortune probably ran. He planted and harvested corn, rye, potatoes, onions, apples, buckwheat, oats, and hay. He cared for the cattle and hogs.

4 Unlike many slaves, who owned little or nothing and were often separated from their families, Fortune owned a small house near Dr. Porter's home. He and Dinah and their children lived together.

5 When Dr. Porter died in 1803, he left an estate that was worth about $7,000—a lot of money for the time. The estate included Fortune's widow, Dinah, and their son Jacob. Fortune had died in 1798.

6 According to Connecticut's Act of Gradual Emancipation, children born to enslaved parents after March 1, 1784, were to be freed when they reached age 21. Jacob was 18. By law, he could be enslaved for another three years.

7 In Dr. Porter's will, he left Dinah to his wife, Lydia. He gave Jacob to his daughter Hannah.

8 No one knows what happened to Africa, Mira, and Roxa.

9 Most slaves who died in Waterbury in the 1700s were buried in one of the town's cemeteries. When Fortune died, he wasn't buried. Instead, Dr. Porter preserved Fortune's skeleton to further the study of human anatomy.[1]

10 Dr. Porter had been a bonesetter for many years, but he'd never had a skeleton to study. He had two sons who were also doctors. They could learn from the skeleton, too.

11 Fortune was about 60 at the time of his death and, in spite of his injuries, in relatively good health. His skeleton was sturdy and complete.

12 Four more generations of Porters became physicians, and the skeleton stayed in the family. Porter children, grandchildren, and great-grandchildren used it to learn the names of the bones. This was their earliest medical training.

13 Sally Porter Law McGlannan, the last Porter doctor, remembered playing with the skeleton as a young girl. . . . Another family member, Leander Law, once brought part of Fortune's skeleton to a college physiology class.

14 At some point—no one knows exactly when—"Larry" was written on the skull. Fortune's name was forgotten for nearly a century.

15 Over the years, the skeleton was lost and found. It was boarded up[2] in an attic, then discovered by a crew of workers hired to renovate an old building.

16 In 1933, Sally Porter Law McGlannan gave the bones to the Mattatuck Museum. The museum sent the bones to Europe to be assembled for display. The skeleton hung in a glass case in the museum for decades, fascinating adults and frightening children.

[1] **anatomy:** the structure and parts of the body.
[2] **boarded up:** packed away.

Don't forget to **Notice & Note** as you read the text.

ANALYZE CHRONOLOGICAL STRUCTURE

Annotate: Mark the time words in paragraph 6.

Draw Conclusions: In what year was Fortune's son Jacob probably emancipated?

NOTICE & NOTE

CONTRASTS AND CONTRADICTIONS

When you notice a sharp contrast between what you would expect and what you observe happening, you've found a **Contrasts and Contradictions** signpost.

Notice & Note: Review paragraph 12. Underline how the Porter family first made use of Fortune's skeleton. Then, circle examples in paragraphs 13–14 of how the Porter family's views toward the skeleton changed.

Interpret: What is the difference, and why does it matter?

A sculptor used information about Fortune's bones to create this reconstruction of Fortune's face.

17 Many stories were invented about the skeleton. Some said that "Larry" was a Revolutionary War hero—maybe even George Washington. Some said he fell to his death. Some said he drowned. Some said he was killed trying to escape. Some thought he had been hanged.

18 One Waterbury resident remembers, "Larry was the thing to see when you go to the museum. I don't think anybody ever envisioned[3] that this was truly a human being."

19 In 1970, the skeleton, still called "Larry," was taken out of its case and put into storage. Times had changed. The museum now believed that displaying the skeleton was disrespectful. It wasn't just a bunch of bones. It was the remains of someone's son, maybe someone's father.

20 The skeleton rested for more than 25 years. Then, in the 1990s, historians searched local records and found a slave named Fortune. Archaeologists and anthropologists studied the bones, which started giving up their secrets. The bones told how Fortune labored, suffered, and died: A quick, sudden injury, like whiplash, may have snapped a vertebra[4] in his neck. He did not drown or fall from a cliff. He was not hanged.

21 But he was free.

[3] **envisioned:** imagined.

[4] **vertebra:** a piece of bone that makes up the spinal column.

TURN AND TALK

At the end of the text, the author raises the question of whether Fortune's death was accidental. Turn to a partner and discuss what you think happened to Fortune.

?

ESSENTIAL QUESTION:

What will people risk to be free?

Review your notes and add your thoughts to your Response Log.

Assessment Practice

Answer these questions before moving on to the **Analyze the Texts** section on the following page.

1. This question has two parts. First, answer **Part A**. Then, answer **Part B**.

Part A

What happened to Fortune's skeleton in 1970?

- (A) It was used in a college physiology class.
- (B) It was removed from display and stored away.
- (C) It was donated to the Mattatuck Museum.
- (D) It was studied to determine how Fortune died.

Part B

Why is this date important to the selection?

- (A) It shows renewed interest in the history of slavery.
- (B) It suggests that the previous owners still wanted the skeleton.
- (C) It refers to a change in thinking about the skeleton.
- (D) It points to a number of medical advances at that time.

2. What is the significance of the last line of the text, "But he was free"?

- (A) Fortune and his family were freed after Dr. Porter's death.
- (B) Fortune managed to escape from slavery before he died.
- (C) Fortune's family reclaimed his bones from the Mattatuck Museum.
- (D) Fortune's true identity and story were finally revealed.

Ed

Test-Taking Strategies

Analyze the Texts

Support your responses with evidence from the texts.

NOTICE & NOTE

Review what you **noticed and noted** as you read the text. Your annotations can help you answer these questions.

1. **ANALYZE** In "Not My Bones," what idea is emphasized through the use of repetition? Support your answer by citing the lines that are repeated most often.

2. **CONNECT** How is the figurative language in lines 25–28 related to the figurative language in lines 37–38?

3. **ANALYZE** Reread paragraph 18 of the notes from *Fortune's Bones*. What do the Waterbury resident's observations reveal about people's feelings and behavior toward Fortune? Cite evidence in your response.

4. **SUMMARIZE** Summarize the excerpt from *Fortune's Bones* by adding the main events described in the text to the timeline below.

5. **EVALUATE** How does the chronological structure of the history writing from *Fortune's Bones* help the author achieve her purpose?

6. **COMPARE** What are the **Contrasts and Contradictions** between the Mattatuck Museum's treatment of Fortune's skeleton in 1933 and its treatment of the skeleton in 1970? What change in attitude or understanding does this contrast reflect?

Choices

Here are some other ways to demonstrate your understanding of the ideas in this lesson.

As you write and discuss, be sure to use the **Academic Vocabulary** words.

access	document
civil	symbolize
demonstrate	

Writing
Write a Letter

Imagine you are a visitor to the Mattatuck Museum in the 1960s who does not approve of Fortune's skeleton being displayed in the museum. Write a letter to the museum to express why you disagree with the museum's choice to display the skeleton and to request that the exhibit be removed.

- Introduce yourself and the reason for your letter.
- Explain why you think it is improper for the museum to display Fortune's skeleton.
- Be sure to maintain a formal tone throughout your letter.

Speaking & Listening
Recite a Poem

With your group, recite part of "Not My Bones" aloud for the class.

- Work with your group to select one stanza of the poem.
- Discuss how you will recite it. Will you recite it together chorally? Will you sing it like a song? Will different members of your group speak different lines? Will you accompany the words with movements or gestures?
- Memorize your lines and rehearse them a few times with your group.
- Present the poem to the class, using appropriate volume, phrasing, and expression.

Social & Emotional Learning
Express Ideas Visually

Create a visual work of some kind—such as a painting, drawing, or video—that is inspired by details you learned about Fortune's life.

- As a group, decide what kind of visual work you will create. Listen respectfully to all group members and give consideration to everyone's ideas.
- Reread the poem and the history notes. Draw on imagery in the poem and details in the history writing to visualize the events of Fortune's story.
- Work together to create your visual work. Consider using digital tools to collaborate.
- As a group, present your work. Explain the aspects of Fortune's life or story on which it focuses or by which it was inspired.

Compare Treatments

Marilyn Nelson and Pamela Espeland both wrote on the same topic—Fortune's bones—but they handled the topic differently. The way a topic is handled is called its **treatment.** To consider a writer's treatment, ask yourself the following questions:

- What form does the text take? For example, is it a poem, a biography, a blog post, or a newspaper article?
- How would you describe the structure of the text? For example, if the text is nonfiction, how is the information organized? If it is fiction or drama, are events presented in a logical sequence? If it is poetry, is there a rhyme scheme, a repeated stanza structure, or any other identifiable patterns?
- For what main purpose was the selection written—to entertain, to express ideas and feelings, to inform, or to persuade?
- What is the writer's **tone,** or attitude toward the subject?

Analyze the Texts

Discuss these questions in your group.

1. **CONNECT** Which text uses more figurative language and imagery? Cite examples. What purpose does it serve?

2. **SYNTHESIZE** Think about the understanding of Fortune that you get from "Not My Bones" and *Fortune's Bones*. What might be the strengths of a book that combines poems with historical notes?

3. **EVALUATE** Think about how the poem and the historical notes were written. Which type of writing allows more freedom in its treatment? Why do you think that is?

4. **CRITIQUE** The full title of Marilyn Nelson's book is *Fortune's Bones: The Manumission Requiem*. (*Manumission* means being freed from slavery, and a *requiem* is music written to honor the dead.) Do you think that is effective as a title for the book? Why or why not? Draw on information from both selections to support your answer.

Decide and Discuss

Now, you can continue exploring the ideas in these texts by discussing with classmates which treatment of Fortune's life and death is more effective. Follow these steps:

1. **CHOOSE A POSITION** Decide for yourself which treatment of Fortune's bones is the most effective or powerful. Ask:
   - Which gives readers a better sense of the man and the issue of slavery in the United States?
   - Which evokes stronger feelings?
   - Which conveys a more universal message?
2. **GATHER INFORMATION** Form a group with others who share the same opinion. Working together, support that opinion with examples from the text.

WHAT I LEARNED OR UNDERSTOOD BETTER	SUPPORT FROM THE TEXT

3. **SELECT INFORMATION** As a group, select three of the strongest examples to present to the class.
4. **SHARE YOUR VIEWS** With your group, present your views to the class. Cite text evidence from both the poem and the historical notes to support your ideas. Listen to what others have to say, ask questions to request and clarify information, and build on the ideas of others as you discuss this topic.

Reader's Choice

Continue your exploration of the Essential Question by doing some independent reading on the Civil War. Read the titles and descriptions shown. Then mark the texts that interest you.

ESSENTIAL QUESTION:
What will people risk to be free?

Short Reads

Available on Ed

These texts are available in your ebook. Choose one to read and rate. Then defend your rating to the class.

I Saw Old General at Bay

Poem by **Walt Whitman**

What kind of leader makes soldiers feel honored to risk their lives?

Rate It ☆☆☆☆☆

from Bloody Times: The Funeral of Abraham Lincoln and the Manhunt for Jefferson Davis

History Writing by **James L. Swanson**

As the city of Richmond burns, one president escapes while another is welcomed like a king.

Rate It ☆☆☆☆☆

A Mystery of Heroism

Short Story by **Stephen Crane**

A soldier struggles with the true meaning of heroism.

Rate It ☆☆☆☆☆

My Friend Douglass

Biography by **Russell Freedman**

Discover why Abraham Lincoln was so eager to speak with Frederick Douglass after his second inauguration.

Rate It ☆☆☆☆☆

Civil War Journal

Journal by **Louisa May Alcott**

Alcott reflects on her experiences as a nurse during the Civil War.

Rate It ☆☆☆☆☆

Long Reads

Here are a few recommended books that connect to this unit topic. For additional options, ask your teacher, school librarian, or peers. Which titles spark your interest?

The Not So Boring Letters of Private Nobody

Novel by **Matthew Landis**

Oliver and Ella—a seemingly odd pair—are given an assignment to research an insignificant Civil War soldier. Just when they think "Private Nobody" is a bust, a mystery unfolds.

March Toward the Thunder

Novel by **Joseph Bruchac**

Louis is a fifteen-year-old Abenaki Indian recruited to fight in the Civil War. Through each battle, he faces prejudice, acceptance, cowardice, and courage.

March Forward, Girl

Memoir by **Melba Pattillo Beals**

Before she was one of the Little Rock Nine, Melba was a warrior. She was told to hold her tongue and know her place, but she wouldn't settle for "separate but equal."

Extension

Connect & Create

SORRY, I CAN EXPLAIN What is an important conflict between characters or people in the text you chose? Is it ever resolved? Write an apology letter from one character or person to another, sharing your understanding of the conflict and the reasons for any actions that caused or inflamed the conflict. Conclude with an attempt at making a connection between the two sides that helps resolve the conflict.

A STUDY IN CONTRASTS Select two major characters from the text you chose to read. What separates them? What do they have in common? Create an illustrated Venn diagram that compares and contrasts these two characters, and include a caption for each illustration. Use the ideas in your Venn diagram to consider the Essential Question: What will people risk to be free? Answer this question in a sentence or two for your two chosen characters.

NOTICE & NOTE

- Pick one of the texts and annotate the Notice & Note signposts you find.
- Then, use the **Notice & Note Writing Frames** to help you write about the significance of the signposts.
- Compare your findings with those of other students who read the same text.

Ed

Notice & Note Writing Frames

Write a Research Report

Writing Prompt

Using ideas, information, and examples from multiple sources, research and write a report about an aspect of the abolition movement in the United States.

Manage your time carefully so that you can

- review the texts in the unit;
- research and plan your report;
- write your report; and
- revise and edit your report.

Be sure to

- clearly introduce the topic of your report;
- develop the topic with evidence;
- use evidence from multiple sources; and
- avoid overly relying on one source.

Review the Mentor Text

For an example of a well-researched and well-written informative text you can use as a mentor text for your report, review:

- from *Fortune's Bones* (pages 326–329).

Make sure to carefully review your notes and annotations about this text. Think about the techniques the author used to make her writing informative, clear, and engaging.

Consider Your Sources

Review the list of texts in the unit and choose at least two that you may want to use as support for the ideas in your report.

As you review potential sources, consult the notes you made on your **Response Log** and make additional notes about any ideas that might be useful as you research and write your report. Include titles and page numbers to help you provide accurate citations when you refer to these texts.

UNIT 4 SOURCES

- ☐ *from* **Narrative of the Life of Frederick Douglass, an American Slave**
- ☐ **The Drummer Boy of Shiloh**
- ☐ **O Captain! My Captain!**
- ☐ *from* **Harriet Tubman: Conductor on the Underground Railroad**
- ☐ **Not My Bones**
- ☐ *from* **Fortune's Bones**

Analyze the Prompt

Review the prompt to make sure you understand the writing task.

1. Mark the sentence in the prompt that identifies the topic of your report. Rephrase this sentence in your own words.
2. Next, look for words that indicate the purpose and audience of your report, and write a sentence describing each.

Consider Your Audience

Ask yourself:

- Who will read my report?
- What do my readers already know about the topic?
- What aspect of the topic might they be interested in learning more about?

What is my topic? What is my writing task?

What is my purpose?

Who is my audience?

Review the Rubric

Your research report will be scored using a rubric. As you write, focus on the characteristics as described in the chart. You will learn more about these characteristics as you work through the lesson.

PURPOSE, FOCUS, AND ORGANIZATION	EVIDENCE AND ELABORATION	CONVENTIONS OF STANDARD ENGLISH
The response includes: • A strongly maintained controlling idea • Use of transitions to connect ideas • Logical progression of ideas • Appropriate style and tone	The response includes: • Effective use of evidence and sources • Effective use of elaboration • Clear and effective expression of ideas • Appropriate vocabulary • Varied sentence structure	The response may include: • Some minor errors in usage but no patterns of errors • Correct punctuation, capitalization, sentence formation, and spelling • Command of basic conventions

1 PLAN YOUR RESEARCH REPORT

Develop Research Questions

To begin, you must take the broad topic of abolition and narrow it. A good way to narrow a topic is to ask questions about it. As you research the answer to each question, you may discover more specific and interesting aspects of the topic to research. Use the chart to help you narrow and refine your topic.

QUESTION	ANSWER AND SOURCE
Initial question: Who were some leading abolitionists?	William Lloyd Garrison founded the American Anti-Slavery Society in 1833. (Encyclopædia Britannica)
Refined question:	
Refined question:	

Ed Help with Planning

Consult **Interactive Writing Lesson: Conducting Research.**

Research Your Report

Search for a variety of print and digital sources to help you answer your research questions. Use the chart to take notes on key ideas and to keep track of your sources. Describe each source and list the title, author, and page number or web address.

Use Primary and Secondary Sources

- **Primary sources** are created by people who witness events. Autobiographies and diaries are examples of primary sources.
- **Secondary sources** are created by people not involved in events. Examples include biographies and reference books.

NOTES	SOURCE INFORMATION

Evaluate and Document Your Sources

Evaluate the sources you locate to ensure they are reliable, credible, and unbiased. Avoid commercial, political, and personal websites. Use the chart to record key facts and quotations you want to use in your report. Include the source for each fact or quotation, and note why you trust this source.

QUOTATION OR FACT AND SOURCE	HOW I KNOW SOURCE IS RELIABLE

Put It in Order

Consider these options for organizing your report:

- If your research question involves how the abolition movement developed over time, present your information in time order.
- If your research question explores different people's perspectives on the movement, compare and contrast perspectives in separate body paragraphs.

Organize Ideas

The answer to your central research question is likely to be your controlling idea. To support it thoroughly, you will need to **synthesize,** or combine information from multiple sources. Create an outline to guide your writing.

INTRODUCTION	• Start your report with a paragraph that clearly introduces your topic and states your controlling idea. • Include an interesting question, quote, or detail to grab the reader's attention.
BODY PARAGRAPHS	• Present evidence to develop your topic, devoting a paragraph to each main point or subtopic. • Let readers know where your key facts and ideas come from, using language such as: Historian ________ explains ________. According to ________'s autobiography ________.
CONCLUSION	• Restate your controlling idea. • Leave readers with a final idea or question to ponder.

2 DEVELOP A DRAFT

Now it is time to draft your essay. It can be helpful to examine how professional authors craft effective informative texts and to use similar techniques in your own research report writing.

Ed

Drafting Online

Check your assignment list for a writing task from your teacher.

Write an Engaging Introduction

EXAMINE THE MENTOR TEXT

In the introduction of your research report, you should state your controlling idea. You should also include something that gets your readers interested in reading your report. Notice how Pamela Espeland captures the reader's attention in her opening sentence from *Fortune's Bones*.

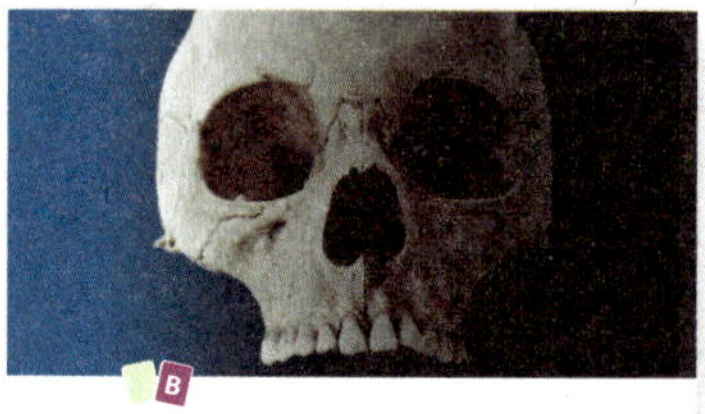

from
Fortune's Bones

The author grabs the audience's attention by making a connection between a real person and his remains in a museum.

> Before Fortune was bones in a Connecticut museum, he was a husband, a father, a baptized Christian, and a slave.

APPLY TO YOUR DRAFT

Use this chart to practice capturing your reader's attention in your introduction. Try several approaches, then decide which one is the most engaging and effective way to begin your report.

Try These Suggestions

Review your research notes with these questions in mind:

- What **fact** surprised me when I first read about it?
- Is there a sentence or phrase from one of my **primary sources** that is especially moving, inspiring, or powerful?
- Is there an **anecdote**—a brief story—that illustrates my controlling idea?

Include a surprising fact or statistic.	
Start off with a famous quotation.	
Provide an interesting anecdote.	

Provide Support by Citing a Source

EXAMINE THE MENTOR TEXT

In *Fortune's Bones*, Pamela Espeland uses a quotation and cites her source to support an idea. In this case, the person quoted may have preferred to be unnamed.

The author cites the source of her quote.

One Waterbury resident remembers, "Larry was the thing to see when you go to the museum. I don't think anybody ever envisioned that this was truly a human being."

Espeland uses a quotation to emphasize the idea that the display of Fortune's bones was dehumanizing.

APPLY TO YOUR DRAFT

Identify a quotation from one of your sources that you'd like to include in your report. Then use this chart to practice different methods of citing the source. Consider using a variety of methods to cite your sources.

Provide the name of the person who said or wrote the quotation.	
Cite the title and author of the book where the quotation appears.	
Include a citation in parentheses at the end of a sentence that includes a quotation or ideas from a source.	

3 REVISE YOUR RESEARCH REPORT

Professional writers rework their language as they write to make sure their ideas are conveyed effectively. Use the guide to help you revise your report.

Ed

Help with Revision

Find a **Peer Review Guide** and **Student Models** online.

REVISION GUIDE		
ASK YOURSELF	**PROVE IT**	**REVISE IT**
Introduction Does my introduction introduce my topic and controlling idea?	**Underline** the controlling idea.	**Add** a controlling idea, or **revise** the controlling idea to clarify your approach.
Controlling Idea Does each paragraph have a main point related to the controlling idea?	**Highlight** the main point of each paragraph.	**Add** a main point if one is missing. **Rewrite** any main points that are unclear.
Supporting Details Are there relevant supporting details for each point?	**Underline** facts, statistics, examples, and quotations that support your points.	**Add** more facts, statistics, examples, and quotations from your notes.
Organization Are ideas organized logically? Do transitions clearly connect ideas?	**Highlight** transitional words and phrases within and between paragraphs.	**Rearrange** sentences and paragraphs to organize ideas logically. **Add** transitions to connect ideas.
Citing Sources Is information gathered from a variety of sources, and are those sources cited correctly?	**Underline** references to sources.	**Add** more sources for variety. **Cite** all sources correctly.
Conclusion Does my conclusion support the information presented?	**Highlight** sentences that support information in the report.	**Add** supporting sentences.

APPLY TO YOUR DRAFT

Consider the following as you look for opportunities to improve your writing.

- Make sure your report has a clear controlling idea.
- Use evidence from sources to support the controlling idea.
- Correct any errors in grammar and punctuation.

Peer Review in Action

Once you have finished revising your research report, you will exchange papers with a partner in a **peer review.** During a peer review, you will give suggestions to improve your partner's draft.

Read this passage from a student's draft and examine the comments made by her peer reviewer.

First Draft

The Role of Education in the Abolition Movement
by Tanzina Salas, Irving Middle School

. . . In all these ways, educating white people in the North about the evils of slavery helped spur the abolition movement.

Reading a book called *The Columbian Orator* shaped young Frederick Douglass's ideas about slavery and emancipation. . .

Can you add a transitional phrase or sentence to connect the paragraphs?

Be sure to cite your source for this fact.

Now read the revised passage below. Notice how the writer has improved her draft by making revisions based on her peer reviewer's comments.

Revision

. . . In all these ways, educating white people in the North about the evils of slavery helped spur the abolition movement.

Education was crucial for enslaved African Americans, too, although it was much harder for them to obtain. Frederick Douglass, who would become a leader among abolitionists, describes in his *Narrative of the Life of Frederick Douglass* how he traded bread for reading lessons with poor white boys (page 269). Later, Douglass tells how reading a book called *The Columbian Orator* shaped his ideas about slavery and emancipation (page 269). . . .

Nice transition! This sentence shows you are shifting to a new topic.

Citing the title of your source and specific page numbers gives readers confidence in your facts.

APPLY TO YOUR DRAFT

During your peer review, give each other specific suggestions for how you could make your reports clearer or more informative. Use your revision guide to help you.

When receiving feedback from your partner, listen attentively and ask questions to make sure you fully understand the revision suggestions.

4 EDIT YOUR RESEARCH REPORT

Apply the finishing touches to your draft. Edit your draft to check for proper use of standard English conventions and to correct any misspellings or grammatical errors.

Watch Your Language!

USE VERB MOODS

The **mood** of a verb shows the writer's attitude toward what is being stated. In a report, most sentences are written in the **indicative mood,** which is used to state facts. The **conditional mood** is used to imagine what might happen if a certain condition is met.

Indicative mood: Frederick Douglass learned to read.

Conditional mood: If Frederick Douglass had not learned to read, the abolition movement would have lost one of its strongest voices.

As the example shows, the conditional mood uses helping verb like *might, could,* or *would* to suggest what might have happened if historical events had been different.

APPLY TO YOUR DRAFT

Now apply what you've learned about the conditional mood to your own work.

1. **Reread your paper** and consider where you might ask readers to think about an alternate outcome in the course of history.
2. **Add a sentence or two** using the conditional mood.
3. **Exchange drafts** with a partner and review each other's work.

5 PUBLISH YOUR RESEARCH REPORT

Share It!

Finalize your research report for a class collection about the abolition movement. You may also use your report as inspiration for other projects.

Ways to Share

- **Give a speech** to the class to present your research findings.
- **Create a multimedia presentation** of your report and post it on a class website.
- **Have a collaborative discussion** with your classmates. See the next task for tips on how.

Speaking & Listening

Participate in a Collaborative Discussion

Imagine you are invited to design a new unit that addresses the essential question: What will people risk to be free? Work collaboratively with group members to choose a topic for such a unit, select materials to teach it, and then present your ideas to the class.

Make a Plan

Working in a small group, make a plan for your collaborative discussion. All group members should contribute so everyone's ideas are considered.

Use the chart to take notes about each step in your group's planning process. Then refer to the chart to guide a group discussion.

Set Some Ground Rules

As you work collaboratively, follow these rules of polite discussion:

- listen closely to one another
- value contributions of all group members
- stay on topic
- express disagreement politely and respectfully
- ask only helpful, relevant questions

DISCUSSION PLANNING STEP	NOTES
Brainstorm With your group, make a list of fights for freedom you know about.	
Vote on a Topic Decide as a group which topic from your list you want to focus on in your discussion.	
Set an Agenda Determine what will be covered in the discussion.	
Create a Schedule Allot an appropriate amount of time for each item to be discussed.	

Prepare to Present

Once you have decided what your unit will focus on, prepare to present your proposal to the class. Everyone in the group should have a role. Practice with each other to improve your performance.

Use this guide to practice each person's speaking part and give specific suggestions for improvement.

Active Listening

When you are listening to other members of your group remember to

- Give each presenter your full attention.
- Suggest ways for presenters to improve their delivery.
- Ask questions to clarify any confusing parts.

SPEAKING GOAL	NOTES FOR IMPROVEMENT
Make your delivery smooth. Practice words that you stumble over and rearrange sentences to clarify ideas.	
Make eye contact with your audience and use natural gestures as you speak.	
Speak clearly at an appropriate volume. Stress important words for dramatic effect or emphasis.	

Present the Unit

Based on the practice session, make any final changes as you get ready for your presentation. Then, groups should take turns presenting their units to the whole class:

- As group members present their unit, they may refer briefly to their notes to recall main points, but they should speak directly to the audience.
- Audience members should listen closely and take notes.
- After each presentation, groups should invite the audience to ask questions about their unit.

Share It!

- **Create a podcast** by recording your discussion and the audience interaction. Review the recording and edit out distracting noises or doubletalk.
- **Take a class poll** on which group's proposal was the most well-received.

Ed

Interactive Speaking & Listening Lesson: Participate in a Collaborative Discussion

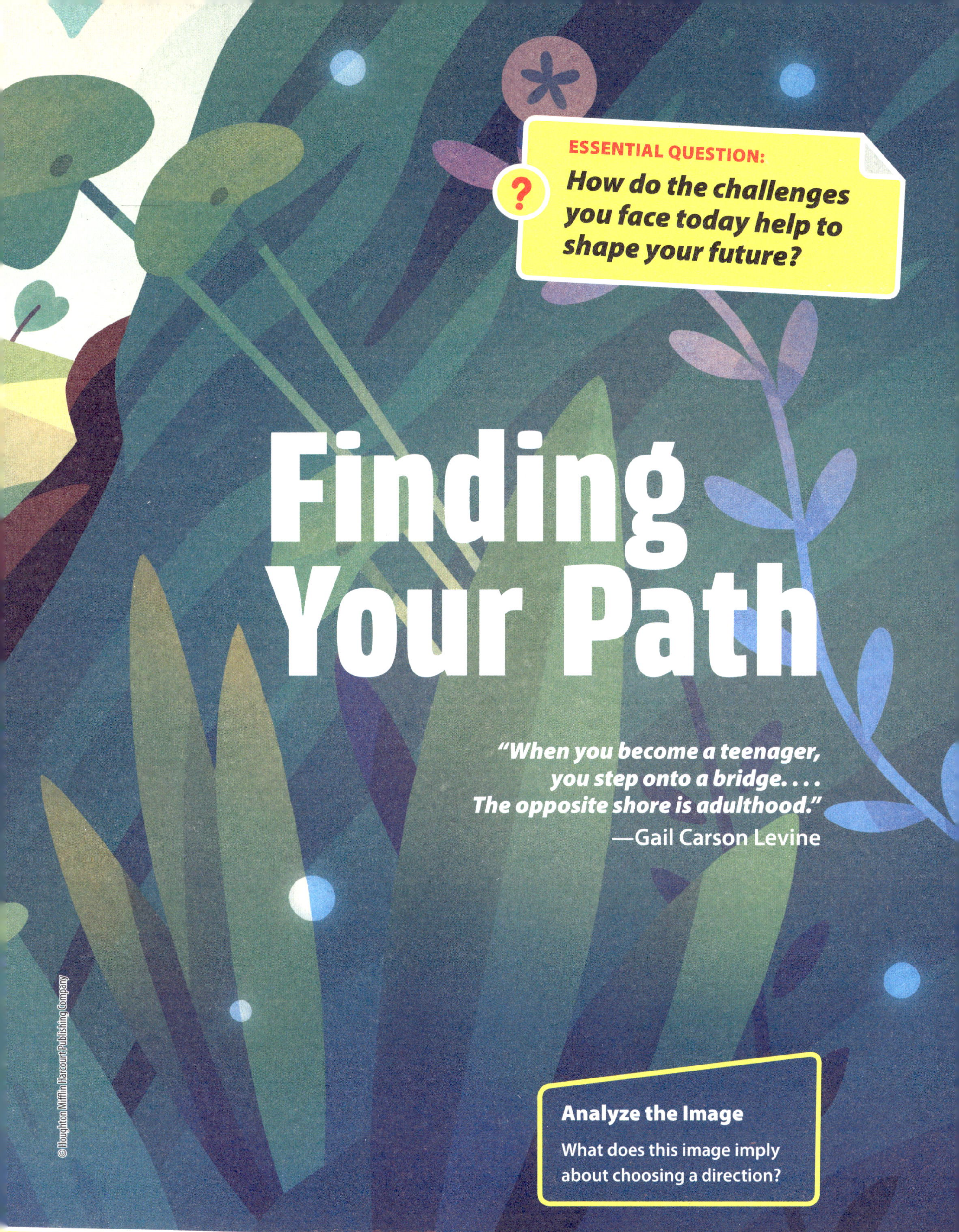

ESSENTIAL QUESTION:

How do the challenges you face today help to shape your future?

Finding Your Path

"When you become a teenager, you step onto a bridge. . . . The opposite shore is adulthood."

—Gail Carson Levine

Analyze the Image

What does this image imply about choosing a direction?

Spark Your Learning

Here are some ways to spark your learning about the topics and themes of **Unit 5: Finding Your Path.**

As you read, you can use the **Response Log** (page R5) to track your thinking about the Essential Question.

Make the Connection

What will your path through life look like? Sketch a picture or write a description of your path in the space below.

Think About the Essential Question

How do the challenges you face today help to shape your future?

Explain your opinion.

Sound Like an Expert

You can use these Academic Vocabulary words to write and talk about the topics and themes in the unit. Which of these words do you already feel comfortable using when speaking or writing?

	I can use it!	I understand it.	I'll look it up.
debate			
deduce			
license			
sufficient			
trend			

Prove It!

Turn to a partner and use one of the words in a sentence about the challenges of being a teenager.

Preview the Texts

Look over the images, titles, and descriptions of the texts in the unit. Mark the title of the text that interests you most.

from Bronx Masquerade

Novel by **Nikki Grimes**

When Mr. Ward's students start reading their poems on "Open Mike Fridays," they're surprised by what they learn about themselves and their classmates.

The Debt We Owe to the Adolescent Brain

Informational Text by **Jeanne Miller**

The teenage years are a time of amazing growth and adaptation for the human brain.

Hanging Fire

Poem by **Audre Lorde**

This poem brilliantly captures the intensity of a fourteen-year-old girl's worries and frustrations.

Summer of His Fourteenth Year

Poem by **Gloria Amescua**

The speaker of this poem watches her son transform into a young man.

from It's Complicated: The Social Lives of Networked Teens

Argument by **dana boyd**

Should adults worry so much about how much time teens spend with technology?

Outsmart Your Smartphone

Argument by **Catherine Steiner-Adair**

This author writes about how teenagers use technology and makes suggestions for using it responsibly.

I Wonder . . .

What's the best thing about being a teenager? Jot down or sketch your answer.

from
Bronx Masquerade

Novel by Nikki Grimes

ESSENTIAL QUESTION:
How do the challenges you face today help to shape your future?

Engage Your Brain

Choose one or two of these activities to start connecting with the narrative you're about to read.

Get to Know the Bronx

The excerpt you are about to read is set at a high school in the Bronx. Do some research to learn more about the Bronx. Make sure to find facts about

- the boroughs of New York City
- famous landmarks in the Bronx
- the population and diversity of the Bronx

Visualize a Masquerade

Think about the title of this text. What do you think of when you read the word *masquerade*? Make a quick drawing or write a brief description.

Let's Talk Poetry

The students in the text you are about to read give poetry readings in their classroom. Have you ever taken part in or attended a poetry reading? Discuss with a partner or small group what you do or do not like about reading, writing, or listening to poetry.

Analyze Perspectives

In literature, the term **perspective** refers to the way in which characters think about their world—its setting, the events that happen in it, and the characters who participate in those events (including themselves). Writers can reveal their characters' perspectives by stating the characters' opinions and thoughts directly. Perspectives can also be suggested by characters' actions.

The excerpt from *Bronx Masquerade* that you are about to read has multiple first-person narrators, each with a unique perspective. As you read, consider how each character's perspective contributes to your understanding of their shared experience.

Focus on Genre

Novel

- is a long work of fiction
- has a plot, or series of events, centered on a conflict that characters try to solve
- has a setting, or time and place of the action, that may affect the characters
- depicts characters who develop and change over time
- develops one or more themes, or messages about life

Analyze Characterization

Readers learn what characters are like through an author's use of **characterization,** the way a writer creates and develops characters. Three story elements used to develop characters are dialogue, the comments of narrators, and plot events. Study the chart below.

STORY ELEMENT USED FOR CHARACTERIZATION	EXPLANATION	EXAMPLE
Dialogue	Characters' spoken words often state or suggest their emotions and motivations.	Tyrone tells Diondra to "Take a deep breath. Ain't nobody going to hurt you here." This suggests that he is kind and wants to help her feel comfortable.
Narrator's comments	Narrated thoughts can give the reader insight into the narrator's personality.	When Devon says, "I've got good height and good hands, and that's a fact," the reader can infer that he is confident about his strengths as a basketball player.
Events	Incidents in a story, and how characters respond to them, can be revealing.	The incident with Devon and Janelle in the library suggests his self-consciousness and her insightfulness.

As you read the excerpt from *Bronx Masquerade*, think about ways in which the author uses characterization to reveal various aspects of each character.

Annotation in Action

Here are one reader's notes about perspective in *Bronx Masquerade.* As you read, note how the author uses different first-person points of view to reveal characters' conflicts, goals, relationships, and values.

If only I was as bold as Raul. The other day, he left one of his paintings out on Mr. Ward's desk where anybody could see it. Which was the point. He sometimes works at Mr. Ward's desk during lunch. The wet paintbrushes sticking up out of the jar are always a sign that he's been at it again.

Diondra admires Raul's confidence. Is she jealous of his artistic talent?

Expand Your Vocabulary

Put a check mark next to the vocabulary words that you feel comfortable using when speaking or writing.

tirade	☐
hunker	☐
snicker	☐
confide	☐

Turn to a partner and use one of the words you already know in a sentence about writing poems.

As you read the excerpt from *Bronx Masquerade,* use the definitions in the side column to learn the vocabulary words you don't already know.

Background

Nikki Grimes (b. 1950) was born in Harlem and spent some of her younger years in foster homes. At age 13, she gave her first public poetry reading at a local library named after the poet Countee Cullen. She was already steeped in the works of Cullen and other Black poets of the era known as the Harlem Renaissance. These poets, she says, have been the primary influences in her work. Grimes has written prose and poetry for adults, children, and young adults, winning many honors and awards for her work.

from

Bronx Masquerade

Novel by **Nikki Grimes**

When Mr. Ward's students start reading their poems on "Open Mike Fridays," they're surprised by what they learn about themselves and their classmates.

NOTICE & NOTE
As you read, use the side margins to make notes about the text.

Diondra Jordan

1 If only I was as bold as Raul. The other day, he left one of his paintings out on Mr. Ward's desk where anybody could see it. Which was the point. He sometimes works at Mr. Ward's desk during lunch. The wet paintbrushes sticking up out of the jar are always a sign that he's been at it again. So of course, anybody who glances over in that direction will be tempted to stop by and look.

2 This particular painting was rough, but anyone could tell it was Raul. A self-portrait. He'll probably hang it in class. Back in September, Mr. Ward covered two of the classroom walls with black construction paper and then scattered paper frames up and down the walls, each one a different size and color. Now half the room looks sort of like an art gallery, which was the

ANALYZE PERSPECTIVES

Annotate: Mark sentences in paragraphs 1–2 that suggest Diondra's perspective regarding Raul.

Infer: What do these sentences suggest about the way that Diondra thinks about Raul?

idea. We're supposed to use the paper frames for our work. Whether we put up poems or photographs or even paintings is up to us, so long as the work is ours and we can tie it in with our study of the Harlem Renaissance.[1] I guess Raul's self-portrait fits, since we've been talking a lot about identity. He'll probably put it up next to his poem. You should have seen him hang that thing. You'd think he was handling a million-dollar masterpiece the way he took his time placing it just so. If you look close, you can see the smudges where he erased a word or two and rewrote it. Mr. Ward must be in shock. He can never get Raul to rewrite a lick of homework or anything else. And don't even talk to him about checking his spelling! He'll launch into a **tirade** on you in a minute. "What?" he'll snap. "You think Puerto Ricans can't spell?" Forget it. Anyway, I dare you to find one misspelled word in that poem of his! Maybe it's a visual thing. Maybe he wants his poem to look as good as his self-portrait. And it is good.

3 I've never tried doing a self-portrait, but why not? I could maybe do one in charcoal. I like drawing faces in charcoal. I've been drawing since I can't remember when. Not that anyone

Ed

Close Read Screencast

Listen to a modeled close read of this text.

tirade

(tī´rād) *n.* A *tirade* is a long, angry speech.

ANALYZE CHARACTERIZATION

Annotate: Mark details in paragraphs 3–4 that help you understand Diondra's character.

Interpret: Why doesn't Diondra want her schoolmates to know about the art she creates?

[1] **Harlem Renaissance:** Between the end of World War I and the 1930s, Black writers, artists, scholars, and musicians fled the repression of the Jim Crow South and moved to Harlem in New York City. The influential literary and cultural movement that began there is known as the Harlem Renaissance.

here knows that, except Tanisha, and she found out by accident when she came to my house to study once and saw a couple of drawings hanging in my room. Mom loves my watercolors and she hung one in the living room, but it isn't signed. Nobody ever mentions it, especially not my father. He's not too wild about my art. Mostly, he's disappointed, first off that I wasn't born a boy, and second that I won't play ball like one. I'm six feet tall, almost as tall as he, and he figures the height is wasted on me since I don't share his dreams of me going to the WNBA. I keep telling him not to hold his breath.

4 I hate always being the tallest girl in school. Everybody expects me to play basketball, so they pick me for their team, throw me the ball, and wait for me to shoot. Big mistake. I fumble it every time. Then they have the nerve to get mad at me, like I did it on purpose! But basketball is not my game. I have no game. I'm an artist, like Raul. The difference is, I don't tell anybody. I refuse to give them new reasons to laugh at me. The Jolly Green Giant jokes are bad enough.

5 Yeah, it's definitely time to try a self-portrait. I think I'll paint myself in front of an easel. With a basketball jersey sticking up out of the trash. Then I could hang it in Mr. Ward's class. See if anybody notices.

Don't forget to **Notice & Note** as you read the text.

ANALYZE PERSPECTIVES

Annotate: In paragraph 5, mark the elements that Diondra plans to include in her self-portrait.

Analyze: How do these elements confirm what you already know about Diondra's perspective regarding herself?

OPEN MIKE
If

By Diondra Jordan

6 *If I stood on tiptoe*
reached up and sculpted
mountains from clouds
would you laugh out loud?

7 *If I dipped my brush in starlight*
painted a ribbon of night
on your windowsill
would you still laugh?

8 *If I drew you adrift*
in a pen and ink sea
in a raging storm
would you laugh at me?

9 *If I planted watercolor roses*
in your garden
would you laugh then?
Or would you breathe deep
to sample their scent?
I wonder.

Tyrone

10 If the sista read any faster, I'd be looking for her Supergirl cape. Talk about nervous! Diondra's hands were shaking the whole time she was holding that poem. She sure spooks easy for somebody so tall.

11 "Yo!" I said. "Take a deep breath. Ain't nobody going to hurt you here." She smiled a little and tried to slow down. But I swear that girl burned rubber getting back to her seat when she was through. I guess she's not exactly used to the limelight.

12 She's got plenty of company. Four more kids read their poetry for the first time today. They were shaking in their boots, but it was all good. I only had to tell one of them to loosen up. Guess you could call that progress!

ANALYZE CHARACTERIZATION

Annotate: Mark the words and phrases that show what Tyrone thinks about the readers.

Draw Conclusions: What do Tyrone's comments reveal about his personality?

Don't forget to **Notice & Note** as you read the text.

Devon Hope

13 Jump Shot. What kind of name is that? Not mine, but try telling that to the brothers at school. That's all they ever call me.

14 You'd think it was written somewhere. Tall guys must be jocks. No. Make that tall *people,* 'cause Diondra's got the same problem. Everybody expects her to shoot hoops. The difference is, she's got no talent in that direction. Ask me, she's got no business playing b-ball. That's my game.

15 I've got good height and good hands, and that's a fact. But what about the rest of me? Forget who I really am, who I really want to be. The law is be cool, be tough, play ball, and use books for weight training—not reading. Otherwise, everybody gives you grief. Don't ask me why I care, especially when the grief is coming from a punk like Wesley. Judging from the company he keeps, he's a gangsta in sheep's clothing. I don't even know why he and Tyrone bother coming to school. It's clear they don't take it seriously, although maybe they're starting to. That's according to Sterling, who believes in praying for everybody and giving them the benefit of the doubt. I love the preacher-man, but I think he may be giving these brothers too much credit. Anyway, when I hang around after school and any of the guys ask me: "Yo, Devon, where you going?" I tell them I'm heading for the gym to meet Coach and work on my layup. Then once they're out the door, I cut upstairs to the library to sneak a read.

16 It's not much better at home. My older brother's always after me to hit the streets with him, calls me a girly man for loving books and jazz.

17 Don't get me wrong. B-ball is all right. Girls like you, for one thing. But it's not you they like. It's Mr. Basketball. And if that's not who you are inside, then it's not you they're liking. So what's the point? Still, I don't mind playing, just not all the time.

VOCABULARY

Use Context Clues: The word *grief* often means "deep sadness." However, by using context clues, the reader can determine that Devon uses the word to mean something other than that in paragraph 15.

Interpret: What does Devon mean by the phrase "everybody gives you grief"?

18 This year is looking better. My English teacher has got us studying the Harlem Renaissance, which means we have to read a lot of poetry. That suits me just fine, gives me a reason to drag around my beat-up volumes of Langston Hughes and Claude McKay. Whenever anybody bugs me about it, all I have to say is "Homework." Even so, I'd rather the brothers not catch me with my head in a book.

19 The other day, I duck into the library, snare a corner table, and **hunker** down with *3000 Years of Black Poetry*. Raynard sees me, but it's not like he's going to tell anybody. He hardly speaks, and he never hangs with any of the brothers I know. So I breathe easy. I'm sure no one else has spotted me until a head pops up from behind the stacks. It's Janelle Battle from my English class. I freeze and wait for the **snickers** I'm used to. Wait for her to say something like: "What? Coach got you *reading* now? Afraid you're gonna flunk out and drop off the team?" But all she does is smile and wave. Like it's no big deal for me to be in a library reading. Like I have a right to be there if I want. Then she pads over, slips a copy of *The Panther & the Lash* on my table, and walks away without saying a word. It's one of my favorite books by Langston Hughes. How could she know? Seems like she's noticed me in the library more often than I thought.

20 Janelle is all right. So what if she's a little plump? At least when you turn the light on upstairs, somebody's at home. She's smart, and she doesn't try hiding it. Which gets me thinking. Maybe it's time I quit sneaking in and out of the library like some thief. Maybe it's time I just started being who I am.

hunker
(hŭng´kər) *v.* To *hunker* down means to stay in a place and focus on a task for a period of time.

snicker
(snĭk´ər) *n.* A *snicker* is a superior, partially suppressed laugh.

NOTICE & NOTE
AHA MOMENT

When you notice a sudden realization that shifts a character's actions or understandings, you've found an **Aha Moment** signpost.

Notice & Note: In paragraphs 19–20, mark words and phrases that show a change in Devon's attitude.

Predict: How might this realization change things for Devon?

OPEN MIKE
Bronx Masquerade

By Devon Hope

21 *I woke up this morning*
exhausted from hiding
the me of me
so I stand here ***confiding***
there's more to Devon
than jump shot and rim.
I'm more than tall
and lengthy of limb.
I dare you to peep
behind these eyes,
discover the poet
in tough-guy disguise.
Don't call me Jump Shot.
My name is Surprise.

confide
(kən-fīd´) *v.* To *confide* means to share private or secret information.

TURN AND TALK

Turn to a partner and discuss how Diondra's and Devon's poems help to express the thoughts and feelings they share in the other parts of the text.

?

ESSENTIAL QUESTION:

How do the challenges you face today help to shape your future?

Review your notes and add your thoughts to your Response Log.

Assessment Practice

Answer these questions before moving on to the **Analyze the Text** section on the following page.

1. This question has two parts. First, answer **Part A**. Then, answer **Part B**.

Part A

What does Diondra want to avoid revealing to others?

(A) how ashamed she is of her basketball skills

(B) how much she sees herself as an artist

(C) how much she wants Raul to be her boyfriend

(D) how embarrassed she is about the way Mom reacts to her art

Part B

Select the statement that best supports the answer to Part A.

(A) "If only I was as bold as Raul." (paragraph 1)

(B) "Mom loves my watercolors. . . ." (paragraph 3)

(C) "Everybody expects me to play basketball. . . ." (paragraph 4)

(D) "I'm an artist. . . . The difference is, I don't tell anybody." (paragraph 4)

2. How does Devon react when he sees Janelle in the library?

(A) He is suspicious of her reason for waving at him.

(B) He tries to hide under his table.

(C) He worries that she will tease him for reading.

(D) He is annoyed that someone from his class is there with him.

Ed

Test-Taking Strategies

Analyze the Text

Support your responses with evidence from the text.

NOTICE & NOTE

Review what you **noticed and noted** as you read the text. Your annotations can help you answer these questions.

1. **ANALYZE** To whom is Tyrone speaking when he says, "Take a deep breath. Ain't nobody going to hurt you here" (paragraph 11)? What aspect of Tyrone's character does this comment reveal?

2. **COMPARE** How does Devon's view of Diondra's playing basketball differ from Diondra's perspective?

3. **CONNECT** Devon shares his thoughts in narrated paragraphs and in a poem—two different structures. What thoughts in his narration are emphasized most clearly in his poem?

4. **EVALUATE** Which character's perspective do you think is presented most effectively? Explain.

5. **INFER** What does the classroom project help Diondra and Devon realize about themselves and others in their struggle for self-expression? Cite examples that suggest the characters are having **Aha Moments.**

6. **ANALYZE** Refer to any notes you took about how the author uses story elements to develop her characters. Give at least one example of how each element is used and provide analysis of each example of characterization.

STORY ELEMENT USED FOR CHARACTERIZATION	EXAMPLE	YOUR ANALYSIS
Dialogue		
Narrator's comments		
Events		

Choices

Here are some other ways to demonstrate your understanding of the ideas in this lesson.

Writing

Write a Poem

Write a poem about identity or the search for identity that you might perform at a poetry reading.

- Review the poems in the excerpt for inspiration, and decide on the message you want to convey in your own poem.
- Think about the form and tone that will best suit your message.
- Consider using repetition to emphasize the most important idea.
- Have a partner read your poem and give you feedback. Make revisions, if necessary.

As you write and discuss, be sure to use the **Academic Vocabulary** words.

debate

deduce

license

sufficient

trend

Speaking & Listening

Present a Poem

Choose a poem to read aloud for your class. It can be any poem—one you've written or one by a published author.

- With a partner, rehearse reading the poem aloud.
- Decide whether you will accompany the words with movement or gestures.
- Present the poem to the class, using appropriate volume, phrasing, and expression.

Social & Emotional Learning

Discuss as a Small Group

In *Bronx Masquerade*, the students who share their writing experience social benefits as well as emotional benefits. Discuss with a small group how poetry readings can help people from diverse backgrounds better understand and respect each other, and how they can help to create a sense of community.

Expand Your Vocabulary

PRACTICE AND APPLY

Use your understanding of the vocabulary words to complete each sentence.

tirade	hunker	snicker	confide

1. A basketball fan might launch into a **tirade** if . . .
2. A serious writer hates to hear **snickers** from the audience during a poetry reading because . . .
3. If you **confide** in a trusted friend, you are . . .
4. When you **hunker** down with a good book, you are . . .

Vocabulary Strategy

Use Context Clues

Context clues can help you clarify the meaning of unfamiliar or ambiguous words. To use context clues, look at surrounding words and phrases to find hints about a word's meaning. Note this example of a multiple-meaning word from *Bronx Masquerade:*

> This particular painting was rough, but anyone could tell it was Raul. A self-portrait. He'll probably hang it in class.

The context clues help you understand that the narrator is referring to what the painting looks like, not how it feels. You can tell from the context that *rough* means "unpolished," not "coarse to the touch."

Ed
Interactive Vocabulary Lesson: Using Context Clues

PRACTICE AND APPLY

Find the following words in paragraphs 2 and 4 of the excerpt from *Bronx Masquerade*. Identify context clues to each word's meaning, and write your guessed definition in the chart. Then look up each word in a dictionary to check your definition.

WORD	CONTEXT CLUES	GUESSED DEFINITION
gallery		
smudge		
launch		
fumble		

Watch Your Language!

Gerunds

Ed Interactive Grammar Lesson: Gerunds and Gerund Phrases

A **verbal** is a word that is formed from a verb but is used as a noun, an adjective, or an adverb. A **gerund** is one kind of verbal—specifically, a verb form ending in *-ing* that is used as a noun.

> I woke up this morning /exhausted from hiding / the me of me.

Not all words ending in *–ing* are gerunds. Some are nouns, as in this sentence from the selection:

> This particular painting was rough, but anyone could tell it was Raul.

Gerunds can perform the same functions as nouns in a sentence:

Subject	**Studying Raul's artwork inspired Diondra.**
Direct Object	**She would try creating her own self-portrait.**
Indirect Object	**She gave drawing her undivided attention.**
Object of a Preposition	**Diondra began by sketching rough features.**
Predicate Noun	**The most difficult part was shading the details correctly.**

PRACTICE AND APPLY

In each sentence, identify each gerund and its function.

1. All our school's art classes began planning an art show.
2. Booking the gym for one weekend was an easy task.
3. We had a harder time with deciding how to arrange and display the various artwork.
4. Assigning sculptures a separate place with special lighting worked well.
5. The artwork in the show made me want to take up painting.

Sleeping is my favorite thing to do.

The Debt We Owe to the Adolescent Brain

Informational Text by Jeanne Miller

ESSENTIAL QUESTION:
How do the challenges you face today help to shape your future?

Engage Your Brain

Choose one or two of these activities to start connecting with the informational text you're about to read.

What's So Great about Your Brain?

Why might we owe the adolescent brain a debt? To answer this question, conduct research and find out more about what makes teenage brains unique. Record your findings below.

Breaking Away

In what ways do teenagers seek independence from their parents? With a partner, have a brief discussion about how teens break away from the influence of their families as they prepare to set out on their own paths.

Pushing the Limits

In the text you are about to read, the author explains that teenagers tend to engage in risky or dangerous behavior. Why do you think this is? Make a list of possible reasons below.

Analyze Structure

The **structure** of a text is the way in which it is put together. In "The Debt We Owe to the Adolescent Brain," the author uses **headings** to divide the article into sections. Headings can help you understand how each section contributes to the overall structure and to the development of key ideas. Authors also use **patterns of organization,** or ways of arranging ideas, to structure their texts.

PATTERN	WHAT IT HIGHLIGHTS	SIGNAL WORDS
main-idea-and-details order	evidence that supports a key idea	*for example, experts say, others agree that*
cause-and-effect order	relationships between causes and effects	*because, so, as a result, therefore*
compare-and-contrast order	ways in which subjects are alike and different	*all, most, similarly, by contrast, but, however*

A pattern of organization may be used to organize an entire piece of writing or single paragraphs or sections within a text. As you read, note the pattern of organization in each section of the article.

Focus on Genre

Informational Text

- provides factual information
- may include headings and subheadings
- uses organizational patterns such as main-idea-and-details to present information clearly
- may appear in a variety of formats, including magazine articles

Analyze Author's Purpose

An **author's purpose** is his or her main reason for writing. In an informational text, the author's purpose is usually to inform or explain. As you read, use the chart below to keep track of how the key ideas in each section of the text help the author achieve her purpose.

SECTION	KEY IDEAS
Introduction (paragraphs 1–2)	
"Brain Under Construction" (paragraphs 3–5)	
"Moving On from Childhood" (paragraphs 6–11)	
"Stone Age Impulses in the Modern World" (paragraphs 12–14)	
Author's Purpose:	

Annotation in Action

Here is an example of notes a student made about the structure of the second paragraph of "The Debt We Owe to the Adolescent Brain." As you read, mark words and phrases that signal which patterns of organization the author is using.

Most mammals have a period of adolescence. But as soon as they're able to reproduce, they begin bearing and caring for children. By contrast, humans, under the protection of their families, take many years to develop and grow into adulthood.

The author compares and contrasts the length of adolescence in humans and other mammals.

Expand Your Vocabulary

Put a check mark next to the vocabulary words that you feel comfortable using when speaking or writing.

- **adaptable** ☐
- **insulate** ☐
- **deplete** ☐
- **lethal** ☐

Turn to a partner and talk about the words you already know. Then, use as many words as you can in a paragraph about becoming an adult. As you read "The Debt We Owe to the Adolescent Brain," use the definitions in the side column to learn the vocabulary words you don't already know.

Background

Jeanne Miller grew up in northwestern Pennsylvania but later settled in Berkeley, California. She writes children's and young adult magazine articles on a variety of science topics. Her book *Food Science* informs young readers about food chemistry, the movement to promote local and traditional foods, and the future of food.

The Debt We Owe to the Adolescent Brain

Informational Text by Jeanne Miller

The teenage years are a time of amazing growth and adaptation for the human brain.

NOTICE & NOTE
As you read, use the side margins to make notes about the text.

1 Polar bears can live above the Arctic Circle but they can't live at the Equator. Gorillas can live at the Equator but they can't live above the Arctic Circle. Humans, however, can live in the Arctic or they can live in the tropics. Why is our species so **adaptable**? We can thank our long period of adolescence for that.

adaptable (ə-dăp´tə-bəl) *adj. Adaptable* means able to survive under a variety of conditions.

2 Most mammals have a period of adolescence. But as soon as they're able to reproduce, they begin bearing and caring for children. By contrast, humans, under the protection of their families, take many years to develop and grow into adulthood.

Brain Under Construction

3 Dr. Jay Giedd, professor of psychiatry[1] at the University of California at San Diego, says, "Nothing is even close to humans in terms of how long we're dependent on caregivers."

[1] **psychiatry** (sĭ-kī´ə-trē): the branch of medicine that deals with the diagnosis, treatment, and prevention of mental and emotional disorders.

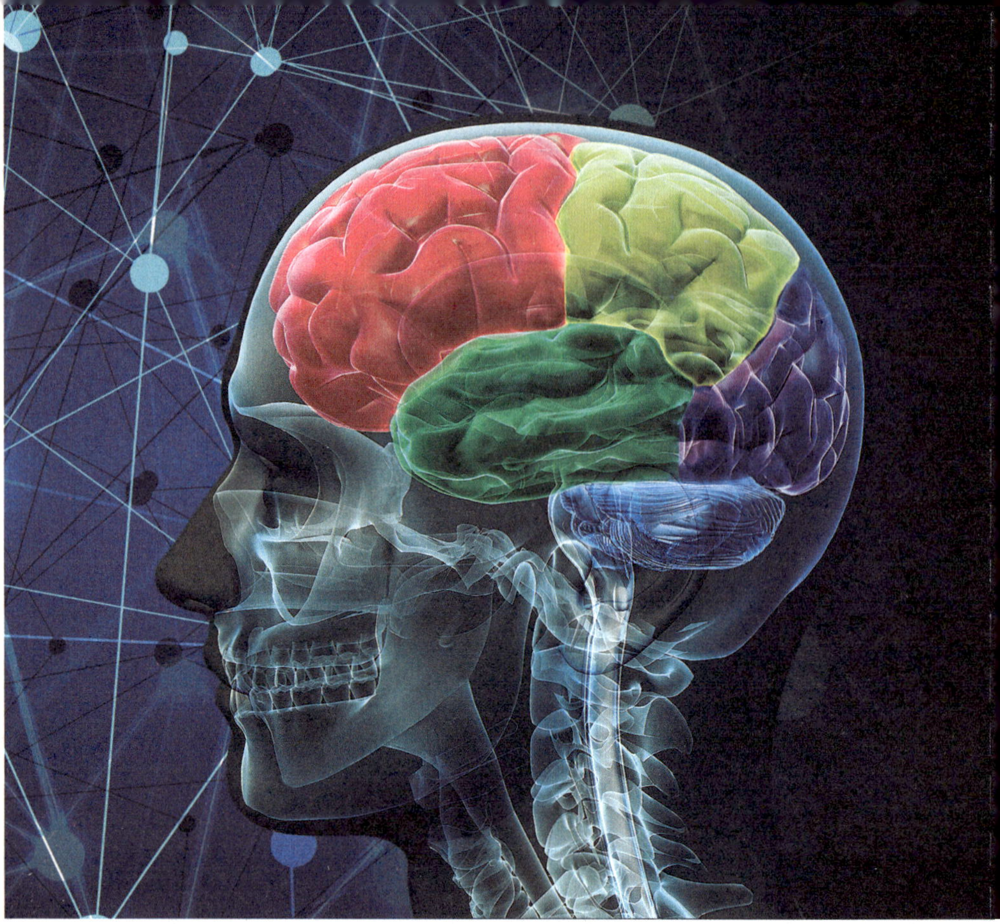

ANALYZE STRUCTURE

Annotate: Mark signal words and phrases that show relationships between ideas in paragraphs 1–3.

Analyze: What is the author's pattern of organization in these paragraphs? How does this pattern help the author introduce and develop main ideas?

He points out that in their early teens, Neanderthals[2] already had children of their own. Neanderthals died out, but our ancestors, *Homo sapiens*, thrived. A large part of that success comes from our brain's taking a long time to mature. This extended period of development lets us build exactly the brain we need in our circumstances. Giedd says, "All the brain's parts have their periods of rapid explosive growth and then rapid pruning back. You have overproduction—more connections than can possibly survive—and then they fight it out. The ones that are used and lead to positive outcomes stay, and those that aren't used, or are used and lead to bad outcomes, are eliminated."

4 We lose "gray matter" and gain "white matter": myelin, which forms an **insulating** sheath around nerve fibers. "We get more and more myelin, which speeds up the communication between nerve cells, as we go through adolescence," says Giedd. "We learn what we need to do and be good at and then the process streamlines that." But the price we pay is that, as myelin is laid down, flexibility diminishes. Adolescence is a kind of golden age when, as Giedd puts it, "You're asking your brain, 'What do I need to be good at? What do I need to do to make it in this world?' Every choice you make trains your brain."

insulate
(ĭn´sə-lāt´) *v.* To *insulate* means to surround or cover to prevent the passage of heat, electricity, or sound.

[2] **Neanderthals** (ne-an´dər-thôlz´): an extinct human species or subspecies.

5 This lets us adjust to our surroundings. Giedd points out, "We all had ancestors that were good at adapting to change. Neanderthals had brains that were about 13 percent bigger than ours and they lived in pretty tough conditions and harsh climates, but they didn't adapt."

Moving On from Childhood

6 Dr. B. J. Casey is a professor of psychology at Weill Cornell Medical College. Her focus on adolescent brains includes those of humans and mice. "There is evidence," she says, "that even adolescent rodents tend to hang out with same-aged peers and tend to have more fights with their parents." Sound familiar? These behaviors—sensitivity to influence from peers, taking risks, and pulling away from parents—are hallmarks of human adolescence. They have their roots in the hunter-gatherer world of our early ancestors, where success meant surviving and reproducing.

7 Finding a mate and passing on your genes means leaving the comfort of your home. Casey says, "If you're getting all your needs met, why in the world would you leave? There needs to be some push-pull tension in evolution to get you to leave that home. Otherwise you'll **deplete** all the resources and it will be difficult to find a mate to partner with."

8 Going out into the world can involve risks, but the adolescent brain is wired for that. Giedd points out that "high risk equals high reward at times." And, compared to children or adults, teens are much more sensitive to rewards.

9 A study in Casey's lab demonstrated that fact when researchers put teenagers in a brain-scanning machine and asked them to complete a simple task. Successfully completing it earned them a lot of money. The resulting brain scans showed an exaggerated response in the reward center of the teens' brains, but only a moderate response in children and adults.

10 Sometimes the reward might be approval by their peers, who will be important to a teenager's future. In another study, Casey's group showed that, unlike children and adults, adolescents found smiling faces to be almost irresistible. She says, "When your peers are smiling it means they're accepting you."

11 Giedd says, "The peer group is the one that will help protect you, who will be your teammates, and who will supply resources. Job one for adolescents is navigating their social world."

NOTICE & NOTE

NUMBERS AND STATS

When you notice the use of specific quantities or comparisons to show amounts, size, or scale, you've found a **Numbers and Stats** signpost.

Notice & Note: In paragraph 5, mark the comparison the author makes using a number.

Infer: What purpose does this number serve in this context?

deplete
(dĭ-plēt´) *v.* To *deplete* means to use up or to reduce to a very small amount.

NOTICE & NOTE

CONTRASTS AND CONTRADICTIONS

When you notice a difference between two or more elements in the text, you've found a **Contrasts and Contradictions** signpost.

Notice & Note: Mark details in paragraphs 8–9 that provide evidence to contrast adolescents with children and adults.

Analyze: Why does the author point out these differences?

ANALYZE AUTHOR'S PURPOSE

Annotate: Circle the subheading of the last section. Then, underline possible effects of "Stone Age impulses in the modern world" in paragraphs 12–14.

Analyze: How does this section help the author achieve her purpose?

Stone Age Impulses in the Modern World

12 In hunter-gatherer societies, success in a risk-taking activity might result in a supply of food, in securing a mate, or in finding new territory. Of course, it can sometimes result in being killed by a predator. Taking certain risks can also pay off for modern teens. Giedd says, "As long as it's not **lethal**—as in the case of foolish risk-taking—it can lead to innovation and creativity."

lethal
(lē´thəl) *adj. Lethal* means causing or capable of causing death.

13 The dangers today's teens face are different from those our early ancestors faced. It's a sad paradox that, relative to children, people in their late adolescence, who are generally the strongest and healthiest they'll ever be, face a 200 percent increase in the chance of dying. The main cause is accidents, with one-third of those being automobile crashes. Reckless driving and other dangerous behaviors put teenagers at risk, but young people also face threats to their health from the considerable stresses of growing up in the 21st century. "Adolescents are dealing with a lot," Casey says, "but they should remember they have greater potential for change now than at any other time. There will be many opportunities for them to change behaviors that they don't want to engage in and to become what they want to be."

VOCABULARY

Use Reference Materials: If you are unfamiliar with the word *paradox* in paragraph 13, use a dictionary or other resource to look it up.

Interpret: How does the author's use of the word *paradox* help get her point across?

14 Giedd agrees. "The challenges adolescents present to their brains now will have effects for decades," he says. The potential for mastering new skills and honing their abilities is phenomenal. "We never lose it completely," Giedd says, "but it's never going to be as good as it is when we're adolescents."

TURN AND TALK

With a partner, discuss the concluding paragraph of the text. Does the information in this paragraph serve as motivation for you?

ESSENTIAL QUESTION:

How do the challenges you face today help to shape your future?

Review your notes and add your thoughts to your Response Log.

Assessment Practice

Answer these questions before moving on to the **Analyze the Text** section on the following page.

1. According to the author, what most distinguishes human adolescence from that of other mammals?

(A) It is shaped mainly by the influence of one's peers.

(B) It lasts longer and includes more dependence on caregivers.

(C) It involves more changes in the brain and body.

(D) It is focused on learning to adapt to one's surroundings.

2. This question has two parts. First answer **Part A**. Then answer **Part B**.

Part A

What is the main idea of paragraphs 6–11?

(A) Human brains develop in a similar way to rodent brains.

(B) Most teenagers' top priority is getting along with their peers.

(C) Adolescents tend to enjoy getting into risky situations.

(D) Adolescent brains react strongly to financial reward.

Part B

Select the sentence that best supports the answer to Part A.

(A) "We can thank our long period of adolescence for that." (paragraph 1)

(B) "Going out into the world can involve risks, but the adolescent brain is wired for that." (paragraph 8)

(C) "[E]ven adolescent rodents tend to hang out with same-aged peers and . . . have more fights with their parents." (paragraph 6)

(D) "Job one for adolescents is navigating their social world." (paragraph 11)

Ed

Test-Taking Strategies

Analyze the Text

Support your responses with evidence from the text.

NOTICE & NOTE

Review what you **noticed and noted** as you read the text. Your annotations can help you answer these questions.

1. **INFER** Why does the author compare humans to Neanderthals in paragraph 3? Cite evidence to support your answer.

2. **CAUSE/EFFECT** What cause-effect relationship does the author identify in the section "Moving On from Childhood"? How does this information relate to the author's purpose?

3. **ANALYZE** What **Contrast or Contradiction** does the author point out in paragraph 13? How does this contradiction relate to the author's purpose?

4. **EVALUATE** What **Numbers and Stats** does the author include in paragraph 13? How effective are these statistics in conveying the key idea of this section of the text?

5. **IDENTIFY PATTERNS** What patterns of organization does the author use to convey information? For each pattern you identify, cite an example and give a reason why she might have used it.

PATTERN	EXAMPLE	REASON FOR USING

6. **ANALYZE** What is the author's main purpose for writing this article? How do the text's structure, headings, and patterns of organization help the author achieve this purpose?

Choices

Here are some other ways to demonstrate your understanding of the ideas in this lesson.

Writing

Explanatory Essay

Write a short essay explaining the evolutionary purpose of some aspect of your teenage behavior.

- Identify an aspect of your behavior that might be explained by current research on brain changes that occur during adolescence.
- Conduct research to learn more about how changes in the brain affect adolescent behavior.
- Cite evidence from the text to support and develop your ideas about the evolutionary purpose of your behavior.

As you write and discuss, be sure to use the **Academic Vocabulary** words.

debate

deduce

license

sufficient

trend

Social & Emotional Learning

Discuss with a Small Group

Have a discussion about how information in "The Debt We Owe to the Adolescent Brain" can help you navigate school and life.

- With a small group, discuss practical ways in which your understanding of adolescent brain changes might influence choices you make or goals that you set at school and at home.
- Be sure to support your views with evidence from the article.
- During your discussion, listen closely and respectfully to all ideas.

Media

Create an Infographic

With a small group, create an infographic that reflects and builds on the ideas and information in the article.

1. Conduct research to gather additional information about the adolescent brain.
2. Decide what kinds of visual aids to include in your infographic. Consider which information will be best conveyed by text and which by charts and graphs.
3. Use digital tools to collaborate and create the final graphic. Make sure the images and text you include work well together.

Expand Your Vocabulary

PRACTICE AND APPLY

Use what you know about the vocabulary words to answer the following questions.

adaptable	insulate	deplete	lethal

1. What would **insulate** a swimmer, a wetsuit or a life jacket? Why?
2. What might **deplete** your energy, a good night's rest or a long soccer practice? Why?
3. If a species is highly **adaptable,** will a change in its environment likely be **lethal**? Why or why not?

Vocabulary Strategy

Use Reference Materials

Ed
Interactive Vocabulary Lesson: Using Reference Sources

When reading an informational text such as a science article, looking up technical terms in reference materials such as dictionaries or glossaries can help you better understand the ideas. Read this passage from "The Debt We Owe to the Adolescent Brain."

> We lose "gray matter" and gain "white matter": myelin, which forms an insulating sheath around nerve fibers. "We get more and more myelin, which speeds up the communication between nerve cells . . ." says Giedd.

You can determine the meaning of *myelin* from context clues such as "white matter" and "speeds up communication between nerve cells." You can also look up *myelin* in a dictionary to confirm its meaning.

PRACTICE AND APPLY

Use context clues to define the following terms from the article. Then use a resource to confirm that your definitions are correct.

TERM	GUESSED DEFINITION	RESOURCE DEFINITION
nerve cell (paragraph 4)		
psychology (paragraph 6)		
gene (paragraph 7)		

Watch Your Language!

Interrogative Mood

Remember that the **mood of a verb** shows the status of the action or condition that it describes. Each mood shapes the purpose of the sentence in which the verb appears. In sentences that use the **interrogative mood,** the purpose is to ask a question. Consider these examples:

> **Why is our species so adaptable?** (paragraph 1)
>
> **Casey says, "If you're getting all your needs met, why in the world would you leave?"** (paragraph 7)

Ed Interactive Grammar Lesson: Sentence Sense

Most often, sentences that use the interrogative mood invert the subject-verb order so that the helping verb comes before the subject. Sometimes a helping verb needs to be added. To make the question flow smoothly, other changes in word order also may occur. Notice how this example of the indicative mood is changed to the interrogative mood:

INDICATIVE MOOD	INTERROGATIVE MOOD
A large part of that success comes from our brain's taking a long time to mature.	Does a large part of that success come from our brain's taking a long time to mature?

PRACTICE AND APPLY

These sentences from "The Debt We Owe to the Adolescent Brain" use the indicative mood. Rewrite each one using the interrogative mood.

1. "We can thank our long period of adolescence for that."

2. "Her focus on adolescent brains includes those of humans and mice."

3. "These behaviors—sensitivity to influence from peers, taking risks, and pulling away from parents—are hallmarks of human adolescence."

Collaborate & Compare

ESSENTIAL QUESTION:

How do the challenges you face today help to shape your future?

Compare Poems

You are about to read two free verse poems that deal with the relationships between teenagers and their parents. As you read, notice how each writer uses the elements of poetry to express the speaker's thoughts and feelings.

A

Hanging Fire

Poem by **Audre Lorde**
pages 382–384

B

Summer of His Fourteenth Year

Poem by **Gloria Amescua**
pages 385–387

After you have read the poems, you will work with your classmates to compare them and give a presentation, following these steps:

- Consider Elements of Structure and Style
- Gather Information
- Compare Structure and Style
- Present to the Class

Hanging Fire

Poem by **Audre Lorde**

Summer of His Fourteenth Year

Poem by **Gloria Amescua**

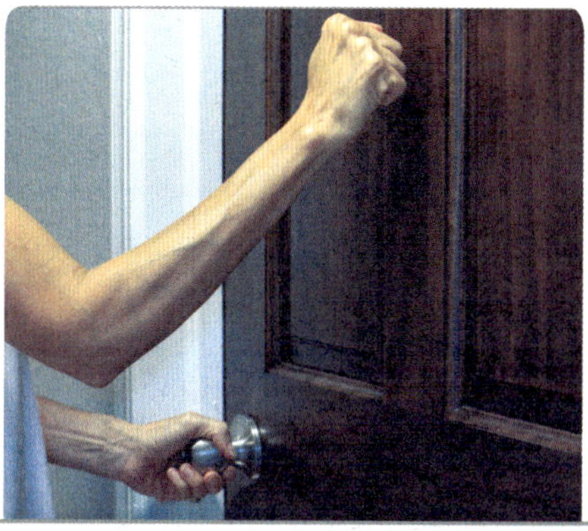

Engage Your Brain

Choose one or two activities to start connecting with the poems you are about to read.

Leaving a Trail

The speaker of "Summer of His Fourteenth Year" says her son leaves "a trail of teenage hunger" around the house. What signs of yourself do you leave behind?

Closed Doors

Every time the speaker of Audre Lorde's poem "Hanging Fire" wants to talk to her mom, the door is closed. Have you ever really needed to talk to a friend or family member, but the person wasn't available? Write a few sentences to describe what happened.

Compare Poetic Structure

When you hear the word *poem*, you might think of writing that has short lines, rhyming words, and a predictable rhythm or pattern of meter. Those are characteristics of many poems—but not all. **Free verse** is poetry that does not have regular patterns of meter or rhyme. Instead, the lines flow more naturally and may sound more like everyday speech.

Compared to poems that follow regular patterns of rhyme and meter, free verse poems can seem unstructured. However, many poets find creative ways to structure their poems without using such patterns.

- **Form:** The form of a poem includes the arrangement of its words and lines on the page. Many free verse poems have unique patterns of line length or stanza structures.
- **Repetition and refrain:** Look for words or phrases that appear more than once in a poem. If the poem is broken into stanzas, see whether there is a **refrain**—a repeated line or group of lines. The use of repetition and refrain can help to emphasize certain details as well as the speaker's ideas and feelings.
- **Organization of ideas:** Sometimes poems describe events in chronological order. Or a series of details or images might be presented to support a poem's overall theme.

As you read "Hanging Fire" and "Summer of His Fourteenth Year," analyze how the poems are structured. Also consider how the poems' structures contribute to their meaning and style. Use a chart like the one below to record your ideas.

Focus on Genre
Free Verse

- uses imagery and figurative language to convey meaning and mood
- may use sound devices such as rhythm and repetition
- sounds like everyday speech, with no regular patterns of rhythm or rhyme
- expresses a theme, or a message about life
- includes a speaker who "talks" to the reader

POEM	FORM	REPETITION AND REFRAIN	ORGANIZATION OF IDEAS
"Hanging Fire"			
"Summer of His Fourteenth Year"			

Annotation in Action

Here is an example of one reader's notes about the structure of "Hanging Fire." As you read each poem, make annotations to record aspects of poetic structure you notice.

I am fourteen
and my skin has betrayed me
the boy I cannot live without
still sucks his thumb
in secret

The poet uses a variety of line lengths to emphasize certain thoughts and feelings of the speaker.

Background

Audre Lorde (1934–1992) was born in New York City and found early success as a poet. One of her poems was published in a popular magazine while she was still in high school. In addition to writing poetry, Lorde also authored acclaimed essays and novels. She won many important awards for her writing and worked to support several social causes close to her heart. Toward the end of her life, Lorde took the African name Gamba Adisa, which is believed to mean "she who makes her meaning clear."

Gloria Amescua has been writing poems and stories since she was a child. Born in Austin, Texas, of Mexican American heritage, she became an inaugural member of Canto Mundo, a national Latino poetry community. Amescua has received numerous awards for her work, including the 2016 New Voices Award Honor. Much of her poetry revolves around the importance of family and community.

Hanging Fire

Poem by **Audre Lorde**

This poem brilliantly captures the intensity of a fourteen-year-old girl's worries and frustrations.

NOTICE & NOTE
As you read, use the side margins to make notes about the text.

I am fourteen
and my skin has betrayed me
the boy I cannot live without
still sucks his thumb
in secret
how come my knees are
always so ashy
what if I die
before morning
and momma's in the bedroom
with the door closed.

Don't forget to **Notice & Note** as you read the text.

I have to learn how to dance
in time for the next party
my room is too small for me
suppose I die before graduation
they will sing sad melodies
but finally
tell the truth about me
There is nothing I want to do
and too much
that has to be done
and momma's in the bedroom
with the door closed.

Nobody even stops to think
about my side of it
I should have been on Math Team
my marks were better than his
why do I have to be
the one
wearing braces
I have nothing to wear tomorrow
will I live long enough
to grow up
and momma's in the bedroom
with the door closed.

COMPARE POETIC STRUCTURE

Annotate: In the second stanza, mark the lines that are exactly the same as lines you saw in the first stanza.

Analyze: Why do you think the author built this thought into the structure of a refrain? Is there a refrain in the third stanza, too?

TURN AND TALK

Turn to a partner and discuss whether you can relate to any of the speaker's complaints or concerns.

ESSENTIAL QUESTION:

How do the challenges you face today help to shape your future?

Review your annotations and notes. Then, add relevant details to your Response Log.

Assessment Practice

Answer these questions about "Hanging Fire" before moving on to the next selection.

1. Which **two** concerns does the speaker in "Hanging Fire" express?

- (A) She worries that she might die young.
- (B) She is making poor grades in school.
- (C) She hates having to wear braces.
- (D) She thinks that nobody will dance with her.
- (E) She is annoyed that her mother has strict rules.

2. This question has two parts. First, answer **Part A**. Then, answer **Part B**.

Part A

In what area of her life does the speaker feel that she has been treated unfairly?

- (A) the lack of respect she gets from her peers
- (B) her disqualification from the Math Team
- (C) her awkwardness as a dancer
- (D) the tiny room that serves as her bedroom

Part B

Select the quotation that best supports the answer to Part A.

- (A) "I have to learn how to dance / in time for the next party" (lines 12–13)
- (B) "suppose I die before graduation / they will sing sad melodies" (lines 15–16)
- (C) "Nobody even stops to think / about my side of it" (lines 24–25)
- (D) "will I live long enough / to grow up" (lines 32–33)

3. What does the image of the closed bedroom door suggest about the speaker?

- (A) She has decided to ignore her problems.
- (B) She wishes she had more privacy.
- (C) She is determined to be independent.
- (D) She craves attention from her mother.

Ed
Test-Taking Strategies

B

Summer of His Fourteenth Year

Poem by **Gloria Amescua**

The speaker of this poem watches her son transform into a young man.

NOTICE & NOTE
As you read, use the side margins to make notes about the text.

A deep, resonant voice answers when I call home.
My child is gone—
In his place is someone who resembles him,
only taller, size ten shoes.

Empty sneakers and dirty socks mark his passage down
vacant halls.
He wanders aimlessly, flexing against walls grown too narrow,
as tensely strung as the tennis racket he grips,
as easily punctured as the deflated hand of the batting glove—
his passions are flung across the hours.

He leaves a trail of teenage hunger—
half empty Coke cans, stale chips in an unclosed bag.
Intermittent impulses, quickly sated,
rarely fill his emptiness,
never end his searching.

COMPARE POETIC STRUCTURE

Annotate: In lines 5–9 (stanza 2), mark the poet's use of repetition.

Analyze: What ideas or feelings of the speaker does this use of repetition suggest?

Wailing guitars weave a cocoon
as he sits cross legged in a recess of his room,
his teeming emotions playing on a muted keyboard.

He tears at the seams
that hold us together
and sees in mother only ties to childhood
Choking him with nagging chores,
Cloying protection,
Closed doors.

Surliness is his knife
Cutting away the bonds.

Silence is his distance
Murmuring goodbye.

TURN AND TALK

With a partner, discuss the tension between the speaker of the poem and her son. What do you think is the cause of this tension?

ESSENTIAL QUESTION:

How do the challenges you face today help to shape your future?

Review your annotations and notes. Then, add relevant details to your Response Log.

Assessment Practice

Answer these questions before moving on to the **Analyze the Texts** section on the following page.

1. The reader can infer that the speaker of the poem believes her son views her as trying to keep him from growing up. Which **two** quotations best support this inference?
   - (A) "My child is gone— / In his place is someone who resembles him" (lines 2–3)
   - (B) "He wanders aimlessly, flexing against walls grown too narrow" (line 6)
   - (C) "his teeming emotions playing on a muted keyboard" (line 17)
   - (D) "and sees in mother only ties to childhood" (line 20)
   - (E) "Surliness is his knife / Cutting away the bonds" (lines 24–25)

2. Which statement best reflects the main theme of the poem?
   - (A) Parents of teenagers are nagging and overprotective.
   - (B) Teenagers tend to be messy and inconsiderate.
   - (C) Communication between teenagers and adults is difficult.
   - (D) Leaving childhood behind is hard for parents and teenagers.

Ed

Test-Taking Strategies

Analyze the Texts

Support your responses with evidence from the texts.

NOTICE & NOTE

Review what you **noticed and noted** as you read the text. Your annotations can help you answer these questions.

1. **INFER** In the first stanza of "Hanging Fire," what does the speaker wish she could change about her appearance? How do you know?

2. **ANALYZE** How does the use of refrain at the end of each stanza in "Hanging Fire" relate to the message of the poem?

3. **ANALYZE** Reread lines 18–19 and 24–25 of "Summer of His Fourteenth Year." How does the mother's insight into her son's behavior create tension for readers?

4. **COMPARE** Read aloud stanzas 1–3 of "Summer of His Fourteenth Year." How does the use of dashes affect the rhythm of those stanzas? How is a similar effect created in "Hanging Fire," where there are no dashes?

5. **CRITIQUE** Which poem's structure is more effective at conveying the relationships between teenagers and their parents? Use the chart to compare and critique the poems' structures.

POEM	POETIC STRUCTURE	YOUR CRITIQUE
"Hanging Fire"		
"Summer of His Fourteenth Year"		

Choices

Here are some other ways to demonstrate your understanding of the ideas in this lesson.

As you write and discuss, be sure to use the **Academic Vocabulary** words.

debate	sufficient
deduce	trend
license	

Writing
Literary Analysis

Think about the teenagers who are the focus of these two poems. Which teenager do you think most readers understand better and find easier to relate to? Write a brief essay in which you analyze the presentation of the two characters. Consider these questions:

- How do readers learn about each character?
- What does each character seem to care about?
- How would you describe each character's relationship with her or his mother?
- How similar or different are the endings of the two poems?

Social & Emotional Learning
Discuss with a Small Group

The teens in both poems have to deal with mood swings and anxiety, which are common during adolescence. With a group of your classmates, discuss mood swings and anxiety, as well as strategies for coping with them. Do some research as needed to learn more about these topics. Address the following questions in your discussion:

- What causes teenage mood swings?
- How do sleep patterns affect mood?
- What are some positive coping techniques for teens?

Speaking & Listening
Give a Dramatic Reading

Work with a partner to create a dramatic reading of one of the poems.

- Begin by discussing the impact of the poet's word choices.
- Practice reading each line of your chosen poem in a way that conveys your personal connection to the poem's meaning.
- Consider how you will accompany the words with movements or gestures.
- Take turns rehearsing with a partner, giving and receiving feedback.
- Present your dramatic reading to the class, using appropriate volume, phrasing, and expression.

Compare Poems

Both "Hanging Fire" and "Summer of His Fourteenth Year" are free verse poems about problems and changes teenagers go through. Ask yourself the following questions to compare the poems.

- How does the speaker's point of view affect the poem's themes?
- How does the structure of the poem contribute to its meaning and style?
- What do literary elements such as word choice, syntax, and imagery contribute to the overall mood or tone?

In a small group, identify similarities and differences between the two poems. Record your thoughts in the chart.

	"HANGING FIRE"	"SUMMER OF HIS FOURTEENTH YEAR"
Point of View		
Structure		
Impact of Literary Elements		

Analyze the Texts

Discuss these questions in your group.

1. **COMPARE** Which poem makes more effective use of figurative language and imagery? Cite text evidence in your discussion.

2. **SYNTHESIZE** Think about the different points of view in the poems. How do these different perspectives help the reader form a fuller understanding of the trials of adolescence?

3. **CITE EVIDENCE** Both poems include the image of a closed door. Discuss what the closed door represents to the teen in each poem.

4. **EVALUATE** Which poem's structure is more effective in expressing its speaker's feelings about the teenage years? Explain.

Create and Present

Now your group can continue exploring these poems by comparing their structures and styles and considering how each poem appeals to teen readers.

1 **CONSIDER ELEMENTS OF STRUCTURE AND STYLE** Think about the elements of each poem that appeal to you. Ask:

- Which poem evokes stronger feelings?
- Which style elements best connect with the reader?
- What insights does each speaker offer?
- How do the structural elements of each poem contribute to its meaning?
- What message about teenage years does each poem convey?

2 **GATHER INFORMATION** With your group, discuss and list examples of the most important elements of structure and style in each poem.

"HANGING FIRE"	"SUMMER OF HIS FOURTEENTH YEAR"

3 **COMPARE STRUCTURE AND STYLE** As a group, examine the structure and style of each poem. Discuss how the poets' structural and stylistic choices help to convey the messages of the poems.

4 **PRESENT TO THE CLASS** Now present your views to the class. Cite text evidence from the poems to support your ideas. Discuss what each poem adds to your understanding about why teenage years can be so difficult. You may use charts or other visuals to help convey information to the class.

Collaborate & Compare

ESSENTIAL QUESTION:
How do the challenges you face today help to shape your future?

Compare Arguments

You are about to read two arguments concerning teenagers and their use of social media and technology. As you read, look for the main claim in each argument and the reasons and evidence given to support it. Then, consider whether your opinion of teens' media use has changed at all as a consequence of reading these arguments.

MENTOR TEXT

A

from It's Complicated: The Social Lives of Networked Teens

Argument by **danah boyd**
pages 396–399

B

Outsmart Your Smartphone

Argument by **Catherine Steiner-Adair**
pages 407–413

After you have read the texts, you will role-play with your classmates, following these steps:

- Choose a Role and a Position
- Gather Information
- Prepare Your Counterclaim
- Role-play the Discussion

from It's Complicated: The Social Lives of Networked Teens

Argument by **danah boyd**

Engage Your Brain

Choose one or two of these activities to start connecting with the argument you're about to read.

Addicted to the Internet?

The text you are about to read mentions Internet addiction. What would you say to someone who had concerns about your relationship with technology? Write a few sentences to respond.

Take a Poll

Poll a small group of friends or classmates to find out how many belong to social media networks. Discuss whether using social media creates a "complicated" social life, and why.

Analyze Claim and Evidence

A strong argument clearly states a **claim,** or position on an issue, and reasons to accept the claim. It provides sufficient relevant evidence to support those reasons. **Evidence** consists of the specific facts, examples, statistics, and expert opinions that support a claim. Evidence is **relevant** if it supports the claim in a logical way.

As you read an argument, determine the writer's claim. Pay attention to the way he or she develops that argument. Decide whether the argument is easy to follow and logical. Also make sure that the writer uses facts (not only opinions) to give the claim reasonable support.

Focus on Genre

Argument

- states a claim and reasons to support the claim
- includes facts and other evidence to support reasons
- may note objections to the claim or alternative viewpoints and explain why they should be dismissed
- takes many forms, such as editorials, feature articles, and essays

Identify Counterclaims

Effective writers acknowledge objections to their point of view and differing opinions about the topic being discussed. Many arguments, therefore, include **counterclaims**—responses to objections or alternative viewpoints. A counterclaim may show that there are ways to explain the opposing point of view or that the view is weak because it lacks convincing evidence. Including a counterclaim thus clears the way for readers to accept a writer's position without reservations.

In the excerpt from *It's Complicated*, the author introduces common parental concerns about teens' media use. She then responds with a counterclaim: she explains why adults really don't need to worry so much about these things. As you read, notice how the author responds to opposing views and note relevant examples in a chart like this one.

PARENTS' CONCERNS ABOUT SOCIAL MEDIA USE	THE AUTHOR'S COUNTERCLAIMS
"Why are my kids tethered to their cell phones or perpetually texting with friends even when they are in the same room?"	"Most teens are not compelled by gadgetry as such—they are compelled by friendship."

Annotation in Action

Here are one reader's notes on how the author responds to an opposing viewpoint with a counterclaim. As you read, note how the author acknowledges possible objections to her argument.

They watch their parents and other adults in their communities for models of adulthood. But they also track celebrities like Kanye West and Kim Kardashian to imagine the freedoms they would have if they were famous. For better or worse, media narratives also help construct broader narratives for how public life works. . . .

The author is addressing some people's concern that teens spend too much time following celebrities online.

Expand Your Vocabulary

Put a check mark next to the vocabulary words that you feel comfortable using when speaking or writing.

relish	☐
dynamic	☐
appease	☐
intimacy	☐

Turn to a partner and talk about the words you already know. Then, use as many words as you can in a paragraph about social media. As you read the excerpt from *It's Complicated,* use the definitions in the side column to learn the vocabulary words you don't already know.

Background

When **danah boyd** (b. 1977) was born, her mother named her "danah michele mattas." Her name was later changed and properly capitalized. As an adult, however, she legally renamed herself "danah boyd," taking her grandfather's last name, honoring her mother's original lowercase spelling, and satisfying her own "political irritation at the importance of capitalization." A Principal Researcher at Microsoft Research and a visiting professor at New York University, she has spent years researching how young people use social media.

from It's Complicated: The Social Lives of Networked Teens

Argument by **danah boyd**

Should adults worry so much about how much time teens spend with technology?

NOTICE & NOTE
As you read, use the side margins to make notes about the text.

Ed
Text in Focus Video
Learn more about comparing arguments.

relish
(rĕl´ĭsh) *v.* To *relish* is to take great joy or pleasure in something.

1 Developing meaningful friendships is a key component of the coming of age process. Friends offer many things—advice, support, entertainment, and a connection that combats loneliness. And in doing so, they enable the transition to adulthood by providing a context[1] beyond that of family and home. Though family is still important, many teens **relish** the opportunity to create relationships that are not simply given but chosen.

2 The importance of friends in social and moral development is well documented. But the fears that surround teens' use of social media overlook this fundamental desire for social connection. All too often, parents project their values onto their children, failing to recognize that school is often not the most

[1] **context:** setting or environment.

pressing concern for most teens. Many parents wonder: Why are my kids tethered to their cell phones or perpetually texting with friends even when they are in the same room? Why do they seem compelled to check Facebook hundreds of times a day? Are they addicted to technology or simply wasting time? How will they get into college if they are constantly distracted? I encounter these questions from concerned adults whenever I give public lectures, and these attitudes figure prominently in parenting guides and in journalistic accounts of teens' engagement with social media.

3 Yet these questions seem far less urgent and difficult when we acknowledge teens' underlying social motivations. Most teens are not compelled by gadgetry as such—they are compelled by friendship. The gadgets are interesting to them primarily as a means to a social end. Furthermore, social interactions may be a distraction from school, but they are often not a distraction from learning. Keeping this basic social **dynamic** firmly in view makes networked teens suddenly much less worrisome and strange.

4 Consider, for example, the widespread concern over internet addiction. Are there teens who have an unhealthy relationship with technology? Certainly. But most of those who are "addicted" to their phones or computers are actually focused on staying connected to friends in a culture where getting together in person is highly constrained.[2] Teens' preoccupation[3] with their friends dovetails[4] with their desire to enter the public spaces that are freely accessible to adults. The ability to access public spaces for sociable purposes is a critical component of the coming of age process, and yet many of the public spaces where adults gather—bars, clubs, and restaurants—are inaccessible to teens.

5 As teens transition from childhood, they try to understand how they fit into the larger world. They want to inhabit public spaces, but they also look to adults, including public figures, to understand what it means to be grown-up. They watch their parents and other adults in their communities for models of adulthood. But they also track celebrities like Kanye West and Kim Kardashian to imagine the freedoms they would have if they were famous. For better or worse, media narratives also help construct broader narratives for how public life works. "Reality" TV shows like Jersey Shore signal the potential fun that can be had by young adults who don't need to **appease** parents and teachers.

ANALYZE CLAIM AND EVIDENCE

Annotate: In paragraph 2, mark the sentence that summarizes the main idea.

Infer: Might this be boyd's claim? If so, what should the rest of the argument show or prove?

dynamic
(dī-năm´ĭk) *n.* A *dynamic* is a system in which conflicting or competing forces are at work.

IDENTIFY COUNTERCLAIMS

Annotate: In paragraph 3, mark all the statements that address the worries the author noted in paragraph 2.

Evaluate: Might a worried parent reading paragraph 3 be convinced by what she says here? Explain.

appease
(ə-pēz´) *v.* To *appease* means to pacify or lessen the anger of, usually by making concessions.

[2] **constrained:** limited.
[3] **preoccupation:** mental absorption or sole focus of attention.
[4] **dovetails:** fits together well, unites, or joins.

NOTICE & NOTE
WORD GAPS

When you notice vocabulary that is unfamiliar, you've found a **Word Gaps** signpost.

Notice & Note: What words or phrases in paragraphs 6–7 are unfamiliar or confusing? Mark these words.

Infer: Can you find clues in the text to help you understand the words or phrases?

6 Some teens may reject the messages of adulthood that they hear or see, but they still learn from all of the signals around them. As they start to envision themselves as young adults, they begin experimenting with the boundaries of various freedoms, pushing for access to cars or later curfews. Teens' determination to set their own agenda can be nerve-racking for some parents, particularly those who want to protect their children from every possible danger. Coming of age is rife with self-determination, risk taking, and tough decision-making.

7 Teens often want to be with friends on their own terms, without adult supervision, and in public. Paradoxically, the networked publics they inhabit allow them a measure of privacy and autonomy that is not possible at home where parents and siblings are often listening in. Recognizing this is important to understanding teens' relationship to social media. Although many adults think otherwise, teens' engagement with public life through social media is not a rejection of privacy. Teens may wish to enjoy the benefits of participating in public, but they also relish **intimacy** and the ability to have control over their social situation. Their ability to achieve privacy is often undermined by nosy adults—notably their parents and teachers—but teens go to great lengths to develop innovative strategies for managing privacy in networked publics.

intimacy
(ĭn´tə-mə-sē) *n. Intimacy* refers to a state of personal closeness that is usually experienced in privacy.

8 Social media enables a type of youth-centric[5] public space that is often otherwise inaccessible. But because that space is highly visible, it can often provoke concerns among adults who are watching teens as they try to find their way.

[5] **youth-centric:** focused on young people's needs, concerns, and interests.

ESSENTIAL QUESTION:
How do the challenges you face today help to shape your future?

Review your notes and add your thoughts to your Response Log.

TURN AND TALK

Do you agree with the author that teens are mainly interested in using gadgets as tools for social interaction? Turn to a partner and discuss.

Assessment Practice

Answer these questions before moving on to the **Analyze the Text** section on the following page.

1. This question has two parts. First, answer **Part A**. Then, answer **Part B**.

Part A

According to paragraph 4, why do teens spend so much time on their phones or computers communicating with friends?

(A) Teens understand that having friends helps them learn to be mature adults.

(B) Teens are obsessed with technology of all kinds.

(C) Teens are compelled to compare their lives with the lives of peers.

(D) Teens have few places where they can meet publicly.

Part B

How does the author make this point clear?

(A) by comparing adults' freedom to meet up with teens' lack of such freedom

(B) by asking readers whether this way of using technology is unhealthy

(C) by assuring readers that time spent in this way does not keep them from learning

(D) by calling teens "addicted" to collecting and keeping friends

2. Which statement best characterizes the author's main message to people who worry about teens' use of social media?

(A) Instead of worrying about teens, you should worry about developing your own social life more fully.

(B) Instead of worrying about teens, you should recognize that it is safer to meet online than to get together in person.

(C) The use of social media by teens is not worrisome when you consider how much they need friends at this age.

(D) The use of social media by teens is not worrisome because following the lives of celebrities is common.

Ed

Test-Taking Strategies

Analyze the Text

Support your responses with evidence from the text.

NOTICE & NOTE

Review what you **noticed and noted** as you read the text. Your annotations can help you answer these questions.

1. **EVALUATE** Reread the final sentence in paragraph 5. Is this statement relevant to the author's argument? Explain.

2. **ANALYZE** Review paragraph 6. Why might the author have chosen to provide this information as part of her counterclaim?

3. **ANALYZE** In paragraph 7, identify the two seemingly contradictory things the author says teens want. How does this idea counter the assumption that many adults make about social media use?

4. **INTERPRET** In paragraph 8, what reason does boyd give to explain why adults may be so concerned about teenagers' use of social media? What counterclaim has she already used to respond to this concern?

5. **CRITIQUE** Does boyd provide sufficient relevant reasons and evidence to support her position? Cite evidence to support your response.

6. **INTERPRET** What, if any, **Word Gaps** did you fill that helped you understand the text?

7. **ANALYZE** What counterclaims does the author make throughout the text to address opposing views? Refer to the chart you filled in as you read.

PARENTS' CONCERNS ABOUT SOCIAL MEDIA USE	THE AUTHOR'S COUNTERCLAIMS

Choices

Here are some other ways to demonstrate your understanding of the ideas in this lesson.

As you write and discuss, be sure to use the **Academic Vocabulary** words.

debate	sufficient
deduce	trend
license	

Writing
Opinion Piece

Write a one- or two-paragraph opinion piece in which you take a position regarding social media use at school. Use evidence from *It's Complicated* to support your points.

- Introduce the topic, state your position on it, and give one good reason to accept your viewpoint. Also state an opposing viewpoint and make a strong counterclaim.
- Alternatively, begin by introducing the topic and the prevailing viewpoint that differs from your own. Present a reason to reject or modify that viewpoint, and conclude by stating your position.
- Use facts, quotations, and other evidence from the text to support your opinions.
- In your conclusion, tell readers what you think they should believe, why they should believe it, and what to do because they now hold this belief.

Speaking & Listening
Media Messages

The author suggests that teenagers look to celebrities and reality TV stars to help them understand what it means to be an adult. What kinds of messages does the media send to teenagers about being grown-up? Have a discussion with a group of your classmates to share your ideas.

- Make sure all group members contribute to the conversation.
- Listen attentively as others are speaking.
- Ask questions to clarify ideas, and respond to each other thoughtfully.

Research
Social Media

Research the amount of time teens spend online and the effects of doing so, if any. Use the chart to record evidence you find and explain whether it supports or contradicts her argument.

EVIDENCE	SUPPORTS OR CONTRADICTS BOYD'S ARGUMENT?

Expand Your Vocabulary

PRACTICE AND APPLY

Demonstrate your understanding of the vocabulary words by answering the following questions.

relish	dynamic	appease	intimacy

1. What would be more likely to **appease** a coach's irritation with you, showing up to practice early or arriving late? Why?
2. If you **relish** a song, are you more likely to want to learn it or forget it? Why?
3. What **dynamic** does boyd think parents ought to keep in mind when evaluating their teens' use of social media? Why?
4. Would **intimacy** be likely to strengthen or weaken a relationship? Why?

Vocabulary Strategy
Context Clues

You know that a word's **context,** or the text around it, can help you figure out its meaning. But did you know that context clues can include synonyms and antonyms? When you notice one of these, it can help you clarify the meaning of an unfamiliar word or one that has multiple meanings. The chart below shows an example.

Ed

Interactive Vocabulary Lesson: Using Context Clues

CONTEXT SENTENCE	ANALYSIS
Teens may wish to enjoy the benefits of participating in public, but they also relish intimacy and the ability to have control over their social situation.	*In public* and *intimacy* are antonyms, as signaled by the word *but*. Since *in public* means "open to the knowledge or judgment of all," you can infer that *intimacy* is the opposite of that, and means something like "privacy."

Any of the following words can be a clue to the presence of a synonym: *similarly, as, like, or*. These words and phrases can signal the presence of an antonym: *but actually, whereas, on the other hand, by contrast*.

PRACTICE AND APPLY

Imagine you need to explain social media and smartphones to a younger person unfamiliar with the technology. Write four sentences that you might use in your explanation. In each sentence, use a synonym or an antonym to clarify the meaning of one unfamiliar or difficult word.

Watch Your Language!

Shifts in Voice and Mood

Interactive Grammar Lesson: Sentence Sense

Verbs have different voices and moods. The **voice** of a verb tells whether its subject performs the action **(active voice)** or receives the action **(passive voice).**

Active Voice	**Teens use social media all the time.**
Passive Voice	**Social media are used by teens all the time.**

The active voice is usually clearer and stronger than the passive voice. To rewrite a passive-voice sentence in the active voice, focus on the verb, and make the original subject the new direct object.

Passive Voice	**Celebrities are often tracked by teenage fans.**
Active Voice	**Teenage fans often track celebrities.**

The **mood** of a verb expresses a writer's intent in the sentence. The **indicative mood** is used when making a statement. The **imperative mood** is used for a polite request or a command.

Indicative Mood	**Teens use their phones often.**
Imperative Mood	**Notice how often teens use their phones.**

A shift, or change, in verb voice or mood within a sentence can make the meaning unclear. It is usually best to make the voice and mood in a sentence consistent.

SHIFT	CORRECTION
From active to passive: **The teens called each other, and plans to meet were made.**	**The teens called each other and made plans to meet.**
From imperative to indicative: **Understand your teens' situation, and it is important to trust them with more decisions.**	**Understand your teens' situation and trust them with more decisions.**

PRACTICE AND APPLY

Rewrite these items. Correct each inappropriate shift in verb voice or mood.

1. This new phone is great, and it will be used a lot by me.
2. When I am called often by my friends, I feel really great.
3. We all love our phones. Be sure to use them responsibly.

Outsmart Your Smartphone

Argument by **Catherine Steiner-Adair**

Engage Your Brain

Choose one or two of these activities to start connecting with the argument you're about to read.

How Can a Phone Be Smart?

Why do they call them "smartphones"? And why would people have to outsmart them? Write a few sentences to respond to these questions.

Text or Talk?

Do you prefer texting or talking on the phone? Discuss the reasons for your preference with a group of your classmates.

Analyze Structure

Every argument presents a writer's position on an issue—that is, the writer makes a **claim.** Writers choose various patterns of organization to develop their claims with reasons and evidence.

In "Outsmart Your Smartphone," the author uses a cause-effect structure. Specifically, she tries to convince readers that five kinds of effects result from social media use. She introduces each effect with a transition such as *first, second,* and *third*. As you read, look for these transitions and the cause-effect relationships they introduce.

Focus on Genre
Argument

- makes a claim
- supports claim with reasons and evidence
- acknowledges opposing claims and provides evidence to refute them
- for topics involving society or psychology, may cite scientific studies as evidence

Analyze Rhetorical Devices

Rhetoric is the art of using language persuasively. **Rhetorical devices** are techniques writers use to enhance their arguments and communicate effectively.

Several rhetorical devices are defined in the chart below. As you read "Outsmart Your Smartphone," add more examples from the text. Then consider why the author might have chosen to use these devices. What impact does each choice have?

RHETORICAL DEVICE	DEFINITION	EXAMPLE
Analogy	A point-by-point comparison of two things that are alike in some respect	Paragraph 11: Learning conversation skills is compared to learning to drive.
Direct address	Talking directly to the reader, often using the pronoun *you*	Paragraph 2: "You can use smartphones and social media to build healthy relationships and a sense of belonging."
Juxtaposition	The placement of two or more things side by side to show their similarities and/or differences	
Rhetorical question	A question that has such an obvious answer that it requires no reply	

Annotation in Action

Here are one reader's notes on the author's use of a rhetorical device. As you read "Outsmart Your Smartphone," note how rhetorical devices help the author get her points across.

Adolescence has always been a hero's journey of growing independence, exploration, and self-discovery. When smartphones swept onto the scene in 2008, teenagers used them for familiar purposes—to connect to each other and share interests out of adults' view. . . .

The author makes an analogy between adolescence and a hero's journey.

Expand Your Vocabulary

Put a check mark next to the vocabulary words that you feel comfortable using when speaking or writing.

- **perspective** ☐
- **stimulant** ☐
- **deliberate** ☐
- **inhibited** ☐

Turn to a partner and talk about the words you already know. Then, use as many words as you can in a paragraph about the things that bother you about using a smartphone. As you read "Outsmart Your Smartphone," use the definitions in the side column to learn the vocabulary words you don't already know.

Background

Catherine Steiner-Adair is an internationally recognized clinical psychologist, consultant, and speaker and the author of the award-winning book *The Big Disconnect*. She has a different perspective on teenagers and technology than danah boyd in *It's Complicated*. In this argument, Steiner-Adair explores problems associated with teenagers' use of social media and smartphones.

B

Outsmart Your Smartphone

Argument by **Catherine Steiner-Adair**

This author writes about how teenagers use technology and makes suggestions for using it responsibly.

NOTICE & NOTE
As you read, use the side margins to make notes about the text.

1 Adolescence has always been a hero's journey of growing independence, exploration, and self-discovery. When smartphones swept onto the scene in 2008, teenagers used them for familiar purposes—to connect to each other and share interests out of adults' view. But was the technology itself significantly changing the landscape of teen life? At first, people took sides on this issue based on their own gut feelings. Now with more than a decade of experience, it's possible to hold a more informed **perspective** on the effects of engaging with social media and life online. In writing my book *The Big Disconnect: Protecting Childhood and Family Relationships in the Digital Age,* I studied the current research and interviewed hundreds of teenagers around the country. I can say without hesitation that though social media is a useful and enticing tool, it poses unique risks to adolescent well-being.

perspective
(pər-spĕk´tĭv) *n.* A *perspective* is a viewpoint on or understanding of something.

ANALYZE STRUCTURE

Annotate: Mark all the positive effects of using social media listed in paragraph 2.

Infer: How might identifying these benefits at the beginning of her argument help the author achieve her purpose?

NOTICE & NOTE

CONTRASTS AND CONTRADICTIONS

When you notice a difference between two or more elements in the text, you've found a **Contrasts and Contradictions** signpost.

Notice & Note: Mark the two sentences in paragraph 3 that introduce a sharp contrast or contradiction.

Analyze: Why does the author point out this contrast?

stimulant
(stĭm´yə-lənt) *n.* A *stimulant* is an agent that excites or temporarily speeds up mental and/or physical functions.

deliberate
(dĭ-lĭb´ər-ĭt) *adj. Deliberate* decision-making activity is the process of making a choice only after carefully considering its likely effects.

2 The benefits of social media are obvious. You can use smartphones and social media to build healthy relationships and a sense of belonging. You can partner with others to help, share, volunteer, collaborate. Never before have middle school students been able to take a class with students in China. You can get in touch with total strangers who like the same rock band, write fan fiction together with people anywhere in the world, or join an online gaming group. Texting and social networking sites make it easier to connect with kids right where you are, too. Social networking lets you get together with friends where your parents aren't around. Expressing yourself, figuring out who you are and developing a sense of self and identity that's separate from your parents and family are important parts of adolescent development.

3 But there's more to the story. While it's tempting to believe that social media is just a new version of what's always been, with the same dangers and benefits, studies suggest that's just not true. A growing body of scientific evidence and everyday experience show that social media is not simply a natural and healthy extension of teens' social lives and development. It can negatively affect the brain and behavior in ways that mimic addiction, adversely affect learning, distort normal aspects of social and emotional development, and increase anxiety. There is too much research and too much everyday evidence now for us to ignore the risks. You have to approach social media with restraint and caution if you want to avoid harm.

4 How and how often you use social media matters. Ninety-two percent of teens report going online daily. Twenty-four percent of them say they are online "almost constantly," according to a 2015 study by the Pew Research Center. More than half (fifty-six percent) of teens, ages thirteen to seventeen, go online several times a day. Most use mobile devices and three-quarters of the teens say they have access to a smartphone. The more time you spend texting or online, the greater the risks of harm. This is especially concerning in adolescence. It's a critical window of time for brain growth, physical development, and social and emotional development.

5 Social media is a **stimulant** to the brain. Texting and other use triggers release of dopamine, a natural chemical that produces a pleasurable sensation that most brains crave to repeat. But the more you use social media, the more you want to use it, and that impulse can override the **deliberate** decision-making activity of the part of the brain called the prefrontal cortex. It also creates a sense of urgency. You feel compelled to react or respond right away and hit send.

6 The combination of the stimulants to the brain and the fact that you feel anonymous or at a distance from the person you're communicating with can lead you to behave differently than you would face to face. You become impulsive, quick to act and react, even when it carries a risk. You feel less **inhibited,** more likely to say mean or careless things without a thought to the impact of your words, or the consequences. It's easy to say things you later wish you hadn't. On the receiving (or waiting) end, you feel anxious when someone doesn't respond right away, or you feel antsy or bored when there's a lull in communication. Every ping, buzz, or text you send or receive keeps you hooked.

7 A false sense of privacy can trick you into thinking it's safe to share anything—or text or post private or inflammatory[1] things. Plenty of teens have found themselves entangled in social drama made worse when posts went viral. At the most tragic extreme, social media has provided a platform for cyberbullying. In a study of teens and social media use, nine out of ten teens reported that they had seen bullying online.

8 Bullying gets a lot of attention and for good reason, but let's look at other common social media behaviors or beliefs with negative consequences.

9 First, texting is easier than talking and seems like the same thing, but it isn't. Social media is no substitute for face-to-face conversation or hanging out, a handshake or comforting hug, shared laughter or even shared quiet time. Texting, tweeting, email and other text-only forms of messaging eliminate two essential aspects of human communication: the power of voice and the ability to see the impact of your words.

[1] **inflammatory:** provocative; likely to provoke a strong reaction.

Don't forget to **Notice & Note** as you read the text.

inhibited
(ĭn-hĭb´ĭt-əd) *adj.* If you feel *inhibited,* you feel restrained, held back, or self-conscious.

ANALYZE RHETORICAL DEVICES

Annotate: Review paragraphs 5 and 6. Mark the sentences in which the author uses direct address.

Analyze: What is the impact of using direct address to convey this particular information?

10 Tone of voice gives meaning to our words. You might use the phrase "I hate you!" jokingly to mean "I'm so jealous of you!" but what if that's not clear? Even a simple text like "sorry" can be difficult to decipher—are you being snarky or sincere? Distanced from the impact your words have on others, you can't see their reaction or correct a misunderstanding.

11 Also, when texting takes the place of face-to-face talking, you don't get the real-time practice of conversation skills and the confidence that goes with it. You can't get a driver's license just by passing an online test. You have to log hours of actual driving time to develop the real-time, real life skills to drive. The same in-real-life practice is required for the social and emotional skills you need to navigate life. Direct communication is one of the most important.

12 Second, social media expands social networks, but not necessarily the deeper stuff of meaningful friendship. Research and life experience tell us that "likes" and casual online "friends" are no substitute for friendship. Friendship includes a deeper knowing of one another, shared respect and trust, and acceptance. It's easy to think that your "street smarts"—your ability to assess if someone is trustworthy or not—work just as well on social media sites as in real life, but research tells us that we tend to trust too easily online. Social media was designed to be a way to connect people. But it also has put a crimp in teens' ability to connect in deep and meaningful ways. Some find it harder to be emotionally vulnerable and emotionally honest with one another. Emotional growth and learning how to be a partner in relationship are hard work, and part of natural development that emerges in adolescence. But it takes time and practice to develop that natural capacity. The default text of *hey what's up?* mutes those moments for more textured conversations. You might find it easier to say things that are serious and important to you by texting, where you don't feel as vulnerable as you might face to face. Ultimately, though, it's important in life to be able to say directly to people what's on your mind and what's in your heart, and have difficult conversations. That takes practice.

ANALYZE STRUCTURE

Annotate: In paragraph 13, mark the effect of "constant connectivity," according to the author. Then mark what that, in turn, can cause.

Evaluate: Does this cause-effect relationship help the author support her argument? Explain.

13 Third, the "everywhere, always on" presence of social media and life online creates new kinds of psychological issues. The constant connectivity can create psychological dependence. This can cause anxiety when you're separated from your phone or unable to go online. Some teens experience a form of separation anxiety if they don't have their phone, or if an adult takes it away.

14 If you are "always on," the fear of missing out often creates anxiety with no relief. On social media, like never before, you can see every party, every event, every "inside joke" that you are

Don't forget to **Notice & Note** as you read the text.

not a part of. You see the endless stream of nasty comments or trending gossip and might start to quietly fear you'll become the target of it. A growing number of studies have also found that looking at "perfect" photos of other people may increase anxiety and make people feel bad about themselves. A 2016 study by researchers at the University of Cologne in Germany described so-called Facebook envy and depression as a serious concern, echoing other studies of social media's negative effects on mental health. Students often tell me that class outings or summer camp where cell phones weren't allowed were "the best ever." Why? Because after a short withdrawal period, classmates enjoyed the freedom from the pressures of social media and the fun of being together.

15 Fourth, social media distraction has a negative effect on learning and on grades. When you multitask on different devices or online activities your brain makes you feel really powerful. It makes you think you can multitask effectively. That's one reason it's so hard to listen to teachers or parents when they say don't do it. But actually, in your brain, multitasking on digital devices takes away from your attention to any one thing with a continuous stream of mini-interruptions.

16 Studies show that multitasking with social media makes homework take longer. It also weakens short-term and long-term memory. Students who used social networking scored twenty percent lower on tests, and had lower grades compared to those that stayed off social media until their work was done. Even when users just go on social media for a "quick" break, the average amount of time off their task is typically twenty to twenty-five minutes. That increases the time it takes to complete a two-hour task by thirty percent. A study conducted by scientists at University of Texas-Austin in 2017 found that just having your smartphone nearby reduces cognitive performance—how well your brain can think and learn—even when the phone is silent or out of sight.

17 Fifth, the distraction of social media can pull you away from your best self, drawing you into the online culture where it's cool to be cruel or disingenuous,[2] and where snarky, mean posts get lots of "likes." This dark side of social networking is not just about meanness. It's that social media cultivates an image-based value system that creates unrealistic expectations and rewards shallowness. As shaming, hate-talk, and other destructive behaviors online get worse, social media becomes increasingly antisocial.

[2] **disingenuous** (dĭs´ĭn-jĕn´yo͞o-əs): insincere, false.

18 A generation ago, parents worried about their kids watching too much TV, which was also seen as spreading poor values. Today's "screen time" is even more problematic. While TV and online entertainment both use screens, our brains don't connect with them in the same ways. TV is at a distance, compared to the close-up visual stimulation on a smartphone or computer screen. Think of how different it feels to binge-watch on the big TV screen versus on your smartphone. TV also tends to be a more social activity. You watch with other people, share the experience, and perhaps talk as you do so.

19 All of this does not mean we must abandon social media entirely, along with those prosocial benefits it does have. But you need self-awareness so that you use this tool to be your best self, make the most of your education, and protect your brain and your own well being. It's important not to let any new app, virtual reality, or whatever the next tech innovation is delete what science has told us for years and still stands true: As a species, we thrive in the context of healthy relationships. We need to manage our use of social media to create supportive connections for learning and life.

ANALYZE RHETORICAL DEVICES

Annotate: An imperative sentence is a direct command, instruction, or request. Mark the imperative sentences In paragraph 20.

Analyze: What rhetorical device are these sentences examples of?

20 For example, you don't have to be part of every social media stream your friends are. Be conscious of how much time you're online and limit yourself. Take breaks. Take off one day a week or at mealtimes. Even when it seems easier to stay home and text with your friends, make an effort to get together somewhere and see them instead. If your school allows students to use phones, exercise restraint. Resist the temptation to multitask when you need to have singular focus on your homework. Educate your peers—remember that just having your phone on your desk or in your backpack interferes with your attention.

21 Adolescents have always been the pioneers in evolving cultures, and today's teens are, too. Given the information and education needed to make sound choices, you'll learn to master the social media tool and be able to share tips with the generations before you and after you, as well.

TURN AND TALK

With a partner, discuss whether you think technology and social media are having a negative impact on your life.

ESSENTIAL QUESTION:

How do the challenges you face today help to shape your future?

Review your notes and add your thoughts to your Response Log.

Assessment Practice

Answer these questions before moving on to the **Analyze the Text** section on the following page.

1. Which is the writer's main claim in "Outsmart Your Smartphone"?

(A) "[S]ocial media . . . poses unique risks to adolescent well-being." (paragraph 1)

(B) "You might find it easier to say things that are serious and important to you by texting. . . ." (paragraph 12)

(C) "The constant connectivity can create psychological dependence." (paragraph 13)

(D) "[W]e thrive in the context of healthy relationships." (paragraph 19)

2. This question has two parts. First, answer **Part A**. Then, answer **Part B**.

Part A

In paragraph 18, what difference does the author suggest between TV and online entertainment, which both use screens?

(A) Watching TV is a more dangerous habit than going online.

(B) Watching TV is not as isolating as being on a screen online.

(C) Dramas on TV feel more real than those seen on smartphones.

(D) Going online does not spread poor values like TV does.

Part B

Which sentence in paragraph 18 most clearly supports the answer in Part A?

(A) "A generation ago, parents worried about their kids watching too much TV, which was also seen as spreading poor values."

(B) "While TV and online entertainment both use screens, our brains don't connect with them in the same ways."

(C) "TV is at a distance, compared to the close-up visual stimulation on a smartphone or computer screen."

(D) "TV also tends to be a more social activity."

Ed

Test-Taking Strategies

Analyze the Text

Support your responses with evidence from the text.

NOTICE & NOTE

Review what you **noticed and noted** as you read the text. Your annotations can help you answer these questions.

1. **IDENTIFY** What is the author's main claim about social media? How does the information in paragraph 2 relate to the claim?

2. **ANALYZE** Are the statistics in paragraph 4 relevant to the author's claim? Explain.

3. **CAUSE/EFFECT** In your own words, explain the cause-effect relationship the author describes in paragraph 5.

4. **COMPARE** How does the author's use of direct address in paragraphs 5–6 differ from her use of that same rhetorical device in paragraph 20?

5. **ANALYZE** What **Contrast or Contradiction** does the author explore in paragraph 12, and why is it important?

6. **CRITIQUE** Refer to the chart you filled in with examples of rhetorical devices you identified as you read the argument. How effective is the author's use of these devices? Critique the author's rhetoric by completing the chart below.

RHETORICAL DEVICE	EXAMPLE	YOUR CRITIQUE
Analogy		
Direct address		
Juxtaposition		
Rhetorical question		

Choices

Here are some other ways to demonstrate your understanding of the ideas in this lesson.

As you write and discuss, be sure to use the **Academic Vocabulary** words.

debate	sufficient
deduce	trend
license	

Writing
Email

Write an email message to the owner or administrator of a social media site that you believe has negatively affected you or someone you know.

- Begin with a professional greeting. Introduce yourself and explain your reason for writing.
- In the body of your email, explain the nature of the negative impact that you have experienced or witnessed. Be sure to support your position with relevant evidence.
- In your final paragraph, make a constructive suggestion for how the site owners might help prevent this problem from occurring again. End the email message with an appropriate closing.

Research
Technology Topics

What topics mentioned in this argument intrigued you? Smartphones, social media sites, the effects of social network addiction? Research one of these or a related topic. Be sure to use credible sources and note those sources for your records.

Speaking & Listening
Critique as a Class

Critique the argument presented in "Outsmart Your Smartphone" to decide whether it is convincing enough to accept as valid.

- Review the text and your notes to identify weaknesses or flaws in the author's argument. Also look for strengths, such as well-used rhetorical devices. Discuss your observations.
- Consider how the author addresses possible objections to her viewpoint. How convincing are her responses to opposing views or evidence that conflicts with her claims?
- As a class, identify points of agreement and draw a conclusion about the effectiveness and soundness of the author's argument.

Expand Your Vocabulary

PRACTICE AND APPLY

Explain how the meanings of the words in each pair are related.

perspective	stimulant	deliberate	inhibited

1. **stimulant** / sedative
2. **perspective** / bias
3. **inhibited** / impulsive
4. **deliberate** / thoughtless

Vocabulary Strategy

Word Families

A **word family** consists of words that have the same root and, thus, related meanings. However, their meanings may be altered by different **affixes**—word parts that are attached before or after the root. For example, the word *perspective* is derived from the Latin root *specere,* meaning "to look at," and the prefix *per-,* meaning "through." Can you see how the meanings of words with this root are similar?

LATIN ROOT	WORD FAMILY
specere: to look at	**inspect:** to examine carefully **perspective:** a viewpoint on something **speculate:** to engage in reasoning based on incomplete evidence

PRACTICE AND APPLY

Complete the word web with words that share the Latin root *ductus,* meaning "to lead." Define each related word. Then infer the meaning of *conducted* as it is used in this sentence:

> A study conducted by scientists at University of Texas-Austin in 2017 found that just having your smartphone nearby reduces cognitive performance—how well your brain can think and learn—even when the phone is silent or out of sight.

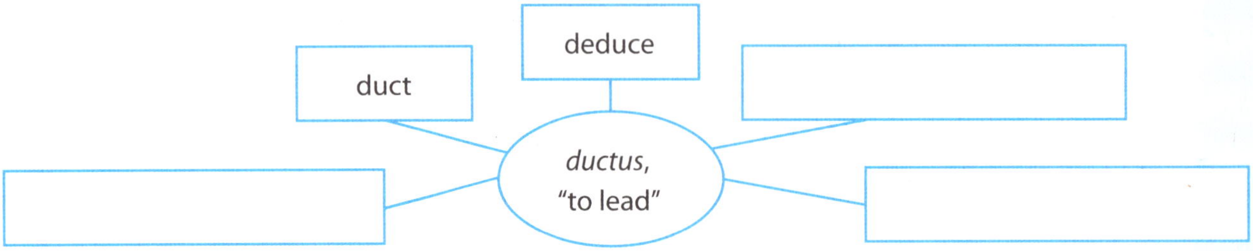

Watch Your Language!

Parallel Structure

One grammatical feature that makes writing effective is the use of parallel structure.

Parallel structure, also called parallelism, is the repetition of similar grammatical constructions to express ideas that are related or equal in importance. Parallel structure can help writers organize and clarify their ideas. It can also affect the meaning or emphasis of a sentence or passage of text.

Consider these examples:

Not parallel: Many teenagers enjoy social media and to communicate with their smartphones.

Parallel: Many teenagers enjoy using social media and communicating with their smartphones.

The second sentence creates parallel structure by repeating the gerund form with the words *using* and *communicating*. This parallelism makes the second sentence easier to understand than the first.

The author of "Outsmart Your Smartphone" uses parallel structure when she lists ways social media can be harmful:

> It can negatively affect the brain and behavior in ways that mimic addiction, adversely affect learning, distort normal aspects of social and emotional development, and increase anxiety.

By using the same grammatical form for each negative effect she lists in this sentence, Steiner-Adair makes it easier for the reader to follow the relationship between her ideas.

PRACTICE AND APPLY

Look back at the last piece of writing you submitted for class. Revise it to add at least two examples of parallel structure within a sentence or between paragraphs. Then, discuss with a partner how each use of parallelism helped you communicate your ideas more clearly or effectively.

Compare Arguments

When you **compare arguments,** you identify similarities and differences between important aspects of each. You might compare and contrast the claims, reasons, and evidence in each. Alternatively, you might focus more deeply on an analysis of one of the following:

- **Fact and interpretation:** Do the arguments introduce conflicting information on the topic? Where do the texts disagree on matters of fact or interpretation?
- **Opposing viewpoints and counterclaims:** Are the most important or common objections raised and addressed? Are opposing claims refuted with effective reasons and evidence?
- **Rhetoric and quality of writing:** Are rhetorical devices used effectively? How persuasive are the authors' writing styles?

In a small group, complete a chart like this one, adjusting the headings in the left column to reflect your particular focus.

EVIDENCE	*IT'S COMPLICATED*	BOTH	"OUTSMART YOUR SMARTPHONE"
Credibility			
Relevancy			
Currency			

Analyze the Texts

Discuss these questions in your group.

1. **COMPARE** How are the authors' points of view alike and different?
2. **COMPARE** How does each selection make use of counterclaims?
3. **ANALYZE** What kind of evidence does each author rely upon most?
4. **CRITIQUE** Which selection do you think presents the stronger argument? Cite evidence from both texts to support your opinion.

Create and Present

With a partner, play the role of an adult and a teenager in a discussion about social media use. The adult may be a parent, a teacher, or someone who is an expert on the topic. The adult and teen should take opposing viewpoints. Follow these steps:

1. **CHOOSE A ROLE AND A POSITION** With your partner, decide who will play the adult and who will play the teenager. Also choose the viewpoint you each plan to promote. This may mean that one of you must adopt a viewpoint that does not match your own.

2. **GATHER INFORMATION** List reasons and evidence from the texts and from your prior research that support your chosen viewpoint.

REASON 1:
Evidence:
REASON 2:
Evidence:

3. **PREPARE YOUR COUNTERCLAIM** Anticipate the other person's claim as well as his or her objections to your points. List reasons and evidence you will cite to challenge the opposing viewpoint.

OTHER'S CLAIM AND/OR OBJECTIONS	YOUR COUNTERCLAIM

4. **ROLE-PLAY THE DISCUSSION** In your chosen roles, have a conversation with your partner in which each of you tries to convince the other to adopt your position. Be on the lookout for flaws in one another's reasoning, and point them out as appropriate. Consider beginning your argument by acknowledging the other's position and its merits and then countering it.

Reader's Choice

Continue your exploration of the Essential Question by doing some independent reading about teenagers and growing up. Read the titles and descriptions shown. Then mark the texts that interest you.

ESSENTIAL QUESTION:
How do the challenges you face today help to shape your future?

Short Reads

Available on Ed

These texts are available in your ebook. Choose one to read and rate. Then defend your rating to the class.

Teenagers

Poem by **Pat Mora**

Parents and teenagers living in the same house feel like strangers behind closed doors.

Rate It ☆☆☆☆☆

Identity

Poem by **Julio Noboa Polanco**

A young poet imagines being free from society's rules.

Rate It ☆☆☆☆☆

Hard on the Gas

Poem by **Janet S. Wong**

Doing things his own way, a grandfather challenges a teen's expectations.

Rate It ☆☆☆☆☆

Marigolds

Short Story by **Eugenia Collier**

The impulsive actions of a young girl change her life forever.

Rate It ☆☆☆☆☆

My Summer of Scooping Ice Cream

Essay by **Shonda Rhimes**

A teenager gets more than a paycheck from her summer job.

Rate It ☆☆☆☆☆

Long Reads

Here are a few recommended books that connect to this unit topic. For additional options, ask your teacher, school librarian, or peers. Which titles spark your interest?

The Outsiders

Novel by **S.E. Hinton**

This novel explores the tensions, fears, and frustrations of gang life from a teenage boy's point of view.

The House on Mango Street

Novel by **Sandra Cisneros**

Told in a series of vignettes, this is the story of twelve-year-old Esperanza Cordero. Growing up in the Hispanic quarter of Chicago, she wonders who she will become.

Hush

Novel by **Jacqueline Woodson**

Evie Thomas's family has been forced to move to a new place and change identities. Her family's drastic behaviors are only adding to her stress as she tries to find her way in a new city.

Extension

Connect & Create

ADVICE COLUMN In the text you chose, what problems do the main characters face? Imagine one of the characters wrote to you to ask for your suggestions. Write an advice column to share your understanding of the situation. Conclude by making recommendations as to what the character should do to find a positive solution for their problems.

CREATE A STORYBOARD Choose a scene from the text you read to adapt into a storyboard. A storyboard is a map used by filmmakers to plan the shooting of a movie. It is made up of a series of frames that combines images and descriptions.

- Create a series of empty frames, either drawing them by hand or using digital tools. In each frame, make a sketch of the characters and settings to show how the scene will be filmed.
- Below each frame, write brief descriptions of the camera angles and any other important aspects of the shot. Include dialogue and describe the action that takes place during the scene.

NOTICE & NOTE

- Pick one of the texts and annotate the Notice & Note signposts you find.
- Then, use the **Notice & Note Writing Frames** to help you write about the significance of the signposts.
- Compare your findings with those of other students who read the same text.

Ed

Notice & Note Writing Frames

Write an Argument

Using ideas, information, and examples from multiple texts in this unit, write an argumentative essay for your school's blog on a topic related to teenagers.

Manage your time carefully so that you can

- review the texts in the unit;
- plan your essay;
- write your essay; and
- revise and edit your essay.

Be sure to

- clearly state the claim of your argument;
- address alternate or opposing claims;
- use and cite evidence from multiple sources; and
- avoid relying too much on one source.

Review the Mentor Text

For an example of a well-written argument you can use as a mentor text and as a source for your essay, review the excerpt from:

- *It's Complicated: The Social Lives of Networked Teens* (pages 396–399).

Make sure to carefully review your notes and annotations about this text. Think about the techniques the author used to make her argument convincing.

Consider Your Sources

Review the list of texts in the unit and choose at least two that you may want to use as a source of ideas or evidence for your argument.

As you review sources, consult the notes you made on your **Response Log** and make additional notes about any ideas that might be useful as you write. Include source titles and page numbers so that you can easily find information later.

UNIT 5 SOURCES

- ☐ *from* **Bronx Masquerade**
- ☐ **The Debt We Owe to the Adolescent Brain**
- ☐ **Hanging Fire**
- ☐ **Summer of His Fourteenth Year**
- ☐ *from* **It's Complicated: The Social Lives of Networked Teens**
- ☐ **Outsmart Your Smartphone**

Analyze the Prompt

Analyze the prompt to make sure you understand the assignment.

1. Mark the phrase in the prompt that identifies the general topic of your argument. Next, decide how you will narrow the topic to focus on a specific issue. Write a sentence that describes your topic and writing task.
2. Determine the purpose and audience of your essay, and write a sentence for each.

Think About Your Audience

Consider the following:

- Who will read my argument?
- What do readers already know about the topic?
- Why might they disagree with my position?

What is my topic? What is my writing task?

What is my purpose?

Who is my audience?

Review the Rubric

Your argument will be scored using a rubric. As you write, focus on the characteristics described in the chart. You will learn more about these characteristics as you work through the lesson.

PURPOSE, FOCUS, AND ORGANIZATION	EVIDENCE AND ELABORATION	CONVENTIONS OF STANDARD ENGLISH
The response includes: • A strongly maintained claim • Effective responses to opposing claims • Use of transitions to connect ideas • Logical progression of ideas • Appropriate style and tone	The response includes: • Effective use of evidence and sources • Effective use of elaboration • Clear and effective expression of ideas • Academic vocabulary • Varied sentence structure	The response may include: • Some minor errors in usage but no patterns of errors • Correct punctuation, capitalization, sentence formation, and spelling • Command of basic conventions

1 PLAN YOUR ARGUMENT

Determine Your Topic

Use the chart to gather information that can help you identify a **topic** (an issue related to teens) and your position on it.

TOPIC:		
PERSONAL INTEREST IN THE TOPIC	BACKGROUND READING	DISCUSSION NOTES

Help with Planning

Consult **Interactive Writing Lesson: Writing Arguments.**

Gather Information

Gather information from:

- notes in your Response Log
- your personal interests
- background reading
- discussion with classmates

Develop a Claim

At the beginning of your argument, you will introduce a **claim,** or your position on the issue related to teenagers that you have chosen. Your claim should:

- be direct and specific
- clearly state your position on the topic
- focus on a single main idea

MY CLAIM

Identify Reasons and Evidence

A strong argument provides relevant **reasons** that support the claim. In your argument, support each of your reasons with multiple pieces of **evidence,** such as facts, statistics, examples, and quotations by experts. Use the chart to outline your support.

REASONS	EVIDENCE	SOURCE

Organize Ideas

Organize your reasons and evidence in logical order.

- Include a response to an opposing claim in which you explain why your position is more valid.
- Think about how to use transitional words and phrases.
- Use techniques such as repetition or parallelism to create a sense of cohesion that holds your argument together.

Determine Structure

Here are two common **organizational patterns:**

- Arrange ideas by **order of importance,** from most important to least important, or vice versa.
- Organize reasons by **order of complexity or familiarity.** Build toward more complex or less familiar ideas.

INTRODUCTION	• Your introduction should grab the reader's attention with an interesting question, quote, or anecdote. • Clearly state your claim, and provide context to help readers understand your position.
BODY PARAGRAPHS	• Present reasons and evidence to support your claim. • Plan a paragraph for each main idea. • Remember to address an opposing claim.
CONCLUSION	• Restate your claim and its significance. • Wrap up your argument with a final thought that follows from the reasons and evidence you presented.

2 DEVELOP A DRAFT

Now it is time to write your essay. Examine how professional authors craft effective arguments and apply similar techniques to your own writing.

Ed

Drafting Online

Check your assignment list for a writing task from your teacher.

Introduce a Claim

EXAMINE THE MENTOR TEXT

Notice how the author of *It's Complicated* introduces her claim about teenagers' use of social media.

The author provides **context** about adolescent development

Developing meaningful friendships is a key component of the coming of age process. Friends offer many things—advice, support, entertainment, and a connection that combats loneliness. And in doing so, they enable the transition to adulthood by providing a context beyond that of family and home. Though family is still important, many teens relish the opportunity to create relationships that are not simply given but chosen.

The importance of friends in social and moral development is well documented. But the fears that surround teens' use of social media overlook this fundamental desire for social connection. . . .

She notes **opposing views** that express concerns about social media use as a way to distinguish her **claim.**

APPLY TO YOUR DRAFT

Answer the questions in the chart to help you draft your introduction.

Try It Out

Why are you interested in your topic? There's a good chance that what interests you might also interest your readers. Don't be afraid to let your passion for your topic show in your introduction.

What about my argument will most concern my readers?	What opinions might readers already have about the topic?	What interesting and relevant background information can I provide?

Address an Opposing Claim

EXAMINE THE MENTOR TEXT

In *It's Complicated*, danah boyd addresses an **opposing claim,** or a viewpoint that expresses disagreement with her position.

The author acknowledges a viewpoint that **opposes** her own position.

The transitional word *but* signals a contrast between concerns about internet addiction and how technology can benefit teens' social-emotional health.

Consider, for example, the widespread concern over internet addiction. Are there teens who have an unhealthy relationship with technology? Certainly. But most of those who are "addicted" to their phones or computers are actually focused on staying connected to friends in a culture where getting together is highly constrained. Teens' preoccupation with their friends dovetails with their desire to enter the public spaces that are freely accessible to adults. The ability to access public spaces for sociable purposes is a critical component of the coming of age process, and yet many of the public spaces where adults gather . . . are inaccessible to teens.

APPLY TO YOUR DRAFT

Including a response to an opposing claim in your essay will strengthen your argument. Use the chart to practice addressing an opposing claim.

Try These Suggestions

Use one of these phrases to introduce an opposing claim:

- Opponents claim . . .
- Some people say . . .
- While others may suggest . . .

Then use one of these phrases to refute the opposing claim:

- However, evidence suggests . . .
- But the truth is . . .
- Yet experts claim . . .

1. INTRODUCE AN OPPOSING CLAIM.

2. STATE WHY YOUR CLAIM IS MORE VALID.

3. USE EVIDENCE TO SUPPORT YOUR REASON.

3 REVISE YOUR ARGUMENT

Experienced writers know the importance of revision. Review your essay and consider how it can be improved. Use the guide to help you revise your argument.

Ed

Help with Revision

Find a **Peer Review Guide** and **Student Models** online.

REVISION GUIDE		
ASK YOURSELF	**PROVE IT**	**REVISE IT**
Introduction Does my introduction contain a clear claim?	**Highlight** the introduction. **Underline** the claim.	**Add** to or **revise** your claim to clarify or strengthen your position on the issue.
Organization Are the paragraphs organized in a logical structure? Do transitions connect ideas throughout the essay?	**Number** the paragraphs and make sure the most important reason comes first or last. **Circle** transitions that connect ideas.	**Rearrange** paragraphs in order of importance. **Add** transitions to connect ideas.
Support Do I include at least two reasons to support my argument? Do I support my reasons with evidence? Do I explain how the evidence supports my claim with elaboration?	**Put a star** (★) next to each reason. **Highlight** the supporting evidence for each reason. **Underline** elaboration that explains how the evidence supports your claim.	**Add** reasons, and/or **include** another specific fact, example, or comparison to further support each reason. **Add** elaboration to clarify how the evidence supports your claim.
Sources Have I cited my sources correctly?	**Put a check mark** (✓) next to references to your sources.	**Add** author names or titles.
Opposing Claims Do I address opposing claims?	**Underline** where you mention opposing claims. **Highlight** sentences that address them.	**Add** possible opposing claims and persuasive responses to refute them.
Conclusion Does my conclusion follow from and support the reasoning of my argument?	**Highlight** the parts of the conclusion that support your claim and reasons.	**Add** or **revise** the conclusion to make sure it logically follows from your argument.

APPLY TO YOUR DRAFT

Consider the following as you look for opportunities to improve your writing.

- Check that you clearly state your claim.
- Make sure an opposing claim is refuted with a compelling reason.
- Review your spelling and grammar and make sure it is correct.

Peer Review in Action

Once you have finished revising your argument, you will exchange papers with a partner in a **peer review.** During a peer review, you will give suggestions to improve your partner's draft.

Read the introduction from a student's draft and examine the comments made by his peer reviewer.

First Draft

Leave Teens' Phones Alone

by Tarek Haddad, Williamstown Middle School

I think kids these days need to learn to manage their screen time themselves. If parents exercise too much control over their teens' phone use, how will they ever learn to navigate life as adults? Sure, they might mess up, but making mistakes is part of the learning process. Kids need space to figure things out for themselves without their helicopter parents swarming around them all the time.

Avoid using the pronoun "I" and slang expressions like "mess up" in a formal essay.

Phrases like "navigate life" and "figure things out" are too general. Try to give more context to help readers better understand the issues you will address.

Now read the revised introduction below. Notice how the writer has improved his draft by making revisions based on the peer reviewer's comments.

Revision

Is it harmful to use your phone too much? Of course. Too much phone use can interfere with your sleep and your ability to concentrate. The risk of negative impacts is greater during adolescence, when the brain is at a crucial stage of development. However, parents who restrict their teens' phone use limit their teens' ability to develop self-control, which is a crucial skill they will need as adults. Teens need to learn to manage their phone use themselves.

Great job! The information you include about the negative impacts of phone use helps me better understand your position, and your claim is direct and clear.

APPLY TO YOUR DRAFT

During your peer review, give each other specific suggestions for how you could make your arguments more compelling. Use the revision guide to help you.

When receiving feedback from your partner, listen attentively and ask questions to make sure you fully understand the revision suggestions.

4 EDIT YOUR ARGUMENT

Edit your final draft to check for proper use of standard English conventions and to correct any grammatical errors.

Ed

Interactive Grammar Lesson

Gerunds and Gerund Phrases

Watch Your Language!

USE GERUNDS CORRECTLY

A **gerund** is verb form ending in *–ing* that functions as a noun. Gerunds may perform any function nouns perform. Avoid confusing gerunds with other kinds of words that end in *–ing*, such as verbs or participles that modify a noun.

Read the following sentences from *It's Complicated:*

All too often, parents project their values onto their children, failing to recognize that school is often not the most pressing concern . . .

In this sentence, *failing* functions as a verb and *pressing* functions as a participle that modifies *concern.*

Furthermore, social interactions may be a distraction from school, but they are often not a distraction from learning.

Learning acts as a gerund in this sentence. It functions as the object of the preposition *from.*

Gerunds

Here are some functions of gerunds:

Subject: *Texting* was the main way the teenagers communicated.

Direct Object: The students stopped *texting* and put their phones away.

Object of Preposition: She didn't see anything wrong with *texting* during class.

Predicate Noun: For many, the main way to communicate was *texting.*

APPLY TO YOUR DRAFT

Now apply what you've learned about gerunds to your own work.

1. **Read your paper aloud** and underline any gerunds.
2. **Check** that each gerund is used correctly.
3. **Exchange drafts** with a peer and discuss the function of gerunds in each other's work.

5 PUBLISH YOUR ARGUMENT

Share It!

Finalize your argument for your writing portfolio. You may also use your argument as inspiration for other projects.

Ways to Share

- **Create a video** for classmates to view and respond to.
- **Write a letter** to a school administrator or other local leader.
- **Participate in a debate** with someone who has an opposing view.

Speaking & Listening

Present an Argument

Now you will adapt your argument for presentation to your classmates. You will also listen to their presentations, ask questions to better understand their ideas, and make suggestions to help them improve their work.

Adapt Your Argument for Presentation

Use the chart below to plan how you will adapt the key elements of your argument to create a script and other presentation materials.

What is the most engaging way to introduce your claim? Use the chart below to generate ideas for your introduction.

Consider Tone

Your tone will affect how your audience receives your argument. Experiment with different tones, such as instructive, serious, or passionate, to figure out which works best for your presentation.

ASK YOURSELF	NOTES
How will you revise your **title** and **introduction** to capture the listener's attention?	
Is there a more concise way to state your **claim?**	
What **tone** will be most persuasive in an oral presentation?	
Which parts of your argument could be clearer? Where can you add **transitions** to better connect **reasons and evidence** that support your claim?	
What **images or graphics** would help clarify your argument? What text should appear on screen?	

Practice with a Partner or Group

Practice your script with a partner or group to improve your presentation.

IF...	TRY...
You stumble over pronouncing certain words.	Rearranging sentences for a smooth delivery.
Listeners at the back of the room can't hear you.	Raising the volume of your voice.
You feel nervous.	Making eye contact briefly with audience members.

Be an Effective Listener

- Make suggestions as to how presenters can improve their presentation techniques.
- Pose questions to clarify any confusing ideas.

Be an Effective Presenter

- Listen closely to questions and respond thoughtfully.
- Try to build on the ideas your group members bring to the discussion.

Deliver Your Presentation

Based on the practice session, make any final changes as you get ready for your presentation. Then, groups should take turns presenting their arguments to the whole class:

- Use the advice you received to make final changes to your argument.
- Using effective verbal and nonverbal techniques, present your argument to your classmates.

Share It!

- **Record your presentation as a podcast** and share it with family members and friends.
- **Create an infographic** that summarizes the main points of your argument.
- **Have a partner discussion** about how your position may have changed after listening to other presentations.

Ed

Interactive Speaking & Listening Lesson: Giving a Presentation

Reflect & Extend

Here are some other ways to show your understanding of the ideas in Unit 5.

Reflect on the Essential Question

How do the challenges you face today help to shape your future?

Has your answer to the question changed after reading the texts in the unit? Discuss your ideas.

You can use these sentence starters to help reflect on your learning.

- **I still have questions about . . .**
- **I've changed my mind about . . .**
- **My opinions shifted because . . .**

Writing

Personal Narrative

Write a personal narrative about an experience that helped you find your path on your journey toward adulthood. Use the chart to jot down or sketch your ideas. Then, write your narrative.

Project-Based Learning

Envision Your Future Self

Create a series of self-portraits to show who you are today and who you hope to become in the future. Include a self-portrait that shows what you look like now. Then use your imagination to create self-portraits of what you'll look like in 10, 20, and 50 years from now. Be as creative as you can. Here are some questions to ask yourself as you get started:

- How do you envision your future? What are your career and personal goals?
- How might challenges you face now affect who you become?
- What colors or symbols might you want to use in your self-portrait?
- What surprising elements might you want to use in the portrait to emphasize certain ideas about yourself?

Ed

Media Projects

To find help with this task online, access **Create a Self-Portrait.**

ASK YOURSELF	MY NOTES
What event or events will you include in your narrative?	
Who played an important role in your experience?	
What did you learn about yourself from the experience?	

UNIT 6

Ed

Get hooked by the unit topic.

Stream to Start Video

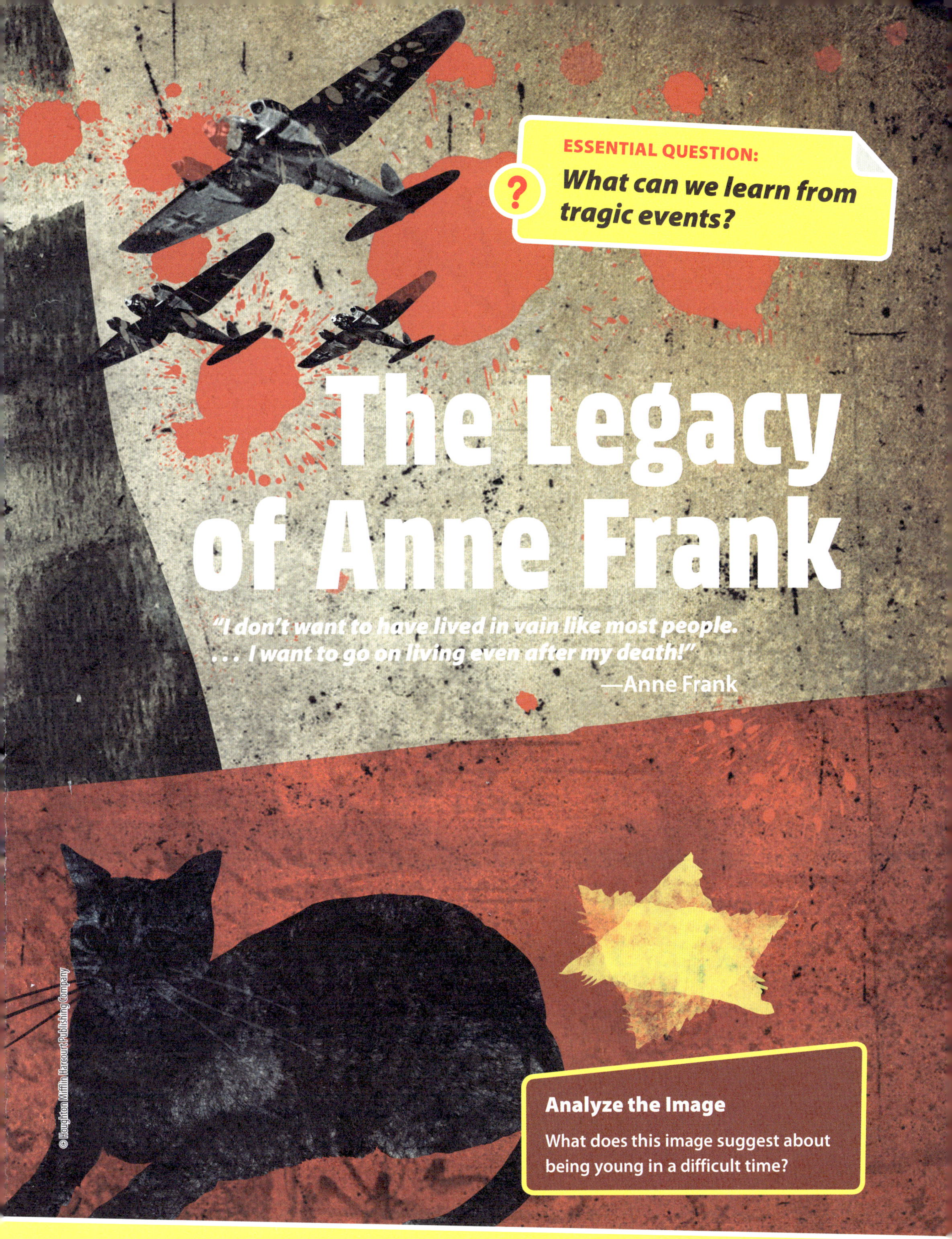

ESSENTIAL QUESTION:

What can we learn from tragic events?

The Legacy of Anne Frank

"I don't want to have lived in vain like most people. . . . I want to go on living even after my death!"
—Anne Frank

Analyze the Image

What does this image suggest about being young in a difficult time?

Spark Your Learning

Here are some ways to spark your learning about the topics and themes of **Unit 6: The Legacy of Anne Frank.**

As you read, you can use the **Response Log** (page R6) to track your thinking about the Essential Question.

Make the Connection

Consider what you already know about Anne Frank. Sketch a picture of her or jot down your ideas about her in the space below.

Think About the Essential Question

What can we learn from tragic events? What lessons do people take away from great tragedy and loss?

Sound Like an Expert

You can use these Academic Vocabulary words to write and talk about the topics and themes in the unit. Which of these words do you already feel comfortable using when speaking or writing?

	I can use it!	I understand it.	I'll look it up.
communicate	☐	☐	☐
draft	☐	☐	☐
liberation	☐	☐	☐
philosophy	☐	☐	☐
publish	☐	☐	☐

Prove It!

Turn to a partner and use one of the words in a sentence about a tragic historical event.

Preview the Texts

Look over the images, titles, and descriptions of the texts in the unit. Mark the title of the text that interests you most.

The Diary of Anne Frank

Drama by **Frances Goodrich and Albert Hackett**

This play provides a fictional account of Anne Frank's experience hiding with her family in the attic rooms behind Mr. Frank's office.

from The Diary of a Young Girl

Diary by **Anne Frank**

These excerpts from her diary give the reader insight into what life was like for Anne and the other people in the Secret Annex.

After Auschwitz

Speech by **Elie Wiesel**

This speech commemorates those who died in the concentration camp at Auschwitz, Poland.

There But for the Grace

Poem by **Wisława Szymborska**

The speaker marvels at the little things that make the difference between survival and death.

Days

Poem by **Billy Collins**

Our lives may be more fragile than we think.

I Wonder . . .

What can we learn from reading about people who experienced tragedy? Jot down or sketch your answer.

The Diary of Anne Frank

Drama by **Frances Goodrich** and **Albert Hackett**

ESSENTIAL QUESTION:
What can we learn from tragic events?

Engage Your Brain

Choose one or two of these activities to start connecting with the drama you're about to read.

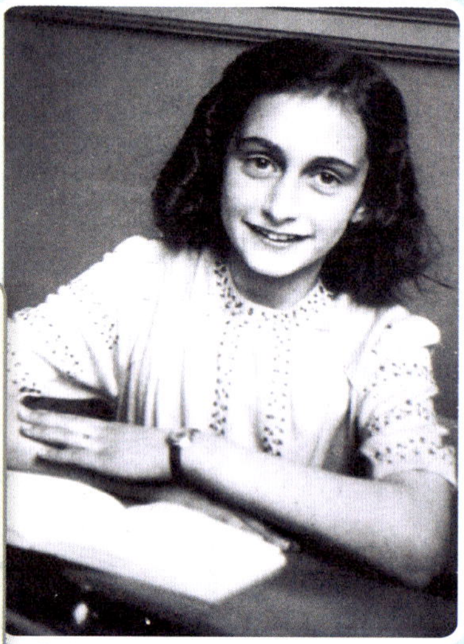

About Anne Frank

Anne Frank is an important figure in world history. What do you know about her? With a small group, make a list of facts about this remarkable girl.

Not Much Room

The people in the play you are about to read have to go into hiding and share a small living space with another family for many months. What would be the hardest parts about living in cramped quarters with others? Write a few sentences to explain your ideas.

Drama vs. Fiction

Have you read many plays? How is reading a drama different than reading a work of fiction? Have a discussion with your classmates to share your opinions about reading drama.

Analyze Drama

A **drama,** or play, is a form of literature meant to be performed on stage. Like other literature, a drama presents a series of events, called the **plot,** and conveys the time and place of those events, called the **setting.** The text of a drama, called a script, usually includes the following elements:

- The **cast of characters** is a list of all the characters in the play.
- **Dialogue,** or written conversation between characters, tells the story and makes up most of the text in a drama. Dialogue can give readers insight into the characters' personality traits. It can also reveal conflicts that prompt characters to make decisions, moving the plot forward.
- **Stage directions,** which often are italicized and in parentheses, are mostly instructions about how to perform the drama. Some stage directions describe the setting and the characters.

A drama is often divided into acts and scenes. Each scene in a drama presents an episode of the play's plot. The events in each scene advance the plot, which usually flows in **chronological order,** the order in which events happen. Playwrights may also use these more complex plot structures to relate events:

- When an author interrupts the chronological order to describe something that took place at an earlier time, the earlier incident or conversation is considered a **flashback.** Flashbacks often help readers better understand a current situation.
- Authors may also provide hints to suggest future events. This is called **foreshadowing.** Foreshadowing creates suspense and makes readers eager to find out what will happen.

As you read *The Diary of Anne Frank*, notice how the playwrights use dialogue and plot events to propel the action of the play and to develop the characters.

Focus on Genre

Drama

- is written to be performed by actors in front of an audience
- tells a story through characters' words and actions
- includes stage directions with important details that explain what's happening
- may be divided into acts, which are in turn divided into scenes
- may show that the time or place of the action has changed by starting a new act or scene

Annotation in Action

Here is an example of notes a student made about this paragraph from *The Diary of Anne Frank*. As you read, make annotations to record your analysis of how dialogue and events in the play reveal the characters' personality traits or advance the plot.

Anne (*as she opens the carton*). You know the way I'm going to think of it here? I'm going to think of it as a boarding house. A very peculiar summer boarding house, like the one that we—(*She breaks off as she pulls out some photographs.*) Father! My movie stars! I was wondering where they were! I was looking for them this morning . . . and Queen Wilhelmina! How wonderful!

This dialogue shows the cheery, positive side of Anne's personality.

Expand Your Vocabulary

Put a check mark next to the vocabulary words that you feel comfortable using when speaking or writing.

- **conspicuous** ☐
- **loathe** ☐
- **indignantly** ☐
- **ostentatiously** ☐
- **appalled** ☐
- **inarticulate** ☐

Turn to a partner and use one of the words you already know in a sentence about Anne Frank.

As you read *The Diary of Anne Frank*, use the definitions in the side column to learn the vocabulary words you don't already know.

Background

Frances Goodrich (1890–1984) and **Albert Hackett** (1900–1995) were a married couple who worked together to write screenplays for movies. They wrote the play called *The Diary of Anne Frank* based on Anne's actual diary entries. Although the play differs from the diary in many ways, Anne's father, who survived the Holocaust, believed that it captured the essence of his daughter's diary. The play won the 1956 Pulitzer Prize for drama. It was later made into an Oscar-winning movie, for which Goodrich and Hackett also wrote the screenplay.

The Diary of Anne Frank

Drama by **Francis Goodrich** and **Albert Hackett**

This play provides a fictional account of Anne Frank's experience hiding with her family in the attic rooms behind Mr. Frank's office.

NOTICE & NOTE
As you read, use the side margins to make notes about the text.

BACKGROUND

Anne Frank and her family were Jewish citizens of Germany. After the Nazi Party, led by Adolf Hitler, came to power in 1933, the Franks moved to the Netherlands to escape persecution. However, the Nazis invaded that country in 1940. In order to survive, Anne's family went into hiding when she was 13 years old. They hid in attic rooms behind Mr. Frank's office, and several other Jews joined them. In this "Secret Annex," Anne kept a diary about her life in hiding. More than two years later, the group's worst fears came true when the Nazis found them. Everyone who had been living there was sent to concentration camps. Anne's diary was discovered later.

ANALYZE DRAMA

Annotate: Review the cast of characters. Circle four members of one family. Underline three members of another.

Analyze: What two families live in the Secret Annex? What other characters are in the play?

ANALYZE DRAMA

Annotate: In paragraphs 3–5, mark details that describe what this scene looks like and sounds like.

Analyze: Why do you think the stage directions include a description of the sounds outside the Annex?

Ed

Text in Focus Video

Learn more about the play's setting.

CHARACTERS

SECRET ANNEX RESIDENTS

Anne Frank	Peter Van Daan
Margot Frank	Mr. Van Daan
Mr. Frank	Mrs. Van Daan
Mrs. Frank	Mr. Dussel

WORKERS IN MR. FRANK'S BUSINESS

Miep Gies (mēp gēs)   Mr. Kraler (krä´lər)

1 **The Time.** *July 1942–August 1944, November 1945*

2 **The Place.** *Amsterdam, the Netherlands*

3 *The scene remains the same throughout the play. It is the top floor of a warehouse and office building in Amsterdam, Holland. The sharply peaked roof of the building is outlined against a sea of other rooftops, stretching away into the distance. Nearby is the belfry of a church tower, the Westertoren, whose carillon rings out the hours. Occasionally faint sounds float up from below: the voices of children playing in the street, the tramp of marching feet, a boat whistle from the canal.*

4 *The three rooms of the top floor and a small attic space above are exposed to our view. The largest of the rooms is in the center, with two small rooms, slightly raised, on either side. On the right is a bathroom, out of sight. A narrow steep flight of stairs at the back leads up to the attic. The rooms are sparsely furnished with a few chairs, cots, a table or two. The windows are painted over, or covered with makeshift blackout curtains. In the main room there is a sink, a gas ring for cooking and a wood-burning stove for warmth.*

5 *The room on the left is hardly more than a closet. There is a skylight in the sloping ceiling. Directly under this room is a small steep stairwell, with steps leading down to a door. This is the only entrance from the building below. When the door is opened we see that it has been concealed on the outer side by a bookcase attached to it.*

ACT ONE Scene 1

6 *The curtain rises on an empty stage. It is late afternoon November, 1945.*

7 *The rooms are dusty, the curtains in rags. Chairs and tables are overturned.*

8 *The door at the foot of the small stairwell swings open.* Mr. Frank

comes up the steps into view. He is a gentle, cultured European in his middle years. There is still a trace of a German accent in his speech.

9 *He stands looking slowly around, making a supreme effort at self-control. He is weak, ill. His clothes are threadbare.*

10 *After a second he drops his rucksack on the couch and moves slowly about. He opens the door to one of the smaller rooms, and then abruptly closes it again, turning away. He goes to the window at the back, looking off at the Westertoren as its carillon strikes the hour of six, then he moves restlessly on.*

11 *From the street below we hear the sound of a barrel organ and children's voices at play. There is a many-colored scarf hanging from a nail.* Mr. Frank *takes it, putting it around his neck. As he starts back for his rucksack, his eye is caught by something lying on the floor. It is a woman's white glove. He holds it in his hand and suddenly all of his self-control is gone. He breaks down, crying.*

12 *We hear footsteps on the stairs.* Miep Gies *comes up, looking for* Mr. Frank. Miep *is a Dutch girl of about twenty-two. She wears a coat and hat, ready to go home. She is pregnant. Her attitude toward* Mr. Frank *is protective, compassionate.*

13 **Miep.** Are you all right, Mr. Frank?

14 **Mr. Frank** (*quickly controlling himself*). Yes, Miep, yes.

15 **Miep.** Everyone in the office has gone home . . . It's after six. (*then pleading*) Don't stay up here, Mr. Frank. What's the use of torturing yourself like this?

16 **Mr. Frank.** I've come to say goodbye . . . I'm leaving here, Miep.

17 **Miep.** What do you mean? Where are you going? Where?

18 **Mr. Frank.** I don't know yet. I haven't decided.

19 **Miep.** Mr. Frank, you can't leave here! This is your home! Amsterdam is your home. Your business is here, waiting for you . . . You're needed here . . . Now that the war is over, there are things that . . .

20 **Mr. Frank.** I can't stay in Amsterdam, Miep. It has too many memories for me. Everywhere there's something . . . the house we lived in . . . the school . . . that street organ playing out there . . . I'm not the person you used to know, Miep. I'm a bitter old man. (*breaking off*) Forgive me. I shouldn't speak to you like this . . . after all that you did for us . . . the suffering . . .

21 **Miep.** No. No. It wasn't suffering. You can't say we suffered. (*As she speaks, she straightens a chair which is overturned.*)

22 **Mr. Frank.** I know what you went through, you and Mr. Kraler. I'll remember it as long as I live. (*He gives one last look around.*) Come, Miep.

Don't forget to **Notice & Note** as you read the text.

ANALYZE DRAMA

Annotate: In paragraphs 8–9, mark details that describe the character of Mr. Frank.

Infer: What details do the stage directions provide about Mr. Frank? What does the description suggest about him?

NOTICE & NOTE

CONTRASTS AND CONTRADICTIONS

When you notice a sharp contrast between what you would expect and what the character actually does, you've found a **Contrasts and Contradictions** signpost.

Notice & Note: Mark what Mr. Frank tells Miep to do with the papers she brings to him.

Compare: Recall what Mr. Frank did with the glove he found. How does his previous reaction contrast with what he says about the papers? Why would Mr. Frank act this way?

Ed

Close Read Screencast

Listen to a modeled close read of this text.

23 (*He starts for the steps, then remembers his rucksack, going back to get it.*)

24 **Miep** (*hurrying up to a cupboard*). Mr. Frank, did you see? There are some of your papers here. (*She brings a bundle of papers to him.*) We found them in a heap of rubbish on the floor after . . . after you left.

25 **Mr. Frank.** Burn them.

26 (*He opens his rucksack to put the glove in it.*)

27 **Miep.** But, Mr. Frank, there are letters, notes . . .

28 **Mr. Frank.** Burn them. All of them.

29 **Miep.** Burn this?

30 (*She hands him a paperbound notebook.*)

31 **Mr. Frank** (*quietly*). Anne's diary. (*He opens the diary and begins to read.*) "Monday, the sixth of July, nineteen forty-two." (*to* Miep) Nineteen forty-two. Is it possible, Miep? . . . Only three years ago. (*As he continues his reading, he sits down on the couch.*) "Dear Diary, since you and I are going to be great friends, I will start by telling you about myself. My name is Anne Frank. I am thirteen years old. I was born in Germany the twelfth of June, nineteen twenty-nine. As my family is Jewish, we emigrated to Holland when Hitler came to power."

32 (*As* Mr. Frank *reads on, another voice joins his, as if coming from the air. It is* Anne's Voice.)

33 **Mr. Frank and Anne.** "My father started a business, importing spice and herbs. Things went well for us until nineteen forty. Then the war came, and the Dutch capitulation, followed by the arrival of the Germans. Then things got very bad for the Jews."

34 (Mr. Frank's Voice *dies out.* Anne's Voice *continues alone. The lights dim slowly to darkness. The curtain falls on the scene.*)

35 **Anne's Voice.** You could not do this and you could not do that. They forced Father out of his business. We had to wear yellow stars.[1] I had to turn in my bike. I couldn't go to a Dutch school any more. I couldn't go to the movies, or ride in an automobile, or even on a streetcar, and a million other things. But somehow we children still managed to have fun. Yesterday Father told me we were going into hiding. Where, he wouldn't say. At five o'clock this morning Mother woke me and told me to hurry and get dressed. I was to put on as many clothes as I could. It would look too suspicious if we walked along carrying suitcases. It wasn't until we were on our way that I learned where we were going. Our hiding place was to be upstairs in the building where Father used to have his business. Three other people were coming in with us . . . the Van Daans and their son Peter . . . Father knew the Van Daans but we had never met them . . .

36 (*During the last lines the curtain rises on the scene. The lights dim on.* Anne's Voice *fades out.*)

Don't forget to **Notice & Note** as you read the text.

NOTICE & NOTE
MEMORY MOMENT

When you notice the narrator has interrupted the forward progress of a story by bringing up something from the past, you've found a **Memory Moment** signpost.

Notice & Note: In paragraphs 31–35, mark time words that indicate this is a Memory Moment.

Infer: Why might these memories be important?

Scene 2

37 *It is early morning, July, 1942. The rooms are bare, as before, but they are now clean and orderly.*

38 Mr. Van Daan, *a tall, portly man in his late forties, is in the main room, pacing up and down, nervously smoking a cigarette. His clothes and overcoat are expensive and well cut.*

39 Mrs. Van Daan *sits on the couch, clutching her possessions, a hatbox, bags, etc. She is a pretty woman in her early forties. She wears a fur coat over her other clothes.*

40 Peter Van Daan *is standing at the window of the room on the right, looking down at the street below. He is a shy, awkward boy of sixteen. He wears a cap, a raincoat, and long Dutch trousers, like "plus fours." At his feet is a black case, a carrier for his cat.*

41 *The yellow Star of David is* ***conspicuous*** *on all of their clothes.*

42 **Mrs. Van Daan** (*rising, nervous, excited*). Something's happened to them! I know it!

43 **Mr. Van Daan.** Now, Kerli!

ANALYZE DRAMA

Annotate: Mark the new date indicated in Scene 2. Then look back at paragraph 6.

Analyze: What indicates that this is a flashback? What do the contrasts between the Annex of the past and the Annex of 1945 suggest may have happened here?

conspicuous
(kən-spĭk´yo͞o-əs) *adj.* Something *conspicuous* is obvious or very easy to see.

[1] **yellow stars:** the six-pointed Stars of David that the Nazis ordered all Jews to wear for identification.

44 **Mrs. Van Daan.** Mr. Frank said they'd be here at seven o'clock. He said . . .

45 **Mr. Van Daan.** They have two miles to walk. You can't expect . . .

46 **Mrs. Van Daan.** They've been picked up. That's what's happened. They've been taken . . .

47 (Mr. Van Daan *indicates that he hears someone coming.*)

48 **Mr. Van Daan.** You see?

49 (Peter *takes up his carrier and his schoolbag, etc., and goes into the main room as* Mr. Frank *comes up the stairwell from below.* Mr. Frank *looks much younger now. His movements are brisk, his manner confident. He wears an overcoat and carries his hat and a small cardboard box. He crosses to the* Van Daans, *shaking hands with each of them.*)

50 **Mr. Frank.** Mrs. Van Daan, Mr. Van Daan, Peter. (*then, in explanation of their lateness*) There were too many of the Green Police[2] on the streets . . . we had to take the long way around.

51 (*Up the steps come* Margot Frank, Mrs. Frank, Miep *[not pregnant now] and* Mr. Kraler. *All of them carry bags, packages, and so forth. The Star of David is conspicuous on all of the* Franks' *clothing.* Margot *is eighteen, beautiful, quiet, shy.* Mrs. Frank *is a young mother, gently bred, reserved. She, like* Mr. Frank, *has a slight German accent.* Mr. Kraler *is a Dutchman, dependable, kindly.*

52 *As* Mr. Kraler *and* Miep *go upstage to put down their parcels,* Mrs. Frank *turns back to call* Anne.)

53 **Mrs. Frank.** Anne?

54 (Anne *comes running up the stairs. She is thirteen, quick in her movements, interested in everything, mercurial in her emotions. She wears a cape, long wool socks and carries a schoolbag.*)

55 **Mr. Frank** (*introducing them*). My wife, Edith. Mr. and Mrs. Van Daan (Mrs. Frank *hurries over, shaking hands with them.*) . . . their son, Peter . . . my daughters, Margot and Anne.

56 (Anne *gives a polite little curtsy as she shakes* Mr. Van Daan's *hand. Then she immediately starts off on a tour of investigation of her new home, going upstairs to the attic room.* Miep *and* Mr. Kraler *are putting the various things they have brought on the shelves.*)

57 **Mr. Kraler.** I'm sorry there is still so much confusion.

58 **Mr. Frank.** Please. Don't think of it. After all, we'll have plenty of leisure to arrange everything ourselves.

[2] **Green Police:** the Nazi police, who wore green uniforms.

59 **Miep** (*to* Mrs. Frank). We put the stores of food you sent in here. Your drugs are here . . . soap, linen here.

60 **Mrs. Frank.** Thank you, Miep.

61 **Miep.** I made up the beds . . . the way Mr. Frank and Mr. Kraler said. (*She starts out.*) Forgive me. I have to hurry. I've got to go to the other side of town to get some ration books[3] for you.

62 **Mrs. Van Daan.** Ration books? If they see our names on ration books, they'll know we're here.

63 **Mr. Kraler.** There isn't anything . . .
64 **Miep.** Don't worry. Your names won't be on them. (*as she hurries out*) I'll be up later.
} *Together*

65 **Mr. Frank.** Thank you, Miep.

66 **Mrs. Frank** (*to* Mr. Kraler). It's illegal, then, the ration books? We've never done anything illegal.

67 **Mr. Frank.** We won't be living here exactly according to regulations. (*As* Mr. Kraler *reassures* Mrs. Frank, *he takes various small things, such as matches, soap, etc., from his pockets, handing them to her.*)

68 **Mr. Kraler.** This isn't the black market,[4] Mrs. Frank. This is what we call the white market . . . helping all of the hundreds and hundreds who are hiding out in Amsterdam.

69 (*The carillon is heard playing the quarter-hour before eight.* Mr. Kraler *looks at his watch.* Anne *stops at the window as she comes down the stairs.*)

70 **Anne.** It's the Westertoren!

71 **Mr. Kraler.** I must go. I must be out of here and downstairs in the office before the workmen get here. (*He starts for the stairs leading out.*) Miep or I, or both of us, will be up each day to bring you food and news and find out what your needs are. Tomorrow I'll get you a better bolt for the door at the foot of the stairs. It needs a bolt that you can throw yourself and open only at our signal. (*to* Mr. Frank) Oh . . .You'll tell them about the noise?

72 **Mr. Frank.** I'll tell them.

Don't forget to **Notice & Note** as you read the text.

ANALYZE DRAMA

Annotate: Mark the stage direction that reveals how Mr. Kraler and Miep respond to Mrs. Van Daan's comment about the ration books.

Interpret: What does that stage direction mean? Why might the playwrights have used it?

[3] **ration books:** books of stamps or coupons issued by the government in wartime. With these coupons, people could purchase scarce items, such as food, clothing, and gasoline.
[4] **black market:** a system for selling goods illegally, in violation of rationing and other restrictions.

73 **Mr. Kraler.** Good-bye then for the moment. I'll come up again, after the workmen leave.

74 **Mr. Frank.** Good-bye, Mr. Kraler.

75 **Mrs. Frank.** (*shaking his hand*). How can we thank you? (*The others murmur their good-byes.*)

76 **Mr. Kraler.** I never thought I'd live to see the day when a man like Mr. Frank would have to go into hiding. When you think— (*He breaks off, going out.* Mr. Frank *follows him down the steps, bolting the door after him. In the interval before he returns,* Peter *goes over to* Margot, *shaking hands with her. As* Mr. Frank *comes back up the steps,* Mrs. Frank *questions him anxiously.*)

77 **Mrs. Frank.** What did he mean, about the noise?

78 **Mr. Frank.** First let us take off some of these clothes. (*They all start to take off garment after garment. On each of their coats, sweaters, blouses, suits, dresses, is another yellow Star of David.* Mr. *and* Mrs. Frank *are underdressed quite simply. The others wear several things, sweaters, extra dresses, bathrobes, aprons, nightgowns, etc.*)

79 **Mr. Van Daan.** It's a wonder we weren't arrested, walking along the streets . . . Petronella with a fur coat in July . . . and that cat of Peter's crying all the way.

80 **Anne** (*as she is removing a pair of panties*). A cat?

81 **Mrs. Frank.** (*shocked*). Anne, please!

82 **Anne.** It's all right. I've got on three more. (*She pulls off two more. Finally, as they have all removed their surplus clothes, they look to* Mr. Frank, *waiting for him to speak.*)

ANALYZE DRAMA

Annotate: Mark details in paragraphs 83–84 about how the residents of the Secret Annex must behave in order to survive.

ret: What is the main problem, in the plot? nk's words add ot?

83 **Mr. Frank.** Now. About the noise. While the men are in the building below, we must have complete quiet. Every sound can be heard down there, not only in the workrooms, but in the offices too. The men come at about eight-thirty, and leave at about five-thirty. So, to be perfectly safe, from eight in the morning until six in the evening we must move only when it is necessary, and then in stockinged feet. We must not speak above a whisper. We must not run any water. We cannot use the sink, or even, forgive me, the w.c.[5] The pipes go down through the workrooms. It would be heard. No trash . . . (Mr. Frank *stops abruptly as he hears the sound of marching feet from the street below. Everyone is motionless, paralyzed with fear.* Mr. Frank *goes quietly into the room on the right to look down out*

w.c.: water closet; toilet.

of the window. Anne *runs after him, peering out with him. The tramping feet pass without stopping. The tension is relieved.* Mr. Frank, *followed by* Anne, *returns to the main room and resumes his instructions to the group.*) . . . No trash must ever be thrown out which might reveal that someone is living up here . . . not even a potato paring. We must burn everything in the stove at night. This is the way we must live until it is over, if we are to survive.

84 (*There is silence for a second.*)

85 **Mrs. Frank.** Until it is over.

86 **Mr. Frank** (*reassuringly*). After six we can move about . . . we can talk and laugh and have our supper and read and play games . . . just as we would at home. (*He looks at his watch.*) And now I think it would be wise if we all went to our rooms, and were settled before eight o'clock. Mrs. Van Daan, you and your husband will be upstairs. I regret that there's no place up there for Peter. But he will be here, near us. This will be our common room, where we'll meet to talk and eat and read, like one family.

87 **Mr. Van Daan.** And where do you and Mrs. Frank sleep?

88 **Mr. Frank.** This room is also our bedroom.

89 **Mrs. Van Daan.** That isn't right. We'll sleep here and you take the room upstairs } *Together*

90 **Mrs. Van Daan.** It's your place. } *Together*

91 **Mr. Frank.** Please. I've thought this out for weeks. It's the best arrangement. The only arrangement.

92 **Mrs. Van Daan** (*to* Mr. Frank). Never, never can we thank you. (*then to* Mrs. Frank) I don't know what would have happened to us, if it hadn't been for Mr. Frank.

93 **Mr. Frank.** You don't know how your husband helped me when I came to this country . . . knowing no one . . . not able to speak the language. I can never repay him for that. (*going to* Van Daan) May I help you with your things?

94 **Mr. Van Daan.** No. No. (*to* Mrs. Van Daan) Come along, *liefje.*[6]

95 **Mrs. Van Daan.** You'll be all right, Peter? You're not afraid?

96 **Peter** (*embarrassed*). Please, Mother.

97 (*They start up the stairs to the attic room above.* Mr. Frank *turns to* Mrs. Frank.)

Don't forget to **Notice & Note** as you read the text.

NOTICE & NOTE

MEMORY MOMENT

When you notice the narrator has interrupted the forward progress of a story by bringing up something from the past, you've found a **Memory Moment** signpost.

Notice & Note: Review paragraphs 92–93. Mark what Mr. Frank recalls when Mrs. Van Daan tries to thank him for taking her family into the Annex.

Analyze: Why might this memory be important?

[6] ***liefje*** (lēf´yə) Dutch: little darling.

98 **Mr. Frank.** You too must have some rest, Edith. You didn't close your eyes last night. Nor you, Margot.

99 **Anne.** I slept, Father. Wasn't that funny? I knew it was the last night in my own bed, and yet I slept soundly.

100 **Mr. Frank.** I'm glad, Anne. Now you'll be able to help me straighten things in here. (*to* Mrs. Frank *and* Margot) Come with me . . . You and Margot rest in this room for the time being. (*He picks up their clothes, starting for the room on the right.*)

101 **Mrs. Frank.** You're sure . . . ? I could help . . . And Anne hasn't had her milk . . .

102 **Mr. Frank.** I'll give it to her. (*to* Anne *and* Peter) Anne, Peter . . . it's best that you take off your shoes now, before you forget. (*He leads the way to the room, followed by* Margot.)

103 **Mrs. Frank.** You're sure you're not tired, Anne?

104 **Anne.** I feel fine. I'm going to help Father.

105 **Mrs. Frank.** Peter, I'm glad you are to be with us.

106 **Peter.** Yes, Mrs. Frank.

107 (Mrs. Frank *goes to* join Mr. Frank *and* Margot.

108 *During the following scene* Mr. Frank *helps* Margot *and* Mrs. Frank *to hang up their clothes. Then he persuades them both to lie down and rest. The* Van Daans *in their room above settle themselves. In the main room* Anne *and* Peter *remove their shoes.* Peter *takes his cat out of the carrier.*)

109 **Anne.** What's your cat's name?

110 **Peter.** Mouschi.[7]

111 **Anne.** Mouschi! Mouschi! Mouschi! (*She picks up the cat, walking away with it. To* Peter.) I love cats. I have one . . . a darling little cat. But they made me leave her behind. I left some food and a note for the neighbors to take care of her . . . I'm going to miss her terribly. What is yours? A him or a her?

112 **Peter.** He's a tom. He doesn't like strangers.

113 (*He takes the cat from her, putting it back in its carrier.*)

114 **Anne** (*unabashed*). Then I'll have to stop being a stranger, won't I? Is he fixed?

115 **Peter** (*startled*). Huh?

116 **Anne.** Did you have him fixed?

[7] **Mouschi** (mo͞o′shē)

Don't forget to **Notice & Note** as you read the text.

117 **Peter.** No.

118 **Anne.** Oh, you ought to have him fixed—to keep him from—you know, fighting. Where did you go to school?

119 **Peter.** Jewish Secondary.

120 **Anne.** But that's where Margot and I go! I never saw you around.

121 **Peter.** I used to see you . . . sometimes . . .

122 **Anne.** You did?

123 **Peter.** . . . in the school yard. You were always in the middle of a bunch of kids. (*He takes a penknife from his pocket.*)

124 **Anne.** Why didn't you ever come over?

125 **Peter.** I'm sort of a lone wolf. (*He starts to rip off his Star of David.*)

126 **Anne.** What are you doing?

127 **Peter.** Taking it off.

128 **Anne.** But you can't do that. They'll arrest you if you go out without your star.

129 (*He tosses his knife on the table.*)

130 **Peter.** Who's going out?

131 **Anne.** Why, of course! You're right! Of course we don't need them any more. (*She picks up his knife and starts to take her star off.*) I wonder what our friends will think when we don't show up today?

132 **Peter.** I didn't have any dates with anyone.

ANALYZE DRAMA

Annotate: In paragraphs 121–125, mark details that reveal something about Anne's personality; then mark details that reveal something about Peter's.

Analyze: What does this conversation reveal about the characters of Anne and Peter? What kind of conflict might you expect to arise between people with such differences?

133 **Anne.** Oh, I did. I had a date with Jopie to go and play ping-pong at her house. Do you know Jopie de Waal?[8]

134 **Peter.** No.

135 **Anne.** Jopie's my best friend. I wonder what she'll think when she telephones and there's no answer? . . . Probably she'll go over to the house . . . I wonder what she'll think . . . we left everything as if we'd suddenly been called away . . . breakfast dishes in the sink . . . beds not made . . . (*As she pulls off her star, the cloth underneath shows clearly the color and form of the star.*) Look! It's still there! (Peter *goes over to the stove with his star.*) What're you going to do with yours?

136 **Peter.** Burn it.

137 **Anne** (*She starts to throw hers in, and cannot.*) It's funny, I can't throw mine away. I don't know why.

138 **Peter.** You can't throw . . . ? Something they branded you with . . . ? That they made you wear so they could spit on you?

139 **Anne.** I know. I know. But after all, it is the Star of David, isn't it?

140 (*In the bedroom, right,* Margot *and* Mrs. Frank *are lying down.* Mr. Frank *starts quietly out.*)

141 **Peter.** Maybe it's different for a girl.

142 (Mr. Frank *comes into the main room.*)

143 **Mr. Frank.** Forgive me, Peter. Now let me see. We must find a bed for your cat. (*He goes to a cupboard.*) I'm glad you brought your cat. Anne was feeling so badly about hers. (*getting a used small washtub*) Here we are. Will it be comfortable in that?

144 **Peter** (*gathering up his things*). Thanks.

145 **Mr. Frank** (*opening the door of the room on the left*). And here is your room. But I warn you, Peter, you can't grow any more. Not an inch, or you'll have to sleep with your feet out of the skylight. Are you hungry?

146 **Peter.** No.

147 **Mr. Frank.** We have some bread and butter.

148 **Peter.** No, thank you.

149 **Mr. Frank.** You can have it for luncheon then. And tonight we will have a real supper . . . our first supper together.

[8] **Jopie de Waal** (yō´pē də väl´)

150 **Peter.** Thanks. Thanks.

151 (*He goes into his room. During the following scene he arranges his possessions in his new room.*)

152 **Mr. Frank.** That's a nice boy, Peter.

153 **Anne.** He's awfully shy, isn't he?

154 **Mr. Frank.** You'll like him, I know.

155 **Anne.** I certainly hope so, since he's the only boy I'm likely to see for months and months.

156 (Mr. Frank *sits down, taking off his shoes.*)

157 **Mr. Frank.** Annele,[9] there's a box there. Will you open it? (*He indicates a carton on the couch.* Anne *brings it to the center table. In the street below there is the sound of children playing.*)

158 **Anne** (*as she opens the carton*). You know the way I'm going to think of it here? I'm going to think of it as a boarding house. A very peculiar summer boarding house, like the one that we—(*She breaks off as she pulls out some photographs.*) Father! My movie stars! I was wondering where they were! I was looking for them this morning . . . and Queen Wilhelmina! How wonderful!

159 **Mr. Frank.** There's something more. Go on. Look further. (*He goes over to the sink, pouring a glass of milk from a thermos bottle.*)

160 **Anne** (*pulling out a pasteboard-bound book*). A diary! (*She throws her arms around her father.*) I've never had a diary. And I've always longed for one. (*She looks around the room.*) Pencil, pencil, pencil, pencil. (*She starts down the stairs.*) I'm going down to the office to get a pencil.

161 **Mr. Frank.** Anne! No! (*He goes after her, catching her by the arm and pulling her back.*)

162 **Anne** (*startled*). But there's no one in the building now.

163 **Mr. Frank.** It doesn't matter. I don't want you ever to go beyond that door.

164 **Anne** (*sobered*). Never . . . ? Not even at nighttime, when everyone is gone? Or on Sundays? Can't I go down to listen to the radio?

165 **Mr. Frank.** Never. I am sorry, Anneke. It isn't safe. No, you must never go beyond that door.

166 (*For the first time* Anne *realizes what "going into hiding" means.*)

Don't forget to **Notice & Note** as you read the text.

ANALYZE DRAMA

Annotate: In paragraphs 158–160, mark the gifts that Mr. Frank gives Anne.

Interpret: What do these gifts reveal about Mr. Frank? How does the diary tie to the events in Scene 1?

[9] **Annele/Anneke:** a nickname for Anne.

NOTICE & NOTE

WORDS OF THE WISER

When you notice a wiser character giving advice about life to the main character, you've found a **Words of the Wiser** signpost.

Notice & Note: Review paragraphs 168–169. Mark the advantages to living in the Secret Annex that Mr. Frank points out to Anne.

Predict: What's the life lesson for Anne, and how might it affect her?

167 **Anne.** I see.

168 **Mr. Frank.** It'll be hard, I know. But always remember this, Anneke. There are no walls, there are no bolts, no locks that anyone can put on your mind. Miep will bring us books. We will read history, poetry, mythology. (*He gives her the glass of milk.*) Here's your milk. (*With his arm about her, they go over to the couch, sitting down side by side.*) As a matter of fact, between us, Anne, being here has certain advantages for you. For instance, you remember the battle you had with your mother the other day on the subject of overshoes? You said you'd rather die than wear overshoes. But in the end you had to wear them? Well now, you see, for as long as we are here you will never have to wear overshoes! Isn't that good? And the coat that you inherited from Margot, you won't have to wear that any more. And the piano! You won't have to practice on the piano. I tell you, this is going to be a fine life for you!

169 (Anne's *panic is gone.* Peter *appears in the doorway of his room, with a saucer in his hand. He is carrying his cat.*)

170 **Peter.** I . . . I . . . I thought I'd better get some water for Mouschi before . . .

171 **Mr. Frank.** Of course.

172 (*As he starts toward the sink the carillon begins to chime the hour of eight. He tiptoes to the window at the back and looks down at the street below. He turns to* Peter, *indicating in pantomime that it is too late.* Peter *starts back for his room. He steps on a creaking board. The three of them are frozen for a minute in fear. As* Peter *starts away again,* Anne *tiptoes over to him and pours some of the milk from her glass into the saucer for the cat.* Peter *squats on the floor, putting the milk before the cat.* Mr. Frank *gives* Anne *his fountain pen, and then goes into the room at the right. For a second* Anne *watches the cat, then she goes over to the center table, and opens her diary.*

173 *In the room at the right,* Mrs. Frank *has sat up quickly at the sound of the carillon.* Mr. Frank *comes in and sits down beside her on the settee, his arm comfortingly around her.*

174 *Upstairs, in the attic room,* Mr. *and* Mrs. Van Daan *have hung their clothes in the closet and are now seated on the iron bed.* Mrs. Van Daan *leans back exhausted.* Mr. Van Daan *fans her with a newspaper.*

175 Anne *starts to write in her diary. The lights dim out, the curtain falls.*

176 *In the darkness* Anne's Voice *comes to us again, faintly at first, and then with growing strength.*)

177 **Anne's Voice.** I expect I should be describing what it feels like to go into hiding. But I really don't know yet myself. I only know it's funny never to be able to go outdoors . . . never to breathe fresh air . . . never to run and shout and jump. It's the silence in the nights that frightens me most. Every time I hear a creak in the house, or a step on the street outside, I'm sure they're coming for us. The days aren't so bad. At least we know that Miep and Mr. Kraler are down there below us in the office. Our protectors, we call them. I asked Father what would happen to them if the Nazis found out they were hiding us. Pim said that they would suffer the same fate that we would . . . Imagine! They know this, and yet when they come up here, they're always cheerful and gay as if there were nothing in the world to bother them . . . Friday, the twenty-first of August, nineteen forty-two. Today I'm going to tell you our general news. Mother is unbearable. She insists on treating me like a baby, which I **loathe.** Otherwise things are going better. The weather is . . .

178 (*As* Anne's Voice *is fading out, the curtain rises on the scene.*)

Don't forget to **Notice & Note** as you read the text.

loathe
(lōth) *v.* To *loathe* something is to dislike it very much.

Scene 3

179 *It is a little after six o'clock in the evening, two months later.*

180 Margot *is in the bedroom at the right, studying.* Mr. Van Daan *is lying down in the attic room above.*

181 *The rest of the "family" is in the main room.* Anne *and* Peter *sit opposite each other at the center table, where they have been doing their lessons.* Mrs. Frank *is on the couch.* Mrs. Van Daan *is seated with her fur coat, on which she has been sewing, in her lap. None of them are wearing their shoes.*

182 *Their eyes are on* Mr. Frank, *waiting for him to give them the signal which will release them from their day-long quiet.* Mr. Frank, *his shoes in his hand, stands looking down out of the window at the back, watching to be sure that all of the workmen have left the building below.*

183 *After a few seconds of motionless silence,* Mr. Frank *turns from the window.*

184 **Mr. Frank** (*quietly, to the group*). It's safe now. The last workman has left. (*There is an immediate stir of relief.*)

185 **Anne** (*Her pent-up energy explodes*). WHEE!

ANALYZE DRAMA

Annotate: Mark the stage direction that tells you how much time has passed since the end of Scene 2.

Infer: During that time, what kinds of tensions do you think have grown among the residents of the Secret Annex, and why?

186 **Mrs. Frank** (*startled, amused*). Anne!

187 **Mrs. Van Daan.** I'm first for the w.c. (*She hurries off to the bathroom.* Mrs. Frank *puts on her shoes and starts up to the sink to prepare supper.* Anne *sneaks* Peter's *shoes from under the table and hides them behind her back.* Mr. Frank *goes in to* Margot's *room.*)

188 **Mr. Frank** (*to* Margot). Six o'clock. School's over.

189 (Margot *gets up, stretching.* Mr. Frank *sits down to put on his shoes. In the main room* Peter *tries to find his.*)

190 **Peter** (*to* Anne). Have you seen my shoes?

191 **Anne** (*innocently*). Your shoes?

192 **Peter.** You've taken them, haven't you?

193 **Anne.** I don't know what you're talking about.

194 **Peter.** You're going to be sorry!

195 **Anne.** Am I? (Peter *goes after her.* Anne, *with his shoes in her hand, runs from him, dodging behind her mother.*)

196 **Mrs. Frank** (*protesting*). Anne, dear!

197 **Peter.** Wait till I get you!

198 **Anne.** I'm waiting! (Peter *makes a lunge for her. They both fall to the floor.* Peter *pins her down, wrestling with her to get the shoes.*) Don't! Don't! Peter, stop it. Ouch!

199 **Mrs. Frank.** Anne! . . . Peter! (*Suddenly* Peter *becomes self-conscious. He grabs his shoes roughly and starts for his room.*)

200 **Anne** (*following him*). Peter, where are you going? Come dance with me.

201 **Peter.** I tell you I don't know how.

202 **Anne.** I'll teach you.

203 **Peter.** I'm going to give Mouschi his dinner.

204 **Anne.** Can I watch?

205 **Peter.** He doesn't like people around while he eats.

206 **Anne.** Peter, please.

207 **Peter.** No! (*He goes into his room.* Anne *slams his door after him.*)

208 **Mrs. Frank**. Anne, dear, I think you shouldn't play like that with Peter. It's not dignified.

209 **Anne.** Who cares if it's dignified? I don't want to be dignified.

210 (Mr. Frank *and* Margot *come from the room on the right.* Margot *goes to help her mother.* Mr. Frank *starts for the center table to correct* Margot's *school papers.*)

Don't forget to **Notice & Note** as you read the text.

211 **Mrs. Frank** (*to* Anne). You complain that I don't treat you like a grownup. But when I do, you resent it.

212 **Anne.** I only want some fun . . . someone to laugh and clown with . . . After you've sat still all day and hardly moved, you've got to have some fun. I don't know what's the matter with that boy.

213 **Mr. Frank.** He isn't used to girls. Give him a little time.

214 **Anne.** Time? Isn't two months time? I could cry. (*catching hold of* Margot) Come on, Margot . . . dance with me. Come on, please.

215 **Margot.** I have to help with supper.

216 **Anne.** You know we're going to forget how to dance . . . When we get out we won't remember a thing.

217 (*She starts to sing and dance by herself.* Mr. Frank *takes her in his arms, waltzing with her.* Mrs. Van Daan *comes in from the bathroom.*)

218 **Mrs. Van Daan.** Next? (*She looks around as she starts putting on her shoes.*) Where's Peter?

219 **Anne** (*as they are dancing*). Where would he be!

220 **Mrs. Van Daan.** He hasn't finished his lessons, has he? His father'll kill him if he catches him in there with that cat and his work not done.

221 (Mr. Frank *and* Anne *finish their dance. They bow to each other with extravagant formality.*) Anne, get him out of there, will you?

222 **Anne** (*at* Peter*'s door*). Peter? Peter?

223 **Peter** (*opening the door a crack*). What is it?

224 **Anne.** Your mother says to come out.

225 **Peter.** I'm giving Mouschi his dinner.

226 **Mrs. Van Daan.** You know what your father says. (*She sits on the couch, sewing on the lining of her fur coat.*)

227 **Peter.** For heaven's sake, I haven't even looked at him since lunch.

228 **Mrs. Van Daan.** I'm just telling you, that's all.

229 **Anne.** I'll feed him.

230 **Peter.** I don't want you in there.

231 **Mrs. Van Daan.** Peter!

232 **Peter** (*to* Anne). Then give him his dinner and come right out, you hear? (*He comes back to the table.* Anne *shuts the door of* Peter*'s room after her and disappears behind the curtain covering his closet.*)

233 **Mrs. Van Daan** (*to* Peter). Now is that any way to talk to your little girl friend?

234 **Peter.** Mother . . . for heaven's sake . . . will you please stop saying that?

235 **Mrs. Van Daan.** Look at him blush! Look at him!

236 **Peter.** Please! I'm not . . . anyway . . . let me alone, will you?

237 **Mrs. Van Daan.** He acts like it was something to be ashamed of. It's nothing to be ashamed of, to have a little girl friend.

238 **Peter.** You're crazy. She's only thirteen.

239 **Mrs. Van Daan.** So what? And you're sixteen. Just perfect. Your father's ten years older than I am. (*to* Mr. Frank) I warn you, Mr. Frank, if this war lasts much longer, we're going to be related and then . . .

240 **Mr. Frank.** *Mazeltov!*[10]

ANALYZE DRAMA

Annotate: In paragraphs 241–249, mark details that show how Anne teases Peter. Then mark what Peter says about Anne.

Draw Conclusions: What do Anne and Peter tease each other about? What conclusions can you draw about Anne and Peter based on this incident?

241 **Mrs. Frank** (*deliberately changing the conversation*). I wonder where Miep is. She's usually so prompt. (*Suddenly everything else is forgotten as they hear the sound of an automobile coming to a screeching stop in the street below. They are tense, motionless in their terror. The car starts away. A wave of relief sweeps over them. They pick up their occupations again.* Anne *flings open the door of* Peter*'s room, making a dramatic entrance. She is dressed in* Peter*'s clothes.* Peter *looks at her in fury. The others are amused.*)

242 **Anne.** Good evening, everyone. Forgive me if I don't stay. (*She jumps up on a chair.*) I have a friend waiting for me in there. My friend Tom. Tom Cat. Some people say that we look alike. But Tom has the most beautiful whiskers, and I have only a little fuzz. I am hoping . . . in time . . .

243 **Peter.** All right, Mrs. Quack Quack!

244 **Anne** (*outraged—jumping down*). Peter!

245 **Peter.** I heard about you . . . How you talked so much in class they called you Mrs. Quack Quack. How Mr. Smitter made you write a composition . . . "'Quack, quack,' said Mrs. Quack Quack."

[10] ***Mazeltov!*** (mä´zəl-tôf´) *Hebrew:* Congratulations!

246 **Anne.** Well, go on. Tell them the rest. How it was so good he read it out loud to the class and then read it to all his other classes!

247 **Peter.** Quack! Quack! Quack . . . Quack . . . Quack . . .

248 (Anne *pulls off the coat and trousers.*)

249 **Anne.** You are the most intolerable, insufferable boy I've ever met!

250 (*She throws the clothes down the stairwell.* Peter *goes down after them.*)

251 **Peter.** Quack, quack, quack!

252 **Mrs. Van Daan** (*to* Anne). That's right, Anneke! Give it to him!

253 **Anne.** With all the boys in the world . . . Why I had to get locked up with one like you! . . .

254 **Peter.** Quack, quack, quack, and from now on stay out of my room!

255 (*As* Peter *passes her,* Anne *puts out her foot, tripping him. He picks himself up, and goes on into his room.*)

256 **Mrs. Frank** (*quietly*). Anne, dear . . . your hair. (*She feels* Anne's *forehead.*) You're warm. Are you feeling all right?

257 **Anne.** Please, Mother. (*She goes over to the center table, slipping into her shoes.*)

258 **Mrs. Frank** (*following her*). You haven't a fever, have you?

259 **Anne** (*pulling away*). No. No.

260 **Mrs. Frank.** You know we can't call a doctor here, ever. There's only one thing to do . . . watch carefully. Prevent an illness before it comes. Let me see your tongue.

261 **Anne.** Mother, this is perfectly absurd.

262 **Mrs. Frank.** Anne, dear, don't be such a baby. Let me see your tongue. (*As* Anne *refuses,* Mrs. Frank *appeals to* Mr. Frank.) Otto . . . ?

263 **Mr. Frank.** You hear your mother, Anne. (Anne *flicks out her tongue for a second, then turns away.*)

264 **Mrs. Frank.** Come on—open up! (*as* Anne *opens her mouth very wide*) You seem all right . . . but perhaps an aspirin . . .

265 **Mrs. Van Daan.** For heaven's sake, don't give that child any pills. I waited for fifteen minutes this morning for her to come out of the w.c.

266 **Anne.** I was washing my hair!

Don't forget to **Notice & Note** as you read the text.

VOCABULARY

Use Prefixes: If you are unsure what the words *intolerable* and *insufferable* in paragraph 249 mean, consider that the prefix *in-* means "not," and the words *tolerable* and *sufferable* both mean "capable of being tolerated." Combine these meanings to determine the definitions of the unfamiliar words.

Interpret: What does Anne's use of the words *intolerable* and *insufferable* indicate about her opinion of Peter?

267 **Mr. Frank.** I think there's nothing the matter with our Anne that a ride on her bike, or a visit with her friend Jopie de Waal wouldn't cure. Isn't that so, Anne?

268 (Mr. Van Daan *comes down into the room. From outside we hear faint sounds of bombers going over and a burst of ack-ack.*)

269 **Mr. Van Daan.** Miep not come yet?

270 **Mrs. Van Daan.** The workmen just left, a little while ago.

271 **Mr. Van Daan.** What's for dinner tonight?

272 **Mrs. Van Daan.** Beans.

273 **Mr. Van Daan.** Not again!

274 **Mrs. Van Daan.** Poor Putti! I know. But what can we do? That's all that Miep brought us.

275 (Mr. Van Daan *starts to pace, his hands behind his back.* Anne *follows behind him, imitating him.*)

276 **Anne.** We are now in what is known as the "bean cycle." Beans boiled, beans en casserole, beans with strings, beans without strings . . .

277 (Peter *has come out of his room. He slides into his place at the table, becoming immediately absorbed in his studies.*)

278 **Mr. Van Daan** (*to* Peter). I saw you . . . in there, playing with your cat.

279 **Mrs. Van Daan**. He just went in for a second, putting his coat away. He's been out here all the time, doing his lessons.

280 **Mr. Frank** (*looking up from the papers*). Anne, you got an excellent in your history paper today . . . and very good in Latin.

281 **Anne** (*sitting beside him*). How about algebra?

282 **Mr. Frank.** I'll have to make a confession. Up until now I've managed to stay ahead of you in algebra. Today you caught up with me. We'll leave it to Margot to correct.

283 **Anne.** Isn't algebra *vile,* Pim!

284 **Mr. Frank.** Vile!

285 **Margot** (*to* Mr. Frank). How did I do?

286 **Anne** (*getting up*). Excellent, excellent, excellent, excellent!

287 **Mr. Frank** (*to* Margot). You should have used the subjunctive here . . .

288 **Margot.** Should I? . . . I thought . . . look here . . . I didn't use it here . . . (*The two become absorbed in the papers.*)

289 **Anne.** Mrs. Van Daan, may I try on your coat?

290 **Mrs. Frank.** No, Anne.

Don't forget to **Notice & Note** as you read the text.

291 **Mrs. Van Daan** (*giving it to* Anne). It's all right . . . but careful with it. (Anne *puts it on and struts with it.*) My father gave me that the year before he died. He always bought the best that money could buy.

292 **Anne.** Mrs. Van Daan, did you have a lot of boy friends before you were married?

293 **Mrs. Frank.** Anne, that's a personal question. It's not courteous to ask personal questions.

294 **Mrs. Van Daan.** Oh I don't mind. (*to* Anne) Our house was always swarming with boys. When I was a girl we had . . .

295 **Mr. Van Daan.** Oh, God. Not again!

296 **Mrs. Van Daan** (*good-humored*). Shut up! (*Without a pause, to* Anne. Mr. Van Daan *mimics* Mrs. Van Daan, *speaking the first few words in unison with her.*) One summer we had a big house in Hilversum. The boys came buzzing round like bees around a jam pot. And when I was sixteen! . . . We were wearing our skirts very short those days and I had good-looking legs. (*She pulls up her skirt, going to* Mr. Frank.) I still have 'em. I may not be as pretty as I used to be, but I still have my legs. How about it, Mr. Frank?

297 **Mr. Van Daan.** All right. All right. We see them.

298 **Mrs. Van Daan.** I'm not asking you. I'm asking Mr. Frank.

299 **Peter.** Mother, for heaven's sake.

300 **Mrs. Van Daan.** Oh, I embarrass you, do I? Well, I just hope the girl you marry has as good. (*then to* Anne) My father used to worry about me, with so many boys hanging round. He told me, if any of them gets fresh, you say to him . . . "Remember, Mr. So-and-So, remember I'm a lady."

301 **Anne.** "Remember, Mr. So-and-So, remember I'm a lady." (*She gives* Mrs. Van Daan *her coat.*)

302 **Mr. Van Daan.** Look at you, talking that way in front of her! Don't you know she puts it all down in that diary?

303 **Mrs. Van Daan.** So, if she does? I'm only telling the truth!

304 (Anne *stretches out, putting her ear to the floor, listening to what is going on below. The sound of the bombers fades away.*)

305 **Mrs. Frank** (*setting the table*). Would you mind, Peter, if I moved you over to the couch?

306 **Anne** (*listening*). Miep must have the radio on.

307 (Peter *picks up his papers, going over to the couch beside* Mrs. Van Daan.)

308 **Mr. Van Daan** (*accusingly, to* Peter). Haven't you finished yet?

309 **Peter.** No.

310 **Mr. Van Daan.** You ought to be ashamed of yourself.

311 **Peter.** All right. All right. I'm a dunce. I'm a hopeless case. Why do I go on?

312 **Mrs. Van Daan.** You're not hopeless. Don't talk that way. It's just that you haven't anyone to help you, like the girls have. (*to* Mr. Frank) Maybe you could help him, Mr. Frank?

313 **Mr. Frank.** I'm sure that his father . . . ?

314 **Mr. Van Daan.** Not me. I can't do anything with him. He won't listen to me. You go ahead . . . if you want.

315 **Mr. Frank** (*going to* Peter). What about it, Peter? Shall we make our school coeducational?

316 **Mrs. Van Daan** (*kissing* Mr. Frank). You're an angel, Mr. Frank. An angel. I don't know why I didn't meet you before I met that one there.

317 Here, sit down, Mr. Frank . . . (*She forces him down on the couch beside* Peter.) Now, Peter, you listen to Mr. Frank.

318 **Mr. Frank.** It might be better for us to go into Peter's room. (Peter *jumps up eagerly, leading the way.*)

319 **Mrs. Van Daan.** That's right. You go in there, Peter. You listen to Mr. Frank. Mr. Frank is a highly educated man. (*As* Mr. Frank *is about to follow* Peter *into his room,* Mrs. Frank *stops him and wipes the lipstick from his lips. Then she closes the door after them.*)

320 **Anne** (*on the floor, listening*). Shh! I can hear a man's voice talking.

321 **Mr. Van Daan** (*to* Anne). Isn't it bad enough here without your sprawling all over the place? (Anne *sits up.*)

322 **Mrs. Van Daan** (*to* Mr. Van Daan). If you didn't smoke so much, you wouldn't be so bad-tempered.

323 **Mr. Van Daan.** Am I smoking? Do you see me smoking?

324 **Mrs. Van Daan.** Don't tell me you've used up all those cigarettes.

325 **Mr. Van Daan.** One package. Miep only brought me one package.

326 **Mrs. Van Daan.** It's a filthy habit anyway. It's a good time to break yourself.

Don't forget to **Notice & Note** as you read the text.

327 **Mr. Van Daan.** Oh, stop it, please.

328 **Mrs. Van Daan.** You're smoking up all our money. You know that, don't you?

329 **Mr. Van Daan.** Will you shut up? (*During this,* Mrs. Frank *and* Margot *have studiously kept their eyes down. But* Anne, *seated on the floor, has been following the discussion interestedly.* Mr. Van Daan *turns to see her staring up at him.*) And what are you staring at?

330 **Anne.** I never heard grownups quarrel before. I thought only children quarreled.

331 **Mr. Van Daan.** This isn't a quarrel! It's a discussion. And I never heard children so rude before.

332 **Anne** (*rising,* ***indignantly***). *I,* rude!

indignantly
(ĭn-dĭg´ nənt-lē) *adv.* Someone who does something *indignantly* acts in a way that shows anger or shock over something that is unjust or unfair.

333 **Mr. Van Daan.** Yes!

334 **Mrs. Frank** (*quickly*). Anne, will you get me my knitting? (Anne *goes to get it.*) I must remember, when Miep comes, to ask her to bring me some more wool.

335 **Margot** (*going to her room*). I need some hairpins and some soap. I made a list. (*She goes into her bedroom to get the list.*)

336 **Mrs. Frank** (*to* Anne). Have you some library books for Miep when she comes?

337 **Anne.** It's a wonder that Miep has a life of her own, the way we make her run errands for us. Please, Miep, get me some starch. Please take my hair out and have it cut. Tell me all the latest news, Miep.

338 (*She goes over, kneeling on the couch beside* Mrs. Van Daan.) Did you know she was engaged? His name is Dirk, and Miep's afraid the Nazis will ship him off to Germany to work in one of their war plants. That's what they're doing with some of the young Dutchmen . . . they pick them up off the streets—

339 **Mr. Van Daan** (*interrupting*). Don't you ever get tired of talking? Suppose you try keeping still for five minutes. Just five minutes. (*He starts to pace again. Again* Anne *follows him, mimicking him.* Mrs. Frank *jumps up and takes her by the arm up to the sink, and gives her a glass of milk.*)

340 **Mrs. Frank.** Come here, Anne. It's time for your glass of milk.

341 **Mr. Van Daan.** Talk, talk, talk. I never heard such a child. Where is my . . . ? Every evening it's the same, talk, talk, talk. (*He looks around.*) Where is my . . . ?

342 **Mrs. Van Daan.** What're you looking for?

343 **Mr. Van Daan.** My pipe. Have you seen my pipe?

344 **Mrs. Van Daan.** What good's a pipe? You haven't got any tobacco.

345 **Mr. Van Daan.** At least I'll have something to hold in my mouth! (*opening* Margot's *bedroom door*) Margot, have you seen my pipe?

346 **Margot.** It was on the table last night.

347 (Anne *puts her glass of milk on the table and picks up his pipe, hiding it behind her back.*)

ANALYZE DRAMA

Annotate: In paragraphs 348–358, mark details that show how Mr. Van Daan expects girls and women to behave. Then mark what Anne wants for herself.

Compare: How do these differences highlight the conflict in values between Mr. Van Daan and Anne?

348 **Mr. Van Daan.** I know. I know. Anne, did you see my pipe? . . . Anne!

349 **Mrs. Frank.** Anne, Mr. Van Daan is speaking to you.

350 **Anne.** Am I allowed to talk now?

351 **Mr. Van Daan.** You're the most aggravating . . . The trouble with you is, you've been spoiled. What you need is a good old-fashioned spanking.

352 **Anne** (*mimicking* Mrs. Van Daan). "Remember, Mr. So-and-So, remember I'm a lady." (*She thrusts the pipe into his mouth, then picks up her glass of milk.*)

353 **Mr. Van Daan** (*restraining himself with difficulty*). Why aren't you nice and quiet like your sister Margot? Why do you have to show off all the time? Let me give you a little advice, young lady. Men don't like that kind of thing in a girl. You know that? A man likes a girl who'll listen to him once in a while . . . a domestic girl, who'll keep her house shining for her husband . . . who loves to cook and sew and . . .

354 **Anne.** I'd cut my throat first! I'd open my veins! I'm going to be remarkable! I'm going to Paris . . .

355 **Mr. Van Daan** (*scoffingly*). Paris!

356 **Anne.** . . . to study music and art.

357 **Mr. Van Daan.** Yeah! Yeah!

358 **Anne.** I'm going to be a famous dancer or singer . . . or something wonderful. (*She makes a wide gesture, spilling the glass of milk on the fur coat in* Mrs. Van Daan's *lap.* Margot *rushes quickly over with a towel.* Anne *tries to brush the milk off with her skirt.*)

359 **Mrs. Van Daan.** Now look what you've done . . . you clumsy little fool! My beautiful fur coat my father gave me . . .

360 **Anne.** I'm so sorry.

361 **Mrs. Van Daan.** What do you care? It isn't yours . . . So go on, ruin it! Do you know what that coat cost? Do you? And now look at it! Look at it!

362 **Anne.** I'm very, very sorry.

363 **Mrs. Van Daan.** I could kill you for this. I could just kill you! (Mrs. Van Daan *goes up the stairs, clutching the coat.* Mr. Van Daan *starts after her.*)

364 **Mr. Van Daan.** Petronella . . . *liefje! Liefje!* . . . Come back . . . the supper . . . come back!

365 **Mrs. Frank.** Anne, you must not behave in that way.

366 **Anne.** It was an accident. Anyone can have an accident.

367 **Mrs. Frank.** I don't mean that. I mean the answering back. You must not answer back. They are our guests. We must always show the greatest courtesy to them. We're all living under terrible tension. (*She stops as* Margot *indicates that* Van Daan *can hear. When he is gone, she continues.*) That's why we must control ourselves . . . You don't hear Margot getting into arguments with them, do you? Watch Margot. She's always courteous with them. Never familiar. She keeps her distance. And they respect her for it. Try to be like Margot.

368 **Anne.** And have them walk all over me, the way they do her? No, thanks!

369 **Mrs. Frank.** I'm not afraid that anyone is going to walk all over you, Anne. I'm afraid for other people, that you'll walk on them. I don't know what happens to you, Anne. You are wild, self-willed. If I had ever talked to my mother as you talk to me . . .

370 **Anne.** Things have changed. People aren't like that any more. "Yes, Mother." "No, Mother." "Anything you say, Mother." I've got to fight things out for myself! Make something of myself!

371 **Mrs. Frank.** It isn't necessary to fight to do it. Margot doesn't fight, and isn't she . . . ?

372 **Anne** (*violently rebellious*). Margot! Margot! Margot! That's all I hear from everyone . . . how wonderful Margot is . . . "Why aren't you like Margot?"

373 **Margot** (*protesting*). Oh, come on, Anne, don't be so . . .

374 **Anne** (*paying no attention*). Everything she does is right, and everything I do is wrong! I'm the goat around here! . . . You're all against me! . . . And you worst of all!

375 (*She rushes off into her room and throws herself down on the settee, stifling her sobs.* Mrs. Frank *sighs and starts toward the stove.*)

Don't forget to **Notice & Note** as you read the text.

NOTICE & NOTE

WORDS OF THE WISER

When you notice a wiser character giving advice about life to the main character, you've found a **Words of the Wiser** signpost.

Notice & Note: Mark the reason that Mrs. Frank gives for why Anne must not answer back or behave rudely to the Van Daans.

Predict: What's the life lesson for Anne, and how might it affect her?

376 **Mrs. Frank** (*to* Margot). Let's put the soup on the stove . . . if there's anyone who cares to eat. Margot, will you take the bread out? (Margot *gets the bread from the cupboard.*) I don't know how we can go on living this way . . . I can't say a word to Anne . . . she flies at me . . .

377 **Margot.** You know Anne. In half an hour she'll be out here, laughing and joking.

378 **Mrs. Frank.** And . . . (*She makes a motion upwards, indicating the* Van Daans.) . . . I told your father it wouldn't work . . . but no . . . no . . . he had to ask them, he said . . . he owed it to him, he said. Well, he knows now that I was right! These quarrels! . . . This bickering!

379 **Margot** (*with a warning look*). Shush. Shush.

380 (*The buzzer for the door sounds.* Mrs. Frank *gasps, startled.*)

381 **Mrs. Frank.** Every time I hear that sound, my heart stops!

382 **Margot** (*starting for* Peter*'s door*). It's Miep. (*She knocks at the door.*) Father?

383 (Mr. Frank *comes quickly from* Peter*'s room.*)

384 **Mr. Frank.** Thank you, Margot. (*as he goes down the steps to open the outer door*) Has everyone his list?

385 **Margot.** I'll get my books. (*giving her mother a list*) Here's your list.

386 (Margot *goes into her and* Anne*'s bedroom on the right.* Anne *sits up, hiding her tears, as* Margot *comes in.*) Miep's here.

387 (Margot *picks up her books and goes back.* Anne *hurries over to the mirror, smoothing her hair.*)

388 **Mr. Van Daan** (*coming down the stairs*). Is it Miep?

389 **Margot.** Yes. Father's gone down to let her in.

390 **Mr. Van Daan.** At last I'll have some cigarettes!

391 **Mrs. Frank** (*to* Mr. Van Daan). I can't tell you how unhappy I am about Mrs. Van Daan's coat. Anne should never have touched it.

392 **Mr. Van Daan**. She'll be all right.

393 **Mrs. Frank.** Is there anything I can do?

394 **Mr. Van Daan.** Don't worry.

395 (*He turns to meet* Miep. *But it is not* Miep *who comes up the steps. It is* Mr. Kraler, *followed by* Mr. Frank. *Their faces are grave.* Anne *comes from the bedroom.* Peter *comes from his room.*)

396 **Mrs. Frank.** Mr. Kraler!

397 **Mr. Van Daan.** How are you, Mr. Kraler?

398 **Margot.** This is a surprise.

399 **Mrs. Frank.** When Mr. Kraler comes, the sun begins to shine.

400 **Mr. Van Daan.** Miep is coming?

401 **Mr. Kraler.** Not tonight.

402 (Kraler *goes to* Margot *and* Mrs. Frank *and* Anne, *shaking hands with them.*)

403 **Mrs. Frank.** Wouldn't you like a cup of coffee? . . . Or, better still, will you have supper with us?

404 **Mr. Frank.** Mr. Kraler has something to talk over with us. Something has happened, he says, which demands an immediate decision.

405 **Mrs. Frank** (*fearful*). What is it?

406 (Mr. Kraler *sits down on the couch. As he talks he takes bread, cabbages, milk, etc., from his briefcase, giving them to* Margot *and* Anne *to put away.*)

407 **Mr. Kraler.** Usually, when I come up here, I try to bring you some bit of good news. What's the use of telling you the bad news when there's nothing that you can do about it? But today something has happened . . . Dirk . . . Miep's Dirk, you know, came to me just now. He tells me that he has a Jewish friend living near him. A dentist. He says he's in trouble. He begged me, could I do anything for this man? Could I find him a hiding place? . . . So I've come to you . . . I know it's a terrible thing to ask of you, living as you are, but would you take him in with you?

408 **Mr. Frank.** Of course we will.

409 **Mr. Kraler** (*rising*). It'll be just for a night or two . . . until I find some other place. This happened so suddenly that I didn't know where to turn.

410 **Mr. Frank.** Where is he?

411 **Mr. Kraler.** Downstairs in the office.

412 **Mr. Frank.** Good. Bring him up.

413 **Mr. Kraler.** His name is Dussel . . . Jan Dussel.

414 **Mr. Frank.** Dussel . . . I think I know him.

415 **Mr. Kraler.** I'll get him. (*He goes quickly down the steps and out.* Mr. Frank *suddenly becomes conscious of the others.*)

Don't forget to **Notice & Note** as you read the text.

ANALYZE DRAMA

Annotate: In paragraphs 407–419, mark the request that Mr. Kraler makes of Mr. Frank and the others.

Interpret: How does Mr. Kraler's request create a new problem for the residents of the Secret Annex?

416 **Mr. Frank.** Forgive me. I spoke without consulting you. But I knew you'd feel as I do.

417 **Mr. Van Daan.** There's no reason for you to consult anyone. This is your place. You have a right to do exactly as you please. The only thing I feel . . . there's so little food as it is . . . and to take in another person . . .

418 (Peter *turns away, ashamed of his father.*)

419 **Mr. Frank.** We can stretch the food a little. It's only for a few days.

420 **Mr. Van Daan.** You want to make a bet?

421 **Mrs. Frank.** I think it's fine to have him. But, Otto, where are you going to put him? Where?

422 **Peter.** He can have my bed. I can sleep on the floor. I wouldn't mind.

423 **Mr. Frank.** That's good of you, Peter. But your room's too small . . . even for you.

424 **Anne.** I have a much better idea. I'll come in here with you and Mother, and Margot can take Peter's room and Peter can go in our room with Mr. Dussel.

425 **Margot.** That's right. We could do that.

426 **Mr. Frank.** No, Margot. You mustn't sleep in that room . . . neither you nor Anne. Mouschi has caught some rats in there. Peter's brave. He doesn't mind.

427 **Anne.** Then how about *this?* I'll come in here with you and Mother, and Mr. Dussel can have my bed.

428 **Mrs. Frank.** No. No. No! Margot will come in here with us and he can have her bed. It's the only way. Margot, bring your things in here. Help her, Anne.

429 (Margot *hurries into her room to get her things.*)

430 **Anne** (*to her mother*). Why Margot? Why can't I come in here?

431 **Mrs. Frank.** Because it wouldn't be proper for Margot to sleep with a . . . Please, Anne. Don't argue. Please. (Anne *starts slowly away.*)

432 **Mr. Frank.** (*to* Anne). You don't mind sharing your room with Mr. Dussel, do you, Anne?

433 **Anne.** No. No, of course not.

434 **Mr. Frank.** Good. (Anne *goes off into her bedroom, helping* Margot. Mr. Frank *starts to search in the cupboards.*) Where's the cognac?

435 **Mrs. Frank.** It's there. But, Otto, I was saving it in case of illness.

436 **Mr. Frank.** I think we couldn't find a better time to use it. Peter, will you get five glasses for me?

437 (Peter *goes for the glasses.* Margot *comes out of her bedroom, carrying her possessions, which she hangs behind a curtain in the main room.* Mr. Frank *finds the cognac and pours it into the five glasses that* Peter *brings him.* Mr. Van Daan *stands looking on sourly.* Mrs. Van Daan *comes downstairs and looks around at all the bustle.*)

438 **Mrs. Van Daan.** What's happening? What's going on?

439 **Mr. Van Daan.** Someone's moving in with us.

440 **Mrs. Van Daan.** In here? You're joking.

441 **Margot.** It's only for a night or two . . . until Mr. Kraler finds him another place.

442 **Mr. Van Daan.** Yeah! Yeah!

443 (Mr. Frank *hurries over as* Mr. Kraler *and* Dussel *come up.* Dussel *is a man in his late fifties, meticulous, finicky . . . bewildered now. He wears a raincoat. He carries a briefcase, stuffed full, and a small medicine case.*)

444 **Mr. Frank.** Come in, Mr. Dussel.

445 **Mr. Kraler.** This is Mr. Frank.

446 **Dussel.** Mr. Otto Frank?

447 **Mr. Frank.** Yes. Let me take your things. (*He takes the hat and briefcase, but* Dussel *clings to his medicine case.*) This is my wife Edith . . . Mr. and Mrs. Van Daan . . . their son, Peter . . . and my daughters, Margot and Anne.

448 (Dussel *shakes hands with everyone.*)

449 **Mr. Kraler.** Thank you, Mr. Frank. Thank you all. Mr. Dussel, I leave you in good hands. Oh . . . Dirk's coat.

450 (Dussel *hurriedly takes off the raincoat, giving it to* Mr. Kraler. *Underneath is his white dentist's jacket, with a yellow Star of David on it.*)

451 **Dussel** (*to* Mr. Kraler). What can I say to thank you . . .?

452 **Mrs. Frank** (*to* Dussel). Mr. Kraler and Miep . . . They're our life line. Without them we couldn't live.

453 **Mr. Kraler.** Please. Please. You make us seem very heroic. It isn't that at all. We simply don't like the Nazis. (*to* Mr. Frank, *who offers him a drink*) No, thanks. (*then going on*) We don't like their methods. We don't like . . .

Don't forget to **Notice & Note** as you read the text.

454 **Mr. Frank** (*smiling*). I know. I know. "No one's going to tell us Dutchmen what to do with our damn Jews!"

455 **Mr. Kraler** (*to* Dussel). Pay no attention to Mr. Frank. I'll be up tomorrow to see that they're treating you right. (*to* Mr. Frank) Don't trouble to come down again. Peter will bolt the door after me, won't you, Peter?

456 **Peter.** Yes, sir.

457 **Mr. Frank.** Thank you, Peter. I'll do it.

458 **Mr. Kraler.** Good night. Good night.

459 **Group.** Good night, Mr. Kraler. We'll see you tomorrow, (*etc., etc.*)

460 (Mr. Kraler *goes out with* Mr. Frank. Mrs. Frank *gives each one of the "grownups" a glass of cognac.*)

461 **Mrs. Frank.** Please, Mr. Dussel, sit down.

462 (Mr. Dussel *sinks into a chair.* Mrs. Frank *gives him a glass of cognac.*)

463 **Dussel.** I'm dreaming. I know it. I can't believe my eyes. Mr. Otto Frank here! (*to* Mrs. Frank) You're not in Switzerland then? A woman told me . . . She said she'd gone to your house . . . the door was open, everything was in disorder, dishes in the sink. She said she found a piece of paper in the wastebasket with an address scribbled on it . . . an address in Zurich. She said you must have escaped to Zurich.

464 **Anne.** Father put that there purposely . . . just so people would think that very thing!

465 **Dussel.** And you've been here all the time?

466 **Mrs. Frank.** All the time . . . ever since July.

467 (Anne *speaks to her father as he comes back.*)

468 **Anne.** It worked, Pim . . . the address you left! Mr. Dussel says that people believe we escaped to Switzerland.

469 **Mr. Frank.** I'm glad . . . And now let's have a little drink to welcome Mr. Dussel. (*Before they can drink,* Mr. Dussel *bolts his drink.* Mr. Frank *smiles and raises his glass.*) To Mr. Dussel. Welcome. We're very honored to have you with us.

470 **Mrs. Frank.** To Mr. Dussel, welcome.

471 (*The* Van Daans *murmur a welcome. The "grown-ups" drink.*)

472 **Mrs. Van Daan.** Um. That was good.

473 **Mr. Van Daan.** Did Mr. Kraler warn you that you won't get much to eat here? You can imagine . . . three ration books among the seven of us . . . and now you make eight.

474 (Peter *walks away, humiliated. Outside a street organ is heard dimly.*)

475 **Dussel** (*rising*). Mr. Van Daan, you don't realize what is happening outside that you should warn me of a thing like that. You don't realize what's going on . . . (*As* Mr. Van Daan *starts his characteristic pacing,* Dussel *turns to speak to the others.*) Right here in Amsterdam every day hundreds of Jews disappear . . . They surround a block and search house by house. Children come home from school to find their parents gone. Hundreds are being deported . . . people that you and I know . . . the Hallensteins . . . the Wessels . . .

476 **Mrs. Frank** (*in tears*). Oh, no. No!

477 **Dussel.** They get their call-up notice . . . come to the Jewish theatre on such and such a day and hour . . . bring only what you can carry in a rucksack. And if you refuse the call-up notice, then they come and drag you from your home and ship you off to Mauthausen.[11] The death camp!

478 **Mrs. Frank.** We didn't know that things had got so much worse.

479 **Dussel.** Forgive me for speaking so.

480 **Anne** (*coming to* Dussel). Do you know the de Waals? . . . What's become of them? Their daughter Jopie and I are in the same class. Jopie's my best friend.

481 **Dussel.** They are gone.

482 **Anne.** Gone?

483 **Dussel.** With all the others.

484 **Anne.** Oh, no. Not Jopie!

485 (*She turns away, in tears.* Mrs. Frank *motions to* Margot *to comfort her.* Margot *goes to* Anne, *putting her arms comfortingly around her.*)

486 **Mrs. Van Daan.** There were some people called Wagner. They lived near us . . . ?

487 **Mr. Frank** (*interrupting, with a glance at* Anne). I think we should put this off until later. We all have many questions we want to ask . . . But I'm sure that Mr. Dussel would like to get settled before supper.

Don't forget to **Notice & Note** as you read the text.

NOTICE & NOTE

CONTRASTS AND CONTRADICTIONS

When you notice a sharp contrast between what you would expect and what a character actually does, you've found a **Contrasts and Contradictions** signpost.

Notice & Note: In paragraph 473, mark dialogue that contrasts with how you would expect someone to act when they meet someone for the first time.

Infer: Why would Mr. Van Daan act this way?

[11] **Mauthausen** (mout´hou´zən): a Nazi concentration camp in Austria.

488 **Dussel.** Thank you. I would. I brought very little with me.

489 **Mr. Frank** (*giving him his hat and briefcase*). I'm sorry we can't give you a room alone. But I hope you won't be too uncomfortable. We've had to make strict rules here . . . a schedule of hours . . . We'll tell you after supper. Anne, would you like to take Mr. Dussel to his room?

490 **Anne** (*controlling her tears*). If you'll come with me, Mr. Dussel? (*She starts for her room.*)

491 **Dussel** (*shaking hands with each in turn*). Forgive me if I haven't really expressed my gratitude to all of you. This has been such a shock to me. I'd always thought of myself as Dutch. I was born in Holland. My father was born in Holland, and my grandfather. And now . . . after all these years . . . (*He breaks off.*) If you'll excuse me.

492 (Dussel *gives a little bow and hurries off after* Anne. Mr. Frank *and the others are subdued.*)

493 **Anne** (*turning on the light*). Well, here we are.

494 (Dussel *looks around the room. In the main room* Margot *speaks to her mother.*)

495 **Margot.** The news sounds pretty bad, doesn't it? It's so different from what Mr. Kraler tells us. Mr. Kraler says things are improving.

496 **Mr. Van Daan.** I like it better the way Kraler tells it.

497 (*They resume their occupations, quietly.* Peter *goes off into his room. In* Anne*'s room,* Anne *turns to* Dussel.)

498 **Anne.** You're going to share the room with me.

499 **Dussel.** I'm a man who's always lived alone. I haven't had to adjust myself to others. I hope you'll bear with me until I learn.

500 **Anne.** Let me help you. (*She takes his briefcase.*) Do you always live all alone? Have you no family at all?

501 **Dussel.** No one. (*He opens his medicine case and spreads his bottles on the dressing table.*)

502 **Anne.** How dreadful. You must be terribly lonely.

503 **Dussel.** I'm used to it.

504 **Anne.** I don't think I could ever get used to it. Didn't you even have a pet? A cat, or a dog?

505 **Dussel.** I have an allergy for fur-bearing animals. They give me asthma.

506 **Anne.** Oh, dear. Peter has a cat.

Don't forget to **Notice & Note** as you read the text.

507 **Dussel.** Here? He has it here?

508 **Anne.** Yes. But we hardly ever see it. He keeps it in his room all the time. I'm sure it will be all right.

509 **Dussel.** Let us hope so.

510 (*He takes some pills to fortify himself.*)

511 **Anne.** That's Margot's bed, where you're going to sleep. I sleep on the sofa there. (*indicating the clothes hooks on the wall*) We cleared these off for your things. (*She goes over to the window.*) The best part about this room . . . you can look down and see a bit of the street and the canal. There's a houseboat . . . you can see the end of it . . . a bargeman lives there with his family . . . They have a baby and he's just beginning to walk and I'm so afraid he's going to fall into the canal some day. I watch him . . .

512 **Dussel** (*interrupting*). Your father spoke of a schedule.

513 **Anne** (*coming away from the window*). Oh, yes. It's mostly about the times we have to be quiet. And times for the w.c. You can use it now if you like.

514 **Dussel** (*stiffly*). No, thank you.

515 **Anne.** I suppose you think it's awful, my talking about a thing like that. But you don't know how important it can get to be, especially when you're frightened . . . About this room, the way Margot and I did . . . she had it to herself in the afternoons for studying, reading . . . lessons, you know . . . and I took the mornings. Would that be all right with you?

516 **Dussel.** I'm not at my best in the morning.

517 **Anne.** You stay here in the mornings then. I'll take the room in the afternoons.

518 **Dussel.** Tell me, when you're in here, what happens to me? Where am I spending my time? In there, with all the people?

519 **Anne.** Yes.

520 **Dussel.** I see. I see.

521 **Anne.** We have supper at half past six.

522 **Dussel** (*going over to the sofa*). Then, if you don't mind . . . I like to lie down quietly for ten minutes before eating. I find it helps the digestion.

523 **Anne.** Of course. I hope I'm not going to be too much of a bother to you. I seem to be able to get everyone's back up.

524 (Dussel *lies down on the sofa, curled up, his back to her.*)

525 **Dussel.** I always get along very well with children. My patients all bring their children to me, because they know I get on well with them. So don't you worry about that.

526 (Anne *leans over him, taking his hand and shaking it gratefully.*)

527 **Anne.** Thank you. Thank you, Mr. Dussel.

528 (*The lights dim to darkness. The curtain falls on the scene.* Anne's Voice *comes to us faintly at first, and then with increasing power.*)

529 **Anne's Voice.** . . . And yesterday I finished Cissy Van Marxvelt's latest book. I think she is a first-class writer. I shall definitely let my children read her. Monday the twenty-first of September, nineteen forty-two. Mr. Dussel and I had another battle yesterday. Yes, Mr. Dussel! According to him, nothing, I repeat . . . nothing, is right about me . . . my appearance, my character, my manners. While he was going on at me I thought . . . sometime I'll give you such a smack that you'll fly right up to the ceiling! Why is it that every grownup thinks he knows the way to bring up children? Particularly the grownups that never had any. I keep wishing that Peter was a girl instead of a boy. Then I would have someone to talk to. Margot's a darling, but she takes everything too seriously. To pause for a moment on the subject of Mrs. Van Daan. I must tell you that her attempts to flirt with Father are getting her nowhere. Pim, thank goodness, won't play.

530 (*As she is saying the last lines, the curtain rises on the darkened scene.* Anne's Voice *fades out.*)

Scene 4

ANALYZE DRAMA

Annotate: In paragraphs 531–535, mark where Mr. Van Daan goes in the dark.

Predict: What do you think Mr. Van Daan is doing? How might his action cause trouble in the future?

531 *It is the middle of the night, several months later. The stage is dark except for a little light which comes through the skylight in* Peter's *room.*

532 *Everyone is in bed.* Mr. *and* Mrs. Frank *lie on the couch in the main room, which has been pulled out to serve as a makeshift double bed.*

533 Margot *is sleeping on a mattress on the floor in the main room, behind a curtain stretched across for privacy. The others are all in their accustomed rooms.*

534 *From outside we hear two drunken soldiers singing "Lili Marlene." A girl's high giggle is heard. The sound of running feet is*

heard coming closer and then fading in the distance. Throughout the scene there is the distant sound of airplanes passing overhead.

535 *A match suddenly flares up in the attic. We dimly see* Mr. Van Daan. *He is getting his bearings. He comes quickly down the stairs, and goes to the cupboard where the food is stored. Again the match flares up, and is as quickly blown out. The dim figure is seen to steal back up the stairs.*

536 *There is quiet for a second or two, broken only by the sound of airplanes, and running feet on the street below.*

537 *Suddenly, out of the silence and the dark, we hear* Anne *scream.*

538 **Anne** (*screaming*). No! No! Don't . . . don't take me!

539 (*She moans, tossing and crying in her sleep. The other people wake, terrified.* Dussel *sits up in bed, furious.*)

540 **Dussel.** Shush! Anne! Anne, for God's sake, shush!

541 **Anne** (*still in her nightmare*). Save me! Save me!

542 (*She screams and screams.* Dussel *gets out of bed, going over to her, trying to wake her.*)

543 **Dussel.** For God's sake! Quiet! Quiet! You want someone to hear?

544 (*In the main room* Mrs. Frank *grabs a shawl and pulls it around her. She rushes in to* Anne, *taking her in her arms.* Mr. Frank *hurriedly gets up, putting on his overcoat.* Margot *sits up, terrified.* Peter*'s light goes on in his room.*)

545 **Mrs. Frank** (*to* Anne, *in her room*). Hush, darling, hush. It's all right. It's all right. (*over her shoulder to* Dussel) Will you be kind enough to turn on the light, Mr. Dussel? (*back to* Anne) It's nothing, my darling. It was just a dream.

546 (Dussel *turns on the light in the bedroom.* Mrs. Frank *holds* Anne *in her arms. Gradually* Anne *comes out of her nightmare, still trembling with horror.* Mr. Frank *comes into the room, and goes quickly to the window, looking out to be sure that no one outside had heard* Anne*'s screams.* Mrs. Frank *holds* Anne, *talking softly to her. In the main room* Margot *stands on a chair, turning on the center hanging lamp. A light goes on in the* Van Daans' *room overhead.* Peter *puts his robe on, coming out of his room.*)

547 **Dussel** (*to* Mrs. Frank, *blowing his nose*). Something must be done about that child, Mrs. Frank. Yelling like that! Who knows but there's somebody on the streets? She's endangering all our lives.

Don't forget to **Notice & Note** as you read the text.

548 **Mrs. Frank.** Anne, darling.

549 **Dussel.** Every night she twists and turns. I don't sleep. I spend half my night shushing her. And now it's nightmares!

550 (Margot *comes to the door of* Anne's *room, followed by* Peter. Mr. Frank *goes to them, indicating that everything is all right.* Peter *takes* Margot *back.*)

551 **Mrs. Frank** (*to* Anne). You're here, safe, you see? Nothing has happened. (*to* Dussel) Please, Mr. Dussel, go back to bed. She'll be herself in a minute or two. Won't you, Anne?

552 **Dussel** (*picking up a book and a pillow*). Thank you, but I'm going to the w.c. The one place where there's peace! (*He stalks out.* Mr. Van Daan, *in underwear and trousers, comes down the stairs.*)

553 **Mr. Van Daan** (*to* Dussel). What is it? What happened?

554 **Dussel.** A nightmare. She was having a nightmare!

555 **Mr. Van Daan.** I thought someone was murdering her.

556 **Dussel.** Unfortunately, no.

557 (*He goes into the bathroom.* Mr. Van Daan *goes back up the stairs.* Mr. Frank, *in the main room, sends* Peter *back to his own bedroom.*)

558 **Mr. Frank.** Thank you, Peter. Go back to bed.

559 (Peter *goes back to his room.* Mr. Frank *follows him, turning out the light and looking out the window. Then he goes back to the main room, and gets up on a chair, turning out the center hanging lamp.*)

560 **Mrs. Frank** (*to* Anne). Would you like some water? (Anne *shakes her head.*) Was it a very bad dream? Perhaps if you told me . . . ?

561 **Anne.** I'd rather not talk about it.

562 **Mrs. Frank.** Poor darling. Try to sleep then. I'll sit right here beside you until you fall asleep.

563 (*She brings a stool over, sitting there.*)

564 **Anne.** You don't have to.

565 **Mrs. Frank.** But I'd like to stay with you . . . very much. Really.

566 **Anne.** I'd rather you didn't.

567 **Mrs. Frank.** Good night, then. (*She leans down to kiss* Anne. Anne *throws her arm up over her face, turning away.* Mrs. Frank, *hiding her hurt, kisses* Anne's *arm.*) You'll be all right? There's nothing that you want?

568 **Anne.** Will you please ask Father to come.

569 **Mrs. Frank** (*after a second*). Of course, Anne dear. (*She hurries out into the other room.* Mr. Frank *comes to her as she comes in.*) *Sie verlangt nach Dir!*[12]

570 **Mr. Frank** (*sensing her hurt*). Edith, *Liebe, schau . . .*[13]

571 **Mrs. Frank.** *Es macht nichts! Ich danke dem lieben Herrgott, dass sie sich wenigstens an Dich wendet, wenn sie Trost braucht! Geh hinein, Otto, sie ist ganz hysterisch vor Angst.*[14] (*as* Mr. Frank *hesitates*) *Geh zu ihr.*[15] (*He looks at her for a second and then goes to get a cup of water for* Anne. Mrs. Frank *sinks down on the bed, her face in her hands, trying to keep from sobbing aloud.* Margot *comes over to her, putting her arms around her.*) She wants nothing of me. She pulled away when I leaned down to kiss her.

572 **Margot.** It's a phase . . . You heard Father . . . Most girls go through it . . . they turn to their fathers at this age . . . they give all their love to their fathers.

573 **Mrs. Frank.** You weren't like this. You didn't shut me out.

574 **Margot.** She'll get over it . . . (*She smooths the bed for* Mrs. Frank *and sits beside her a moment as* Mrs. Frank *lies down. In* Anne's *room* Mr. Frank *comes in, sitting down by* Anne. Anne *flings her arms around him, clinging to him. In the distance we hear the sound of ack-ack.*)

575 **Anne.** Oh, Pim. I dreamed that they came to get us! The Green Police! They broke down the door and grabbed me and started to drag me out the way they did Jopie.

576 **Mr. Frank.** I want you to take this pill.

577 **Anne.** What is it?

578 **Mr. Frank.** Something to quiet you.

579 (*She takes it and drinks the water. In the main room* Margot *turns out the light and goes back to her bed.*)

580 **Mr. Frank** (*to* Anne). Do you want me to read to you for a while?

581 **Anne.** No. Just sit with me for a minute. Was I awful? Did I yell terribly loud? Do you think anyone outside could have heard?

ANALYZE DRAMA

Annotate: In paragraphs 569–571, notice the lines that Mr. and Mrs. Frank speak in German. Mark the English translations in the footnotes.

Infer: Why might the playwrights have chosen to have the characters speak German in this part of the script?

[12] ***Sie verlangt nach Dir*** (zē fer-längt´näkh dîr) *German:* She is asking for you.
[13] ***Liebe, schau*** (lē´bə shou´) *German:* Dear, look.
[14] ***Es macht . . . vor Angst*** (ĕs mäkht´ nĭkhts´! ĭkh dängk´ə dām lē´bən hĕr´gôt´, däs zē zĭkh´ vān´ĭkhshtənz än dĭkh´ vĕn´dət, vĕn zē trôst´ broukht´! gā hĭn-īn´, ôt´tô, zē ĭst gänts hüstĕr´ĭsh fôr ängst´) *German:* It's all right. I thank dear God, that at least she turns to you, when she needs comfort. Go in, Otto, she is hysterical with fear.
[15] ***Geh zu ihr*** (gā´ tso͞o îr´) *German:* Go to her.

582 **Mr. Frank.** No. No. Lie quietly now. Try to sleep.

583 **Anne.** I'm a terrible coward. I'm so disappointed in myself. I think I've conquered my fear . . . I think I'm really grown-up . . . and then something happens . . . and I run to you like a baby . . . I love you, Father. I don't love anyone but you.

584 **Mr. Frank** (*reproachfully*). Annele!

585 **Anne.** It's true. I've been thinking about it for a long time. You're the only one I love.

586 **Mr. Frank.** It's fine to hear you tell me that you love me. But I'd be happier if you said you loved your mother as well . . . She needs your help so much . . . your love . . .

587 **Anne.** We have nothing in common. She doesn't understand me. Whenever I try to explain my views on life to her she asks me if I'm constipated.

588 **Mr. Frank.** You hurt her very much just now. She's crying. She's in there crying.

589 **Anne.** I can't help it. I only told the truth. I didn't want her here . . . (*then, with sudden change*) Oh, Pim, I was horrible, wasn't I? And the worst of it is, I can stand off and look at myself doing it and know it's cruel and yet I can't stop doing it. What's the matter with me? Tell me. Don't say it's just a phase! Help me.

590 **Mr. Frank.** There is so little that we parents can do to help our children. We can only try to set a good example . . . point the way. The rest you must do yourself. You must build your own character.

591 **Anne.** I'm trying. Really I am. Every night I think back over all of the things I did that day that were wrong . . . like putting the wet mop in Mr. Dussel's bed . . . and this thing now with Mother. I say to myself, that was wrong. I make up my mind, I'm never going to do *that* again. Never! Of course I may do something worse . . . but at least I'll never do that again! . . . I have a nicer side, Father . . . a sweeter, nicer side. But I'm scared to show it. I'm afraid that people are going to laugh at me if I'm serious. So the mean Anne comes to the outside and the good Anne stays on the inside, and I keep on trying to switch them around and have the good Anne outside and the bad Anne inside and be what I'd like to be . . . and might be . . . if only . . . only . . . (*She is asleep.* Mr. Frank *watches her for a moment and then turns off the light, and starts out. The lights dim out. The curtain falls on the scene.* Anne's Voice *is heard dimly at first, and then with growing strength.*)

Don't forget to **Notice & Note** as you read the text.

592 **Anne's Voice.** . . . The air raids are getting worse. They come over day and night. The noise is terrifying. Pim says it should be music to our ears. The more planes, the sooner will come the end of the war. Mrs. Van Daan pretends to be a fatalist. What will be, will be. But when the planes come over, who is the most frightened? No one else but Petronella! . . . Monday, the ninth of November, nineteen forty-two. Wonderful news! The Allies have landed in Africa. Pim says that we can look for an early finish to the war. Just for fun he asked each of us what was the first thing we wanted to do when we got out of here. Mrs. Van Daan longs to be home with her own things, her needle-point chairs, the Beckstein piano her father gave her . . . the best that money could buy. Peter would like to go to a movie. Mr. Dussel wants to get back to his dentist's drill. He's afraid he is losing his touch. For myself, there are so many things . . . to ride a bike again . . . to laugh till my belly aches . . . to have new clothes from the skin out . . . to have a hot tub filled to overflowing and wallow in it for hours . . . to be back in school with my friends . . .

593 (*As the last lines are being said, the curtain rises on the scene. The lights dim on as* Anne's Voice *fades away.*)

Scene 5

594 *It is the first night of the Hanukkah*[16] *celebration.* Mr. Frank *is standing at the head of the table on which is the Menorah.*[17] *He lights the Shamos, or servant candle, and holds it as he says the blessing. Seated listening is all of the "family," dressed in their best. The men wear hats,* Peter *wears his cap.*

595 **Mr. Frank** (*reading from a prayer book*). "Praised be Thou, oh Lord our God, Ruler of the universe, who has sanctified us with Thy commandments and bidden us kindle the Hanukkah lights. Praised be Thou, oh Lord our God, Ruler of the universe, who has wrought wondrous deliverances for our fathers in days of old. Praised be Thou, oh Lord our God, Ruler of the universe, that Thou has given us life and sustenance and brought us to this happy season." (Mr. Frank *lights the one candle of the Menorah as he continues.*) "We kindle this Hanukkah light to

[16] **Hanukkah** (hä´nə-kə): a Jewish holiday, celebrated in December and lasting eight days.

[17] **Menorah** (mə-nôr´ə): a candleholder with nine branches, used in the celebration of Hanukkah.

celebrate the great and wonderful deeds wrought through the zeal with which God filled the hearts of the heroic Maccabees, two thousand years ago. They fought against indifference, against tyranny and oppression, and they restored our Temple to us. May these lights remind us that we should ever look to God, whence cometh our help." Amen. [Pronounced O-mayn.]

596 **All.** Amen.

597 (Mr. Frank *hands* Mrs. Frank *the prayer book.*)

598 **Mrs. Frank** (*reading*). "I lift up mine eyes unto the mountains, from whence cometh my help. My help cometh from the Lord who made heaven and earth. He will not suffer thy foot to be moved. He that keepeth thee will not slumber. He that keepeth Israel doth neither slumber nor sleep. The Lord is thy keeper. The Lord is thy shade upon thy right hand. The sun shall not smite thee by day, nor the moon by night. The Lord shall keep thee from all evil. He shall keep thy soul. The Lord shall guard thy going out and thy coming in, from this time forth and forevermore." Amen.

599 **All.** Amen.

600 (Mrs. Frank *puts down the prayer book and goes to get the food and wine.* Margot *helps her.* Mr. Frank *takes the men's hats and puts them aside.*)

601 **Dussel** (*rising*). That was very moving.

602 **Anne** (*pulling him back*). It isn't over yet!

603 **Mrs. Van Daan.** Sit down! Sit down!

604 **Anne.** There's a lot more, songs and presents.

605 **Dussel.** Presents?

606 **Mrs. Frank.** Not this year, unfortunately.

607 **Mrs. Van Daan.** But always on Hanukkah everyone gives presents . . . everyone!

608 **Dussel.** Like our St. Nicholas's Day.[18] (*There is a chorus of "no's" from the group.*)

609 **Mrs. Van Daan.** No! Not like St. Nicholas! What kind of a Jew are you that you don't know Hanukkah?

610 **Mrs. Frank** (*as she brings the food*). I remember particularly the candles . . . First one, as we have tonight. Then the second night you light two candles, the next night three . . . and so on until

[18] **St. Nicholas's Day:** December 6, the day that Christian children in the Netherlands receive gifts.

Don't forget to **Notice & Note** as you read the text.

you have eight candles burning. When there are eight candles it is truly beautiful.

611 **Mrs. Van Daan.** And the potato pancakes.

612 **Mr. Van Daan.** Don't talk about them!

613 **Mrs. Van Daan.** I make the best *latkes*[19] you ever tasted!

614 **Mrs. Frank.** Invite us all next year . . . in your own home.

615 **Mr. Frank.** God willing!

616 **Mrs. Van Daan.** God willing.

617 **Margot.** What I remember best is the presents we used to get when we were little . . . eight days of presents . . . and each day they got better and better.

618 **Mrs. Frank** (*sitting down*). We are all here, alive. That is present enough.

619 **Anne.** No, it isn't. I've got something . . .

620 (*She rushes into her room, hurriedly puts on a little hat improvised from the lamp shade, grabs a satchel bulging with parcels and comes running back.*)

621 **Mrs. Frank.** What is it?

622 **Anne.** Presents!

[19] ***latkes*** (lät´kəz): potato pancakes.

623 **Mrs. Van Daan.** Presents!

624 **Dussel.** Look!

625 **Mr. Van Daan.** What's she got on her head?

626 **Peter.** A lamp shade!

627 **Anne** (*She picks out one at random*). This is for Margot. (*She hands it to* Margot, *pulling her to her feet.*) Read it out loud.

628 **Margot** (*reading*).
"You have never lost your temper.
You never will, I fear,
You are so good.
But if you should,
Put all your cross words here."
(*She tears open the package.*)
A new crossword puzzle book!
Where did you get it?

629 **Anne.** It isn't new. It's one that you've done. But I rubbed it all out, and if you wait a little and forget, you can do it all over again.

630 **Margot** (*sitting*). It's wonderful, Anne. Thank you. You'd never know it wasn't new.

631 (*From outside we hear the sound of a streetcar passing.*)

632 **Anne** (*with another gift*). Mrs. Van Daan.

633 **Mrs. Van Daan** (*taking it*). This is awful . . . I haven't anything for anyone . . . I never thought . . .

634 **Mr. Frank.** This is all Anne's idea.

635 **Mrs. Van Daan** (*holding up a bottle*). What is it?

636 **Anne.** It's hair shampoo. I took all the odds and ends of soap and mixed them with the last of my toilet water.

637 **Mrs. Van Daan.** Oh, Anneke!

638 **Anne.** I wanted to write a poem for all of them, but I didn't have time. (*offering a large box to* Mr. Van Daan) Yours, Mr. Van Daan, is really something . . . something you want more than anything. (*as she waits for him to open it*) Look! Cigarettes!

639 **Mr. Van Daan.** Cigarettes!

640 **Anne.** Two of them! Pim found some old pipe tobacco in the pocket lining of his coat . . . and we made them . . . or rather, Pim did.

641 **Mrs. Van Daan.** Let me see . . . Well, look at that! Light it, Putti! Light it.

Don't forget to **Notice & Note** as you read the text.

642 (Mr. Van Daan *hesitates.*)

643 **Anne.** It's tobacco, really it is! There's a little fluff in it, but not much.

644 (*Everyone watches intently as* Mr. Van Daan *cautiously lights it. The cigarette flares up. Everyone laughs.*)

645 **Peter.** It works!

646 **Mrs. Van Daan.** Look at him.

647 **Mr. Van Daan** (*spluttering*). Thank you, Anne. Thank you.

648 (Anne *rushes back to her satchel for another present.*)

649 **Anne** (*handing her mother a piece of paper*). For Mother, Hanukkah greeting. (*She pulls her mother to her feet.*)

650 **Mrs. Frank** (*She reads.*) "Here's an I.O.U. that I promise to pay. Ten hours of doing whatever you say. Signed, Anne Frank." (Mrs. Frank, *touched, takes* Anne *in her arms, holding her close.*)

651 **Dussel** (*to* Anne). Ten hours of doing what you're told? *Anything* you're told?

652 **Anne.** That's right.

653 **Dussel.** You wouldn't want to sell that, Mrs. Frank?

654 **Mrs. Frank.** Never! This is the most precious gift I've ever had!

655 (*She sits, showing her present to the others.* Anne *hurries back to the satchel and pulls out a scarf, the scarf that* Mr. Frank *found in the first scene.*)

656 **Anne** (*offering it to her father*). For Pim.

657 **Mr. Frank.** Anneke . . . I wasn't supposed to have a present! (*He takes it, unfolding it and showing it to the others.*)

658 **Anne.** It's a muffler . . . to put round your neck . . . like an ascot, you know. I made it myself out of odds and ends . . . I knitted it in the dark each night, after I'd gone to bed. I'm afraid it looks better in the dark!

659 **Mr. Frank** (*putting it on*). It's fine. It fits me perfectly. Thank you, Annele.

660 (Anne *hands* Peter *a ball of paper, with a string attached to it.*)

661 **Anne.** That's for Mouschi.

662 **Peter** (*rising to bow*). On behalf of Mouschi, I thank you.

663 **Anne** (*hesitant, handing him a gift*). And . . . this is yours . . . from Mrs. Quack Quack. (*as he holds it gingerly in his hands*) Well . . . open it . . . Aren't you going to open it?

664 **Peter.** I'm scared to. I know something's going to jump out and hit me.

ANALYZE DRAMA

Annotate: In the stage directions, mark the gift that Anne gives her father.

Connect: How is the scarf connected to Act One, Scene 1? Why is it important for the audience to make the connection?

665 **Anne.** No. It's nothing like that, really.

666 **Mrs. Van Daan** (*as he is opening it*). What is it, Peter? Go on. Show it.

667 **Anne** (*excitedly*). It's a safety razor!

668 **Dussel.** A what?

669 **Anne.** A razor!

670 **Mrs. Van Daan** (*looking at it*). You didn't make that out of odds and ends.

671 **Anne** (*to* Peter). Miep got it for me. It's not new. It's second-hand. But you really do need a razor now.

672 **Dussel.** For what?

673 **Anne.** Look on his upper lip . . . you can see the beginning of a mustache.

674 **Dussel.** He wants to get rid of that? Put a little milk on it and let the cat lick it off.

675 **Peter** (*starting for his room*). Think you're funny, don't you.

676 **Dussel.** Look! He can't wait! He's going in to try it!

677 **Peter.** I'm going to give Mouschi his present! (*He goes into his room, slamming the door behind him.*)

678 **Mr. Van Daan** (*disgustedly*). Mouschi, Mouschi, Mouschi.

679 (*In the distance we hear a dog persistently barking.* Anne *brings a gift to* Dussel.)

680 **Anne.** And last but never least, my roommate, Mr. Dussel.

681 **Dussel.** For me? You have something for me? (*He opens the small box she gives him.*)

682 **Anne.** I made them myself.

683 **Dussel** (*puzzled*). Capsules! Two capsules!

684 **Anne.** They're ear-plugs!

685 **Dussel.** Ear-plugs?

686 **Anne.** To put in your ears so you won't hear me when I thrash around at night. I saw them advertised in a magazine. They're not real ones . . . I made them out of cotton and candle wax. Try them . . . See if they don't work . . . see if you can hear me talk . . .

687 **Dussel** (*putting them in his ears*). Wait now until I get them in . . . so.

688 **Anne.** Are you ready?

689 **Dussel.** Huh?

690 **Anne.** Are you ready?

691 **Dussel.** Good God! They've gone inside! I can't get them out! (*They laugh as* Mr. Dussel *jumps about, trying to shake the plugs out of his ears. Finally he gets them out. Putting them away.*) Thank you, Anne! Thank you!

692 **Mr. Van Daan.** A real Hanukkah!
693 **Mrs. Van Daan.** Wasn't it cute of her?
694 **Mrs. Frank.** I don't know when she did it.
695 **Margot.** I love my present.

Together

696 **Anne** (*sitting at the table*). And now let's have the song, Father . . . please . . . (*to* Dussel) Have you heard the Hanukkah song, Mr. Dussel? The song is the whole thing! (*She sings.*) "Oh, Hanukkah! Oh Hanukkah! The sweet celebration . . ."

697 **Mr. Frank** (*quieting her*). I'm afraid, Anne, we shouldn't sing that song tonight. (*to* Dussel) It's a song of jubilation, of rejoicing. One is apt to become too enthusiastic.

698 **Anne.** Oh, please, please. Let's sing the song. I promise not to shout!

699 **Mr. Frank.** Very well. But quietly now . . . I'll keep an eye on you and when . . .

700 (*As* Anne *starts to sing, she is interrupted by* Dussel, *who is snorting and wheezing.*)

701 **Dussel** (*pointing to* Peter). You . . . You! (Peter *is coming from his bedroom,* ***ostentatiously*** *holding a bulge in his coat as if he were holding his cat, and dangling* Anne's *present before it.*) How many times . . . I told you . . . Out! Out!

702 **Mr. Van Daan** (*going to* Peter). What's the matter with you? Haven't you any sense? Get that cat out of here.

703 **Peter** (*innocently*). Cat?

704 **Mr. Van Daan.** You heard me. Get it out of here!

705 **Peter.** I have no cat. (*Delighted with his joke, he opens his coat and pulls out a bath towel. The group at the table laugh, enjoying the joke.*)

706 **Dussel** (*still wheezing*). It doesn't need to be the cat . . . his clothes are enough . . . when he comes out of that room . . .

707 **Mr. Van Daan.** Don't worry. You won't be bothered any more. We're getting rid of it.

708 **Dussel.** At last you listen to me. (*He goes off into his bedroom.*)

709 **Mr. Van Daan** (*calling after him*). I'm not doing it for you. That's all in your mind . . . all of it! (*He starts back to his place at*

Don't forget to **Notice & Note** as you read the text.

ostentatiously
(ŏs tĕn´-tā´shəs-lē) *adv.* Someone who does something *ostentatiously* acts in an exaggerated way in order to attract attention.

the table.) I'm doing it because I'm sick of seeing that cat eat all our food.

710 **Peter.** That's not true! I only give him bones . . . scraps . . .

711 **Mr. Van Daan.** Don't tell me! He gets fatter every day! Damn cat looks better than any of us. Out he goes tonight!

712 **Peter.** No! No!

713 **Anne.** Mr. Van Daan, you can't do that! That's Peter's cat.

714 **Mrs. Frank** (*quietly*). Anne.

715 **Peter** (*to* Mr. Van Daan). If he goes, I go.

716 **Mr. Van Daan.** Go! Go!

717 **Mrs. Van Daan.** You're not going and the cat's not going! Now please . . . this is Hanukkah . . . Hanukkah . . . this is the time to celebrate . . . What's the matter with all of you? Come on, Anne. Let's have the song.

718 **Anne** (*singing*). "Oh, Hanukkah! Oh, Hanukkah! The sweet celebration."

719 **Mr. Frank** (*rising*). I think we should first blow out the candle . . . then we'll have something for tomorrow night.

720 **Margot.** But, Father, you're supposed to let it burn itself out.

721 **Mr. Frank.** I'm sure that God understands shortages. (*before blowing it out*) "Praised be Thou, oh Lord our God, who hast sustained us and permitted us to celebrate this joyous festival."

722 (*He is about to blow out the candle when suddenly there is a crash of something falling below. They all freeze in horror, motionless. For a few seconds there is complete silence.* Mr. Frank *slips off his shoes. The others noiselessly follow his example.* Mr. Frank *turns out a light near him. He motions to* Peter *to turn off the center lamp.* Peter *tries to reach it, realizes he cannot and gets up on a chair. Just as he is touching the lamp he loses his balance. The chair goes out from under him. He falls. The iron lamp shade crashes to the floor. There is a sound of feet below, running down the stairs.*)

723 **Mr. Van Daan** (*under his breath*). God Almighty! (*The only light left comes from the Hanukkah candle.* Dussel *comes from his room.* Mr. Frank *creeps over to the stairwell and stands listening. The dog is heard barking excitedly.*) Do you hear anything?

724 **Mr. Frank** (*in a whisper*). No. I think they've gone.

725 **Mrs. Van Daan.** It's the Green Police. They've found us.

726 **Mr. Frank.** If they had, they wouldn't have left. They'd be up here by now.

Ed

Close Read Screencast

Listen to a modeled close read of this text.

Don't forget to **Notice & Note** as you read the text.

727 **Mrs. Van Daan.** I know it's the Green Police. They've gone to get help. That's all. They'll be back!

728 **Mr. Van Daan.** Or it may have been the Gestapo,[20] looking for papers . . .

729 **Mr. Frank** (*interrupting*). Or a thief, looking for money.

730 **Mrs. Van Daan.** We've got to do something . . . Quick! Quick! Before they come back.

731 **Mr. Van Daan.** There isn't anything to do. Just wait.

732 (Mr. Frank *holds up his hand for them to be quiet. He is listening intently. There is complete silence as they all strain to hear any sound from below. Suddenly* Anne *begins to sway. With a low cry she falls to the floor in a faint.* Mrs. Frank *goes to her quickly, sitting beside her on the floor and taking her in her arms.*)

733 **Mrs. Frank.** Get some water, please! Get some water!

734 (Margot *starts for the sink.*)

735 **Mr. Van Daan** (*grabbing* Margot). No! No! No one's going to run water!

736 **Mr. Frank.** If they've found us, they've found us. Get the water. (Margot *starts again for the sink.* Mr. Frank, *getting a flashlight*) I'm going down.

737 (Margot *rushes to him, clinging to him.* Anne *struggles to consciousness.*)

738 **Margot.** No, Father, no! There may be someone there, waiting . . . It may be a trap!

739 **Mr. Frank.** This is Saturday. There is no way for us to know what has happened until Miep or Mr. Kraler comes on Monday morning. We cannot live with this uncertainty.

740 **Margot.** Don't go, Father!

741 **Mrs. Frank.** Hush, darling, hush. (Mr. Frank *slips quietly out, down the steps and out through the door below.*) Margot! Stay close to me.

742 (Margot *goes to her mother.*)

743 **Mr. Van Daan.** Shush! Shush!

744 (Mrs. Frank *whispers to* Margot *to get the water.* Margot *goes for it.*)

[20] **Gestapo** (gə-stä´pō): the Nazi secret police force, known for its terrorism and brutality.

745 **Mrs. Van Daan.** Putti, where's our money? Get our money. I hear you can buy the Green Police off, so much a head. Go upstairs quick! Get the money!

746 **Mr. Van Daan.** Keep still!

747 **Mrs. Van Daan** (*kneeling before him, pleading*). Do you want to be dragged off to a concentration camp? Are you going to stand there and wait for them to come up and get you? Do something, I tell you!

748 **Mr. Van Daan** (*pushing her aside*). Will you keep still! (*He goes over to the stairwell to listen.* Peter *goes to his mother, helping her up onto the sofa. There is a second of silence, then* Anne *can stand it no longer.*)

749 **Anne.** Someone go after Father! Make Father come back!

750 **Peter** (*starting for the door*). I'll go.

751 **Mr. Van Daan.** Haven't you done enough?

752 (*He pushes* Peter *roughly away. In his anger against his father* Peter *grabs a chair as if to hit him with it, then puts it down, burying his face in his hands.* Mrs. Frank *begins to pray softly.*)

753 **Anne.** Please, please, Mr. Van Daan. Get Father.

754 **Mr. Van Daan.** Quiet! Quiet!

755 (Anne *is shocked into silence.* Mrs. Frank *pulls her closer, holding her protectively in her arms.*)

756 **Mrs. Frank** (*softly, praying*). "I lift up mine eyes unto the mountains, from whence cometh my help. My help cometh from the Lord who made heaven and earth. He will not suffer thy foot to be moved . . . He that keepeth thee will not slumber . . ." (*She stops as she hears someone coming. They all watch the door tensely.* Mr. Frank *comes quietly in.* Anne *rushes to him, holding him tight.*)

757 **Mr. Frank.** It was a thief. That noise must have scared him away.

758 **Mrs. Van Daan.** Thank God.

759 **Mr. Frank.** He took the cash box. And the radio. He ran away in such a hurry that he didn't stop to shut the street door. It was swinging wide open. (*A breath of relief sweeps over them.*) I think it would be good to have some light.

760 **Margot.** Are you sure it's all right?

761 **Mr. Frank.** The danger has passed. (Margot *goes to light the small lamp.*) Don't be so terrified, Anne. We're safe.

ANALYZE DRAMA

Annotate: In paragraphs 757–768, mark Mr. Frank's explanation for what caused the noise downstairs. Then mark Mr. Dussel's fears about what will happen as a result.

Predict: Remember that when a writer hints at future events, it is called foreshadowing. Do you think the playwrights are foreshadowing what will actually happen in the future—that the Annex residents will be caught because of the thief? Explain your prediction.

762 **Dussel.** Who says the danger has passed? Don't you realize we are in greater danger than ever?

763 **Mr. Frank.** Mr. Dussel, will you be still!

764 (Mr. Frank *takes* Anne *back to the table, making her sit down with him, trying to calm her.*)

765 **Dussel** (*pointing to* Peter). Thanks to this clumsy fool, there's someone now who knows we're up here! Someone now knows we're up here, hiding!

766 **Mrs. Van Daan** (*going to* Dussel). Someone knows we're here, yes. But who is the someone? A thief! A thief! You think a thief is going to go to the Green Police and say . . . I was robbing a place the other night and I heard a noise up over my head? You think a thief is going to do that?

767 **Dussel.** Yes. I think he will.

768 **Mrs. Van Daan** (*hysterically*). You're crazy! (*She stumbles back to her seat at the table.* Peter *follows protectively, pushing* Dussel *aside.*)

769 **Dussel.** I think some day he'll be caught and then he'll make a bargain with the Green Police . . . if they'll let him off, he'll tell them where some Jews are hiding!

770 (*He goes off into the bedroom. There is a second of* ***appalled*** *silence.*)

771 **Mr. Van Daan.** He's right.

772 **Anne.** Father, let's get out of here! We can't stay here now . . . Let's go . . .

773 **Mr. Van Daan.** Go! Where?

774 **Mrs. Frank** (*sinking into her chair at the table*). Yes. Where?

775 **Mr. Frank** (*rising, to them all*). Have we lost all faith? All courage? A moment ago we thought that they'd come for us. We were sure it was the end. But it wasn't the end. We're alive, safe. (Mr. Van Daan *goes to the table and sits.* Mr. Frank *prays.*) "We thank Thee, oh Lord our God, that in Thy infinite mercy Thou hast again seen fit to spare us." (*He blows out the candle, then turns to* Anne.) Come on, Anne. The song! Let's have the song! (*He starts to sing.* Anne *finally starts falteringly to sing, as* Mr. Frank *urges her on. Her voice is hardly audible at first.*)

776 **Anne** (*singing*). "Oh, Hanukkah! Oh, Hanukkah! The sweet . . . celebration . . . " (*As she goes on singing, the others gradually join in, their voices still shaking with fear.* Mrs. Van Daan *sobs as she sings.*)

Don't forget to **Notice & Note** as you read the text.

appalled (ə-pôld′) *adj.* To be *appalled* is to feel horror and shock about something.

ANALYZE DRAMA

Annotate: Review paragraphs 775–784. Mark details in the stage directions that reveal how the characters sing the Hanukkah song.

Interpret: How does the gradual change in the way the characters are singing reveal their feelings? How does this change affect the mood, or emotional atmosphere, at the end of Act One?

777 **Group.** "Around the feast . . . we . . . gather
In complete . . . jubilation . . .
Happiest of sea . . . sons
Now is here. Many are the reasons for good cheer."

778 (Dussel *comes from the bedroom. He comes over to the table, standing beside* Margot, *listening to them as they sing.*)

779 "Together
We'll weather
Whatever tomorrow may bring."

780 (*As they sing on with growing courage, the lights start to dim.*)

781 "So hear us rejoicing
And merrily voicing
The Hanukkah song that we sing.
Hoy!"

782 (*The lights are out. The curtain starts slowly to fall.*)

783 "Hear us rejoicing
And merrily voicing
The Hanukkah song that we sing."

784 (*They are still singing, as the curtain falls.*)

785 *The Curtain Falls.*

TURN AND TALK

Turn to a partner and discuss the playwrights' choice to end Act One with a scene in which the characters celebrate Hanukkah. What is the impact of this choice?

ESSENTIAL QUESTION:

What can we learn from tragic events?

Review your notes and add your thoughts to your Response Log.

Assessment Practice

Answer these questions before moving on to the **Analyze the Text** section on the following page.

1. Which detail from the stage directions in Act One, Scene 1, hints at the fact that an upsetting event took place in the Secret Annex?

- (A) *"Chairs and tables are overturned."* (paragraph 7)
- (B) *"He is weak, ill. His clothes are threadbare."* (paragraph 9)
- (C) *"Her attitude toward Mr. Frank is protective. . . ."* (paragraph 12)
- (D) *"She hands him a paperbound notebook."* (paragraph 30)

2. This question has two parts. First, answer **Part A**. Then, answer **Part B**.

Part A

Which sentence reflects how Anne and Peter first get along?

- (A) Anne has a crush on Peter, but he only wants to be friends.
- (B) They form a strong bond over their love of cats.
- (C) Anne is lively and sociable, which distresses shy Peter.
- (D) They both keep to themselves and study hard.

Part B

Which sentence best supports the answer in Part A?

- (A) "I love cats. I have one . . . a darling little cat. . . ." (paragraph 111)
- (B) "Anne *and* Peter *sit opposite each other at the center table . . . doing their lessons."* (paragraph 181)
- (C) "Peter . . . ? Come dance with me." (paragraph 200)
- (D) "I only want some fun. . . . I don't know what's the matter with that boy." (paragraph 212)

Ed Test-Taking Strategies

Analyze the Text

Support your responses with evidence from the text.

1. **IDENTIFY PATTERNS** How many scenes are there in Act One of this play? Why might the playwright have begun a new scene after paragraph 178?

2. **DRAW CONCLUSIONS** Examine paragraphs 351–363. What do the stage directions and dialogue reveal about the characters?

3. **CAUSE/EFFECT** One incident that both propels action and reveals more about the characters in the Annex is the arrival of Mr. Dussel. How does his arrival affect life in the Annex? What does the impact of his presence reveal about Mr. Van Daan's character?

4. **ANALYZE** Review paragraph 589. What might explain the **Contrasts and Contradictions** in Anne's feelings and behavior toward her mother?

5. **PREDICT** Reread the stage directions in paragraph 722. What effects could the events described in these stage directions have on future events in the plot?

NOTICE & NOTE

Review what you **noticed and noted** as you read the text. Your annotations can help you answer these questions.

Choices

Here are some other ways to demonstrate your understanding of Act One.

Research

Create a Timeline

Most of the events in *The Diary of Anne Frank* focus on a two-year period toward the end of the Second World War. World War II began in 1939, but the Nazis' rise to power had begun 20 years earlier. Using several sources, research key events in the rise of the Nazi regime and the effects those events had on Jewish people. Then present your findings on a timeline and share with the rest of the class.

Writing

Character Analysis

Write a character analysis of one of the characters in the play. Include quotations from the text that illustrate the character's personality. Your analysis should address:

- the words, thoughts, and actions of the character
- the physical appearance of the character
- how others respond to the character
- how the character changes in the first act

ACT TWO Scene 1

Don't forget to **Notice & Note** as you read the text.

1 *In the darkness we hear* Anne's Voice, *again reading from the diary.*

2 **Anne's Voice.** Saturday, the first of January, nineteen forty-four. Another new year has begun and we find ourselves still in our hiding place. We have been here now for one year, five months and twenty-five days. It seems that our life is at a standstill.

3 *The curtain rises on the scene. It is late afternoon. Everyone is bundled up against the cold. In the main room* Mrs. Frank *is taking down the laundry which is hung across the back.* Mr. Frank *sits in the chair down left, reading.* Margot *is lying on the couch with a blanket over her and the many-colored knitted scarf around her throat.* Anne *is seated at the center table, writing in her diary.* Peter, Mr. *and* Mrs. Van Daan, *and* Dussel *are all in their own rooms, reading or lying down.*

4 *As the lights dim on,* Anne's Voice *continues, without a break.*

5 **Anne's Voice.** We are all a little thinner. The Van Daans' "discussions" are as violent as ever. Mother still does not understand me. But then I don't understand her either. There is one great change, however. A change in myself. I read somewhere that girls of my age don't feel quite certain of themselves. That they become quiet within and begin to think of the miracle that is taking place in their bodies. I think that what is happening to me is so wonderful . . . not only what can be seen, but what is taking place inside. Each time it has happened I have a feeling that I have a sweet secret. (*We hear the chimes and then a hymn being played on the carillon outside.*) And in spite of any pain, I long for the time when I shall feel that secret within me again.

6 (*The buzzer of the door below suddenly sounds. Everyone is startled,* Mr. Frank *tiptoes cautiously to the top of the steps and listens. Again the buzzer sounds, in* Miep's *V-for-Victory signal.*)

7 **Mr. Frank.** It's Miep! (*He goes quickly down the steps to unbolt the door. Mrs. Frank calls upstairs to the* Van Daans *and then to* Peter.)

8 **Mrs. Frank.** Wake up, everyone! Miep is here! (Anne *quickly puts her diary away.* Margot *sits up, pulling the blanket around her shoulders.* Mr. Dussel *sits on the edge of his bed, listening, disgruntled.* Miep *comes up the steps, followed by* Mr. Kraler.

ANALYZE DRAMA

Annotate: Mark the date of Anne's diary entry at the beginning of Act Two, Scene 1.

Draw Conclusions: How much time has passed between the end of Act One and the beginning of Act Two? What does this suggest about the suspected thief who may have heard noise from the Annex?

They bring flowers, books, newspapers, etc. Anne rushes to Miep, throwing her arms affectionately around her.) Miep . . . *and* Mr. Kraler . . . What a delightful surprise!

9 **Mr. Kraler.** We came to bring you New Year's greetings.

10 **Mrs. Frank.** You shouldn't . . . you should have at least one day to yourselves. (*She goes quickly to the stove and brings down teacups and tea for all of them.*)

11 **Anne.** Don't say that, it's so wonderful to see them! (*sniffing at Miep's coat*) I can smell the wind and the cold on your clothes.

12 **Miep** (*giving her the flowers*). There you are. (*then to Margot, feeling her forehead*) How are you, Margot? . . . Feeling any better?

13 **Margot.** I'm all right.

14 **Anne.** We filled her full of every kind of pill so she won't cough and make a noise. (*She runs into her room to put the flowers in water.* Mr. *and* Mrs. Van Daan *come from upstairs. Outside there is the sound of a band playing.*)

15 **Mrs. Van Daan.** Well, hello, Miep. Mr. Kraler.

16 **Mr. Kraler** (*giving a bouquet of flowers to* Mrs. Van Daan). With my hope for peace in the New Year.

17 **Peter** (*anxiously*). Miep, have you seen Mouschi? Have you seen him anywhere around?

18 **Miep.** I'm sorry, Peter. I asked everyone in the neighborhood had they seen a gray cat. But they said no.

19 (Mrs. Frank *gives* Miep *a cup of tea.* Mr. *Frank comes up the steps, carrying a small cake on a plate.*)

20 **Mr. Frank.** Look what Miep's brought for us!

21 **Mrs. Frank** (*taking it*). A cake!

22 **Mr. Van Daan.** A cake! (*He pinches* Miep's *cheeks gaily and hurries up to the cupboard.*) I'll get some plates.

23 (Dussel, *in his room, hastily puts a coat on and starts out to join the others.*)

24 **Mrs. Frank.** Thank you, Miepia. You shouldn't have done it. You must have used all of your sugar ration for weeks. (*giving it to* Mrs. Van Daan) It's beautiful, isn't it?

25 **Mrs. Van Daan.** It's been ages since I even saw a cake. Not since you brought us one last year. (*without looking at the cake, to* Miep) Remember? Don't you remember, you gave us one on New Year's Day? Just this time last year? I'll never forget it

because you had "Peace in nineteen forty-three" on it. (*She looks at the cake and reads.*) "Peace in nineteen forty-four!"

26 **Miep.** Well, it has to come sometime, you know. (*as* Dussel *comes from his room*) Hello, Mr. Dussel.

27 **Mr. Kraler.** How are you?

28 **Mr. Van Daan** (*bringing plates and a knife*). Here's the knife, *liefje*. Now, how many of us are there?

29 **Miep.** None for me, thank you.

30 **Mr. Frank.** Oh, please. You must.

31 **Miep.** I couldn't.

32 **Mr. Van Daan.** Good! That leaves one . . . two . . . three . . . seven of us.

33 **Dussel.** Eight! Eight! It's the same number as it always is!

34 **Mr. Van Daan.** I left Margot out. I take it for granted Margot won't eat any.

35 **Anne.** Why wouldn't she!

36 **Mrs. Frank.** I think it won't harm her.

37 **Mr. Van Daan.** All right! All right! I just didn't want her to start coughing again, that's all.

38 **Dussel.** And please, Mrs. Frank should cut the cake.

39 **Mr. Van Daan.** What's the difference?

40 **Mrs. Van Daan.** It's not Mrs. Frank's cake, is it, Miep? It's for all of us.

Together

41 **Dussel.** Mrs. Frank divides things better.

42 **Mrs. Van Daan** (*going to* Dussel). What are you trying to say?

43 **Mr. Van Daan.** Oh, come on! Stop wasting time!

Together

44 **Mrs. Van Daan** (*to* Dussel). Don't I always give everybody exactly the same? Don't I?

45 **Mr. Van Daan.** Forget it, Kerli.

46 **Mrs. Van Daan.** No. I want an answer! Don't I?

47 **Dussel.** Yes. Yes. Everybody gets exactly the same . . . except Mr. Van Daan always gets a little bit more.

48 (Mr. Van Daan *advances on* Dussel, *the knife still in his hand.*)

49 **Mr. Van Daan.** That's a lie!

50 (Dussel *retreats before the onslaught of the* Van Daans.)

Don't forget to **Notice & Note** as you read the text.

ANALYZE DRAMA

Annotate: Review paragraphs 38–51. Mark the lines that reveal who Mr. Dussel thinks should cut the cake and why.

Interpret: Think about Mr. and Mrs. Van Daan's reaction to Dussel's comments, and what Mr. Frank says. What does the characters' dialogue reveal about them?

51 **Mr. Frank.** Please, please! (*then to Miep*) You see what a little sugar cake does to us? It goes right to our heads!

52 **Mr. Van Daan** (*handing* Mrs. Frank *the knife*). Here you are, Mrs. Frank.

53 **Mrs. Frank.** Thank you. (*then to Miep as she goes to the table to cut the cake*) Are you sure you won't have some?

54 **Miep** (*drinking her tea*). No, really, I have to go in a minute.

55 (*The sound of the band fades out in the distance.*)

56 **Peter** (*to* Miep). Maybe Mouschi went back to our house . . . they say that cats . . . Do you ever get over there . . . ? I mean . . . do you suppose you could . . . ?

57 **Miep.** I'll try, Peter. The first minute I get I'll try. But I'm afraid, with him gone a week . . .

58 **Dussel.** Make up your mind, already someone has had a nice big dinner from that cat!

inarticulate
(ĭn´är-tĭk´yə-lĭt) *adj.* Someone who is *inarticulate* is unable to speak in a clear way.

59 (Peter *is furious, **inarticulate.** He starts toward* Dussel *as if to hit him.* Mr. Frank *stops him.* Mrs. Frank *speaks quickly to ease the situation.*)

60 **Mrs. Frank** (*to* Miep). This is delicious, Miep!

61 **Mrs. Van Daan** (*eating hers*). Delicious!

62 **Mr. Van Daan** (*finishing it in one gulp*). Dirk's in luck to get a girl who can bake like this!

63 **Miep** (*putting down her empty teacup*). I have to run. Dirk's taking me to a party tonight.

64 **Anne.** How heavenly! Remember now what everyone is wearing, and what you have to eat and everything, so you can tell us tomorrow.

65 **Miep.** I'll give you a full report! Good-bye, everyone!

66 **Mr. Van Daan** (*to* Miep). Just a minute. There's something I'd like you to do for me. (*He hurries off up the stairs to his room.*)

67 **Mrs. Van Daan** (*sharply*). Putti, where are you going? (*She rushes up the stairs after him, calling hysterically.*) What do you want? Putti, what are you going to do?

68 **Miep** (*to* Peter). What's wrong?

69 **Peter** (*his sympathy is with his mother*). Father says he's going to sell her fur coat. She's crazy about that old fur coat.

70 **Dussel.** Is it possible? Is it possible that anyone is so silly as to worry about a fur coat in times like this?

71 **Peter.** It's none of your darn business . . . and if you say one more thing . . . I'll, I'll take you and I'll . . . I mean it . . . I'll . . .

72 (*There is a piercing scream from* Mrs. Van Daan *above. She grabs at the fur coat as* Mr. Van Daan *is starting downstairs with it.*)

73 **Mrs. Van Daan.** No! No! No! Don't you dare take that! You hear? It's mine! (*Downstairs* Peter *turns away, embarrassed, miserable.*) My father gave me that! You didn't give it to me. You have no right. Let go of it . . . you hear?

74 (Mr. Van Daan *pulls the coat from her hands and hurries downstairs.* Mrs. Van Daan *sinks to the floor, sobbing.* As Mr. Van Daan *comes into the main room the others look away, embarrassed for him.*)

75 **Mr. Van Daan** (*to* Mr. Kraler). Just a little—discussion over the advisability of selling this coat. As I have often reminded Mrs. Van Daan, it's very selfish of her to keep it when people outside are in such desperate need of clothing . . . (*He gives the coat to* Miep.) So if you will please to sell it for us? It should fetch a good price. And by the way, will you get me cigarettes. I don't care what kind they are . . . get all you can.

76 **Miep.** It's terribly difficult to get them, Mr. Van Daan. But I'll try. Good-bye.

77 (*She goes.* Mr. Frank *follows her down the steps to bolt the door after her.* Mrs. Frank *gives* Mr. Kraler *a cup of tea.*)

78 **Mrs. Frank.** Are you sure you won't have some cake, Mr. Kraler?

79 **Mr. Kraler.** I'd better not.

80 **Mr. Van Daan.** You're still feeling badly? What does your doctor say?

81 **Mr. Kraler.** I haven't been to him.

82 **Mrs. Frank.** Now, Mr. Kraler! . . .

83 **Mr. Kraler** (*sitting at the table*). Oh, I tried. But you can't get near a doctor these days . . . they're so busy. After weeks I finally managed to get one on the telephone. I told him I'd like an appointment . . . I wasn't feeling very well. You know what he answers . . . over the telephone . . . Stick out your tongue! (*They laugh. He turns to* Mr. Frank *as* Mr. Frank *comes back.*) I have some contracts here . . . I wonder if you'd look over them with me . . .

84 **Mr. Frank** (*putting out his hand*). Of course.

85 **Mr. Kraler** (*He rises*). If we could go downstairs . . . (Mr. Frank *starts ahead,* Mr. Kraler *speaks to the others.*) Will you forgive

Don't forget to **Notice & Note** as you read the text.

us? I won't keep him but a minute. (*He starts to follow* Mr. Frank *down the steps.*)

86 **Margot** (*with sudden foreboding*). What's happened? Something's happened! Hasn't it, Mr. Kraler?

87 (Mr. Kraler *stops and comes back, trying to reassure* Margot *with a pretense of casualness.*)

88 **Mr. Kraler.** No, really. I want your father's advice . . .

89 **Margot.** Something's gone wrong! I know it!

90 **Mr. Frank** (*coming back, to* Mr. Kraler). If it's something that concerns us here, it's better that we all hear it.

91 **Mr. Kraler** (*turning to him, quietly*). But . . . the children . . . ?

92 **Mr. Frank.** What they'd imagine would be worse than any reality.

93 (*As* Mr. Kraler *speaks, they all listen with intense apprehension.* Mrs. Van Daan *comes down the stairs and sits on the bottom step.*)

ANALYZE DRAMA

Annotate: Mark the incident that Mr. Kraler tells the group about in paragraphs 94–96.

Analyze: What decision does this incident force the characters to make?

94 **Mr. Kraler.** It's a man in the storeroom . . . I don't know whether or not you remember him . . . Carl, about fifty, heavy-set, near-sighted . . . He came with us just before you left.

95 **Mr. Frank.** He was from Utrecht?

96 **Mr. Kraler.** That's the man. A couple of weeks ago, when I was in the storeroom, he closed the door and asked me . . . how's Mr. Frank? What do you hear from Mr. Frank? I told him I only knew there was a rumor that you were in Switzerland. He said he'd heard that rumor too, but he thought I might know something more. I didn't pay any attention to it . . . but then a thing happened yesterday . . . He'd brought some invoices to the office for me to sign. As I was going through them, I looked up. He was standing staring at the bookcase . . . your bookcase. He said he thought he remembered a door there . . . Wasn't there a door there that used to go up to the loft? Then he told me he wanted more money. Twenty guilders[1] more a week.

97 **Mr. Van Daan.** Blackmail!

98 **Mr. Frank.** Twenty guilders? Very modest blackmail.

99 **Mr. Van Daan.** That's just the beginning.

100 **Dussel** (*coming to* Mr. Frank). You know what I think? He was the thief who was down there that night. That's how he knows we're here.

[1] **guilders** (gĭl´dərz): the basic monetary unit of the Netherlands at the time.

Don't forget to **Notice & Note** as you read the text.

101 **Mr. Frank** (*to* Mr. Kraler). How was it left? What did you tell him?

102 **Mr. Kraler.** I said I had to think about it. What shall I do? Pay him the money? . . Take a chance on firing him . . . or what? I don't know.

103 **Dussel** (*frantic*). For God's sake don't fire him! Pay him what he asks . . . keep him here where you can have your eye on him.

104 **Mr. Frank.** Is it so much that he's asking? What are they paying nowadays?

105 **Mr. Kraler.** He could get it in a war plant. But this isn't a war plant. Mind you, I don't know if he really knows . . . or if he doesn't know.

106 **Mr. Frank.** Offer him half. Then we'll soon find out if it's blackmail or not.

107 **Dussel.** And if it is? We've got to pay it, haven't we? Anything he asks we've got to pay!

108 **Mr. Frank.** Let's decide that when the time comes.

109 **Mr. Kraler.** This may be all my imagination. You get to a point, these days, where you suspect everyone and everything. Again and again . . . on some simple look or word, I've found myself . . . (*The telephone rings in the office below.*)

110 **Mrs. Van Daan** (*hurrying to* Mr. Kraler). There's the telephone! What does that mean, the telephone ringing on a holiday?

111 **Mr. Kraler.** That's my wife. I told her I had to go over some papers in my office . . . to call me there when she got out of church. (*He starts out.*) I'll offer him half then. Good-bye . . . we'll hope for the best!

112 (*The group call their good-byes half-heartedly.* Mr. Frank *follows* Mr. Kraler, *to bolt the door below. During the following scene,* Mr. Frank *comes back up and stands listening, disturbed.*)

113 **Dussel** (*to* Mr. Van Daan). You can thank your son for this . . . smashing the light! I tell you, it's just a question of time now. (*He goes to the window at the back and stands looking out.*)

114 **Margot.** Sometimes I wish the end would come . . . whatever it is.

115 **Mrs. Frank** (*shocked*). Margot!

116 (Anne *goes to* Margot, *sitting beside her on the couch with her arms around her.*)

117 **Margot.** Then at least we'd know where we were.

118 **Mrs. Frank.** You should be ashamed of yourself! Talking that way! Think how lucky we are! Think of the thousands dying in the war, every day. Think of the people in concentration camps.

119 **Anne** (*interrupting*). What's the good of that? What's the good of thinking of misery when you're already miserable? That's stupid!

120 **Mrs. Frank.** Anne!

121 (*As* Anne *goes on raging at her mother,* Mrs. Frank *tries to break in, in an effort to quiet her.*)

122 **Anne.** We're young, Margot and Peter and I! You grownups have had your chance! But look at us . . . If we begin thinking of all the horror in the world, we're lost! We're trying to hold onto some kind of ideals . . . when everything . . . ideals, hopes . . . everything, are being destroyed! It isn't our fault that the world is in such a mess! We weren't around when all this started! So don't try to take it out on us!

123 (*She rushes off to her room, slamming the door after her. She picks up a brush from the chest and hurls it to the floor. Then she sits on the settee, trying to control her anger.*)

124 **Mr. Van Daan.** She talks as if we started the war! Did we start the war? (*He spots* Anne's *cake. As he starts to take it,* Peter *anticipates him.*)

ANALYZE DRAMA

Annotate: In paragraphs 125–128, mark details in the stage directions and dialogue that reveal Peter's changing feelings toward Anne.

Infer: What do you infer from Peter's actions and words?

125 **Peter.** She left her cake. (*He starts for* Anne's *room with the cake. There is silence in the main room.* Mrs. Van Daan *goes up to her room, followed by* Van Daan. Dussel *stays looking out the window.* Mr. Frank *brings* Mrs. Frank *her cake. She eats it slowly, without relish.* Mr. Frank *takes his cake to* Margot *and sits quietly on the sofa beside her.* Peter *stands in the doorway of* Anne's *darkened room, looking at her, then makes a little movement to let her know he is there.* Anne *sits up, quickly, trying to hide the signs of her tears.* Peter *holds out the cake to her.*) You left this.

126 **Anne** (*dully*). Thanks.

127 (Peter *starts to go out, then comes back.*)

128 **Peter.** I thought you were fine just now. You know just how to talk to them. You know just how to say it. I'm no good . . . I never can think . . . especially when I'm mad . . . That Dussel . . . when he said that about Mouschi . . . someone eating him . . . all I could think is . . . I wanted to hit him. I wanted to give him such a . . . a . . . that he'd . . . That's what I used to do when there was an argument at school . . . That's the way I . . . but here . . . And an old man like that . . . it wouldn't be so good.

Don't forget to **Notice & Note** as you read the text.

129 **Anne.** You're making a big mistake about me. I do it all wrong. I say too much. I go too far. I hurt people's feelings . . .

130 (Dussel *leaves the window, going to his room.*)

131 **Peter.** I think you're just fine . . . What I want to say . . . if it wasn't for you around here, I don't know. What I mean . . .

132 (Peter *is interrupted by* Dussel's *turning on the light.* Dussel *stands in the doorway, startled to see* Peter. Peter *advances toward him forbiddingly.* Dussel *backs out of the room.* Peter *closes the door on him.*)

133 **Anne.** Do you mean it, Peter? Do you really mean it?

134 **Peter.** I said it, didn't I?

135 **Anne.** Thank you, Peter!

136 (*In the main room* Mr. *and* Mrs. Frank *collect the dishes and take them to the sink, washing them.* Margot *lies down again on the couch.* Dussel, *lost, wanders into* Peter's *room and takes up a book, starting to read.*)

137 **Peter** (*looking at the photographs on the wall*). You've got quite a collection.

138 **Anne.** Wouldn't you like some in your room? I could give you some. Heaven knows you spend enough time in there . . . doing heaven knows what . . .

139 **Peter.** It's easier. A fight starts, or an argument . . . I duck in there.

140 **Anne.** You're lucky, having a room to go to. His lordship is always here . . . I hardly ever get a minute alone. When they start in on me, I can't duck away. I have to stand there and take it.

141 **Peter.** You gave some of it back just now.

142 **Anne.** I get so mad. They've formed their opinions . . . about everything . . . but we . . . we're still trying to find out . . . We have problems here that no other people our age have ever had. And just as you think you've solved them, something comes along and bang! You have to start all over again.

ANALYZE DRAMA

Annotate: In paragraphs 143–146, mark details in the dialogue that reveal Anne's relationship with her mother. Then mark details that reveal her relationship with her father.

Compare: Contrast these two relationships. Why do you think Anne has such different relationships with her father and mother?

143 **Peter.** At least you've got someone you can talk to.

144 **Anne.** Not really. Mother . . . I never discuss anything serious with her. She doesn't understand. Father's all right. We can talk about everything . . . everything but one thing. Mother. He simply won't talk about her. I don't think you can be really intimate with anyone if he holds something back, do you?

145 **Peter.** I think your father's fine.

146 **Anne.** Oh, he is, Peter! He is! He's the only one who's ever given me the feeling that I have any sense. But anyway, nothing can take the place of school and play and friends of your own age . . . or near your age . . . can it?

147 **Peter.** I suppose you miss your friends and all.

148 **Anne.** It isn't just . . . (*She breaks off, staring up at him for a second.*) Isn't it funny, you and I? Here we've been seeing each other every minute for almost a year and a half, and this is the first time we've ever really talked. It helps a lot to have someone to talk to, don't you think? It helps you to let off steam.

149 **Peter** (*going to the door*). Well, any time you want to let off steam, you can come into my room.

Don't forget to **Notice & Note** as you read the text.

150 **Anne** (*following him*). I can get up an awful lot of steam. You'll have to be careful how you say that.

151 **Peter.** It's all right with me.

152 **Anne.** Do you mean it?

153 **Peter.** I said it, didn't I?

154 (*He goes out.* Anne *stands in her doorway looking after him. As* Peter *gets to his door he stands for a minute looking back at her. Then he goes into his room.* Dussel *rises as he comes in, and quickly passes him, going out. He starts across for his room.* Anne *sees him coming, and pulls her door shut.* Dussel *turns back toward* Peter's *room.* Peter *pulls his door shut.* Dussel *stands there, bewildered, forlorn.*

155 *The scene slowly dims out. The curtain falls on the scene.* Anne's Voice *comes over in the darkness . . . faintly at first, and then with growing strength.*)

156 **Anne's Voice.** We've had bad news. The people from whom Miep got our ration books have been arrested. So we have had to cut down on our food. Our stomachs are so empty that they rumble and make strange noises, all in different keys. Mr. Van Daan's is deep and low, like a bass fiddle. Mine is high, whistling like a flute. As we all sit around waiting for supper, it's like an orchestra tuning up. It only needs Toscanini[2] to raise his baton and we'd be off in the Ride of the Valkyries.[3] Monday, the sixth of March, nineteen forty-four. Mr. Kraler is in the hospital. It seems he has ulcers. Pim says we are his ulcers. Miep has to run the business and us too. The Americans have landed on the southern tip of Italy. Father looks for a quick finish to the war. Mr. Dussel is waiting every day for the warehouse man to demand more money. Have I been skipping too much from one subject to another? I can't help it. I feel that spring is coming. I feel it in my whole body and soul. I feel utterly confused. I am longing . . . so longing . . . for everything . . . for friends . . . for someone to talk to . . . someone who understands . . . someone young, who feels as I do . . .

157 (*As these last lines are being said, the curtain rises on the scene. The lights dim on.* Anne's Voice *fades out.*)

[2] **Toscanini** (tŏs´kə-nē´nē): Arturo Toscanini, a famous Italian orchestral conductor.

[3] **Ride of the Valkyries** (văl-kîr´əz): an exciting passage from an opera by Richard Wagner, a German composer.

Scene 2

158 *It is evening, after supper. From outside we hear the sound of children playing. The "grownups," with the exception of* Mr. Van Daan, *are all in the main room.* Mrs. Frank *is doing some mending,* Mrs. Van Daan *is reading a fashion magazine.* Mr. Frank *is going over business accounts.* Dussel, *in his dentist's jacket, is pacing up and down, impatient to get into his bedroom.* Mr. Van Daan *is upstairs working on a piece of embroidery in an embroidery frame.*

159 *In his room* Peter *is sitting before the mirror, smoothing his hair. As the scene goes on, he puts on his tie, brushes his coat and puts it on, preparing himself meticulously for a visit from* Anne. *On his wall are now hung some of* Anne's *motion picture stars.*

160 *In her room* Anne *too is getting dressed. She stands before the mirror in her slip, trying various ways of dressing her hair.* Margot *is seated on the sofa, hemming a skirt for* Anne *to wear.*

161 *In the main room* Dussel *can stand it no longer. He comes over, rapping sharply on the door of his and* Anne's *bedroom.*

ANALYZE DRAMA

Annotate: Mark details in paragraphs 159–161 that reveal what Peter and Anne are doing at the beginning of Scene 2.

Predict: What do these stage directions suggest will happen next? Why did the playwrights choose to include those details about Peter and Anne?

162 **Anne** (*calling to him*). No, no, Mr. Dussel! I am not dressed yet. (Dussel *walks away, furious, sitting down and burying his head in his hands.* Anne *turns to* Margot.) How is that? How does that look?

163 **Margot** (*glancing at her briefly*). Fine.

164 **Anne.** You didn't even look.

165 **Margot.** Of course I did. It's fine.

166 **Anne.** Margot, tell me, am I terribly ugly?

167 **Margot.** Oh, stop fishing.

168 **Anne.** No. No. Tell me.

169 **Margot.** Of course you're not. You've got nice eyes . . . and a lot of animation, and . . .

170 **Anne.** A little vague, aren't you?

171 (*She reaches over and takes a brassière out of* Margot's *sewing basket. She holds it up to herself, studying the effect in the mirror. Outside,* Mrs. Frank, *feeling sorry for* Dussel, *comes over, knocking at the girls' door.*)

172 **Mrs. Frank** (*outside*). May I come in?

173 **Margot.** Come in, Mother.

174 **Mrs. Frank** (*shutting the door behind her*). Mr. Dussel's impatient to get in here.

175 **Anne** (*still with the brassière*). Heavens, he takes the room for himself the entire day.

176 **Mrs. Frank** (*gently*). Anne, dear, you're not going in again tonight to see Peter?

177 **Anne** (*dignified*). That is my intention.

178 **Mrs. Frank.** But you've already spent a great deal of time in there today.

179 **Anne.** I was in there exactly twice. Once to get the dictionary, and then three-quarters of an hour before supper.

180 **Mrs. Frank.** Aren't you afraid you're disturbing him?

181 **Anne.** Mother, I have some intuition.

182 **Mrs. Frank.** Then may I ask you this much, Anne. Please don't shut the door when you go in.

183 **Anne.** You sound like Mrs. Van Daan! (*She throws the brassière back in* Margot's *sewing basket and picks up her blouse, putting it on.*)

184 **Mrs. Frank.** No. No. I don't mean to suggest anything wrong. I only wish that you wouldn't expose yourself to criticism . . . that you wouldn't give Mrs. Van Daan the opportunity to be unpleasant.

185 **Anne.** Mrs. Van Daan doesn't need an opportunity to be unpleasant!

186 **Mrs. Frank.** Everyone's on edge, worried about Mr. Kraler. This is one more thing . . .

187 **Anne.** I'm sorry, Mother. I'm going to Peter's room. I'm not going to let Petronella Van Daan spoil our friendship.

188 (Mrs. Frank *hesitates for a second, then goes out, closing the door after her. She gets a pack of playing cards and sits at the center table, playing solitaire. In* Anne's *room* Margot *hands the finished skirt to* Anne. *As* Anne *is putting it on,* Margot *takes off her high-heeled shoes and stuffs paper in the toes so that* Anne *can wear them.*)

189 **Margot** (*to* Anne). Why don't you two talk in the main room? It'd save a lot of trouble. It's hard on Mother, having to listen to those remarks from Mrs. Van Daan and not say a word.

190 **Anne.** Why doesn't she say a word? I think it's ridiculous to take it and take it.

Don't forget to **Notice & Note** as you read the text.

NOTICE & NOTE
WORDS OF THE WISER

When you notice a wiser character giving advice about life to the main character, you've found a **Words of the Wiser** signpost.

Notice & Note: In paragraphs 189–191, mark the explanation Margot gives Anne for why Mrs. Frank doesn't react to Mrs. Van Daan's remarks.

Infer: What's the life lesson for Anne, and how might it affect her?

191 **Margot.** You don't understand Mother at all, do you? She can't talk back. She's not like you. It's just not in her nature to fight back.

192 **Anne.** Anyway . . . the only one I worry about is you. I feel awfully guilty about you.

193 (*She sits on the stool near* Margot, *putting on* Margot's *high-heeled shoes.*)

194 **Margot.** What about?

195 **Anne.** I mean, every time I go into Peter's room, I have a feeling I may be hurting you. (Margot *shakes her head.*) I know if it were me, I'd be wild. I'd be desperately jealous, if it were me.

196 **Margot.** Well, I'm not.

197 **Anne.** You don't feel badly? Really? Truly? You're not jealous?

198 **Margot.** Of course I'm jealous . . . jealous that you've got something to get up in the morning for . . . But jealous of you and Peter? No.

199 (Anne *goes back to the mirror.*)

200 **Anne.** Maybe there's nothing to be jealous of. Maybe he doesn't really like me. Maybe I'm just taking the place of his cat . . . (*She picks up a pair of short white gloves, putting them on.*) Wouldn't you like to come in with us?

201 **Margot.** I have a book.

202 (*The sound of the children playing outside fades out. In the main room* Dussel *can stand it no longer. He jumps up, going to the bedroom door and knocking sharply.*)

203 **Dussel.** Will you please let me in my room!

204 **Anne.** Just a minute, dear, dear Mr. Dussel. (*She picks up her Mother's pink stole and adjusts it elegantly over her shoulders, then gives a last look in the mirror.*) Well, here I go . . . to run the gauntlet.[4] (*She starts out, followed by* Margot.)

205 **Dussel** (*as she appears—sarcastic*). Thank you so much.

206 (Dussel *goes into his room.* Anne *goes toward* Peter's *room, passing* Mrs. Van Daan *and her parents at the center table.*)

207 **Mrs. Van Daan.** My God, look at her! (Anne *pays no attention. She knocks at* Peter's *door.*) I don't know what good it is to have a son. I never see him. He wouldn't care if I killed myself. (Peter *opens the door and stands aside for* Anne *to come in.*) Just

[4] **to run the gauntlet:** to endure a series of troubles or difficulties.

a minute, Anne. (*She goes to them at the door.*) I'd like to say a few words to my son. Do you mind? (Peter *and* Anne *stand waiting.*) Peter, I don't want you staying up till all hours tonight. You've got to have your sleep. You're a growing boy. You hear?

Don't forget to **Notice & Note** as you read the text.

208 **Mrs. Frank.** Anne won't stay late. She's going to bed promptly at nine. Aren't you, Anne?

209 **Anne.** Yes, Mother . . . (*to* Mrs. Van Daan) May we go now?

210 **Mrs. Van Daan.** Are you asking me? I didn't know I had anything to say about it.

211 **Mrs. Frank.** Listen for the chimes, Anne dear.

212 (*The two young people go off into* Peter's *room, shutting the door after them.*)

213 **Mrs. Van Daan** (*to* Mrs. Frank). In my day it was the boys who called on the girls. Not the girls on the boys.

214 **Mrs. Frank.** You know how young people like to feel that they have secrets. Peter's room is the only place where they can talk.

215 **Mrs. Van Daan.** Talk! That's not what they called it when I was young.

216 (Mrs. Van Daan *goes off to the bathroom.* Margot *settles down to read her book.* Mr. Frank *puts his papers away and brings a chess game to the center table. He and* Mrs. Frank *start to play. In* Peter's *room,* Anne *speaks to* Peter, *indignant, humiliated.*)

217 **Anne.** Aren't they awful? Aren't they impossible? Treating us as if we were still in the nursery.

218 (*She sits on the cot.* Peter *gets a bottle of pop and two glasses.*)

219 **Peter.** Don't let it bother you. It doesn't bother me.

220 **Anne.** I suppose you can't really blame them . . . they think back to what *they* were like at our age. They don't realize how much more advanced we are . . . When you think what wonderful discussions we've had! . . . Oh, I forgot. I was going to bring you some more pictures.

221 **Peter.** Oh, these are fine, thanks.

222 **Anne.** Don't you want some more? Miep just brought me some new ones.

223 **Peter.** Maybe later. (*He gives her a glass of pop and, taking some for himself, sits down facing her.*)

NOTICE & NOTE
MEMORY MOMENT

When you notice the narrator has interrupted the forward progress of a story by bringing up something from the past, you've found a **Memory Moment** signpost.

Notice & Note: Mark the memories that Anne has as she looks at the photos that Miep brought her.

Interpret: Why might these memories be important?

224 **Anne** (*looking up at one of the photographs*). I remember when I got that . . . I won it. I bet Jopie that I could eat five ice-cream cones. We'd all been playing ping-pong . . . We used to have heavenly times . . . we'd finish up with ice cream at the Delphi, or the Oasis, where Jews were allowed . . . there'd always be a lot of boys . . . we'd laugh and joke . . . I'd like to go back to it for a few days or a week. But after that I know I'd be bored to death. I think more seriously about life now. I want to be a journalist . . . or something. I love to write. What do you want to do?

225 **Peter.** I thought I might go off some place . . . work on a farm or something . . . some job that doesn't take much brains.

226 **Anne.** You shouldn't talk that way. You've got the most awful inferiority complex.

227 **Peter.** I know I'm not smart.

228 **Anne.** That isn't true. You're much better than I am in dozens of things . . . arithmetic and algebra and . . . well, you're a million times better than I am in algebra. (*with sudden directness*) You like Margot, don't you? Right from the start you liked her, liked her much better than me.

229 **Peter** (*uncomfortably*). Oh, I don't know.

230 (*In the main room* Mrs. Van Daan *comes from the bathroom and goes over to the sink, polishing a coffee pot.*)

231 **Anne.** It's all right. Everyone feels that way. Margot's so good. She's sweet and bright and beautiful and I'm not.

232 **Peter.** I wouldn't say that.

233 **Anne.** Oh, no, I'm not. I know that. I know quite well that I'm not a beauty. I never have been and never shall be.

234 **Peter.** I don't agree at all. I think you're pretty.

235 **Anne.** That's not true!

236 **Peter.** And another thing. You've changed . . . from at first, I mean.

237 **Anne.** I have?

238 **Peter.** I used to think you were awful noisy.

239 **Anne.** And what do you think now, Peter? How have I changed?

240 **Peter.** Well . . . er . . . you're . . . quieter.

241 (*In his room* Dussel *takes his pajamas and toilet articles and goes into the bathroom to change.*)

Don't forget to **Notice & Note** as you read the text.

242 **Anne.** I'm glad you don't just hate me.

243 **Peter.** I never said that.

244 **Anne.** I bet when you get out of here you'll never think of me again.

245 **Peter.** That's crazy.

246 **Anne.** When you get back with all of your friends, you're going to say . . . now what did I ever see in that Mrs. Quack Quack.

247 **Peter.** I haven't got any friends.

248 **Anne.** Oh, Peter, of course you have. Everyone has friends.

249 **Peter.** Not me. I don't want any. I get along all right without them.

250 **Anne.** Does that mean you can get along without me? I think of myself as your friend.

251 **Peter.** No. If they were all like you, it'd be different.

252 (*He takes the glasses and the bottle and puts them away. There is a second's silence and then* Anne *speaks, hesitantly, shyly.*)

253 **Anne.** Peter, did you ever kiss a girl?

254 **Peter.** Yes. Once.

255 **Anne** (*to cover her feelings*). That picture's crooked. (Peter *goes over, straightening the photograph.*) Was she pretty?

256 **Peter.** Huh?

257 **Anne.** The girl that you kissed.

258 **Peter.** I don't know. I was blindfolded. (*He comes back and sits down again.*) It was at a party. One of those kissing games.

259 **Anne** (*relieved*). Oh. I don't suppose that really counts, does it?

260 **Peter.** It didn't with me.

261 **Anne.** I've been kissed twice. Once a man I'd never seen before kissed me on the cheek when he picked me up off the ice and I was crying. And the other was Mr. Koophuis, a friend of Father's who kissed my hand. You wouldn't say those counted, would you?

262 **Peter.** I wouldn't say so.

263 **Anne.** I know almost for certain that Margot would never kiss anyone unless she was engaged to them. And I'm sure too that Mother never touched a man before Pim. But I don't know . . . things are so different now . . . What do you think? Do

you think a girl shouldn't kiss anyone except if she's engaged or something? It's so hard to try to think what to do, when here we are with the whole world falling around our ears and you think . . . well . . . you don't know what's going to happen tomorrow and . . . What do you think?

264 **Peter.** I suppose it'd depend on the girl. Some girls, anything they do's wrong. But others . . . well . . . it wouldn't necessarily be wrong with them. (*The carillon starts to strike nine o'clock.*) I've always thought that when two people . . .

265 **Anne.** Nine o'clock. I have to go.

266 **Peter.** That's right.

267 **Anne** (*without moving*). Good night.

268 (*There is a second's pause, then* Peter *gets up and moves toward the door.*)

269 **Peter.** You won't let them stop you coming?

270 **Anne.** No. (*She rises and starts for the door.*) Sometime I might bring my diary. There are so many things in it that I want to talk over with you. There's a lot about you.

271 **Peter.** What kind of things?

ANALYZE DRAMA

Annotate: Reread paragraphs 253–264 and mark what Anne and Peter conclude about whether their previous kisses counted.

Infer: What are Anne and Peter trying to determine in this conversation? Can you infer what they both actually want?

272 **Anne.** I wouldn't want you to see some of it. I thought you were a nothing, just the way you thought about me.

273 **Peter.** Did you change your mind, the way I changed my mind about you?

274 **Anne.** Well . . . You'll see . . .

275 (*For a second* Anne *stands looking up at* Peter, *longing for him to kiss her. As he makes no move she turns away. Then suddenly* Peter *grabs her awkwardly in his arms, kissing her on the cheek.* Anne *walks out dazed. She stands for a minute, her back to the people in the main room. As she regains her poise she goes to her mother and father and* Margot, *silently kissing them. They murmur their good nights to her. As she is about to open her bedroom door, she catches sight of* Mrs. Van Daan. *She goes quickly to her, taking her face in her hands and kissing her first on one cheek and then on the other. Then she hurries off into her room.* Mrs. Van Daan *looks after her, and then looks over at* Peter's *room. Her suspicions are confirmed.*)

276 **Mrs. Van Daan** (*She knows*). Ah hah!

277 (*The lights dim out. The curtain falls on the scene. In the darkness* Anne's Voice *comes faintly at first and then with growing strength.*)

278 **Anne's Voice.** By this time we all know each other so well that if anyone starts to tell a story, the rest can finish it for him. We're having to cut down still further on our meals. What makes it worse, the rats have been at work again. They've carried off some of our precious food. Even Mr. Dussel wishes now that Mouschi was here. Thursday, the twentieth of April, nineteen forty-four. Invasion fever is mounting every day. Miep tells us that people outside talk of nothing else. For myself, life has become much more pleasant. I often go to Peter's room after supper. Oh, don't think I'm in love, because I'm not. But it does make life more bearable to have someone with whom you can exchange views. No more tonight. P.S. . . . I must be honest. I must confess that I actually live for the next meeting. Is there anything lovelier than to sit under the skylight and feel the sun on your cheeks and have a darling boy in your arms? I admit now that I'm glad the Van Daans had a son and not a daughter. I've outgrown another dress. That's the third. I'm having to wear Margot's clothes after all. I'm working hard on my French and am now reading *La Belle Nivernaise.*

279 (*As she is saying the last lines—the curtain rises on the scene. The lights dim on, as* Anne's Voice *fades out.*)

Don't forget to **Notice & Note** as you read the text.

Scene 3

ANALYZE DRAMA

Annotate: In paragraphs 280–299, mark details in the stage directions and dialogue that introduce a new conflict to the drama.

Connect: What conflict arises in this scene? What event earlier in the play foreshadowed this conflict?

280 *It is night, a few weeks later. Everyone is in bed. There is complete quiet. In the* Van Daans' *room a match flares up for a moment and then is quickly put out.* Mr. Van Daan, *in bare feet, dressed in underwear and trousers, is dimly seen coming stealthily down the stairs and into the main room, where* Mr. *and* Mrs. Frank *and* Margot *are sleeping. He goes to the food safe and again lights a match. Then he cautiously opens the safe, taking out a half-loaf of bread. As he closes the safe, it creaks. He stands rigid.* Mrs. Frank *sits up in bed. She sees him.*

281 **Mrs. Frank** (*screaming*). Otto! Otto! *Komme schnell!*[5]

282 (*The rest of the people wake, hurriedly getting up.*)

283 **Mr. Frank.** *Was ist los? Was ist passiert?*[6]

284 (Dussel, *followed by* Anne, *comes from his room.*)

285 **Mrs. Frank** (*as she rushes over to* Mr. Van Daan). *Er stiehlt das Essen!*[7]

286 **Dussel** (*grabbing* Mr. Van Daan). You! You! Give me that.

287 **Mrs. Van Daan** (*coming down the stairs*). Putti . . . Putti . . . what is it?

288 **Dussel** (*his hands on* Van Daan's *neck*). You dirty thief . . . stealing food . . . you good-for-nothing . . .

289 **Mr. Frank.** Mr. Dussel! For God's sake! Help me, Peter!

290 (Peter *comes over, trying, with* Mr. Frank, *to separate the two struggling men.*)

291 **Peter.** Let him go! Let go!

292 (Dussel *drops* Mr. Van Daan, *pushing him away. He shows them the end of a loaf of bread that he has taken from* Van Daan.)

293 **Dussel.** You greedy, selfish . . . !

294 (Margot *turns on the lights.*)

295 **Mrs. Van Daan.** Putti . . . what is it?

296 (*All of* Mrs. Frank's *gentleness, her self-control, is gone. She is outraged, in a frenzy of indignation.*)

297 **Mrs. Frank.** The bread! He was stealing the bread!

[5] ***Komme schnell!*** (kôm´e shnĕl´) *German:* Come quickly!
[6] ***Was ist los? Was ist passiert?*** (väs ĭst lôs´? väs ĭst pä-sērt´?) *German:* What's the matter? What has happened?
[7] ***Er stiehlt das Essen!*** (ĕr shtēlt´ däs ĕs´ən) *German:* He is stealing food!

298 **Dussel.** It was you, and all the time we thought it was the rats!

299 **Mr. Frank.** Mr. Van Daan, how could you!

300 **Mr. Van Daan.** I'm hungry.

301 **Mrs. Frank.** We're all of us hungry! I see the children getting thinner and thinner. Your own son Peter . . . I've heard him moan in his sleep, he's so hungry. And you come in the night and steal food that should go to them . . . to the children!

302 **Mrs. Van Daan** (*going to* Mr. Van Daan *protectively*). He needs more food than the rest of us. He's used to more. He's a big man.

303 (Mr. Van Daan *breaks away, going over and sitting on the couch.*)

304 **Mrs. Frank** (*turning on* Mrs. Van Daan). And you . . . you're worse than he is! You're a mother, and yet you sacrifice your child to this man . . . this . . . this . . .

305 **Mr. Frank.** Edith! Edith!

306 (Margot *picks up the pink woolen stole, putting it over her mother's shoulders.*)

307 **Mrs. Frank** (*paying no attention, going on to* Mrs. Van Daan). Don't think I haven't seen you! Always saving the choicest bits for him! I've watched you day after day and I've held my tongue. But not any longer! Not after this! Now I want him to go! I want him to get out of here!

308 **Mr. Frank.** Edith!

309 **Mr. Van Daan.** Get out of here?

} *Together*

310 **Mrs. Van Daan.** What do you mean?

311 **Mrs. Frank.** Just that! Take your things and get out!

312 **Mr. Frank** (*to* Mrs. Frank). You're speaking in anger. You cannot mean what you are saying.

313 **Mrs. Frank.** I mean exactly that!

314 (Mrs. Van Daan *takes a cover from the* Franks' *bed, pulling it about her.*)

315 **Mr. Frank.** For two long years we have lived here, side by side. We have respected each other's rights . . . we have managed to live in peace. Are we now going to throw it all away? I know this will never happen again, will it, Mr. Van Daan?

316 **Mr. Van Daan.** No. No.

317 **Mrs. Frank.** He steals once! He'll steal again!

Don't forget to **Notice & Note** as you read the text.

NOTICE & NOTE

CONTRASTS AND CONTRADICTIONS

When you notice behavior that contradicts a character's previous behavior, you've found a **Contrasts and Contradictions** signpost.

Notice & Note: In paragraphs 301–313, mark dialogue that contradicts how you would expect Mrs. Frank to act.

Analyze: Why would Mrs. Frank act this way?

318 (Mr. Van Daan, *holding his stomach, starts for the bathroom.* Anne *puts her arms around him, helping him up the step.*)

319 **Mr. Frank.** Edith, please. Let us be calm. We'll all go to our rooms . . . and afterwards we'll sit down quietly and talk this out . . . we'll find some way . . .

320 **Mrs. Frank.** No! No! No more talk! I want them to leave!

321 **Mrs. Van Daan.** You'd put us out, on the streets?

322 **Mrs. Frank.** There are other hiding places.

323 **Mrs. Van Daan.** A cellar . . . a closet. I know. And we have no money left even to pay for that.

324 **Mrs. Frank.** I'll give you money. Out of my own pocket I'll give it gladly. (*She gets her purse from a shelf and comes back with it.*)

325 **Mrs. Van Daan.** Mr. Frank, you told Putti you'd never forget what he'd done for you when you came to Amsterdam. You said you could never repay him, that you . . .

326 **Mrs. Frank** (*counting out money*). If my husband had any obligation to you, he's paid it, over and over.

327 **Mr. Frank.** Edith, I've never seen you like this before. I don't know you.

328 **Mrs. Frank.** I should have spoken out long ago.

329 **Dussel.** You can't be nice to some people.

330 **Mrs. Van Daan** (*turning on* Dussel). There would have been plenty for all of us, if you hadn't come in here!

331 **Mr. Frank.** We don't need the Nazis to destroy us. We're destroying ourselves.

332 (*He sits down, with his head in his hands.* Mrs. Frank *goes to* Mrs. Van Daan.)

333 **Mrs. Frank** (*giving* Mrs. Van Daan *some money*). Give this to Miep. She'll find you a place.

334 **Anne.** Mother, you're not putting *Peter* out. Peter hasn't done anything.

335 **Mrs. Frank.** He'll stay, of course. When I say I must protect the children, I mean Peter too.

336 (Peter *rises from the steps where he has been sitting.*)

337 **Peter.** I'd have to go if Father goes.

338 (Mr. Van Daan *comes from the bathroom.* Mrs. Van Daan *hurries to him and takes him to the couch. Then she gets water from the sink to bathe his face.*)

339 **Mrs. Frank** (*while this is going on*). He's no father to you . . . that man! He doesn't know what it is to be a father!

340 **Peter** (*starting for his room*). I wouldn't feel right. I couldn't stay.

341 **Mrs. Frank.** Very well, then. I'm sorry.

342 **Anne** (*rushing over to* Peter). No, Peter! No! (Peter *goes into his room, closing the door after him.* Anne *turns back to her mother, crying.*) I don't care about the food. They can have mine! I don't want it! Only don't send them away. It'll be daylight soon. They'll be caught . . .

343 **Margot** (*putting her arms comfortingly around* Anne). Please, Mother!

344 **Mrs. Frank.** They're not going now. They'll stay here until Miep finds them a place. (*to* Mrs. Van Daan) But one thing I insist on! He must never come down here again! He must never come to this room where the food is stored! We'll divide what we have . . . an equal share for each! (Dussel *hurries over to get a sack of potatoes from the food safe.* Mrs. Frank *goes on, to* Mrs. Van Daan.) You can cook it here and take it up to him.

345 (Dussel *brings the sack of potatoes back to the center table.*)

346 **Margot.** Oh, no. No. We haven't sunk so far that we're going to fight over a handful of rotten potatoes.

347 **Dussel** (*dividing the potatoes into piles*). Mrs. Frank, Mr. Frank, Margot, Anne, Peter, Mrs. Van Daan, Mr. Van Daan, myself . . . Mrs. Frank . . .

348 (*The buzzer sounds in Miep's signal.*)

349 **Mr. Frank.** It's Miep! (*He hurries over, getting his overcoat and putting it on.*)

350 **Margot.** At this hour?

351 **Mrs. Frank.** It is trouble.

352 **Mr. Frank** (*as he starts down to unbolt the door*). I beg you, don't let her see a thing like this!

353 **Mr. Dussel** (*counting without stopping*). . . . Anne, Peter, Mrs. Van Daan, Mr. Van Daan, myself . . .

Don't forget to **Notice & Note** as you read the text.

354 **Margot** (*to Dussel*). Stop it! Stop it!

355 **Dussel.** . . . Mr. Frank, Margot, Anne, Peter, Mrs. Van Daan, Mr. Van Daan, myself, Mrs. Frank . . .

356 **Mrs. Van Daan.** You're keeping the big ones for yourself! All the big ones . . . Look at the size of that! . . . And that! . . .

357 (Dussel *continues on with his dividing.* Peter, *with his shirt and trousers on, comes from his room.*)

358 **Margot.** Stop it! Stop it!

359 (*We hear* Miep's *excited voice speaking to* Mr. Frank *below.*)

ANALYZE DRAMA

Annotate: In paragraphs 360–373, mark details that reveal what Miep has come to tell everyone about.

Summarize: Why do the residents of the Annex go "crazy" and have a "wild demonstration"?

360 **Miep.** Mr. Frank . . . the most wonderful news! . . . The invasion has begun!

361 **Mr. Frank.** Go on, tell them! Tell them!

362 (Miep *comes running up the steps, ahead of* Mr. Frank. *She has a man's raincoat on over her nightclothes and a bunch of orange-colored flowers in her hand.*)

363 **Miep.** Did you hear that, everybody? Did you hear what I said? The invasion has begun! The invasion!

364 (*They all stare at* Miep, *unable to grasp what she is telling them.* Peter *is the first to recover his wits.*)

365 **Peter.** Where?

366 **Mrs. Van Daan.** When? When, Miep?

367 **Miep.** It began early this morning . . .

368 (*As she talks on, the realization of what she has said begins to dawn on them. Everyone goes crazy. A wild demonstration takes place.* Mrs. Frank *hugs* Mr. Van Daan.)

369 **Mrs. Frank.** Oh, Mr. Van Daan, did you hear that? (Dussel *embraces* Mrs. Van Daan. Peter *grabs a frying pan and parades around the room, beating on it, singing the Dutch National Anthem.* Anne *and* Margot *follow him, singing, weaving in and out among the excited grownups.* Margot *breaks away to take the flowers from* Miep *and distribute them to everyone. While this pandemonium is going on* Mrs. Frank *tries to make herself heard above the excitement.*)

370 **Mrs. Frank** (*to* Miep). How do you know?

371 **Miep.** The radio . . . The B.B.C.! They said they landed on the coast of Normandy!

372 **Peter.** The British?

Don't forget to **Notice & Note** as you read the text.

373 **Miep.** British, Americans, French, Dutch, Poles, Norwegians . . . all of them! More than four thousand ships! Churchill spoke, and General Eisenhower! D-Day they call it!

374 **Mr. Frank.** Thank God, it's come!

375 **Mrs. Van Daan.** At last!

376 **Miep** (*starting out*). I'm going to tell Mr. Kraler. This'll be better than any blood transfusion.

377 **Mr. Frank** (*stopping her*). What part of Normandy did they land, did they say?

378 **Miep.** Normandy . . . that's all I know now . . . I'll be up the minute I hear some more! (*She goes hurriedly out.*)

379 **Mr. Frank** (*to* Mrs. Frank). What did I tell you? What did I tell you?

380 (Mrs. Frank *indicates that he has forgotten to bolt the door after* Miep. *He hurries down the steps.* Mr. Van Daan, *sitting on the couch, suddenly breaks into a convulsive sob. Everybody looks at him, bewildered.*)

381 **Mrs. Van Daan** (*hurrying to him*). Putti! Putti! What is it? What happened?

382 **Mr. Van Daan.** Please. I'm so ashamed.

383 (Mr. Frank *comes back up the steps.*)

384 **Dussel.** Oh, for God's sake!

385 **Mrs. Van Daan.** Don't, Putti.

386 **Margot.** It doesn't matter now!

387 **Mr. Frank** (*going to* Mr. Van Daan). Didn't you hear what Miep said? The invasion has come! We're going to be liberated! This is a time to celebrate!

388 (*He embraces* Mrs. Frank *and then hurries to the cupboard and gets the cognac and a glass.*)

389 **Mr. Van Daan.** To steal bread from children!

390 **Mrs. Frank.** We've all done things that we're ashamed of.

391 **Anne.** Look at me, the way I've treated Mother . . . so mean and horrid to her.

392 **Mrs. Frank.** No, Anneke, no.

393 (Anne *runs to her mother, putting her arms around her.*)

394 **Anne.** Oh, Mother, I was. I was awful.

395 **Mr. Van Daan.** Not like me. No one is as bad as me!

396 **Dussel** (*to* Mr. Van Daan). Stop it now! Let's be happy!

397 **Mr. Frank** (*giving* Mr. Van Daan *a glass of cognac*). Here! Here! *Schnapps! L'chaim!*[8] (Van Daan *takes the cognac. They all watch him. He gives them a feeble smile.* Anne *puts up her fingers in a V-for-Victory sign. As* Van Daan *gives an answering V-sign, they are startled to hear a loud sob from behind them. It is* Mrs. Frank, *stricken with remorse. She is sitting on the other side of the room.*)

398 **Mrs. Frank** (*through her sobs*). When I think of the terrible things I said . . .

399 (Mr. Frank, Anne, *and* Margot *hurry to her, trying to comfort her.* Mr. Van Daan *brings her his glass of cognac.*)

400 **Mr. Van Daan.** No! No! You were right!

401 **Mrs. Frank.** That I should speak that way to you! . . . Our friends! . . . Our guests! (*She starts to cry again.*)

402 **Dussel.** Stop it, you're spoiling the whole invasion!

403 (*As they are comforting her, the lights dim out. The curtain falls.*)

ANALYZE DRAMA

Annotate: In paragraph 404, mark details that show how the mood in the Annex changes immediately after the residents learn about D-Day (the Allied invasion on June 6, 1944) and a month later.

Interpret: What has happened in the month since D-Day? How has this affected people's spirits?

404 **Anne's Voice** (*faintly at first and then with growing strength*). We're all in much better spirits these days. There's still excellent news of the invasion. The best part about it is that I have a feeling that friends are coming. Who knows? Maybe I'll be back in school by fall. Ha, ha! The joke is on us! The warehouse man doesn't know a thing and we are paying him all that money! . . . Wednesday, the second of July, nineteen forty-four. The invasion seems temporarily to be bogged down. Mr. Kraler has to have an operation, which looks bad. The Gestapo have found the radio that was stolen. Mr. Dussel says they'll trace it back and back to the thief, and then, it's just a matter of time till they get to us. Everyone is low. Even poor Pim can't raise their spirits. I have often been downcast myself . . . but never in despair. I can shake off everything if I write. But . . . and that is the great question . . . will I ever be able to write well? I want to so much. I want to go on living even after my death. Another birthday has gone by, so now I am fifteen. Already I know what I want. I have a goal, an opinion.

405 (*As this is being said—the curtain rises on the scene, the lights dim on, and* Anne's Voice *fades out.*)

[8] ***Schnapps!*** (shnäps) *German:* Brandy!
L'chaim! (lə khä´yĭm) *Hebrew:* To life!

Scene 4

Don't forget to **Notice & Note** as you read the text.

406 *It is an afternoon a few weeks later . . . Everyone but* Margot *is in the main room. There is a sense of great tension.*

407 *Both* Mrs. Frank *and* Mr. Van Daan *are nervously pacing back and forth,* Dussel *is standing at the window, looking down fixedly at the street below.* Peter *is at the center table, trying to do his lessons.* Anne *sits opposite him, writing in her diary.* Mrs. Van Daan *is seated on the couch, her eyes on* Mr. Frank *as he sits reading.*

408 *The sound of a telephone ringing comes from the office below. They all are rigid, listening tensely.* Mr. Dussel *rushes down to* Mr. Frank.

409 **Dussel.** There it goes again, the telephone! Mr. Frank, do you hear?

410 **Mr. Frank** (*quietly*). Yes. I hear.

411 **Dussel** (*pleading, insistent*). But this is the third time, Mr. Frank! The third time in quick succession! It's a signal! I tell you it's Miep, trying to get us! For some reason she can't come to us and she's trying to warn us of something!

412 **Mr. Frank.** Please. Please.

413 **Mr. Van Daan** (*to* Dussel). You're wasting your breath.

414 **Dussel.** Something has happened, Mr. Frank. For three days now Miep hasn't been to see us! And today not a man has come to work. There hasn't been a sound in the building!

415 **Mrs. Frank.** Perhaps it's Sunday. We may have lost track of the days.

416 **Mr. Van Daan** (*to* Anne). You with the diary there. What day is it?

417 **Dussel** (*going to* Mrs. Frank). I don't lose track of the days! I know exactly what day it is! It's Friday, the fourth of August. Friday, and not a man at work. (*He rushes back to* Mr. Frank, *pleading with him, almost in tears.*) I tell you Mr. Kraler's dead. That's the only explanation. He's dead and they've closed down the building, and Miep's trying to tell us!

418 **Mr. Frank.** She'd never telephone us.

419 **Dussel** (*frantic*). Mr. Frank, answer that! I beg you, answer it!

420 **Mr. Frank.** No.

421 **Mr. Van Daan.** Just pick it up and listen. You don't have to

speak. Just listen and see if it's Miep.

422 **Dussel** (*speaking at the same time*). For God's sake . . . I ask you.

423 **Mr. Frank.** No. I've told you, no. I'll do nothing that might let anyone know we're in the building.

424 **Peter.** Mr. Frank's right.

425 **Mr. Van Daan.** There's no need to tell us what side you're on.

426 **Mr. Frank.** If we wait patiently, quietly, I believe that help will come.

427 (*There is silence for a minute as they all listen to the telephone ringing.*)

428 **Dussel.** I'm going down. (*He rushes down the steps.* Mr. Frank *tries ineffectually to hold him.* Dussel *runs to the lower door, unbolting it. The telephone stops ringing.* Dussel *bolts the door and comes slowly back up the steps.*) Too late. (Mr. Frank *goes to* Margot *in* Anne's *bedroom.*)

429 **Mr. Van Daan.** So we just wait here until we die.

430 **Mrs. Van Daan** (*hysterically*). I can't stand it! I'll kill myself! I'll kill myself!

431 **Mr. Van Daan.** For God's sake, stop it!

432 (*In the distance, a German military band is heard playing a Viennese waltz.*)

433 **Mrs. Van Daan.** I think you'd be glad if I did! I think you want me to die!

434 **Mr. Van Daan.** Whose fault is it we're here? (Mrs. Van Daan *starts for her room. He follows, talking at her.*) We could've been safe somewhere . . . in America or Switzerland. But no! No! You wouldn't leave when I wanted to. You couldn't leave your things. You couldn't leave your precious furniture.

435 **Mrs. Van Daan.** Don't touch me!

436 (*She hurries up the stairs, followed by* Mr. Van Daan. Peter, *unable to bear it, goes to his room.* Anne *looks after him, deeply concerned.* Dussel *returns to his post at the window.* Mr. Frank *comes back into the main room and takes a book, trying to read.* Mrs. Frank *sits near the sink, starting to peel some potatoes.* Anne *quietly goes to* Peter's *room, closing the door after her.* Peter *is lying face down on the cot.* Anne *leans over him, holding him in her arms, trying to bring him out of his despair.*)

437 **Anne.** Look, Peter, the sky. (*She looks up through the skylight.*) What a lovely, lovely day! Aren't the clouds beautiful? You know

what I do when it seems as if I couldn't stand being cooped up for one more minute? I *think* myself out. I think myself on a walk in the park where I used to go with Pim. Where the jonquils and the crocus and the violets grow down the slopes. You know the most wonderful part about *thinking* yourself out? You can have it any way you like. You can have roses and violets and chrysanthemums all blooming at the same time . . . It's funny . . . I used to take it all for granted . . . and now I've gone crazy about everything to do with nature. Haven't you?

Don't forget to **Notice & Note** as you read the text.

438 **Peter.** I've just gone crazy. I think if something doesn't happen soon . . . if we don't get out of here . . . I can't stand much more of it!

439 **Anne** (*softly*). I wish you had a religion, Peter.

440 **Peter.** No, thanks! Not me!

441 **Anne.** Oh, I don't mean you have to be Orthodox[9] . . . or believe in heaven and hell and purgatory and things . . . I just mean some religion . . . it doesn't matter what. Just to believe in something! When I think of all that's out there . . . the trees . . . and flowers . . . and seagulls . . . when I think of the dearness of you, Peter . . . and the goodness of the people we know . . . Mr. Kraler, Miep, Dirk, the vegetable man, all risking their lives for us every day . . . When I think of these good things, I'm not afraid any more . . . I find myself, and God, and I . . . (Peter *interrupts, getting up and walking away.*)

442 **Peter.** That's fine! But when I begin to think, I get mad! Look at us, hiding out for two years. Not able to move! Caught here like . . . waiting for them to come and get us . . . and all for what?

443 **Anne.** We're not the only people that've had to suffer. There've always been people that've had to . . . sometimes one race . . . sometimes another . . . and yet . . .

444 **Peter.** That doesn't make me feel any better!

445 **Anne** (*going to him*). I know it's terrible, trying to have any faith . . . when people are doing such horrible . . . But you know what I sometimes think? I think the world may be going through a phase, the way I was with Mother. It'll pass, maybe not for hundreds of years, but some day . . . I still believe, in spite of everything, that people are really good at heart.

446 **Peter.** I want to see something now . . . Not a thousand years from now! (*He goes over, sitting down again on the cot.*)

[9] **Orthodox:** Orthodox Jews who strictly observe Jewish laws and traditions.

447 **Anne.** But, Peter, if you'd only look at it as part of a great pattern . . . that we're just a little minute in the life . . . (*She breaks off.*) Listen to us, going at each other like a couple of stupid grownups! Look at the sky now. Isn't it lovely? (*She holds out her hand to him.* Peter *takes it and rises, standing with her at the window looking out, his arms around her.*) Some day, when we're outside again, I'm going to . . .

448 (*She breaks off as she hears the sound of a car, its brakes squealing as it comes to a sudden stop. The people in the other rooms also become aware of the sound. They listen tensely. Another car roars up to a screeching stop.* Anne *and* Peter *come from* Peter's *room.* Mr. *and* Mrs. Van Daan *creep down the stairs.* Dussel *comes out from his room. Everyone is listening, hardly breathing. A doorbell clangs again and again in the building below.* Mr. Frank *starts quietly down the steps to the door.* Dussel *and* Peter *follow him. The others stand rigid, waiting, terrified.*

449 *In a few seconds* Dussel *comes stumbling back up the steps. He shakes off* Peter's *help and goes to his room.* Mr. Frank *bolts the door below, and comes slowly back up the steps. Their eyes are all on him as he stands there for a minute. They realize that what they feared has happened.* Mrs. Van Daan *starts to whimper.* Mr. Van Daan *puts her gently in a chair, and then hurries off up the stairs to their room to collect their things.* Peter *goes to comfort his mother. There is a sound of violent pounding on a door below.*)

450 **Mr. Frank** (*quietly*). For the past two years we have lived in fear. Now we can live in hope.

451 (*The pounding below becomes more insistent. There are muffled sounds of voices, shouting commands.*)

452 **Men's Voices.** *Auf machen! Da drinnen! Auf machen! Schnell! Schnell! Schnell! etc., etc.*[10]

453 (*The street door below is forced open. We hear the heavy tread of footsteps coming up.* Mr. Frank *gets two school bags from the shelves, and gives one to* Anne *and the other to* Margot. *He goes to get a bag for* Mrs. Frank. *The sound of feet coming up grows louder.* Peter *comes to* Anne, *kissing her good-bye, then he goes to his room to collect his things. The buzzer of their door starts to ring.* Mr. Frank *brings* Mrs. Frank *a bag. They stand together, waiting. We hear the thud of gun butts on the door, trying to break it down.*

[10] **Auf machen! . . . Schnell!** (ouf´ mäkh´ən! dä drĭn´ən! ouf´ mäkh´ən! shnĕl! shnĕl! shnĕl!) *German:* Open up! Inside there! Open up! Quick! Quick! Quick!

454 Anne *stands, holding her school satchel, looking over at her father and mother with a soft, reassuring smile. She is no longer a child, but a woman with courage to meet whatever lies ahead.*

455 *The lights dim out. The curtain falls on the scene. We hear a mighty crash as the door is shattered. After a second* Anne's Voice *is heard.*)

456 **Anne's Voice.** And so it seems our stay here is over. They are waiting for us now. They've allowed us five minutes to get our things. We can each take a bag and whatever it will hold of clothing. Nothing else. So, dear Diary, that means I must leave you behind. Good-bye for a while. P.S. Please, please, Miep, or Mr. Kraler, or anyone else. If you should find this diary, will you please keep it safe for me, because some day I hope . . .

457 (*Her voice stops abruptly. There is silence. After a second the curtain rises.*)

VOCABULARY

Use Prefixes: If you are unfamiliar with the word *reassuring* in paragraph 454, consider that the prefix *re-* means "again," and the word *assure* means "to give confidence to." By putting these meanings together, you can figure out the definition of *reassuring*.

Interpret: What does the word *reassuring* suggest about Anne's character?

Scene 5

458 *It is again the afternoon in November, 1945. The rooms are as we saw them in the first scene.* Mr. Kraler *has joined* Miep *and* Mr. Frank. *There are coffee cups on the table. We see a great change in* Mr. Frank. *He is calm now. His bitterness is gone. He slowly turns a few pages of the diary. They are blank.*

459 **Mr. Frank.** No more. (*He closes the diary and puts it down on the couch beside him.*)

460 **Miep.** I'd gone to the country to find food. When I got back the block was surrounded by police . . .

461 **Mr. Kraler.** We made it our business to learn how they knew. It was the thief . . . the thief who told them.

462 (Miep *goes up to the gas burner, bringing back a pot of coffee.*)

463 **Mr. Frank** (*after a pause*). It seems strange to say this, that anyone could be happy in a concentration camp. But Anne was happy in the camp in Holland where they first took us. After two years of being shut up in these rooms, she could be out . . . out in the sunshine and the fresh air that she loved.

464 **Miep** (*offering the coffee to* Mr. Frank). A little more?

ANALYZE DRAMA

Annotate: Mark details in the stage directions at the opening of Scene 5 that reveal the time and place of that scene.

Interpret: How does the setting of Scene 5 complete the structure of the play?

465 **Mr. Frank** (*holding out his cup to her*). The news of the war was good. The British and Americans were sweeping through France. We felt sure that they would get to us in time. In September we were told that we were to be shipped to Poland . . . The men to one camp. The women to another. I was sent to Auschwitz. They went to Belsen. In January we were freed, the few of us who were left. The war wasn't yet over, so it took us a long time to get home. We'd be sent here and there behind the lines where we'd be safe. Each time our train would stop . . . at a siding, or a crossing . . . we'd all get out and go from group to group . . . Where were you? Were you at Belsen? At Buchenwald? At Mauthausen? Is it possible that you knew my wife? Did you ever see my husband? My son? My daughter? That's how I found out about my wife's death . . . of Margot, the Van Daans . . . Dussel. But Anne . . . I still hoped . . . Yesterday I went to Rotterdam. I'd heard of a woman there . . . She'd been in Belsen with Anne . . . I know now.

466 (*He picks up the diary again, and turns the pages back to find a certain passage. As he finds it we hear* Anne's Voice.)

467 **Anne's Voice.** In spite of everything, I still believe that people are really good at heart.

468 (Mr. Frank *slowly closes the diary.*)

469 **Mr. Frank.** She puts me to shame. (*They are silent.*)

470 *The Curtain Falls.*

ESSENTIAL QUESTION:

What can we learn from tragic events?

Review your notes and add your thoughts to your Response Log.

TURN AND TALK

Anne wrote: "In spite of everything, I still believe that people are really good at heart." With a partner, discuss whether you think this true, based on your reading of the play.

Assessment Practice

Answer these questions before moving on to the **Analyze the Text** section on the following page.

1. Which of the following scenes take place after World War II has ended?

- (A) Act One, Scenes 1 and 2
- (B) Act One, Scenes 2–5 and Act Two, Scenes 1–4
- (C) Act One, Scenes 1–5
- (D) Act One, Scene 1 and Act Two, Scene 5

2. Read the excerpt from the play. Then, answer the question.

> "**Margot** (*with sudden foreboding*). . . . Something's happened! Hasn't it, Mr. Kraler?" (Act Two, paragraph 86)

What inference can you make about Margot from the excerpt?

- (A) Margot is suspicious of Mr. Kraler.
- (B) Margot senses that Mr. Kraler has bad news.
- (C) Margot fears that a thief has broken into the office.
- (D) Margot is afraid that someone has informed on them.

3. Select **two** examples of dialogue that best explain why tensions in the Annex are temporarily relieved in Act Two.

- (A) "**Mrs. Frank.** I should have spoken out long ago." (paragraph 328)
- (B) "**Mrs. Frank.** He'll stay, of course. When I say I must protect the children, I mean Peter too." (paragraph 335)
- (C) "**Miep.** . . . The invasion has begun! The invasion!" (paragraph 363)
- (D) "**Mr. Frank** (*going to* Mr. Van Daan). . . . We're going to be liberated! This is a time to celebrate!" (paragraph 387)
- (E) "**Anne's Voice** (*faintly at first and then with growing strength*). . . . We're all in much better spirits these days. . . ." (paragraph 404)

Ed
Test-Taking Strategies

Analyze the Text

Support your responses with evidence from the text.

NOTICE & NOTE

Review what you **noticed and noted** as you read the text. Your annotations can help you answer these questions.

1. **ANALYZE** Briefly summarize Act One and then Act Two, identifying the main focus of each. How do the two acts work together to develop the action in this drama?

2. **CONNECT** In Act Two, Scene 5, Mr. Kraler reveals who told the police about the Franks' hiding place. How was this reason for their being discovered foreshadowed earlier in the play?

3. **ANALYZE** Examine the dialogue in Act Two, paragraphs 281–307, that reveals Mrs. Frank's reaction to Mr. Van Daan stealing bread. What decision does this incident cause Mrs. Frank to reach? What actions does she take as a result?

4. **EVALUATE** How do the playwrights make the drama seem like one long flashback? Does this use of flashback add to or detract from the overall impact of the play? Explain.

5. **CONNECT** How do the **Words of the Wiser** that Anne speaks in Act Two, paragraph 437, relate to her father's words to her in Act One, Scene 2? Why did the playwrights have Anne tell Peter these words in Act Two?

6. **ANALYZE** Refer to any notes you took about how the playwrights use dialogue and plot events to develop the play's characters or to move the action of the play forward. Give at least one example of how each element is used and provide analysis of each example you provide.

DRAMA ELEMENT	EXAMPLE	YOUR ANALYSIS
Dialogue		
Events		

Choices

Here are some other ways to demonstrate your understanding of the ideas in this lesson.

Writing

Start Some Drama

With a small group, write a short script for a dramatic scene. Consider what you've learned about drama from reading *The Diary of Anne Frank*.

- Brainstorm and decide as a group what situation your script will depict. What conflict will the characters need to resolve?
- Provide a cast of characters. Each group member should have a role to play.
- Write dialogue that reveals the conflict the characters are facing. Also use the dialogue to make the characters seem like real people with unique personalities.
- Use stage directions to explain how the dialogue should be spoken or what actions the characters should take as they perform the script.

As you write and discuss, be sure to use the **Academic Vocabulary** words.

- communicate
- draft
- liberation
- philosophy
- publish

Media

Make a Poster

Create a poster to convey how the characters in the drama were affected by their time in the Secret Annex.

- As a group, choose three Annex residents to depict.
- Analyze how the conditions in the Annex affected each character. Explain each character's motivations, actions, and reactions in relation to others and to the historical context.
- Create a poster to show the effects of setting on each character. As a group, present your poster to the class.

Social & Emotional Learning

Dramatize a Relationship

Act out (or do a dramatic reading of) two sections of the drama to demonstrate how a relationship between two characters change.

- As a group, discuss how Anne's relationship with Peter develops throughout the play. How does each character's personality and perspective affect the way the relationship develops?
- Choose two short sections of the play that show how Anne and Peter's relationship changes over time. Rehearse the lines. Then act them out for the class.

Expand Your Vocabulary

PRACTICE AND APPLY

Complete each sentence in a way that shows the meaning of the vocabulary word.

1. If you wanted to be **conspicuous** in a crowd, you might . . .
2. My friends **loathe** that TV show because . . .
3. The player spoke **indignantly** to the coach when . . .
4. The pop star dressed **ostentatiously** because . . .
5. The hostess of the party was **appalled** when . . .
6. The politician suddenly became **inarticulate** because . . .

Vocabulary Strategy

Use Prefixes

A **prefix** is a word part that has been added to the beginning of a base word to form a new word. You can sometimes use prefixes to figure out the meanings of unfamiliar words. Imagine, for example, that you aren't sure what *inarticulate* means but you know that someone who is articulate speaks clearly and you know that the prefix *in-* means "not." Then you can figure out that someone who is inarticulate does not speak clearly. Here are some common prefixes and their meanings:

Ed

Interactive Vocabulary Lesson: Common Roots, Prefixes, and Suffixes

PREFIX	MEANING
dis-, in-, im-, non-, un-	"not"
pre-	"before"
re-	"back" or "again"

PRACTICE AND APPLY

Choose a prefix to add to each base word below (more than one is possible). Then, use each new word in an original sentence.

1. view
2. arrange
3. committed

Watch Your Language!

Capitalization

Ed
Interactive Grammar Lessons: Capital Letters

You already know a lot about correct capitalization. For example, you know that the first word in a sentence is always capitalized. You also know that certain proper nouns, such as a person's name and the city in which you live, are always capitalized. But there are other types of words—many having to do with government and culture—that also need to be capitalized. The chart lists types of words to capitalize, along with examples.

TYPES OF WORDS TO CAPITALIZE	EXAMPLES
Languages	English, Spanish, German, Japanese
Countries and continents	Holland (the Netherlands), Mexico; Europe, North America
Nationalities and regional affiliations	American, Dutch, Chinese; European, Asian
Ethnicities	Hispanic, Native American, Jewish, Asian
Political parties	Democrats, Republicans, Nazis, Socialists
Religions	Judaism, Islam, Christianity, Buddhism
Religious words (texts, symbols, and words referring to a deity)	Bible, Koran; Menorah, Star of David; Thou, God, Ruler

PRACTICE AND APPLY

Rewrite the following sentences, correcting any errors in capitalization. A sentence may contain more than one error.

1. Not all germans wanted the nazis to be in control.
2. Because they were jewish, the Franks fled to holland to escape persecution.
3. Anne Frank's diary was translated into many languages, including english.

When you have finished, share your sentences with a partner and compare your use of capitalization.

"To them, capital punishment means making them use proper capitalization."

from

The Diary of a Young Girl

Diary by **Anne Frank**

ESSENTIAL QUESTION:
What can we learn from tragic events?

Engage Your Brain

Choose one or two of these activities to start connecting with the text you're about to read.

Dear Diary

Have you ever kept a diary or journal? What did you learn from doing it? Share your experiences with keeping a diary or journal with a group of your classmates.

A Prized Possession

In one of her diary entries, Anne describes losing a prized possession—a fountain pen that was a gift from her grandmother. Have you ever lost something that was special to you? Describe what happened.

Mood Swings

Like many teenagers, Anne Frank experienced frequent changes in her temperament. With a partner, have a brief discussion about mood swings.

Analyze a Diary

People sometimes write to explore and reflect on events in their daily lives. The result is often a **diary**—a record of the person's experiences, thoughts, and feelings during a certain time. When world events affect the person, diary entries may reveal what she or he has witnessed and may make connections between those events and the person's life.

Diary entries are sometimes composed as letters addressed to the diary itself, often with headings and salutations, as shown below. As you read the excerpt from Anne Frank's diary, consider what you learn about life during World War II.

Focus on Genre
Diary

- is a type of autobiographical writing
- uses first-person point of view
- records a writer's thoughts, experiences, and feelings
- uses text features to help organize the writing

MONDAY EVENING, NOVEMBER 8, 1943

Dearest Kitty,

If you were to read all my letters in one sitting, you'd be struck by the fact that they were written in a variety of moods.

The **heading** contains the date on which the entry was made.

The **salutation** reveals to whom the entry has been addressed.

Make Inferences

Since Anne does not explain everything she writes about, readers must fill in gaps in their understanding by making **inferences,** or logical guesses, from clues in the text and their prior knowledge. For example, in this passage, readers must infer why the doorbell frightens Anne:

> This evening, when Bep was still here, the doorbell rang long and loud. I instantly turned white, my stomach churned, and my heart beat wildly—and all because I was afraid.

What the text says:	+	What I know:	=	Inference:
The doorbell rang.		The Franks are hiding from the Nazis.		Anne is afraid they have been discovered.

As you read *The Diary of a Young Girl,* use clues in the text, as well as what you know of the Franks' situation and what it's like to be a teen, to make inferences about experiences that Anne does not fully explain.

Annotation in Action

Here are one reader's comments about the elements of a diary. As you read, notice how the elements of her diary help you learn about Anne Frank.

MONDAY EVENING, NOVEMBER 8, 1943

Dearest Kitty,

If you were to read all my letters in one sitting, you'd be struck by the fact that they were written in a variety of moods. It annoys me to be so dependent on the moods here in the Annex, but I'm not the only one: we're all subject to them. . . .

Anne addresses her diary as "Kitty" and uses "you."

Expand Your Vocabulary

Put a check mark next to the vocabulary words that you feel comfortable using when speaking or writing.

- **implore** ☐
- **splendid** ☐
- **conjecture** ☐

Turn to a partner and talk about the words you already know. Then, use as many words as you can in a paragraph about keeping a diary or journal. As you read *The Diary of a Young Girl,* use the definitions in the side column to learn the vocabulary words you don't already know.

Background

Anne Frank (1929–1945) was 13 years old when she and her family went into hiding to avoid being sent to concentration camps by the Nazis. During the two years she spent living in an attic, she kept a diary. After the war, Anne's father, the only family member to survive the concentration camps to which the family was eventually sent, chose to publish the diary. The selection you are about to read consists of entries taken from throughout the work.

from

The Diary of a Young Girl

Diary by **Anne Frank**

These excerpts from her diary give the reader insight into what life was like for Anne and the other people in the Secret Annex.

NOTICE & NOTE
As you read, use the side margins to make notes about the text.

MONDAY EVENING, NOVEMBER 8, 1943

Dearest Kitty,

1 If you were to read all my letters in one sitting, you'd be struck by the fact that they were written in a variety of moods. It annoys me to be so dependent on the moods here in the Annex, but I'm not the only one: we're all subject to them. If I'm engrossed in a book, I have to rearrange my thoughts before I can mingle with other people, because otherwise they might think I was strange. As you can see, I'm currently in the middle of a depression. I couldn't really tell you what set it off, but I think it stems from my cowardice, which confronts me at every turn. This evening, when Bep was still here, the doorbell rang long and loud. I instantly turned white, my stomach churned, and my heart beat wildly—and all because I was afraid.

2 At night in bed I see myself alone in a dungeon, without Father and Mother. Or I'm roaming the streets, or the Annex is on fire, or they come in the middle of the night to take us away

MAKE INFERENCES

Annotate: In paragraph 4, mark what Anne compares to "a castle in the air."

Infer: What reasons might Anne have for making this comparison?

implore
(ĭm-plôr´) *v.* To *implore* is to beg for something urgently.

VOCABULARY

Connotation and Denotation: All words have a **denotation,** or dictionary definition. Many words also have **connotations,** or ideas and feelings associated with the words. Consider the connotation of the word *howled* in paragraph 8.

Interpret: How does Anne's choice of the word *howled* help to convey her ideas?

splendid
(splĕn´dĭd) *adj.* If something is *splendid*, it is magnificent or very good.

and I crawl under my bed in desperation. I see everything as if it were actually taking place. And to think it might all happen soon!

3 Miep often says she envies us because we have such peace and quiet here. That may be true, but she's obviously not thinking about our fear.

4 I simply can't imagine the world will ever be normal again for us. I do talk about "after the war," but it's as if I were talking about a castle in the air, something that can never come true.

5 I see the eight of us in the Annex as if we were a patch of blue sky surrounded by menacing black clouds. The perfectly round spot on which we're standing is still safe, but the clouds are moving in on us, and the ring between us and the approaching danger is being pulled tighter and tighter. We're surrounded by darkness and danger, and in our desperate search for a way out we keep bumping into each other. We look at the fighting down below and the peace and beauty up above. In the meantime, we've been cut off by the dark mass of clouds, so that we can go neither up nor down. It looms before us like an impenetrable wall, trying to crush us, but not yet able to. I can only cry out and **implore**, "Oh, ring, ring, open wide and let us out!"

Yours, Anne

THURSDAY, NOVEMBER 11, 1943

Dearest Kitty,

6 I have a good title for this chapter:

Ode to My Fountain Pen
In Memoriam

7 My fountain pen was always one of my most prized possessions; I valued it highly, especially because it had a thick nib, and I can only write neatly with thick nibs. It has led a long and interesting fountain-pen life, which I will summarize below.

8 When I was nine, my fountain pen (packed in cotton) arrived as a "sample of no commercial value" all the way from Aachen,[1] where my grandmother (the kindly donor) used to live. I lay in bed with the flu, while the February winds howled around the apartment house. This **splendid** fountain pen came in a red leather case, and I showed it to my girlfriends the first chance I got. Me, Anne Frank, the proud owner of a fountain pen.

9 When I was ten, I was allowed to take the pen to school, and to my surprise, the teacher even let me write with it.

[1] **Aachen** (ä´kən): a city in Germany.

Don't forget to **Notice & Note** as you read the text.

When I was eleven, however, my treasure had to be tucked away again, because my sixth-grade teacher allowed us to use only school pens and inkpots. When I was twelve, I started at the Jewish Lyceum and my fountain pen was given a new case in honor of the occasion. Not only did it have room for a pencil, it also had a zipper, which was much more impressive. When I was thirteen, the fountain pen went with me to the Annex, and together we've raced through countless diaries and compositions. I'd turned fourteen and my fountain pen was enjoying the last year of its life with me when . . .

10 It was just after five on Friday afternoon. I came out of my room and was about to sit down at the table to write when I was roughly pushed to one side to make room for Margot and Father, who wanted to practice their Latin. The fountain pen remained unused on the table, while its owner, sighing, was forced to make do with a very tiny corner of the table, where she began rubbing beans. That's how we remove mold from the beans and restore them to their original state. At a quarter to six I swept the floor, dumped the dirt into a newspaper, along with the rotten beans, and tossed it into the stove. A giant flame shot up, and I thought it was wonderful that the stove, which had been gasping its last breath, had made such a miraculous recovery.

11 All was quiet again. The Latin students had left, and I sat down at the table to pick up where I'd left off. But no matter where I looked, my fountain pen was nowhere in sight. I took another look. Margot looked, Mother looked, Father looked, Dussel looked. But it had vanished.

12 "Maybe it fell into the stove, along with the beans!" Margot suggested.

13 "No, it couldn't have!" I replied.

MAKE INFERENCES

Annotate: Mark details in paragraph 10 that describe Anne's actions.

Infer: What can you infer about Anne's relationship with her family based on these details?

14 But that evening, when my fountain pen still hadn't turned up, we all assumed it had been burned, especially because celluloid is highly inflammable. Our darkest fears were confirmed the next day when Father went to empty the stove and discovered the clip, used to fasten it to a pocket, among the ashes. Not a trace of the gold nib was left. "It must have melted into stone," Father **conjectured**.

conjecture
(kən-jĕk´chər) *v.* If you *conjecture*, you guess or suppose.

15 I'm left with one consolation, small though it may be: my fountain pen was cremated,[2] just as I would like to be someday!

SATURDAY, JANUARY 15, 1944

My dearest Kitty,

16 There's no reason for me to go on describing all our quarrels and arguments down to the last detail. It's enough to tell you that we've divided many things like meat and fats and oils and are frying our own potatoes. Recently we've been eating a little extra rye bread because by four o'clock we're so hungry for dinner we can barely control our rumbling stomachs.

ANALYZE A DIARY

Annotate: Mark names and third-person pronouns in paragraphs 17–19.

Draw Conclusions: Although diaries are written from the first-person point of view, clues in the text may provide insight into the character traits and feelings of others. What conclusions can you draw about the people Anne mentions based on the details she includes?

17 Mother's birthday is rapidly approaching. She received some extra sugar from Mr. Kugler, which sparked off jealousy on the part of the van Daans, because Mrs. van D. didn't receive any on her birthday. But what's the point of boring you with harsh words, spiteful conversations and tears when you know they bore us even more?

18 Mother has expressed a wish, which isn't likely to come true any time soon: not to have to see Mr. van Daan's face for two whole weeks. I wonder if everyone who shares a house sooner or later ends up at odds with their fellow residents. Or have we just had a stroke of bad luck? At mealtime, when Dussel helps himself to a quarter of the half-filled gravy boat and leaves the rest of us to do without, I lose my appetite and feel like jumping to my feet, knocking him off his chair and throwing him out the door.

19 Are most people so stingy and selfish? I've gained some insight into human nature since I came here, which is good, but I've had enough for the present. Peter says the same.

20 The war is going to go on despite our quarrels and our longing for freedom and fresh air, so we should try to make the best of our stay here.

21 I'm preaching, but I also believe that if I live here much longer, I'll turn into a dried-up old beanstalk. And all I really want is to be an honest-to-goodness teenager!

Yours, Anne

[2] **cremated** (krē´māt´əd): burned to ashes.

TURN AND TALK

With a partner, discuss what you have learned about Anne from reading her diary entries.

ESSENTIAL QUESTION:

What can we learn from tragic events?

Review your notes and add your thoughts to your Response Log.

Assessment Practice

Answer these questions before moving on to the **Analyze the Text** section on the following page.

1. What is most likely Anne's purpose for telling the story of her fountain pen?
   - (A) to express frustration about having to share space at the table
   - (B) to explain how angry she was about having lost her pen
   - (C) to pay tribute to her pen by reflecting on her time with it
   - (D) to describe her thoughts about school before going into hiding

2. This question has two parts. First answer **Part A**. Then, answer **Part B**.

   Part A

   According to Anne, which word best expresses how Mrs. Frank feels toward Mr. van Daan?
   - (A) furious
   - (B) accommodating
   - (C) understanding
   - (D) envious

   Part B

   Which quotation best supports the answer in Part A?
   - (A) "[W]e've divided many things. . . ." (paragraph 16)
   - (B) "She received some extra sugar from Mr. Kugler, which sparked off jealousy on the part of the van Daans. . . ." (paragraph 17)
   - (C) "Mother has expressed a wish . . . not to have to see Mr. van Daan's face for two whole weeks." (paragraph 18)
   - (D) "I've gained some insight into human nature. . . ." (paragraph 19)

Ed

Test-Taking Strategies

Analyze the Text

Support your responses with evidence from the text.

NOTICE & NOTE

Review what you **noticed and noted** as you read the text. Your annotations can help you answer these questions.

1 **INFER** What is Anne Frank's view of the tension among all eight people living in the Annex? Cite evidence to support your response.

2 **INTERPRET** A simile makes a comparison between two unlike things using the word *like* or *as*. Reread paragraph 5. What does Anne reveal about her perspective with her use of the simile "I see the eight of us in the Annex as if we were a patch of blue sky surrounded by menacing black clouds"?

3 **DRAW CONCLUSIONS** Review the introduction to the entry for Thursday, November 11, 1943. Notice that the elements of this entry differ from the others. Why might Anne have used a slightly different form here?

4 **COMPARE** How does Anne's emotional state in paragraphs 1–2 compare with her feelings in paragraphs 18–21? Does your comparison support Anne's statement that her reader would be "struck by the fact" that her entries are "written in a variety of moods"? Explain.

5 **DRAW CONCLUSIONS** Over what span of time are the entries in this excerpt from the diary written? What does Anne reveal has been happening during this period?

6 **SUMMARIZE** Use the chart below to briefly summarize the text. Describe the main topics and ideas Anne relates in each of the three diary entries included in the selection.

NOVEMBER 8, 1943	NOVEMBER 11, 1943	JANUARY 15, 1944

Watch Your Language!

Transitions

Transitions are words and phrases that show how ideas, events, experiences, and pieces of information are related to one another. Consider what the transitions in this passage from the selection help to clarify:

> This evening, when Bep was still here, the doorbell rang long and loud. I instantly turned white, my stomach churned, and my heart beat wildly—and all because I was afraid.

These transitions show how events and experiences are related in time. Other useful time-order transitions include *later that day, after dinner, then, meanwhile,* and *afterward.*

To show a relationship of contrast, you can use transitions such as *on the other hand, however,* or *by contrast.* Anne does that here while also indicating how the events are related in time:

> When I was ten, I was allowed to take the pen to school, and to my surprise, the teacher even let me write with it. When I was eleven, however, my treasure had to be tucked away again. . . .

Other kinds of relationships that can be signaled with transitions include similarity (*similarly, likewise*), a cause-effect relationship (*as a result, because, consequently*), and sequential order (*first, second, last*).

PRACTICE AND APPLY

Link each pair of sentences below with one or more transitions that show how the ideas, events, experiences, or pieces of information expressed in each are related.

1. Anne found that she had too little space at the table to write. She cleaned beans instead. (cause-effect)

2. Anne rubbed mold off the beans. She swept up the garbage. (time)

3. Anne was upset when she realized that she had destroyed her pen. She was pleased with the lovely ode she wrote for it. (contrast)

After Auschwitz

Speech by **Elie Wiesel**

ESSENTIAL QUESTION:
What can we learn from tragic events?

Engage Your Brain

Choose one or both of these activities to start connecting with the speech you're about to read.

Talk About It

The speech you are about to read was given at a ceremony to mark the 50th anniversary of the liberation of Auschwitz, a Nazi concentration camp. With your class, discuss why people take the time to hold such ceremonies. Why is it important to remember tragic events from the past?

Fact Finding

Elie Wiesel was a survivor of the Auschwitz concentration camp. With a partner, do some research to learn about Wiesel and other Holocaust survivors. Record your findings below.

Analyze Appeals

In "After Auschwitz," Elie Wiesel's purpose is to persuade, or convince, his audience to adopt a particular viewpoint and to accept his claim. To do so, he uses **rhetoric,** or the art of using language effectively and persuasively. This includes making specific word choices that appeal to the feelings and values of his audience.

Rhetorical appeals are used to make an argument more persuasive.

- An **emotional appeal,** or an appeal to **pathos,** is a message that creates strong feelings in order to make an impact. These appeals can tap into people's feelings, such as fear, pity, or vanity.
- In an **ethical appeal,** or an appeal to **ethos,** a speaker or writer links a claim to a widely accepted value in order to gain moral support for the claim and to establish a bond with the audience as someone who shares their values.

Review the chart below for examples of each kind of appeal. As you read the speech, consider how Wiesel appeals to his audience's emotions and ethics.

Focus on Genre
Speech

- is a talk or public address presented to an audience
- may have one or more purposes, such as to entertain, to explain, or to persuade
- is often delivered on a special occasion
- may be recorded or transcribed for later reading and analysis

TYPE OF APPEAL	EXAMPLE FROM THE SPEECH	PERSUASIVE EFFECT
Emotional appeal	Close your eyes and listen. Listen to the silent screams of terrified mothers, the prayers of anguished old men and women. Listen to the tears of children, Jewish children. . . .	Appeals to people's feelings of sympathy and compassion for others
Ethical appeal	And it worked. The killers killed, the victims died and the world was the world and everything else was going on, life as usual.	Appeals to the established beliefs that people should not kill each other and that victims shouldn't suffer in silence

Analyze Rhetorical Devices

Rhetorical devices are techniques writers use to enhance their arguments.

- **Repetition** is a rhetorical device in which a sound, word, phrase, clause, or line is repeated for emphasis or to give a text or speech a sense of unity. Repetition also helps reinforce meaning and can create an appealing rhythm, as in this example.

  After Auschwitz, the human condition is no longer the same. After Auschwitz, nothing will ever be the same.

- **Parallelism** is the use of words, phrases, clauses, or lines that have a similar structure or grammatical form. Like repetition, parallelism can emphasize meaning and also produce an engaging rhythm.

  In this place of darkness and malediction we can but stand in awe and remember its stateless, faceless and nameless victims.

- **Figurative language** communicates meaning beyond the literal meaning of the words. Writers use figurative language to create effects and to evoke emotions.

  Look and listen as they quietly walk towards dark flames so gigantic that the planet itself seemed in danger.

Annotation in Action

Here are one reader's notes about Wiesel's use of repetition. As you read, mark parts of the speech that use rhetorical devices.

I speak to you as a man, who 50 years and nine days ago had no name, no hope, no future and was known only by his number, A7713.

The three phrases that begin with "no" emphasize Wiesel's despair.

Background

Elie Wiesel (1928–2016) was born in Romania. After the Germans invaded his town, he and his family were sent to Auschwitz, a concentration camp. Only Wiesel and two of his sisters survived. Wiesel wrote about his experiences in the book *Night,* which has sold millions of copies in many different languages. After its publication, Wiesel devoted himself to ensuring that the deaths of millions of Jews would never be forgotten. In 1986, Wiesel was awarded the Nobel Peace Prize for his life's work.

After Auschwitz

Speech by Elie Wiesel

This speech commemorates those who died in the concentration camp at Auschwitz, Poland.

NOTICE & NOTE
As you read, use the side margins to make notes about the text.

BACKGROUND

The Auschwitz concentration camp complex opened in 1940 in southern Poland. Concentration camps were used to incarcerate Jews and other supposed enemies of the state. Auschwitz played a major role in the Nazi plan to exterminate all the Jews in Europe. Inside, Nazis forced prisoners into hard labor. Anyone unable to work was executed upon arrival. Between 1940 and 1945, more than one million Jews and others including Poles, Roma, and Soviet prisoners of war were sent to Auschwitz. Few survived. Auschwitz was finally abandoned by German soldiers as the Soviet army advanced upon it in 1945.

NOTICE & NOTE
EXTREME OR ABSOLUTE LANGUAGE

When you notice language that leaves no doubt about a situation or an event, you've found an **Extreme or Absolute Language** signpost.

Notice & Note: In paragraphs 1–3, mark words and phrases that suggest certainty or completeness.

Infer: What does this language reveal about Wiesel's purpose?

ANALYZE APPEALS

Annotate: Mark the words in paragraph 6 in which Wiesel asks the audience to do something.

Analyze: Does this paragraph appeal to the audience's emotions or ethics? Explain.

1 *"After Auschwitz, the human condition is not the same, nothing will be the same."*

2 Here heaven and earth are on fire.

3 I speak to you as a man, who 50 years and nine days ago had no name, no hope, no future and was known only by his number, A7713.[1]

4 I speak as a Jew who has seen what humanity has done to itself by trying to exterminate an entire people and inflict suffering and humiliation and death on so many others.

5 In this place of darkness and malediction[2] we can but stand in awe and remember its stateless, faceless and nameless victims. Close your eyes and look: endless nocturnal processions are converging here, and here it is always night. Here heaven and earth are on fire.

6 Close your eyes and listen. Listen to the silent screams of terrified mothers, the prayers of anguished old men and women. Listen to the tears of children, Jewish children, a beautiful little girl among them, with golden hair, whose vulnerable tenderness has never left me. Look and listen as they quietly walk towards dark flames so gigantic that the planet itself seemed in danger.

[1] **A7713:** the identification number tattooed on Wiesel at Auschwitz.

[2] **malediction** (măl´ĭ-dĭk´shən): curse.

Don't forget to **Notice & Note** as you read the text.

7 All these men and women and children came from everywhere, a gathering of exiles drawn by death.

8 **Yitgadal veyitkadash, Shmay Rabba.**[3]

9 In this kingdom of darkness there were many people. People who came from all the occupied lands of Europe. And then there were the Gypsies and the Poles and the Czechs … It is true that not all the victims were Jews. But all the Jews were victims.

10 Now, as then, we ask the question of all questions: what was the meaning of what was so routinely going on in this kingdom of eternal night. What kind of demented mind could have invented this system?

11 And it worked. The killers killed, the victims died and the world was the world and everything else was going on, life as usual. In the towns nearby, what happened? In the lands nearby, what happened? Life was going on where God's creation was condemned to blasphemy[4] by their killers and their accomplices.

12 **Yitgadal veyitkadash, Shmay Rabba.**

[3] **Yitgadal veyitkadash, Shmay Rabba:** the words that begin a Jewish prayer for the dead.
[4] **blasphemy** (blăs´fə-mē): a disrespect for religion.

ANALYZE RHETORICAL DEVICES

Annotate: Mark the question Wiesel poses in paragraph 17.

Compare: The question in paragraph 17 is a device called a rhetorical question—one that author does not expect the audience to answer. Compare this question to the statement in the next paragraph. What impact does each have on the audience?

ESSENTIAL QUESTION:
What can we learn from tragic events?

Review your notes and add your thoughts to your Response Log.

13 Turning point or watershed,[5] Birkenau[6] produced a mutation[7] on a cosmic scale, affecting man's dreams and endeavours. After Auschwitz, the human condition is no longer the same. After Auschwitz, nothing will ever be the same.

14 **Yitgadal veyitkadash, Shmay Rabba.**

15 As we remember the solitude and the pain of its victims, let us declare this day marks our commitment to commemorate their death, not to celebrate our own victory over death.

16 As we reflect upon the past, we must address ourselves to the present and the future. In the name of all that is sacred in memory, let us stop the bloodshed in Bosnia, Rwanda and Chechnia; the vicious and ruthless terror attacks against Jews in the Holy Land.[8] Let us reject and oppose more effectively religious fanaticism and racial hate.

17 Where else can we say to the world "*Remember the morality of the human condition,*" if not here?

18 For the sake of our children, we must remember Birkenau, so that it does not become their future.

19 **Yitgadal veyitkadash, Shmay Rabba:** Weep for Thy children whose death was not mourned then: weep for them, our Father in heaven, for they were deprived of their right to be buried, for heaven itself became their cemetery.

[5] **watershed:** a place that marks a change of course or direction.
[6] **Birkenau:** the sub-camp at Auschwitz where prisoners were killed.
[7] **mutation** (myo͞o-tā´shən): change.
[8] **Holy Land:** the ancient kingdom of Israel.

TURN AND TALK

Turn to a partner and discuss why you think Wiesel chose the 50th anniversary of the liberation of Auschwitz to deliver this message.

Assessment Practice

Answer these questions before moving on to the **Analyze the Text** section on the following page.

1. Why does Wiesel use the present tense in paragraph 2, "Here heaven and earth are on fire"?

   (A) He is telling a story about the concentration camp.

   (B) He wants Auschwitz to be burned down and forgotten.

   (C) He believes Auschwitz still affects us today.

   (D) He is still bitter and angry about what happened to him.

2. This question has two parts. First answer **Part A**. Then answer **Part B**.

   Part A

   What does the speech's title, "After Auschwitz," mean?

   (A) The author survived Auschwitz and became successful.

   (B) The world is haunted by those who died at Auschwitz.

   (C) Former enemies can be friends by accepting past wrongdoing.

   (D) People must take a stand against injustice and hate.

   Part B

   Which **two** sentences best support the answer in Part A?

   (A) "I speak to you as a man, who 50 years and nine days ago had no name, no hope, no future. . . ." (paragraph 3)

   (B) "All these men and women and children came from everywhere, a gathering of exiles drawn by death." (paragraph 7)

   (C) "After Auschwitz, nothing will ever be the same." (paragraph 13)

   (D) "In the name of all that is sacred in memory, let us stop the bloodshed in Bosnia, Rwanda and Chechnia; the vicious and ruthless terror attacks against Jews in the Holy Land." (paragraph 16)

   (E) "For the sake of our children, we must remember Birkenau, so that it does not become their future." (paragraph 18)

Ed Test-Taking Strategies

Analyze the Text

Support your responses with evidence from the text.

NOTICE & NOTE

Review what you noticed and noted as you read the text. Your annotations can help you answer these questions.

1. **CONNECT** Wiesel's speech begins: "After Auschwitz, the human condition is not the same, nothing will be the same." Identify where similar language is repeated later in his speech. What is the effect of this repetition?

2. **ANALYZE** Reread paragraphs 3–4 and identify the examples of parallelism. What impact does the parallelism create? How does it contribute to the writer's **tone,** or the attitude he expresses?

3. **INTERPRET** Wiesel writes: "Here heaven and earth are on fire." What effect might this figurative language have on his audience?

4. **EVALUATE** The sentence *Yitgadal veyitkadash, Shmay Rabba* is stated four times in the speech. Is Wiesel's repetition of this prayer effective as a rhetorical device? Why or why not?

5. **INTERPRET** Review Wiesel's ethical appeal in paragraphs 16–18. What values is he asking his audience to consider? What impact does his use of **Absolute Language** have on this appeal?

6. **ANALYZE** Refer to the chart you filled in with examples of Wiesel's use of rhetorical appeals. Provide at least one example of each type of appeal, and analyze the persuasive effect of each example.

TYPE OF APPEAL	EXAMPLE FROM THE SPEECH	PERSUASIVE EFFECT
Emotional appeal		
Ethical appeal		

Choices

Here are some other ways to demonstrate your understanding of the ideas in this lesson.

Writing

Speech

Choose an issue that you feel strongly about. Prepare a persuasive speech to convince your audience to adopt your view of the issue.

- Remember, this speech is an argument. Form a claim and state it in early in your speech.
- Support your claim with reasons, and support each reason with strong, relevant evidence.
- Use clear transitions to help listeners follow how your claim, reasons, and evidence are related.
- Use rhetorical appeals and rhetorical devices to be as convincing as possible.

As you write and discuss, be sure to use the **Academic Vocabulary** words.

- communicate
- draft
- liberation
- philosophy
- publish

Media

Make a Poster

Choose a quotation from "After Auschwitz" that moved you. You might find it by reading the notes you took on the selection or by rereading the speech. Then create a poster that amplifies the message of this quotation.

- Write the quotation prominently on your poster.
- Research the Holocaust and/or current events to find facts, dates, and other details that support the message expressed by the quotation you chose.
- Add to your poster the most powerful pieces of relevant information and visual details you found during your research.
- Explain your completed work to the class in an oral presentation.

Social & Emotional Learning

Discuss with a Group

In a small group, discuss how you might follow Wiesel's direction to "reject and oppose more effectively religious fanaticism and racial hate." What successful efforts do you know of? What problems exist today, and how might you help solve them?

- Choose a persecuted group that you know of from reading the news or doing research.
- Discuss these questions: Why is the group being persecuted? What global or national groups are helping the persecuted?
- Using your knowledge of how conflicts between groups of people have been resolved before, discuss how you think the current conflict can come to a just resolution.

Collaborate & Compare

ESSENTIAL QUESTION:
What can we learn from tragic events?

Compare Poems

You are about to read two poems that convey messages about the delicate nature of life. As you read, compare the ways in which each poet uses techniques such as sound devices or figurative language to convey themes in his or her poem.

A

There But for the Grace

Poem by **Wisława Szymborska**
pages 556–557

B

Days

Poem by **Billy Collins**
pages 558–559

After you have read the poems, you will work with your classmates to compare the poems and to analyze their connections to the other texts in this unit, following these steps:

- Identify Connections
- Discuss Ideas
- Select Information
- Draft and Share
- Publish Your Analysis

There But for the Grace

Poem by Wisława Szymborska

Days

Poem by Billy Collins

Engage Your Brain

Choose one or two of these activities to start connecting with the poems you're about to read.

Close Call

Think of a "close call" you had. It could be a time when you narrowly avoided an accident or almost made a mistake. Write down how you felt during and after the close call.

Where Have I Heard That Before?

The title of the poem "There But for the Grace" comes from a famous quotation. Do some research to learn about this quotation. Who said it, and under what circumstances? What does the quotation mean? Record your findings below.

Analyze Sound Devices

Sound devices are uses of certain words for their connection to the sense of hearing. Poets use a wide variety of sound devices to convey meaning and **tone** (the writer's attitude toward the subject). Poets also use sound devices to draw attention to certain lines or images, to engage readers, or to unify a work.

As you read each poem, notice the impact of the sound devices listed in the chart below. How do they help convey meaning and express the poet's message? How do these word choices affect you as a reader?

Focus on Genre

Poetry

- uses imagery and figurative language to convey meaning and tone
- uses sound devices such as alliteration and assonance
- expresses a theme or message about life
- includes a speaker who "talks" to the reader; the speaker is not necessarily the poet

SOUND DEVICE	DEFINITION	EXAMPLE FROM THE POEMS
alliteration	repetition of consonant sounds at the beginnings of words	What would have happened had not a hand . . .
assonance	repetition of vowel sounds within non-rhyming words	or set upon your forehead moments before you open your eyes.
consonance	repetition of consonant sounds within and at the ends of words	It happened sooner. Later. Nearer. Farther.
onomatopoeia	the use of words whose sounds echo their meanings	place this cup on yesterday's saucer without the slightest clink.
repetition	a technique in which a sound, word, phrase, or line is repeated for emphasis or unity	It could have happened. It had to happen. It happened sooner. Later.

Analyze Figurative Language

Writers—especially poets—use **figurative language** to help readers see things in new ways. A **simile** is one type of figurative language in which two unlike things are compared using the word *like* or *as*. A **metaphor** is also a comparison between things that are basically dissimilar. However, unlike a simile, a metaphor does not contain the word *like* or *as*. In the example below from "Days," the poet uses a metaphor to compare a window to a "calm eye."

EXAMPLE FROM "DAYS"	EFFECT
Through the calm eye of the window	emphasizes the peacefulness of the scene

While reading "There But for the Grace" and "Days," consider the impact of the poets' use of figurative language. In what ways does the figurative language add interest and support meaning?

Annotation in Action

Here are one reader's comments on the figurative language in "Days." As you read the poems, look for examples of figurative language.

Each one is a gift, no doubt,
mysteriously placed in your waking hand
or set upon your forehead
moments before you open your eyes.

The poem is called "Days," so "each one" means "each day." Comparing each day to a gift highlights the idea each day is special.

Background

Poet **Wisława Szymborska** (1923–2012) was born in a small town in western Poland. She was in high school when Germany invaded her country, and she was fortunate to avoid imprisonment and death. She won the Nobel Prize for Literature in 1996.

Billy Collins (b. 1941) is perhaps the most popular poet in North America. When he served as the U.S. Poet Laureate, he created the 180 Project which provided high schools with poems to be read with daily announcements.

There But for the Grace

Poem by **Wisława Szymborska**

This speaker marvels at the little things that make the difference between survival and death.

NOTICE & NOTE
As you read, use the side margins to make notes about the text.

ANALYZE SOUND DEVICES

Annotate: Mark the repetition in lines 6–11.

Analyze: How does the repetition in these lines impact the rhythm and meaning of the poem?

It could have happened.
It had to happen.
It happened sooner. Later.
Nearer. Farther.
It happened not to you.

You survived because you were the first.
You survived because you were the last.
Because you were alone. Because of people.
Because you turned left. Because you turned right.
Because rain fell. Because a shadow fell.
Because sunny weather prevailed.[1]
Luckily there was a wood.
Luckily there were no trees.
Luckily there was a rail, a hook, a beam, a brake,
a frame, a bend, a millimeter, a second.
Luckily a straw was floating on the surface.

[1] **prevailed:** was common or frequent.

Thanks to, because, and yet, in spite of.
What would have happened had not a hand, a foot,
by a step, a hairsbreadth[2]
by sheer coincidence.

So you're here? Straight from a moment still ajar?
The net had one eyehole, and you got through it?
There's no end to my wonder, my silence.
Listen
how fast your heart beats in me.

[2] **hairsbreadth:** a tiny space.

ANALYZE FIGURATIVE LANGUAGE

Annotate: Mark the metaphor that relates to survival in lines 21–25.

Analyze: What does this metaphor mean? What ideas does this use of figurative language emphasize?

TURN AND TALK

The speaker suggests that luck or chance plays a big part in survival. Do you agree? Discuss with a partner.

ESSENTIAL QUESTION:
What can we learn from tragic events?

Review your notes and add your thoughts to your Response Log.

Assessment Practice

Answer this question before moving on to the next selection.

1. This question has two parts. First, answer **Part A**. Then, answer **Part B**.

Part A

What sound device does the poet use in lines 12–16?

- (A) assonance
- (B) onomatopoeia
- (C) repetition
- (D) rhythm

Part B

What idea does the poet emphasize by using this sound device?

- (A) People should admit that the world is a lucky place.
- (B) Survival often depends on luck.
- (C) People should focus on the positive.
- (D) Certain steps can be taken to survive a tragedy.

Ed
Test-Taking Strategies

Days

Poem by **Billy Collins**

NOTICE & NOTE
As you read, use the side margins to make notes about the text.

Our lives may be more fragile than we think.

Each one is a gift, no doubt,
mysteriously placed in your waking hand
or set upon your forehead
moments before you open your eyes.

Today begins cold and bright,
the ground heavy with snow
and the thick masonry of ice,
the sun glinting off the turrets of clouds.

Through the calm eye of the window
everything is in its place
but so precariously
this day might be resting somehow

on the one before it,
all the days of the past stacked high
like the impossible tower of dishes
entertainers used to build on stage.

No wonder you find yourself
perched on the top of a tall ladder

ANALYZE FIGURATIVE LANGUAGE

Annotate: Mark the simile in lines 12–16.

Analyze: What two unlike things does the speaker compare? How does this comparison impact the meaning of the poem?

hoping to add one more.
Just another Wednesday

you whisper,
then holding your breath,
place this cup on yesterday's saucer
without the slightest clink.

TURN AND TALK

Have a discussion with a partner about the comparison Collins makes in this poem. Do you think it's a good comparison? Explain.

?

ESSENTIAL QUESTION:

What can we learn from tragic events?

Review your notes and add your thoughts to your Response Log.

Assessment Practice

Answer this question before moving on to the **Analyze the Texts** section on the following page.

1. This question has two parts. First, answer **Part A**. Then, answer **Part B**.

Part A

What does the figurative language in the poem suggest about the days in a person's life?

(A) They are beautiful and limitless.

(B) They are cold yet calm.

(C) They are precious but fragile.

(D) They are boring and repetitive.

Part B

Which **two** lines best support the answer to Part A?

(A) "Each one is a gift, no doubt," (line 1)

(B) "Today begins cold and bright," (line 5)

(C) "Through the calm eye of the window" (line 9)

(D) "perched on the top of a tall ladder" (line 18)

(E) "Just another Wednesday" (line 20)

Ed

Test-Taking Strategies

Analyze the Texts

Support your responses with evidence from the texts.

NOTICE & NOTE

Review what you **noticed and noted** as you read the text. Your annotations can help you answer these questions.

1. **IDENTIFY PATTERNS** Choose an example of repetition in "There But for the Grace," and explain how it emphasizes the poem's message.

2. **ANALYZE** In line 16 of "There But for the Grace," identify the sound device used. Then, explain how it affects the ending of the stanza.

3. **COMPARE** How does the message conveyed in lines 1–4 of "Days" compare with the message conveyed in lines 21–24? Cite examples of the word choices the poet uses in your response.

4. **EVALUATE** What other words and phrases in "Days" relate to the simile in lines 14–16? What impact does this extended comparison have on the poem's overall meaning?

5. **ANALYZE** Use the chart below to identify at least one sound device from each poem, and provide analysis of how the use of these devices affects each poem's meaning and tone.

SOUND DEVICE	EXAMPLE	YOUR ANALYSIS

Choices

Here are some other ways to demonstrate your understanding of the ideas in this lesson.

As you write and discuss, be sure to use the **Academic Vocabulary** words.

communicate	philosophy
draft	publish
liberation	

Writing
Literary Analysis

Write a two- to three-paragraph essay in which you analyze "There But for the Grace" or "Days."

- Reread the background information and the poem.
- Develop a clear thesis statement. In other words, what main point do you want to address in your analysis?
- Cite examples from the poem. Describe how specific instances of figurative language and sound devices help support your analysis.
- End by briefly summarizing your thesis statement and supporting evidence.
- Ask another student or small group to review your analysis.

Research
Pick a Poet

Which poet would you like to find out more about? Do some research to learn more about Wisława Szymborska or Billy Collins. Include the following information in your research:

- how and when the poet started writing poetry
- interesting biographical details about the poet
- literary awards or honors the poet has received

Speaking & Listening
Recite a Poem

With a small group, present a recitation of "There But for the Grace" or "Days" for the class.

- Work with your group to select which poem you will present.
- Plan how you will present the poem. Will you take turns reciting different stanzas, or recite stanzas in unison?
- Memorize your lines and rehearse with your group.
- Present the poem with appropriate rate, volume, and expression.

Compare Poems

To compare the structure of "Days" and "There But for the Grace," think about the following elements:

- **Stanzas** How are the stanzas organized? Does each stanza include the same number of lines?
- **Line lengths** Are the line lengths similar throughout the poem, or does the poet include both short and longer lines?

"There But for the Grace" and "Days" also have similar themes—that is, similar messages about life. Now that you have thought about both poems, compare how their structures impact their style, meaning, and themes. Record your thoughts below.

	"THERE BUT FOR THE GRACE"	"DAYS"
Stanzas and Line Lengths		
Style		
Meaning and Theme		

Analyze the Texts

Discuss these questions in your group.

1. **COMPARE** Together, review details in your charts. In what ways do the structures of the poems differ? How are they similar? Explain.
2. **CRITIQUE** Briefly describe the theme of each poem. Which poem do you believe has a stronger or a more compelling theme? How does the structure help to reinforce its theme?
3. **COMPARE** Does the tone of each poem remain the same, or change? Explain.
4. **INTERPRET** How does the figurative language in each poem emphasize its theme? Cite text evidence to support your answer.

Analyze and Share

Continue exploring the ideas in these poems by analyzing their connections to the other selections in this unit. Follow these steps:

1. **IDENTIFY CONNECTIONS** Think about similarities between these poems and the other Unit 6 selections. Ask yourself:
   - How are the themes (messages about life) related?
   - What ideas do they share?
   - How are their explicit and implicit meanings similar?
   - Which poem connects more closely to the other selections in the unit? Why?

   Use this chart to record your thoughts.

OTHER UNIT SELECTIONS	CONNECTIONS TO "THERE BUT FOR THE GRACE"	CONNECTIONS TO "DAYS"
The Diary of Anne Frank		
The Diary of a Young Girl		
"After Auschwitz"		

2. **DISCUSS IDEAS** Join a group and compare the connections you have made. Discuss your interpretations of the themes. Listen carefully, and make sure to speak respectfully even if you disagree with others' interpretations. Be willing to adjust your responses to the poems based on what others say.

3. **SELECT INFORMATION** Working independently, use the information you generated on your own and in the group to decide which poem is a better fit for the unit.

4. **DRAFT AND SHARE** Write an analysis that explains which poem best captures the spirit of the unit and why. Cite text evidence to support your ideas. Share your analysis with a partner, and use your partner's feedback to revise your analysis.

5. **PUBLISH YOUR ANALYSIS** Include your analysis in a collection you can share with the whole class.

Reader's Choice

Continue your exploration of the Essential Question by doing some independent reading about the impact of tragic events. Read the titles and descriptions shown. Then mark the texts that interest you.

ESSENTIAL QUESTION:
What can we learn from tragic events?

Short Reads

Available on Ed

These texts are available in your ebook. Choose one to read and rate. Then defend your rating to the class.

Peace Can Happen

Essay by **Christine Kingery**

Forgiveness and compassion can heal all wounds—one person at a time.

Rate It ☆☆☆☆☆

The Butterfly/On a Sunny Evening

Poems by **Pavel Friedmann/Anonymous**

Young prisoners in a concentration camp hunger for the natural world.

Rate It ☆☆☆☆☆

The Singing Women

Short Story by **Rebecca Makkai**

An attempt to preserve a fragile culture puts it in harm's way.

Rate It ☆☆☆☆☆

from A Tragedy Revealed: A Heroine's Last Days

Article by **Ernst Schnabel**

This historical account details the fate of Anne and the other residents of the Secret Annex.

Rate It ☆☆☆☆☆

Nobel Prize Acceptance Speech

Speech by **Elie Wiesel**

A survivor of the Holocaust argues for our common humanity and against injustice.

Rate It ☆☆☆☆☆

Long Reads

Here are three recommended books that connect to this unit topic. For additional options, ask your teacher, school librarian, or peers. Which titles spark your interest?

The Book Thief

Novel by **Mark Zusak**

Death narrates this story. Sometimes distracted from the never-ending work of collecting souls, Death tells the story of Liesel, a nine-year-old living with foster parents outside of Munich.

The Diary of a Young Girl

Diary by **Anne Frank**

This is the heart-rending diary of a young Jewish girl who hid from the Nazis in an attic with her family for two years.

Tropical Secrets

Novel in Verse by **Margarita Engle**

Fleeing Nazi Germany, Daniel's ship full of refugees is turned away from New York and sent to Cuba. The island seems magical at first, but the darkness lingering in other parts of the world manages to reach Daniel.

Extension

Connect & Create

INSPIRATION BOARD Create an inspiration board based on the text or texts you chose.

- Think about the impact that the writing had on you. What did you learn from the text you read?
- Choose visuals (or draw your own images) that represent the people/characters in your text.
- Add memorable quotations or excerpts from the text.
- Present your inspiration board to the rest of the class with a short explanation.

LESSONS LEARNED Think again about the Essential Question of this unit: What can we learn from tragic events? In what ways did the text or texts you chose help to answer this question? What themes or lessons did the text convey, and what actions might readers take to demonstrate that they've understood those themes or lessons? Have a discussion with your classmates to exchange your ideas.

NOTICE & NOTE

- Pick one of the texts and annotate the **Notice & Note** signposts you find.
- Then, use the **Notice & Note Writing Frames** to help you write about the significance of the signposts.
- Compare your findings with those of other students who read the same text.

Ed

Notice & Note Writing Frames

Write a Personal Narrative

Writing Prompt

Using ideas, information, and examples from multiple texts in this unit, including the November 11, 1943, entry from *The Diary of a Young Girl,* in which Anne Frank writes about a pen she values, write a personal narrative about an experience involving a treasured object.

Manage your time carefully so that you can

- review the texts in the unit;
- plan your narrative;
- write your narrative; and
- revise and edit your narrative.

Be sure to

- establish a context and engage readers;
- develop the narrative with a logical sequence of events;
- include descriptive details and sensory language;
- use narrative techniques; and
- use transitions to clarify sequence and connect ideas.

Review the Mentor Text

For an example of a well-written personal narrative you can use as a mentor text, review:

- *The Diary of a Young Girl* (pages 533–537).

Review your notes and annotations about this text. Think about how Anne Frank expresses emotions and ideas.

Consider Your Sources

Review the list of texts in the unit and choose at least two that you may want to use as sources of ideas or inspiration for your personal narrative.

As you review selections, consult the notes you made on your **Response Log** and make additional notes about any ideas that might be useful as you write your personal narrative. Especially consider how the writers use narrative techniques to describe events or experiences.

UNIT 6 SOURCES

- ☐ **The Diary of Anne Frank**
- ☐ *from* **The Diary of a Young Girl**
- ☐ **After Auschwitz**
- ☐ **There But for the Grace**
- ☐ **Days**

Analyze the Prompt

Review the prompt to make sure you understand the assignment.

1. Mark the phrase in the prompt that identifies the general topic of your personal narrative. Restate the topic in your own words.
2. Next, look for words that suggest the purpose and audience of your personal narrative, and write a sentence describing each.

Find a Purpose

Two common purposes of a personal narrative are

- to **entertain** readers
- to convey a **theme,** or a message about life or human nature

What is my topic? What is my writing task?

What is my purpose?

Who is my audience?

Review the Rubric

Your personal narrative will be scored using a rubric. As you write, focus on the characteristics described in the chart. You will learn more about these characteristics as you work through the lesson.

PURPOSE, FOCUS, AND ORGANIZATION	NARRATIVE TECHNIQUE	CONVENTIONS OF STANDARD ENGLISH
The response includes: • An engaging introduction • A well-developed plot structure • Use of transitions to convey sequence and connect ideas • Logical sequence of events • A conclusion that follows from the narrated events	The response includes: • Use of descriptive details and sensory language • Effective use of narrative techniques • Varied sentence structure	The response may include: • Some minor errors in usage but no patterns of errors • Correct punctuation, capitalization, sentence formation, and spelling • Command of basic conventions

1 PLAN YOUR NARRATIVE

Choose a Topic

Use the chart to brainstorm ideas for your narrative. Jot down details about experiences involving an object that was meaningful to you. Then circle the experience that you would like to focus on for your narrative.

Brainstorm Topic Ideas

Remember, an interesting **personal narrative** might explore

- how you faced a **problem** or challenge
- how a **realization** shaped your actions or understandings

EXPERIENCE	HOW I FELT ABOUT IT

Brainstorm Details

Brainstorm **descriptive details** that will help bring your narrative to life. List words and phrases that will help readers imagine events. Include **sensory language** that appeals to the senses of sight, hearing, touch, smell, or taste.

EVENT	DETAILS

Organize Ideas

Think about the most logical and interesting way to structure your narrative. Use the chart to help you plan your draft.

INTRODUCTION (establish context and engage readers)

↓

MAIN NARRATIVE (sequence of events)

↓

CONCLUSION (reflect on what happened)

Determine Narrative Techniques

Here are some **narrative techniques** that can add interest to your writing:

- Use **flashback** to recall past events.
- Use **foreshadowing** to hint at events that occur later.
- Speed up or slow down the **pacing** to build tension or emphasize ideas.

2 DEVELOP A DRAFT

Now it is time to write your essay. Examining published works can help you develop your own writing skills. Read about techniques you might use as you draft your personal narrative.

Drafting Online

Check your assignment list for a writing task from your teacher.

Use Transitions

EXAMINE THE MENTOR TEXT

Notice how Anne Frank uses varied transitions to show connections between events and experiences in *The Diary of a Young Girl* (page 535).

Transitions signaling Anne Frank's age help make the sequence of events clear.

When I was ten, I was allowed to take the pen to school, and to my surprise, the teacher even let me write with it. When I was eleven, however, my treasure had to be tucked away again, because my sixth-grade teacher allowed us to use only school pens and inkpots. When I was twelve, I started at the Jewish Lyceum and my fountain pen was given a new case in honor of the occasion. Not only did it have room for a pencil, it also had a zipper, which was much more impressive.

The transitions "however" and "not only" signal a contrast and an additional detail.

APPLY TO YOUR DRAFT

Your personal narrative should include transitions that make the sequence of events clear and show the connections between ideas. Practice using the transitions in the chart below to describe your responses to events in your narrative. As you write, apply this technique to your draft.

TRANSITION	EVENT → MY RESPONSE
Before...	
After...	
Because of...	
As a result of...	

Use Narrative Techniques

EXAMINE THE MENTOR TEXT

In *The Diary of a Young Girl*, Anne Frank uses narrative techniques to build tension and convey emotion about the loss of her pen.

All was quiet again. The Latin students had left, and I sat down at the table to pick up where I'd left off. But no matter where I looked, my fountain pen was nowhere in sight. I took another look. Margot looked, Mother looked, Father looked, Dussel looked. But it had vanished.

"Maybe it fell into the stove, along with the beans!" Margot suggested.

"No, it couldn't have!" I replied.

Short sentences and repetition of the verb *look* help build tension.

Dialogue helps show Anne's frantic response.

Try These Suggestions

Vary the way you develop your narrative. Try these out:

- Share your thoughts and feelings using sensory details.
- Vary pacing using shorter or longer sentences to describe action.
- Use dialogue to advance action and reveal motivations and traits.

APPLY TO YOUR DRAFT

Use this chart to practice using narrative techniques. Draft a few sentences that reveal your unique perspective of events through description and dialogue. Then apply these techniques to your draft.

Thoughts	
Actions	
Words	

3 REVISE YOUR PERSONAL NARRATIVE

Even experienced writers rework their ideas and language during their writing process. Use the guide to help you revise your personal narrative.

Help with Revision
Find a **Peer Review Guide** and **Student Models** online.

REVISION GUIDE		
ASK YOURSELF	**PROVE IT**	**REVISE IT**
Introduction Does my introduction establish context and engage readers?	**Circle** key details that establish context. **Highlight** words and phrases that hint at what might happen.	**Add** key details to help readers understand the context of the narrative. **Reword** phrases to spark readers' curiosity about what happens next.
Point of View Do I establish and develop a first-person narrative voice?	**Put a star** (★) next to pronouns that show your point of view. **Underline** words and phrases that describe your thoughts and feelings.	**Change** third-person pronouns to first-person pronouns as necessary. **Add** descriptions to convey your thoughts and feelings.
Narrative Techniques Do I use narrative techniques to add interest and draw in readers?	**Put a check mark** (✓) next to dialogue. **Number** (1, 2, 3...) the sequence of events.	**Add** or **rearrange** details to vary the pacing or to convey a more natural or logical sequence.
Transitions Do I use transitions to clarify sequence and to show connections between ideas?	**Circle** transitions between sentences and paragraphs.	**Add** transitions as necessary.
Conclusion Does my conclusion reveal why the experience was significant?	**Underline** statements that tell why the experience was meaningful.	**Add** statements that explain the event's importance.

APPLY TO YOUR DRAFT

Consider the following as you look for opportunities to improve your writing.

- Make sure your narrative follows a logical sequence.
- Use dialogue and description to help readers imagine events.
- Correct any errors in grammar and punctuation.

Peer Review in Action

Once you have finished revising your personal narrative, you will exchange papers with a partner in a **peer review.** During a peer review, you will give suggestions to improve your partner's draft.

Read the introduction from a student's draft and examine the comments made by the peer reviewer to see how it's done.

First Draft

My Heirloom Mug
by Shay Fernandes, Franklin High School

I heard my grandmother telling me to be careful. Then I dropped her favorite mug on the floor. The handle broke off. I worried about how upset she would be. I looked up at her. She was smiling. She told me not to worry. She picked up the pieces and held them together. She got some glue from the cupboard. Then I noticed a mark in the handle where it had been glued together before.

I like how you start in the middle of a scene. This could also be a good place to use dialogue.

Good job describing events in order, but try combining sentences to make the story sound more interesting.

Now read the revised introduction below. Notice how the writer has improved the draft by making revisions based on the reviewer's comments.

Revision

"Cuidado, es mi favorita," said my grandmother. Right after she warned me to be careful, I dropped my grandmother's favorite mug on the floor, and the handle broke off. I still remember worrying about how upset she would be as I looked up at her. Instead, her face lit up into a warm smile. "Mira, no problema!" she said, as she picked up the pieces and held them together. Then she set the pieces on the counter and walked over to the cupboard to get some special glue. As we worked together to repair the mug, I noticed a mark in the handle where it had been glued together before.

Nice dialogue! I like how I can figure out the meaning even though I don't know Spanish!

Great job using connecting words to combine sentences!

APPLY TO YOUR DRAFT

During your peer review, give each other specific suggestions for how you could make your personal narratives more vivid or engaging. Use your revision guide to help you.

When receiving feedback from your partner, listen attentively and ask questions to make sure you fully understand the revision suggestions.

4 EDIT YOUR PERSONAL NARRATIVE

Ed
Interactive Grammar Lessons: Capital Letters

Edit your final draft to check for proper use of standard English conventions and to correct any misspellings or grammatical errors.

Watch Your Language!

USE CORRECT CAPITALIZATION

Capitalizing certain words is important to provide clarity in your writing. Take the time to check that your personal narrative follows the rules of capitalization.

Here are some examples of correct capitalization.

Correct Capitalization

Remember to capitalize:

- words in titles except articles, conjunctions, and prepositions shorter than five letters
- names and titles before names
- proper nouns and adjectives formed from proper nouns

CAPITALIZATION TYPE	EXAMPLE
Titles of literary works	*The Diary of a Young Girl*, "After Auschwitz"
Titles before names	Mr. Frank, Mrs. Van Daan
Place names	Amsterdam, the Netherlands, the Annex
Nationalities, ethnicities, languages	Dutch, British, Jewish
Organizations, government bodies	Jewish Lyceum, Nazis, Green Police, Allies
Historical periods and events	World War II, the Holocaust

APPLY TO YOUR DRAFT

Now apply what you've learned about capitalization to your own work.

1. Read your paper aloud and circle any titles, names, proper nouns, or proper adjectives.
2. Correct capitalization errors.
3. Exchange drafts with a peer and edit each other's work, looking for capitalization errors.

5 PUBLISH YOUR NARRATIVE

Share It!

The prompt asks you to write a personal narrative. You may also adapt your narrative to other formats.

Ways to Share

- **Present your narrative as a speech** to the class.
- **Record an interview** to answer a classmate's questions about your experience.
- **Create a podcast** based on your narrative.

Reflect & Extend

Here are some other ways to show your understanding of the ideas in Unit 6.

Reflect on the Essential Question

What can we learn from tragic events?

Has your answer to the question changed after reading the texts in the unit? Discuss your ideas.

You can use these sentence starters to help you reflect on your learning.

- **My thoughts changed because...**
- **Now that I've considered..., I realize...**
- **I've also gained insight about...**

Writing

Write a Persuasive Essay

Write an essay in which you take a position on the best way for people to avoid repeating tragic events of the past.

- Introduce the topic and clearly state your viewpoint or claim.
- Develop your claim with key ideas and evidence from the selections in Unit 6 and other sources.
- In your conclusion, restate your claim and make a call to action, asking your readers to accept your position and to act accordingly.

Project-Based Learning

Create a Theme Song

You've read about the life of Anne Frank. Now, create a theme song for a television version of *The Diary of Anne Frank*.

Here are some questions to ask yourself as you get started.

- What details about Anne Frank's character and which scenes or events from the play will the song lyrics reflect?
- What overall message will the song convey?
- How will I combine the lyrics, melody, and rhythm to convey my intended mood?

Work with your class to create the theme song. One group may want to work on lyrics, while others work on music. Use digital media and tools to aid your collaboration with your classmates.

Ed

Media Projects

To find help with this task online, access **Create a Theme Song.**

Resources

HMH *Into Literature* Resources Ed

For more instruction and practice, access the *Into Literature* Resources and Interactive Lessons.

- Reading Resources
- Student Edition
- Media Projects
- Vocabulary Resources
- Current Events
- Grammar Resources
- Intervention, Review, & Extension
- Speaking & Listening Resources
- Text Library
- Writing Resources
- Graphic Organizers

UNIT 1

Response Log

ESSENTIAL QUESTION:
Does technology improve or control our lives?

Use this Response Log to record your ideas about how each of the texts in Unit 1 relates to or comments on the **Essential Question.**

The Brave Little Toaster	
Are Bionic Superhumans on the Horizon?	
Interflora	
The Automation Paradox	
Heads Up, Humans	

UNIT 2

Response Log

Use this Response Log to record your ideas about how each of the texts in Unit 2 relates to or comments on the **Essential Question.**

ESSENTIAL QUESTION:
Why do we sometimes like to feel frightened?

What Is the Horror Genre?	
The Tell-Tale Heart	
The Monkey's Paw (short story)	
from The Monkey's Paw (film clip)	
from The Aeneid of Virgil	
from Hades: Lord of the Dead	

UNIT 3

Response Log

ESSENTIAL QUESTION: ***What are the places that shape who you are?***

Use this Response Log to record your ideas about how each of the texts in Unit 3 relates to or comments on the **Essential Question.**

from The Book of Unknown Americans	
My Favorite Chaperone	
Spirit Walking in the Tundra	
New Immigrants Share Their Stories	
A Common Bond: Teens Forge Friendships Despite Differences	

UNIT 4

Response Log

Use this Response Log to record your ideas about how each of the texts in Unit 4 relates to or comments on the **Essential Question.**

?

ESSENTIAL QUESTION:
What will people risk to be free?

from Narrative of the Life of Frederick Douglass, an American Slave	
The Drummer Boy of Shiloh	
O Captain! My Captain!	
from Harriet Tubman: Conductor on the Underground Railroad	
Not My Bones	
from Fortune's Bones	

UNIT 5

Response Log

Use this Response Log to record your ideas about how each of the texts in Unit 5 relates to or comments on the **Essential Question.**

ESSENTIAL QUESTION:
How do the challenges you face today help to shape your future?

from Bronx Masquerade	
The Debt We Owe to the Adolescent Brain	
Hanging Fire	
Summer of His Fourteenth Year	
from It's Complicated: The Social Lives of Networked Teens	
Outsmart Your Smartphone	

UNIT 6

Response Log

Use this Response Log to record your ideas about how each of the texts in Unit 6 relates to or comments on the **Essential Question.**

ESSENTIAL QUESTION:
What can we learn from tragic events?

The Diary of Anne Frank	
from The Diary of a Young Girl	
After Auschwitz	
There But for the Grace	
Days	

NOTICE & NOTE Handbook

Get More Out of What You Read

Answer your own questions!

Two educators spent years working with students and reading and rereading the books that students read most. They identified a handful of common things authors include in literary and informational texts that signal the reader to pay attention. They call them **signposts.** When you notice a signpost and think about it, you can take control of your own reading.

Learn more about the signposts below.

SIGNPOSTS FOR LITERARY TEXTS
(such as poetry, plays, and fiction)

SIGNPOSTS FOR INFORMATIONAL TEXTS
(such as articles and arguments)

Contrasts and Contradictions

LITERARY ANALYSIS CONNECTION

Paying attention to Contrasts and Contradictions can help you analyze

- character development
- internal conflict
- theme
- relationship between setting and plot
- mood

Contrasts and Contradictions occur either when there is a sharp contrast between what we would expect and what we observe happening, or when the character behaves in a way that contradicts previous behavior or well-established patterns. Contrasts and Contradictions can occur with setting, too.

Read carefully and be alert for moments when a character begins acting or thinking in a new way, or in a way that surprises you because it's not how most people would react. Words like *but* or *despite* can provide clues to these differences.

When you notice Contrasts and Contradictions, pause. Think about what this unexpected or unusual behavior tells you about the character or setting.

A good question to ask is . . .

One day, Mister Toussaint came home to find an extra 300 euros' worth of groceries on his doorstep. So he called up Miz Rousseau, the grocer, and said, "Why have you sent me all this food? My fridge is already full of delicious things. I don't need this stuff and besides, I can't pay for it."

But Miz Rousseau told him that he had ordered the food. His refrigerator had sent in the list, and she had the signed order to prove it.

—from "The Brave Little Toaster," p. 7

Aha Moment

Ed Notice & Note Peer Coach Videos

An **Aha Moment** occurs when characters realize something that shifts the way they act or what they understand about themselves, others, or the world.

Be alert for these realizations, because they often mark important turning points.

Some phrases that can signal an Aha Moment are:

She realized . . .

He suddenly noticed . . .

In that instant, I understood . . .

It gets me thinking . . .

When you notice an Aha Moment, pause. Think about what effect the character's new knowledge might have on the story.

A good question to ask is . . .

I'm sure no one else has spotted me until a head pops up from behind the stacks. It's Janelle Battle from my English class. I freeze and wait for the snickers I'm used to . . . But all she does is smile and wave. Like it's no big deal for me to be in a library reading. Like I have a right to be there if I want. . . .

. . . She's smart, and she doesn't try hiding it. Which gets me thinking. Maybe it's time I quit sneaking in and out of the library like some thief. Maybe it's time I just started being who I am.

—from *Bronx Masquerade*, p. 360

LITERARY ANALYSIS CONNECTION

Paying attention to Aha Moments can help you analyze

- character development
- internal conflict
- plot

T? Tough Questions

LITERARY ANALYSIS CONNECTION

Paying attention to Tough Questions can help you analyze

- *internal conflict*
- *theme*
- *character development*

Tough Questions are questions characters raise that reveal their inner struggles.

Be alert to the times when characters ask themselves difficult questions, or when others ask questions that make the character think hard or feel deeply. At these moments, you can learn about characters' internal conflicts and gain insight into the theme of the story.

Tough Questions are sometimes expressed as statements, but ones that reveal uncertainty or confusion. Some phrases that can signal Tough Questions are:

What if she . . .

Would he be able to . . .

Why should I . . .

She wasn't sure if . . .

When you notice Tough Questions, pause. Think about what the questions suggest about the character or the theme and how these struggles might affect the rest of the story.

A good question to ask is . . .

In homeroom when Mr. Horswill handed out the permission slip for the Spring Fling, the all-school dance, I almost didn't take one. Why should I bother when I was sure the answer would be the same? Even though I'm in ninth grade now, it would still be the same. No. *Nyet* is what they say, and I don't want to hear this again. But I took a permission slip anyway. I don't know why I didn't just shake my head when this very popular girl Marcia Egness was handing them out. And even after I took one, I don't know why I didn't throw it away. Maybe I just couldn't give up hope. . . .

—from "My Favorite Chaperone," p. 193

Words of the Wiser

Ed
Notice & Note Peer Coach Videos

Words of the Wiser are pieces of advice or insights a wiser character, who is usually older, offers about life to the main character.

Look for moments when a character is receiving advice or wisdom about how to deal with a difficult problem or decision. These moments often occur when a character is wrestling with an inner conflict, and the advice can offer clues to the theme of the story.

When you notice Words of the Wiser, pause. Think about what the advice or insight suggests about the story's theme and how it is likely to affect the way the character deals with a problem or decision.

A good question to ask is . . .

"Why am I telling you this? That's what you wanted to ask, eh? Well, when you got a bunch of wild horses on a loose rein somewhere, somehow you got to bring order, rein them in. These lads, fresh out of the milkshed, don't know what I know, and I can't tell them: men actually die, in war. So each is his own army. I got to make *one* army of them. And for that, boy, I need you."

"Me!" The boy's lips barely twitched.

"Now, boy," said the General quietly, "you are the heart of the army. Think of that. You're the heart of the army. Listen, now."

—from "The Drummer Boy of Shiloh," p. 283

LITERARY ANALYSIS CONNECTION

Paying attention to Words of the Wiser can help you analyze

- theme
- internal conflict
- relationship between character and plot

Again and Again

LITERARY ANALYSIS CONNECTION

Paying attention to Again and Again can help you analyze

- plot
- setting
- symbolism
- theme
- character development
- conflict
- mood

Again and Again is when events, images, or particular words recur over a portion of the story or novel.

Authors include these words, images, or events Again and Again to

- reveal things about character motivation
- offer insight into the story's theme
- make connections between elements of the plot
- help create the story's mood

When you notice the Again and Again signpost, pause. Think about the meaning the repeated words, images, or events might have and how it relates to the setting, plot, theme, or character development.

A good question to ask is . . .

. . . Yet the sound increased—and what could I do? It was *a low, dull, quick sound—much such a sound as a watch makes when enveloped in cotton.* I gasped for breath—and yet the officers heard it not. I talked more quickly—more vehemently; but the noise steadily increased. I arose and argued about trifles, in a high key and with violent gesticulations, but the noise steadily increased. Why *would* they not be gone? I paced the floor to and fro with heavy strides, as if excited to fury by the observation of the men—but the noise steadily increased. . .

—from "The Tell-Tale Heart," p. 102

Memory Moment

Ed
Notice & Note Peer Coach Videos

A **Memory Moment** occurs when a character has a recollection that interrupts the forward progress of the story.

Be alert for places where the character is thinking about something that occurred at an earlier time. These moments can

- provide insight into the current situation
- explain character motivation
- offer insight into the theme of the story

Some phrases that can signal a Memory Moment are:

One winter they . . .
It reminded her of . . .
She remembered when . . .
When I was a girl . . .

When you notice a Memory Moment, pause. Think about why the author included this detail from the past.

A good question to ask is . . .

LITERARY ANALYSIS CONNECTION

Paying attention to Memory Moments can help you analyze

- character development
- theme
- plot
- relationship between character and plot

Mrs. Van Daan. Oh I don't mind. (*to* Anne) Our house was always swarming with boys. When I was a girl we had . . .

Mr. Van Daan. Oh, God. Not again!

Mrs. Van Daan (*good-humored*). Shut up! (*Without a pause, to* Anne. Mr. Van Daan *mimics* Mrs. Van Daan, *speaking the first few words in unison with her.*) One summer we had a big house in Hilversum. The boys came buzzing round like bees around a jam pot. . . .

—from *The Diary of Anne Frank,* p. 461

Q? Big Questions

When you read any informational text or argument, it's important to remember that the author is presenting only one version of the truth. This version may be factual and mostly free of bias, or it may include slanted, overstated, or even untrue claims or descriptions. Either way, you have to think critically about the author's relationship to the topic. That's why it's important to approach these texts from a **Questioning Stance,** or position. To do that, keep these three **Big Questions** in mind as you read:

- What surprised me?
- What did the author think I already knew?
- What changed, challenged, or confirmed what I already knew?

These questions will not only help you evaluate what you read and avoid falling for things that aren't entirely true, they will also help make the things you read more interesting. In addition, they can help you get to the root of things that might confuse you. The chart below gives more detail about each of the Big Questions.

What surprised me?	Look for parts of the text that make you think "really!?", and put an exclamation point there. **You might think:** • *"I didn't know that!"* • *"Really? Is that true?"* • *"Oh! Now I get it."* • *"How could anyone think that way?"* or *"I hadn't thought of it that way."*
What did the author think I already knew?	Look for places where the language is tough or where the author is writing about things you don't know much about, and put a question mark there. **You might think:** • *"The author thought I'd know what this word means."* • *"The author thought I could picture this."* • *"The author thought I'd know something about this."* • *"The author thought I'd get how this happens."*
What changed, challenged, or confirmed what I already knew?	Look for ideas that change your thinking. Put a C by those places. **You might think:** • *"I realize now . . ."* • *"This makes me rethink my opinion about . . ."* • *"That supports what I already thought."*

Contrasts and Contradictions

Notice & Note Peer Coach Videos

Contrasts and Contradictions occur either when the author shows you how ideas, things, events, or people differ from one another, or when you come across something that goes against what you would have expected.

To help you find Contrasts and Contradictions within the text, look for signal words and phrases such as

- yet
- however
- on the other hand
- unlike
- as opposed to
- instead of

For Contrasts and Contradictions between the text and your own expectations, be on the lookout for things that surprise you as you read.

When you notice Contrasts and Contradictions, pause. Think about why the author may have chosen to focus on these differences or how your knowledge contrasts with what's described in the text.

A good question to ask is . . .

Now, as then, we ask the question of all questions: what was the meaning of what was so routinely going on in this kingdom of eternal night. What kind of demented mind could have invented this system?

And it worked. The killers killed, the victims died and the world was the world and everything else was going on, life as usual. In the towns nearby, what happened? In the lands nearby, what happened? Life was going on where God's creation was condemned to blasphemy by their killers and their accomplices.

—from "After Auschwitz," p. 547

RELATED READING SKILLS

- Compare and contrast
- Generalize
- Identify main idea
- Infer
- Identify cause and effect
- Identify details
- Understand author's purpose or bias

Extreme or Absolute Language

RELATED READING SKILLS

- Draw conclusions
- Generalize
- Identify author's point of view
- Identify main idea
- Infer
- Recognize hyperbole
- Identify cause and effect
- Understand author's purpose or bias

Extreme or Absolute Language occurs when the author uses language that leaves no room for doubt, allows for no questions, and may seem to exaggerate or overstate a claim.

This language includes words such as

- all
- every
- always
- no one
- never
- totally
- perfectly
- unarguably

It can also include dramatic phrases intended to cause a strong reaction, such as "obliterate life as we know it," "our safety is at stake," or "despicable actions."

When you notice Extreme or Absolute Language, pause and think. The author might be expressing strong feelings, or they may be overstating things or even trying to mislead the reader. This language can reveal things about the author's purpose or bias.

A good question to ask is . . .

A growing body of scientific evidence and everyday experience show that social media is not simply a natural and healthy extension of teens' social lives and development. It can negatively affect the brain and behavior in ways that mimic addiction, adversely affect learning, distort normal aspects of social and emotional development, and increase anxiety. There is too much research and too much everyday evidence now for us to ignore the risks. You have to approach social media with restraint and caution if you want to avoid harm.

—from "Outsmart Your Smartphone," p. 408

Numbers and Stats

Ed
Notice & Note Peer Coach Videos

Numbers and Stats occur either when authors use specific figures to show amounts, size, or scale, or when they are vague when you would have expected more details.

Some key words that may show when an author is being vague include

- many
- most
- some
- longer
- bigger
- farther
- oldest

When you notice Numbers and Stats, pause. Think about why the author may have chosen to use or leave out specific figures in describing something.

A good question to ask is . . .

Why did the author use these numbers or amounts?

RELATED READING SKILLS

- Draw conclusions
- Find facts
- Generalize
- Identify details
- Infer
- Make comparisons
- Recognize evidence
- Understand author's purpose or bias

There is no argument that many jobs now held by humans will be replaced by some form of advanced technology. According to a new report by a multi-national accounting and consulting firm based in London, 38% of U.S. jobs are at high risk of being replaced by robots and artificial intelligence over the next 15 years. The report estimates the percentage of jobs lost to automation in Britain will be 30%, with 35% in Germany, and 21% in Japan.

—from "Heads Up, Humans," p. 54

“ ” Quoted Words

RELATED READING SKILLS

- Compare and contrast
- Draw conclusions
- Identify author’s point of view
- Infer
- Identify cause and effect
- Separate fact from opinion
- Understand author’s purpose or bias

Quoted Words occur when the author cites or quotes a person or group to provide support for a point. Authors often include opinions or conclusions from people who are experts on a topic or from people who were participants in or witnesses to events.

When you notice Quoted Words, pause. Think about why the author may have chosen to quote this particular person or group.

A good question to ask is . . .

For many students, the International High School at Prospect Heights is kind of like a second home in the city. “What makes our school a welcoming place and feel like home is in the importance we put on relationships: You can only develop a relationship with a people if you spend time with them and do things together,” says the school principal, Nedda de Castro. Students and teachers get to know each other in small groups and different settings both inside and outside of school, on field trips, for instance.

—from “A Common Bond,” p. 235

W Word Gaps

Notice & Note Peer Coach Videos

Word Gaps occur either when authors use vocabulary that is unfamiliar or when they use familiar words in ways that are new to you. Authors of informational texts often use words with multiple meanings, technical or scientific words, or words that are unique to specific subjects.

Sometimes authors provide clues to these words, such as putting them in boldfaced or italic font or highlighting them. Other times, authors follow a less-known word with the phrase *is like* to help explain it. Many times, however, the way you identify a Word Gap is simply by noticing that you've come across a word that you don't understand.

When you notice Word Gaps, pause. Ask yourself the following questions. The answers will help you decide if you need to look the word up or keep reading for more information.

Do I know this word from someplace else?

Does this seem like technical talk for experts on this topic?

RELATED READING SKILLS

- Generalize
- Identify details
- Infer
- Make comparisons
- Understand author's purpose or bias
- Use context clues

We lose "gray matter" and gain "white matter": myelin, which forms an insulating sheath around nerve fibers. "We get more and more myelin, which speeds up the communication between nerve cells, as we go through adolescence," says Giedd. "We learn what we need to do and be good at and then the process streamlines that." But the price we pay is that, as myelin is laid down, flexibility diminishes. . . .

—from "The Debt We Owe to the Adolescent Brain," p. 370

Using a Glossary

A glossary is an alphabetical list of vocabulary words. Use a glossary just as you would a dictionary—to determine the meanings, parts of speech, pronunciation, and syllabification of words. (Some technical, foreign, and more obscure words in this book are defined for you in the footnotes that accompany many of the selections.)

Many words in the English language have more than one meaning. This glossary gives the meanings that apply to the words as they are used in the selections in this book.

The following abbreviations are used to identify parts of speech of words:

adj. adjective   *adv.* adverb   *n.* noun   *v.* verb

Each word's pronunciation is given in parentheses. A guide to the pronunciation symbols appears in the Pronunciation Key below. The stress marks in the Pronunciation Key are used to indicate the force given to each syllable in a word. They can also help you determine where words are divided into syllables.

For more information about the words in this glossary or for information about words not listed here, consult a dictionary.

Pronunciation Key

Symbol	Examples
ă	**pat**
ā	**pay**
ä	f**a**ther, h**a**rd
âr	**care**
b	**b**i**b**
ch	**ch**ur**ch**
d	**d**ee**d**, mi**ll**ed
ĕ	p**e**t
ē	b**ee**
f	**f**i**f**e, **ph**ase, rou**gh**
g	**g**a**g**
h	**h**at
hw	**wh**ich
ĭ	p**i**t
ī	p**ie**, b**y**
îr	p**ier**
j	**j**u**dg**e
k	**k**ick, **c**at, pi**qu**e
l	**l**id, need**le*** (nēd′l)
m	**m**u**m**
n	**n**o, sudde**n*** (sŭd′n)
ng	thi**ng**
ŏ	p**o**t
ō	t**oe**
ô	c**au**ght, p**aw**
oi	n**oi**se
o͝o	t**oo**k
o͞o	b**oo**t
o͝or	l**ure**
ôr	c**ore**
ou	**ou**t
p	**p**o**p**
r	**r**oa**r**
s	**s**au**c**e
sh	**sh**ip, di**sh**
t	**t**igh**t**, stopp**ed**
th	**th**in
th	**th**is
ŭ	c**u**t
ûr	**ur**ge, t**er**m, f**ir**m, w**or**d, h**ear**d
v	**v**al**v**e
w	**w**ith
y	**y**es
z	**z**ebra, **x**ylem
zh	vi**s**ion, plea**s**ure, gara**ge**
ə	**a**bout, it**e**m, ed**i**ble, gall**o**p, circ**u**s
ər	butt**er**

Sounds in Foreign Words

Symbol	Examples
KH	*German* i**ch**, a**ch**; *Scottish* lo**ch**
N	*French*, bo**n** (bôN)
œ	*French* f**eu**, **œ**uf; *German* sch**ö**n
ü	*French* t**u**; *German* **ü**ber

*In English the consonants *l* and *n* often constitute complete syllables by themselves.

Stress Marks

The relevant emphasis with which the syllables of a word or phrase are spoken, called stress, is indicated in three different ways. The strongest, or primary, stress is marked with a bold mark (′). An intermediate, or secondary, level of stress is marked with a similar but lighter mark (′). The weakest stress is unmarked. Words of one syllable show no stress mark.

Glossary of Academic Vocabulary

access (ăk´sĕs) *n.* a way of approaching or making use of

civil (sĭv´əl) *adj.* of, or related to, citizens and their relations with each other and the state

commentary (kŏm´ən-tĕr´ē) *n.* explanation or interpretation in the form of comments or observations

communicate (kə-myōō´nĭ-kāt´) *v.* to convey information or exchange ideas

contribute (kən-trĭb´yōōt) *v.* to give or supply for a common purpose

convention (kən-vĕn´shən) *n.* a practice or procedure widely used by a group; a custom

debate (dĭ-bāt´) *v.* to engage in arguments by discussing opposing points

deduce (dĭ-dōōs´) *v.* to reach a conclusion or decision through reasoning

demonstrate (dĕm´ən-strāt´) *v.* to show clearly and deliberately

document (dŏk´yə-mənt) *n.* a written or printed paper that provides evidence or information

draft (drăft) *n.*; *v.* an early version or stage of a written document or plan; to write such a version

immigrate (ĭm´ĭ-grāt´) *v.* to enter and settle in a new country

liberation (lĭb´ə-rā´shən) *n.* the act of freeing or the state of being free

license (lī´səns) *n.* a document that is issued as proof of legal permission to do something

network (nĕt´wûrk´) *n.* a complex, interconnected group or system

occupation (ŏk´yə-pā´shən) *n.* an activity that serves as one's source of income

option (ŏp´shən) *n.* something chosen or available as a choice

philosophy (fĭ-lŏs´ə-fē) *n.* an underlying theory or set of ideas relating to life as a whole

predict (prĭ-dĭkt´) *v.* to tell about in advance, especially on the basis of special knowledge

psychology (sī-kŏl´ə-jē) *n.* the study of mental processes and behaviors

publish (pŭb´lĭsh) *v.* to prepare and issue a book or other material to the public

reaction (rē-ăk´shən) *n.* a response to something

relocate (rē-lō´kāt) *v.* to move to a new place

shifting (shĭft´ĭng) *adj.* changing attitudes, judgments, or emphases

speculate (spĕk´yə-lāt´) *v.* to reason or form a theory about something based on available evidence

sufficient (sə-fĭsh´ənt) *adj.* being enough, or as much as needed

summary (sŭm´ə-rē) *n.* a condensed, or shorter, report that includes the main points of a text or event

symbolize (sĭm´bə-līz´) *v.* to serve as a symbol of, or represent, something else

technique (tĕk-nēk´) *n.* the systematic or orderly procedure by which a task is accomplished

trend (trĕnd) *n.* the general direction of something; a current style

Glossary of Critical Vocabulary

abode (ə-bōd´) *n.* An *abode* is a home.

adaptable (ə-dăp´tə-bəl) *adj.* *Adaptable* means able to survive under a variety of conditions.

ample (ăm´pəl) *adj.* To be *ample* is to be plentiful or enough.

anonymous (ə-nŏn´ə-məs) *adj.* To be *anonymous* means to be unknown or unidentified by name.

appalled (ə-pôld´) *adj.* To be *appalled* is to feel horror and shock about something.

appease (ə-pēz´) *v.* To *appease* means to pacify or lessen the anger of, usually by making concessions.

apprehension (ăp´rĭ-hĕn´shən) *n.* *Apprehension* is the fear or dread of the future.

askew (ə-skyōō´) *adj.* When something is *askew*, it is off center.

assimilate (ə-sĭm´ə-lāt´) *v.* To *assimilate* means to blend into or become similar to the prevailing culture.

assure (ə-shŏŏr´) *v.* To *assure* is to state something positively, so as to remove doubt about it.

audacity (ô-dăs´ĭ-tē) *n.* *Audacity* is shameless daring or boldness.

cajole (kə-jōl´) *v.* When you *cajole*, you coax or urge gently.

capitalize (kăp´ĭ-tl-īz´) *v.* To *capitalize* on something means to use it to one's advantage.

chafe (chāf) *v.* To *chafe* is to annoy or bother someone.

collaborate (kə-lăb´ə-rāt´) *v.* To *collaborate* means to work together.

commence (kə-mĕns´) *v.* When things *commence*, they begin or start.

compensation (kŏm´pən-sā´shən) *n.* *Compensation* is something, such as money, that is received as payment.

conceive (kən-sēv´) *v.* When you *conceive* an idea, you think of it.

condole (kən-dōl´) *v.* If you *condole* with someone, you express sympathy or sorrow.

confer (kən-fûr´) *v.* To *confer* is to share ideas or make a decision with one or more other people.

confide (kən-fīd´) *v.* To *confide* means to share private or secret information.

conjecture (kən-jĕk´chər) *v.* If you *conjecture*, you guess or suppose.

conspicuous (kən-spĭk´yōō-əs) *adj.* Something *conspicuous* is obvious or very easy to see.

convene (kən-vēn´) *v.* To *convene* is to come together for a purpose.

credulity (krĭ-dōō´lĭ-tē) *n.* *Credulity* is a tendency to believe too readily.

crevice (krĕv´ĭs) *n.* A *crevice* is a narrow crack.

deliberate (dĭ-lĭb´ər-ĭt) *adj.* *Deliberate* decision-making activity is the process of making a choice only after carefully considering its likely effects.

denunciation (dĭ-nŭn´sē-ā´shən) *n.* A *denunciation* is the public condemnation of something as wrong or evil.

dependent (dĭ-pĕn´dənt) *adj.* *Dependent* means relying on or requiring the aid or support of another.

deplete (dĭ-plēt´) *v.* To *deplete* means to use up or to reduce to a very small amount.

derision (dĭ-rĭzh´ən) *n.* *Derision* is jeering laughter or ridicule.

disheveled (dĭ-shĕv´əld) *adj.* When something is *disheveled*, it is messy or untidy.

dispatcher (dĭs-păch´ər) *n.* A *dispatcher* is a person who sends out vehicles according to a schedule.

dispel (dĭ-spĕl´) *v.* When you ***dispel*** something, you drive it away.

dynamic (dī-năm´ĭk) *n.* A ***dynamic*** is a system in which conflicting or competing forces are at work.

eligible (ĕl´ĭ-jə-bəl) *adj.* ***Eligible*** means qualified to be selected.

eloquence (ĕl´ə-kwəns) *n.* ***Eloquence*** is the ability to speak powerfully and persuasively.

embrace (ĕm-brās´) *v.* To ***embrace*** an idea means to accept and support it.

enhancement (ĕn-hăns´mənt) *n.* An ***enhancement*** improves or adds to the quality or function of something.

evoke (ĭ-vōk´) *v.* When you ***evoke*** something, you bring it to mind.

exotic (ĕg-zŏt´ĭk) *adj.* Something that is ***exotic*** is unusual or different.

expansive (ĭk-spăn´sĭv) *adj.* ***Expansive*** means broad in size, range, or degree of openness.

froth (frôth) *n.* A ***froth*** is a fit of frustration or excitement.

grimace (grĭm´ĭs) *n.* A ***grimace*** is a facial expression of pain or disgust.

hunker (hŭng´kər) *v.* To ***hunker*** down means to stay in a place and focus on a task for a period of time.

hypocritical (hĭp´ə-krĭt´ĭ-kəl) *adj.* If someone is ***hypocritical***, the person is false or deceptive.

implant (ĭm-plănt´) *v.* To ***implant*** a device means to place it inside the body through surgery.

implore (ĭm-plôr´) *v.* To ***implore*** is to beg for something urgently.

impulsive (ĭm-pŭl´sĭv) *adj.* To be ***impulsive*** means to act quickly, before thinking about the consequences.

inarticulate (ĭn´är-tĭk´yə-lĭt) *adj.* Someone who is ***inarticulate*** is unable to speak in a clear way.

indignantly (ĭn-dĭg´nənt-lē) *adv.* Someone who does something ***indignantly*** acts in a way that shows anger or shock over something that is unjust or unfair.

inhibited (ĭn-hĭb´ĭt-əd) *adj.* If you feel ***inhibited*** you feel restrained, held back, or self-conscious.

instill (ĭn-stĭl´) *v.* When you ***instill*** something, you establish or implant it gradually.

insulate (ĭn´sə-lāt´) *v.* To ***insulate*** means to surround or cover to prevent the passage of heat, electricity, or sound.

integrity (ĭn-tĕg´rĭ-tē) *n.* ***Integrity*** is following a strict code of ethical conduct.

intensify (ĭn-tĕn´sə-fī´) *v.* If you ***intensify*** something, you make it grow in strength.

intimacy (ĭn´tə-mə-sē) *n.* ***Intimacy*** refers to a state of personal closeness that is usually experienced in privacy.

justify (jŭs´tə-fī´) *v.* If you ***justify*** something, you prove it is right or valid.

legitimately (lə-jĭt´ə-mĭt-lē) *adv.* When you do something ***legitimately***, you do it lawfully.

lethal (lē´thəl) *adj.* ***Lethal*** means causing or capable of causing death.

linger (lĭng´gər) *v.* To ***linger*** is to remain or stay longer.

loathe (lōth) *v.* To ***loathe*** something is to dislike it very much.

melodrama (mĕl´ə-drä´mə) *n.* ***Melodrama*** is behavior characterized by exaggerated emotions.

muted (myo͞o´tĭd) *adj.* When something is ***muted***, it is softened or muffled.

ostentatiously (ŏs´tĕn-tā´shəs-lē) *adv.* Someone who does something ***ostentatiously*** acts in an exaggerated way in order to attract attention.

paradox (păr´ə-dŏks´) *n.* A ***paradox*** is a person, thing, or situation that is contradictory.

parallel (păr´ə-lĕl´) *adj.* If things are ***parallel***, they have comparable or similar parts.

Glossary of Critical Vocabulary

peril (pĕr´əl) *n.* A *peril* is something that is dangerous.

perspective (pər-spĕk´tĭv) *n.* A *perspective* is a viewpoint on or understanding of something.

predominantly (prĭ-dŏm´ə-nənt-lē) *adv.* *Predominantly* refers to the most important, obvious, or typical aspect(s) of something.

prosaic (prō-zā´ĭk) *adj.* If something is *prosaic*, it is dull or ordinary.

prudence (pro͞od´ns) *n.* *Prudence* is the wise handling of practical matters.

quest (kwĕst) *n.* A *quest* is a search.

ravage (răv´ĭj) *v.* To *ravage* is to cause serious damage or destruction.

redistribute (rē´dĭ-strĭb´yo͞ot) *v.* To *redistribute* means to distribute again but differently.

reintegrate (rē-ĭn´tĭ-grāt´) *v.* To *reintegrate* is to come together, as when similar materials are collected for recycling.

relevant (rĕl´ə-vənt) *adj.* Something is *relevant* to a topic when it is related or important to that topic.

relish (rĕl´ĭsh) *v.* To *relish* is to take great joy or pleasure in something.

reminisce (rĕm´ə-nĭs´) *v.* When you *reminisce*, you think or talk about past experiences.

renowned (rĭ-nound´) *adj.* Someone or something that is *renowned* is famous.

resignation (rĕz´ĭg-nā´shən) *n.* *Resignation* is the acceptance of something that is inescapable.

resolute (rĕz´ə-lo͞ot´) *adj.* If you are *resolute*, you are firm or determined.

retract (rĭ-trăkt´) *v.* To *retract* is to pull in.

robustly (rō-bŭst´lē) *adv.* *Robustly* means in a strong, healthy way.

scrutinize (skro͞ot´n-īz´) *v.* To *scrutinize* is to examine or inspect with great care.

scuffle (skŭf´əl) *n.* A *scuffle* is a disorderly fight.

sector (sĕk´tər) *n.* A *sector* is a part or division, as of a city or a national economy.

snicker (snĭk´ər) *n.* A *snicker* is a superior, partially suppressed laugh.

solemn (sŏl´əm) *adj.* If an event is *solemn*, it is deeply serious.

splendid (splĕn´dĭd) *adj.* If something is *splendid*, it is magnificent or very good.

sponsor (spŏn´sər) *v.* If you *sponsor* someone, you support his or her admission into a group.

stifle (stī´fəl) *v.* If you *stifle* something, you smother it.

stimulant (stĭm´yə-lənt) *n.* A *stimulant* is an agent that excites or temporarily speeds up mental and/or physical functions.

strewn (stro͞on) *v.* Something *strewn* is spread here and there, or scattered.

stun (stŭn) *v.* To *stun* someone is to make him or her feel shocked or dazed.

sullen (sŭl´ən) *adj.* *Sullen* people show silent resentment.

tirade (tī´rād) *n.* A *tirade* is a long, angry speech.

unabated (ŭn´ə-bā´tĭd) *adj.* If something is *unabated*, it keeps its full force without decreasing.

unrest (ŭn-rĕst´) *n.* *Unrest* refers to an unstable or turbulent condition that is often marked by protests or riots.

vehemently (vē´ə-mənt-lē) *adv.* If you do something *vehemently*, you do it with intense emotion.

vex (vĕks) *v.* If you *vex* someone, you annoy that person.

vindication (vĭn´dĭ-kā´shən) *n.* *Vindication* is the evidence or proof that someone's claim is correct.

vindictive (vĭn-dĭk´tĭv) *adj.* Something is *vindictive* if it is intended to hurt or punish someone.

whimper (hwĭm´pər) *v.* To *whimper* is to sob or let out a soft cry.

Index of Skills

D

E

Index of Titles and Authors

Acknowledgments

Excerpt from *The Aeneid of Virgil* by Virgil, translated by Allen Mandelbaum. Text copyright © 1971 by Allen Mandelbaum. Reprinted by permission of Bantam Books, an imprint of Random House, a division of Penguin Random House LLC. All rights reserved.

"After Auschwitz" by Elie Wiesel. Text copyright © 1995 by Elie Wiesel. Reprinted by permission of Georges Borchardt, Inc.

Excerpts from *The American Heritage Dictionary of The English Language, Fifth Edition.* Text copyright © 2016 by Houghton Mifflin Harcourt Publishing Company. Reprinted by permission of Houghton Mifflin Harcourt Publishing Company.

"Are Bionic Superhumans on the Horizon?" by Ramez Naam from CNN.com April 25, 2013. Text copyright © 2013 by Turner Broadcast Systems. Reprinted by permission of PARS International on behalf of Turner Broadcast Systems. All rights reserved. Protected by the Copyright Laws of the United States. The printing, copying, redistribution, or retransmission of this Content without express written permission is prohibited.

"The Automation Paradox" by James Bessen, from *The Atlantic Monthly*, January 19, 2016. Text copyright © 2016 by The Atlantic Monthly. Reprinted by permission of Tribune Content Agency.

Excerpt from *The Book of Unknown Americans* by Cristina Henríquez. Text copyright © 2014 by Cristina Henríquez. Reprinted by permission of Alfred A. Knopf, an imprint of the Knopf Doubleday Publishing Group, a division of Penguin Random House LLC and Canongate Books. All rights reserved. Any third-party use of this material, outside this publication, is prohibited. Interested parties must apply directly to Penguin Random House LLC for permission.

"The Brave Little Toaster" from *TRSF* by Cory Doctorow. Text copyright © 2014 by Cory Doctorow. Reprinted by permission of Cory Doctorow.

"Days" from *The Art of Drowning* by Billy Collins. Text copyright © 1995 by Billy Collins. Reprinted by permission of University of Pittsburgh Press.

"The Debt We Owe to the Adolescent Brain" by Jeanne Miller from *Odyssey,* March 2015. Text copyright © 2015 by Carus Publishing Company. Reprinted by permission of Carus Publishing Company. All Cricket Media material is copyrighted by Carus Publishing Company d/b/a Cricket Media, and/or various authors and illustrators. Any commercial use or distribution of material without permission is strictly prohibited. Please visit http://cricketmedia.com/licensing for licensing and http://www.cricketmedia.com for subscriptions.

"Devon Hope" by Nikki Grimes; "Open Mike: Bronx Masquerade" by Devon Hope; "Open Mike: If" by Diondra Jordan; "Diondra Jordan," and "Tyrone" from *Bronx Masquerade* by Nikki Grimes. Text copyright © 2002 by Nikki Grimes. Reprinted by permission of Dial Books for Young Readers, an imprint of Penguin Young Readers Group, a division of Penguin Random House LLC, Curtis Brown, Ltd., and Recorded Books. All rights reserved. Any third-party use of this material, outside this publication, is prohibited. Interested parties must apply directly to Penguin Random House LLC for permission.

Entire Play from *The Diary of Anne Frank* by Frances Goodrich and Albert Hackett. Text copyright © 1956 by Albert Hackett, Frances Goodrich Hackett and Otto Frank, renewed 1984 by Albert Hackett. Adapted from *Anne Frank: Diary of a Young Girl* by Anne Frank. Reprinted by permission of Random House, an imprint and division of Penguin Random House LLC and Flora Roberts, Inc. All rights reserved. Any third-party use of this material, outside of this publication, is prohibited. Interested parties must apply directly to Penguin Random House LLC for permission.

Excerpts from *The Diary of a Young Girl: The Definitive Editions* by Anne Frank, edited by Otto H. Frank and Mirjam Pressler, translated by Susan Massotty. Text copyright © 1991 by The Anne Frank-Fonds, Basle, Switzerland. Translation copyright © 1995 by Doubleday, a division of Bantam Doubleday Dell Publishing Group Inc. Reprinted by permission of Penguin Books Ltd. Translation copyright © 1995 by Penguin Random House LLC. All rights reserved. Any third-party use of this material, outside of this publication, is prohibited. Interested parties must apply directly to Penguin Random House LLC for permission. Reprinted by permission of Doubleday, an imprint of the Knopf Doubleday Publishing Group, a division of Penguin Random House LLC.

"The Drummer Boy of Shiloh" from *The Saturday Evening Post,* April 30, 1960, by Ray Bradbury. Text copyright © 1960 by the Curtis Publishing Company, renewed 1988 by Ray Bradbury. Reprinted by permission of Don Congdon Associates, Inc.

"Fortune's Bones" from *Fortune's Bones: The Manumission Requiem* by Marilyn Nelson. Text copyright © 2004 by Pamela Espeland. Reprinted by permission of Highlights for Children, Inc.

Excerpt from *Hades: Lord of the Dead* by George O'Connor. Text copyright © 2012 by George O'Connor. Reprinted by permission of Macmillan Publishing.

"Hanging Fire" from *The Collected Poems of Audre Lorde* by Audre Lorde. Text copyright © 1978 by The Audre Lorde Estate. Reprinted by permission of W. W. Norton and Company and Charlotte Sheedy Literary Agency.

Harriet Tubman: Conductor on the Underground Railroad by Ann Petry. Text copyright © 1955, © 1983 by Ann Petry. Reprinted by permission of Hannigan Salky Getzler Agency as agents for the author.

"Interflora" by Susan Hamlyn. Text copyright and permission by Susan Hamlyn.

Excerpt from *It's Complicated: The Social Lives of Networked Teens* by danah boyd. Text copyrighted © 2014 by danah boyd. Reprinted by permission of Yale University Press.

"My Favorite Chaperone" by Jean Davies Okimoto. Text copyright © 2004 by Jean Davies Okimoto. Reprinted with permission of Jean Davies Okimoto.

"Not My Bones" from *Fortune's Bones: The Manumission Requiem* by Marilyn Nelson. Text copyright © 2003 by Marilyn Nelson. Reprinted by permission of Highlights for Children, Inc.

Quote by Henning Mankell from "All along the watchtower" by Nick Hasted from *The Guardian*, January 11, 2002. Text copyright © 2002 by Guardian News & Media Limited. Reprinted courtesy of Guardian News & Media Limited.

"Spirit Walking in the Tundra" from *Conflict Resolution for Holy Beings: Poems* by Joy Harjo. Text copyright © 2015 by Joy Harjo. This selection may not be reproduced, stored in a retrieval system, or transmitted in any form or by any means without the prior written permission of the publisher. Reprinted by permission of W. W. Norton & Company, Inc.

"Summer of His Fourteenth Year" from *Wind Chimes* by Gloria Amescua. Text copyright © 2004 by Altura Press. Reprinted by permission of Gloria Amescua.

"There But for the Grace" from *Sounds, Feelings, Thoughts: Seventy Poems by Wisława Szymborska* by Wisława Szymborska translated by Magnus J. Krynski and Robert A. Maguire. Text copyright © 1981 by Princeton University Press. Reprinted by permission Copyright Clearance Center on behalf of Princeton University Press.

Excerpt from "What Is the Horror Genre?" by Stephen King from *Stephen King: A Critical Companion* by Sharon A. Russell. Text copyright © 1996 by Sharon A. Russell. Reprinted by permission of Copyright Clearance Center.

Unit Opener Image Credits

The Fight for Freedom: face in profile ©Alexander Porter/Image Source/Media Bakery, union soldier uniform Sewall Shattuck/ Library of Congress Prints & Photographs Division [LC-DIG-ppmsca-37118], African American soldiers William Morris Smith/Library of Congress Prints & Photographs Division [LC-DIG-cwpb-04294], face National Archives, eyes of main soldier ©Bettmann/Getty Images, American flag ©MindStorm/Shutterstock, union soldiers ©Michael Turner/iStock Editorial/Getty Images Plus/ Getty Images.

Legacy of Anne Frank: Anne Frank ©United Archives GmbH/ Alamy; cat ©adogslifephoto/Fotolia; German planes ©FLHC/Alamy; diary ©Heritage Image Partnership Ltd./Alamy.